Practical PostgreSQL

John C. Worsley and Joshua D. Drake

O'REILLY®

Beijing · Cambridge · Farnham · Köln · Paris · Sebastopol · Taipei · Tokyo

Practical PostgreSQL

by John C. Worsley and Joshua D. Drake

Copyright © 2002 Command Prompt, Inc. All rights reserved.
Printed in the United States of America.

Published by O'Reilly & Associates, Inc., 1005 Gravenstein Highway North, Sebastopol, CA 95472.

O'Reilly & Associates books may be purchased for educational, business, or sales promotional use. Online editions are also available for most titles (*safari.oreilly.com*). For more information, contact our corporate/institutional sales department: 800-998-9938 or *corporate@oreilly.com*.

Editor: Jonathan Gennick

Cover Designer: Ellie Volckhausen

Printing History:

January 2002:   First Edition.

ISBN: 1-56592-846-6

[M]

Practical PostgreSQL

Table of Contents

Preface

PostgreSQL is one of the most successful open source databases available. It is arguably also the most advanced, with a wide range of features that challenge even many closed-source databases.

This book is intended to be a practical guide to PostgreSQL v7.1.x, though most of the book should also apply to earlier and future releases of PostgreSQL. The content is focused on getting you comfortable with PostgreSQL in the most expedient fashion possible. Although we will touch on some academic database subjects, such discussion will be kept brief. Our core focus is to provide the reader with enough of an understanding of PostgreSQL to manage a fully operational PostgreSQL database. Our hope is that by introducing this book to the community we will provide a better understanding of PostgreSQL and its functionality.

Who Is the Intended Audience?

This book is for anyone interested in utilizing the PostgreSQL object-relational database-management system (ORDBMS). The reader should be familiar with Linux- and Unix-based systems, but is not expected to be a database guru. Although the test operating system for this book is Red Hat Linux, the tasks in this book that apply to Linux should apply to most Unix variants without much modification.

Structure of This Book

This book is divided into four parts, each focused on a different aspect of a PostgreSQL database system. It also includes a complete command reference, and a small set of technical appendixes.

Part 1, *Introduction & Installation*, is a general overview of PostgreSQL. It documents what it is, where you can obtain it, and how to install it on your system. It also covers a wide variety of compilation options which allow you to customize PostgreSQL to your needs.

Part 2, *Using PostgreSQL*, includes everything from general information on relational databases and the structured query language (SQL), to advanced extensibility of PostgreSQL's functions and operators. Chapter 3, *Understanding SQL*, begins with relational database and table concepts, and introduces the basics of statements, keywords, identifiers, and data types. Chapter 4, *Using SQL with PostgreSQL*, delves deeper into the use of SQL, covering how to perform essential database functions such as creating and altering tables, inserting rows into tables, copying data, retrieving result sets, and using views.

Chapter 5, *Operators and Functions*, expands on the variety of operators and functions built into PostgreSQL, while Chapter 6, *PostgreSQL Clients*, includes extra information on the use of the *psql* and PgAccess database clients. Concluding the part is Chapter 7, *Advanced Features*, which details the more advanced PostgreSQL features such as indices, inheritance, arrays, constraints, triggers, sequences and cursors. This chapter also documents PostgreSQL's advanced extensibility with user-defined operators and functions.

Part 3, *Administrating PostgreSQL*, explores topics with which you should be familiar if you are (or plan to be) the administrator of a PostgreSQL database. This part begins with Chapter 8, *Authentication and Encryption*, which describes PostgreSQL's authentication methods and the types of encryption available for use. Chapter 9, *Database Management* details the fundamental management of a PostgreSQL database, including initialization of the filesystem, and how to start and stop the backend. This chapter also contains information on database creation, removal, backup, and restoration of a backup. Chapter 10, *User and Group Management* documents how to add and remove user accounts and groups, and manage database privileges.

Part 4, *PostgreSQL Programming*, is a foray into the world of programming for PostgreSQL, covering the PL/pgSQL procedural language, JDBC (*Java DataBase Connectivity*), and LXP. Chapter 11, *PL/pgSQL* includes information about the PL/pgSQL language, how to add it into a PostgreSQL database, and how to use its various programmatic features. Chapter 12, *JDBC*, shows how to build the JDBC interface to PostgreSQL, and introduces the basics of using it. Chapter 13, *LXP* wraps up the part by documenting the installation, configuration and use of the LXP PostgreSQL application server for the Apache HTTP server.

Finally, Part 5 contains a comprehensive command reference guide, which documents each of the standard and extended SQL commands supported by PostgreSQL.

Platform and Version Used

At the time of this book's writing, version 7.1.3 is the most current release of Post-greSQL. This is the version used in all examples, and for the construction of our example database, booktown. All examples should be compatible with any of the PostgreSQL 7.1 versions, which is the reason you will see the version referred to as 7.1.x within our text.

What Is Included on the CD?

The CD included with this book contains the complete source for PostgreSQL 7.1.3. The CD also includes the PostgreSQL application server LXP. The following is a listing of what is on the CD, including a short description of each package:

postgresql-7.1.3.tar.gz

The community version of PostgreSQL in compressed source form. This is the most actively developed PostgreSQL distribution. We do not provide binaries of PostgreSQL, as you may want to compile different features.

The source is available as a single compressed file (*postgresql-7.1.3.tar.gz*). Its contents are not extracted on the CD, as you must copy and extract the files onto your hard drive before installing PostgreSQL.

lxp-eval-0.8.0.tgz

An evaluation/developer-use copy of the LXP PostgreSQL application server for Apache 1.3.x. LXP is a good tool for integrating PostgreSQL (and other technologies) with the web. This package is a binary distribution intended for x86-based systems. It must be copied to your hard drive before it can be extracted.

lxp/

A directory containing the extracted contents of the *lxp-eval-0.8.0.tgz* file. LXP can be installed directly from the *lxp* directory on the CD. See Chapter 13 for information on installing LXP.

booktown.sql

The PostgreSQL dump of the example booktown database used throughout this book. This file contains both commands to re-create the database schema, as well as some sample data.

To install this database after you have installed PostgreSQL, type from the command line *psql -U postgres template1 -f /mnt/cdrom/booktown.sql* (where */mnt/cdrom* is the path to your mounted CD, and *postgres* is your PostgreSQL superuser).

Conventions Used in This Book

Italic

> Used for filenames, directory names, string-bound constants, and URLs. It is also used for emphasis, and for the first use of a technical term.

`Constant width`

> Used for keywords, identifiers (such as tables and columns), data types, examples, and to show the contents of files, and the output of commands.

`Constant width italic`

> Used in syntax descriptions to indicated user-defined items.

`Constant width bold`

> Indicates user input within examples.

`UPPERCASE`

> Used within syntax descriptions, uppercase usually indicates keywords.

`lowercase`

> Used within syntax descriptions, lowercase usually indicates user-defined items, such as variables and identifiers.

`[ ]`

> Used within syntax descriptions, square brackets enclose optional items, which are separated from one another by pipes (|).

`{ }`

> Used within syntax descriptions, curly brackets enclose a set of items from which you *must* choose one.

`. . .`

> Used within syntax descriptions, ellipses indicate repeating information. Used within examples, ellipses indicate that a section of unimportant information was removed from the example output to improve readability and conserve space.

 The owl icon indicates a tip, suggestion, or general note. For example, we'll let you know that PostgreSQL supports the use of all ISO standard time zone abbreviations in the section on time zones.

 The turkey icon indicates a warning or caution. For example, we'll warn you ahead of time that using the `DELETE` command without a `WHERE` clause can delete all of your data from a table.

Acknowledgments

Command Prompt would like to express our thanks to the following people: Andrew Brookins for his contributions and editing support, Michael Holloway for clutch editing, Corwin Light-Williams for his JDBC chapter, and of course, a chubby little Penguin named Tux. We would also like to take a moment to thank our families; it has been a long road and we appreciate your love and patience.

John would like to thank his parents for their lifelong support, and for purchasing him computer equipment in his formative years for better reasons than playing Wolfenstein 3D until 2:00 in the morning.

Joshua would like to thank God for providing a family with enough patience to tolerate the long hours needed to complete this book, and specifically his son, Joshua A, for being the coolest kid on the planet.

Last but not least, we would like to thank O'Reilly & Associates for their help in creating this book, and the PostgreSQL community for their technical assistance (particularly Tom Lane), and for providing such a great product.

Comments and Questions

We have tested and verified the information in this book to the best of our ability, but you may find that features have changed or that we have made mistakes. If so, please notify us by writing to:

O'Reilly & Associates
101 Morris Street
Sebastopol, CA 95472
(800) 998-9938 (in the U.S. or Canada)
(707) 829-0515 (international or local)
(707) 829-0104 (FAX)

You can also send messages electronically. To be put on the mailing list or request a catalog, send email to:

info@oreilly.com

To ask technical questions or comment on the book, send email to:

bookquestions@oreilly.com

There is a web page for this book, which lists errata, examples, and any additional information. You can access this page at:

http://www.oreilly.com/catalog/ppostgresql/

You may view a constantly developed version of this book at the authors website. The authors' website is available at:

http://www.commandprompt.com/ppbook/
http://www.postgresql.info/

I

Introduction & Installation

1

What Is PostgreSQL?

PostgreSQL is an Object-Relational Database Management System (ORDBMS) that has been developed in various forms since 1977. It began as a project named Ingres at the University of California at Berkeley. Ingres itself was later developed commercially by Relational Technologies/Ingres Corporation.

In 1986 another team led by Michael Stonebraker from Berkeley continued the development of the Ingres code to create an object-relational database system called Postgres. In 1996, due to a new open source effort and the enhanced functionality of the software, Postgres was renamed to PostgreSQL, after a brief stint as Postgres95. The PostgreSQL project is still under very active development worldwide from a team of open source developers and contributors.

PostgreSQL is widely considered to be the most advanced open source database system in the world. It provides many features (which are discussed in more detail in the section titled "PostgreSQL Feature Set") that are traditionally seen only in enterprise-caliber commercial products.

Open Source Free Version

PostgreSQL is an open source project. Open source by definition means that you can obtain the source code, use the program, and modify it freely without the confines of proprietary software. In the database world, open source means that you have honest access to benchmarking numbers and performance statistics, which companies such as Oracle prohibit. Open source also means that you are free to modify PostgreSQL to fit your particular needs.

However, there is a misconception that since open source software is free from distribution restrictions, it is always free of cost to your company. This is not necessarily the case. It is true that you can, without external cost, download and install open source software, but there will always be costs associated with the time and energy your company puts into support and research of the application. As such, if you do not have those resources to spend, there are several commercial vendors and consultants who deal specifically with PostgreSQL.

Commercial PostgreSQL Products

The Red Hat version of PostgreSQL is called Red Hat Database and is a very new product to the database market. Red Hat Database is based on the community-released open source version, PostgreSQL 7.1. Red Hat Database currently supports Linux only, preferably Red Hat Linux 7.1.

Open Source Versus Commercial Products

The open source version of PostgreSQL only includes the database-management system and the associated programming interfaces. The Red Hat version of PostgreSQL includes a graphical installer and limited support for the installation.

The main factor in deciding whether to use the open source version of PostgreSQL or a commercially packaged version should be your business requirements. If you have a knowledgeable on-site technical-support staff, the community version may do well for you. However, if you need installation, configuration, and management support, you may be better served by purchasing a commercial version of PostgreSQL.

If you prefer to do business with smaller consulting companies, we have compiled a modest list of professional companies providing support for PostgreSQL in the section titled "Commercial Support."

The Bottom Line

Marketing would suggest that a commercial version of PostgreSQL is somehow objectively superior to an open source version of PostgreSQL. In reality, this is not the case. When deciding what version of PostgreSQL you are going to run, you need only be aware of your own needs. For example, are you going to need installation support? Is a graphical installation important to you? If they are, then you should probably purchase a commercial version of PostgreSQL. However, if you or one of your staff are comfortable with compiling and configuring source code, the open source version could be more applicable to you.

There are two additional questions you may want to ask. Do you need printed documentation and are you willing to pay for PostgreSQL? The commercial distribution comes with printed documentation. However, if you are reading this book, we hope you won't need the additional documentation. The other question relates to cost. Red Hat Database is priced at $2,295.00.

The most important thing to remember when deciding on which version of Post-greSQL to use is this (from a perspective of general usage and feature availability): *there is no practical difference between the open source and the commercial versions.*

Commercial Support

Outside of Red Hat, there are many companies that provide consulting services to the PostgreSQL community. The following is a small list of consultants providing commercial support for PostgreSQL.

Command Prompt, Inc. (http://www.commandprompt.com/)
> Command Prompt, Inc. is a Linux managed-services and PostgreSQL-support company. They provide Linux and PostgreSQL support, including custom programming in C & C++, Java, PHP, Perl, and their own LXP application server for PostgreSQL.

> Command Prompt, Inc. is the author of this book.

Cybertec Geschwinde & Schvnig OEG (http://postgres.cybertec.at/)
> Cybertec provides training courses, support, consulting, and cost-effective high-end systems. Cybertec services the German-speaking region (Austria, Germany, and Switzerland).

dbExperts (http://www.dbexperts.com.br/)
> dbExperts offers training courses, specialized support for development, and commercial products for PostgreSQL. dbExperts is located in Brazil and provides services in the Portuguese language.

PostgreSQL, Inc. (http://www.pgsql.com/)
> PostgreSQL, Inc. offers support for PostgreSQL, database hosting, and promotional materials.

Software Research Associates (http://osb.sra.co.jp/)
> Software Research Associates offers a range of services to aid customers with open source software-based systems. Support from this company is also available in Japanese.

Community Support

The PostgreSQL community provides active support to users of PostgreSQL via a number of mailing lists. There are several user mailing lists to which you can subscribe, segregated by topic (e.g., *pgsql-general, pgsql-hackers*, etc.). The mailing lists for PostgreSQL users are quite thorough, covering everything from general discussion to support on developing with PostgreSQL programming interfaces. For a complete list of mailing lists with associated descriptions, please visit the Post-greSQL website at *http://www.postgresql.org*.

PostgreSQL Feature Set

As stated previously in this chapter, PostgreSQL is widely considered the most advanced open source database in the world. PostgreSQL provides a wealth of features that are usually only found in commercial databases such as DB2 or Oracle. The following is a brief listing of some of these core features, as of PostgreSQL 7.1.x.

Object-Relational DBMS

PostgreSQL approaches data with an object-relational model, and is capable of handling complex routines and rules. Examples of its advanced functionality are declarative SQL queries, multi-version concurrency control, multi-user support, transactions, query optimization, inheritance, and arrays.

Highly extensible

PostgreSQL supports user-defined operators, functions, access methods, and data types.

Comprehensive SQL support

PostgreSQL supports the core SQL99 specification and includes advanced features such as SQL92 joins.

Referential integrity

PostgreSQL supports referential integrity, which is used to insure the validity of a database's data.

Flexible API

The flexibility of the PostgreSQL API has allowed vendors to provide development support easily for the PostgreSQL RDBMS. These interfaces include Object Pascal, Python, Perl, PHP, ODBC, Java/JDBC, Ruby, TCL, C/C++, and Pike.

Procedural languages

PostgreSQL has support for internal procedural languages, including a native language called PL/pgSQL. This language is comparable to the Oracle procedural language, PL/SQL. Another advantage to PostgreSQL is its ability to use Perl, Python, or TCL as an embedded procedural language.

MVCC

MVCC, or Multi-Version Concurrency Control, is the technology that PostgreSQL uses to avoid unnecessary *locking*. If you have ever used another SQL capable DBMS, such as MySQL or Access, you have probably noticed that there are times when a reader has to wait for access to information in the database. The waiting is caused by people who are writing to the database. In short, the reader is blocked by writers who are updating records.

By using MVCC, PostgreSQL avoids this problem entirely. MVCC is considered better than row-level locking because a reader is never blocked by a writer. Instead, PostgreSQL keeps track of all transactions performed by the database users. PostgreSQL is then able to manage the records without causing people to wait for records to become available.

Client/server

PostgreSQL uses a process-per-user client/server architecture. This is similar to the Apache 1.3.x method of handling processes. There is a master process that forks to provide additional connections for each client attempting to connect to PostgreSQL.

Write Ahead Logging (WAL)

The PostgreSQL feature known as *Write Ahead Logging* increases the reliability of the database by logging changes *before* they are written to the database. This ensures that, in the unlikely occurrence of a database crash, there will be a record of transactions from which to restore. This can be greatly beneficial in the event of a crash, as any changes that were not written to the database can be recovered by using the data that was previously logged. Once the system is restored, a user can then continue to work from the point that they were at before the crash occurred.

Where to Proceed from Here

Now that your introduction to PostgreSQL is complete, there are several places to proceed. We have provided the following list as a synopsis of the rest of the book. This is a guideline, so to speak, of what you need to read next.

- If you would like to install PostgreSQL 7.1.x at this time, then you may continue to Chapter 2, *Installing PostgreSQL*.

- If you are new to the SQL language and database queries, then you may continue to Chapter 3, *Understanding SQL*. Note that although many of the concepts introduced in Chapter 3 are of a general nature, some of the techniques and concepts presented are specific to PostgreSQL, and should not be overlooked if you want a comprehensive understanding of the software.

- If you are already familiar with the SQL language and statement structure, you may be more interested in Chapter 4, *Using SQL with PostgreSQL*, Chapter 5, *Operators and Functions*, or Chapter 7, *Advanced Features*.

- If you have a working knowledge of PostgreSQL as an end user and you would like to begin setting up the database server, database users and groups, and authentication, then you may skip to Part 3, *Administrating PostgreSQL*. This part was written to aid system administrators in initializing, configuring, and managing newly installed or existing PostgreSQL databases.

- If you are familiar with PostgreSQL as a database-management system and would like to move directly into technical programming concepts and techniques, read through Part 4, *PostgreSQL Programming*. This part of the book contains documentation on PL/pgSQL, the native PostgreSQL procedural language, as well as information and examples on the JDBC interface and the LXP web-based application server.

2

Installing PostgreSQL

This chapter focuses on the requirements and steps involved in installing and configuring PostgreSQL. Many of the PostgreSQL capabilities are not enabled, by default. For example, support for the TCL language is a feature that must be explicitly requested during compile-time. As there are many other features that are not configured by default, we will cover the various flags and options you may use to enable them when compiling PostgreSQL. It is important that you carefully read through all the steps in this process before beginning installation.

This chapter will walk you through the installation steps on a Linux/Unix-style platform. Our installation platform is Linux, but these instructions should be compatible with most current Unix platforms.

 Although PostgreSQL is capable of running on a Win32 platform, this book does not cover installation on Windows. The Win32 version of PostgreSQL requires the Cygwin environment and will not operate independently within Win32. Although Cygwin can be useful in many situations, the use of PostgreSQL in a Cygwin environment is not recommended.

Preparing for Installation

The installation of PostgreSQL is not difficult. However, there are some software requirements that you will need for the PostgreSQL compilation. All of the requirements—outside of the PostgreSQL source code—are GNU tools. If you are running Linux, there is a good chance that the tools are already installed. If you are running a BSD derivative, such as FreeBSD or MacOS X, you may have to download the tools.

If you find that you are missing any of the required components, first check your vendor's web site for the packages; otherwise, you may download them from *http://www.gnu.org*. It is also essential that you have enough disk space available to unpack and compile the source code on the filesystem to which you install. Disk-space requirements are discussed in the section titled "Disk Space."

Required Software Packages

You will most likely have some of the required software packages already installed on your system, if not all of them. These packages are as follows:

GNU make

GNU make is commonly known as *gmake* on non-GNU based systems, but is normally referred to as just *make* on GNU-based systems such as Linux. For consistency, we will refer to it as *gmake* throughout the majority of this book.

We recommend that you use at least *gmake* version 3.76.1 or higher when compiling PostgreSQL. To verify the existence and correct version number of *gmake*, type the command shown in Example 2-1.

Example 2-1: Verifying GNU make

```
$ gmake --version

GNU Make version 3.79.1, by Richard Stallman and Roland McGrath.
Built for i386-redhat-linux-gnu
Copyright (C) 1988, 89, 90, 91, 92, 93, 94, 95, 96, 97, 98, 99, 2000
        Free Software Foundation, Inc.
This is free software; see the source for copying conditions.
There is NO warranty; not even for MERCHANTABILITY or FITNESS FOR A
PARTICULAR PURPOSE.

Report bugs to <bug-make@gnu.org>.
```

ISO/ANSI C Compiler

There are numerous ISO/ANSI C compilers available. The recommended compiler for PostgreSQL is the GNU C Compiler, although PostgreSQL has been known to build with compilers from different vendors. At the time of this writing, the most commonly distributed versions of GCC are 2.95 and 2.96 (Red-Hat Linux 7.x and Mandrake Linux 8.x). If you do not currently have GCC installed, you can download it by visiting the GNU website at *http://gcc.gnu.org*.

To check for the existence and version of GCC, enter the command shown in Example 2-2.

Example 2-2: Verifying GCC

```
$ gcc --version
2.95.3
```

GNU zip and tar

GNU zip is also called *gzip*. GNU zip is a compression utility that can compress as well as decompress files. All compressed, or *zipped*, files made with *gzip* have a *.gz* extension. You can test for the existence of the *gzip* program with the *gzip --version* command.

In addition to *gzip*, you will require a copy of *tar*, a utility used to group several files and directories into a single archive, as well as to unpack these archives onto the filesystem. An archived *tar* output file will typically contain a *.tar* extension. Files that are both archived by *tar* and compressed by *gzip* often have a *.tar.gz* compound extension, as is the case with the included PostgreSQL source distribution. You can test for *tar* with the *tar --version* command.

Example 2-3: Verifying gzip and tar

```
$ gzip --version
gzip 1.3
(1999-12-21)
Copyright 1999 Free Software Foundation
Copyright 1992-1993 Jean-loup Gailly
This program comes with ABSOLUTELY NO WARRANTY.
You may redistribute copies of this program
under the terms of the GNU General Public License.
For more information about these matters, see the file named COPYING.
Compilation options:
DIRENT UTIME STDC_HEADERS HAVE_UNISTD_H HAVE_MEMORY_H HAVE_STRING_H
Written by Jean-loup Gailly.

$ tar --version
tar (GNU tar) 1.13.17
Copyright 2000 Free Software Foundation, Inc.
This program comes with NO WARRANTY, to the extent permitted by law.
You may redistribute it under the terms of the GNU General Public License;
see the file named COPYING for details.
Written by John Gilmore and Jay Fenlason.
```

Optional Packages

The following are some optional packages that you may want to have installed:

GNU Readline library

The GNU Readline library greatly increases the usability of *psql*, the standard PostgreSQL command-line console client. It adds all of the standard functionality of the GNU Readline library to the *psql* command line, such as being able to easily modify, edit, and retrieve command-history information with the arrow keys and the ability to search the command history (also known as a *reverse-i-search*). If the Readline library is already installed on your system, the configuration process should automatically compile readline support with *psql*.

 You may not need this package if you have NetBSD, as NetBSD has a *libedit* library, which provides Readline compatibility.

OpenSSL

OpenSSL is an Open Source implementation of the SSL/TLS protocols. OpenSSL is commonly used with utilities such as OpenSSH and Apache-SSL. PostgreSQL can make use of OpenSSL for encrypted connectivity between the *psql* client application and the PostgreSQL backend. You may also want to consider OpenSSL if you wish to use Stunnel. More information on OpenSSL is located at *http://www.openssl.org*. Installing and configuring Stunnel for use with PostgreSQL is discussed in Chapter 8, *Authentication and Encryption*.

Tcl/Tk

Tcl/Tk is a combination programming language and graphical toolkit. Although we don't cover the use of Tcl with PostgreSQL, we do cover the use of PgAccess, which is written in Tcl. If you wish to utilize the PgAccess application you will need to install the Tcl/Tk software. The website for Tcl/Tk is *http://tcl.activestate.com*.

Ant/JDK

The JDK is the Java Development Kit. It is required for Java development; hence, it is required by PostgreSQL if you wish to enable JDBC support. *Ant* is a Java-based build tool (somewhat like *gmake*) that is also required for JDBC support. The JDK can be downloaded from *http://java.sun.com/j2se/index.html*, and *Ant* can be downloaded from *http://jakarta.apache.org/ant/index.html*.

Disk Space

PostgreSQL does not require the extensive use of disk resources. In fact, in comparison to products such as Oracle, PostgreSQL could be considered fat free. However, PostgreSQL is a database, and as with any database, the requirements will grow as you continue to use PostgreSQL.

On an average Linux machine, you will need approximately 50 MB of hard-drive space to unpack the source and another 60 MB of hard drive space to compile the source. If you choose to run the regression tests, you will need an additional 30 MB. Depending on the configuration options you choose, PostgreSQL can take anywhere from 8 to 15 MB of hard drive space once installed.

 Remember that PostgreSQL's space requirements will grow as you use the system! Be sure to plan ahead for the amount of data you will be storing.

Trying to install on a system lacking in disk space is potentially dangerous! Before installing PostgreSQL, we recommend that you check your filesystem to be sure you have enough disk space in your intended installation partition (e.g., */usr/local*). If you have a GNU-based system, the *df* command should be at your disposal. Example 2-4 checks for free disk space, reported in 1k blocks.

Example 2-4: Verifying disk space

```
$ df -k
Filesystem       1k-blocks      Used Available Use% Mounted on
/dev/hda1         2355984     932660   1303644  42% /
/dev/hdb1         4142800    2133160   1799192  54% /home
/dev/hda6         1541680     272540   1190828  19% /usr/local
```

10 Steps to Installing PostgreSQL

PostgreSQL is included on the CD distributed with this book, but you may want to visit the PostgreSQL website to see if there is a newer version available. Many FTP sites make the source files for PostgreSQL available for download; a complete list of FTP mirrors can be found at *http://www.postgresql.org*.

Once you have connected to a PostgreSQL FTP mirror, you will see the stable releases located within a directory beginning with *v* followed by a version (such as *v7.1.3/*). There should also be a symbolic link to the most recent stable release's directory called *latest/*.

Within this sub-directory is a list of package files. The complete PostgreSQL installation package is named *postgresql-[version].tar.gz* and should be the largest file in the list. The following sub-packages are also made available for download, and may be installed in any combination (though at least *base* is required):

postgresql-base-[version].tar.gz
> The *base* package contains the bare minimum of source code required to build and run PostgreSQL.

postgresql-docs-[version].tar.gz
> The *docs* package contains the PostgreSQL documentation in HTML format. Note that the PostgreSQL *man* pages are automatically installed with the *base* package.

postgresql-opt-[version].tar.gz
> The *opt* package contains several optional extensions to PostgreSQL, such as the interfaces for C++ (*libpq++*), JDBC, ODBC, Perl, Python, and Tcl. It also contains the source required for multibyte support.

postgresql-test-[version].tar.gz
> The *test* package contains the regression test suite. This package is required to run regression tests after compiling PostgreSQL.

Step 1: Creating the "postgres" User

Create a Unix user account to own and manage the PostgreSQL database files. Typically, this user is named *postgres*, but it can be named anything that you choose. For consistency throughout the book, the user *postgres* is considered the PostgreSQL root or superuser.

You will need to have root privileges to create the PostgreSQL superuser. On a Linux machine, you can use the command shown in Example 2-5 to add the *postgres* user.

Example 2-5: Adding the postgres user

```
$ su - -c "useradd postgres"
```

> Do not try to use the *root* user as the PostgreSQL superuser. Doing so presents a large security hole.

Step 2: Installing the PostgreSQL Source Package

Once you have acquired the source for PostgreSQL, you should copy the PostgreSQL source package to a temporary compilation directory. This directory will be the path where you install and configure PostgreSQL. Within this path, you will extract the contents from the *tar.gz* file and proceed with installation.

Bear in mind that this will not be the location of the installed database files. This is a temporary location for configuration and compilation of the source package itself. If you have downloaded the PostgreSQL package from the Internet, it is probably not saved in your intended compilation directory (unless you explicitly chose to save there). A common convention for building source on Unix and Linux machines is to build within the */usr/local/src* path. You will most likely need root privileges to access this path. As such, the remaining examples in this chapter will involve the *root* user until otherwise specified.

If you are a user of a commercial Linux distribution, we strongly suggest that you verify whether or not you have PostgreSQL already installed. On RPM-based systems, such as SuSe, Mandrake, or Red-Hat, this can be done by using the following command: *rpm -qa | grep -i postgres*. If you do have PostgreSQL installed, there is a good chance that it is outdated. You will want to download and install the latest version of PostgreSQL available. An RPM installation of PostgreSQL will sometimes install scripts and programs such as *postmaster* and *psql* into globally accessible directories. This can cause conflicts with source-built versions, so before installing a new version, be sure to remove the RPM by using the *rpm -e <package name>* command.

To unpack PostgreSQL source code on a Linux system, first move (or copy, from the CD) the compressed source file into */usr/local/src* (most people move their source files here to keep them separate from their home directories and/or other locations they may keep downloaded files). After moving it to the filesystem location where you wish to unpack it, use *tar* to unpack the source files. The commands to perform these actions are shown in Example 2-6.

Example 2-6: Unpacking the PostgreSQL source package

```
[root@host root]# cp postgresql-7.1.3.tar.gz /usr/local/src
[root@host root]# cd /usr/local/src
[root@host src]# tar -xzvf postgresql-7.1.3.tar.gz
postgresql-7.1.3/
postgresql-7.1.3/ChangeLogs/
postgresql-7.1.3/ChangeLogs/ChangeLog-7.1-7.1.1
postgresql-7.1.3/ChangeLogs/ChangeLog-7.1RC1-to-7.1RC2
postgresql-7.1.3/ChangeLogs/ChangeLog-7.1RC2-to-7.1RC3
postgresql-7.1.3/ChangeLogs/ChangeLog-7.1RC3-to-7.1rc4
postgresql-7.1.3/ChangeLogs/ChangeLog-7.1beta1-to-7.1beta3
postgresql-7.1.3/ChangeLogs/ChangeLog-7.1beta3-to-7.1beta4
postgresql-7.1.3/ChangeLogs/ChangeLog-7.1beta4-to-7.1beta5
postgresql-7.1.3/ChangeLogs/ChangeLog-7.1beta5-to-7.1beta6
postgresql-7.1.3/ChangeLogs/ChangeLog-7.1beta6-7.1RC1
postgresql-7.1.3/ChangeLogs/ChangeLog-7.1rc4-7.1
postgresql-7.1.3/ChangeLogs/ChangeLog-7.1.1-7.1.2
postgresql-7.1.3/ChangeLogs/ChangeLog-7.1.2-7.1.3
postgresql-7.1.3/COPYRIGHT
[...]
[root@host root]# chown -R postgres.postgres postgresql-7.1.3
```

Notice the last command used in Example 2-6. The command is *chown -R postgres.postgres postgresql-7.1.3*. This command grants the ownership of the PostgreSQL source directory tree to *postgres*, which in turn enables you to compile PostgreSQL as the *postgres* user. Once the extraction and ownership change has completed, you can switch to the *postgres* user to compile PostgreSQL, resulting in all compiled files automatically being owned by *postgres*.

For reference purposes, the following list is a description of the *tar* options used to extract the PostgreSQL source distribution:

x (extract)

> *tar* will extract from the passed filename (as opposed to creating a new file).

v (verbose)

> *tar* will print verbose output as files are extracted. You may omit this flag if you do not wish to see each file as it is unpacked.

z (zipped)

> *tar* will use *gunzip* to decompress the source. This option assumes that you are using the GNU tools; other versions of *tar* may not support the *z* flag. In the event that you are not using the GNU tools, you will need to manually unzip the file using *gunzip* before you can unpack it with *tar*.

f (file)

> *tar* will use the filename following the *f* parameter to determine from which file to extract. In our examples, this file is *postgresql-7.1.3.tar.gz*.

After you have completed the extraction of the files, switch to the *postgres* user and change into the newly created directory (e.g., */usr/local/src/postgres-7.1.3*). The remaining installation steps will take place in that directory.

Step 3: Configuring the Source Tree

Before compilation, you must configure the source, and specify installation options specific to your needs. This is done with the *configure* script.

The *configure* script is also used to check for software dependencies that are required to compile PostgreSQL. As *configure* checks for dependencies, it will create the necessary files for use with the *gmake* command.

To use the default installation script, issue the following command: *./configure*. To specify options that will enable certain non-default features, append the option to the *./configure* command. For a list of all the available configuration options, use *./configure --help*

There is a good chance that the default source configuration that *configure* uses will not be the setup you require. For a well-rounded PostgreSQL installation, we recommend you use at least the following options:

--with-CXX

Allows you to build C++ programs for use with PostgreSQL by building the *libpq++* library.

--enable-odbc

Allows you to connect to PostgreSQL with programs that have a compatible ODBC driver (such as Microsoft Access).

--enable-multibyte

Allows multibyte characters to be used, such as non-English language characters (e.g., Kanji).

--with-maxbackends=NUMBER

Sets NUMBER as the maximum number of allowed connections (32, by default).

You can also specify anything from the following complete list of configuration options:

--prefix=PREFIX

Specifies that files should be installed under the directory provided with PREFIX, instead of the default installation directory (*/usr/local/pgsql*).

--exec-prefix=EXEC-PREFIX

Specifies that architecture-dependent executable files should be installed under the directory supplied with EXEC-PREFIX.

--bindir=DIRECTORY

Specifies that user executable files (such as *psql*) should be installed into the directory supplied with DIRECTORY.

--datadir=DIRECTORY

Specifies that the database should install data files used by PostgreSQL's program suite (as well as sample configuration files) into the directory supplied with DIRECTORY. Note that the directory here is *not* used as an alternate database data directory; it is merely the directory where read-only files used by the program suite are installed.

--sysconfdir=DIRECTORY

Specifies that system configuration files should be installed into the directory supplied with DIRECTORY. By default, these are put into the *etc* folder within the specified base installation directory.

--libdir=DIRECTORY

Specifies that library files should be stored in the directory supplied with DIRECTORY. If you are running Linux, this directory should also be entered into the *ld.so.conf* file.

--includedir=DIRECTORY

Specifies that C and C++ header files should be installed into the directory supplied with *DIRECTORY*. By default, include files are stored in the *include* folder within the base installation directory.

--docdir=DIRECTORY

Specifies that documentation files should be installed into the directory supplied with *DIRECTORY*. This does not include PostgreSQL's *man* files.

--mandir=DIRECTORY

Specifies that *man* files should be installed into the directory supplied with *DIRECTORY*.

--with-includes=DIRECTORIES

Specifies that the colon-separated list of directories supplied with *DIRECTORIES* should be searched with the purpose of locating additional header files.

--with-libraries=DIRECTORIES

Specifies that the colon-separated list of directories supplied with *DIRECTORIES* should be searched with the purpose of locating additional libraries.

--enable-locale

Enables locale support. The use of locale support will incur a performance penalty and should only be enabled if you are are not in an English-speaking location.

--enable-recode

Enables the use of the *recode* translation library.

--enable-multibyte

Enables multibyte encoding. Enabling this option allows the support of non-ASCII characters; this is most useful with languages such as Japanese, Korean, and Chinese, which all use nonstandard character encoding.

--with-pgport=NUMBER

Specifies that the the port number supplied with *NUMBER* should be used as the default port by PostgreSQL. This can be changed when starting the *postmaster* application.

--with-maxbackends=NUMBER

Sets *NUMBER* as the maximum number of allowed connections (32, by default).

--with-CXX

Specifies that the C++ interface library should be compiled during installation. You will need this library if you plan to develop C++ applications for use with PostgreSQL.

--with-perl

Specifies that the PostgreSQL Perl interface module should be compiled during installation. This module will need to be installed in a directory that is usually owned by *root*, so you will most likely need to be logged in as the *root* user to complete installation with this option chosen. This configuration option is only required if you plan to use the pl/Perl procedural language.

--with-python

Specifies that the PostgreSQL Python interface module should be compiled during installation. As with the *--with-perl* option, you will most likely need to log in as the *root* user to complete installation with this option. This option is only required if you plan to use the pl/Python procedural language.

--with-tcl

Specifies that Tcl support should be included in the installation. This option will install PostgreSQL applications and extensions that require Tcl, such as *pgaccess* (a popular graphical database client) and the pl/Tcl procedural language.

--without-tk

Specifies that Tcl support should be compiled without additional support for Tk, the graphical application tool kit. Using this option with the *--with-tcl* option specifies that PostgreSQL Tcl applications that require Tk (such as *pgtksh* and *pgaccess*) should not be installed.

--with-tclconfig=DIRECTORY, --with-tkconfig=DIRECTORY

Specifies that the Tcl or Tk (depending on the option) configuration file (either *tclConfig.sh* or *tkConfig.sh*) is located in the directory supplied with DIRECTORY, instead of the default directory. These two files are installed by Tcl/Tk, and the information within them is required by PostgreSQL's Tcl/Tk interface modules.

--enable-odbc

Enables support for ODBC.

--with-odbcinst=DIRECTORY

Specifies that the ODBC driver should look in the directory supplied with DIRECTORY for its *odbcinst.ini* file. By default, this file is held in the *etc* directory, which is located in the installation directory.

--with-krb4=DIRECTORY, --with-krb5=DIRECTORY

Enables support for the Kerberos authentication system. The use of Kerberos is not covered in this book.

--with-krb-srvnam=NAME

> Specifies the name of the Kerberos service principal. By default, *postgres* is set as the service principal name.

--with-openssl=DIRECTORY

> Enables the use of SSL to support encrypted database connections. To build support for SSL, OpenSSL must be configured correctly and installed in the directory supplied with *DIRECTORY*. This option is required if you plan on using the *stunnel* tool.

--with-java

> Enables Java/JDBC support. The *Ant* and JDK packages are required for Post-greSQL to compile correctly with this feature enabled.

--enable-syslog

> Enables the use of the *syslog* daemon for logging. You will need to specify that you wish to use *syslog* for logging at runtime if you wish to use it.

--enable-debug

> Enables the compilation of all PostgreSQL libraries and applications with debugging symbols. This will slow down performance and increase binary file size, but the debugging symbols are useful for developers to help diagnose bugs and problems that can be encountered with PostgreSQL.

--enable-cassert

> Enables assertion checking. This feature slows down performance and should be used only during development of the PostgreSQL system itself.

If you compile PostgreSQL and find that you are missing a feature, you can return to this step, reconfigure, and continue with the subsequent steps to build and install PostgreSQL. If you choose to come back to this step and reconfigure the PostgreSQL source before installing, be sure to use the *gmake clean* command from the top-level directory of the source tree (usually, */usr/local/src/postgresql-[version]*). This will remove any leftover object files and partially compiled files.

Step 4: Compiling the Source

After using the *configure* command, you may begin compiling the PostgreSQL source by entering the *gmake* command.

> On Linux machines, you should be able to use *make* instead of *gmake*. BSD users should use *gnumake*.

Example 2-7: Compiling the source with GNU make

```
[postgres@host postgresql-7.1.3]# gmake
gmake -C doc all
gmake[1]: Entering directory /usr/local/src/postgresql-7.1.3/doc'
gmake[1]: Nothing to be done for all'.
gmake[1]: Leaving directory /usr/local/src/postgresql-7.1.3/doc'
gmake -C src all
gmake[1]: Entering directory /usr/local/src/postgresql-7.1.3/src'
gmake -C backend all
gmake[2]: Entering directory /usr/local/src/postgresql-7.1.3/src/backend'
gmake -C utils fmgroids.h
gmake[3]: Entering directory /usr/local/src/postgresql-7.1.3/src/backend/utils'
[...]
```

At this point, depending on the speed of your machine, you may want to get some coffee because the PostgreSQL compilation could take 10 minutes, an hour, or even more. After the compilation has finished, the following message should appear:

```
All of PostgreSQL is successfully made.  Ready to install.
```

Step 5: Regression Testing

Regression tests are an optional but recommended step. The regression tests help verify that PostgreSQL will run as expected after you have compiled the source. The tests check tasks such as standard SQL operations, as well as extended capabilities of PostgreSQL. The regression tests can point out possible (but not necessarily probable) problems which may arise when running PostgreSQL.

If you decide you would like to run the regression tests, do so by using the following command: *gmake check*, as shown in Example 2-8.

Example 2-8: Making regression tests

```
[postgres@host postgresql-7.1.3]# gmake check
gmake -C doc all
gmake[1]: Entering directory /usr/local/src/postgresql-7.1.3/doc'
gmake[1]: Nothing to be done for all'.
gmake[1]: Leaving directory /usr/local/src/postgresql-7.1.3/doc'
[...]
```

The *gmake check* command will build a test installation of PostgreSQL within the source tree, and display a list of all the checks it is running. As each test completes, the success or failure will be reported. Items that fail the check will have a failed message printed, rather than the successful ok message. If any checks fail, *gmake check* will display output similar to that found in Example 2-9, though the number of tests failed may be higher on your system than the number in the example.

Example 2-9: Regression check output

```
========================
1 of 76 tests failed.
========================

The differences that caused some tests to fail can be viewed in the
file ./regression.diffs'. A copy of the test summary that you see
above is saved in the file ./regression.out'.
```

The files referenced in Example 2-9 (*regression.diffs* and *regression.out*) are placed within the source tree at *src/test/regress*. If the source tree is located in */usr/local/src*, the full path to the directory files would be */usr/local/src/postgresql-[version]/src/test/regress*.

The regression tests will not always pick up every possible error. This can be due to inconsistencies in locale settings (such as time zone support), or hardware-specific issues (such as floating-point results). As with any application, be sure to perform your own requirements testing while developing with PostgreSQL.

You cannot run the regression tests as the *root* user. Be sure to run *gmake check* as the *postgres* user.

Step 6: Installing Compiled Programs and Libraries

After you have configured and compiled the PostgreSQL source code, it is time to install the compiled libraries, binaries, and data files into a more appropriate home on the system. If you are upgrading from a previous version of PostgreSQL, be sure to back up your database before beginning this step. Information on performing PostgreSQL database backups can be found in Chapter 9, *Database Management*.

Installation of the compiled files is accomplished with the commands demonstrated in Example 2-10. When executed in the manner shown in Example 2-10, the *su* command temporarily logs you in as the *root* user to execute the required commands. You must have the *root* password to execute both of the commands shown in Example 2-10.

If you specified a non-default installation directory in Step 3, use the directory you specified instead of */usr/local/pgsql*.

Example 2-10: The gmake install command

```
$ su -c "gmake install"
Password:
gmake -C doc install
gmake[1]: Entering directory /usr/local/src/postgresql-7.1.3/doc'
mkdir /usr/local/pgsql
mkdir /usr/local/pgsql/man
mkdir /usr/local/pgsql/doc
mkdir /usr/local/pgsql/doc/html
[...]
$ su -c "chown -R postgres.postgres /usr/local/pgsql"
Password:
```

The *su -c "gmake install"* command will install the freshly compiled source either into the directory structure you chose in Step 3 with the *--prefix* configuration option, or, if this was left unspecified, into the default directory of */usr/local/pgsql*. The use of the *su -c "chown -R postgres.postgres /usr/local/pgsql"* command will ensure that the *postgres* user owns the PostgreSQL installation directories. Using the *su -c* command lets you save a step by only logging you in as the *root* user for the duration of the command's execution.

If you chose to configure the PostgreSQL source with the Perl or Python interface, but did not have root access, you can still install the interfaces manually. Use the commands demonstrated in Example 2-11 to install the Perl and Python modules manually.

Example 2-11: Installing Perl and Python modules manually

```
$ su -c "gmake -C src/interfaces/perl5 install"
Password:
Password:
gmake: Entering directory /usr/local/src/postgresql-7.1.3/src/interfaces/perl5'
perl Makefile.PL
Checking if your kit is complete...
Looks good
Writing Makefile for Pg
gmake -f Makefile clean
[...]
$ su -c "gmake -C src/interfaces/python install"
Password:
gmake: Entering directory /usr/local/src/postgresql-7.1.3/src/interfaces/python'
sed -e 's,@libpq_srcdir@,../../../src/interfaces/libpq,g' \
    -e 's,@libpq_builddir@,../../../src/interfaces/libpq,g' \
    -e 's%@EXTRA_LIBS@% -lz -lcrypt -lresolv -lnsl -ldl -lm -lbsd -lreadline -ltermcap %g' \
    -e 's%@INCLUDES@%-I../../../src/include%g' \
[...]
```

You may also want to install the header files for PostgreSQL. This is important, because the default installation will only install the header files for client application development. If you are going to be using some of PostgreSQL's advanced functionality, such as user-defined functions or developing applications in C that use the *libpq* library, you will need the header files. To install the required header files, perform the commands demonstrated in Example 2-12.

Example 2-12: Installing all headers

```
$ su -c "gmake install-all-headers"
Password:
gmake -C src install-all-headers
gmake[1]: Entering directory /usr/local/src/postgresql-7.1.3/src'
gmake -C include install-all-headers
[...]
```

Step 7: Setting Environment Variables

The use of the PostgreSQL environment variables is not required. However, they are helpful when performing tasks within PostgreSQL, including starting and shutting down the *postmaster* processes. The environment variables that should be set are for the *man* pages and the *bin* directory. You can do so by adding the following statements into the */etc/profile* file. This should work for any *sh*-based shell, including bash and ksh.

```
PATH=$PATH:/usr/local/pgsql/bin
MANPATH=$MANPATH:/usr/local/pgsql/man
export PATH MANPATH
```

 You must login to the system *after* the */etc/profile* file has had environment variables added to it in order for your shell to utilize them.

Depending on how your system handles shared libraries, you may need to inform the operating system of where your PostgreSQL shared libraries are located. Systems such as Linux, FreeBSD, NetBSD, OpenBSD, Irix, HP/UX, and Solaris will most likely not need to do this.

In a default installation, shared libraries will be located in */usr/local/pgsql/lib* (this may be different, depending on whether you changed it with the - -*prefix* configuration option). One of the most common ways to accomplish this is to set the LD_LIBRARY_PATH environment variable to */usr/local/pgsql/lib*. See Example 2-13 for an example of doing this in Bourne-style shells and Example 2-14 for an example of doing this in *csh* and *tcsh*.

Example 2-13: Setting LD_LIBRARY_PATH in a bash shell

```
$ LD_LIBRARY_PATH=/usr/local/pgsql/lib
$ export LD_LIBRARY_PATH
```

Example 2-14: Setting LD_LIBRARY_PATH in csh and tcsh

```
$ setenv LD_LIBRARY_PATH /usr/local/pgsql/lib
```

Step 8: Initializing and Starting PostgreSQL

If you are logged in as the *root* user, instead of using the *su -c* command in the previous steps, you will now need to login as the *postgres* user you added in step 1. Once you are logged in as the *postgres* user, issue the command shown in Example 2-15.

Example 2-15: Initializing the database

```
$ /usr/local/pgsql/bin/initdb -D /usr/local/pgsql/data
```

The *-D* option in the previous command is the location where the data will be stored. This location can also be set with the PGDATA environment variable. If you have set PGDATA, the *-D* option is unnecessary. If you would like to use a different directory to hold these data files, make sure the *postgres* user account can write to that directory. When you execute *initdb* you will see something similar to what is shown in Example 2-16.

Example 2-16: Output from initdb

```
$ /usr/local/pgsql/bin/initdb -D /usr/local/pgsql/data
This database system will be initialized with username "postgres."
This user will own all the data files and must also own the server process.

Creating directory /usr/local/pgsql/data
Creating directory /usr/local/pgsql/data/base
Creating directory /usr/local/pgsql/data/global
Creating directory /usr/local/pgsql/data/pg_xlog
Creating template1 database in /usr/local/pgsql/data/base/1
DEBUG:  database system was shut down at 2001-08-24 16:36:35 PDT
DEBUG:  CheckPoint record at (0, 8)
DEBUG:  Redo record at (0, 8); Undo record at (0, 8); Shutdown TRUE
DEBUG:  NextTransactionId: 514; NextOid: 16384
DEBUG:  database system is in production state
Creating global relations in /usr/local/pgsql/data/global
DEBUG:  database system was shut down at 2001-08-24 16:36:38 PDT
DEBUG:  CheckPoint record at (0, 108)
DEBUG:  Redo record at (0, 108); Undo record at (0, 0); Shutdown TRUE
DEBUG:  NextTransactionId: 514; NextOid: 17199
DEBUG:  database system is in production state
Initializing pg_shadow.
Enabling unlimited row width for system tables.
Creating system views.
```

Example 2-16: Output from initdb (continued)

```
Loading pg_description.
Setting lastsysoid.
Vacuuming database.
Copying template1 to template0.

Success. You can now start the database server using:

/usr/local/pgsql/bin/postmaster -D /usr/local/pgsql/data
or
/usr/local/pgsql/bin/pg_ctl -D /usr/local/pgsql/data -l logfile start
```

 You can indicate that PostgreSQL should use a different data directory by specifying the directory location with the *-D* option. This
path must be initialized through *initdb*.

When the *initdb* command has completed, it will provide you with information on
starting the PostgreSQL server. The first command displayed will start *postmaster* in
the foreground. After entering the command as it is shown in Example 2-17, the
prompt will be inaccessible until you press CTRL-C on the keyboard to shut down
the *postmaster* process.

Example 2-17: Running postmaster in the foreground

```
$ /usr/local/pgsql/bin/postmaster -D /usr/local/pgsql/data
DEBUG:   database system was shut down at 2001-10-12 23:11:00 PST
DEBUG:   CheckPoint record at (0, 1522064)
DEBUG:   Redo record at (0, 1522064); Undo record at (0, 0); Shutdown TRUE
DEBUG:   NextTransactionId: 615; NextOid: 18720
DEBUG:   database system is in production state
```

Starting PostgreSQL in the foreground is not normally required. We suggest the use
of the second command displayed. The second command will start *postmaster* in
the background. It uses *pg_ctl* to start the postmaster service, as shown in Example
2-18.

Example 2-18: Running postmaster in the background

```
$ /usr/local/pgsql/bin/pg_ctl -D /usr/local/pgsql/data -l /tmp/pgsql.log start
postmaster successfully started
```

The major difference between the first command and the second command is that
the second runs *postmaster* in the background, as well as redirects any debugging
information to */tmp/pgsql.log*. For normal operation, it is generally better to run
postmaster in the background, with logging enabled.

The *pg_ctl* application can be used to start and stop the PostgreSQL server. See Chapter 9 for more on this command.

Step 9: Configuring the PostgreSQL SysV Script

The SysV script will allow the graceful control of the PostgreSQL database through the use of the SysV runlevel system. The SysV script can be used for starting, stopping, and status-checking of PostgreSQL. It is known to work with most Red Hat based versions of Linux, including Mandrake; however, it should work with other SysV systems (e.g., UnixWare, Solaris, etc.) with little modification. The script is named *linux*. To use it, you will first need to copy the *linux* script to your *init.d* directory. You may require root access to do this.

First, change to the directory where you unpacked the PostgreSQL source. In our case, the path to that directory is */usr/local/src/postgresql-7.1.3/*. Then, issue a *cp* command to copy the script from *contrib/start-scripts* into the *init.d* directory. Example 2-19 demonstrates how to do this on a Red Hat Linux system.

Example 2-19: Copying the linux script

```
$ cd /usr/local/src/postgresql-7.1.3/
$ su -c "cp contrib/start-scripts/linux /etc/rc.d/init.d/postgresql"
```

Example 2-19 arbitrarily re-names the new copy to *postgresql*; you may call it whatever you prefer, though it is typically named either *postgresql*, or *postgres*.

You will need to make the script file *executable* after copying it. To do so, use the command shown in Example 2-20.

Example 2-20: Making the linux script executable

```
$ su -c "chmod a+x /etc/rc.d/init.d/postgresql"
```

There are no additional requirements to use the SysV script with Red Hat, if you do not intend on using it to start PostgreSQL automatically (i.e., if you wish to use the script manually). However, if you do wish for the script to startup PostgreSQL automatically when the machine boots up (or changes runlevels), you will need to have the *chkconfig* program installed. If *chkconfig* is installed, you will also need to add the following two lines, including the hash (#) symbol, at the beginning of the */etc/rc.d/init.d/postgresql* file:

```
# chkconfig: 345 85 15
# description: PostgreSQL RDBMS
```

These example numbers should work on your system; however, it is good to know what role they perform. The first group of numbers (345) represent which runlevels PostgreSQL should be started at. The example shown would start PostgreSQL at runlevels 3, 4, and 5. The second group of numbers (85) represent the order in which PostgreSQL should be started within that runlevel, relative to other programs. You should probably keep the second number high, to indicate that it should be started later in the runlevel. The third number (15) represents the order in which PostgreSQL should be shutdown. It is a good idea to keep this number low, representing a shutdown order that is inverse from the startup order. As previously mentioned, the script should work on your system with the numbers provided, but you can change them if it is necessary.

Once these two lines have been added to the script, you can use the commands shown in Example 2-21 on Red Hat and Mandrake Linux distributions to start the PostgreSQL database. Be sure to execute these as the *root* user.

Example 2-21: Starting PostgreSQL with the SysV script

```
$ service postgresql start
Starting PostgreSQL: ok
$ service postgresql stop
Stopping PostgreSQL: ok
```

The SysV script logs redirects all PostgreSQL debugging output to */usr/local/pgsql/data/serverlog*, by default.

Step 10: Creating a Database

Now that the PostgreSQL database system is running, you have the option of using the default database, template1. If you create a new database, and you would like all of your consecutive databases to have the same system-wide options, then you should first configure the template1 database to have those options enabled. For instance, if you plan to use the PL/pgSQL language to program, then you should install the PL/pgSQL language into template1 before using *createdb*. Then when you use the *createdb* command, the database created will inherit template1's objects, and thus, inherit the PL/pgSQL language. For more information on installing the PL/pgSQL language into a database, refer to Chapter 11, *PL/pgSQL*.

The next step will be to create a new database. This will be a simple test database. We do not recommend using the default template1 database for testing purposes. As you have not created any users with database-creation rights, you will want to make sure that you are logged in as the *postgres* user when adding a new database. You can also create users that are allowed to add databases, which is discussed later in Chapter 10, *User and Group Management*. To create a new database named testdb, enter the command shown in Example 2-22.

Example 2-22: Creating a database

```
$ createdb testdb
CREATE DATABASE
```

You should receive a message that says CREATE DATABASE, indicating that creation of the database was successful. You can now use PostgreSQL's command line interface, *psql*, to access the newly created database. To do so, enter the command shown in Example 2-23.

Example 2-23: Accessing a database with psql

```
$ psql testdb
```

You can now start entering SQL commands (e.g., such as SELECT) at the *psql* prompt. If you are unfamiliar with *psql*, please see Chapter 4, *Using SQL with Post-greSQL* for an introduction.

To verify that the database is working correctly, you can issue the command shown in Example 2-24, which should give you a listing of the languages installed in the database.

Example 2-24: Querying a system table

```
testdb=# SELECT * FROM pg_language;
  lanname | lanispl | lanpltrusted | lanplcallfoid | lancompiler
----------+---------+--------------+---------------+-------------
  internal | f       | f            |             0 | n/a
  C        | f       | f            |             0 | /bin/cc
  sql      | f       | f            |             0 | postgres
(3 rows)
```

II

Using PostgreSQL

3

Understanding SQL

This chapter discusses the history and fundamental concepts of SQL and forms the foundation for the next chapter, which is about applying SQL with PostgreSQL. It addresses the basics of relational databases, object-related database extensions, the structure of a SQL statement, and provides an overview of PostgreSQL-supported data types, operators and functions.

Introduction to SQL

SQL, the *Structured Query Language*, is a mature, powerful, and versatile relational query language. The history of SQL extends back to IBM research begun in 1970. The next few sections discuss the history of SQL, its predecessors, and the various SQL standards that have developed over the years.

A Brief History of SQL

The relational model, from which SQL draws much of its conceptual core, was formally defined in 1970 by Dr. E. F. Codd, a researcher for IBM, in a paper entitled *A Relational Model of Data for Large Shared Data Banks*. This article generated a great deal of interest in both the feasibility and practical commercial application of such a system.

In 1974 IBM began the System/R project and with the work of Donald Chamberlin and others, developed SEQUEL, or *Structured English Query Language*. System/R was implemented on an IBM prototype called SEQUEL-XRM in 1974–75. It was then completely rewritten in 1976–1977 to include multi-table and multiuser features. When the system was revised it was briefly called "SEQUEL/2," and then renamed "SQL" for legal reasons.

In 1978, methodical testing commenced at customer test sites. Demonstrating both the usefulness and practicality of the system, this testing proved to be a success for IBM. As a result, IBM began to develop commercial products that implemented SQL based on their System R prototype, including SQL/DS (introduced in 1981), and DB2 (in 1983).

Several other software vendors accepted the rise of the relational model and announced SQL-based products. These included Oracle (who actually beat IBM to market by two years by releasing their first commercial RDBMS, in 1979), Sybase, and Ingres (based on the University of California's Berkeley Ingres project).

 PostgreSQL's name is, as you might have guessed, a play on the name Ingres. Both PostgreSQL and Ingres trace their roots back to the UC Berkeley's Ingres RDBMS system.

SQL and Its Predecessors

SQL is based largely on relational algebra and tuple relational calculus. Relational algebra, introduced by E. F. Codd in 1972, provided the basic concepts behind computing SQL syntax. It is a procedural way to construct data-driven queries, and it addresses the *how* logic of a structured query. The tuple relational calculus (*TRC*), on the other hand, affects the underlying appearance of SQL. Relational calculus uses declarative expressions, addressing the *what* logic of a structured query.

There are additional features that set SQL apart from those that merely implement features that are part of relational algebra or calculus. These features include:

Support for data insertion, modification and deletion
  Users are allowed to insert, delete, and modify stored data records.

Arithmetic operators
  Arithmetic operations such as addition, subtraction, multiplication, and division (e.g., (value1 * 5) + value2) are allowed, as well as comparison operators (e.g., value3 >= value4).

Display of data
  Users may display query-generated relationships (such as a table's contents).

Assignment
  Users may rename a relation that is computed by a query instead of forcing the use of the default relationship name, which may be derived from a column or function name, depending on the query.

Aggregate functions

User may group related rows together and calculate averages, sums, counts, maximums, and minimums.

SQL Standards

The American National Standards Institute (ANSI) standardized SQL in 1986 (X3.135) and the International Standards Organization (ISO) standardized it in 1987. The United States government's Federal Information Processing Standard (*FIPS*) adopted the ANSI/ISO standard. In 1989, a revised standard known commonly as *SQL89* or *SQL1*, was published.

Due partially to conflicting interests from commercial vendors, much of the SQL89 standard was intentionally left incomplete, and many features were labeled implementor-defined. In order to strengthen the standard, the ANSI committee revised its previous work with the *SQL92* standard ratified in 1992 (also called *SQL2*). This standard addressed several weaknesses in SQL89 and set forth conceptual SQL features which at that time exceeded the capabilities of any existing RDBMS implementation. In fact, the SQL92 standard was approximately six times the length of its predecessor. As a result of this disparity, the authors defined three levels of SQL92 compliance: *Entry-level conformance* (only the barest improvements to SQL89), *Intermediate-level conformance* (a generally achievable set of major advancements), and *Full conformance* (total compliance with the SQL92 features).

More recently, in 1999, the ANSI/ISO released the *SQL99* standard (also called *SQL3*). This standard addresses some of the more advanced and previously ignored areas of modern SQL systems, such as object-relational database concepts, call level interfaces, and integrity management. SQL99 replaces the SQL92 levels of compliance with its own degrees of conformance: *Core SQL99* and *Enhanced SQL99*.

PostgreSQL presently conforms to most of the Entry-level SQL92 standard, as well as many of the Intermediate- and Full-level features. Additionally, many of the features new in SQL99 are quite similar to the object-relational concepts pioneered by PostgreSQL (arrays, functions, and inheritance).

Introduction to Relational Databases

PostgreSQL is a sophisticated *Object-Relational Database Management System* (ORDBMS). An ORDBMS is an extension of the more traditional *Relational Database Management Systems* (RDBMS). An RDBMS enables users to store related pieces of data in two-dimensional data structures called *tables*. This data may consist of many defined *types*, such as integers, floating-point numbers, character strings, and timestamps. Data inserted in a table is categorized using a grid-like system of vertical columns, and horizontal rows. The relational model was built on a strong premise of conceptual simplicity, which is arguably both its most prominent strength and weakness.

The object-relational aspect of PostgreSQL adds numerous enhancements to the straight relational data model. These include support for *arrays* (multiple values in a single column), *inheritance* (child-parent relationships between tables), and *functions* (programmatic methods invoked by SQL statements). For the advanced developer, PostgreSQL even supports extensibility of its data types and procedural languages.

Due to this object-relational concept, tables are sometimes called classes, while rows and columns can be referred to as object-instances and object-attributes, respectively. We will use this terminology interchangeably in this book. Other SQL data structures, such as indices and views, can be referred to as database objects.

 Take care to observe that *object-relational* is not synonymous with *object-oriented*, a term pertaining to many modern programming languages. While PostgreSQL supports several objective improvements to the relational model, it is still accurate to refer to PostgreSQL as a Relational Database Management System (RDBMS).

Understanding Databases

While PostgreSQL is commonly considered an RDBMS, or a "database," it may not be commonly understood what is meant specifically by the word *database*. A database within PostgreSQL is an object-relational implementation of what is formally called a *schema* in SQL99.

Put simply, a database is a stored set of data that is logically interrelated. Typically, this data can be accessed in a multiuser environment. This is the case with PostgreSQL, though there are well-defined rights and restrictions enforced with that access.

It may not be commonly understood that PostgreSQL can have *several* databases concurrently available, each with their own owner, and each with their own unique tables, views, indices, sequences, and functions.

In order to create a table, function, or any other database object, you must connect to a specific database via a PostgreSQL *client*. Once connected, you can create an object, which is then *owned* by the connected database, and therefore is inaccessible from any other database (though a client may have several connections open to different databases).

By keeping fundamental data objects segregated into their own databases in this fashion, you run a smaller risk of running into a naming collision by choosing a table name already chosen for another purpose (e.g., if two users each wanted to have a table called products for two separate applications). This is because neither database has any knowledge of the other database's components, and will not attempt to make any kind of logical relationship between them. Furthermore, as the same rule applies to object-relational data objects, users may even create functions and language definitions within their database that are inaccessible to other users connected to other databases running within PostgreSQL.

By default, PostgreSQL installs only one functional database, which is called template1 to represent the template nature of the database. Any database created after template1 is essentially a clone, inheriting any of its database objects, including table structure, functions, languages, etc. It is not uncommon to create a default database for new PostgreSQL users with the same name as their PostgreSQL username, as PostgreSQL will attempt to connect to a database with the same name as the connecting user if a database name is not specified.

Understanding Tables

Tables are quite possibly the most important aspect of SQL to understand inside and out, as all of your data will reside within them. In order to be able to correctly plan and design your SQL data structures, and any programmatic routines toward accessing and applying that data, a thorough understanding of tables is an absolute pre-requisite.

A table is composed of *columns* and *rows*, and their intersections are *fields*. If you have ever used spreadsheet software before (such as Excel), these two terms are visually represented in the same manner, and the fields within a table are equivalent to the cells within a spreadsheet. From a general perspective, columns within a table describe the name and type of data that will be found (and can be entered) by row for that column's fields. Rows within a table represent *records* composed of fields that are described from left to right by their corresponding column's name and type. Each field in a row is implicitly correlated with each other field in that row. In this sense, columns can be thought of as descriptors for the discrete, sequential elements of a row, and each row can be thought of as a stored record matching that description.

Table 3-1 illustrates a simple table called books, used by our imaginary bookstore, *Book Town*. We will frequently refer to this table in later examples. Each of its stored records describes a book by a numeric identifier, title, author identifier, and subject identifier. These characteristics, from left to right, are described by its columns (id, title, author_id, and subject_id).

Table 3-1. An example SQL table

id	title	author_id	subject_id
7808	The Shining	4156	9
156	The Tell-Tale Heart	15	9
4513	Dune	1866	15
4267	2001: A Space Odyssey	2001	15
1608	The Cat in the Hat	1809	2
1590	Bartholomew and the Oobleck	1809	2

As you can see, this describes a table with four columns, in a fixed, left-to-right order, currently populated by six rows (also known as tuples, or records). It is essential to understand that in a relational database, while a table has a fixed column order, rows themselves are inherently unordered. You will see later, as the SQL's query structure is explained in Chapter 4, *Using SQL with PostgreSQL,* that there are ways within SQL to order selected rows. However, the rows in the database itself are not automatically ordered in any consistently predictable way. When order is meaningful for a SQL query, you must carefully consider and explicitly order records.

Every table must have at least one column, but tables may at times contain no rows, because each vertical column corresponds to a relatively fixed *attribute* of the data represented in that table (such as the `title` column in the previous example's `books` table). Without a column, a row's contents would be ambiguous; without a row, a table is merely lacking recorded data. As of PostgreSQL 7.1, there is a maximum of 1600 columns to a table, and an unlimited number of rows (i.e., you are limited only by hardware limitations, such as disk space).

In Table 3-1, the column names fairly clearly indicate the significance of each column. The decision of how to name columns is fairly arbitrary, though, and care must be taken in planning table names and conventions to avoid ambiguity.

Though it may not be immediately obvious, each of the columns of a table have an associated *data type*. While a column's data type helps to further describe the sort of information it contains, it *constrains* the kind of data that may be inserted into the column. For example, the `author_id` column is of type `integer`; this signifies that any insertion attempts not consisting of pure a integer (e.g., 110a) will fail. These types are described in more detail in the section titled "Data Types."

This section introduced the general concepts of how data is logically arranged in a relational database and within tables. The next section explains why statements are the basis for *all interactions* with the database.

SQL Statements

Conceptual information on relational databases and tables is of course entirely moot if you don't have any idea of how to directly interact with your data. From a general perspective, SQL consists entirely of structured *statements*, with which all data in the database is added, modified, and removed. These statements form the basis for your communication with the PostgreSQL server.

The following sections dissect the anatomy of a SQL statement into its structural pieces, explaining the significance of each, and their relation to one another. The standard PostgreSQL command-line client, *psql*, provides output to display example PostgreSQL statements.

Our SQL examples commonly take place within an example database called booktown, the database for our imaginary bookstore, Book Town. The output from *psql* is consistently prefixed with a default prompt style, which looks like this:

```
booktown=#
```

Some simpler examples may use our generic test database, testdb, if not specific to the Book Town examples. By default, the *psql* prompt displays only the name of the connected database and the =# characters indicating that the system is ready for a new command (though you will see that the = symbol will change dynamically as *psql* tracks the status of SQL input). We display this prompt along with the SQL input and output in order to help familiarize you with the *psql* output.

Chapter 4 documents *psql* in more detail, and it is only mentioned here to explain the source and style of this book's SQL examples using PostgreSQL.

The schema (with sample data) for the booktown database can be found in the *booktown.sql* file, on the CD-ROM. To install this database, type *psql -U postgres template1 -f /mnt/cdrom/booktown.sql* from the command line (where */mnt/cdrom* is the path to your mounted CD, and *postgres* is your PostgreSQL superuser).

The Anatomy of a SQL Statement

SQL statements always begin with a *command* (a word, or group of words, that describes *what* action the statement will initiate). The command can be called the *verb* of the SQL statement, as it always describes an action to be taken. Statements typically contain one or more *clauses*, which are formal modifiers that further describe the function of the SQL statement.

Table 3-2 contains a list of some of the most commonly used PostgreSQL commands.

Table 3-2. Fundamental PostgreSQL commands

Command	Description
CREATE DATABASE	Creates a new database
CREATE INDEX	Creates a new index on a table column
CREATE SEQUENCE	Creates a new sequence in an existing database
CREATE TABLE	Creates a new table in an existing database
CREATE TRIGGER	Creates a new trigger definition
CREATE VIEW	Creates a new view on an existing table
SELECT	Retrieves records from a table
INSERT	Adds one or more new records into a table
UPDATE	Modifies the data in existing table records
DELETE	Removes existing records from a table
DROP DATABASE	Destroys an existing database
DROP INDEX	Removes a column index from an existing table
DROP SEQUENCE	Destroys an existing sequence generator
DROP TABLE	Destroys an existing table
DROP TRIGGER	Destroys an existing trigger definition
DROP VIEW	Destroys an existing table view
CREATE USER	Adds a new PostgreSQL user account to the system
ALTER USER	Modifies an existing PostgreSQL user account
DROP USER	Removes an existing PostgreSQL user account
GRANT	Grant rights on a database object to a user
REVOKE	Deny rights on a database object from a user
CREATE FUNCTION	Creates a new SQL function within a database
CREATE LANGUAGE	Creates a new language definition within a database
CREATE OPERATOR	Creates a new SQL operator within a database
CREATE TYPE	Creates a new SQL data type within a database

While obviously code-like in nature, SQL was designed with ease of use and readability in mind. As a result, SQL statements often bear a strong resemblance to simple, instructional English sentences. A strong feature of SQL is that its statements are designed to instruct the server *what* data to find, not literally *how* to find it, as you would be forced to do in an ordinary programming language. Reading a well-designed SQL query should be nearly as easy as reading an ordinary sentence.

In SQL texts, the word *query* is frequently used interchangeably with *statement*. In order to be clear, within this book the term *query* is used only to refer to statements which *return data* (e.g., SELECT statements), rather than general SQL statements, which may instead create, add, or modify data.

Internally, PostgreSQL interprets structured SQL statements as a sequence of *tokens*, usually delimited by whitespace (spaces or newlines, outside of quotes), though some tokens may be placed adjacently if there is no chance of ambiguity (such as when operators are placed directly next to identifiers). A token in this context is a word or character that can be identified meaningfully by the server when the SQL statement is *parsed*, or interpreted.

Technically, each token can either be considered a *keyword*, an *identifier*, a *quoted identifier*, a *constant* (also called a *literal*), or one of several special character symbols. Keywords are words PostgreSQL recognizes as words with pre-defined SQL or PostgreSQL-specific meanings; these include SQL commands, clauses, function names, and special *noise* terms, which are often accompanied optionally with SQL commands (e.g., the noise term WORK in the COMMIT command). In contrast, identifiers represent variable names for tables, columns, and any other database object.

Both keywords and identifiers reference internally defined functions, values, or records, as far as PostgreSQL is concerned. Constants, on the other hand, describe pieces of data that are interpreted literally, such as a number or character string.

Finally, a SQL statement contains special character symbols. These are reserved characters (such as parentheses, the semicolon, and square brackets) that logically affect the meaning and arrangement of your keywords, identifiers, and literals. You can think of these characters as the punctuation for your SQL statements.

Operators fall under the category of special character symbols; they can be used to imply logical operations or evaluations between data values (either literals, or represented by identifiers), and are generally between one and four characters in length.

The following sections explain and expand upon the nature of these elementary components of SQL.

Token Formatting Considerations

As described in the preceding section, each sequential element of a SQL statement is considered a token. What may not be immediately clear, however, is that tokens may be kept all on the same line, or they may be split across several lines, as extra whitespace is ignored by PostgreSQL's parser.

Consider the SQL statement in Example 3-1, which is executed first on a single line, and then executed again, split across two separate lines. Both SELECT statements instruct the database to display the entire contents of the my_list table:

Example 3-1: Spaces and newlines

```
testdb=# SELECT * FROM my_list;
                     todos
-------------------------------------------------
 Pick up laundry.
 Send out bills.
 Wrap up Grand Unifying Theory for publication.
(3 rows)


testdb=# SELECT *
testdb-#        FROM
testdb-#        my_list;
                     todos
-------------------------------------------------
 Pick up laundry.
 Send out bills.
 Wrap up Grand Unifying Theory for publication.
(3 rows)
```

In Example 3-1 there are several newlines and spaces between the second statement's tokens. As you can see by the identical output, PostgreSQL ignores the extra newlines and spaces, making both statements semantically equivalent. You can take advantage of this behavior by splitting a long string of tokens across numerous lines for improved readability of your SQL statement. This probably isn't necessary for statements as simple as those in Example 3-1, but it can be quite helpful when dealing with complex SQL statements with numerous clauses, expressions, and conditions. Throughout this book we will periodically split some statements over several lines to help show what each part of the statement is intended to accomplish.

Keywords and Identifiers

Keywords are any reserved SQL terms which have a reserved syntactic meaning to the server. Some common keywords are INSERT, UPDATE, SELECT, and DELETE.

All SQL commands are keywords, though many keywords themselves are not complete commands. For instance, the command INSERT INTO is a valid SQL command, and the word INTO is a reserved keyword. As you might guess, however, the word INTO has no particular significance when used out of context.

Identifiers, as described earlier, are variable names that reference database objects. These names are arbitrarily designated by the creator of the database object upon creation. The objects which can be referred to by identifiers in PostgreSQL may be databases, tables, columns, indices, views, sequences, rules, triggers, or functions.

Example 3-2 adds three pieces of information about Oregon into a simple table called states.

Example 3-2: Keywords and commands

```
booktown=# INSERT INTO states VALUES (33, 'Oregon', 'OR');
INSERT 3389701 1
```

In Example 3-2, the INSERT INTO SQL command makes use of the SQL keywords INSERT, INTO, and VALUES.

The INSERT INTO command modifies the table referenced by the states identifier. The modification in this case is the insertion of a new record.

Quoted identifiers

While not normally required, quotes can be used around identifiers, meaning they should be interpreted literally. For example, if we want to view each of the columns from a table called states, a simple statement to achieve this would ordinarily read:

```
booktown=# SELECT * FROM states;
 id |    name    | abbreviation
----+------------+--------------
 33 | Oregon     | OR
 42 | Washington | WA
(2 rows)
```

The keywords in this statement are SELECT and FROM, while the identifiers are the asterisk * (indicating all columns), and states (the table name). With this command, we are selecting all columns from a table named states and thereby viewing its contents.

You can accomplish the same thing by putting quotes around the identifier, with the following statement:

```
booktown=# SELECT * FROM "states";
 id |    name    | abbreviation
----+------------+--------------
 33 | Oregon     | OR
 42 | Washington | WA
(2 rows)
```

As you can see, the output is identical when applying quotes to a lowercase identifier. However, the following statement, which uses quotes around the stAtEs identifier, will fail:

```
booktown=# SELECT * FROM "stAtEs";
ERROR: Relation 'stAtEs' does not exist
```

This statement fails because it instructs PostgreSQL to look for a table called, literally, stAtEs (rather than states). In other words, with the use of quotes, the statement has explicitly requested that PostgreSQL interpret the identifier name *literally*.

All non-quoted identifiers are *folded*, or converted, to lowercase. When specifying stAtEs, or STATES (i.e., any combination of uppercase or lowercase letters) *without* quotes, PostgreSQL automatically converts the identifier to lowercase (states) before processing the statement.

The folding of unquoted identifiers to lowercase names is a PostgreSQL-specific convention. The SQL92 standard specifies that unquoted identifiers always be converted to uppercase. For both legacy and readability reasons, PostgreSQL does not intend to move to this part of the SQL92 standard.

This should be of special note to database administrators familiar with other SQL products, such as Oracle, who expect case to automatically change to uppercase. If you are a developer, and you are interested in writing easily portable applications, be sure to consider this case issue to avoid conflicts over this convention.

Since the parser can still read and understand mixed-case statements (provided that they are formed with the correct syntax), you should use uppercase and lowercase terminology carefully. Your use of case can both help and hinder your efficiency when working with a large amount of SQL.

We recommend that, for readability, you try typing identifiers in lowercase and keywords in uppercase, the convention used throughout this book. By visually separating the fixed, systematic terminology from the user-defined data objects, you make it a great deal easier to quickly read and understand complex SQL statements.

When quotes are required

The only instances where you are *required* to use quotes are either when a database object's identifier is identical to a keyword, or when the identifier has at least one capitalized letter in its name. In either of these circumstances, you must remember to quote the identifier both when creating the object, as well as in any subsequent references to that object (e.g., in SELECT, DELETE, or UPDATE statements).

If you do not quote an identifier that is spelled identically to an existing keyword, PostgreSQL will return an error message because it interprets the intended identifier *as a keyword.* For instance, if you had a table whose name was literally select, you would get an error message if you tried querying it with the following statement:

```
testdb=# SELECT * FROM select;
ERROR: parser: parse error at or near "select"
```

As you can see, an unquoted query on a table called select produces an error message. To specify that select is in fact a table, and not a keyword, it needs to be placed inside of quotes. Therefore, the correct syntax to view a table named select is as follows.

```
testdb=# SELECT * FROM "select";
 selected
-----------
        0
        1
       52
      105
(4 rows)
```

Remember that any identifiers with at least one capitalized letter must be treated similarly. For example, if you've for some reason created a table named ProDucts (notice the capitalized "P" and "D"), and you want to destroy it (as you probably should, with a name like that!), then once again the identifier needs to be quoted in order to accurately describe its name to PostgreSQL, as follows:

```
booktown=# DROP TABLE ProDucts;
ERROR: table "products" does not exist
booktown=# DROP TABLE "ProDucts";
DROP
```

This technique can be extremely useful in some circumstances, even if you never name database objects with these criteria yourself. For example, importing data through an external ODBC connection (e.g., via Microsoft Access) can result in table names with all capitalized letters. Without the functionality of quoted identifiers, you would have no way to accurately reference these tables.

Identifier validity

Both keywords and identifier names in PostgreSQL have a maximum length limit of 31 characters. Parsed keywords or identifiers over that length limit are automatically truncated. Identifiers may begin with any letter (a through z), or with an underscore, and may then be followed by letters, numbers (0 through 9), or underscores. While keywords are not permitted to start or end with an underscore, identifier names *are* permitted to do so. Neither keywords nor identifiers should ever begin with a number.

In the section titled "When quotes are required" we described how quoted identifiers could be used to "overrule" the case insensitivity of identifiers by placing quotes around them. The same rule-bending can apply to the assertion that an identifier cannot begin with a number. While PostgreSQL will not allow you to create a table using the name 1st_bent_rule without quotes, the name is acceptable if it is surrounded with quotes.

Example 3-3 first fails in trying to create an illegally named table. It then proceeds to bend the rules with quotes.

Example 3-3: Bending rules

```
booktown=# CREATE TABLE 1st_bent_rule (rule_name text);
ERROR:  parser: parse error at or near "1"
booktown=# CREATE TABLE "1st_bent_rule" (rule_name text);
CREATE
```

Furthermore, while quotes themselves are, of course, not allowed within the set of quotes to refer to a table name, other normally illegal characters are allowed, such as spaces and ampersands. Take note that while the ANSI/ISO SQL standard forbids using identifiers with the same names as SQL keywords, PostgreSQL (like many other SQL implementations) has a similarly relaxed view on this, allowing you to force such names with quoted identifiers.

Remember that while the use of quotes can be a useful trick to know for unusual circumstances, if you wish to design portable, standard SQL statements and relations, it is best to adhere to ANSI/ISO standards whenever possible.

Constants

While much of the data in working with a database is stored on the disk and referred to via identifiers (e.g., table names, column names, and functions), there are obviously times when new data must be introduced to the system. This may be observed when inserting new records, when forming clauses to specify criteria to delete or modify, or even when performing calculations on existing records. This data is input through constants, which are sometimes called literals because they literally represent a value in a SQL statement (rather than referencing an existing value by identifier).

An *implicitly typed* constant is one whose *type* is recognized automatically by PostgreSQL's parser merely by its syntax. PostgreSQL supports five types of implicitly typed constants:

- *String*

- *Bit string*

- *Integer*

- *Floating point*

- *Boolean*

String constants

A string constant is an arbitrary sequence of characters bound by single quotes (apostrophes). These are typically used when inserting character data into a table or passing character data to any other database object. A practical example of the necessity of string constants is updating the first and last names of authors in Book Town's authors table:

```
booktown=# SELECT * FROM authors;
   id  | last_name |    first_name
-------+-----------+------------------
  1809 | Geisel    | Theodor Seuss
  1111 | Denham    | Ariel
 15990 | Bourgeois | Paulette
 25041 | Bianco    | Margery Williams
    16 | Alcott    | Luoisa May
   115 | Poe       | Edgar Allen
(6 rows)
```

Looking at this table's contents, it might stand out to you that the first_name with id 16, *Louisa May* has been misspelled as *Luoisa May*. To correct this, an UPDATE statement can be made with a string constant, as shown in Example 3-4.

Example 3-4: Using string constants

```
booktown=# UPDATE authors
booktown-#      SET first_name = 'Louisa May'
booktown-#      WHERE first_name = 'Luoisa May';
UPDATE 1
booktown=# SELECT * FROM authors;
   id  | last_name |    first_name
-------+-----------+------------------
  1809 | Geisel    | Theodor Seuss
  1111 | Denham    | Ariel
 15990 | Bourgeois | Paulette
 25041 | Bianco    | Margery Williams
    15 | Poe       | Edgar Allen
    16 | Alcott    | Louisa May
(6 rows)
```

The UPDATE statement made in Example 3-4 uses the string constants *Louisa May* and *Luoisa May* in conjunction with the SET and WHERE keywords. This statement updates the contents of the table referenced by the authors identifier and, as shown, corrects the misspelling.

The fact that string constants are bound by single quotes presents an obvious semantic problem, however, in that if the sequence itself contains a single quote, the literal bounds of the constant are made ambiguous. To *escape* (make literal) a single quote within the string, you may type two adjacent single quotes. The parser will interpret the two adjacent single quotes within the string constant as a single, literal quote. PostgreSQL will also allow single quotes to be embedded by using a C-style backslash:

```
testdb=# SELECT 'PostgreSQL''s great!' AS example;
       example
---------------------
 PostgreSQL's great!
(1 row)

booktown=# SELECT 'PostgreSQL\'s C-style slashes are great!' AS example;
                  example
-----------------------------------------
 PostgreSQL's C-style slashes are great!
(1 row)
```

PostgreSQL also supports the C-style "backslash escape" sequences, which are listed in Table 3-3.

Table 3-3. PostgreSQL supported C-style escape sequences

Escape sequence	Description
\\	Literal backslash
\'	Literal apostrophe
\b	Backspace
\f	Form feed
\n	Newline
\r	Carriage return
\t	Tab
\xxx	ASCII character with the corresponding octal number *xxx*

As a result of the backslashes' special meaning described in Table 3-3, in order to include a backslash in the string you *must* escape it using a another backslash (e.g., `'A single backslash is: \\'` will transform the pair of backslashes into a single backslash).

When entering two quoted character strings to PostgreSQL that are separated by some amount of whitespace, and where that whitespace includes at least one newline, the strings are concatenated and viewed as if they had been typed as one constant. This is illustrated in Example 3-5.

Example 3-5: Multiline string constants

```
booktown=# SELECT 'book'
booktown-#
booktown-# 'end' AS example;
 example
---------
 bookend
(1 row)


booktown=# SELECT 'bookend' AS example;
 example
---------
 bookend
(1 row)
```

As you can see, the semantics of the two statements is equivalent. However, at least one newline is *required* for this interpretation to be possible, as spaces alone would result in the following error:

```
booktown=# SELECT 'book' 'end' AS mistake;
ERROR:  parser: parse error at or near "'"
```

This error occurs because without a newline, PostgreSQL will assume that you are referring to two separate constants. If you wish to concatenate two string constants this way on a single line, PostgreSQL supports the || operator for text concatenation (see Chapter 5, *Operators and Functions*, for more details on this operator).

```
booktown=# SELECT 'book' || 'end' AS example;
 example
---------
 bookend
(1 row)
```

Bit string constants

Bit string constants provide a way to directly represent a binary value with an arbitrary sequence of ones and zeroes. Similarly to string constants, they are bound by single quotes, but they also must be preceded by a leading B character (which may be uppercase or lowercase). This character identifies to PostgreSQL that the forthcoming constant is a bit string, and not a normal string of character data.

Syntactically, the opening single quote must follow immediately after the leading B, and the bit string may not contain any character other than 0 or 1. While there cannot be whitespace within this string of bits, it can be continued across multiple lines just like regular string constants, as documented in the section titled "String constants."

Bit string constants are generally only useful when working with tables or functions that require binary values. Example 3-6 demonstrates the use of a bit string constant upon a simple table containing raw bytes. A bit string byte is inserted into a list of bytes in the my_bytes table, and insertion is verified with a simple query.

Example 3-6: Using bit string constants

```
testdb=# INSERT INTO my_bytes VALUES (B'00000000');
testdb=# SELECT my_byte FROM my_bytes;
 my_byte
----------
 10000000
 10000001
 10000101
 11111111
 00000000
(5 rows)
```

Integer constants

Integer constants are far more frequently used than bit string constants. PostgreSQL identifies an integer constant as any token that consists solely of a sequence of numbers (without a decimal point) and that is outside of single-quotes. Technically, SQL defines integer constants as a sequence of decimal digits with no decimal point. The range of values available for an integer constant depends largely on the context within which it is used, but PostgreSQL's default for the integer data type is a 4-byte signed integer, with range from –2147483648 to 2147483647.

Integer constants are used anywhere you wish to represent a literal integer value. They are used frequently within mathematical operations, as well as in SQL commands that reference a column with an integer data type. Example 3-7 is a simple demonstration of the use of integer constants to update an author's numeric identifier via an UPDATE command.

Consider once again the authors table used in previous sections, which correlates a numeric author identifier with two character strings representing the author's first and last name. Suppose that, for administrative reasons, it has been deemed necessary that any author with an identifier of less than 100 must be modified to a value of more than 100.

The first step to correct this would be to locate any author with such an id value. An integer constant can first be used in a SELECT statement's WHERE clause to perform a less-than comparison to check.

Example 3-7: Using integer constants

```
booktown=# SELECT * FROM authors WHERE id < 100;
   id  | last_name |     first_name
-------+-----------+------------------
    16 | Alcott    | Louisa May
(1 row)

booktown=# SELECT * FROM authors WHERE id = 116;
   id  | last_name |     first_name
-------+-----------+------------------
(0 rows)

booktown=# UPDATE authors
booktown-#     SET id = 116
booktown-#   WHERE id = 16;
UPDATE 1
booktown=# SELECT * FROM authors WHERE id = 116;
   id  | last_name |     first_name
-------+-----------+------------------
   116 | Alcott    | Louisa May
(1 row)
```

In Example 3-7, the WHERE clause in the SELECT statement compares the id column identifier against an integer constant of 100, returning one row. Once the author with the offending id is found, a second SELECT statement is issued to check for an existing author with an id of 116. This is to verify that the new id is not in use by another author within the authors table, as this column has been specified as requiring a unique identifier. Finally, an UPDATE statement is executed, again using integer constants in both the SET and WHERE clauses.

Floating-point constants

A floating-point constant is similar to an integer constant, but it is used to represent decimal values as well as whole integers. These are required whenever such a floating-point value must be represented literally within a SQL statement.

A floating-point constant can be represented in several forms, as shown in Table 3-4. Each occurrence of ## represents one or more digits.

Table 3-4. Floating-point representations

Representation	Example
##.##	6.4
##e[+-]##	8e-8
[##].##e[+-]##	.04e8
##.[##][e[+-]##]	4.e5

In the first form, there must be at least one digit before or after the decimal point for PostgreSQL to recognize the value as a floating-point constant versus an integer constant. The other options involve having at least one digit before or after an *exponent clause*, denoted by the *e* in the list. The presence of either the decimal point, the exponent clause, or both, distinguishes an integer constant from a floating-point.

Each of these valid formats is represented in Example 3-8 through a simple SQL SELECT statement illustrating a variety of floating-point conventions.

Example 3-8: Valid floating-point values

```
booktown=# SELECT .04 AS small_float,
booktown-#     -16.63 AS negative_float,
booktown-#        4e3 AS exponential_float,
booktown-#    6.1e-2 AS negative_exponent;
 small_float | negative_float | exponential_float | negative_exponent
-------------+----------------+-------------------+-------------------
        0.04 |         -16.63 |              4000 |             0.061
(1 row)
```

Boolean constants

Boolean constants are much simpler than any other constant values recognized by PostgreSQL, as they may consist only of two possible values: true and false. When PostgreSQL encounters either of these terms outside of single quotes, they are implicitly interpreted as Boolean constants, rather than as string constants. Example 3-9 shows this important distinction.

Example 3-9: The difference between true and 'true'

```
testdb=# SELECT true AS boolean_t,
testdb-#           'true' AS string_t,
testdb-#           false AS boolean_f,
testdb-#           'false' AS string_f;
 bool_t | string_t | bool_f | string_f
--------+----------+--------+----------
 t      | true     | f      | false
(1 row)
```

When the terms true and false are parsed by PostgreSQL outside of single quotes, they are implied Boolean values. As shown in Example 3-9, PostgreSQL displays values which are literally of the type boolean as t or f, though be careful not to try to use only t or f as Boolean constant values, as this will not be interpreted correctly by PostgreSQL, and will cause an error.

Special Character Symbols

Special character symbols are characters with a pre-defined syntactic meaning in PostgreSQL. They are typically disallowed from being used in identifier names for this reason, though as mentioned in the section on quoted identifiers, this restriction can usually be worked around with quotes if need be.

Punctuation symbols

Some special character symbols help to make up the "punctuation" of a SQL statement, much like parentheses, periods and commas do in the English language. Table 3-5 shows some common PostgreSQL-recognized syntactic symbols.

Table 3-5. Punctuation symbols

Character	Definition
* (asterisk)	Used with the SELECT command to query all columns in the table, and with the count() aggregate function to count all rows in a table.
() (parentheses)	Used to group expressions, enforce operator precedence, and to make function calls. The use of parentheses is highly subjective to the context in which they are used.
[] (brackets)	Used in the selection of specific elements in an array, or in the declaration of an array type (e.g., with the CREATE TABLE command).
; (semicolon)	Used to terminate a SQL command. The only place it can be used within a statement is within a string constant or quoted identifier.
, (comma)	Some commands use the comma to separate elements within a list.
. (period)	Used in floating-point constants (e.g., 3.1415), as well as to reference column names as children of tables (e.g., table_name.column_name).
: (colon)	Used to select *slices* from arrays.
$ (dollar sign)	Used in the body of a function definition to represent a positional parameter, or argument.

Operator symbols

An operator is another type of special character symbol; it is used to perform *operations* on identifiers or constants, returning resultant values. Operators can be used for mathematical operations, such as addition, as well as to perform comparison and logical operations.

Consider again the books table, and its numeric author_id field. Recall that the author_id column is an integer used to identify an author. Now imagine that, due to a system modification, all author identifiers must be incremented by 1,500. This can be achieved by evaluating the result of an operation (an *operator expression*) in an UPDATE statement upon the author_id column. This requires use of the addition (+) operator. An example of this can be seen in Example 3-10.

Example 3-10: Operators in statements

```
booktown=# SELECT * FROM books;
   id   |            title             | author_id | subject_id
--------+-----------------------------+-----------+------------
   7808 | The Shining                 |      4156 |          9
    156 | The Tell-Tale Heart         |        15 |          9
   4513 | Dune                        |      1866 |         15
   4267 | 2001: A Space Odyssey       |      2001 |         15
   1608 | The Cat in the Hat          |      1809 |          2
   1590 | Bartholomew and the Oobleck |      1809 |          2
(6 rows)

booktown=# UPDATE books SET author_id = author_id + 1500;
UPDATE 6
booktown=# SELECT * FROM books;
   id   |            title             | author_id | subject_id
--------+-----------------------------+-----------+------------
   7808 | The Shining                 |      5656 |          9
    156 | The Tell-Tale Heart         |      1515 |          9
   4513 | Dune                        |      3366 |         15
   4267 | 2001: A Space Odyssey       |      3501 |         15
   1608 | The Cat in the Hat          |      3309 |          2
   1590 | Bartholomew and the Oobleck |      3309 |          2
(6 rows)
```

As you can see in Example 3-10, each author_id record is modified with the results of the + operator's operation upon the previous author_id value.

Common operators that you may already be familiar with include the basic mathematical operators: the + sign for the addition of two numeric values, the – sign for the subtraction of one numeric value from another, etc. Some of the more esoteric operators include the bitwise & and | operators, which modify binary values at the bit level.

In addition to these character symbol operators, it's important to remember the SQL keywords, which are frequently called operators as well. Most notably, this includes the logical operators AND, OR, and NOT. While technically keywords, these terms are grouped with the operators because of their operational effect upon constants and identifiers.

Table 3-6 lists some fundamental PostgreSQL operators.

Table 3-6. Fundamental PostgreSQL operators

Category	Operator	Definition
Mathematical operators	+ (addition)	Adds two numeric types
	– (subtraction)	Subtracts one numeric type from another
	/ (division)	Divides one numeric type by another
	* (multiplication)	Multiplies one numeric type by another
	! (factorial)	Returns an integer's factorial
	@ (absolute value)	Returns the absolute value of a numeric value
Comparison operators	= (equivalence)	Compares two values for equivalence
	< (less than)	Evaluates whether or not one number is less than another
	> (greater than)	Evaluates whether or not one number is larger than another
	~ (regular expression)	Performs a regular expression comparison on text values
Logical operators	NOT	Returns the opposite of a Boolean condition
	AND	Returns true if both Boolean conditions are true
	OR	Returns true if at least one of two Boolean conditions is true

While many operators have various connotations depending on their context, the = operator is an especially important one due to its meaning when used with an UPDATE statement's SET clause.

While in most expressions the = operator is an equivalence operator (used to compare two values for equivalence), when following the SET clause and an identifier name in an UPDATE statement, the = is read as an *assignment* operator. This means that it is used to assign a new value to an existing identifier, as the SET term implies.

For more information on operators, see the section titled "Operators."

Comments

Comments are blocks of text that, through special character sequences, can embed non-SQL text within SQL code. These can be used within blocks of code, because PostgreSQL removes the commented areas from the input stream and treats them as whitespace. There are two styles of comments available: single-line comments, and multiline comments.

Single-line comments are preceded by two dashes (--) and may either be on a line by themselves, or they may follow valid SQL tokens. (The comments themselves are not considered tokens to PostgreSQL's parser, as any character data following the -- sequence, up to the end of the line, is treated as whitespace.) This is demonstrated in Example 3-11.

Example 3-11: Single-line comments

```
testdb=# SELECT 'Test' -- This can follow valid SQL tokens,
testdb=#               -- or be on a line of it own.
testdb=# AS example;
 example
 ---------
 Test
(1 row)
```

Multiline comments begin with a sequential slash-asterisk (/*) sequence, and terminate with a sequential asterisk-slash (*/) sequence. This style of commenting may already be familiar to C programmers, but there is one key difference between PostgreSQL's interpreter and the C language interpreter: PostgreSQL comments may be *nested*. Therefore, when you create a multiline comment within another multiline comment, the */ used to close the inner comment does not also close the outer comment. Example 3-12 provides a comment explanation.

Example 3-12: Multiline comments

```
testdb=# SELECT 'Multi' /* This comment extends across
testdb*#                 * numerous lines, and can be
testdb*#                 * /* nested safely */ */
testdb-# || '-test' AS example;
 example
 ------------
 Multi-test
(1 row)
```

Nesting comments can be useful if you have a file containing SQL syntax of which you wish to comment a large portion before sending to PostgreSQL for interpreting and execution. If you have already used multiline comments within that document and you wish to comment a large section which includes those comments, PostgreSQL is intelligent enough to recognize that a closing comment sequence (*/) closes only the most recently opened comment, not the entire commented region.

The asterisk character by itself (without an adjacent slash character) has no special meaning within a comment. The extra asterisks in Example 3-12 on multiline comments are provided only for aesthetic purposes and readability.

Putting It All Together

In summary, a SQL statement is comprised of tokens, where each token can represent either a keyword, identifier, quoted identifier, constant, or special character symbol. Table 3-7 uses a simple SELECT statement to illustrate a basic, but complete, SQL statement and its components.

Table 3-7. A simple SQL query

	SELECT	id, name	FROM	states
Token Type	Keyword	Identifiers	Keyword	Identifier
Description	Command	Id and name columns	Clause	Table name

As shown in the table, the SELECT statement contains the keywords SELECT and FROM. Together, the FROM keyword and states token compose a clause, as they modify and further describe the SELECT command.

The id, name, and states tokens are the identifiers of the statement. The id and name identifiers specify the selected columns, while the states identifier specifies the table name to select from. Therefore, with the preceding SQL query, you are instructing PostgreSQL to display the columns named id and name for each row from the states table. Example 3-13 shows the output this query generates within the booktown database.

Example 3-13: Example SQL query

```
booktown=# SELECT id, name FROM states;
 id |    name
----+------------
 42 | Washington
 51 | Oregon
(2 rows)

booktown=#
```

Getting more complicated, Table 3-8 and Table 3-9 break down another example statement. This statement uses the UPDATE command, along with SET and WHERE clauses, which respectively specify with *what* to update the records, and *how* to find the records to update.

Table 3-8. UPDATE example: the SET clause

UPDATE	states	SET	id	=	51
keyword	identifier	keyword	identifier	operator	integer constant
command	table name	clause	column	assignment	new id value

Table 3-9. UPDATE example: the WHERE clause

WHERE	name	=	'Oregon'
keyword	identifier	operator	string constant
clause	column name	equivalence	string value to match

When executed, this statement examines each record's `name` column to find matches for the `WHERE` clause's stated condition (equivalence to the string constant 'Oregon'). Then, for each row which matches that condition, it updates the `id` column with the value 51.

Breaking it down, this `UPDATE` statement has three keywords, three identifiers, two operators, and two constants. The keywords are `UPDATE` (the SQL command), `SET` (specifies the updates to make), and `WHERE` (identifies the rows to update). The identifiers are the `states` table name, the `id` column name, and the `name` column name.

The operators are both represented by the = operator. When used with the `SET` clause, this operator is used for assignment (to assign a new value to an existing record's identified column); this is a special use which is unique to the `SET` clause. In contrast, when used with the `WHERE` clause, the = operator is used to check equivalence between values. In this case, this means that the equivalence operator will check the value of a record's `name` column against a string constant with the value of *Oregon*.

Finally, the constants in this statement are the integer constant 51 (the new value for the `id` column), and the string constant *Oregon* (compared to the `name` column through the `WHERE` clause).

Example 3-14 therefore updates the `states` table by setting the `id` column to 51 whenever the `name` column matches the value *Oregon*. It then checks the results of that `UPDATE` statement with another `SELECT` statement.

Example 3-14: A SQL update

```
booktown=# UPDATE states
booktown-#    SET id = 51
booktown-#  WHERE name = 'Oregon';
UPDATE 1
booktown=# SELECT * FROM states
```

Example 3-14: A SQL update (continued)

```
booktown-# WHERE name = 'Oregon';
 id |  name  | abbreviation
----+--------+--------------
 51 | Oregon | OR
(1 row)

booktown=#
```

Data Types

SQL is considered a *strongly typed language*. This means that any piece of data represented by PostgreSQL has an associated data type, even if it is not plainly obvious. A data value's type both defines and constrains the kinds of operations which may be performed on it.

Not only is every piece of data associated with a type, but types play a large part in the construction of tables. As stated in the section titled "Introduction to Relational Databases," tables are made up of one or more columns. These columns must, in addition to having a name, have a specific data type.

 While PostgreSQL provides a wide variety of built-in data types, you also have the option to add new data types to PostgreSQL using the CREATE TYPE command. See the reference entry on CREATE TYPE for more on this command.

Table 3-10 lists the data types officially supported by PostgreSQL, as well as any PostgreSQL recognized *aliases* (alternative names that are identical in connotation). There are many other internal (meaning they are no longer intended for normal use) or deprecated (outdated, and discouraged) data types available that are unlisted.

Additionally, while most of the data types implemented in PostgreSQL are directly derived from SQL standards, there are some actively maintained data types that are non-standard (such as the geometric and spacial types). Therefore, you will not always be able to find equivalent types on other SQL-capable database management systems.

Table 3-10. PostgreSQL supported data types

Category	Data type	Description	Standardization
Boolean & binary types	`boolean, bool`	A single true or false value.	SQL99
	`bit(n)`	An *n*-length bit string (exactly *n* binary bits).	SQL92
	`bit varying(n)`, `varbit(n)`	A variable *n*-length bit string (up to *n* binary bits)	SQL92
Character types	`character (n)`, `char(n)`	A fixed *n*-length character string.	SQL89
	`character varying(n)`, `varchar(n)`	A variable length character string of up to *n* characters.	SQL92
	`text`	A variable length character string, of unlimited length.	PostgreSQL-specific
Numeric types	`smallint, int2`	A signed 2-byte integer.	SQL89
	`integer, int, int4`	A signed 4-byte integer.	SQL92
	`bigint, int8`	A signed 8-byte integer, up to 18 digits in length.	PostgreSQL-specific
	`real, float4`	A 4-byte floating-point number.	SQL89
	`double precision, float8, float`	An 8-byte floating-point number.	SQL89
	`numeric(p,s)`, `decimal(p,s)`	An exact numeric type with arbitrary precision *p*, and scale *s*.	SQL99
	`money`	A fixed precision, U.S.-style currency.	PostgreSQL-specific, deprecated.
	`serial`	An auto-incrementing 4-byte integer.	PostgreSQL-specific
Date and time types	`date`	The calendar date (day, month and year).	SQL92
	`time`	The time of day.	SQL92
	`time with time zone`	The time of day, including time zone information.	SQL92
	`timestamp (includes time zone)`	Both the date and time.	SQL92
	`interval`	An arbitrarily specified length of time.	SQL92
Geometric types	`box`	A rectangular box in a 2D plane.	PostgreSQL-specific

Table 3-10. PostgreSQL supported data types (continued)

Category	Data type	Description	Standardization
	line	An infinite line in a 2D plane.	PostgreSQL-specific
	lseg	A finite line segment in a 2D plane.	PostgreSQL-specific
	circle	A circle with center and radius.	PostgreSQL-specific
	path	Open and closed geometric paths in a two-dimensional plane.	PostgreSQL-specific
	point	geometric point in a 2D plane	PostgreSQL-specific
	polygon	A closed geometric path in a 2D plane.	PostgreSQL-specific
Network types	cidr	An IP network specification.	PostgreSQL-specific
	inet	A network IP address, with optional subnet bits.	PostgreSQL-specific
	macaddr	A MAC address (e.g., an Ethernet card's hardware address).	PostgreSQL-specific
System types	oid	An object (row) identifier.	PostgreSQL-specific
	xid	A transaction identifier.	PostgreSQL-specific

Remaining true to theme, the following sections on data types will describe in further detail each of the most widely used and practical types. This book will not go into detail on the non-standard and/or more esoteric types, such as the geometric, network and bitwise types. These sections include information on valid usage, storage considerations, input and output formats and general syntactic conventions. Before we go much further on specific data types there are a couple of topics worth discussing, including the NULL keyword.

NULL Values

Despite the previously discussed rule that a column can have only one data type and logically accept only that type, there is a value that *all* columns can be defined as, no matter what their data type. This is the value a column is set to when you use the SQL keyword NULL. Essentially, NULL has no data value, so it is not considered a type; it is a system value that indicates to the database that the field it is located within contains no value. The only exception to the rule that any column can contain a NULL is when the NOT NULL constraint is specified for a column.

NULL is often used in places where a value is optional. It can be a convenient way of omitting data without having to resort to strange or arbitrary conventions, such as storing negative values in an integer field to represent omitted data. While your system requirements may change over time, the connotation of NULL is always NULL.

NULL can be thought of as a meta-value: a value that represents a *lack of a value*, which will *never* be equivalent to a non-NULL value. One problem often encountered when working with NULL values is that they are easily confused with empty character strings, which return a blank value to the client when selected. The reason this can be confusing is that NULL values also return a blank value when selected; however, they are completely different than empty character strings and this must be understood in order to avoid creating faulty queries or code. A character string column that contains a blank value still contains a string of characters, though the characters that compose the string are blank; thus, there is still a value in the column. A NULL value represents the complete absence of value within the column, not that it is merely blank.

This is an important distinction, as the rules for SQL operations involving the NULL value are quite different than the rules for operations involving empty string values. This internal distinction is especially important in reference to *joins*, which are discussed in Chapter 4.

The return of both NULL and empty values is shown in Example 3-15, which retrieves a set of five books from the books table. The first SELECT query shows that there appear to be two books which have been inserted without titles. Upon successive querying, however, it becomes clear that while neither have visible titles, one of the books has an *empty* value for its title (id 100), while the other has a NULL value.

Example 3-15: Observing NULL values

```
booktown=# SELECT id, title FROM books;
   id  |        title
------+---------------------
 7808 | The Shining
  156 | The Tell-Tale Heart
 4513 | Dune
  100 |
  101 |
(5 rows)

booktown=# SELECT id, title FROM books WHERE title = '';
 id | title
----+-------
```

Example 3-15: Observing NULL values (continued)

```
  100 |
(1 row)


booktown=# SELECT id, title FROM books WHERE title IS NULL;
 id | title
-----+-------
 101 |
(1 row)
```

Example 3-16 demonstrates a more practical (and likely) use of NULL in a table called editions, which relates a book's ISBN number to its publication date.

Example 3-16: Using NULL values

```
booktown=# SELECT isbn, publication FROM editions;
    isbn     | publication
------------+-------------
 039480001X | 1957-03-01
 0394800753 | 1949-03-01
 0385121679 |
(3 rows)

booktown=# SELECT isbn, publication FROM editions WHERE publication IS NULL;
    isbn     | publication
------------+-------------
 0385121679 |
(1 row)
```

NULL might be used in this manner in order to represent books with editions that are not yet published, or for books whose publication date was unknown when entered into the database. It could be misleading to supply some arbitrarily illogical date for a book fitting either of these criteria, and in both cases, NULL makes sense as a solution.

Boolean Values

A *Boolean* value is a simple data structure which can only represent values of true or false. PostgreSQL supports the SQL99-defined boolean data type, with a PostgreSQL-specific alias of bool.

Like all other data types, Boolean values can also be set to NULL. If a Boolean is set to NULL, it will never be interpreted as either true or false; it will be interpreted as NULL. This may seem obvious, but it is significant in situations where you may think to check for NULL Booleans by checking for false values (which won't work). You must use IS NULL to check for NULL Booleans. The ability to be true, false, or NULL (and its related rules regarding the designation of NULL as not being true or false) is known as three-valued logic.

Table 3-11 shows the valid constant values for a true or false state that are recognized by PostgreSQL. Which convention you choose to employ is dependent solely on your own preference. All variations of true, as well as all variations of false, are interpreted identically by the server.

Table 3-11. Supported true or false constants

True	False
true	false
't'	'f'
'true'	'false'
'y'	'n'
'yes'	'no'
'1'	'0'

If you decide to use the constants listed in Table 3-11, every value (except for true and false) must be enclosed within single quotes. Failure to do so will result in a server error.

Example 3-17 creates a table named daily_inventory that logs what books are stock and which are not, correlating an ISBN number with a Boolean value. Once created, the table is populated with data via a series of INSERT statements involving a string constant (the ISBN number), and a variety of valid Boolean constants.

Example 3-17: Simple Boolean table

```
booktown=# CREATE TABLE daily_inventory (isbn text, in_stock boolean);
CREATE
booktown=# INSERT INTO daily_inventory VALUES ('0385121679', true);
INSERT 3390926 1
booktown=# INSERT INTO daily_inventory VALUES ('039480001X', 't');
INSERT 3390927 1
booktown=# INSERT INTO daily_inventory VALUES ('044100590X', 'true');
INSERT 3390928 1
booktown=# INSERT INTO daily_inventory VALUES ('0451198492', false);
INSERT 3390929 1
booktown=# INSERT INTO daily_inventory VALUES ('0394900014', '0');
INSERT 3390930 1
booktown=# INSERT INTO daily_inventory VALUES ('0441172717', '1');
INSERT 3390931 1
booktown=# INSERT INTO daily_inventory VALUES ('0451160916');
INSERT 3390932 1
```

Now that the table has been populated with records, a SELECT query may be issued to easily check which books are in stock, as shown in Example 3-18.

Example 3-18: Checking Boolean values

```
booktown=# SELECT * FROM daily_inventory WHERE in_stock = 'yes';
    isbn    | in_stock
------------+----------
 0385121679 | t
 039480001X | t
 044100590X | t
 0441172717 | t
(4 rows)
```

With a Boolean column you have the ability to *imply* a true value by referencing the column name without any kind of operator or modifying keyword. This can lead to more intuitive looking queries for well-designed tables, as shown in Example 3-19.

Example 3-19: Implying Boolean 'true'

```
booktown=# SELECT * FROM daily_inventory WHERE in_stock;
    isbn    | in_stock
------------+----------
 0385121679 | t
 039480001X | t
 044100590X | t
 0441172717 | t
(4 rows)
```

Although the second query does not specify 'true' or 'false', it implicitly looks for a value of 'true' by omitting a comparison operator.

Similarly, if you want to search for false values, you may either compare the named column's value against any of the valid `boolean` constants in Table 3-11, or you may use the SQL keyword `NOT` just before the column name. Each method is demonstrated in Example 3-20.

Example 3-20: Checking for 'false' Boolean values

```
booktown=# SELECT * FROM daily_inventory WHERE in_stock = 'no';
    isbn    | in_stock
------------+----------
 0451198492 | f
 0394900014 | f
(2 rows)


booktown=# SELECT * FROM daily_inventory WHERE NOT in_stock;
    isbn    | in_stock
------------+----------
 0451198492 | f
 0394900014 | f
(2 rows)
```

In this way, you can see how SQL was designed with human readability in mind. By naming your tables and columns in well-designed terms, a SQL query can read almost as plainly as an English sentence.

For the more programming-oriented readers, it may be of interest that you can use the inequality (!=) operator to compare the value of a boolean field against any of the values in Table 3-11 (e.g., WHERE in_stock != 't'). As such, the following three syntactic variations are each equivalent:

```
SELECT * FROM daily_inventory WHERE NOT in_stock;
SELECT * FROM daily_inventory WHERE in_stock = 'no';
SELECT * FROM daily_inventory WHERE in_stock != 't';
```

You may have noticed that while seven rows were inserted into the table in Example 3-17, only six rows were returned between the books found in stock, and those found out of stock. This is due to the last insertion in Example 3-17 not supplying a value at all for the in_stock column, leaving the record for the book with ISBN *0451160916* with a NULL value in the in_stock column.

As stated previously, NULL will not register as either true or false. As such, you may use the SQL phrase IS NULL to check for rows with NULL values. Alternatively, you may use != but you will risk portability issues with other databases. The following syntax demonstrates a SQL query which uses the IS NULL phrase:

```
booktown=# SELECT * FROM daily_inventory WHERE in_stock IS NULL;
     isbn    | in_stock
-------------+----------
 0451160916  |
(1 row)
```

Since IS NULL is a general SQL phrase, you can use the same WHERE clause in an UPDATE statement to correct any accidental NULL values.

Example 3-21: Correcting NULL values

```
booktown=# UPDATE daily_inventory SET in_stock = 'f' WHERE in_stock IS NULL;
UPDATE 1
```

Character Types

Character types are required any time that you wish to reference character data, such as blocks of ASCII text. They are commonly used for storing names, addresses, and so on.

SQL provides two character types called character, and character varying. In addition to these, a general text type is supported by PostgreSQL, which does not require an explicitly declared upper limit on the size of the field. Columns of type text are automatically re-sized according to the data you put in them, and they may re-size without boundaries (discounting, of course, the 1GB limit for a single field). Table 3-12 shows the available character data types within PostgreSQL.

Table 3-12. Character types

Type	Storage	Description
character(n), char(n)	(4 + n) bytes	A fixed-length character string, padded with spaces so that it is n characters in length.
character varying(n), varchar(n)	Up to (4 + n) bytes	A variable-length character string with a limit of n characters
text	Variable	A variable, unlimited-length character string

The *n* in Table 3-12 represents an arbitrarily specified number of characters. This number is specified for a column when a table is created.

Although the text data type is not part of the ANSI/ISO SQL standards, many other Relational Database Management Systems (RDBMS) provide this functionality, including Sybase and MS SQL Server.

Numeric Types

PostgreSQL's numeric types are used to represent both integers and decimal floating-point values. From a general perspective, PostgreSQL's supported numeric types consist of:

- Two-, four-, and eight-byte integers
- Four- and eight-byte floating-point numbers
- Fixed precision decimals

PostgreSQL has support for special types which fall under the family of numeric types, including the deprecated money type, and the special serial construct.

Table 3-13. Numeric types overview

Data type	Storage	Range
bigint, int8	8 bytes	Whole integer values, −9,223,372,036,854,775,807 to +9,223,372,036,854,775,807
double precision, float8, float	8 bytes	Floating-point integer values, 15 significant digits, unlimited size (with limited precision)

Table 3-13. Numeric types overview (continued)

Data type	Storage	Range
`integer`, `int`, `int4`	4 bytes	Whole integer values, –2147483648 to +2147483647
`numeric(p,s)`, `decimal (p,s)`	Variable	Whole or floating point integers defined as *p* total digits (including digits to the right of the decimal) with *s* digits to the right of the decimal point
`real`, `float4`	4 bytes	Floating-point integer values, six significant digits, unlimited size (with limited precision)
`smallint`, `int2`	2 bytes	Whole integers, –32768 to +32767
`money`	4 bytes	Floating-point integer values with a scale of two digits to the right of the decimal, —21474836.48 to +21474836.47
`serial`	4 bytes	Whole integers, 0 to 2147483647

As shown in Table 3-13, several of PostgreSQL's data types have aliases that are equivalent to their associated data types. This was done for ease of use, but at times it can be confusing, due to the fact that some of the aliases sound familiar. If you are not careful to understand what data type an alias you are using is associated with, you may accidentally reference the wrong data type. For example, in PostgreSQL the `real` and `double precision` data types represent values that in many other languages are referred to as float values; however, they both have aliases that contain the word "float" (`float` and `float8` link to `double precision`; `float4` links to `real`). Problems may result if if you attempt to use the `float` alias, thinking it is linked to `real`, when in fact it is associated with `double precision`.

The numeric type

The `numeric` (also known as `decimal`) type is a specially designed numeric data type that can represent arbitrarily large and precise values within a fixed length that is given by the user. When you create a table with a column of type `numeric`, you may specify in parentheses two values: the *precision* and the *scale*.

The precision is the maximum number of digits that the numeric value may hold (including digits to the right of the decimal point), while the scale describes how many of those digits of precision are to be to the right of the decimal point. If left unspecified, the precision will default to 30 digits, and scale to 6 digits. The maximum precision (and, hence, the maximum scale) you can set this to is 1,000. Setting the precision to 1,000 would allow a maximum 1,000 digits, which should be fairly adequate for most needs.

PostgreSQL will not always return an error if you violate the precision and scale of a numeric column.

Unlike the floating-point data types, you will receive an overflow error if you attempt to insert a number that is larger than the allotted precision range. Beside this limitation, you should be able to insert any number that fits within the provided precision and scale of the numeric type column.

For example, in a numeric(11,6) column, you may safely insert the value 9.999999 with two digits too many to the right of the decimal point (though the value is rounded up to 10.000000). However, an attempt to insert the value 99999.99999999 will fail, as shown in Example 3-22.

Problems that arise from trying to insert values that are two large can be avoided by using the trunc() numeric truncating function within an INSERT command to make sure a number is truncated to a size suitable for the column it is being inserted into. You must provide the length it should be truncated to, which means you'll have to be aware of the precisions you've previously specified. The use of trunc() is also illustrated within Example 3-22.

Example 3-22: Avoiding overflow errors

```
booktown=# INSERT INTO numbers VALUES (9.99999999);
INSERT 3390697 1
booktown=# SELECT * FROM numbers;
    number
--------------
     10.000000
(1 row)


booktown=# INSERT INTO numbers VALUES (99999.99999999);
ERROR:  overflow on numeric ABS(value) >= 10^5 for field with precision 11 scale 6
booktown=# INSERT INTO numbers VALUES (trunc(99999.99999999, 6));
INSERT 3390698 1
booktown=# SELECT * FROM numbers;
    number
--------------
     10.000000
  99999.999999
(2 rows)


booktown=# INSERT INTO numbers VALUES (trunc(9.99999999, 6));
INSERT 3390699 1
booktown=# SELECT * FROM numbers;
    number
--------------
```

Example 3-22: Avoiding overflow errors (continued)

```
    10.000000
99999.999999
     9.999999
(3 rows)
```

The money type

The money type stores U.S.-style currency notation and plain numeric values. As of the writing of this book, the money type is deprecated, and is discouraged from being actively used. It is only presented here as it is still a functional data type, and may be in use on existing PostgreSQL systems.

The suggested alternative to the money type is the numeric type, with a scale of 2 to represent coin values, and a precision large enough to store the largest necessary monetary value (including two digits for the coin precision). Formatting similar to that of the money type can be achieved with the to_char() function, as shown in Example 3-23. This example demonstrates the text concatenation operator, and the ltrim() text formatting function, each described in Chapter 4.

Example 3-23: A numeric alternative to money

```
booktown=# CREATE TABLE money_example (money_cash money,
booktown(#                           numeric_cash numeric(10,2));
CREATE
booktown=# INSERT INTO money_example VALUES ('$12.24', 12.24);
INSERT 3391095 1
booktown=# SELECT * FROM money_example;
 money_cash | numeric_cash
------------+--------------
     $12.24 |        12.24
(1 row)

booktown=# SELECT money_cash,
booktown-#        '$' || ltrim(to_char(numeric_cash, '9999.99'))
booktown-#        AS numeric_cashified
booktown-#        FROM money_example;
 money_cash | numeric_cashified
------------+--------------------
     $12.24 | $12.24
(1 row)
```

The serial type

The serial type is a non-standard but useful shortcut which allows you to easily create an identifier column within a table that contains a unique value for each row. The serial type literally combines the functionality of a 4-byte integer data type, an index, and a sequence. Example 3-24 shows the serial type being used to generate a unique identifier for each row in a table named auto_identified.

Example 3-25 shows the same thing being accomplished using an integer column, the nextval() function , and a sequence. As of the writing of this book, these two methods are functionally identical.

See Chapter 7, *Advanced Features*, for more information on using sequences.

Example 3-24: Using the serial data type

```
booktown=# CREATE TABLE auto_identified (id serial);
NOTICE:  CREATE TABLE will create implicit sequence 'auto_identified_id_seq'
for SERIAL column 'auto_identified.id'
NOTICE:  CREATE TABLE/UNIQUE will create implicit index 'auto_identified_id_key'
for table 'auto_identified'
CREATE
```

Example 3-25: Accomplishing the same goal manually

```
booktown=# CREATE SEQUENCE auto_identified_id_seq;
CREATE
booktown=# CREATE TABLE auto_identified
booktown-# (id integer UNIQUE DEFAULT nextval('auto_identified_id_seq'));
NOTICE:  CREATE TABLE/UNIQUE will create implicit index 'auto_identified_id_key'
for table 'auto_identified'
CREATE
```

 Upon dropping a table, the implicit sequence created for the serial types are not automatically dropped. You must clean up after these types of sequences if you destroy a table which had a serial column, as shown in Example 3-24, with the DROP SEQUENCE command.

Date and Time Types

Date and time types are a convenient way to store date and time related data in a uniform SQL data structure, without having to worry about the conventions involved with storage (e.g., if you were to try to store such information in a character data type). PostgreSQL uses Julian dates for all date and time calculations. Julian date representation is the commonly used January through December calendar that you are most likely familiar with. By fixing the length of a year at about 365.24 days, Julian dates can correctly calculate any date after 4713 BC, as well as far into the future.

PostgreSQL supports all of the SQL92-defined date and time types shown in Table 3-14, as well as some PostgreSQL-specific extensions to help with SQL92's time-zone limitations.

Table 3-14. Date and time types

Data type	Storage	Description	Range
date	4 bytes	A calendar date (year, month, and day)	4713 BC to 32767 AD
time	4 bytes	The time of day only, without time zone information	00:00:00.00 to 23:59:59.99
time with time zone	4 bytes	The time of day only, including a time zone	00:00:00.00+12 to 23:59:59.99-12
timestamp with time zone, timestamp	8 bytes	Both the calendar date and time, with time zone information	1903 AD to 2037 AD
interval	12 bytes	A general time span interval	−1780000000 years to 17800000 years

Backward compatibility

To ensure compatibility with earlier versions of PostgreSQL, the developers have continued to provide the datetime and timespan data types. The datetime type is equivalent to timestamp, while the timespan is equivalent to the interval type.

Other date/time data types include abstime and reltime, which are lower precision types. However, these types are internal to PostgreSQL, and any or all of these types may disappear in a future release. It is advised therefore to design new applications with the SQL-compliant data types in mind, and to convert older applications from any of these data types as soon as is possible.

Date conventions

Date input can be accepted by PostgreSQL in many common formats, including the ISO-8601 format, the traditional SQL format, the original PostgreSQL format, and more. Table 3-15 lists several of these date formats.

These formats are relevant to the date and the timestamp data types.

Table 3-15. Valid date formats

Format Example	Description
July 1, 2001	Named month, day and year
Sunday July 1, 2001	Named day, named month, day and year
July 15, 01 BC	Named month, day and year before the Common Era
2001-07-01	Standard ISO-8601 format: numeric year, month and day
20010715	ISO-8601: formatted numerically as complete year, month, day

Table 3-15. Valid date formats (continued)

Format Example	Description
010715	ISO-8601: formatted numerically as 2-digit year, month, day
7/01/2001	Non-European (U.S.) format: numeric month, day and year
1/7/2001	European format: numeric day, month and year
2001.182	Numeric format, with complete year, and sequential day of the year

When specifying a named month in a date value to PostgreSQL, you may either type the complete month name, or choose from a set of defined abbreviations for each month. These abbreviations are listed in Table 3-16.

Table 3-16. Month abbreviations

Month	Abbreviation
January	Jan
February	Feb
March	Mar
April	Apr
May	May
June	Jun
July	Jul
August	Aug
September	Sep, Sept
October	Oct
November	Nov
December	Dec

Similarly, Table 3-17 lists recognized abbreviations for weekday names.

Table 3-17. Day of the week abbreviations

Day	Abbreviation
Sunday	Sun
Monday	Mon
Tuesday	Tue, Tues
Wednesday	Wed, Weds
Thursday	Thu, Thur, Thurs
Friday	Fri
Saturday	Sat

Despite the wide variety of ways in which PostgreSQL can interpret date values, the values are always stored uniformally, and will be returned in a consistent format. As such, you have a variety of methods available to you to customize the default behavior with which date and time values are returned to you.

 While date values can always be formatted during selection via several formatting functions (e.g., to_char()), it is more efficient to configure your defaults as close to the most commonly used conventions as you can before having to resort to manual type conversion and text formatting.

To set the general date/time output format, the SET command can be applied to the run-time variable DATESTYLE. This variable may be set to one of four available general styles shown in Table 3-18.

Table 3-18. Date output formats

General format	Description	Example
ISO	ISO-8601 standard	2001-06-25 12:24:00-07
SQL	Traditional SQL style	06/25/2001 12:24:00.00 PDT
Postgres	Original PostgreSQL style	Mon 25 Jun 12:24:00 2001 PDT
German	Regional style for Germany	25.06.2001 12:24:00.00 PDT

As an example, you can use the following SQL statement to set the date style to *SQL*:

```
booktown=# SET DATESTYLE TO SQL;
SET VARIABLE
```

If you perform a SELECT current_timestamp query after setting this variable, PostgreSQL should return the current time using the ISO format as instructed:

```
booktown=# SELECT current_timestamp;
        timestamp
---------------------------
 08/10/2001 13:25:55.00 PDT
(1 row)
```

The SHOW command can be used to display the current value of the DATESTYLE variable while PostgreSQL is running.

```
booktown=# SHOW DATESTYLE;
NOTICE:  DateStyle is SQL with US (NonEuropean) conventions
SHOW VARIABLE
```

In addition to these general formats, PostgreSQL's date output format has two other variants which further describe how to display the date, shown in Table 3-19: European and non-European (U.S.). These determine whether the format is day followed by month, or vice versa. This variation can be applied on top of the previous four general formats with the same syntax to SET DATESTYLE and will not modify your chosen format except for the arrangement of the month and day.

Table 3-19. Extended date output formats

Month/day format	Description	Example
European	day/month/year	12/07/2001 17:34:50.00 MET
U.S., or Non-European	month/day/year	07/12/2001 17:34:50.0 PST

Furthermore, you may set both the general format and day/month convention by supplying both variables to the SET command, comma delimited. The order of these variables is not important to the SET command as long as the variables are not mutually exclusive (e.g., *SQL* and *ISO*), as shown in Example 3-26.

Example 3-26: Setting date formats

```
booktown=# SET DATESTYLE TO ISO,US;
SET VARIABLE
booktown=# SHOW DATESTYLE;
NOTICE:  DateStyle is ISO with US (NonEuropean) conventions
SHOW VARIABLE
booktown=# SET DATESTYLE TO NONEUROPEAN, GERMAN;
SET VARIABLE
booktown=# SHOW DATESTYLE;
NOTICE:  DateStyle is German with European conventions
SHOW VARIABLE
```

If you do not specify a month/day format, a reasonable default will usually be chosen (e.g., European is the default for the German regional format).

While SET DATESTYLE is a convenient way to set the output format, it is important to note that this is a *run-time variable*, which means that it exists only for the lifespan of your connected session. There are two methods available that allow you to provide a default value for the DATESTYLE variable, which lets you avoid explicitly setting the variable for each new session you begin:

• You may change the PGDATESTYLE environment variable on the server running *postmaster*. For example, with the bash shell, you could add the export PGDATESTYLE="SQL US" line to the *postgres* user's *.bash_profile* file. When the *postgres* user starts *postmaster*, the PGDATESTYLE variable will be read and applied globally to all date and time formatting performed by PostgreSQL.

- You may change the PGDATESTYLE environment variable used by a client application (assuming it was written with the *libpq* library) on its session start-up, if you wish the client rather than the server to configure the output. For example, setting the PGDATESTYLE variable at a bash prompt with the export command before starting *psql* sets the format for *psql* to use.

Time conventions

Time values, like date values, may be entered in to a table in a number of ways. Commonly used formats are listed in Table 3-20. These apply to values of type time and time with time zone.

Table 3-20. Valid time formats

Format example	Description
01:24	ISO-8601, detailed to minutes
01:24 AM	Equivalent to 01:24 (the "AM" attached is for readability only, and does not affect the value)
01:24 PM	Equivalent to 13:24 (the hour must be less-than or equal to 12 to use "PM")
13:24	24-hour time, equivalent to 01:24 PM
01:24:11	ISO-8601, detailed to seconds
01:24:11.112	ISO-8601, detailed to microseconds
012411	ISO-8601, detailed to seconds, formatted numerically

In addition to these formats, PostgreSQL allows for further description of a time value which is defined as time with time zone by supporting extra time zone parameters following the time value. Supported formats are shown in Table 3-21.

Table 3-21. Valid time zone formats

Format example	Description
01:24:11-7	ISO-8601, 7 hours behind GMT
01:24:11-07:00	ISO-8601, 7 hours, zero minutes behind GMT
01:24:11-0700	ISO-8601, 7 hours, zero minutes behind GMT
01:24:11 PST	ISO-8601, Pacific Standard Time (7 hours behind GMT)

PostgreSQL supports the use of all ISO standard time zone abbreviations.

The `time with time zone` data type is mainly supported by PostgreSQL to adhere to existing SQL standards and for portability with other database management systems. If you need to work with time zones, it is recommended that you use the `timestamp` data type discussed in the section titled "Timestamps." This is primarily because of the fact that, due to daylight savings, time zones cannot always be meaningfully interpreted without an associated date.

Internally, PostgreSQL keeps track of all time zone information as a numeric offset of GMT (Greenwich Mean Time), which is also known as UTC (Universal Coordinated Time). By default, PostgreSQL's time display will use the time zone that your server's operating system is configured for. If you wish the time value to operate under a different time zone, there are four ways in which you can modify the output:

Set the `TZ` environment variable on the server

This variable is found by the backend server as the default time zone when the *postmaster* starts up. It can be set, for example, in the postgres user's *.bash_profile* file with a bash `export TZ='zone'` command.

Set the `PGTZ` environment variable on the client

If the `PGTZ` environment variable is set, it can be read by any client written with *libpq* and interpreted as the client's default time zone.

Use the `SET TIMEZONE TO` SQL statement

This SQL command sets the time zone for the session to *zone* (e.g., `SET TIMEZONE TO UTC`)

Use the `AT TIME ZONE` SQL clause

This SQL92 clause can be used to specify *zone* as a text time zone (e.g., *PST*) or as an interval (e.g., `interval('-07:00')`). This clause may be applied in the middle of a SQL statement following a value which contains a timestamp (e.g., `SELECT my_timestamp AT TIME ZONE 'PST'`).

 Most systems will default to GMT when a time zone variable is set to an invalid time zone. Additionally, if the compiler option *USE_AUS-TRALIAN_RULES* was set when PostgreSQL was built, the *EST* time zone will refer to Australian Eastern Standard Time (with an offset of +10:00 hours from GMT) rather than U.S. Eastern Standard Time.

Timestamps

The PostgreSQL `timestamp` combines the functionality of the PostgreSQL `date` and `time` types into a single data type. The syntax of a timestamp value consists of a valid date format, followed by at least one whitespace character, and a valid time format. It can be followed optionally by a time zone value, if specified.

Combinations of all date and time formats listed in Table 3-15 and Table 3-20 are each supported in this fashion. Table 3-22 illustrates some examples of valid timestamp input.

Table 3-22. Some valid timestamp formats

Format Example	Description
1980-06-25 11:11-7	ISO-8601 date format, detailed to minutes, and PST time zone
25/06/1980 12:24:11.112	European date format, detailed to microseconds
06/25/1980 23:11	U.S. date format, detailed to minutes in 24-hour time
25.06.1980 23:11:12 PM	German regional date format, detailed to seconds, and PM attached

   While PostgreSQL supports the syntax of creating a column or value with the type timestamp without time zone, as of PostgreSQL 7.1.2 the resultant data type still contains a time zone.

Intervals

The SQL92 standard specifies a data typed called an *interval*, which represents a fixed span of time. By itself, an interval represents only a *quantity of time*, and does not begin or end at any set date or time. These intervals can be useful when applied to date and time values to calculate a new date or time, either by subtracting or adding the quantity. They can also be handy for quickly determining the precise interval between two date or time values. This can be achieved by subtracting date values, time values or timestamps from one another.

The two syntax variations below can specify an interval within PostgreSQL:

```
qty unit   [ ago ]
qty1 unit [, qty2 unit2 ... ] [ ago ]
```
Where:

qty

Specifies the quantity of your interval, which may be any whole integer, or floating-point number in the case of microseconds. The literal meaning of this number is qualified by the subsequent *unit*.

unit

Qualifies the *qty* provided. The *unit* may be any one of the following keywords: second, minute, hour, day, week, month, year, decade, century, millen-
nium. It can also be an abbreviation (as short as you want, as long as it cannot
be confused with another keyword) or plurals of the previously mentioned
units.

ago

The optional ago keyword of the interval determines whether or not you are
describing a period of time *before* the associated time, rather than after. You
can think of it as a negative sign for date and time types.

Example 3-27 shows functional syntax for date and interval values being meaningfully combined. You can see that subtracting an inverted time interval (e.g., one
with the term ago) is functionally identical to adding a normal interval. This can be
thought of as similar to the effect of adding negative numbers to integer values.

Example 3-27: Interpreting interval formats

```
booktown=# SELECT date('1980-06-25');
    date
------------
 1980-06-25
(1 row)

booktown=# SELECT interval('21 years 8 days');
     interval
------------------
 21 years 8 days
(1 row)

booktown=# SELECT date('1980-06-25') + interval('21 years 8 days')
booktown-# AS spanned_date;
      spanned_date
------------------------
 2001-07-03 00:00:00-07
(1 row)

booktown=# SELECT date('1980-06-25') - interval('21 years 8 days ago')
booktown-# AS twice_inverted_interval_date;
  twice_inverted_interval_date
------------------------------
 2001-07-03 00:00:00-07
(1 row)
```

Built-in date and time constants

PostgreSQL supports many special constants for use when referencing dates and
times. These constants represent common date/time values, such as *now, tomorrow,* and *yesterday.* The predefined date and time constants supported by

PostgreSQL are listed in Table 3-23.

PostgreSQL also provides three built-in functions for retrieving the current time, date, and timestamp. These are aptly named `current_date`, `current_time`, and `current_timestamp`.

Table 3-23. Date and time constants

Constant	Description
current	The current transaction time, deferred. Unlike a *now*, *current* is not a timestamp; it represents the current system time and can be used to reference whatever that time may be.
epoch	1970-01-01 00:00:00+00 (Unix's "Birthday")
infinity	An abstract constant later than all other valid dates and times
-infinity	An abstract constant earlier than all other valid dates and times
now	The current transaction timestamp
today	Midnight, on the current day
tomorrow	Midnight, on the day after the current day
yesterday	Midnight on the day before the current day

The *now* and *current* timestamp constants may seem to be identical, looking solely at their names. They are, however, very different in terms of storing them in a table. The *now* constant is *translated* into the timestamp of the system time at the execution of whichever command referenced it (e.g., the time of insertion, if *now* had been referenced in an INSERT statement). In contrast, the *current* constant, as it is a deferred identifier, will actually appear as the phrase *current* in the database. From there, it can be translated (e.g., via the to_char() function) to the timestamp associated with the transaction time of *any query which requests that value*.

In other words, *current* will always tell you the "current" time when queried, regardless of when it was stored to the table. The *current* constant can be used in special situations, such as process tracking, where you may need to calculate the difference between a timestamp made with *now* and the current date and time to find the total time the process has been running. Example 3-28 demonstrates using the *now* and *current* constants to create a log of tasks. First, a table is created to house the task's name, its start date and time, and its finished date and time. Two tasks are then added to the table, using the *now* constant to set the start date and *current* to set the completed date. The reason this is done is to show that both of these tasks are uncompleted. If a task were to be completed, the table could be updated to show a *now* timestamp for that task's timefinished column.

The use of time/date constants requires the use of single-quotes around their respective names. See Example 3-28 for a valid representation of single-quoted time/date constants.

Example 3-28: Using the current and now constants

```
booktown=# CREATE TABLE tasklog
booktown=#    (taskname char(15),
booktown=#     timebegun timestamp,
booktown=#     timefinished timestamp);
CREATE
booktown=# INSERT INTO tasklog VALUES
booktown=#    ('delivery', 'now', 'current');
INSERT 169936 1
booktown=# INSERT INTO tasklog VALUES
booktown=#    ('remodeling', 'now', 'current');
INSERT 169937 1
booktown=# SELECT taskname, timefinished - timebegun AS timespent FROM tasklog;
    taskname     | timespent
-----------------+-----------
 delivery        | 00:15:32
 remodeling      | 00:04:42
(2 rows)
```

Therefore, you generally want to use *now* when storing a transaction timestamp in a table, or even the current_timestamp function, which is equivalent to the output of *now*. Example 3-29 shows how this could be a potentially disastrous SQL design issue if not properly understood. It shows a pair of INSERT statements; one which uses *now*, another which uses current. If you watch the first row returned from the two queries (the row with a *current* timestamp), you'll notice it changes in each query to show the updated system time, while the second row remains the same (this is the row in which *now* was used).

Example 3-29: Comparing now to current

```
booktown=# INSERT INTO shipments (customer_id, isbn, ship_date)
booktown-#        VALUES (1, '039480001X', 'current');
INSERT 3391221 1
booktown=# INSERT INTO shipments (customer_id, isbn, ship_date)
booktown-#        VALUES (2, '0394800753', 'now');
INSERT 3391222 1
booktown=# SELECT isbn, ship_date FROM shipments;
    isbn    |          ship_date
------------+-------------------------
 039480001X | current
 0394800753 | 2001-08-10 18:17:49-07
(2 rows)

booktown=# SELECT isbn,
```

Example 3-29: Comparing now to current (continued)

```
    booktown-#        to_char(ship_date, 'YYYY-MM-DD HH24:MI:SS')
    booktown-#        AS value
    booktown-#    FROM shipments;
       isbn      |        value
    ------------+--------------------
     039480001X | 2001-08-10 18:21:22
     0394800753 | 2001-08-10 18:17:49
    (2 rows)

    booktown=# SELECT isbn, to_char(ship_date, 'YYYY-MM-DD HH24:MI:SS') AS value
    booktown-#    FROM shipments;
       isbn      |        value
    ------------+--------------------
     039480001X | 2001-08-10 18:22:35
     0394800753 | 2001-08-10 18:17:49
    (2 rows)
```

Geometric Types

Geometric types in PostgreSQL represent two dimensional spatial objects. These types are not standard SQL data types, and will not be discussed in depth in this book. Table 3-24 gives a brief overview of each of the available geometric types.

Table 3-24. Geometric types

Type Name	Storage	Description	Syntax
point	16 bytes	A dimensionless object with no properties except for its location, where x and y are floating-point numbers.	(x, y)
lseg	32 bytes	Finite line segment. The points specified are the end points of the line segment.	$((x1, y1), (x2, y2))$
box	32 bytes	Rectangular box. The points specified are the opposite corners of the box.	$((x1, y1), (x2, y2))$
path	$4 + 32 * n$ bytes	Closed path (similar to polygon). A connected set of n points.	$((x1, y1), \ldots)$
path	$4 + 32 * n$ bytes	Open path. A connected set of n points.	$[(x1, y1), \ldots]$
polygon	$4 + 32 * n$ bytes	Polygon (similar to closed path), with n end points defining line segments that makes up the boundary of the polygon.	$((x1, y1), \ldots)$

Table 3-24. Geometric types (continued)

Type Name	Storage	Description	Syntax
circle	24 bytes	The point (x, y) is the center, while r is the radius of the circle.	$<(x, y), r>$

Arrays

The original relational model specifies that the values represented by columns within a table be an atomic piece of data, object-relational database systems such as PostgreSQL allow non-atomic values to be used through data structures called *arrays*.

An array is a collection of data values referenced through a single identifier. The array may be a collection of values of a built-in data type or a user-defined data type, but every value in the array must be of the same type. Arrays can be accessed from a table through subscript notation via square brackets (e.g., my_array[0]). You can also use an array constant via curly braces within single quotes (e.g., '{value_one,value_two,value_three}').

Arrays in tables

When defining an array, the syntax allows for the array to be defined either as fixed-length or variable-length; however as of PostgreSQL 7.1.2, the fixed-length size restriction is not enforced. This means that you may treat the array as having a fixed number of elements at all times, but it can still be dynamically sized. For example, it is perfectly acceptable for a single column defined as an array to contain three values in one record, four values in another, and no values in a third.

Additionally, arrays may be defined as being *multi-dimensional*, meaning that each element of the array may actually represent *another array*, rather than an atomic value. Values that are selected from a multi-dimensional array will consist of nested curly braces in order to show an array within an array, as follows:

```
booktown=# SELECT editions FROM my_notes WHERE title='The Cat in the Hat';
                        editions
-------------------------------------------------------------
 {{"039480001X","1st Ed, Hard Cover"},{"0394900014","1st Ed"}}
(1 row)
```

Array constants

In order to actually insert array values into a table column, you need a way to refer to several values as an array in a SQL statement. The formal syntax of an array constant is a grouping of values, separated by delimiters (commas, for built-in data types), enclosed by curly braces ({}), which are in turn enclosed by single quotes, as follows:

```
'{ value1 , value2 [, ...] }'
```

The *values* in this syntax can be any valid PostgreSQL data type. As the entire array is constrained by single quotes, the use of single quotes *within* an array value must be escaped, just as they must be within a string constant. The use of commas to delimit the values, however, poses an interesting problem pertaining to the use of character strings which contain commas themselves, as the commas will be interpreted as delimiters if not within single-quotes. However, as just mentioned, the singles quotes constrain the *array*, not the array's *values*.

PostgreSQL's method of handling this is to use *double-quotes* to quote string constants where single-quotes would ordinarily be used outside of an array context, as follows:

```
'{"value1" , "value 2, which contains a comma" }'
```

It's vital to remember that arrays *require* the single quotes surrounding the curly braces in order to be interpreted correctly by PostgreSQL. You can think of array constants as being akin to a special type of string constant, which is interpreted as an array based on where it is used (e.g., when used to add records to a target column which is of an array data type). This is because unless used in an array context, a constant of the this format will be interpreted by PostgreSQL as a normal string constant (as it is bound by single quotes) which just happens to include curly braces.

Type Coercion

PostgreSQL supports three separate conventions for type coercion (also called *type casting*, or *explicit type casting*). Type coercion is a somewhat ugly looking term which refers to a PostgreSQL method for changing a value from one data type to another. In the middle of a SQL statement, this has the net effect of explicitly creating a constant of an arbitrary type.

Generally any of the following three methods can be used in order to cast the value contained within a string constant to another type:

- *type* `'value'`
- `'value'`::*type*
- CAST (`'value'` AS *type*)

In the case of maintained numeric constants that you wish to cast to a character string, you will need to use one of the following syntax forms:

- *value* :: *type*

- CAST (*value* AS *type*)

The *value* in this syntax represents the constant whose data type you wish to modify, and *type* represents the type that you wish to coerce, or cast, the value to.

> Remember that the money type is deprecated, and therefore not easily cast.

Constants are not the only data values that may be coerced to different types. Columns of a data set returned by a SQL query may be cast by using its identifier in one of the following syntax forms:

- *identifier* :: *type*

- CAST (*identifier* AS *type*)

Bear in mind that not every data type can be coerced into every other data type. For example, there is no meaningful way to convert the character string *abcd* into a binary bit type. Invalid casting will result in an error from PostgreSQL. Common valid casts are from character string, date/time type, or a numeric type to text, or character strings to numeric values.

In addition to these type casting conventions, there are some functions that can be called to achieve essentially the same effect as an explicit cast of any of the previously mentioned forms. These often bear the name of the type itself (such as the text() function), though others are named more specifically (such as bitfromint4()). Example 3-30 shows such a function, converting the integer 1000 to a character string of type text representing the characters *1000*.

Example 3-30: Using type conversion functions

```
booktown=# SELECT text(1000)
booktown-# AS explicit_text;
 explicit_text
---------------
 1000
(1 row)
```

Because of conflicting semantics recognized by PostgreSQL's parser, the type coercion format of *type* '*value*' can only be used to specify the data type of a single value (e.g., a string constant bound by single quotes). In contrast, the other available methods of type coercion ('*value*'::*type*, CAST('*value*' AS *type*) and type conversion functions, where applicable) can be used to to specify the type of arbitrary expressions.

This is partially because attempting to follow a data type with a grouped expression (e.g., in parentheses) will cause PostgreSQL to expect a *function* with the name of the provided data type (which will often cause an error) while each of the other methods are syntactically valid upon grouped expressions.

```
booktown=# SELECT 1 + integer ('1' || '2') AS add_one_to_twelve;
ERROR:  Function 'integer(text)' does not exist
        Unable to identify a function that satisfies the given argument types
        You may need to add explicit typecasts
booktown=# SELECT 1 + ('1' || '2')::integer AS add_one_to_twelve;
 add_one_to_twelve
-------------------
                13
(1 row)

booktown=# SELECT 1 + CAST('1' || '2' AS integer) AS add_on_to_twelve;
 add_on_to_twelve
------------------
                13
(1 row)
```

Tables in PostgreSQL

If you are already familiar with SQL or other RDBMS packages, you probably already have a solid understanding of many of the relational database concepts put forth in this chapter. However, each RDBMS handles tables differently at the system level. This section takes a closer look at tables as they are implemented in PostgreSQL.

System Columns

PostgreSQL defines a series of *system columns* in all tables, which are normally invisible to the user (e.g., they will not be shown by queries unless explicitly requested). These columns contain *meta-data* about the content of the table's rows. Many of these contain data that can help to differentiate between *tuples* (an individual state of a row) when working with transaction blocks. (See Chapter 7 for more about transactions.)

As a result of these system-defined columns, in addition to the user-defined columns of a table, any inserted row will have values in each of the columns described in Table 3-25.

Table 3-25. System columns

Column	Description
oid (object identifier)	The unique object identifier of a row. PostgreSQL automatically adds this 4-byte number to all rows. It is never re-used within the same table.
tableoid (table object identifier)	The oid of the table that contains a row. The name and oid of a table are related by the pg_class system table.
xmin (transaction minimum)	The transaction identifier of the inserting transaction of a tuple.
cmin (command minimum)	The command identifier, starting at 0, associated with the inserting transaction of a tuple.
xmax (transaction maximum)	The transaction identifier of a tuple's deleting transaction. If a tuple is visible (has not been deleted) this is set to zero.
cmax (command maximum)	The command identifier associated with the deleting transaction of a tuple. Like xmax, if a tuple is visible, this is set to zero.
ctid (tuple identifier)	The identifier which describes the physical location of the tuple within the database. A pair of numbers are represented by the ctid: the block number, and tuple index within that block.

Object Identifiers

As described in the section titled "Understanding Tables," a database is used to store tables, and a table consists of at least one named column. A table may contain rows of data, but does not necessarily at any given time. For each stored row, there is a data value (or a NULL value) for each column.

One table management concern can be how to distinguish between two rows whose column values are identical. A very useful PostgreSQL feature is that every row has its own *object identifier* number, or *OID*, which is unique within that table. In other words, no two rows within the same table should ever have the same OID. This means that even if a table were designed in such a way that two rows might be identical, there is still a programmatic way to discern between them: through the OID. This technique is demonstrated in Example 3-31.

Example 3-31: Differentiating rows with the OID

```
testdb=# SELECT * FROM my_list;
           todos
-----------------------------------
```

Example 3-31: Differentiating rows with the OID (continued)

```
    Correct redundancies in my list.
    Correct redundancies in my list.
    (2 rows)

    testdb=# SELECT *,oid FROM my_list;
                  todos                |   oid
    ----------------------------------+---------
     Correct redundancies in my list. | 3391263
     Correct redundancies in my list. | 3391264
    (2 rows)

    testdb=# DELETE FROM my_list
    testdb=#         WHERE oid = 3391264;
    DELETE 1
    testdb=# SELECT *,oid FROM my_list;
                  todos                |   oid
    ----------------------------------+---------
     Correct redundancies in my list. | 3391263
    (1 row)
```

Planning Ahead

Before you start creating any tables, we suggest that you take some extra time to plan out your intended database objects by deciding the names, types, and purposes of all columns within each table. This can help you to be consistent with table naming structures, which in turn helps you more easily read and construct "legible" queries and statements.

In addition to taking the somewhat semantic considerations just described (names, types, and purposes), it is important to be sure that each table's relationship to each other table is clearly defined. This can be an important point of table design, as you do not wish to redundantly represent large amounts of data, nor do you want to end up omitting important data from one table by misunderstanding the needs that must be satisfied by your implementation.

As an example, consider again the Book Town books table, from Table 3-1. This table holds an internal Book Town identification number for each book, the title, author identification number, and a subject identification number. Notice that rather than storing the name of the author, and rather than storing a text representation of the subject of the book, simple identification integers are stored. These identification numbers are used to create relationships to two other tables: the authors, and subjects tables, whose partial contents are shown in Table 3-26 and Table 3-27.

Table 3-26. The authors table

id	last_name	first_name
1809	Geisel	Theodor Seuss
1111	Denham	Ariel
15990	Bourgeois	Paulette
2031	Brown	Margaret Wise
25041	Margery Williams	Bianco
16	Alcott	Louisa May
115	Poe	Edgar Allen

Table 3-27. The subjects table

id	subject	location
0	Arts	Creativity St
2	Children's Books	Kids Ct
3	Classics	Academic Rd
4	Computers	Productivity Ave
6	Drama	Main St
9	Horror	Black Raven Dr
15	Science Fiction	Main St

By keeping the author and subject-specific data separate from the books table, the data is stored more efficiently. When multiple books need to be correlated with a particular subject, only the subject_id needs to be stored, rather than all of the data associated with that subject. This also makes for simpler maintenance of data associated with book subjects, such as the location in the store. Such data can be updated in a single, small table, rather than having to update all affected book records with such a modification. The same general principle applies to the authors table, and its relationship to the books table via the author_id.

Thoughtful planning can also help to avoid mistakes in choosing appropriate data types. For example, in the editions table, ISBN numbers are associated with Book Town book identification numbers. At first glance, it might seem that the ISBN number could be represented with a column of type integer. The design oversight in this case would be that not only can ISBNs sometimes contain character data, but a value of type integer would lose any leading zeroes in the ISBN (e.g., *0451160916* would become 451160916).

For all of these reasons, good table design is not an issue to be overlooked in database administration.

4

Using SQL with PostgreSQL

In this chapter we continue to discuss SQL, this time with a practical focus. We'll address creating tables, populating tables with data, and managing that data via SQL statements.

Like most network-capable database systems, PostgreSQL fits into a client-server paradigm. The heart of PostgreSQL is the server backend, or the *postmaster* process. It is called a "backend" because it is not meant to directly interface with a user; rather, it can be connected to with a variety of clients.

When you start the PostgreSQL service, the *postmaster* process starts running in the background, listening to a specific TCP/IP port for connections from clients. Unless explicitly configured, *postmaster* will bind to, and listen on, port 5432.

There are several interfaces available through which clients may connect to the *postmaster* process. The examples in this book use *psql*, the most portable and readily accessible client distributed with PostgreSQL.

This chapter covers *psql* basics, how to create and use tables, and how to retrieve and manage data within those tables. It also addresses SQL sub-queries and views.

Introduction to psql

The *psql* client is a command-line client distributed with PostgreSQL. It is often called the *interactive monitor* or *interactive terminal*. With *psql*, you get a simple yet powerful tool with which you can directly interface with the PostgreSQL server, and thereby begin exploring SQL.

Starting psql

Before starting *psql*, be sure that you have either copied the *psql* binary into a path in your system PATH variable (e.g., */usr/bin*), or that you have placed the PostgreSQL binary path (e.g., */usr/local/pgsql/bin*) within your list of paths in your PATH environment variable (as shown in Chapter 2, *Installing PostgreSQL*).

How you set the appropriate PATH variable will depend on your system shell. An example in either bash or ksh might read:

```
$ export PATH=$PATH:/usr/local/pgsql/bin
```

An example in either csh or tcsh might read:

```
$ set path=($path /usr/local/pgsql/bin)
```

Example 4-1: Setting system path for psql

```
[user@host user]$ psql
bash: psql: command not found
[user@host user]$ echo $PATH
/bin:/usr/bin:/usr/local/bin:/usr/bin/X11:/usr/X11R6/bin
[user@host user]$ export PATH=$PATH:/usr/local/pgsql/bin
[user@host user]$ psql testdb
Welcome to psql, the PostgreSQL interactive terminal.

Type:  \copyright for distribution terms
       \h for help with SQL commands
       \? for help on internal slash commands
       \g or terminate with semicolon to execute query
       \q to quit

testdb=#
```

Note that Example 4-1 takes place within a bash shell.

Once you have appropriately set your PATH variable, you should be able to type *psql*, along with a database name, to start up the PostgreSQL interactive terminal.

Shell environment variables are erased after you have logged out. If you wish for your changes to the PATH variable to be retained upon logging in, you need to enter the appropriate PATH declaration into your shell-specific start-up scripts (e.g., *˜/.bash_profile*).

Introduction to psql Syntax

Upon starting *psql*, you are greeted with a brief synopsis of four essential *psql slash commands*: \h for SQL help, \? for help on *psql*-specific commands, \g for executing queries and \q for actually exiting *psql* once you are done. Every *psql*-specific command is prefixed by a backslash; hence the term "slash command."

Example 4-2: Listing psql slash commands

```
booktown=# \?
 \a              toggle between unaligned and aligned mode
 \c[onnect] [dbname|- [user]]
                 connect to new database (currently 'booktown')
 \C <title>      table title
 \copy ...       perform SQL COPY with data stream to the client machine
 \copyright      show PostgreSQL usage and distribution terms
 \d <table>      describe table (or view, index, sequence)
 \d{t|i|s|v}     list tables/indices/sequences/views
 \d{p|S|l}       list permissions/system tables/lobjects
 \da             list aggregates
 \dd [object]    list comment for table, type, function, or operator
 \df             list functions
 \do             list operators
 \dT             list data types
 \e [file]       edit the current query buffer or [file] with external editor
 \echo <text>    write text to stdout
 \encoding <encoding>  set client encoding
 \f <sep>        change field separator
 \g [file]       send query to backend (and results in [file] or |pipe)
 \h [cmd]        help on syntax of sql commands, * for all commands
 \H              toggle HTML mode (currently off)
 \i <file>       read and execute queries from <file>
 \l              list all databases
 \lo_export, \lo_import, \lo_list, \lo_unlink
                 large object operations
 \o [file]       send all query results to [file], or |pipe
 \p              show the content of the current query buffer
 \pset <opt>     set table output  <opt> = {format|border|expanded|fieldsep|
                 null|recordsep|tuples_only|title|tableattr|pager}
 \q              quit psql
 \qecho <text>   write text to query output stream (see \o)
 \r              reset (clear) the query buffer
 \s [file]       print history or save it in [file]
 \set <var> <value>  set internal variable
 \t              show only rows (currently off)
 \T <tags>       HTML table tags
 \unset <var>    unset (delete) internal variable
 \w <file>       write current query buffer to a <file>
 \x              toggle expanded output (currently off)
 \z              list table access permissions
 \! [cmd]        shell escape or command
```

Executing Queries

Entering and executing a query (*psql*'s generic term for SQL input) within *psql* can be done two different ways. When using the client in interactive mode, the normal method is to directly enter queries into the prompt (i.e., standard input, or stdin). However, through the use of *psql*'s \i slash command, you can have *psql* read and interpret a file on your local filesystem as the input.

Entering queries at the psql prompt

To enter queries directly into the prompt, open *psql* and make sure you are connected to the correct database (and logged in as the correct user). You will be presented with a prompt that, by default, is set to display the name of the database you are currently connected to. The prompt will look like this:

```
testdb=#
```

To pass SQL statements to PostgreSQL, simply type them into the prompt. Anything you type (barring a slash command) will be queued until you terminate the query with a semicolon. This is the case even if you start a new line of type, thus allowing you to spread query statements across multiple lines. Examine Example 4-3 to see how this is done.

Example 4-3: Entering statements into psql

```
testdb=# SELECT * FROM employees
testdb-#            WHERE firstname = 'Michael';
```

The query entered in Example 4-3 will return a table that consists of all employees whose first name is Michael. The query could be broken up over multiple lines to improve readability, and *psql* would not send it to the backend until the terminating semicolon was sent. The prompt will show the end-character of a previous line if the character requires a closing character, such as a parenthesis or a quote (this is not shown in the example). If you were to issue a CREATE TABLE command to start a statement, and then hit enter to begin a new line for readability purposes, you would see a prompt similar to the one displayed in Example 4-4.

Example 4-4: Leaving end-characters open

```
testdb=# CREATE TABLE employees (
testdb(#
```

At this point you could continue the statement. The *psql* prompt is informing you of the open parenthesis by inserting an open parenthesis symbol into the prompt.

Editing the query buffer

Use the \e command to edit the current query buffer with the editor that your EDI-TOR environment variable is set to. Doing so can be very useful when entering queries and statements in *psql*, as you can easily view and modify all lines of your query or statement before it is committed. Example 4-5 shows how to set the EDITOR variable. The *vi* editor will be used if EDITOR is not set.

Example 4-5: Setting the EDITOR variable

```
$ set EDITOR='joe'
$ export EDITOR
```

You can also use this command to save your current buffer as a file. Issue the \e command to enter editing mode. This will open your editor and load the buffer as if it were a file. Complete whatever work you wish to do with the buffer, then use your editor's save function to save the buffer and return to *psql*. To save the query as a normal file, use your editor's save-as function and save it as a file other than the *.tmp* created by \e.

Using Tables

Tables are the fundamental building blocks with which to store data within your database. Before you can begin to add, retrieve, or modify data within your database, you will first have to construct your tables to house that data.

This section covers how to create, modify and destroy tables, using the CREATE TABLE, ALTER TABLE, and DROP TABLE SQL commands. (If you need information about creating a database within which to work, see Chapter 9, *Database Management.*)

Creating Tables with CREATE TABLE

The SQL command to create a table is CREATE TABLE. This command requires, at a minimum, the name for the new table and a description for each column, which consists of the column name and data type. The CREATE TABLE command accepts several optional parameters: *column constraints* (rules on what data is or is not allowed within a column), and *table constraints* (general limitations and relationships defined on the table itself).

CREATE TABLE syntax

The following is the syntax for CREATE TABLE with a detailed explanation of the terms used:

```
CREATE [ TEMPORARY | TEMP ] TABLE table_name (
    { column_name type [ column_constraint [ ... ] ] | table_constraint }
    [, ... ]
    ) [ INHERITS ( inherited_table [, ... ] ) ]
```

TEMPORARY | TEMP

The TEMPORARY or TEMP SQL keyword causes the created table to be automatically destroyed at the end of the active session to PostgreSQL. A temporary table may have the same name as an existing table, and until the temporary table is destroyed, any references to that table name will utilize the temporary table. Any indices placed on this table are temporary and will be destroyed in the same fashion at the end of the session.

table_name

table_name identifies your table's name (once created).

column_name type [*column_constraint*] | *table_constraint*

Each table column and table constraint is defined within the parentheses following the table name, separated by commas. Column definitions must contain a valid identifier for a *column_name*, followed by a valid data *type*, and may optionally include a *column_constraint*. The requirements of column constraint definitions are dependent on the constraints, described in the section titled "Using Constraints" in Chapter 7, *Advanced Features*. Table constraints and columns may be mixed in this grouped list, though it is common practice to list columns first, followed by any table constraints.

[, ...]

Each column definition may be followed by a comma in order to define a subsequent column after it. The ellipses denote that you may enter as many columns as you wish (up to the limit of 1,600). Be sure that you do not follow the last column or constraint in the list with a comma, as is allowed in languages like Perl; this will cause a parsing error.

INHERITS (*inherited_table* [, ...])

The object-relational capabilities of PostgreSQL allow you to specify one or more tables (in a grouped, comma-delimited list) from which your table will *inherit*. This optional specification creates an implied parent-child relationship between tables. This relatively new technique to RDBMSs is discussed in more detail in the section titled "Inheritance" within Chapter 7.

 The terms *column_constraint* and *table_constraint* in the above syntax definition refer to sets of potentially complex constraint definitions. The syntax for these various constraints is listed in detail in the section titled "Using Constraints" within Chapter 7.

Creating an example table

Example 4-6 demonstrates the syntax to create Book Town's books table.

Example 4-6: Creating the books table

```
booktown=# CREATE TABLE books (
booktown(#              id integer UNIQUE,
booktown(#              title text NOT NULL,
booktown(#              author_id integer,
booktown(#              subject_id integer,
booktown(#              CONSTRAINT books_id_pkey PRIMARY KEY (id));
NOTICE:  CREATE TABLE/PRIMARY KEY will create implicit index 'books_id_pkey'
for table 'books'
CREATE
```

The CREATE output following the execution of the statement indicates that the table was successfully created. If you receive an error message, check your punctuation and spelling to make sure you have entered the correct syntax. Receiving no message at all means that you probably left open a quote, parenthesis, or other special character symbol.

Additionally, the NOTICE statement serves to inform you that in order to properly complete the creation of this table as described, an implicit index called books_id_pkey will be created.

Examining a created table

Once created, you may use the \d describe command (followed by the table name) within *psql* to display the structure of the table and its constraints (if any). Example 4-7 shows the output of \d when it is used to describe the books table created in the last section.

Notice that this format does not show actual row data, but instead places each column and its attributes in its own *row*, essentially turning the table on its side. This is done for the sake of clarity, as many tables can grow too large to fit on a screen (or on a page) horizontally. We'll use this format throughout the book when examining table structure without data.

Example 4-7: The \d command's output

```
booktown=#  \d books
          Table "books"
  Attribute  |  Type   | Modifier
-------------+---------+----------
 id          | integer | not null
 title       | text    | not null
 author_id   | integer |
 subject_id  | integer |
Index: books_id_pkey
```

The following list provides a more detailed explanation of the fields and terms shown in Example 4-7:

id The id column is a numeric identifier unique to each book. It is defined as being of the data type integer, and has on it the following constraints:

UNIQUE

This constraint ensures that the column always has a unique value. A column with the UNIQUE constraint set may ordinarily contain empty (NULL values, but any attempt to insert duplicate values will fail. The id column is also designed to be used as the PRIMARY KEY.

PRIMARY KEY

While not displayed in the \d breakdown, you can see in our original CRE-ATE TABLE statement that this table's primary key is defined on the id column. Placing the constraint of PRIMARY KEY on a column implicitly sets both the NOT NULL and UNIQUE constraints as well.

NOT NULL

This constraint is set automatically by setting the PRIMARY KEY constraint. It ensures that the ID column always has a value. Data for this column can never be empty, and any attempt to insert NULL values will fail.

title

The title column of the table must contain character strings of type text. The text type is more flexible than varchar, and is a good choice for this column as it does not require that you specify the maximum number of characters allowed. This column has the NOT NULL constraint set, indicating that a row's title column cannot ever be set to NULL.

author_id

The author_id column must contain values of type integer, and relates to the authors table. There are no constraints placed on this column, as sometimes an author may not be known for a title (making NOT NULL inappropriate), and an author may show up more than once (making UNIQUE inappropriate as well).

subject_id

The subject_id is similar to the author_id column, as it may contain values of type integer, and relates to the subjects table. Again, there are no constraints on the contents of this column, as many books may be uncategorized, or fall under the same subject.

While a table's structure can be modified after it has been created, the available modifications are limited. These include, for example, renaming the table, renaming its columns, and adding new columns. PostgreSQL 7.1.x does not support dropping columns from a table. It is therefore good practice to thoughtfully and carefully plan your table structures before creating them.

Altering Tables with ALTER TABLE

Most mature RDBMSs allow you to alter the properties of existing tables via the
ALTER TABLE command. The PostgreSQL implementation of ALTER TABLE allows for
six total types of table modifications as of version 7.1.x:

- Adding columns
- Setting and removing default column values
- Renaming the table
- Renaming columns
- Adding constraints
- Changing ownership

Adding columns

You can add a new column to a table using the ALTER TABLE command's ADD COL-
UMN clause. Here is the syntax for the ALTER TABLE command's ADD COLUMN clause:

```
ALTER TABLE table
        ADD [ COLUMN ] column_name column_type
```

table_name
> The name of the table to modify.

column_name
> The name of the column to add.

column_type
> The data type of the new column.

Technically, the COLUMN keyword may be omitted; it is considered a noise term and
is only useful for your own readability.

As an example of adding a column, imagine that an industrious employee at Book
Town decides that the books table requires another column, specifically, a date
column to represent the publication date. Example 4-8 demonstrates such a procedure.

Example 4-8: Adding a column

```
booktown=# ALTER TABLE books
booktown-#         ADD publication date;
ALTER
booktown=# \d books
          Table "books"
   Attribute  |  Type  | Modifier
```

Example 4-8: Adding a column (continued)

```
--------------+---------+----------
 id           | integer | not null
 title        | text    | not null
 author_id    | integer |
 subject_id   | integer |
 publication  | date    |
Index: books_id_pkey
```

Example 4-8 successfully adds a new column to Book Town's books table with the name of publication, and a data type of date. It also demonstrates a pitfall of uncoordinated table design among developers: in our examples, the Book Town editions table already stores the publication date, so the column should not have been added to the books table. See the section titled "Restructuring Existing Tables" for information on how to restructure a table after such a mistake has been made.

Setting and removing default values

The most flexible table modification pertains to the default values of columns. These values may be both set and removed from a column with relative ease via the ALTER TABLE command's ALTER COLUMN clause.

The following syntax passed to PostgreSQL describes how to use ALTER TABLE in order to either set, or remove a default value of *value* from a column named *column_name*:

```
ALTER TABLE table
      ALTER [ COLUMN ] column_name
      { SET DEFAULT value | DROP DEFAULT }
```

Again, the COLUMN keyword is considered noise, and is an optional term used only for improved readability of the statement. Example 4-9 demonstrates setting and dropping a simple default sequence value on the books table's id column.

Example 4-9: Altering column defaults

```
booktown=# ALTER TABLE books
booktown-#       ALTER COLUMN id
booktown-#       SET DEFAULT nextval('book_ids');
ALTER
booktown=# \d books
                      Table "books"
 Attribute  | Type    |               Modifier
------------+---------+------------------------------------------
 id         | integer | not null default nextval('book_ids'::text)
 title      | text    | not null
 author_id  | integer |
 subject_id | integer |
Index: books_id_pkey
```

Example 4-9: Altering column defaults (continued)

```
booktown=# ALTER TABLE books
booktown-#        ALTER id
booktown-#        DROP DEFAULT;
ALTER
booktown=# \d books
             Table "books"
  Attribute  |  Type   | Modifier
-------------+---------+----------
 id          | integer | not null
 title       | text    | not null
 author_id   | integer |
 subject_id  | integer |
Index: books_id_pkey
```

Renaming a table

A table may be safely renamed by passing the RENAME clause with the ALTER TABLE command. The following is the syntax to rename a table:

```
ALTER TABLE table
      RENAME TO new_table
```

A table may be arbitrarily renamed as many times as you like without affecting the data. This could, of course, be a dangerous thing to do if you are dealing with a table on which an external application relies.

Example 4-10: Renaming a table

```
booktown=# ALTER TABLE books RENAME TO literature;
ALTER
booktown=# ALTER TABLE literature RENAME TO books;
ALTER
```

Renaming columns

A table's columns may be safely renamed in PostgreSQL without modifying the data contained in the table. Renaming a column is a dangerous thing to do because existing applications may use explicit references to column names. If an existing program references a column by name and the column is renamed, the program could cease functioning correctly.

The following syntax describes how to rename a column:

```
ALTER TABLE table
      RENAME [ COLUMN ] column_name TO new_column_name;
```

As with the other ALTER TABLE commands, the COLUMN keyword is considered noise, and may be optionally omitted. The existence of two identifiers separated by the TO keyword provides enough information for PostgreSQL to determine that you are renaming a column, and not a table, as demonstrated in Example 4-11.

Example 4-11: Renaming a column

```
booktown=# \d daily_inventory
      Table "daily_inventory"
  Attribute |  Type  | Modifier
-----------+---------+----------
  isbn      | text    |
  in_stock  | boolean |

booktown=# ALTER TABLE daily_inventory
booktown-#        RENAME COLUMN in_stock TO is_in_stock;
ALTER
booktown=# ALTER TABLE daily_inventory
booktown-#        RENAME is_in_stock TO is_stocked;
ALTER
```

Adding constraints

Constraints may be added in a limited fashion after a table has been created. As of PostgreSQL 7.1.x, only foreign key and check constraints may be added to an existing table column with ALTER TABLE. The following is the syntax to add a constraint to a table:

```
ALTER TABLE table
      ADD CONSTRAINT constraint_name constraint_definition
```

The syntax of the *constraint_definition* is dependent on the type of constraint you wish to add. As foreign keys and checks are the only supported constraints with the ADD CONSTRAINT clause (as of PostgreSQL 7.1.x), the syntax for adding a foreign key to the editions table (which references the books table's id column) and a check condition on the type column is demonstrated in Example 4-12.

Example 4-12: Adding constraints to a table

```
booktown=# ALTER TABLE editions
booktown-#        ADD CONSTRAINT foreign_book
booktown-#        FOREIGN KEY (book_id) REFERENCES books (id);
NOTICE: ALTER TABLE ... ADD CONSTRAINT will create implicit trigger(s)
for FOREIGN KEY check(s)
CREATE
booktown=# ALTER TABLE editions
booktown-#        ADD CONSTRAINT hard_or_paper_back
booktown-#        CHECK (type = 'p' OR type = 'h');
ALTER
```

Due to the foreign key constraint, any book_id value in the editions table will now also have to exist in the books table. Additionally, due to the check constraint, the type values within the editions table may only be set to either *p* or *h*.

To implicitly add a unique constraint, a workaround is to create a unique index using the CREATE INDEX command (see the section titled "Indices" in Chapter 7).

See the section titled "Using Constraints" in Chapter 7 for more detailed information about constraints, their purpose, and their syntax.

Changing ownership

By default, the creator of a table is automatically its *owner*. The owner has all rights that can be associated with a table, in addition to the ability to *grant* and *revoke* rights with the GRANT and REVOKE commands (for more information see Chapter 10, *User and Group Management*). If ownership must be changed, you can use the ALTER TABLE command's OWNER clause. The syntax to change the ownership of a table from one user to another is:

```
ALTER TABLE table
       OWNER TO new_owner
```

Example 4-13 demonstrates altering a table's ownership with the ALTER TABLE command's OWNER clause. In it, corwin is set as the owner of the employees table.

Example 4-13: Changing table ownership

```
booktown=# ALTER TABLE employees
booktown-#        OWNER TO corwin;
ALTER
```

 In order to change the ownership of a table, you must either be the owner of that table or a PostgreSQL superuser.

Restructuring Existing Tables

While you have the ability to arbitrarily add new columns to existing tables, remember that (as of PostgreSQL 7.1.x) *you cannot drop columns from existing tables*. There are two fairly painless workarounds for restructuring existing tables. The first involves the CREATE TABLE AS command, while the second combines the CREATE TABLE command with the INSERT INTO command.

Each of these methods, in essence, involves creating a new table with your desired structure, filling it up with the data from your existing table, and renaming the tables so that the new table takes the place of your old table.

When "restructuring" a table in this fashion, it is important to notice that old indices placed on the original table will not automatically be applied to the newly created table, nor will the OIDs (object identifiers) be the same. Any indices must be dropped and recreated.

Restructuring with CREATE TABLE AS

One common technique of restructuring a table is to use the CREATE TABLE command in conjunction with the AS clause and a valid SQL query. This allows you to restructure your existing table into a temporary table, which can then be renamed. Doing this also allows you to both remove and re-arrange columns to a table by physically re-creating it, and simultaneously re-populating it with data from the original table.

The following syntax describes this limited version of CREATE TABLE, where *query* is the valid SELECT statement that selects the data to populate the new table with. The data type of each created column is implied by the type of each corresponding column selected by *query*:

```
CREATE [ TEMPORARY | TEMP ] TABLE table
    [ ( column_name [, ...] ) ]
    AS query
```

The advantage to this technique is that you may create the new table and populate it in a single SQL command. The most notable limitation of this technique is that there is no comprehensive way to set constraints on the newly created table; the only constraints that may be added to the table after is has been created are the foreign key and check constraints. Once the new table has been created, the old one can be renamed (or destroyed), and the new one can be renamed to the name of the original table.

Suppose, for example, that you wanted to modify the books table in order to drop the superfluous publication column which was created in the section titled "Adding columns." You can create a limited copy of the table (designating only the desired columns) by passing a valid SELECT statement to the AS clause of CREATE TABLE, and dropping the old table with DROP TABLE, as shown in Example 4-14.

Example 4-14: Restructuring a table with CREATE TABLE AS

```
booktown=# \d books
          Table "books"
  Attribute  |  Type   | Modifier
-------------+---------+----------
 id          | integer | not null
 title       | text    | not null
 author_id   | integer |
```

Example 4-14: Restructuring a table with CREATE TABLE AS (continued)

```
subject_id | integer |
publication | date    |
Index: books_id_pkey

booktown=# CREATE TABLE new_books
booktown-#         (id, title, author_id, subject_id)
booktown-#         AS SELECT id, title, author_id, subject_id
booktown-#             FROM books;
SELECT
booktown=# ALTER TABLE books RENAME TO old_books;
ALTER
booktown=# ALTER TABLE new_books RENAME TO books;
ALTER
booktown=# \d books
         Table "books"
 Attribute  |  Type   | Modifier
------------+---------+----------
 id         | integer |
 title      | text    |
 author_id  | integer |
 subject_id | integer |

booktown=# DROP TABLE books;
DROP
```

As of PostgreSQL 7.1.x, if you specify the optional column list within parentheses, you cannot use the asterisk (*) in the *query* statement. This behavior is scheduled to be corrected in PostgreSQL 7.2.

Restructuring with CREATE TABLE and INSERT INTO

If you require a more specifically defined table than that created by CREATE TABLE AS (e.g., one with column constraints), you can replicate the effect of the CREATE TABLE AS technique by issuing two SQL statements rather than one. You can achieve this by first creating the new table as you ordinarily would with CREATE TABLE, and then populating the table with data via the INSERT INTO command and a valid SELECT statement.

Example 4-15: Restructuring a table with CREATE TABLE and INSERT INTO

```
booktown=# CREATE TABLE new_books (
booktown(#    id integer UNIQUE,
booktown(#    title text NOT NULL,
booktown(#    author_id integer,
booktown(#    subject_id integer,
booktown(#    CONSTRAINT books_id_pkey PRIMARY KEY (id)
booktown(# );
```

Example 4-15: Restructuring a table with CREATE TABLE and INSERT INTO (continued)

```
NOTICE:  CREATE TABLE/PRIMARY KEY will create implicit index 'books_id_pkey'
for table 'new_books'
CREATE
booktown=# INSERT INTO new_books
booktown-#                SELECT id, title, author_id, subject_id
booktown-#                     FROM books;
INSERT 0 12
booktown=# ALTER TABLE books RENAME TO old_books;
ALTER
booktown=# ALTER TABLE new_books RENAME TO books;
ALTER
booktown=# \d books
          Table "books"
 Attribute  |  Type   | Modifier
------------+---------+----------
 id         | integer | not null
 title      | text    | not null
 author_id  | integer |
 subject_id | integer |
Index: books_id_pkey
```

See the section titled "Inserting Values from Other Tables with SELECT" for more information about using the INSERT INTO command with a SELECT statement, and the section titled "Retrieving Rows with SELECT" for more information about valid SELECT statements.

Destroying Tables with DROP TABLE

The SQL command to permanently destroy a table is DROP TABLE. The following is the syntax for DROP TABLE, where *tablename* is the table that you wish to destroy:

```
DROP TABLE tablename
```

Use caution when dropping a table, as doing so destroys all data associated with the table.

Destroying a table with an implicitly-created index will destroy any associated indices.

Adding Data with INSERT and COPY

Once you have created your table with the necessary specifications, the next logical step is to fill the table with data. There are generally three methods in PostgreSQL with which you can fill a table with data:

- Use the INSERT INTO command with a grouped set of data to insert new values.

- Use the INSERT INTO command in conjunction with a SELECT statement to insert existing values from another table.

- Use the COPY (or \copy) command to insert values from a system file.

Inserting New Values

The following is the syntax of the INSERT INTO command, when used to insert new values, which is subsequently described in detail:

```
INSERT INTO table_name
       [ ( column_name [, ...] ) ]
       VALUES ( value [, ...] )
```

table_name

The INSERT SQL command initiates an insertion of data into the table called *table_name*.

(*column_name* [, . . .])

An optional grouped expression which describes the targeted columns for the insertion.

VALUES

The SQL clause which instructs PostgreSQL to expect a grouped expression of values to follow.

(*value* [, . . .])

The required grouped expression that describes the values to be inserted. There should be one *value* for each specified column, separated by commas. These values may be expressions themselves (e.g., an operation between two values), or constants.

Each *value* following the VALUES clause must be of the same data type as the column it is being inserted into. If the optional column-target expression is omitted, PostgreSQL will expect there to be one value for each column in the literal order of the table's structure. If there are fewer values to be inserted than columns, PostgreSQL will attempt to insert a default value (or the NULL value, if there is no default) for each omitted value.

To demonstrate, Example 4-16 illustrates the insertion of a new book into Book Town's books table.

Example 4-16: Inserting new values into the books table

```
booktown=# INSERT INTO books (id, title, author_id, subject_id)
booktown-#        VALUES (41472, 'Practical PostgreSQL', 1212, 4);
INSERT 3574037 1
```

The SQL statement in Example 4-16 inserts a new book with an id of 41472, a title of *Practical PostgreSQL*, an author identifier of 1212, and a subject identifier of 4. Note the feedback beginning with INSERT, which indicates that the insertion was successful. The first number following INSERT is the OID (object identifier) of the freshly inserted row. The second number following INSERT represents the number of rows inserted (in this case, 1).

Notice that the optional column target list is specified identically to the physical structure of the table, from left to right. In this case, omitting the grouped expression would have no effect on the statement since the INSERT statement assumes that you are inserting values in the natural order of the table's columns. You can re-arrange the names of the columns in the grouped column target list if you wish to specify the values in a different order following the VALUES clause, as demonstrated in Example 4-17.

Example 4-17: Changing the order of target columns

```
booktown=# INSERT INTO books (subject_id, author_id, id, title)
booktown-#        VALUES (4, 7805, 41473, 'Programming Python');
INSERT 3574041 1
```

Inserting Values from Other Tables with SELECT

If you already have values within one table (or across several other tables) that you wish to insert into a separate table, this can also be achieved with the INSERT INTO command. The following syntax is used for this technique:

```
INSERT INTO table_name
       [ ( column_name [, ...] ) ]
       query
```

Similar to the syntax of INSERT INTO presented in the previous section, you may optionally specify which columns you wish to insert into, and in what order the *query* returns their values. However, with this form of INSERT INTO, you provide a complete SQL SELECT statement in the place of the VALUES keyword.

For example, imagine that Book Town keeps a table called book_queue, which holds books waiting to be approved for sale. When approved, those values need to be moved from the queue, into the normal books table. This can be achieved with the syntax demonstrated in Example 4-18.

Example 4-18: Inserting values from another table

```
booktown=# INSERT INTO books (id, title, author_id, subject_id)
booktown-#         SELECT nextval('book_ids'), title, author_id, subject_id
booktown-#             FROM book_queue WHERE approved;
INSERT 0 2
```

The preceding example demonstrates the insertion of two rows from the table book_queue into the books table by way of a SELECT statement that is passed to the INSERT INTO command. Any valid SELECT statement may be used in this context. In this case, the query selects the result of a function called nextval() from a sequence called book_ids, followed by the title, author_id and subject_id columns from the book_queue table.

Since more than one row is being inserted, the INSERT result indicating success returns 0 in place of the OID that would be returned if a single row had been inserted. The second number, as with a normal INSERT INTO command, returns the number of rows inserted (in this case, 2).

Copying Values from External Files with COPY

A useful technique within PostgreSQL is to use the COPY command to insert values directly into tables from external files. Files used for input by COPY must either be in standard ASCII text format, whose fields are delimited by a uniform symbol, or in PostgreSQL's binary table format. Common delimiters for ASCII files are tabs and commas. When using an ASCII formatted input file with COPY, each line within the file will be treated as a row of data to be inserted and each delimited field will be treated as a column value.

The COPY FROM command operates much faster than a normal INSERT command because the data is read as a single transaction directly to the target table. On the other hand, it is a very strict format, and the entire COPY procedure will fail if just one line is malformed.

The following is the syntax for using the COPY FROM command, where *table_name* is the table that you wish to insert values into and *filename* is the absolute system path to the file to be read:

```
COPY [ BINARY ] table_name [ WITH OIDS ]
    FROM { 'filename' | stdin }
    [ [USING] DELIMITERS 'delimiter' ]
    [ WITH NULL AS 'null_string' ]
```

BINARY
> Indicates that input will come from a binary file previously created by the COPY
> TO command.

table_name
> The name of the table you are copying.

WITH OIDS
> Instructs PostgreSQL to retrieve all of the OIDs of the table represented by
> *filename* from the first line of the file.

FROM { '*filename*' | stdin }
> Indicates that either the file specified with *filename* or standard input (stdin)
> should be read by PostgreSQL.

[USING] DELIMITERS '*delimiter*'
> Indicates the character provided with *delimiter* should be used as a delimiter
> when parsing input. This clause is not applicable to files that were output in
> PostgreSQL's binary format.

WITH NULL AS '*null_string*'
> Indicates that the character(s) provided with *null_string* should be inter-
> preted as NULL values. This clause is not applicable to files that were output in
> PostgreSQL's binary format.

When preparing to copy a file from the underlying operating system, remember
that the file specified must be readable by the *postmaster* process (i.e., the user
which PostgreSQL is running as), since the backend reads the file directly. Additionally, the filename must be provided with an absolute path; an attempt to use a
relative path will result in an error.

If you are using an ASCII formatted input file, a *delimiter* value may be passed to
the DELIMITERS clause, which defines the character which delimits columns on a
single line in the filename. If omitted, PostgreSQL will assume that the ASCII file is
tab-delimited. The optional WITH NULL clause allows you to specify in what form to
expect NULL values. If omitted, PostgreSQL interprets the \N sequence as a NULL
value to be inserted (e.g., blank fields in a source file will be treated as blank
string constants, rather than NULL, by default).

The stdin term may be supplied as the source for the FROM clause if you wish to
type values in manually or paste from another location directly into a terminal session. If you choose to enter values from stdin, you must terminate the input stream
with a \. sequence (backslash-period) followed immediately by a newline.

Example 4-19 shows the contents of a file that was output in ASCII format by PostgreSQL. The file in Example 4-19 is comma-delimited and uses \null to represent
NULL values. It contains row data from the Book Town subjects table.

Example 4-19: An example ASCII copy file

```
1,Business,Productivity Ave
2,Children's Books,Kids Ct
3,Classics,Academic Rd
4,Computers,Productivity Ave
5,Cooking,Creativity St
12,Religion,\null
8,History,Academic Rd
9,Horror,Black Raven Dr
10,Mystery,Black Raven Dr
11,Poetry,Sunset Dr
13,Romance,Main St
14,Science,Productivity Ave
15,Science Fiction,Main St
0,Arts,Creativity St
6,Drama,Main St
7,Entertainment,Main St
```

The statement in Example 4-20 copies the file (*/tmp/subjects.sql*) into a table within the booktown database's subjects table.

Example 4-20: Copying an ASCII file

```
booktown=# COPY subjects FROM '/tmp/subjects.sql'
booktown-#               USING DELIMITERS ',' WITH NULL AS '\null';
COPY
```

Binary format

The COPY command can also input and output binary formatted data. Specifying to the COPY FROM command the BINARY keyword requires that the input file specified was created with the COPY TO command in PostgreSQL's binary format. Binary files can be read more quickly than ASCII files, but are not readable or modifiable with plain-text editors as ASCII files are.

Example 4-21 uses the COPY command to insert the rows in the binary output file from the subjects table within the booktown database.

Example 4-21: Copying a binary file

```
booktown=# COPY BINARY subjects FROM '/tmp/subjects.sql';
COPY
```

The difference between COPY and \copy

The COPY command is *not* the same as the *psql* \copy command. The \copy command accepts the same syntax (though without a terminating semicolon), and therefore performs the operation via the *psql* client, rather than the *postmaster* server. The result is that \copy operates with the permissions of the user running *psql* rather than of the user the *postmaster* is running as.

COPY TO

The syntax of COPY FROM may be used with nearly identical syntax to send a table's data to a file. You need only replace the FROM keyword with the TO keyword. Additionally, the stdin keyword may be replaced with stdout if you wish to redirect to standard output rather than to a file (e.g., to the screen, in *psql*). Example 4-22 shows how you would copy the books table to an ASCII formatted file.

Example 4-22: Copying the books table to an ASCII file

```
booktown=# COPY books TO 'filename';
COPY
```

Copying WITH OIDS

Files containing row data with object identifier values (created with the COPY TO command, involving the WITH OIDS clause) can be read by a COPY FROM command, if the WITH OIDS clause is specified. Attempts to use the COPY FROM command with the WITH OIDS clause on a file that wasn't given OIDs during its creation will fail.

The ability to copy values into a table with object-identifiers is a special capability reserved for COPY. These values cannot be modified by INSERT or UPDATE, as they are system values. If you are not careful, you may end up with two rows which have the same OID, which potentially negates their usefulness.

Retrieving Rows with SELECT

The heart of all SQL queries is the SELECT command. SELECT is used to build queries (also known as SELECT statements). Queries are the only SQL instructions by which your data can be retrieved from tables and views. The data returned via a query is called a *result set* and consists of rows, with columns, similar to a table.

The columns of a result set are not stored on the disk in any fixed form. They are purely a temporary result of the query's requested data. A query on a table may return a result set with the same column structure as the table, or it may differ drastically. Result sets may even have columns which are drawn from several other tables by a single query.

Since it is central to PostgreSQL, SELECT is easily the most complicated single command, having the most available clauses and parameters. The following is the syntax for SELECT. The terms used are summarized and described in greater detail within the following sections. The term *expression* is used to refer to either a column name, or a general expression (such as a column being operated upon by a constant, or another column).

```
SELECT [ ALL | DISTINCT [ ON ( expression [, ...] ) ] ]
    target [ AS name ] [, ...]
    [ FROM source [, ...] ]
            [ [ NATURAL ] join_type source
            [ ON condition | USING ( column_list ) ] ]
            [, ...]
    [ WHERE condition ]
    [ GROUP BY expression [, ...] ]
    [ HAVING condition [, ...] ]
    [ { UNION | INTERSECT | EXCEPT } [ ALL ] sub-query ]
    [ ORDER BY expression
            [ ASC | DESC | USING operator ]
            [, ...] ]
    [ FOR UPDATE [ OF table [, ...] ] ]
    [ LIMIT { count | ALL } [ { OFFSET | , } start ] ]
```

In this syntax diagram, *source* may be either a table name or a subselect. The syntax for these general forms is as follows:

```
FROM { [ ONLY ] table [ [ AS ] alias [ ( column_alias [, ...] ) ] ] |
    ( query ) [ AS ] alias [ ( column_alias [, ...] ) ] ] }
```

ALL

The ALL keyword may be specified as a noise term to make it clear that all rows should be returned.

DISTINCT [ON (*expression* [, . . .])]

The DISTINCT clause specifies a column (or expression) for which to retrieve only one row per unique value of *expression*.

target [AS *name*] [, . . .]

The SELECT targets are usually column names, though they can be constants, identifiers, functions or general expressions. Each *target* requested must be separated by commas, and may be named dynamically to *name* via the AS clause. Supplying the asterisk symbol (*) as a target is shorthand for requesting all non-system columns, and may be listed along with other targets.

FROM *source* [, . . .]

The FROM clause dictates the *source* that PostgreSQL will look in for the specified *targets*. The *source*, in this case, may be a table name or a sub-query. You can specify numerous sources, separated by commas. (This is roughly equivalent to a cross join). The syntax for the FROM clause is described in more detail later in this section.

[NATURAL] *join_type source* [ON *condition* | USING (*column_list*)]

The FROM sources may be joined together via the JOIN clause, which requires a *join_type* (e.g., INNER, FULL OUTER, CROSS) and may require a *condition* or *column_list* to further define the nature of the join, depending on the *join_type*.

WHERE *condition*

The WHERE clause constrains the result set from the SELECT statement to speci-fied criteria, which are defined by *condition*. Conditions must return a single Boolean value (true or false), but may consist of several checks combined with logical operators (e.g., with AND, and OR) to indicate that available rows must meet all supplied conditions to be included in the statement's results.

GROUP BY *expression* [, . . .]

The GROUP BY clause aggregates (groups) rows together by the criteria described in *expression*. This can be as simple as a column name (and often is) or an arbitrary expression applied to values of the result set.

HAVING *condition* [, . . .]

The HAVING clause is similar to the WHERE clause, but checks its conditions on aggregated (grouped) sets instead of atomic rows.

{ UNION | INTERSECT | EXCEPT } [ALL] *sub-query*

Performs one of three *set operations* between the SELECT statement and a sec-ond query, returning their result sets in uniform column structure (which must be compatible). Duplicate rows are removed from the resultant set unless the ALL keyword is used.

UNION

Returns the set of collected rows.

INTERSECT

Returns the set of rows where the values of the two sets overlap.

EXCEPT

Returns the set of rows which are found in the SELECT statement, but not found in the secondary query.

ORDER BY *expression*

Sorts the results of the SELECT statement by *expression*.

[ASC | DESC | USING operator]

Determines whether or not the ORDER BY *expression* proceeds in ascending order (ASC), or descending order (DESC). An *operator* may alternatively be specified with the USING keyword (e.g., < or >).

FOR UPDATE [OF *table* [, . . .]]

Allows for exclusive locking of the returned rows. When used within a trans-action block, FOR UPDATE locks the rows of the specified table until the transac-tion is committed. While locked, the rows cannot be updated by other transac-tions.

LIMIT { *count* | ALL }

Limits the number of rows returned to a maximum of *count*, or explicitly allows ALL rows.

{ OFFSET | , } *start*

Instructs the LIMIT clause at what point to begin limiting the results. For example, a LIMIT with a *count* set to 100, and an OFFSET clause with a *start* value of 50 would return the rows from 50 to 150 (if there are that many results to return).

Terms used in the FROM clause's syntax description are as follows:

[ONLY] *table*

The *table* name specifies what table to use as a source for the SELECT statement. Specifying the ONLY clause causes the rows of any child's table to be omitted from the query.

[AS] *alias*

An *alias* may optionally be assigned to a FROM source, in order to simplify a query (e.g., books might be temporarily referenced with an alias of b). The AS term is considered noise, and is optional.

(*query*) [AS] *alias*

Any valid SELECT statement may be placed in parentheses as the *query*. This causes the result set created by the query to be used as a FROM source, as if it had been a static table. This use of a sub-query requires a specified *alias*.

(*column_alias* [, ...])

The FROM sources which have assigned aliases may also alias columns by specifying arbitrary column aliases. Each *column_alias* must be separated by commas, and grouped within parentheses following the FROM source's alias. These aliases must match the order of the defined columns in the table to which it is applied.

A Simple SELECT

A SELECT statement may be as simple as a request for all rows and all columns from a specified table. Use the following syntax to retrieve all rows and columns from a table:

```
SELECT * FROM table_name;
```

The asterisk (*) character, as mentioned in the explanation of SELECT's syntax, is short-hand for all non-system columns. In essence, the SELECT * requests all non-system data in the table named *table_name*; this retrieves all columns and all rows, because no row limit is specified. To demonstrate, Example 4-23 requests all columns (*) from Book Town's books table.

Example 4-23: Selecting all from the books table

```
booktown=# SELECT * FROM books;
   id  |            title             | author_id | subject_id
-------+-----------------------------+-----------+------------
  7808 | The Shining                 |      4156 |          9
  4513 | Dune                        |      1866 |         15
  4267 | 2001: A Space Odyssey       |      2001 |         15
  1608 | The Cat in the Hat          |      1809 |          2
  1590 | Bartholomew and the Oobleck |      1809 |          2
 25908 | Franklin in the Dark        |     15990 |          2
  1501 | Goodnight Moon              |      2031 |          2
   190 | Little Women                |        16 |          6
  1234 | The Velveteen Rabbit        |     25041 |          3
  2038 | Dynamic Anatomy             |      1644 |          0
   156 | The Tell-Tale Heart         |       115 |          9
 41472 | Practical PostgreSQL        |      1212 |          4
 41473 | Programming Python          |      7805 |          4
 41477 | Learning Python             |      7805 |          4
 41478 | Perl Cookbook               |      7806 |          4
(15 rows)
```

Specifying Target Columns

While SELECT * is a good example of a basic query, and is sometimes very useful, you will probably be interested in retrieving only a few columns worth of information at a time. To stay efficient, and to keep your queries clear, it is a good idea to explicitly specify the intended target columns rather than to use the asterisk. This is especially true when using the JOIN clause, as will be discussed in the section titled "Joining Data Sets with JOIN."

To specify the target columns for a query, list the names of the columns following the *SELECT* keyword. The query will return data for only those columns that you list. The order of these columns need not match their literal order in the table, and columns may be listed more than once, or not at all, as shown in Example 4-24.

Example 4-24: Re-ordering columns

```
booktown=# SELECT id, author_id, title, id
booktown-#        FROM books;
   id  | author_id |            title            |   id
-------+-----------+-----------------------------+-------
  7808 |      4156 | The Shining                 |  7808
  4513 |      1866 | Dune                        |  4513
  4267 |      2001 | 2001: A Space Odyssey       |  4267
  1608 |      1809 | The Cat in the Hat          |  1608
  1590 |      1809 | Bartholomew and the Oobleck |  1590
 25908 |     15990 | Franklin in the Dark        | 25908
  1501 |      2031 | Goodnight Moon              |  1501
   190 |        16 | Little Women                |   190
  1234 |     25041 | The Velveteen Rabbit        |  1234
```

Example 4-24: Re-ordering columns (continued)

```
    2038 |      1644 | Dynamic Anatomy              |    2038
     156 |       115 | The Tell-Tale Heart          |     156
   41472 |      1212 | Practical PostgreSQL         |   41472
   41473 |      7805 | Programming Python           |   41473
   41477 |      7805 | Learning Python              |   41477
   41478 |      7806 | Perl Cookbook                |   41478
  (15 rows)
```

As you can see, the data sets returned in both Example 4-24 and Example 4-23 are nearly identical. The second set is returned in a different column arrangement, (omitting the subject_id column, and repeating the id column twice) as a result of the target list.

Expressions, Constants, and Aliases

In addition to plain column names, targets in the SELECT statement may be arbitrary expressions (e.g., involving functions, or operators acting upon identifiers), or constants. The syntax is simple, and only requires that each identifier, expression, or constant be separated by commas. Conveniently, different types of targets may be arbitrarily mixed in the target list.

In fact, the SELECT command may be used to retrieve expressions and constants without the use of a FROM clause or specified columns, as in Example 4-25.

Example 4-25: Using expressions and constants

```
    testdb=# SELECT 2 + 2,
    testdb-#        pi(),
    testdb-#        'PostgreSQL is more than a calculator!';
     ?column? |        pi        |                ?column?
    ----------+------------------+----------------------------------------
            4 | 3.14159265358979 | PostgreSQL is more than a calculator!
    (1 row)
```

The target list allows the use of an optional AS clause for each specified target, which re-names a column in the returned result set to an arbitrary name specified in the clause. The rules and limitations for the specified name are the same as for normal identifiers (e.g., they may be quoted to contain spaces, may not be keywords unless quoted, and so on).

Using AS has no lasting effect on the column itself, but only on the result set which is returned by the query. AS can be particularly useful when selecting expressions or constants, rather than plain columns. Naming result set columns with AS can clarify the meaning of an otherwise ambiguous expression or constant. This technique is demonstrated in Example 4-26, which shows the same results as Example 4-25, but with different column headings.

Example 4-26: Using the AS clause with expressions and constants

```
booktown=# SELECT 2 + 2 AS "2 plus 2",
booktown-#        pi() AS "the pi function",
booktown-#        'PostgreSQL is more than a calculator!' AS comments;
 2 plus 2 | the pi function |                 comments
----------+-----------------+-----------------------------------------
        4 | 3.14159265358979 | PostgreSQL is more than a calculator!
(1 row)
```

Selecting Sources with the FROM Clause

The FROM clause allows you to choose either a table or a result set as a source for your specified target list. Multiple sources may be entered following the FROM clause, separated by commas. Specifying multiple sources in this fashion is functionally similar to a CROSS JOIN, discussed in the section titled "Joining Data Sets with JOIN."

Take care when specifying multiple FROM sources to PostgreSQL. The result of performing a SELECT on several comma-delimited sources without a WHERE or JOIN clause to qualify the relationship between the sources is that the complete *Cartesian product* of the sources will be returned. This is a result set where each column from each source is combined in every possible combination of rows between each other source.

Typically a WHERE clause is used to define the relationship between comma-delimited FROM sources, as shown in Example 4-27 (see the section titled "Qualifying with the WHERE Clause" for more information about the WHERE clause).

You must be careful when identifying column names and using multiple sources in the FROM clause, as it can introduce ambiguity between identifiers. Consider a SELECT that draws from both the books table and the authors table. Each of these tables has a column called id. If specified, PostgreSQL will be unable to determine if the id column refers to the book, or the author:

```
booktown=# SELECT id FROM books, authors;
ERROR:  Column reference "id" is ambiguous
```

As a result of the potential for ambiguity, "complete" column names can be referenced through a special syntax called *dot-notation*. Dot-notation refers to the placement of a dot, or period, between the table name and a column name, in order to explicitly reference a particular column. For example, books.id refers to the id column within the books table.

Dot-notation is only *required* in instances of ambiguity between data sets. As shown in Example 4-27, you can use the column name as an identifier source, as long as it is unique among the available sets defined by the FROM clause. (In this case, the title column, which is unique to the books table, and the last_name column, which is unique to the authors tables).

Example 4-27: Selecting from multiple table sources

```
booktown=# SELECT books.id, title, authors.id, last_name
booktown-#        FROM books, authors
booktown-#        WHERE books.author_id = authors.id;
   id   |            title             |  id   | last_name
--------+------------------------------+-------+-------------
    190 | Little Women                 |    16 | Alcott
    156 | The Tell-Tale Heart          |   115 | Poe
  41472 | Practical PostgreSQL         |  1212 | Worsley
   2038 | Dynamic Anatomy              |  1644 | Hogarth
   1608 | The Cat in the Hat           |  1809 | Geisel
   1590 | Bartholomew and the Oobleck  |  1809 | Geisel
   4513 | Dune                         |  1866 | Herbert
   4267 | 2001: A Space Odyssey        |  2001 | Clarke
   1501 | Goodnight Moon               |  2031 | Brown
   7808 | The Shining                  |  4156 | King
  41473 | Programming Python           |  7805 | Lutz
  41477 | Learning Python              |  7805 | Lutz
  41478 | Perl Cookbook                |  7806 | Christiansen
  25908 | Franklin in the Dark         | 15990 | Bourgeois
   1234 | The Velveteen Rabbit         | 25041 | Bianco
(15 rows)
```

If you wish to use a sub-query to generate a result set as a source for your FROM clause, the entire query must be surrounded by parentheses. This instructs Post-greSQL to correctly interpret the query as a sub-SELECT statement and to execute it before the SELECT statement within which it resides.

Example 4-28 demonstrates a peculiar query which retrieves all column values (*) from the books table via a sub-query. The query then retrieves a string constant of *test* and the id values from that result set (derived from the sub-query).

Example 4-28: Selecting from a sub-query

```
booktown=# SELECT 'test' AS test, id
booktown-#        FROM (SELECT * FROM books)
booktown-#        AS example_sub_query;
 test |  id
------+-------
 test |  7808
 test |  4513
 test |  4267
 test |  1608
 test |  1590
 test | 25908
 test |  1501
 test |   190
 test |  1234
 test |  2038
 test |   156
```

Example 4-28: Selecting from a sub-query (continued)

```
test | 41472
test | 41473
test | 41477
test | 41478
(15 rows)
```

The query in Example 4-28 is rather peculiar because the net effect is no different than if you had selected from the books table. This occurs because the result set from the sub-query is identical to the set of values in the books table. The use of this query demonstrates the combination of a string constant from one SELECT statement with a value drawn from the result set of a second SELECT statement. See the section titled "Using Sub-Queries" for more realistic examples of sub-queries once you have a better understanding of the SELECT statement itself.

When specifying a table that is inherited by other tables, you may provide the optional ONLY keyword before the table name to indicate that you do not want to draw from any sub-tables. (See Chapter 7 for more information on inheritance.)

Aliasing FROM Sources

Like columns, FROM sources (e.g., tables, or sub-queries) may be aliased with the AS clause. This is usually applied as a convenient shorthand for the dot-notation described in the preceding section. Aliasing a data set allows you to refer to it via dot-notation, which provides a more succinct and readable SQL statement. Example 4-29 demonstrates the same query used in Example 4-27, however you can see that it simplifies the dot-notation with the AS clause.

Example 4-29: Aliasing FROM sources

```
booktown=# SELECT b.id, title, a.id, last_name
booktown-#     FROM books AS b, authors AS a
booktown-#     WHERE b.author_id = a.id;
  id   |            title             |  id  | last_name
-------+-----------------------------+------+--------------
   190 | Little Women                |   16 | Alcott
   156 | The Tell-Tale Heart         |  115 | Poe
 41472 | Practical PostgreSQL        | 1212 | Worsley
  2038 | Dynamic Anatomy             | 1644 | Hogarth
  1608 | The Cat in the Hat          | 1809 | Geisel
  1590 | Bartholomew and the Oobleck | 1809 | Geisel
  4513 | Dune                        | 1866 | Herbert
  4267 | 2001: A Space Odyssey       | 2001 | Clarke
  1501 | Goodnight Moon              | 2031 | Brown
  7808 | The Shining                 | 4156 | King
```

Example 4-29: Aliasing FROM sources (continued)

```
     41473 | Programming Python          |  7805 | Lutz
     41477 | Learning Python             |  7805 | Lutz
     41478 | Perl Cookbook               |  7806 | Christiansen
     25908 | Franklin in the Dark        | 15990 | Bourgeois
      1234 | The Velveteen Rabbit        | 25041 | Bianco
    (15 rows)
```

In addition to placing aliases on the FROM clause's data sources, you can place
aliases on the *columns* within that source. This is done by following a valid data
source's alias with a list of *column aliases*, grouped in parentheses and separated
by commas. A column alias list therefore consists of a sequence of identifier
aliases for each column, which correspond to the literal columns in the order that
the table is defined with (from left to right).

When describing a column alias list, you do not need to specify each column; any
column that is left unspecified is accessible via its normal name within such a
query. If the only column you wish to alias is to the right of any other columns
that you do not necessarily wish to alias, you will need to explicitly list the preceding columns (it is valid to list the same name for an existing column as its
"alias"). Otherwise, PostgreSQL will have no way of knowing which column you
were attempting to alias and will assume you were addressing the first column
from the left.

     The AS keyword is technically considered noise, and may be omitted
        in practice; PostgreSQL determines that any stray identifiers follow-
        ing a FROM source may be used as aliases.

Example 4-30 illustrates the same query that is used in Example 4-29 but aliases
the id columns in each table to unique identifiers in order to reference them
directly (i.e., without dot-notation). The syntax is functionally identical, aliasing
only the books table's id column, thus making the authors table's id column non-
ambiguous:

Example 4-30: Aliasing columns

```
booktown=# SELECT the_book_id, title, id, last_name
booktown-#        FROM books AS b (the_book_id), authors
booktown-#        WHERE author_id = id;
 the_book_id |           title            |  id  | last_name
-------------+----------------------------+------+------------
         190 | Little Women               |   16 | Alcott
         156 | The Tell-Tale Heart        |  115 | Poe
       41472 | Practical PostgreSQL       | 1212 | Worsley
        2038 | Dynamic Anatomy            | 1644 | Hogarth
```

Example 4-30: Aliasing columns (continued)

```
     1608 | The Cat in the Hat             |  1809 | Geisel
     1590 | Bartholomew and the Oobleck   |  1809 | Geisel
     4513 | Dune                          |  1866 | Herbert
     4267 | 2001: A Space Odyssey         |  2001 | Clarke
     1501 | Goodnight Moon                |  2031 | Brown
     7808 | The Shining                   |  4156 | King
    41473 | Programming Python            |  7805 | Lutz
    41477 | Learning Python               |  7805 | Lutz
    41478 | Perl Cookbook                 |  7806 | Christiansen
    25908 | Franklin in the Dark          | 15990 | Bourgeois
     1234 | The Velveteen Rabbit          | 25041 | Bianco
(15 rows)
```

Removing Duplicate Rows with DISTINCT

The optional DISTINCT keyword excludes duplicate rows from the result set. If supplied without the ON clause, a query that specifies DISTINCT will exclude any row whose target columns have already been retrieved identically. Only columns in the SELECT's target list will be evaluated.

For example, the books table has 15 rows, each with an author_id. Some authors may have several entries in the books table, causing there to be several rows with the same author_id. Supplying the DISTINCT clause, as shown in the first query in Example 4-31, ensures that the result set will not have two identical rows.

Example 4-31: Using DISTINCT

```
booktown=# SELECT DISTINCT author_id
booktown-#        FROM books;
 author_id
-----------
        16
       115
      1212
      1644
      1809
      1866
      2001
      2031
      4156
      7805
      7806
     15990
     25041
(13 rows)

booktown=# SELECT DISTINCT ON (author_id)
booktown-#        author_id, title
booktown-#        FROM books;
 author_id |         title
```

Example 4-31: Using DISTINCT (continued)

```
-----------+--------------------
        16 | Little Women
       115 | The Tell-Tale Heart
      1212 | Practical PostgreSQL
      1644 | Dynamic Anatomy
      1809 | The Cat in the Hat
      1866 | Dune
      2001 | 2001: A Space Odyssey
      2031 | Goodnight Moon
      4156 | The Shining
      7805 | Programming Python
      7806 | Perl Cookbook
     15990 | Franklin in the Dark
     25041 | The Velveteen Rabbit
    (13 rows)
```

As you can see, the first query in Example 4-31 returns only 13 rows from the books table, even though there are 15 total rows within it. Two authors with two books each end up being displayed only once.

The second query in Example 4-31 uses a different form of DISTINCT, which specifies the columns (or expressions) to be checked for redundancies. In this case, 13 rows are still returned, as the ON clause specifies to use the author_id column as the basis for determining if a row is redundant or not. Without the ON clause, the second query would return all 15 rows, because the DISTINCT clause would cause PostgreSQL to look for rows that are completely unique.

The titles that are omitted from the resultant data set by ON are arbitrarily determined by PostgreSQL, unless an ORDER BY clause is specified. If the ORDER BY clause is used with DISTINCT, you can specify the order in which columns are selected; hence, you can select which rows will be considered distinct first. See the section titled "Sorting Rows with ORDER BY" for information about sorting rows.

If you are interested in grouping rows which have non-unique criteria, rather than omitting all rows but one, see the description of the GROUP BY clause in the section titled "Grouping Rows with GROUP BY."

Qualifying with the WHERE Clause

The WHERE clause allows you to provide Boolean (true or false) conditions that rows must satisfy to be included in the resulting row set. In practice, a SELECT statement will almost always contain at least one qualification via the WHERE clause.

Suppose that you want to see all of the books in Book Town's Computers section. The subject_id for the Computers subject is 4. Therefore, the WHERE clause can be applied with an equivalence operation (the = operator) to check for rows in the books table with a subject_id equal to 4. This is shown in Example 4-32.

Example 4-32: A simple WHERE clause

```
booktown=# SELECT * FROM books
booktown-#           WHERE subject_id = 4;
  id  |        title        | author_id | subject_id
------+---------------------+-----------+------------
 41472 | Practical PostgreSQL |    1212 |          4
 41473 | Programming Python   |    7805 |          4
 41477 | Learning Python      |    7805 |          4
 41478 | Perl Cookbook        |    7806 |          4
(4 rows)
```

The query in Example 4-32 returns only rows whose subject_id column matches the integer constant value of 4. Thus, only the four rows for computer books are returned, rather than the 15 rows shown by the simple query in Example 4-23.

The WHERE clause accepts numerous conditions, provided that they are joined by valid logical keywords (e.g., the AND, and OR keywords) and returns a single Boolean condition. For example, you may be interested in seeing all Book Town titles that fall under the Computers subject which are *also* by the author Mark Lutz, thus joining two conditions to narrow the focus of your query. Alternatively, you might be interested in seeing each of Book Town's titles that fall under either the Computers subject or the Arts subject, thereby joining two conditions to broaden the focus of your intended result set. Example 4-33 demonstrates each of these scenarios using the AND keyword and OR keyword, respectively.

Example 4-33: Combining conditions in the WHERE clause

```
booktown=# SELECT title FROM books
booktown-#             WHERE subject_id = 4
booktown-#             AND author_id = 7805;
     title
--------------------
 Programming Python
 Learning Python
(2 rows)

booktown=# SELECT title FROM books
booktown-#             WHERE subject_id = 4
booktown-#             OR subject_id = 0;
      title
----------------------
 Dynamic Anatomy
 Practical PostgreSQL
 Programming Python
 Learning Python
 Perl Cookbook
(5 rows)
```

The first SELECT statement in Example 4-33 combines one condition, which checks for titles in the Computers subject (with a subject_id of 4), with another condition, which checks if the author is Mark Lutz (with an `author_id` of 7805) via the `AND` keyword. The result is a smaller data set, constrained to two rows that fit *both* specified conditions.

The second `SELECT` statement in Example 4-33 combines the same first condition (books in the Computers subject) with a second condition: if the title falls under the Arts subject (with a `subject_id` of 0). The result is a slightly larger data set of five rows that matched *at least one* of these conditions.

`WHERE` conditions may be grouped together indefinitely, though after two conditions you may wish to group the conditions with parentheses. Doing so explicitly indicates how the conditions are interrelated. As a demonstration, the two statements in Example 4-34 have different effects based merely on the addition of parentheses.

Example 4-34: Grouping WHERE conditions with parentheses

```
booktown=# SELECT * FROM books
booktown-#            WHERE author_id = 1866
booktown-#            AND subject_id = 15
booktown-#            OR subject_id = 3;
  id  |        title        | author_id | subject_id
------+---------------------+-----------+------------
 4513 | Dune                |      1866 |         15
 1234 | The Velveteen Rabbit|     25041 |          3
(2 rows)

booktown=# SELECT * FROM books
booktown-#            WHERE author_id = 1866
booktown-#            AND (subject_id = 15
booktown(#                OR subject_id = 3);
  id  | title | author_id | subject_id
------+-------+-----------+------------
 4513 | Dune  |      1866 |         15
(1 row)
```

The preceding example demonstrates two attempts to look up Book Town titles with an `author_id` of 1866. The titles also have a `subject_id` of either 15, or 3. As you can see from the first statement, when the three conditions are used without parentheses, the intent of the statement is ambiguous, and interpreted incorrectly. The addition of parentheses will cause the evaluations within parentheses to be considered before any surrounding condition.

Joining Data Sets with JOIN

As demonstrated by the use of the `WHERE` clause on two table sources in the section titled "Selecting Sources with the FROM Clause," you have the ability to retrieve data from different data sources by combining their columns into joined rows. In SQL, this process is formally called a *join*.

The essential concept behind a join is that two or more data sets, when joined, have their columns combined into a *new* set of rows containing each of the columns requested from each of the data sets. The foundation of all joins is the *Cartesian product*, which is the set of all possible combinations between two data sets. That product may then be refined into a smaller subset by a set of criteria in the JOIN syntax. These criteria describe a relationship between data sets, though such a definition is not required.

There are three general types of joins:

Cross joins

> Creates a Cartesian product (or cross product) between two sets of data. It is called a product because it does not define a relationship between the sets; instead, it returns every possible combination of rows between the joined sets, essentially multiplying the sources by one another.

Inner joins

> Creates a subset of the Cartesian product between two sets of data, requiring a conditional clause to specify criteria upon which to join records. The condition must return a Boolean value to determine whether or not a row is included in the joined set.

Outer joins

> Similar to an inner join, in that it accepts criteria which will match rows between two sets of data, but returns at least one instance of each row from a specified set. This is either the left set (the data source to the left of the JOIN keyword), the right set (the data source to the right of the JOIN keyword), or both sets, depending on the variety of outer join employed. The missing column values for the empty half of the row which does not meet the join condition are returned as NULL values.

Cross joins

A cross join is functionally identical to listing comma-delimited sources. It therefore should almost always be accompanied by a WHERE clause to qualify the relationship between the joined data sets. Example 4-35 demonstrates the same functional query used in Example 4-27, substituting the formal JOIN syntax for the comma.

Example 4-35: A simple CROSS JOIN

```
booktown=# SELECT b.id, title, a.id, last_name
booktown-#        FROM books AS b CROSS JOIN authors AS a
booktown-#        WHERE b.author_id = a.id;
   id  |            title             |  id  |  last_name
-------+-----------------------------+------+--------------
   190 | Little Women                |   16 | Alcott
```

Example 4-35: A simple CROSS JOIN (continued)

```
   156 | The Tell-Tale Heart          |   115 | Poe
 41472 | Practical PostgreSQL         |  1212 | Worsley
  2038 | Dynamic Anatomy              |  1644 | Hogarth
  1608 | The Cat in the Hat           |  1809 | Geisel
  1590 | Bartholomew and the Oobleck  |  1809 | Geisel
  4513 | Dune                         |  1866 | Herbert
  4267 | 2001: A Space Odyssey        |  2001 | Clarke
  1501 | Goodnight Moon               |  2031 | Brown
  7808 | The Shining                  |  4156 | King
 41473 | Programming Python           |  7805 | Lutz
 41477 | Learning Python              |  7805 | Lutz
 41478 | Perl Cookbook                |  7806 | Christiansen
 25908 | Franklin in the Dark         | 15990 | Bourgeois
  1234 | The Velveteen Rabbit         | 25041 | Bianco
(15 rows)
```

This syntax is merely a more formal way of stating the relationship between the two data sets. There is no functional difference between the CROSS JOIN syntax and using a simple comma delimited list of tables.

Inner and outer join syntax

More useful are the inner and outer joins, which *require* a qualification of the relationship between joined data sets in the JOIN syntax itself. The following is the syntax for an inner or outer join:

```
source1 [ NATURAL ] join_type source2
[ ON ( condition [, ...] ) | USING ( column [, ...] ) ]
```

source1

Identifies the first data set that is being joined (i.e., a table name or subquery).

[NATURAL]

Implies that the two data sets should be joined on equivalent values between like-named columns (e.g., if two tables have a column called id, it will join rows where the id values are equivalent). The NATURAL clause will respect column aliases, if applied. The use of the NATURAL clause makes it both unnecessary and invalid to try to specify either of the ON or USING clauses.

join_type

Specifies the type of JOIN intended. Valid values in this context are [INNER] JOIN (specifying just JOIN implies an INNER JOIN), LEFT [OUTER] JOIN, RIGHT [OUTER] JOIN, and FULL [OUTER] JOIN.

source2

Identifies the second data set that is being joined (i.e., a table name, or sub-query).

ON (*condition* [, ...])

Identifies the second data set that is being joined (i.e., a table name, or sub-query).

Specifies the relationship between source1 and source2. Any arbitrary criteria may be specified within the ON clause, just as you would specify conditions following a WHERE clause. Column and table aliases are allowed in this criteria.

USING (*column* [, ...])

Specifies like-named columns between source1 and source2 with which to join rows by equivalent values. Similar to a NATURAL JOIN, but allows you to indicate what specific columns to join on, whereas NATURAL will join on *all* like-named columns. Similar to NATURAL joins, column aliases are respected in the USING clause's parameters.

Inner joins

The SQL92 INNER JOIN syntax is a tool that helps differentiate the conditions with which you are joining data sources (the JOIN conditions) from the conditions with which you are evaluating rows for inclusion in your data set (the WHERE conditions). For example, consider the two SELECT statements in Example 4-36.

Example 4-36: Comparing INNER JOIN to WHERE

```
booktown=# SELECT title, last_name, first_name
booktown-#        FROM books, authors
booktown-#        WHERE (books.author_id = authors.id)
booktown-#        AND last_name = 'Geisel';
            title             | last_name |  first_name
--------------------------------+-----------+---------------
 The Cat in the Hat             | Geisel    | Theodor Seuss
 Bartholomew and the Oobleck    | Geisel    | Theodor Seuss
(2 rows)

booktown=# SELECT title, last_name, first_name
booktown-#        FROM books AS b INNER JOIN authors AS a
booktown-#        ON (b.author_id = a.id)
booktown-#        WHERE last_name = 'Geisel';
            title             | last_name |  first_name
--------------------------------+-----------+---------------
 The Cat in the Hat             | Geisel    | Theodor Seuss
 Bartholomew and the Oobleck    | Geisel    | Theodor Seuss
(2 rows)
```

The two forms of syntax in Example 4-36 are functionally identical, and return the same results. The INNER JOIN syntax allows you to segregate the relational criteria from your evaluation criteria by only defining the set relationships in the ON clause. This can make involved queries much easier to read and maintain, as you do not need to interpret what each condition described by the WHERE clause is conceptually achieving.

Notice that the second query demonstrates the use of aliases b and a in the ON clause for the books and authors tables, respectively. The use of these aliases in the ON clause is perfectly valid, and often preferable from a perspective of improved readability.

In cases of simple equivalence joins, it may be more convenient for you to use either the USING or NATURAL clauses instead of the ON clause. These are only applicable on data sets with identically named columns. If you have columns that define a relationship between two sets that are not identically named, you may still use the USING or NATURAL clauses by employing column aliases, as demonstrated in Example 4-37, to re-name one or both of the columns to a uniform name.

Example 4-37: The NATURAL and USING clauses

```
booktown=# SELECT title, last_name, first_name
booktown-#        FROM books INNER JOIN authors AS a (author_id)
booktown-#        USING (author_id)
booktown-#        WHERE last_name = 'Geisel';
            title             | last_name |  first_name
--------------------------+-----------+---------------
 The Cat in the Hat           | Geisel    | Theodor Seuss
 Bartholomew and the Oobleck  | Geisel    | Theodor Seuss
(2 rows)


booktown=# SELECT title, last_name, first_name
booktown-#        FROM books NATURAL INNER JOIN authors AS a (author_id)
booktown-#        WHERE last_name = 'Geisel';
            title             | last_name |  first_name
--------------------------+-----------+---------------
 The Cat in the Hat           | Geisel    | Theodor Seuss
 Bartholomew and the Oobleck  | Geisel    | Theodor Seuss
(2 rows)
```

The first SELECT statement in Example 4-37 assigns the alias of author_id to the first column in the authors table (which is actually named id). By passing the author_id identifier to the USING clause, PostgreSQL then searches for a column identifier in each data set with that name to join rows on values found to be equivalent.

Inner joins are adequate for a wide variety of queries, but there are times when an outer join is required to get all of the data you need. The key to understanding the difference between inner and outer joins is in knowing how each type of join handles rows that do not meet their defined relationship.

In short, an inner join will discard any row for which it cannot find a corresponding value between the sets being joined (as specified by either the ON or USING clause).

Outer joins

In contrast to inner joins, an outer join *can* retain rows where corresponding values between sets are not found, populating the missing columns with NULL values. Whether or not the outer join *does* retain that row depends on which set is missing the value and the kind of outer join that is specified.

There are three forms of outer joins:

Left outer joins
> Will always return at least one instance of each row in the set of rows to the left of the JOIN keyword. Missing columns in the right set are populated with NULL values.

Right outer joins
> Will always return at least one instance of each row in the set of rows to the right of the JOIN keyword. Missing columns in the left set are populated with NULL values.

Full outer joins
> Will always return at least one instance of each row in each joined set. Missing columns on either side of the new set will be populated with NULL values.

Consider again Book Town's books table, and another Book Town table called editions. While the books table stores general information on a given title, the editions table stores specific information pertaining to each edition, such as an the book's ISBN, publisher, and publication date. The editions table has a column called book_id which corresponds to the books table's primary key column, id.

Suppose that you want to retrieve each of Book Town's titles, along with its isbn, if applicable. Performing a query with an inner join between the books and editions tables will correctly return a data set with title and isbn columns. However, as demonstrated in Example 4-38, if a book does not yet have a printed edition (or if that edition has not yet been entered into Book Town's database), those titles will not be displayed.

In contrast, the statement immediately following the inner join in Example 4-38 employs an outer join, returning 20 rows. Three of the returned rows do not have ISBN numbers, but are not omitted due to the definition of the join.

Example 4-38: Inner joins versus outer joins

```
booktown=# SELECT title, isbn
booktown-#        FROM books INNER JOIN editions
booktown-#        ON (books.id = editions.book_id);
            title            |    isbn
-----------------------------+------------
 The Tell-Tale Heart         | 1885418035
 The Tell-Tale Heart         | 0929605942
 Little Women                | 0760720002
 The Velveteen Rabbit        | 0679803335
 Goodnight Moon              | 0694003611
 Bartholomew and the Oobleck | 0394800753
 The Cat in the Hat          | 039480001X
 The Cat in the Hat          | 0394900014
 Dynamic Anatomy             | 0823015505
 2001: A Space Odyssey       | 0451457994
 2001: A Space Odyssey       | 0451198492
 Dune                        | 0441172717
 Dune                        | 044100590X
 The Shining                 | 0451160916
 The Shining                 | 0385121679
 Franklin in the Dark        | 0590445065
 Programming Python          | 0596000855
(17 rows)

booktown=# SELECT title, isbn
booktown-#        FROM books LEFT OUTER JOIN editions
booktown-#        ON (books.id = editions.book_id);
            title            |    isbn
-----------------------------+------------
 The Tell-Tale Heart         | 1885418035
 The Tell-Tale Heart         | 0929605942
 Little Women                | 0760720002
 The Velveteen Rabbit        | 0679803335
 Goodnight Moon              | 0694003611
 Bartholomew and the Oobleck | 0394800753
 The Cat in the Hat          | 039480001X
 The Cat in the Hat          | 0394900014
 Dynamic Anatomy             | 0823015505
 2001: A Space Odyssey       | 0451457994
 2001: A Space Odyssey       | 0451198492
 Dune                        | 0441172717
 Dune                        | 044100590X
 The Shining                 | 0451160916
 The Shining                 | 0385121679
 Franklin in the Dark        | 0590445065
 Practical PostgreSQL        |
 Programming Python          | 0596000855
 Learning Python             |
 Perl Cookbook               |
(20 rows)
```

The join specified by the second query in Example 4-38 uses the LEFT OUTER JOIN clause to define its join type. This is because the query focuses on titles from the books table that have ISBN numbers, and not those editions having ISBN numbers that do not correspond to titles. As the books table is to the left of the JOIN keyword, it is defined as a left outer join to achieve this. If the focus of the query was to see both ISBN numbers without titles as well as titles without ISBN numbers, the same query could instead be modified to be a full outer join with the FULL OUTER JOIN clause.

The difference between inner and outer joins illustrated in Example 4-38 is a vital concept to understand, as misuse of joins can lead to both omitted and unexpected rows.

The actual OUTER keyword is an optional term in a PostgreSQL outer join. Specifying a join as either a LEFT JOIN, RIGHT JOIN or FULL JOIN implicitly defines it as an outer join.

Intricate joins

It should be understood that while a single JOIN clause connects only two sets of data, in practice, joins are not restricted to only two data sources. You may arbitrarily specify numerous JOIN clauses following sets that are themselves constructed from joins, just as you may specify numerous data sources separated by commas.

When connecting several joins together, it is a good practice to group each join and sub-join within parentheses. Explicitly grouping joins in this fashion insures that there is no ambiguity, to either PostgreSQL or a developer, as to which data sets are joined, and in what order.

Example 4-39: Joining many data sources

```
booktown=# SELECT a.last_name, p.name AS publisher, e.isbn, s.subject
booktown-#        FROM ((((authors AS a INNER JOIN books AS b
booktown(#              ON (a.id = b.author_id))
booktown(#        INNER JOIN editions AS e ON (e.book_id = b.id))
booktown(#        INNER JOIN publishers AS p ON (p.id = e.publisher_id))
booktown(#        INNER JOIN subjects AS s ON (s.id = b.subject_id));
  last_name |         publisher         |   isbn    |     subject
-----------+---------------------------+-----------+------------------
  Hogarth   | Watson-Guptill Publications | 0823015505 | Arts
  Brown     | HarperCollins             | 0694003611 | Children's Books
  Geisel    | Random House              | 0394800753 | Children's Books
  Geisel    | Random House              | 039480001X | Children's Books
  Geisel    | Random House              | 0394900014 | Children's Books
  Bourgeois | Kids Can Press            | 0590445065 | Children's Books
```

Example 4-39: Joining many data sources (continued)

```
     Bianco    | Penguin                     | 0679803335 | Classics
     Lutz      | O'Reilly & Associates       | 0596000855 | Computers
     Alcott    | Henry Holt & Company, Inc.  | 0760720002 | Drama
     Poe       | Mojo Press                  | 1885418035 | Horror
     Poe       | Books of Wonder             | 0929605942 | Horror
     King      | Doubleday                   | 0451160916 | Horror
     King      | Doubleday                   | 0385121679 | Horror
     Clarke    | Roc                         | 0451457994 | Science Fiction
     Clarke    | Roc                         | 0451198492 | Science Fiction
     Herbert   | Ace Books                   | 0441172717 | Science Fiction
     Herbert   | Ace Books                   | 044100590X | Science Fiction
     (17 rows)
```

An interesting observation to be made about Example 4-39 is that, while the `books` table is itself deeply involved in the join, none of its columns are retrieved in the final result set. The `books` table is included in the `JOIN` clauses in order to provide criteria through which other tables are joined together. Each of the tables whose columns are retrieved in the query rely on the books table in order to draw relationships with any other table through the `id` column (with the exception of the `publishers` table, which relates to the `publisher_id` column in the `editions` table).

Grouping Rows with GROUP BY

The `GROUP BY` clause introduces a powerful SQL concept: *aggregation*. To aggregate means to gather into a sum, or whole. The practical effect of aggregating in a SQL query is that any rows whose results from the `GROUP BY` expression match identically are grouped together into a *single aggregate row*. The `GROUP BY` expression may define a column, but it may also be any operation upon a column as well. If several columns or expressions are specified (delimited by commas), the entire set of specified criteria must be identical for rows to be grouped together.

To effectively use aggregation you must understand that any target columns requested by an aggregating query which are *not* specified in the `GROUP BY` clause will be inaccessible, unless selected through an *aggregate function*. An aggregate function accepts a column name (or expression involving at least one column name) which can represent *several values* (i.e., from several grouped rows), performs an operation on those values, and returns a single value.

Common aggregate functions include `count()`, which returns the number of rows in the set, `max()`, which returns the maximum value in the column, and `min()`, which returns the minimum value in the column. An aggregate function operates only on rows in the query's result set, and is therefore executed *after* conditional joins and `WHERE` conditions have been processed.

Imagine that you wanted to know how many books Book Town stores in its database for each known publisher. You could perform a simple join between the editions and publishers tables in order to associate each publisher name with a title that they publish. It would be tedious to manually count how many titles each publisher maintained, and in cases of larger data sets, it can become difficult to manage larger result sets.

Example 4-40 demonstrates a join between these two Book Town tables, but also introduces two new elements: the count() function, and the GROUP BY clause.

Example 4-40: Using GROUP BY

```
booktown=# SELECT count(e.isbn) AS "number of books",
booktown-#        p.name AS publisher
booktown-#        FROM editions AS e INNER JOIN publishers AS p
booktown-#            ON (e.publisher_id = p.id)
booktown-#        GROUP BY p.name;
 number of books |          publisher
-----------------+-----------------------------
               2 | Ace Books
               1 | Books of Wonder
               2 | Doubleday
               1 | HarperCollins
               1 | Henry Holt & Company, Inc.
               1 | Kids Can Press
               1 | Mojo Press
               1 | O'Reilly & Associates
               1 | Penguin
               3 | Random House
               2 | Roc
               1 | Watson-Guptill Publications
(12 rows)
```

The GROUP BY clause in Example 4-40 instructs PostgreSQL to group the rows in the joined data set by p.name, which in this query is a reference to the name column in the publishers table. Therefore, any rows that have the same publisher name will be grouped together, or aggregated. The count() function then counts the number of isbn values from the editions table that are in each aggregated row, and returns a single numeric value representing the number of rows that were aggregated for each unique publisher.

Note that in Example 4-40 the argument of the editions table's isbn column is chosen simply to indicate the objective of the example (to count how many books there are per publisher). Any column name will return the same number, as count() will always return the number of rows grouped in the current aggregate row.

Something to watch out for when designing aggregate queries is that the WHERE clause cannot accept criteria involving aggregate functions. Instead, use the HAVING clause. It functions identically to the WHERE clause, but its conditions must be on aggregate functions rather than single-row conditions. Syntactically, the HAVING clause follows the GROUP BY clause, as demonstrated in Example 4-41.

Example 4-41: Using the HAVING clause

```
booktown=# SELECT count(e.isbn) AS "number of books",
booktown-#        p.name AS publisher
booktown-#        FROM editions AS e INNER JOIN publishers AS p
booktown-#           ON (e.publisher_id = p.id)
booktown-#        GROUP BY publisher
booktown-#        HAVING count(e.isbn) > 1;
 number of books | publisher
-----------------+--------------
               2 | Ace Books
               2 | Doubleday
               3 | Random House
               2 | Roc
(4 rows)
```

Both Example 4-40 and Example 4-41 create a data set through an inner join between the editions and publishers table. However, Example 4-41 constrains the final result to publishers having more than a single book in the Book Town database, as set by the HAVING clause.

If a result set's column is aliased via an AS clause to a name that overlaps with a real column in one of the source data sets, and used in the GROUP BY clause, PostgreSQL will assume that you are referring to the input column, not the output alias.

Sorting Rows with ORDER BY

As described in Chapter 3, *Understanding SQL*, row data is not stored in a consistent order within tables. In fact, an identical query executed twice is in no way guaranteed to return the rows in the same order each time. As order is commonly an important part of retrieving data for database-dependent applications, use the ORDER BY clause to allow flexible sorting of your result set.

The ORDER BY clause accepts as its parameters a list of comma-delimited column names (or expressions upon columns), which are used as sorting criteria. For each sort criteria, you may optionally apply either the ASC, DESC, or USING keywords to control the type of sorting employed:

ASC

> Causes the rows to sort by the related criteria in an ascending fashion (e.g., numbers will be sorted lowest to highest, text will be sorted alphabetically from a to z). ASC is equivalent to specifying USING <. Since it is the default behavior, specifying ASC is only useful for explicit readability.

DESC

Causes the rows to sort by the related criteria in a descending fashion (e.g., numbers will be sorted highest to lowest, text will be sorted alphabetically from z to a). DESC is equivalent to specifying USING >.

USING *operator*

Allows the specification of the operator *operator* to be used to compare each column for precedence. This can be particularly useful for custom operators.

Example 4-42 demonstrates the use of the ORDER BY clause on the editions table. It specifies the publication column as the source of values to sort by, and explicitly declares the ordering method as an ascending (ASC) sort.

Example 4-42: Using ORDER BY

```
booktown=# SELECT isbn, edition, publication
booktown-#        FROM editions
booktown-#        ORDER BY publication ASC;
    isbn    | edition | publication
------------+---------+-------------
 0760720002 |       1 | 1868-01-01
 0679803335 |       1 | 1922-01-01
 0694003611 |       1 | 1947-03-04
 0394800753 |       1 | 1949-03-01
 0394900014 |       1 | 1957-01-01
 039480001X |       1 | 1957-03-01
 0823015505 |       1 | 1958-01-01
 0451160916 |       1 | 1981-08-01
 0590445065 |       1 | 1987-03-01
 0385121679 |       2 | 1993-10-01
 1885418035 |       1 | 1995-03-28
 0441172717 |       2 | 1998-09-01
 0929605942 |       2 | 1998-12-01
 044100590X |       3 | 1999-10-01
 0451198492 |       3 | 1999-10-01
 0451457994 |       3 | 2000-09-12
 0596000855 |       2 | 2001-03-01
(17 rows)
```

As you can see in the result set from Example 4-42, the rows return in ascending order, from the oldest date to the newest. It should be noted that even columns and expressions that do not appear in the target list of the SELECT statement may be used to sort the retrieved rows. Furthermore, aggregate functions and expressions are allowed by the ORDER BY clause if the query involves aggregation. The ability to sort by such a wide scope of sources thus allows for a great deal of flexibility in ordering results from a variety of query approaches.

If a column alias in the result set has the same name as a literal column in an input source from which it is drawing rows, and it is used in the ORDER BY clause, PostgreSQL will assume that it is a reference to the named column in the result set, not the column in the source set. This is an accepted inconsistency compared against the default behavior of the GROUP BY clause, as specified by the SQL92 standard.

When specifying multiple expressions to sort by, the result set will be ordered by the first criteria (from left to right), and will only process subsequent sorting criteria if the first condition's sort is inconclusive. For example, consider the sorting performed in Example 4-43.

Example 4-43: Using ORDER BY with multiple expressions

```
booktown=# SELECT edition, publication
booktown-#        FROM editions
booktown-#        ORDER BY edition ASC,
booktown-#                 publication DESC;
 edition | publication
---------+-------------
       1 | 1995-03-28
       1 | 1987-03-01
       1 | 1981-08-01
       1 | 1958-01-01
       1 | 1957-03-01
       1 | 1957-01-01
       1 | 1949-03-01
       1 | 1947-03-04
       1 | 1922-01-01
       1 | 1868-01-01
       2 | 2001-03-01
       2 | 1998-12-01
       2 | 1998-09-01
       2 | 1993-10-01
       3 | 2000-09-12
       3 | 1999-10-01
       3 | 1999-10-01
(17 rows)
```

The query in Example 4-43 selects the numeric edition and publication date of each book from the editions table. The ORDER BY clause then specifies two columns to sort by: edition, in ascending order, and publication, in descending order.

As you can see in the result set for Example 4-43, each row is first sorted by edition, proceeding from the lower editions to the higher editions. Subsequently, wherever the editions are identical, the publication date is used to then sort again, from the most recent publication date to the least recent.

Sorting is extremely relevant when using the DISTINCT keyword, as discussed in the section titled "Removing Duplicate Rows with DISTINCT." If you are only interested in seeing the most recently published copy of each edition in the editions table, the ORDER BY and DISTINCT clauses can be combined to achieve an effect somewhat similar to the GROUP BY clause, as shown in Example 4-44.

Example 4-44: Using DISTINCT with ORDER BY

```
booktown=# SELECT DISTINCT ON (edition)
booktown-#        edition, publication
booktown-#        FROM editions
booktown-#        ORDER BY edition ASC,
booktown-#                 publication DESC;
 edition | publication
---------+-------------
       1 | 1995-03-28
       2 | 2001-03-01
       3 | 2000-09-12
(3 rows)

booktown=# SELECT edition, max(publication)
booktown-#        FROM editions
booktown-#        GROUP BY edition;
 edition |    max
---------+-------------
       1 | 1995-03-28
       2 | 2001-03-01
       3 | 2000-09-12
(3 rows)
```

Since the ORDER BY occurring before the DISTINCT clause eliminates duplicate rows, the net effect can be very similar to using the max() or min() with a GROUP BY clause. This technique can sometimes be more efficient, depending on the complexity of the aggregation and sorting involved.

 While never strictly necessary, PostgreSQL can accept integer constants as expressions in the ORDER BY clause, instead of column names or expressions. Such a constant will be interpreted as representing the column that is at the numbered position in the target list, from left to right, starting at 1 (e.g., ORDER BY 1 ASC references the first column in the result set).

Setting Row Range with LIMIT and OFFSET

PostgreSQL enforces no limit upon the number of rows retrievable from a SQL query. If you attempt to execute a query that returns several million rows, it may take a while, but the server will not stop until it has returned the entire result set (or until it is interrupted).

Applications could conceivably be written to programmatically "page" through large sets of data after retrieval, but SQL provides as a convenience the LIMIT and OFFSET clauses, which allow for the retrieval of a specified portion of the generated result set.

When the LIMIT clause is specified, no more than the requested number of rows will be returned (though there may be fewer if the result set is smaller than the passed parameter). When the OFFSET clause is specified, it skips the number of rows defined by its parameters before returning rows. If both are specified, the number of rows to be included as per the LIMIT clause will not be counted until the number of rows dictated by the OFFSET clause have been skipped.

Example 4-45: Using LIMIT and OFFSET

```
booktown=# SELECT isbn, title, publication
booktown-#        FROM editions NATURAL JOIN books AS b (book_id)
booktown-#        ORDER BY publication DESC
booktown-#        LIMIT 5;
    isbn    |        title         | publication
------------+----------------------+-------------
 0596000855 | Programming Python   | 2001-03-01
 0451457994 | 2001: A Space Odyssey | 2000-09-12
 0451198492 | 2001: A Space Odyssey | 1999-10-01
 044100590X | Dune                 | 1999-10-01
 0929605942 | The Tell-Tale Heart  | 1998-12-01
(5 rows)

booktown=# SELECT isbn, title, publication
booktown-#        FROM editions NATURAL JOIN books AS b (book_id)
booktown-#        ORDER BY publication DESC
booktown-#        LIMIT 5
booktown-#        OFFSET 2;
    isbn    |        title         | publication
------------+----------------------+-------------
 0451198492 | 2001: A Space Odyssey | 1999-10-01
 044100590X | Dune                 | 1999-10-01
 0929605942 | The Tell-Tale Heart  | 1998-12-01
 0441172717 | Dune                 | 1998-09-01
 1885418035 | The Tell-Tale Heart  | 1995-03-28
(5 rows)
```

Example 4-45 demonstrates, in the first query, a simple use of LIMIT, by retrieving only 5 rows from the joined set of the editions and books table. Ordinarily, such a join would result in 17 rows.

The second query in Example 4-45 shows the use of the OFFSET clause, to shift the scope of the result set down by two rows. You can see that the last three rows of the first query's result set overlap with the first three rows of the second query's result set. The ORDER BY clause in each of these queries insures the consistency of the sets returned.

> The ORDER BY clause can be a helpful tool for making sure that the results of a limited query are relevant. This is because sorting occurs before limiting, allowing you to determine which rows end up being limited.

Comparing Sets with UNION, INTERSECT and EXCEPT

While joins are used in SQL to combine column values into a single row, the UNION, INTERSECT and EXCEPT clauses exist to merge or omit row data by comparing column values, returning a new result set based on this comparison. Each of these keywords may be used at the end of a valid SQL query and followed by a second query, in order to compare the resultant data sets, and then either merge or omit rows based on that comparison.

When comparing data sets in this manner, it is required that they each have the same number of columns, as well as the same column type. Note that they do not need to have the same name, or be queried from the same table or data source.

UNION

    A pair of queries merged with the UNION keyword will combine all non-distinct rows into a single data set. Like rows will not be duplicated.

INTERSECT

    A pair of queries merged with the INTERSECT keyword will cause any rows not found in both data sets to be omitted. As such, the only rows returned are those that overlap between the two query result sets.

EXCEPT

    A pair of queries merged with the EXCEPT keyword will cause any rows found in both data sets to be omitted from the returned data set. As such, only rows found in the query to the *left* of the EXCEPT clause that are *not* found in the query to the right of the clause will be returned.

Example 4-46, Example 4-47, and Example 4-48 each demonstrate these keywords by combining and omitting rows from comparative data sets. Example 4-46 creates a result set by combining several authors' last names with book titles via the UNION keyword.

Example 4-47 demonstrates the selection of ISBN numbers from the books table, limited to rows which intersect with the query on the shipments table for books which have records of more than two shipments. Finally, Example 4-48 demonstrates the removal of any rows from the first query which are matched completely in the second.

Example 4-46: Using UNION

```
booktown=# SELECT title FROM books
booktown-#        UNION
booktown-#        SELECT last_name FROM authors
booktown-#        LIMIT 11;
             title
----------------------------
 2001: A Space Odyssey
 Alcott
 Bartholomew and the Oobleck
 Bianco
 Bourgeois
 Brautigan
 Brite
 Brown
 Christiansen
 Clarke
 Denham
(11 rows)
```

Example 4-47: Using INTERSECT

```
booktown=# SELECT isbn FROM editions
booktown-#        INTERSECT
booktown-#        SELECT isbn FROM shipments
booktown-#            GROUP BY isbn
booktown-#            HAVING count(id) > 2;
    isbn
------------
 039480001X
 0394800753
 0451160916
 0590445065
 0694003611
(5 rows)
```

Example 4-48: Using EXCEPT

```
booktown=# SELECT last_name, first_name
booktown-#        FROM authors
booktown-#        EXCEPT
booktown-#        SELECT last_name, first_name
booktown-#            FROM authors AS a (author_id)
booktown-#            NATURAL INNER JOIN books
booktown-#        ORDER BY first_name ASC;
 last_name | first_name
```

Example 4-48: Using EXCEPT (continued)

```
-----------+-------------
  Denham   | Ariel
  Gorey    | Edward
  Brite    | Poppy Z.
  Brautigan | Richard
(4 rows)
```

In Example 4-48, only rows that do not match the second query are returned. Notice that the effective result of this is that only authors who do not have a book in the books table are returned. This is due to the INNER JOIN clause, which causes the second query to omit any authors whose author_id is not found in the books table.

While the use of these keywords in a single SQL query precludes the ability to use the LIMIT clause, this limitation can be circumvented by PostgreSQL's support for sub-queries. By grouping in parentheses each of the queries involved between a UNION, EXCEPT, or EXCEPT clause, the returned result sets from the sub-queries are compared, as demonstrated in Example 4-49.

Example 4-49: Comparing sub-query result sets

```
booktown=# (SELECT title FROM books ORDER BY title DESC LIMIT 7)
booktown-#      EXCEPT
booktown-#      (SELECT title FROM books ORDER BY title ASC LIMIT 11)
booktown-#      ORDER BY title DESC;
         title
----------------------
 The Velveteen Rabbit
 The Tell-Tale Heart
 The Shining
 The Cat in the Hat
(4 rows)
```

Notice that the query used in Example 4-49 creates a set from the books table that is constrained to the last seven rows and sorted alphabetically by title. The EXCEPT clause then removes from that data set the first eleven rows, sorted alphabetically in an ascending fashion. The result consists of the last four rows from the table, sorted from the bottom by the final ORDER BY clause on the new exception set.

Using Case Expressions

In order to achieve simple programmatic transformations without having to call out to a procedural language, PostgreSQL supports standard SQL *case expressions*. These use the SQL keywords CASE, WHEN, THEN, and END to allow basic conditional transformations per each row.

The entirety of a case expression is syntactically placed within the SELECT statement's target list. A case expression's result column is named case by default, but it may be aliased in the same manner as any normal target list. The general syntax for a case expression in a SELECT statement's target list is as follows:

```
CASE WHEN condition1 THEN result1
     WHEN condition2 THEN result2
     [ ... ]
     [ ELSE default_result ]
END [ AS alias ]
```

The CASE, WHEN, THEN, and ELSE keywords are somewhat similar to the if-then-else logic in programming languages. The *condition* of a WHEN clause must return a Boolean result.

When a WHEN condition is met, the result from its corresponding THEN clause will return in the result column for that row. If no conditions are met, the ELSE clause may be used to specify a default result value. If there are no results found for a case expression, NULL is returned.

Example 4-50: Using case expressions in statements

```
booktown=# SELECT isbn,
booktown-#        CASE WHEN cost > 20 THEN 'over $20.00 cost'
booktown-#             WHEN cost = 20 THEN '$20.00 cost'
booktown-#             ELSE 'under $20.00 cost'
booktown-#        END AS cost_range
booktown-#        FROM stock
booktown-#        LIMIT 8;
    isbn     |     cost_range
-------------+--------------------
 0385121679  | over $20.00 cost
 039480001X  | over $20.00 cost
 044100590X  | over $20.00 cost
 0451198492  | over $20.00 cost
 0394900014  | over $20.00 cost
 0441172717  | under $20.00 cost
 0451160916  | over $20.00 cost
 0679803335  | $20.00 cost
(8 rows)
```

Adding to the power of case expressions are PostgreSQL's sub-queries, described in the section titled "Using Sub-Queries." As demonstrated in Example 4-51, a sub-query may be provided as a *result* within a conditional expression.

Example 4-51: Using case expressions with sub-queries

```
booktown=# SELECT isbn,
booktown-#        CASE WHEN cost > 20 THEN 'N/A - (Out of price range)'
booktown-#             ELSE (SELECT title FROM books b JOIN editions e
booktown(#                         ON (b.id = e.book_id)
booktown(#                   WHERE e.isbn = stock.isbn)
booktown-#        END AS cost_range
booktown-#        FROM stock
```

Example 4-51: Using case expressions with sub-queries (continued)

```
booktown-#        ORDER BY cost_range ASC
booktown-#        LIMIT 8;
   isbn    |         cost_range
-----------+------------------------------
 0451457994 | 2001: A Space Odyssey
 0394800753 | Bartholomew and the Oobleck
 0441172717 | Dune
 0760720002 | Little Women
 0385121679 | N/A - (Out of price range)
 039480001X | N/A - (Out of price range)
 044100590X | N/A - (Out of price range)
 0451198492 | N/A - (Out of price range)
(8 rows)
```

In Example 4-51, any book found to have a cost of less than 20 has its title returned via a sub-select to the books table, along with its ISBN from the main query to the stock table.

Creating Tables from Other Tables

The INTO TABLE clause may be used with any valid SELECT query in order to create a new table with the column structure and row data of the returned result set. The syntax for this is as follows:

```
SELECT select_targets
       INTO [ TABLE ] new_table
       FROM old_table;
```

This syntax performs an implicit CREATE TABLE command, creating a table with the same column names, value types, and row data as the result set from the original table. When the message SELECT is returned, you will know that the statement was successfully performed, and the new table created. This is demonstrated in Example 4-52, which creates a backup table called stock_backup out of the data in the stock table.

Example 4-52: Using SELECT INTO

```
booktown=# SELECT * INTO stock_backup
booktown-#        FROM stock;
SELECT
```

The table specified by the INTO clause must not exist, or else an error will be returned. Upon the error, the values of the query will not be inserted and the query will fail. Note that the TABLE keyword, in this query, is an optional noise term.

Modifying Rows with UPDATE

Once data has been inserted into rows within the database, those rows can have one or more of their column values modified through use of the SQL UPDATE command. Column values may be updated either with constants, identifiers to other data sets, or expressions. They may apply to an entire column, or a subset of a column's values through specified conditions. The UPDATE command uses the following syntax:

```
UPDATE [ ONLY ] table SET
       column = expression [, ...]
       [ FROM source ]
       [ WHERE condition ]
```

UPDATE [ONLY] table

> The ONLY keyword may be used to indicate that only the table *table* should be updated, and none of its sub-tables. This is only relevant if *table* is inherited by any other tables.

SET column = expression [, . . .]

> The required SET clause is followed by an update expression for each column name that needs to have its values modified, separated by commas. This expression is always of the form *column = expression*, where *column* is the name of the column to be updated (which may not be aliased, or dot-notated), and where *expression* describes the new value to be inserted into the column.

FROM source

> The FROM clause is a non-standard PostgreSQL extension that allows table columns from other data sets to update a column's value.

WHERE condition

> The WHERE clause describes the *condition* upon which a row in *table* will be updated. If unspecified, *all values* in *column* will be modified. This may be used to qualify sources in the FROM clause, as you would in a SELECT statement.

Example 4-53 demonstrates a simple UPDATE statement. It instructs PostgreSQL to update the value in the stock table's retail column with the floating-point constant value of 29.95. The WHERE clause constrains any modifications to rows that match the criteria described by it.

Example 4-53: A simple UPDATE

```
booktown=# SELECT retail FROM stock
booktown-#         WHERE isbn = '0590445065';
 retail
--------
  23.95
```

Example 4-53: A simple UPDATE (continued)

```
(1 row)

booktown=# UPDATE stock
booktown-#        SET retail = 25.95
booktown-#        WHERE isbn = '0590445065';
UPDATE 1
booktown=# SELECT retail FROM stock
booktown-#        WHERE isbn = '0590445065';
 retail
--------
  25.95
(1 row)
```

The resultant UPDATE 1 message from Example 4-53 indicates that one record was successfully updated. Even if the value that is modified is identical to the record previously stored, it is considered an update, and the database files on disk are still modified as a result of the statement.

Updating Entire Columns

If the WHERE clause is omitted, an UPDATE statement will modify each of the values within the entire specified column. This is generally most useful when updating columns with an *expression* rather than a constant value. When an expression is specified in the SET clause, it is re-evaluated just before updating each row. Thus, each row is updated to a value determined dynamically by the interpreted expression's value for each row. This is demonstrated in Example 4-54.

Example 4-54 demonstrates using an UPDATE statement on the stock table's retail column. It uses a mathematical expression to raise the retail price of each stocked book. The expression itself has several components, separated by parentheses to enforce order of execution.

The (retail / cost) sub-expression determines the current profit margin of the book, which is then incremented by one tenth with the + operator and a floating-point constant of 0.1. The 0.1::numeric syntax explicitly casts the floating point constant to a value of type numeric. This is necessary due to the result of the division sub-expression returning a value of type numeric. Finally, this new profit margin is multiplied by the base cost from the cost column, resulting in the new price with which the retail column should be updated.

Example 4-54: Updating entire columns

```
booktown=# SELECT isbn, retail, cost
booktown-#        FROM stock
booktown-#        ORDER BY isbn ASC
booktown-#        LIMIT 3;
    isbn    | retail | cost
```

Example 4-54: Updating entire columns (continued)

```
------------+--------+-------
 0385121679 |  36.95 | 29.00
 039480001X |  32.95 | 30.00
 0394800753 |  16.95 | 16.00
(3 rows)
```

```
booktown=# UPDATE stock
booktown-#        SET retail =
booktown-#            (cost * ((retail / cost) + 0.1::numeric));
UPDATE 16

booktown=# SELECT isbn, retail, cost
booktown-#        FROM stock
booktown-#        ORDER BY isbn ASC
booktown-#        LIMIT 3;
    isbn    | retail | cost
------------+--------+-------
 0385121679 |  39.85 | 29.00
 039480001X |  35.95 | 30.00
 0394800753 |  18.55 | 16.00
(3 rows)
```

Since the UPDATE statement in Example 4-54 has no WHERE clause, all rows within the stock table are modified by this statement.

Updating Several Columns

By separating assignment expressions in the SET clause with commas, you may execute updates to several columns of a table in a single statement. Example 4-55 illustrates updating both the name and address column of the publishers table for the Publisher with the id of 113.

Example 4-55: Using UPDATE on several columns

```
booktown=# UPDATE publishers
booktown-#        SET name = 'O\'Reilly & Associates',
booktown-#            address = 'O\'Reilly & Associates, Inc. '
booktown-#                || '101 Morris St, Sebastopol, CA 95472'
booktown-#        WHERE id = 113;
UPDATE 1
booktown=# SELECT name, substr(address, 1, 40) || '...' AS short_address
booktown-#        FROM publishers
booktown-#        WHERE id = 113;
         name         |                short_address
----------------------+---------------------------------------------
 O'Reilly & Associates | O'Reilly & Associates, Inc. 101 Morris S...
(1 row)
```

The UPDATE statement in Example 4-55 shows both the name and address columns assigned through string constants. Notice that several backslashes within the string constants escape the input apostrophes. The SELECT statement following the update verifies that the desired information was updated.

Example 4-55 also demonstrates the use of the || text concatenation operator, and the substr() function, in practical usage. The address column is set with two string constants that are attached through the || operator in order to prevent the query from wrapping past the edge of the terminal. The substr() function is then used in the SELECT verification to prevent the output from wrapping. Each of these are used here to maintain readability of the output (of course, you would not want to display only a substring of the address field if you were interested in verifying its complete contents).

Updating from Several Sources

PostgreSQL supports a powerful non-standard enhancement to the SQL UPDATE statement in the form of the FROM clause. By using the FROM clause, you can apply your knowledge of the SELECT statement to draw input data from other existing data sets, such as tables, or sub-selects.

Example 4-56 uses an UPDATE statement in conjunction with a FROM clause to modify the row data within the stock table via the stock_backup table. The WHERE clause describes the relationship between the table to be updated and its source. Wherever the isbn column is found to match, the value in the stock table is modified to the value from the previously populated stock_backup table.

Example 4-56: Using UPDATE with several sources

```
booktown=# UPDATE stock
booktown-#        SET retail = stock_backup.retail
booktown-#        FROM stock_backup
booktown-#        WHERE stock.isbn = stock_backup.isbn;
UPDATE 16
```

The FROM clause supports each of the JOIN syntax options described in the section titled "Retrieving Rows with SELECT," enabling a wide variety of update methods from existing data sets. Further, as stated previously, sub-selects may be used as a data source to the FROM clause, just as is possible with the SELECT command.

Removing Rows with DELETE

Existing row data within PostgreSQL can be removed with the standard SQL DELETE command. Unless carefully working within transaction blocks, removal via the DELETE command is *permanent*, and *extreme caution* should therefore be taken before attempting to remove data from your database.

The syntax to remove one or more rows from a table is as follows:

```
DELETE FROM [ ONLY ] table
     [ WHERE condition ]
```

`DELETE FROM [ ONLY ] table`

The ONLY keyword may be used to indicate that only the table `table` should have rows removed from it, and none of its sub-tables. This is only relevant if `table` is inherited by any other tables.

`WHERE condition`

The WHERE clause describes under what `condition` to delete rows from `table`. If unspecified, *all rows in the table will be deleted.*

The WHERE clause is almost always part of a DELETE statement. It specifies which rows in the target table are to be deleted based on its specified conditions, which may be expressed syntactically in the same form as in the SELECT statement.

It is a good habit to execute a SELECT statement with the intended WHERE clause for your DELETE statement. This allows you to review the data to be deleted before the DELETE statement is actually executed. This technique and a simple DELETE statement are demonstrated in Example 4-57.

Example 4-57: Deleting rows from a table

```
booktown=# SELECT * FROM stock
booktown=#             WHERE stock = 0;
    isbn    | cost  | retail | stock
------------+-------+--------+-------
 0394800753 | 16.00 |  16.95 |     0
 0394900014 | 23.00 |  23.95 |     0
 0451198492 | 36.00 |  46.95 |     0
 0451457994 | 17.00 |  22.95 |     0
(4 rows)

booktown=# DELETE FROM stock
booktown=#          WHERE stock = 0;
DELETE 4
```

If a WHERE condition is not specified, the DELETE command removes *all rows* within that table, as shown in Example 4-58.

Example 4-58: Deleting all table rows

```
booktown=# DELETE FROM stock_backup;
DELETE 16
```

Using Sub-Queries

Sub-queries, first introduced to PostgreSQL in version 6.3, add a tremendous amount of flexibility to your SQL statements. Sub-queries are often referred to as sub-selects, as they allow a SELECT statement to be executed arbitrarily within the body of another SQL statement. A sub-query is executed by enclosing it in a set of parentheses. Sub-queries are generally used to return a single row as an atomic value, though they may be used to compare values against multiple rows with the IN keyword.

Sub-queries are allowed at nearly any meaningful point in a SQL statement, including the target list, the WHERE clause, and so on. A simple sub-query could be used as a search condition. For example, between a pair of tables. Example 4-59 demonstrates such a use of a sub-query.

Example 4-59: A simple sub-query

```
booktown=# SELECT title FROM books
booktown-#          WHERE author_id = (SELECT id FROM authors
booktown(#                             WHERE last_name='Geisel'
booktown(#                             AND first_name='Theodor Seuss');
              title
-----------------------------
 The Cat in the Hat
 Bartholomew and the Oobleck
(2 rows)
```

Example 4-59 uses the equal-to operator to compare the one row result of a sub-query on the authors table with the author_id column in the books table. In a single statement, the author identification number is acquired from the authors table by a WHERE clause specifying the name of *Theodor Seuss Geisel*, and the single identifier field returned is compared against the author_id column of the books table to return any books by Dr. Seuss.

Note that caution should be taken with this sort of sub-query: to use a normal value operator on the results of a sub-query, *only one field* must be returned. For example, if a more general sub-query were used to check for an author identifier, and several rows were found, you might see an error such as the following:

```
booktown=# SELECT title FROM books
booktown-#          WHERE author_id = (SELECT id FROM authors
booktown(#                             WHERE last_name ~ 'G');
ERROR:  More than one tuple returned by a subselect used as an
expression.
```

Normal comparison operators cannot check for a single value being equal to multiple values, so a check for equivalence between the author_id column and multiple rows causes an error. This could be solved with a LIMIT 1 clause to ensure that the sub-query never returns more than a single row.

If you are interested in checking for the existence of a single value within a set of other values, use the IN keyword as an operator upon the result set from a sub-query. Example 4-60 illustrates comparing a sub-query which produces several results (the authors whose names begin with *A* through *E*) to the author_id column via the IN keyword (see the section titled "Operators" in Chapter 5, *Operators and Functions*, for more about the regular expression being employed).

Example 4-60: A sub-query using IN

```
booktown=# SELECT title FROM books
booktown-#         WHERE author_id IN (SELECT id FROM authors
booktown(#                             WHERE last_name ~ '^[A-E]');
        title
-----------------------
 2001: A Space Odyssey
 Franklin in the Dark
 Goodnight Moon
 Little Women
 The Velveteen Rabbit
 Perl Cookbook
(6 rows)
```

As a result of the use of IN, books from several authors may be found in the books table through a comparison against several rows from a sub-query. Note that while the IN keyword allows you to compare against multiple rows, the number of columns against which to be match must be identical.

If you wish to use IN to compare several columns, you may group column names together in the WHERE clause with parentheses immediately preceding IN. The number of columns grouped must be the same as those in the target list of the sub-query, and of the same data type for comparison.

Example 4-61 demonstrates a sub-query which targets the isbn column of the editions table, and an integer constant of 0, for each paperback book (with a type value of *p*). Those rows are then returned and compared against the isbn column and the stock column of the stock table with the IN keyword, effectively selecting any paperback book that is out of stock.

Example 4-61: A multi-column sub-query using IN

```
booktown=# SELECT isbn, cost, retail FROM stock
booktown-#         WHERE (isbn, stock)
booktown-#         IN (SELECT isbn, 0 FROM editions
booktown(#             WHERE type = 'p');
    isbn    | cost  | retail
------------+-------+--------
 0394800753 | 16.00 |  16.95
 0394900014 | 23.00 |  23.95
```

Example 4-61: A multi-column sub-query using IN (continued)

```
0451457994 | 17.00 |  22.95
(3 rows)
```

Using Views

While working with SQL, times will often arise when you would like your statements to be re-usable. This is especially the case when working with large or intricate queries. There are few things more frustrating then having to re-type a long query over and over again within *psql*. Furthermore, it can be highly inefficient to pass excessively large queries over a network to your PostgreSQL server for commonly executed routines.

This is where *views* can come in handy. Views can be thought of as stored queries, which allow you to create a database object that functions very similarly to a table, but whose contents are dynamically and directly reflective only of the rows which it is defined to select. Views are quite flexible in practice, in that they may address common, simple queries to a single table, as well as extraordinarily complicated ones which may span across several tables.

Creating a View

The following is the syntax for creating a view:

```
CREATE VIEW view
        AS query
```

view

The name (identifier) of the view that you wish to create.

query

The complete SQL SELECT query that defines the content of the view.

Imagine that you have a table called shipments that relates a unique shipping identifier with a customer identifier, a book ISBN, and a timestamp reflecting when the book was shipped. This table is shown in Table 4-1.

Table 4-1. The shipments table

Column	Type	Modifier
id	integer	NOT NULL DEFAULT nextval('shipments_ship_id_seq')
customer_id	integer	
isbn	text	
ship_date	timestamp	

Now, imagine that you are interested in seeing how many shipments have been made and logged into this table. There are several ways that you can achieve the results you are looking for, but to keep things simple, you can begin with a query like this:

```
booktown=# SELECT COUNT(*) FROM shipments;
 count
-------
    32
(1 row)
```

Remember that the asterisk (*) symbol in this query simply indicates to PostgreSQL that all rows should be counted, regardless of NULL values that may exist in an otherwise specified column name. The query counts the number of total rows that return from the query, and thus the number of logged shipments.

Increasing the complexity of this query, a JOIN clause can be attached to join the shipments information with the editions and books tables, in order to retrieve the title of each shipped book. Furthermore, a GROUP BY clause can be added to the query in order to aggregate the shipments by their titles.

Recall that by aggregating by the title column, the count() function will count the number of rows per aggregated row (in this case, per unique title). Finally, a max() function can be applied to the ship_date column of the shipments table in order to see the most recently shipped copy of each book, along with the counted number shipped:

```
booktown=# SELECT count(*) AS num_shipped, max(ship_date), title
booktown-#        FROM shipments
booktown-#        JOIN editions USING (isbn)
booktown-#        NATURAL JOIN books AS b (book_id)
booktown-#        GROUP BY b.title
booktown-#        ORDER BY num_shipped DESC;
 num_shipped |         max          |           title
-------------+----------------------+---------------------------
           5 | 2001-08-13 09:47:04-07 | The Cat in the Hat
           5 | 2001-08-14 13:45:51-07 | The Shining
           4 | 2001-08-11 09:55:05-07 | Bartholomew and the Oobleck
           3 | 2001-08-14 13:49:00-07 | Franklin in the Dark
           3 | 2001-08-15 11:57:40-07 | Goodnight Moon
           3 | 2001-08-14 13:41:39-07 | The Tell-Tale Heart
           2 | 2001-08-15 14:02:01-07 | 2001: A Space Odyssey
           2 | 2001-08-14 08:42:58-07 | Dune
           2 | 2001-08-07 13:00:48-07 | Little Women
           2 | 2001-08-09 09:30:46-07 | The Velveteen Rabbit
           1 | 2001-08-14 07:33:47-07 | Dynamic Anatomy
(11 rows)
```

While obviously an informative query, the syntax can be somewhat too unwieldy to repeat frequently. Example 4-62 demonstrates creating a view on this same query with the CREATE VIEW command.

Example 4-62: Creating a view

```
booktown=# CREATE VIEW recent_shipments
booktown-#         AS SELECT count(*) AS num_shipped, max(ship_date), title
booktown-#         FROM shipments
booktown-#         JOIN editions USING (isbn)
booktown-#         NATURAL JOIN books AS b (book_id)
booktown-#         GROUP BY b.title
booktown-#         ORDER BY num_shipped DESC;
CREATE
```

The CREATE server response in Example 4-62 confirms that the view was accurately created. As a result, the Book Town database should now have a view called recent_shipments that will show each title that has been shipped from Book Town, how many of each title was shipped, and when the most recent shipment of that title occurred.

Applying Views

The key difference in the functionality of a view is that instead of having to type a long query, only a simple SELECT command is needed, as shown in Example 4-63.

Example 4-63: Using a view

```
booktown=# SELECT * FROM recent_shipments;
 num_shipped |          max          |          title
-------------+-----------------------+----------------------------
           5 | 2001-08-13 09:47:04-07 | The Cat in the Hat
           5 | 2001-08-14 13:45:51-07 | The Shining
           4 | 2001-08-11 09:55:05-07 | Bartholomew and the Oobleck
           3 | 2001-08-14 13:49:00-07 | Franklin in the Dark
           3 | 2001-08-15 11:57:40-07 | Goodnight Moon
           3 | 2001-08-14 13:41:39-07 | The Tell-Tale Heart
           2 | 2001-08-15 14:02:01-07 | 2001: A Space Odyssey
           2 | 2001-08-14 08:42:58-07 | Dune
           2 | 2001-08-07 13:00:48-07 | Little Women
           2 | 2001-08-09 09:30:46-07 | The Velveteen Rabbit
           1 | 2001-08-14 07:33:47-07 | Dynamic Anatomy
(11 rows)

booktown=# SELECT * FROM recent_shipments
booktown-#         ORDER BY max DESC
booktown-#         LIMIT 3;
 num_shipped |          max          |         title
-------------+-----------------------+----------------------
           2 | 2001-08-15 14:02:01-07 | 2001: A Space Odyssey
           3 | 2001-08-15 11:57:40-07 | Goodnight Moon
           3 | 2001-08-14 13:49:00-07 | Franklin in the Dark
(3 rows)
```

Example 4-63 further demonstrates that, even though the view was created with an ORDER BY clause, the order of the view's result set itself can be re-sorted. This is achieved by passing an ORDER BY clause to the SELECT command which is querying the view.

Any attempt to use DELETE or UPDATE on a view will result in an error, as a view itself does not contain data. The view is merely a window to another set of data, despite its similar functional appearance to a table, and is not itself a modifiable data set.

Destroying a view

The syntax to permanently destroy a view is entered as follows, where *view* is the name of the view to be destroyed:

```
DROP VIEW view
```

The destruction of a view will have no effect on the data that the view utilizes. A view exists purely as a means to observe data in other tables, and may be safely destroyed without losing data (though the query described by the view will, of course, be lost). Thus any attempts to alter or delete from a view will fail.

Further SQL Application

This chapter has provided the fundamental concepts of applying SQL within Post-greSQL. You should now have a solid understanding of how to create and manage tables, as well as how to retrieve, modify, and generally manage the data within those tables. Chapter 5 covers in more detail the functions and operators already alluded to and used in this chapter.

5

Operators and Functions

This chapter expands on the operators and functions available to PostgreSQL. These character symbols and identifiers allow you to flexibly modify and compare results within SQL statements. The results of these operations can be used in a variety of ways, from updating existing row data, to constraining query results to only rows matching particular conditions.

PostgreSQL supports the usual variety of standard SQL operators and functions as defined by the ANSI/ISO SQL standards, such as mathematical operators, basic text formatting functions, and date and time value extraction. PostgreSQL also comes with a rich set of custom PostgreSQL extensions, such as regular expression comparison operators, and the flexible to_char() text conversion function.

Take note that these sections describe the *native* operators and functions available to PostgreSQL. An excellent feature of PostgreSQL is its extensibility in this area. Once you have a solid understanding of operators and functions, you may be interested in developing your own. These techniques are described in Chapter 7, *Advanced Features*.

Operators

In Chapter 3, *Understanding SQL*, operators are defined syntactically as tokens that are used to perform operations on values (e.g., constants, or identifiers), and return the results of those operations. In addition to these syntactic character symbols, there are some SQL keywords that are considered operators due to their effect on values in a SQL statement. Throughout this section, both these symbols and keywords will be referred to as operators.

The function of each operator is highly dependent on its context. Applications of operators range from performing mathematical operations and concatenating character strings, to performing a wide variety of comparisons yielding Boolean results. This section describes the general usage of operators in SQL, with successive sections on the following families of operators:

- Character string
- Numeric
- Logical

For an up-to-date and complete list of PostgreSQL supported operators, you can use *psql*'s \do slash command to view a list of available operators. Understand that many of the listed operators are PostgreSQL-specific, and therefore may not exist in other SQL-capable databases implementations.

Following the discussions of the various types of operators, you'll find information on dealing with NULL values in expressions, and on the order in which operators are evaluated.

Using Operators

Operators operate on either a single value or a pair of values. The majority of operators operate on two values, with the operator placed between the values it is to operate upon (e.g., a - b). Operators that affect only one value are called *unary operators*, and either precede or follow the value they affect (e.g., the @ operator preceding a value is a unary operator indicating the absolute value).

Many operators, while invoked with the same keyword or character symbol, will have different effects depending on the data types to which they are applied. Further, operators will not always have a relevant use to every data type (see Chapter 3 for more information about what data types are available to PostgreSQL).

For example, you can use the addition operator (+) to add two integer values together, but you cannot use it to add an integer to a text type. This is an undefined (and therefore ambiguous and disallowed) use of the operator. The operator character itself (+, in this case) will still be recognized, but you will receive an error such as the one shown in Example 5-2 if you try to misuse an operator:

Consider the Book Town authors table, which correlates author's names with numeric identifiers.

```
           Table "authors"
    Attribute |  Type   | Modifier
   -----------+---------+----------
       id     | integer | not null
```

```
    last_name | text    |
    first_name | text   |
    Index: authors_pkey
```

Two identifiers in this table are the columns id, and last_name, which are types integer (a 4-byte integer) and text, respectively. Since the id column is type integer, it may be used with a mathematical operator along with another numeric value.

Example 5-1 demonstrates correct usage of the addition (+) operator.

Example 5-1: Correct operator usage

```
booktown=# SELECT id + 1 AS id_plus_one, last_name
booktown-#        FROM authors
booktown-#        ORDER BY id DESC LIMIT 5;
 id_plus_one |  last_name
-------------+--------------
       25042 | Bianco
       15991 | Bourgeois
        7807 | Christiansen
        7806 | Lutz
        4157 | King
(5 rows)
```

Notice the result of trying to add incompatible types in Example 5-2.

Example 5-2: Incorrect operator usage

```
booktown=# SELECT id + last_name AS mistake
booktown-#        FROM authors;
ERROR:  Unable to identify an operator '+' for types 'int4' and 'text'
        You will have to retype this query using an explicit cast
```

Fortunately, as you can see in Example 5-2, PostgreSQL's operator-misuse error messages supply a reason for failure, rather than blindly failing. These can be helpful in determining the next step in developing your statement, in order to make it a valid query.

Character String Operators

PostgreSQL contains a comprehensive set of character string operators, from simple text concatenation and string comparison, to a strong set of regular expression matching. Character string operators are valid upon values of types char, varchar, and PostgreSQL's own text type.

The following sections describe the basic comparison and concatenation operators, as well as the implementation of case-sensitive and case-insensitive *regular expression* operators.

Basic comparison

Each of the basic character string comparison and concatenation operators supported by PostgreSQL are listed in Table 5-1.

 Note that the LIKE and ILIKE keywords, which call to the like( ) function, are sometimes referred to as string comparison *operators*. These keywords are covered in the section titled "Functions".

Table 5-1. Basic character string operators

Operator	Usage	Description
=	'string' = 'comparison'	A comparison returning true if *string* matches *comparison* identically
!=	'string' != 'comparison'	A comparison returning true if *string* does not match *comparison* identically
<>	'string' <> 'comparison'	Identical to the != operator
<	'string' < 'comparison'	A comparison returning true if *string* should be sorted alphabetically before *comparison*
<=	'string' <= 'comparison'	A comparison returning true if *string* should be sorted alphabetically before *comparison*, or if the values are identical
>	'string' > 'comparison'	A comparison returning true if *string* should be sorted alphabetically after *comparison*
>=	'string' >= 'comparison'	A comparison returning true if *string* should be sorted alphabetically after *comparison*, or if the values are identical

Each of the string comparison operators returns a Boolean result of either true or false. The alphabetical sorting referred to by Table 5-1 compares each sequential character in a string, determining if one character is considered 'greater than' or 'less than' the other. If the leading characters in two strings are at all identical, each character is checked from left to right until two different characters are found for comparison. In this sorting scheme, characters are determined to be higher than one another based on their ASCII value, as demonstrated in the following example:

```
booktown=# SELECT letter, ascii(letter)
booktown-#        FROM text_sorting
booktown-#        ORDER BY letter ASC;
 letter | ascii
--------+-------
   0    |    48
```

```
        1       |    49
        2       |    50
        3       |    51
        A       |    65
        B       |    66
        C       |    67
        D       |    68
        a       |    97
        b       |    98
        c       |    99
        d       |   100
(12 rows)
```

If you are unsure of how a character will be sorted, you can use the ascii() function to determine the ASCII value of the character. This function is described further in the section titled "Functions." Example 5-3 illustrates a comparative check on the books table, and returns all titles whose first letter would be sorted before the letter *D*.

Example 5-3: Comparing strings

```
booktown=# SELECT title FROM books
booktown-#                 WHERE substr(title, 1, 1) < 'D';
              title
----------------------------
 2001: A Space Odyssey
 Bartholomew and the Oobleck
(2 rows)
```

String concatenation

The text concatenation operator (||) is an invaluable tool for formatting output results. Like all operators, it may be used anywhere a constant value is allowed in a SQL statement. Values may be repeatedly concatenated in a single statement by simply appending the || operator after each appended string constant or identifier.

As an example, it might be used in the WHERE clause in order to constrain rows by comparing against a character string. Example 5-4 demonstrates how to use this operator.

Example 5-4: Concatenating strings

```
booktown=# SELECT 'The Title: ' || title || ', by ' ||
booktown-#        first_name || ' ' || last_name AS book_info
booktown-#        FROM books NATURAL JOIN authors AS a (author_id) LIMIT 3;
                 book_info
-----------------------------------------------------------
 The Title: The Shining, by Stephen King
 The Title: Dune, by Frank Herbert
 The Title: 2001: A Space Odyssey, by Arthur C. Clarke
(3 rows)
```

Regular expression matching operators

For times when normal equivalence comparisons are inadequate, PostgreSQL has several operators designed to perform pattern matching against regular expressions. A regular expression is similar to any other string to be matched against, with the exception that some characters (such as the square braces, pipe, and backslash) have special meaning in a comparison. If you have used Unix programs such as *sed*, *grep*, or *perl*, you may already be familiar with this kind of syntax.

For more detailed information on regular expressions in general, refer to O'Reilly's *Mastering Regular Expressions*, by Jeffrey E. F. Friedl.

When a value is compared against a regular expression, the expression itself (or *regex*) may match both literal character sequences, as well as several variable character sequences. Both literal and variable sequences may be specified throughout the expression. Example 5-5 illustrates an example of such a sequence. It searches the Book Town authors table for names beginning with either *A* or *T*.

Example 5-5: An example regular expression

```
booktown=# SELECT first_name, last_name
booktown-#        FROM authors
booktown-#        WHERE first_name ~ '^A|^T';
  first_name   |  last_name
---------------+--------------
 Ariel         | Denham
 Tom           | Christiansen
 Arthur C.     | Clarke
 Andrew        | Brookins
 Theodor Seuss | Geisel
(5 rows)
```

The ~ symbol is the regular expression operator, within the WHERE clause, and the regular expression sequence itself in Example 5-5 is ^A | ^T. The special characters in this sequence are the caret (^), and the pipe (|), while the literal characters are *A* and *T*. The special characters used in regular expressions are explained in detail later in this section.

The most important syntactic difference between the use of the like() function and regular expression operators is that like() uses wild-card symbols (e.g., %) at the beginning and end of its expression in order to match a substring. In contrast, (with the beginning and end-line symbols found in Table 5-3) regular expression operators will implicitly look for the regular expression sequence *anywhere in the compared character string* unless otherwise instructed.

Table 5-2 lists the regular expression operators. These operators compare a text value (either an identifier or a constant) to a regular expression. Each operator provides a Boolean result, depending on the nature of the operator.

Table 5-2. Regular expression comparison operators

Operator	Usage	Description
~	`'string' ~ 'regex'`	A regular expression comparison, yielding true if the expression matches
!~	`'string' !~ 'regex'`	A regular expression comparison, yielding true if the expression *does not* match
~*	`'string' ~* 'regex'`	A case-insensitive regular expression, yielding true if the expression matches
!~*	`'string' !~* 'regex'`	not equal to regular expression, case insensitive

The special characters available to a regular expression are listed in Table 5-3. These are the characters which may be used in a regular expression string to represent special meaning.

Table 5-3. Regular expression symbols

Symbol(s)	Usage	Description
^	`^expression`	Matches the beginning (^) of the character string
$	`expression $`	Matches the end ($) of the character string
.	`.`	Matches any single character
[]	`[abc]`	Matches any single character which is between brackets (e.g., *a, b,* or *c*)
[^]	`[^abc]`	Matches any single character not between brackets, following caret (e.g., not *a, b,* or *c*)
[-]	`[a-z]`	Matches any character which is between the range of characters between brackets and separated by the dash (e.g., within *a* through *z*)
[^-]	`[^a-z]`	Matches any characters *not* between the range of characters between brackets and separated by the dash (e.g., not within *a* through *z*)
?	`a?`	Matches zero or one instances of the character (or regex sequence) preceding it
*	`a*`	Matches zero or more instances of the character (or regex sequence) preceding it
+	`a+`	Matches one or more instances of the character (or regex sequence) preceding it

Table 5-3. Regular expression symbols (continued)

Symbol(s)	Usage	Description
|	*expr1* | *expr2*	Matches character sequences to the left *or* right of it (e.g., either *expr1*, or *expr2*)
()	(*expr1*) *expr2*	Explicitly groups expressions, to clarify precedence of special character symbols

Note that in order to use a literal version of any of the characters in Table 5-3, they must be prefixed with *two* backslashes (e.g., \\$ represents a literal dollar sign).

A common use of regular expressions is to search for a literal substring within a larger string. This can be achieved either with the ~ operator, if case is important, or with the ~* operator if the comparison should be case-insensitive. These operators are each demonstrated in Example 5-6.

Example 5-6: A simple regular expression comparison

```
booktown=# SELECT title FROM books
booktown-#         WHERE title ~ 'The';
         title
----------------------
 The Shining
 The Cat in the Hat
 The Velveteen Rabbit
 The Tell-Tale Heart
(4 rows)

booktown=# SELECT title FROM books
booktown-#         WHERE title ~* 'The';
           title
----------------------------
 The Shining
 The Cat in the Hat
 Bartholomew and the Oobleck
 Franklin in the Dark
 The Velveteen Rabbit
 The Tell-Tale Heart
(6 rows)
```

As you can see in Example 5-6, two more rows are returned when using the ~* operator, as it matches not just "the" sequence, but modification of case on the same sequence (including *the*, *tHe*, *ThE*, and so on).

The same regular expression sequence can be modified to use the ^ symbol, to match only the character string *The* when it is at the beginning of the comparison string, as shown in Example 5-7. Additionally, the *.** sequence is then appended, to indicate any number of characters may match until the next following grouped expression. In this case, the *.** sequence is followed by a parenthetically grouped pair of strings (*rabbit* and *heart*), which are separated by the | symbol, indicating that either of the strings will be considered a match.

Example 5-7: A more involved regular expression comparison

```
booktown=# SELECT title FROM books
booktown-#          WHERE title ~* '^The.*(rabbit|heart)';
        title
----------------------
 The Velveteen Rabbit
 The Tell-Tale Heart
(2 rows)
```

In Example 5-7, the results should fairly clearly indicate the effect of the regular expression comparison. Translated into English, the expression *^The.*(rabbit|heart)* states that a match will be found only if the compared string begins with the character sequence *The* and, any amount of any characters thereafter, contain either the character sequence *rabbit*, or *heart*. The use of the *~** operator (rather than just the *~* operator) makes the comparison case-insensitive.

Example 5-8 executes an even more complicated regular expression comparison.

Example 5-8: A complicated regular expression comparison

```
booktown=# SELECT title FROM books
booktown-#          WHERE title ~* '(^t.*[ri]t)|(ing$|une$)';
        title
----------------------
 The Shining
 Dune
 The Velveteen Rabbit
 The Tell-Tale Heart
(4 rows)

booktown=#
```

The regular expression used in Example 5-8 is a good example of how regular expressions can be intimidating! Breaking it down an element at a time, you can see that there are two parenthetically grouped expressions, separated by a | symbol. This means that if either of these expressions are found to match the title, the comparison will be considered a match.

Breaking it down further, you can see that the expression to the left of the | symbol consists of, from left to right: a caret (^) followed by the character *t*, a period (.) followed by an asterisk (*), and a pair of square brackets (*[]*) enclosing the characters *r* and *i*, followed by the character *t*. Translated into English, this subexpression essentially says that in order to match, the compared string must begin with the letter *t*, and be followed by a sequence of zero or more characters until either the letter *r*, or *i* is found, which must be followed immediately by the letter *t*. If any of these conditions is not found, the comparison will not be considered a match.

The expression to the right of the | symbol is a bit simpler, consisting of two character string sequences (*ing* and *une*), each followed by the *$* character, and separated by another | symbol. This sub-expression, translated into English, describes a match as a relationship in which either ends with the value *ing*, or *une*. If either of these are found, the expression is considered a match, because of the | symbol.

Numeric Operators

PostgreSQL's numeric operator support can be divided into three general groups:

Mathematical operators
> Mathematical operators affect one or two values, perform a mathematical operation, and return a value of a numeric data type.

Numeric comparison operators
> Numeric comparison operators draw a conclusion based on two numeric values (such as whether one is larger than the other) and return a value of type boolean, set to either true or false.

Binary (or bit string) operators
> Binary, or bit string, operators manipulate numeric values at the bit level of zeroes and ones. The following sections address each of these operator groups.

Mathematical operators

Mathematical operators can be used in the target list, in the WHERE clause of a SELECT statement, or anywhere else a numeric result may be appropriate. This sometimes will include the ORDER BY clause, a JOIN qualifier, or a GROUP BY clause.

Table 5-4 describes each of the mathematical operators available in PostgreSQL, along with example usage.

Table 5-4. Mathematical operators

Operator	Usage	Description
+	*a* + *b*	Addition of numeric quantities *a* and *b*
−	*a* − *b*	Subtraction of numeric quantity *b* from *a*
*	*a* * *b*	Multiplication of numeric quantities *a* and *b*
/	*a* / *b*	Division of numeric quantity *a* by *b*

Table 5-4. Mathematical operators (continued)

Operator	Usage	Description
%	a % b	Modulus, or remainder, from dividing a by b
^	a ^ b	Exponential operator, the value of a to the power of b
|/	|/ a	Square root of a
||/	||/ a	Cube root of a
!	a!	Factorial of a
!!	!! a	Factorial prefix, factorial of a, different only in syntactic placement from !
@	@ a	Absolute value of a

As an example of mathematical operators in the target list, the statement in Example 5-9 takes the retail price for each book and divides the cost with the / operator in order to determine the profit margin. This value is then typecast to a truncated numeric value with only two digits of precision. Finally, the integer constant 1 is subtracted from the division result, to yield only the percentage points over 100.

Example 5-9: Using mathematical operators

```
booktown=# SELECT isbn,
booktown-#        (retail / cost)::numeric(3, 2) - 1 AS margin
booktown-#        FROM stock
booktown-#        ORDER BY margin DESC
booktown-#        LIMIT 4;
    isbn    | margin
------------+--------
 0451457994 |   0.35
 0760720002 |   0.33
 0451198492 |   0.30
 0441172717 |   0.29
(4 rows)
```

Notice that the column name is temporarily aliased to margin by using the AS keyword. Remember that the column name created by the AS keyword is a temporary name, and used only for the duration of the query.

Numeric comparison operators

Comparison operators are used to compare values of types such as integer or text to one another, but they will always return a value of type boolean. These operators are most commonly used in the WHERE clause, but may be used anywhere in a SQL statement where a value of type boolean would be valid.

Table 5-5 shows the available comparison operators.

Table 5-5. Comparison operators

Operator	Description
<	Less-than, returns true if the value to the left is smaller in quantity than the value to the right
>	Greater-than, returns true if the value to the left is greater in quantity than the value to the right
<=	Less-than or equal-to, returns true if the value to the left is smaller, or equal to, in quantity than the value to the right
>=	Greater-than or equal-to, returns true if the value to the left is greater, or equal to, in quantity than the value to the right
=	Equal-to, returns true if the values to the left and right of the operator are equivalent
<> or !=	Not-equal, returns true if the values to the left and right of the operator not equivalent

The <> operator exists as an alias to the != operator for functional compatibility with other SQL-capable database implementations. They are effectively identical.

For an example of mathematical comparison operator usage, observe Example 5-10. The query involved uses the <= operator first, to check if the retail value is less-than or equal-to 25. Subsequently, the != operator is employed with the AND keyword to ensure that only books which are in stock (whose stock value are not equal to 0) are returned.

Example 5-10: Using comparison operators

```
booktown=# SELECT isbn, stock
booktown-#        FROM stock
booktown-#        WHERE retail <= 25
booktown-#        AND stock != 0;
    isbn    | stock
------------+-------
 0441172717 |    77
 0590445065 |    10
 0679803335 |    18
 0760720002 |    28
 0929605942 |    25
 1885418035 |    77
(6 rows)
```

Numeric comparison keywords

The BETWEEN keyword (sometimes called an operator) allows you to check a value for existence within a range of values. For instance, Example 5-11 shows a SELECT statement that looks for books with cost between 10 and 17 dollars.

Example 5-11: Using BETWEEN

```
booktown=# SELECT isbn FROM stock
booktown-#        WHERE cost BETWEEN 10 AND 17;
   isbn
------------
 0394800753
 0441172717
 0451457994
(3 rows)
```

You can achieve the same output using the less-than-or-equal-to operator (<=) in conjunction with the greater-than-or-equal-to (>=) operator. See Example 5-12.

Example 5-12: Operator equivalents to BETWEEN

```
booktown=# SELECT isbn FROM stock
booktown-#        WHERE cost >= 10 AND cost <= 17;
   isbn
------------
 0394800753
 0441172717
 0451457994
(3 rows)
```

The BETWEEN syntax simply adds to the readability of an SQL statement. Since both the keyword and operator forms are equally valid to PostgreSQL, it's mostly a matter of user preference.

Binary operators

Binary operators perform bitwise operations on the literal bits of a bit string or integer. These operators may affect integer values, or bit string values. Each of PostgreSQL's binary operators are described in Table 5-6.

Table 5-6. Bit-string operators

Operator	Usage	Description
&	a & b	Binary AND between bit string values of a and b (which may be provided as integers)
|	a | b	Binary OR between bit string values of a and b (which may be provided as integers)

Table 5-6. Bit-string operators (continued)

Operator	Usage	Description
#	a # b	Binary XOR between bit string values of *a* and *b* (which may be provided as integers)
~	~ b	Binary NOT, returns the inverted bit string of *b*
<<	b << n	Binary shifts *b* to the left by *n* bits
>>	b >> n	Binary shifts *b* to the right by *n* bits

Example 5-13 demonstrates shifting a numeric value, and its equivalent bit string, two bits to the right with the >> operator. It also demonstrates the use of the binary to integer bittoint4() function, which is described later in the section titled "Functions."

Example 5-13: Shifting bit strings

```
booktown=# SELECT b'1000' >> 2 AS "8 shifted right",
booktown-#        bittoint4(b'1000' >> 2) AS integer,
booktown-#        8 >> 2 AS likewise;
 8 shifted right | integer | likewise
-----------------+---------+----------
 0010            |       2 |        2
(1 row)
```

 When shifting bit strings, the original length of the string does not change, and any digits pushed either to the left or right of the bit string will be truncated. When using &, |, or #, the bit strings operated on must be of equal length in order to properly compare each bit on a one-to-one basis.

Logical Operators

The AND, OR, and NOT keywords are PostgreSQL's Boolean operators. They are commonly used to join or invert conditions in a SQL statement, particularly in the WHERE clause and the HAVING clause.

Table 5-7 illustrates the Boolean values returned for the AND, OR, and NOT keywords, with each possible value for a Boolean field (true, false, or NULL).

Table 5-7. The AND, OR, and NOT operators

a	b	a AND b	a OR b	NOT a	NOT b
true	true	true	true	false	false
true	false	false	true	false	true
true	NULL	NULL	true	false	NULL
false	false	false	false	true	true
false	NULL	false	NULL	true	NULL
NULL	NULL	NULL	NULL	NULL	NULL

Example 5-14 sequentially uses the OR and AND keywords in two queries to combine a pair of conditions by which rows should be retrieved. In the first query, if a book has either a cost of greater than thirty dollars, or is out of stock, its information will be returned. As you can see from the result set, matching one or both of these conditions causes a row to be returned.

The second query in Example 5-14 uses the same conditions, but combines them with the AND keyword. This results in a stricter condition, as both criteria must be met. As such, only one row is returned, since only one book is found which both has a cost of greater than thirty dollars, and is out of stock.

Example 5-14: Combining comparisons with Boolean operators

```
booktown=# SELECT isbn, cost, stock
booktown-#        FROM stock
booktown-#        WHERE cost > 30
booktown-#          OR stock = 0;
    isbn    | cost  | stock
------------+-------+-------
 0394900014 | 23.00 |     0
 044100590X | 36.00 |    89
 0451198492 | 36.00 |     0
 0451457994 | 17.00 |     0
(4 rows)

booktown=# SELECT isbn, cost, stock
booktown-#        FROM stock
booktown-#        WHERE cost > 30
booktown-#          AND stock = 0;
    isbn    | cost  | stock
------------+-------+-------
 0451198492 | 36.00 |     0
(1 row)
```

Using Operators with NULL

If a table has NULL values in it, a special pair of comparison operators that can be used to include or omit NULL valued fields. You can check for fields set to NULL using the IS NULL keyword phrase. In order to check for a non-NULL value, use the IS NOT NULL keyword phrase.

Example 5-15 uses the IS NULL keyword to check for authors whose first_name column value are set to NULL.

Example 5-15: Comparisons using IS NULL

```
booktown=# SELECT last_name, first_name
booktown-#        FROM authors
booktown-#          WHERE first_name IS NULL;
 last_name | first_name
-----------+------------
 Geisel    |
(1 row)
```

Examining Example 5-15 and Example 5-16, you might think that the syntax in the two statements provided are identical. There is, however, a key difference.

Example 5-16: Comparisons equal to NULL

```
booktown=# SELECT last_name, first_name
booktown-#        FROM authors
booktown-#          WHERE first_name = NULL;
 last_name | first_name
-----------+------------
 Geisel    |
(1 row)
```

PostgreSQL provides a translation from = NULL to IS NULL, and likewise for the != NULL operation with IS NOT NULL. This is provided only for compatibility with existing client applications (such as Microsoft Access).

When comparing a value to NULL in an expression, be in the habit of using the IS NULL and IS NOT NULL keyword operators rather than the = or != math-style operators. While this translation is provided for the sake of compatibility with other systems, it may be discontinued in the future, as it is not a standard SQL procedure (and it is certainly not guaranteed to be a portable procedure to other SQL-based database systems for the same reason).

Any as-yet undiscussed comparison operator used on a NULL value will return a NULL value, as NULL will never be larger, smaller, or otherwise related to any non-NULL value. (See Example 5-17.) A direct query on the result of a comparison against a NULL value will therefore return NULL. You can think of a NULL value as being a sort of SQL black hole, from which no comparison (outside of IS NULL, and its special = translation) may return true, and to which no values may be added, or concatenated.

Example 5-17: Using operators with NULL values

```
booktown=# \pset null *null* Null display is '*null*'.
booktown=# SELECT 5 > NULL;
 ?column?
----------

 *null*
(1 row)

booktown=# SELECT NULL IS NULL;
 ?column?
----------

 t
(1 row)

booktown=# SELECT NULL || 'Test';
 ?column?
----------

 *null*
(1 row)
```

Operator Precedence

When utilizing several operators in large expressions, it can be helpful to know in what order PostgreSQL processes operators. It is not, as you might think, strictly from left to right. If not properly understood, the order of execution can introduce potential for accidental side-effects, such as those shown in Example 5-18.

Example 5-18: Operator precedence

```
booktown=# SELECT 60 + 12 * 5 AS "sixty plus twelve times five",
booktown-#          12 + 60 * 5 AS "twelve plus sixty times five";
 sixty plus twelve times five | twelve plus sixty times five
------------------------------+------------------------------
                          120 |                          312
(1 row)
```

As you can see by the two column values returned in Example 5-18, the use of several operators without parentheses to enforce precedence can return very different results, despite the same numbers being manipulated in only a slightly different order. In this example, the multiplication is actually executed first (regardless of the fact that the addition sign (+) precedes it sequentially, from left to right).

Table 5-8 lists, in order of PostgreSQL's execution from the top down, the precedence of each group of operators.

Table 5-8. Operator precedence

Operator	Usage	Description
`::`	`value::type`	Explicit typecast
`[]`	`value[index]`	Array element index
`.`	`table.column`	Table and column name separator
`-`	`-value`	Unary minus
`^`	`value ^ power`	Exponent
`* / %`	`value1 * value2`	Multiplication, division, and modulus
`+ -`	`value1 + value2`	Addition and subtraction
`IS`	`value IS boolean`	Compares against true or false
`ISNULL`	`value ISNULL`	Compares against NULL
`IS NOT NULL`	`value IS NOT NULL`	Checks for *value* inequivalent to NULL
Other	*Variable*	Includes all other native and user-defined character operators
`IN`	`value IN set`	Checks for membership of *value* in *set*
`BETWEEN`	`value BETWEEN a AND b`	Checks for *value* in range between values *a* and *b*
`LIKE, ILIKE`	`string LIKE comparison`	Checks for matching pattern *comparison* in *string*
`< > <= >=`	`value1 < value2`	Quantity comparisons for less than, greater than, less than or equal to, and greater than or equal to.
`=`	`value1 = value2`	Equality comparison
`NOT`	`NOT value`	Logical NOT inversion
`AND`	`value1 AND value2`	Logical AND conjunction
`OR`	`value1 OR value2`	Logical OR conjunction

 The operator precedence listed in Table 5-8 applies to user-defined operators that have the same character sequence as built-in operators. For example, if you define the plus symbol (+) operator for your own user-defined data type, it has the same precedence as the built in plus (+) operator, regardless of its function.

Functions

A *function* is an identifier that instructs PostgreSQL to perform a programmatic operation within a SQL statement. A function returns a single value from its operation, and that value is then used in the SQL statement where the function was invoked. This process is similar to the way operators return their results in the location from which they were called in the query. (In fact, operators are technically pointers to built-in system functions, and are sometimes called "syntactic sugar" for functions, as they are a syntactically convenient way to call underlying functions.)

Using Functions

To use a function in a SQL statement, type the function's name, followed by its list of parameters (called *arguments*), if any. The arguments passed to a function are enclosed in parentheses. There are two general styles of entering arguments: the standard SQL92 functions are generally implemented so that they accept their arguments delimited by special SQL keywords, such as FROM, FOR, and USING. PostgreSQL-style functions, on the other hand, accept arguments delimited by commas (which you might expect if you have experience with a programming language such as C).

Arguments may be constants, valid identifiers, or expressions. The particular arguments you need to pass to a function will depend completely on the function being used, and its requirements: especially with regards to data types. With a couple of exceptions, all functions require the open and closing parentheses following the function name, even if no arguments are passed.

```
sql92_style_function ( { argument | KEYWORD } [...] )
pgsql_style_function ( argument [, ...] )
```

The exceptions to the parenthetical function syntax are the SQL92 functions current_date, current_time, and current_timestamp. These lack parentheses to remain compatible with the SQL92 specification.

A powerful use of functions is that they may be nested, provided that the data type returned by a nested function is compatible with the argument accepted by the function it is nested within. Functions may be nested to any depth:

```
function_name ( nested_function_name ( arguments [, ...] ) [, ...] )
```

PostgreSQL defines a rich set of functions for its built-in data types. To view a complete list of functions available, execute the \df slash command within *psql*. PostgreSQL also supports extensibility of its function set through the CREATE FUNC-TION command. See Chapter 7 for more on this topic.

The default name for a column that is described by a function in the target list will be the name of the function, without trailing parentheses, or arguments (e.g., to_char).

Mathematical Functions

The mathematical functions provided for PostgreSQL operate on a variety of numeric data types, and generally return a value of the same type as the function's arguments. They can perform many useful and common arithmetic and trigonometric operations; Table 5-9 provides an overview of some of the most common mathematical functions in PostgreSQL.

Table 5-9. Mathematical functions in PostgreSQL

Function	Description
abs(x)	Returns the absolute value of x
acos(x)	Returns the inverse cosine of x
asin(x)	Returns the inverse sine of x
atan(x)	Returns the inverse tangent of x
atan2(x, y)	Returns the inverse tangent of the quotient of x and y
cbrt(x)	Returns the cube root of x
ceil(x)	Returns the smallest whole integer not less than argument (rounds up)
cos(x)	Returns the cosine of x
cot(x)	Returns the cotangent of x
degrees(r)	Returns degrees from radians r
exp(x)	Returns the e constant (2.71828 . . .), to the power of x
floor(x)	Returns the largest whole integer not greater than x (rounds down)
ln(x)	Returns the natural logarithm of x (the inverse of the exp( ) function)
log(b, x)	Returns the base b logarithm of x
log(x)	Returns the base 10 logarithm of x
mod(x, y)	Returns the remainder (modulus) when dividing x / y
pi( )	Returns the *pi* constant (3.14159 . . .)
pow(x, y)	Returns value of x to the exponential power of y
radians(d)	Returns radian equivalent to d degrees

Table 5-9. Mathematical functions in PostgreSQL (continued)

Function	Description
random()	Returns a pseudo-random value from 0.0 to 1.0
round(x)	Returns x rounded to the nearest whole integer
round(x, s)	Returns the value of x, optionally rounded to s decimal places
sin(x)	Returns the sine of x
sqrt(x)	Returns the square root of x
tan(x)	Returns the tangent of x
trunc(x)	Returns the value of x, with any digits past the decimal point truncated
trunc(x, s)	Returns the value of x, with any digits past s decimal points truncated

The following sections elaborate on each of the functions described in Table 5-9, detailing required arguments, data types, and functionality. Note that while a function will usually only accept one of a set of data types as its arguments, PostgreSQL will attempt to implicitly convert supplied arguments to the required types, if necessary. If an implicit type conversion fails, PostgreSQL will supply the appropriate error message, and you may need to use an explicit type conversion. See Chapter 3 for more information on explicitly converting types.

abs()

```
abs(x)
```

The abs() function accepts a single numeric argument x, and returns its absolute value (distance from zero). It therefore has no effect on positive numbers, but inverts the sign of a negative number to a positive number.

It can accept an argument which is of any of the numeric data types (numeric, bigint, smallint, real, or double precision), and returns the result in the form of the same data type which was passed to it.

Example

```
testdb=# SELECT abs(100) AS abs_positive,
testdb-#        abs(-100) AS abs_negative;
 abs_positive | abs_negative
--------------+--------------
          100 |          100
(1 row)
```

acos()

```
acos(x)
```

The acos() function accepts a valid cosine, and returns the inverse (or arc) cosine of the double precision argument x (between −1 and 1) passed to it. This

effectively returns the inverse of the cos() function. The result is a double precision value of an angle, in radians, between 0 and *pi*.

Example

```
testdb=# SELECT acos(1), acos(0), acos(-1),
testdb=#        acos(cos(1)) AS inverse_example;
 acos |      acos       |      acos        | inverse_example
------+-----------------+------------------+-----------------
    0 | 1.5707963267949 | 3.14159265358979 |               1
(1 row)
```

asin()

```
asin(x)
```

The asin() function returns the inverse (or arc) sine of the double precision
argument *x* (between –1 and 1) passed to it. Like acos(), this effectively returns
the inverse of the sin() function. The result is a double precision value of an
angle, in radians, between *pi / 2* and *–pi / 2*.

Example

```
testdb=# SELECT asin(1), asin(0), asin(-1),
testdb=#        asin(sin(1)) AS inverse_example;
      asin       | asin |       asin        | inverse_example
-----------------+------+-------------------+-----------------
 1.5707963267949 |    0 | -1.5707963267949 |               1
(1 row)
```

atan()

```
atan(x)
```

The atan() function returns the inverse (or arc) tangent of a double precision
argument *x* passed to it, which effectively returns the inverse of the tan() function. The result is a double precision value of an angle, in radians, between *pi / 2*
and *–pi / 2*.

Example

```
testdb=# SELECT atan(1), atan(0), atan(-1),
testdb=#        atan(tan(1)) AS inverse_example;
       atan        | atan |        atan         | inverse_example
-------------------+------+---------------------+-----------------
 0.785398163397448 |    0 | -0.785398163397448 |               1
(1 row)
```

atan2()

```
atan2(x, y)
```

Similar to the atan() function, atan2() returns the inverse (or arc) tangent in the form of a double precision value of an angle, in radians, between *pi / 2* and *–pi / 2*. Unlike atan(), atan2() accepts two double precision arguments rather than one, and returns the inverse tangent of the quotient of the first argument divided into the second argument.

In general, atan2(x, y) is functionally identical to atan(x / y), though specifying a *y* value of 0 will not cause a divide by zero error with atan2(), as it would if specifying x / y to the atan() function. If *y* is specified to atan2() as zero, the resultant value will be *pi / 2* for a positive value of *x*, *–pi / 2* for a negative value of *x*, or 0 for a zero value of *x*.

Example

```
testdb=# SELECT atan2(0, 1), atan2(1, 1),
testdb-#        atan(0 / 1) AS functionally,
testdb-#        atan(1 / 1) AS identical;
 atan2 |      atan2       | functionally |     identical
-------+------------------+--------------+-------------------
     0 | 0.785398163397448 |            0 | 0.785398163397448
(1 row)

testdb=# SELECT atan2(1, 0) AS positive_x,
testdb-#        atan2(-1, 0) AS negative_x,
testdb-#        atan2(0, 0) AS zero_x,
testdb-#        pi() / 2 AS pi_over_two;
    positive_x     |    negative_x     | zero_x |    pi_over_two
------------------+-------------------+--------+------------------
 1.5707963267949 | -1.5707963267949 |      0 | 1.5707963267949
(1 row)
```

cbrt()

```
cbrt(x)
```

The cbrt() function accepts a single double precision argument *x*, and returns its cubed root as a double precision value. This function is effectively the inverse of raising a number by the power of 3 with the pow function.

Example

```
testdb=# SELECT pow(2.0, 3) AS "two cubed",
testdb-#        cbrt(8.0) AS "eight's cube root";
 two cubed | eight's cube root
-----------+-------------------
         8 |                 2
(1 row)
```

ceil()

```
ceil(x)
```

The ceil() function accepts a value *x* of any numeric data type (numeric, bigint, smallint, real, or double precision), and rounds it up to the smallest whole integer greater than the passed value. If a whole integer is passed, ceil() has no effect.

Example

```
testdb=# SELECT ceil(1.0), ceil(1.1), ceil(1.5);
 ceil | ceil | ceil
------+------+------
    1 |    2 |    2
(1 row)
```

cos()

```
cos(x)
```

The cos() function accepts a single double precision value *x* representing an angle (in radians), and returns its cosine as a double precision value.

Example

```
testdb=# SELECT cos(pi()) AS cos_pi,
testdb-#        cos(0) AS cos_zero;
 cos_pi | cos_zero
--------+----------
     -1 |        1
(1 row)
```

cot()

```
cot(x)
```

The cot() function accepts a single double precision value *x* representing an angle (in radians), and returns its cotangent as a double precision value. The argument passed must be non-zero.

Example

```
testdb=# SELECT cot(1), cot(-1);
       cot        |        cot
------------------+--------------------
 0.642092615934331 | -0.642092615934331
(1 row)
```

degrees()

```
degrees(r)
```

The degrees() function accepts a double precision argument *r* representing a value expressed in radians, and converts them into degrees. The result is returned as a value of type double precision. degrees() is effectively the inverse of the radians() function.

Example

```
testdb=# SELECT degrees(acos(-1)) AS half_circle,
testdb-#        degrees(pi() * 2) AS full_circle;
 half_circle | full_circle
-------------+-------------
         180 |         360
(1 row)
```

exp()

```
exp(x)
```

The exp() function accepts a single double precision or numeric argument *x*, and returns the special *e* constant, raised to the power passed to the function.

Example

```
testdb=# SELECT exp(0.0) AS one,
testdb-#        exp(1.0) AS e,
testdb-#        exp(2.0) AS "e squared";
 one |        e         |     e squared
-----+------------------+------------------
   1 | 2.71828182845905 | 7.38905609893065
(1 row)
```

floor()

```
floor(x)
```

The floor() function accepts a single numeric value *x*, and rounds it down to the largest whole integer not greater than the passed argument. It therefore has no effect on a whole integer.

Example

```
testdb=# SELECT floor(1.0) AS one,
testdb-#        floor(1.1) AS "one point one",
testdb-#        floor(1.8) AS "one point eight";
 one | one point one | one point eight
-----+---------------+-----------------
   1 |             1 |               1
(1 row)
```

ln()

```
ln(x)
```

ln() accepts a single numeric or double precision value *x* and returns the natural logarithm of that argument. This is effectively the inverse of the exp() function, as well as the equivalent of selecting the log() of the argument, with base *e*.

Example

```
testdb=# SELECT ln(10.0) AS natural_log,
testdb=#        log(exp(1.0), 10.0) AS natural_log,
testdb=#        ln(exp(10.0)) AS inverse_example;
   natural_log    |    natural_log    | inverse_example
------------------+-------------------+-----------------
 2.30258509299405 | 2.30258509299404 |              10
(1 row)
```

log()

```
log(x)
log(b, x)
```

The log() function accepts either one or two arguments of type numeric. If one argument is specified, log(*x*) returns the base 10 logarithm of *x*. If two arguments are specified, log(*b*, *x*) returns the base *b* logarithm of *x*.

Example

```
testdb=# SELECT log(12.0) AS log_12,
testdb=#        log(10, 12.0) AS log_12,
testdb=#        log(3, 12.0) AS "log 12, base 3";
      log_12      |    log_12     | log 12, base 3
------------------+---------------+----------------
 1.07918124604762 | 1.0791812460 |   2.2618595071
(1 row)
```

mod()

```
mod(x, y)
```

The mod() function accepts two numeric arguments, *x* and *y*, which may be of type numeric, integer, smallint, or bigint. The value returned is the remainder, or modulus, left over from dividing *x* / *y*.

Example

```
testdb=# SELECT mod(5, 5) AS no_remainder,
testdb=#        mod(6, 5) AS remainder_one, mod(19, 5) AS remainder_four;
 no_remainder | remainder_one | remainder_four
--------------+---------------+----------------
            0 |             1 |              4
(1 row)
```

pi()

```
pi()
```

The pi() function requires no arguments, and returns the *pi* constant of roughly 3.14159265358979.

Example

```
testdb=# SELECT pi() AS "the pi constant";
 the pi constant
------------------
 3.14159265358979
(1 row)
```

pow()

```
pow(x, y)
```

The pow() function accepts two arguments, *x* and *y*, of type numeric or double precision. It returns the value of *x* raised to the exponent of *y*. The result is returned as a value of the same data type as the passed arguments. Note that the arguments must contain decimal points.

Example

```
testdb=# SELECT pow(2.0, 3.0) AS "two cubed",
testdb-#        pow(2.0, 2.0) AS "two squared",
testdb-#        pow(2.0, 1.0) AS "just two";
 two cubed | two squared | just two
-----------+-------------+----------
         8 |           4 |        2
(1 row)
```

radians()

```
radians(d)
```

The radians() function accepts a single argument *d* of type double precision, specifying degrees. The function returns the equivalent number of radians, as a value of type double precision. radians() is effectively the inverse of the degrees() function.

Example

```
testdb=# SELECT radians(180) AS half_circle,
testdb-#        radians(360) AS full_circle;
   half_circle    |   full_circle
------------------+------------------
 3.14159265358979 | 6.28318530717959
(1 row)
```

random()

```
random()
```

The `random()` function accepts no arguments, and returns a pseudo-random value between 0.0 and 1.0, of type `double precision`. Each invocation of `random()` returns a different value, even when used in multiple places within the same query.

Typically this function is used in conjunction with mathematical operators (e.g., + and *) to set a range of random numbers, and then rounded with an appropriate rounding function (e.g., `round()`, `trunc()`).

Example

```
testdb=# SELECT random() AS natural_random,
testdb-#        round(random() * 9) + 1 AS one_through_ten,
testdb-#        trunc(random() * 99) + 1 AS one_through_one_hundred;
  natural_random  | one_through_ten | one_through_one_hundred
------------------+-----------------+-------------------------
 0.478887704424042 |             2 |                      37
(1 row)
```

round()

```
round(x)
round(x,s)
```

The `round()` function may accept either one or two arguments. The first argument, *x*, of type `numeric` or `double precision`, is the number that you intend to round. The second optional argument, *s*, of type `integer`, specifies how many digits past the decimal to round from. The result is returned as a value of the same type as the first argument.

If there are more digits specified by *s* than by *x*, the extra digits will be padded with zeroes.

Example

```
testdb=# SELECT round(1.0) AS one,
testdb-#        round(1.1) AS "one point one",
testdb-#        round(1.5) AS "one point five",
testdb-#        round(1.8) AS "one point eight";
 one | one point one | one point five | one point eight
-----+---------------+----------------+-----------------
   1 |             1 |              2 |               2
(1 row)

testdb=# SELECT round(1.4949, 1) AS one_digit_scale,
testdb-#        round(1.4949, 3) AS three_digit_scale,
testdb-#        round(1.4949, 10) AS ten_digit_scale,
testdb-#        round(1.4949, 0) AS rounded;
```

```
        one_digit_scale | three_digit_scale | ten_digit_scale | rounded
     -----------------+-------------------+-----------------+---------
                  1.5 |             1.495 |    1.4949000000 |       1
     (1 row)
```

sin()

```
    sin(x)
```

The sin() function accepts a single argument *x* of type double precision, representing an angle described in radians. The sine of the argument is returned as a value of type double precision.

Example

```
    testdb=# SELECT sin(pi() / 4) AS quarter_pi,
    testdb-#        sin(pi() / 2) AS half_pi;
        quarter_pi     | half_pi
    -------------------+---------
     0.707106781186547 |       1
    (1 row)
```

sqrt()

```
    sqrt(x)
```

The sqrt() function accepts a single argument *x*, of either type double precision, or numeric, and returns its square root. The returned value is of the same data type passed to it. The sqrt function is effectively the inverse of the pow() function, used with a power of 2.

Example

```
    testdb=# SELECT sqrt(2.0), sqrt(4.0),
    testdb-#        sqrt(pow(2.0, 2)) AS inverse_example;
          sqrt       | sqrt | inverse_example
    -----------------+------+-----------------
     1.4142135623731 |    2 |               2
    (1 row)
```

tan()

```
    tan(x)
```

The tan() function accepts a single argument *x*, of type double precision, representing an angle described in radians. The tangent of the argument is returned as a value of type double precision.

Example

```
    testdb=# SELECT tan(pi() / 8),
    testdb-#        tan(0);
         tan        | tan
```

```
--------------------+-----
 0.414213562373095 |   0
(1 row)
```

trunc()

```
trunc(x)
trunc(x, s)
```

The trunc() function accepts one or two arguments, *x* and *s*. The *x* argument may be of the numeric or double precision type, and represents the value to be truncated. The *s* argument may be of the integer type.

If specified, *s* dictates the number of digits allowed to the right of the decimal before truncation. If unspecified, any digits past the decimal in *x* are truncated. If more digits are specified by *s* than there are represented by *x*, the extra digits will be padded with zeroes.

Example

```
testdb=# SELECT trunc(1.598) AS natural_truncation,
testdb=#        trunc(1.598, 1) AS one_decimal_point,
testdb=#        trunc(1.598, 8) AS extra_places;
 natural_truncation | one_decimal_point | extra_places
--------------------+-------------------+--------------
                  1 |               1.5 |   1.59800000
(1 row)
```

Character String Functions

PostgreSQL supports a wide variety of text formatting, analysis and comparison functions. These include both SQL92 standard functions, such as substring() and trim(), as well as PostgreSQL-specific extensions, such as ltrim(), rtrim() and substr(). Table 5-10 lists the functions available to PostgreSQL for use with character strings. In general, when referring to a value of type text, it is functionally synonymous with a value of type character, or varchar.

Table 5-10. Character string functions

Function	Description
ascii(*s*)	Returns the ascii code of the first character passed to it in character string *s*
btrim(*s* [, *t*])	Returns character string *s*, trimmed on the left and right of any substrings consisting solely of letters in character string *t* (or whitespace, if *t* is not specified)
char_length(*s*)	Returns the numeric length of character string *s*

Table 5-10. Character string functions (continued)

Function	Description
chr(*n*)	Returns the character whose ascii value corresponds to the number *n*
s ilike(*f*)	Returns true if the expression *f* is found to match (case-insensitively) *s*
initcap(*s*)	Returns the character string *s*, with each word's first letter capitalized
length(*s*)	Returns the numeric length of character string *s*
s like(*f*)	Returns true if the expression *f* is found to match *s*
lower(*s*)	Returns the string *s*, in all lowercase
lpad(*s*, *n* [, *c*])	Returns the character string *s*, padded to the left with character string *c* (or whitespace, if *c* is not defined) to length of *n* characters (or truncated on the right to *n* characters)
ltrim(*s* [, *f*])	Returns character string *s*, trimmed on the left of a substring consisting solely of letters in character string *f* (or whitespace, if *f* is not specified)
octet_length(*s*)	Returns the number of 8-bit bytes in character string *s*
position(*b* IN *s*)	Returns the location of character sub-string *b* in character string *s* (counting from 1)
repeat(*s*, *n*)	Returns the character string *s*, repeated *n* times
rpad(*s*, *n* [, *c*])	Returns the character string *s*, padded to the right with character string *c* (or whitespace, if *c* is not specified) to length of *n* characters (or truncated on the left to *n* characters)
rtrim(*s* [, *f*])	Returns character string *s*, trimmed on the right of a substring consisting solely of letters in character string *f* (or whitespace, if *f* is not specified)
strpos(*s*, *b*)	Returns the location of character sub-string *b* in character string *s* (counting from 1). This is a PostgreSQL specific function which duplicates the effect of the SQL position() function, using C style arguments.
substr(*s*, *n* [, *l*])	Returns a character sub-string of the character string *s*, starting at digit *n* (counting from 1), with optional maximum length *l* characters
substring(*s* FROM *n* FOR *l*)	Returns a character sub-string of the character string *s*, starting at digit *n* (counting from 1), with optional maximum length *l* characters
to_ascii(*s*, *f*)	Returns text *s* converted from multibyte encoding format *f* to plain ASCII

Table 5-10. Character string functions (continued)

Function	Description
translate(*s*, *f*, *r*)	Returns the character string *s*, with any found characters from string *f* replaced with corresponding character in string *r*
trim(*side f* FROM *s*)	Returns character string *s*, trimmed of leading and/or trailing substrings which consist solely of letters in character string *f*, as dictated by the *side* keyword (which is either LEADING, TRAILING or BOTH)
upper(*s*)	Returns the character string *s*, converted to all uppercase

The following sections describe each of these character string functions, detailing their argument requirements, return types, and general usage.

ascii()

```
ascii(s)
```

The ascii() function accepts a single argument of either a single character, or a character string of type text, and returns the numeric ASCII value of the first character interpreted. The result is returned as a value of type integer.

Examples

```
booktown=# SELECT ascii('T');
 ascii
-------
    84
(1 row)


booktown=# SELECT DISTINCT ON (substr)
booktown-#        title, substr(title, 1, 1),
booktown-#        ascii(title)
booktown-#        FROM books
booktown-#        ORDER BY substr ASC;
            title            | substr | ascii
-----------------------------+--------+-------
 2001: A Space Odyssey       | 2      |    50
 Bartholomew and the Oobleck | B      |    66
 Dune                        | D      |    68
 Franklin in the Dark        | F      |    70
 Goodnight Moon              | G      |    71
 Little Women                | L      |    76
 Practical PostgreSQL        | P      |    80
 The Shining                 | T      |    84
(8 rows)
```

btrim()

```
btrim(s)
btrim(s, t)
```

The btrim() function accepts one or two arguments s, and (optionally) t, each of type text. If t is specified, the function trims the string value s of any leading or trailing strings consisting solely of characters described in t. If t is not specified, leading and trailing whitespace is trimmed. The resultant trimmed value is returned as type text.

It is important to understand that the order of the characters described by t is not relevant to btrim(). Any strings at the beginning or end of s that consecutively match *any* of the characters described in t will be trimmed.

Example

```
booktown=# SELECT btrim('  whitespace example  ') AS trim_blanks,
booktown-#        btrim('123example 332', '123') AS trim_numbers;
     trim_blanks     | trim_numbers
---------------------+--------------
 whitespace example | example
(1 row)
```

char_length()

```
char_length(s)
```

The char_length() SQL92 function accepts a single argument of type text, var-char, or character, and returns the number of characters in the character string s passed to it. The returned value is of type integer.

Example

```
booktown=# SELECT char_length(title), title
booktown-#        FROM books
booktown-#        LIMIT 3;
 char_length |          title
-------------+------------------------
          11 | The Shining
           4 | Dune
          21 | 2001: A Space Odyssey
(3 rows)
```

chr()

```
chr(n)
```

The chr() function accepts a single numeric argument n of type integer, and returns the corresponding character value for that ASCII value of n. The resultant value is of type text.

The chr() function is effectively the inverse of the ascii function.

Examples

```
booktown=# SELECT chr(65), ascii('A');
 chr | ascii
-----+-------
 A   |    65
(1 row)
```

initcap()

```
initcap(s)
```

The initcap() function accepts a single argument *s* of type text, and returns its value, with the first letter of each word capitalized. In this context, a "word" is a string of characters separated from other words by whitespace.

Example

```
booktown=# SELECT initcap('a prospective book title');
          initcap
--------------------------
 A Prospective Book Title
(1 row)
```

length()

```
length(s)
```

Functionally identical to the char_length() SQL92 function. Accepts a single argument *s* of type text, character, or varchar, and returns its length as a value of type integer.

Example

```
booktown=# SELECT length(title), title
booktown-#        FROM books
booktown-#        LIMIT 3;
 length |        title
--------+----------------------
     11 | The Shining
      4 | Dune
     21 | 2001: A Space Odyssey
(3 rows)
```

The length evaluation functions for character strings defined in SQL92 are char_length() and octet_length(). Therefore, these functions are more likely to exist within other RDBMS systems than the length() function.

like() and ilike()

```
s like(f)
s LIKE f
like(s, f)
s ilike(f)
s ILIKE f
```

The like() function checks the expression described by *f*, and attempts to see if it matches the character string *s*. It may either accept two arguments of type text, *s* and *f*, or it may be used in a special SQL syntax format where the argument *s* precedes the function name, adding to the readability of the statement. The ilike() function is a non-standard, case-insensitive version of like(), and may only be invoked through the SQL-style syntax.

> The SQL keyword LIKE actually invokes the like() function with PostgreSQL. The ability to use the LIKE keyword without parentheses to invoke this functionality is a syntactic convenience, and there is no different in practice.

The use of like() differs from a normal equivalence operation in that the character string *f* may contain either an underscore (_) or percent (%) symbol to indicate special meaning in matching character values. PostgreSQL interprets the _ symbol as indicating that any single character should be considered a match, while the % symbol is interpreted as indicating that zero or more characters of any value will be considered a match. These special characters may be interspersed throughout the character string *f*.

For more advanced pattern matching capabilities within PostgreSQL, see the section titled "Regular expression matching operators" earlier in this chapter.

Examples

```
booktown=# SELECT * FROM books
booktown-#        WHERE title LIKE ('%Rabbit');
  id  |        title         | author_id | subject_id
------+----------------------+-----------+------------
 1234 | The Velveteen Rabbit |     25041 |          3
(1 row)

booktown=# SELECT * FROM books
booktown-#        WHERE title LIKE '%D___';
  id   |        title        | author_id | subject_id
-------+---------------------+-----------+------------
  4513 | Dune                |      1866 |         15
 25908 | Franklin in the Dark |     15990 |          2
(2 rows)
```

```
booktown=# SELECT * FROM books
booktown-#        WHERE title ILIKE '%python%';
  id   |       title        | author_id | subject_id
-------+--------------------+-----------+------------
 41473 | Programming Python |      7805 |          4
 41477 | Learning Python    |      7805 |          4
(2 rows)
```

lower()

```
lower(s)
```

The `lower()` SQL92 function accepts a single character string argument *s* of type text, and returns the same value with all characters converted to lowercase. The resultant value is returned as type text.

Example

```
booktown=# SELECT lower(title)
booktown-#        FROM books
booktown-#        LIMIT 3;
       lower
----------------------
 the shining
 dune
 2001: a space odyssey
(3 rows)
```

lpad()

```
lpad(s, n)
lpad(s, n, c)
```

The `lpad()` function accepts either two or three arguments *s*, *n*, and optionally *c*, of types text, integer, and text, respectively. The function "pads" the left side of the character string *s* with either whitespace, or the optional character string defined by *c*, until it is exactly *n* characters in length.

If the character string *s* is initially longer than *n*, *s* will be truncated from the right until it is exactly the length of *n*.

Example

```
booktown=# SELECT title, lpad(title, 12, '-') AS dashed,
booktown-#        lpad(title, 12, '-+-') AS plus_dashed
booktown-#        FROM books LIMIT 4;
         title         |    dashed    | plus_dashed
-----------------------+--------------+--------------
 The Shining           | -The Shining | -The Shining
 Dune                  | --------Dune | -+--+--+Dune
 2001: A Space Odyssey | 2001: A Spac | 2001: A Spac
 The Cat in the Hat    | The Cat in t | The Cat in t
(4 rows)
```

ltrim( )

```
ltrim(s)
ltrim(s, f)
```

The ltrim( ) function accepts either one or two arguments, *s* and optionally *f*, each of type text. If *f* is unspecified, the function returns the value of *s*, with any leading whitespace trimmed off. Otherwise, the function returns the character string *s*, with any leading substring containing exclusively characters contained in *f* removed. If no such substring is found, no change is made.

Examples

```
booktown=# SELECT ltrim('    whitespace example');
       ltrim
--------------------
 whitespace example
(1 row)

booktown=# SELECT title, ltrim(title, 'TD2he ')
booktown-#        FROM books
booktown-#        LIMIT 4;
        title          |       ltrim
-----------------------+---------------------
 The Shining           | Shining
 Dune                  | une
 2001: A Space Odyssey | 001: A Space Odyssey
 The Cat in the Hat    | Cat in the Hat
(4 rows)
```

octet_length( )

```
char_length(s)
```

The octet_length( ) SQL92 function accepts a single argument of type text, varchar or, character, and returns the number of 8-bit character bytes in the character string *s* passed to it. The returned value is of type integer.

In most circumstances, there will be the same number of octets as there are characters to a character string, though this may not necessarily be the case with multibyte characters. This is because a multibyte character may consist of more than a single octet (byte), by definition.

Example

```
booktown=# SELECT title, octet_length(title)
booktown-#        FROM books
booktown-#        ORDER BY title ASC
booktown-#        LIMIT 3;
         title          | octet_length
------------------------+--------------
 2001: A Space Odyssey  |           21
```

```
Bartholomew and the Oobleck |              27
Dune                        |               4
(3 rows)
```

position()

```
position(b IN s)
```

The position() SQL92 function accepts two arguments, *b* and *s*, each of type text. The position of the string *b* within the string *s* is returned as a value of type integer (counting from 1). If the string is not found, zero is returned.

Example

```
booktown=# SELECT title, position('the' IN title) AS the_pos
booktown-#          FROM books
booktown-#          WHERE position('the' IN title) != 0;
            title             | the_pos
------------------------------+---------
 The Cat in the Hat           |    12
 Bartholomew and the Oobleck  |    17
 Franklin in the Dark         |    13
(3 rows)
```

repeat()

```
repeat(s, n)
```

The repeat() function accepts two arguments *s* and *n*, of types text and integer, respectively. The function returns the character string described by *s*, repeated *n* consecutive times, as a value of type text.

Example

```
booktown=# SELECT repeat(last_name, 2)
booktown-#          FROM authors
booktown-#          LIMIT 3;
      repeat
--------------------
 DenhamDenham
 BourgeoisBourgeois
 BiancoBianco
(3 rows)
```

rpad()

```
rpad(s, n)
rpad(s, n, c)
```

The rpad() function is essentially the same as the lpad function, but operates on the *right* side of the string *s*, rather than the left. It accepts either two or three arguments *s*, *n*, and optionally *c*, of types text, integer, and text, respectively. The function pads the right side of the character string *s* with either whitespace, or the optional character string defined by *c*, until it is exactly *n* characters in length.

If the character string *s* is longer than *n* characters long to begin with, it will be truncated from the *left* until it is exactly *n* characters in length.

Examples

```
booktown=# SELECT rpad('whitespace example', 30);
             rpad
-------------------------------
 whitespace example
(1 row)

booktown=# SELECT title, rpad(title, 12, '-') AS right_dashed,
booktown-#        rpad(title, 12, '-+-') AS right_plus_dashed
booktown-#        FROM books
booktown-#        LIMIT 3;
         title        | right_dashed | right_plus_dashed
----------------------+--------------+-------------------
 The Shining          | The Shining- | The Shining-
 Dune                 | Dune-------- | Dune-+--+--+
 2001: A Space Odyssey | 2001: A Spac | 2001: A Spac
(3 rows)
```

rtrim()

```
rtrim(s)
rtrim(s, f)
```

The rtrim() function accepts either one or two arguments, *s* and optionally *f*, each of type text. If *f* is unspecified, the function returns the value of *s*, with any trailing whitespace trimmed off. Otherwise, the function returns the character string *s*, with any trailing substring containing exclusively characters contained in *f* removed. If no such substring is found, no change is made.

Examples

```
booktown=# SELECT rtrim('whitespace example ');
       rtrim
--------------------
 whitespace example
(1 row)

booktown=# SELECT title, rtrim(title, 'yes')
booktown-#        FROM books
booktown-#        LIMIT 4;
         title        |        rtrim
----------------------+----------------------
 The Shining          | The Shining
 Dune                 | Dun
 2001: A Space Odyssey | 2001: A Space Od
 The Cat in the Hat   | The Cat in the Hat
(4 rows)
```

strpos()

```
strpos(s, b)
```

The `strpos()` function is functionally identical to the SQL92 `position()` function, but accepts C-style arguments *b* and *s*, each of type `text`. The position of the string *b* within the string *s* is returned as a value of type `integer` (counting from 1). If the string is not found, zero is returned.

Example

```
booktown=# SELECT title, strpos(lower(title), 'rabbit')
booktown-#        FROM books
booktown-#        WHERE strpos(lower(title), 'rabbit') != 0;
       title        | strpos
--------------------+--------
 The Velveteen Rabbit |     15
(1 row)
```

substr()

```
substr(s, n)
substr(s, n, l)
```

The `substr()` function is effectively equivalent to the SQL92 function `substring()`, but accepts C-style arguments *s*, *n*, and optionally *l*, of types `text`, `integer`, and `integer`, respectively. The function returns the substring of *s*, beginning at character index *n*, and optionally stopping after *l* characters.

If the length of the substring to be selected is longer than the available characters, only the available substring will be returned. In other words, it will not be padded as it would be with a trim function.

Example

```
booktown=# SELECT title, substr(title, 15), substr(title, 5, 9)
booktown-#        FROM books
booktown-#        ORDER BY title DESC
booktown-#        LIMIT 3;
       title        | substr |  substr
--------------------+--------+-----------
 The Velveteen Rabbit | Rabbit | Velveteen
 The Tell-Tale Heart  | Heart  | Tell-Tale
 The Shining          |        | Shining
(3 rows)
```

substring()

```
substring(s FROM n)
substring(s FROM n FOR l)
```

The `substring()` function is the SQL92 equivalent to the PostgreSQL-specific `substr()` function. It accepts two or three arguments, *s*, *n*, and optionally *l*, of types text, integer, and integer, respectively. The function returns the substring of *s*, beginning at character index *n*, and optionally stopping after *l* characters.

Examples

```
booktown=# SELECT title, substring(title FROM 15)
booktown-#        FROM books
booktown-#        ORDER BY title DESC
booktown-#        LIMIT 3;
        title         | substring
----------------------+-----------
 The Velveteen Rabbit | Rabbit
 The Tell-Tale Heart  | Heart
 The Shining          |
(3 rows)

booktown=# SELECT title, substring(title FROM 5 FOR 9)
booktown-#        FROM books
booktown-#        ORDER BY title DESC
booktown-#        LIMIT 3;
        title         | substring
----------------------+-----------
 The Velveteen Rabbit | Velveteen
 The Tell-Tale Heart  | Tell-Tale
 The Shining          | Shining
(3 rows)
```

to_ascii()

```
to_ascii(s, f)
```

The to_ascii() function accepts a single argument *s* of type text containing multibyte text with format *f*, and returns normal ASCII text as a value of type text.

The available multibyte encoding formats are *LATIN1* (ISO 8859-1), *LATIN2* (ISO 8859-2), and *WIN1250* (Windows CP1250, or WinLatin2). This function requires that multibyte encoding be enabled (which is a compile-time option when building and installing PostgreSQL).

Example

```
booktown=# SELECT to_ascii('Multibyte Source', 'LATIN1');
     to_ascii
-------------------
 Multibyte Source
(1 row)
```

translate()

```
translate(s, f, r)
```

The translate() function accepts three arguments, *s*, *f* and *r*, each of type text. It replaces any instance of a character in the string *s* that matches any character in *f* with the corresponding character at the same index from string *r*. The result is returned as a value of type text.

Note that this function does not replace only complete instances of the character string *f*, but replaces *any character* within *s* that matches *any character* in *f* with the corresponding character from *r*. If there are more characters in *f* than in *r*, any character in *f* without a corresponding character in *r* will simply be omitted (this can be a useful way to remove unwanted characters).

The important thing to remember about this method of replacement is that there is always a one-to-one relationship between the character found and its replacement character (though its replacement may be empty, if omitted).

The following examples replace all question marks with exclamation points.

Examples

```
booktown=# SELECT translate('I am an example?', '?', '!');
     translate
-------------------
 I am an example!
(1 row)
```

The next example replaces all instances of the character *i* with the character *w*, and all instances of the character *s* with the character *a*. The extra *s* at the end of "was" is ignored.

```
booktown=# SELECT translate('This is a mistake.', 'is', 'was');
      translate
--------------------
 Thwa wa a mwatake.
(1 row)
```

This final example replaces all vowels with nothing, effectively removing all vowels from the input strings.

```
booktown=# SELECT title,
booktown-#        translate(title, 'aeiouAEIOU', '') AS vowelless
booktown-#        FROM books
booktown-#        LIMIT 5;
            title             |      vowelless
------------------------------+--------------------
 The Shining                  | Th Shnng
 Dune                         | Dn
 2001: A Space Odyssey        | 2001:  Spc dyssy
 The Cat in the Hat           | Th Ct n th Ht
 Bartholomew and the Oobleck  | Brthlmw nd th blck
(5 rows)
```

trim()

```
trim(side f FROM s)
```

The trim() function is the SQL92 function used to achieve the same effects as PostgreSQL's rtrim(), ltrim(), and btrim() functions. It accepts three arguments, including a leading keyword *side* (which may be either LEADING, TRAILING, or BOTH), and two character strings, *f* and *s*.

When specified as LEADING, trim() behaves as ltrim(), trimming the longest substring from the beginning of the string *s* which consist solely of characters contained within *f*.

When specified as TRAILING, trim() behaves as rtrim(), trimming the longest substring from the end of the string *s* which consists solely of characters contained within *f*.

When specified as BOTH, trim() behaves as btrim(), trimming the longest substrings from both the beginning and end of the string *s* which consists solely of characters contained within *f*.

Examples

```
booktown=# SELECT isbn, trim(LEADING '0' FROM isbn)
booktown-#        FROM editions
booktown-#        LIMIT 2;
    isbn    |   ltrim
------------+-----------
 039480001X | 39480001X
 0451160916 | 451160916
(2 rows)

booktown=# SELECT isbn, trim(TRAILING 'X' FROM isbn)
booktown-#        FROM editions
booktown-#        LIMIT 2;
    isbn    |   rtrim
------------+-----------
 039480001X | 039480001
 0451160916 | 0451160916
(2 rows)

booktown=# SELECT isbn, trim(BOTH '0X' FROM isbn)
booktown-#        FROM editions
booktown-#        LIMIT 2;
    isbn    |   btrim
------------+-----------
 039480001X | 39480001
 0451160916 | 451160916
(2 rows)
```

upper()

```
upper(s)
```

The upper() SQL92 function accepts a single argument *s* of type text, and returns the character string with each character converted to lowercase as a value of type text.

Example

```
booktown=# SELECT title, upper(title)
booktown-#        FROM books
booktown-#        ORDER BY id ASC
booktown-#        LIMIT 3;
        title        |        upper
---------------------+---------------------
 The Tell-Tale Heart | THE TELL-TALE HEART
 Little Women        | LITTLE WOMEN
 The Velveteen Rabbit| THE VELVETEEN RABBIT
(3 rows)
```

Date and Time Functions

The standard SQL92 date and time functions (current_date, current_time, current_timestamp, and extract()) are each supported by PostgreSQL, as well as a variety of PostgreSQL-specific extensions. Each of PostgreSQL's date and time retrieval and extraction functions are listed in Table 5-11.

Table 5-11. Date and time functions

Function	Description
current_date	Returns the current date as a value of type date
current_time	Returns the current time as a value of type time
current_timestamp	Returns the current date and time as a value of type timestamp
date_part(*s*, *t*)	Returns a date or time element from timestamp *t* as specified by character string *s*
date_part(*s*, *i*)	Returns a date or time element from interval *i* as specified by character string *s*
date_trunc(*s*, *t*)	Returns timestamp *t* truncated to the degree specified by *s*
extract(*k* FROM *t*)	Returns a date or time element from timestamp *t* as specified by the keyword *k*
extract(*k* FROM *i*)	Returns a date or time element from interval *i* as specified by the keyword *k*
isfinite(*t*)	Returns true if the timestamp *t* is a finite value (neither *invalid*, nor *infinity*)
isfinite(*i*)	Returns true if the interval *i* is a finite value (not *infinity*)

Table 5-11. Date and time functions (continued)

Function	Description
now()	Returns the date and time as a timestamp value. This is equivalent to the *now* timestamp constant.
timeofday()	Returns the current date and time as a text value

The following sections elaborate on each of PostgreSQL's date and time functions described in Table 5-11. Note that the syntax for the current_date, current_time and current_timestamp functions omits the parentheses. This is done to remain compliant with the SQL92 standard requirements.

current_date

```
current_date
```

The current_date function accepts no arguments, and returns the current date as a value of type date. This is identical to casting the special *now* constant to a value of type date.

Example

```
booktown=# SELECT current_date,
booktown=#        'now'::date AS date;
    date    |    date
------------+------------
 2001-08-31 | 2001-08-31
(1 row)
```

current_time

```
current_time
```

The current_time function accepts no arguments, and returns the current time as a value of type time. This is identical to casting the special *now* constant to a value of type time.

Example

```
booktown=# SELECT current_time,
booktown=#        'now'::time AS time;
   time   |   time
----------+----------
 11:36:52 | 11:36:52
(1 row)
```

current_timestamp

```
current_timestamp
```

The `current_timestamp` function accepts no arguments, and returns the current date and time as a value of type `timestamp`. This is identical to casting the special *now* constant to a value of type `timestamp`, or to calling the `now()` function.

Example

```
booktown=# SELECT current_timestamp,
booktown-#        now() AS timestamp;
       timestamp          |        timestamp
--------------------------+--------------------------
 2001-08-31 11:39:42-07   | 2001-08-31 11:39:42-07
(1 row)
```

date_part()

```
date_part(s, t)
date_part(s, i)
```

The `date_part()` function accepts two arguments, *s* of type `text`, and either *t* of type `timestamp`, or *i* of type `interval`. The function removes the part of the time length specified by *s*, and returns it as a value of type `double precision`.

To understand the function of `date_part()`, it can be helpful to think of a `timestamp` or `interval` value as being broken up into several *fields*. These fields each describe a discrete component of the temporal value, such as the number of days, hours, or minutes described. The valid values for time field units described by *s* are detailed in Table 5-12. Notice that some values are only appropriate for use with a `timestamp` value, and not with an `interval`.

Table 5-12. Timestamp and interval units

Unit	Description
century	Describes the year field, divided by 100 (will not describe the literal century)
day	Describes the day field, from 1 to 31, for a `timestamp`, or the total number of days for an `interval`
decade	Describes the year field, divided by 10
dow	Describes the day of the week field, from 0 to 6 (beginning on Sunday), for a `timestamp`, not applicable to an `interval`
doy	Describes the day of the year field, from 1 to 365 or 366 for a `timestamp` value, not application to an `interval`
epoch	Describes the number of seconds since the *epoch* (Jan 1, 1970) for a `timestamp`, or total number of seconds for an `interval`

Table 5-12. *Timestamp and interval units (continued)*

Unit	Description
hour	Describes the hour represented by a `timestamp`
microseconds	Describes the millionths of seconds following the decimal in the seconds field of a `timestamp` value
millennium	Describes the year field, divided by 1000 (will not describe the literal millennium)
milliseconds	Describes the thousandths of seconds following the decimal in the seconds field of a `timestamp` value
minute	Describes the minutes field of a `timestamp` or `interval` value
month	Describes the month of the year for a `timestamp` value, or the number of months modulo 12 for `interval` values
quarter	Describes the quarter of the year, from 1 to 4, for `timestamp` values
second	Describes the seconds field of a `timestamp` or `interval` value
week	Describes the week of the year of a `timestamp` value. ISO-8601 defines the first week of the year to be the week containing January 4.
year	Describes the year field of a `timestamp` or `interval` value

Examples

```
booktown=# SELECT date_part('minute',
booktown(#                  interval('3 days 4 hours 12 minutes'));
 date_part
-----------
        12
(1 row)

booktown=# SELECT isbn,
booktown-#        date_part('year', publication)
booktown-#        FROM editions
booktown-#        ORDER BY date_part ASC
booktown-#        LIMIT 3;
    isbn    | date_part
------------+-----------
 0760720002 |      1868
 0679803335 |      1922
 0694003611 |      1947
(3 rows)
```

The standard SQL function for achieving the same function as the `date_part()` function is the `extract()` function.

date_trunc()

```
date_trunc(s, t)
```

The date_trunc() function accepts two arguments *s* and *t*, of types text and timestamp, respectively. The character string *s* defines the degree to which the timestamp value *t* should be truncated. In this context, truncation means eliminating an amount of detail in the value represented.

See Table 5-12 for valid values for time unit *s*.

Example

```
booktown=# SELECT date_trunc('minute', now());
      date_trunc
------------------------
 2001-08-31 09:59:00-07
(1 row)

booktown=# SELECT date_trunc('hour', now());
      date_trunc
------------------------
 2001-08-31 09:00:00-07
(1 row)

booktown=# SELECT date_trunc('year', now());
      date_trunc
------------------------
 2001-01-01 00:00:00-08
(1 row)
```

extract()

```
extract(k FROM t)
extract(k FROM i)
```

The extract() function is the SQL92 equivalent to PostgreSQL's date_part() function, with a slightly modified syntax. The SQL syntax for this function uses the FROM keyword, rather than a comma. The arguments are similar to those for the date_part() function, though it differs in that its first argument is a SQL *keyword*, rather than a character string, and should therefore not be quoted. Valid values for *k* are the same as those listed in Table 5-12.

Note that the extract() function exists as a SQL92 syntax "alias" for the PostgreSQL date_part() function; for this reason, the output column name from PostgreSQL is, by default, date_part.

Examples

```
booktown=# SELECT extract(MINUTE FROM interval('3 days 12 minutes'));
 date_part
-----------
```

```
            12
 (1 row)

 booktown=# SELECT extract(MONTH FROM now());
  date_part
 -----------
            8
 (1 row)
```

isfinite()

```
 isfinite(t)
 isfinite(i)
```

The isfinite() function accepts one argument, of type timestamp or type interval. It returns true if the value passed to it is not found to be an infinite value, which would be one set with either the special constant *infinity* or *invalid* (a special timestamp constant only).

Example

```
 booktown=# SELECT isfinite('now'::timestamp) AS now_is_finite,
 booktown-#          isfinite('infinity'::timestamp) AS infinity,
 booktown-#          isfinite('invalid'::timestamp) AS invalid;
  now_is_finite | infinity | invalid
 ---------------+----------+---------
  t             | f        | f
 (1 row)
```

now()

```
 now()
```

The now() function accepts no arguments, and returns the time and date of when now() is executed by PostgreSQL, in the form of a timestamp value.

Example

```
 booktown=# SELECT now();
          now
 ------------------------
  2001-08-31 10:31:18-07
 (1 row)
```

timeofday()

```
 timeofday()
```

The timeofday() function accepts no arguments. It returns the time and date of when the function is executed by PostgreSQL. The timeofday() function is similar in use to the now() function. However, the timeofday() function returns a value of the type text. This means that it is less flexible to work with, as you cannot use the date_part() or to_char() functions to break down elements of the value without casting it first to another type. It can be useful for applications that require a Unix style timestamp, as well as providing extended precision for the seconds value.

Example

```
booktown=# SELECT timeofday();
              timeofday
-------------------------------------
 Fri Aug 31 10:33:00.837338 2001 PDT
(1 row)
```

Type Conversion Functions

While PostgreSQL is able to explicitly cast between most commonly used data types, some conversions require a function in order to meaningfully translate values. Some of PostgreSQL's commonly used type conversion functions are listed in Table 5-13. These are detailed in the following sections.

Table 5-13. Type conversion functions

Function	Description
bitfromint4(n)	Converts numeric value n to a binary bit string
bittoint4(b)	Converts bit string b to its numeric decimal representation
to_char(n, f)	Converts numeric value n to a character string with format f
to_char(t, f)	Converts timestamp t to a character string with format f
to_date(s, f)	Converts character string s with date format f to a date value
to_number(s, f)	Converts character string s with format f to a numeric value
to_timestamp(s, f)	Converts character string s with format f to a timestamp value
timestamp(d)	Returns the date d as a value of type timestamp
timestamp(d, t)	Returns a timestamp value derived from date d and time t

bitfromint4()

```
bitfromint4(n)
```

The bitfromint4() function accepts a single argument n of type integer and returns its binary bit string equivalent. As explicit casts between binary and integer types do not exist, this function is required to transform decimal values to their binary counterparts.

The returned value is of type bit, and may not exceed 32 bits. Therefore, since the integer argument is signed, valid input values are between −2147483648 and 2147483647.

Example

```
booktown=# SELECT bitfromint4(16385);
          bitfromint4
-----------------------------------
 0000000000000000100000000000001
(1 row)
```

bittoint4()

```
bittoint4(b)
```

The `bittoint4()` function is essentially the inverse of the `bitfromint4()` function; it accepts a single argument *b* of type `bit` and returns its decimal numeric value as type `integer`.

The bounds of input and output are the reverse of the `bitfromint4` function, in that it accepts up to 32 binary digits, and will thus not return more than 2147483647 or less than −2147483648 as its result value.

Example

```
booktown=# SELECT bittoint4(B'101010'),
booktown-#           bittoint4(bitfromint4(99)) AS inverse_example;
 bittoint4 | inverse_example
-----------+-----------------
        42 |              99
(1 row)
```

to_char() with numbers

```
to_char(n, f)
```

The `to_char()` function, when used with argument *n* of type `numeric` and argument *f*, of type `text`, formats the numeric value of n to a character string returned as type `text`. The character string *f* describes the character string format within which to place the value of *n*.

The *f* format string consists of a series of *meta-characters*, which PostgreSQL translates into the literal values they represent. Valid meta-characters that may be used within this format string for a numeric conversion are outlined in Table 5-14.

Table 5-14. Numeric conversion formatting characters

Character	Description
9	The next sequential digit in the value *n*
0	The next sequential digit in *n*, or a leading or trailing zero if more digits are specified by *f* than are in *n*; may thus be used to force significant digits to the left or right of a value

Table 5-14. Numeric conversion formatting characters (continued)

Character	Description
.	A decimal point (there can be only one)
,	A comma (there can be several, for separating thousands, millions, etc.)
D	A decimal point (e.g., a period) derived from locale
G	A group separator (e.g., a comma) derived from locale
PR	If n is a negative value, placing *PR* at the end of f surrounds the returned string in angle brackets
SG	A plus or minus sign, depending on the value of n
MI	A minus sign, if the n is negative
PL	A plus sign, if n is positive
S	A plus or minus sign, derived from locale
L	A currency symbol, derived from locale
RN	The Roman Numeral characters for numeric values of n between 1 and 3999
TH, th	The appropriate ordinal suffix for n (e.g., *4th*, *2nd*)
V	Adds a zero to the right for each *9* following *V*, effectively shifting up by exponents of ten
FM	Sets format to "fill mode," causing leading and trailing zeroes (created by the *9* character, but not *0*), and extra whitespace, to be omitted

When more digits are specified with the *9* character in the format string than are within the numeric value n, the extra digits will be padded with whitespace. When more digits are specified with the *0* character, the extra digits will be padded with zeroes.

If *fewer* digits are specified then are necessary to represent the digits to the left of the decimal, the meaning of the conversion becomes ambiguous, as significant digits must be omitted. Since it is unclear which digits should be omitted, the to_char() function will enter the # character in place of each specified digit. It is therefore important to specify the maximum number of digits that you expect to receive back from the translation. You should also use a function such as translate() or one of the trim functions to remove unwanted whitespace from the translation.

Literal versions of meta-characters may be used within the format string by surrounding them with double quotes. Doing this within the format string changes the quoted meta-characters so they are interpreted literally. Note that in order to use a literal double-quote within this scheme, *two backslashes* must prefix the double-quote, as it is essentially twice escaped.

Any character that is not a meta-character may be safely used in a format string (e.g., the *$* symbol). Such characters will appear in the formatted string unchanged.

Examples

```
booktown=# SELECT to_char(123456789, '999G999G999D99') AS formatted,
booktown-#        to_char(123456789, '999999999') AS just_digits,
booktown-#        to_char(123456789, '00999999999') AS with_zeroes;
   formatted    | just_digits | with_zeroes
----------------+-------------+--------------
 123,456,789.00 |  123456789  | 00123456789
(1 row)
```

```
booktown=# SELECT cost * 100 AS cost_to_order,
booktown-#        to_char(cost * 100, '$99,999.99') AS monetary,
booktown-#        translate(to_char(cost * 100, '$9,999.99'),' ','')
booktown-#          AS translated
booktown-#        FROM stock
booktown-#        LIMIT 3;
 cost_to_order |  monetary  | translated
---------------+------------+------------
       2900.00 | $ 2,900.00 | $2,900.00
       3000.00 | $ 3,000.00 | $3,000.00
       1600.00 | $ 1,600.00 | $1,600.00
(3 rows)
```

```
booktown=# SELECT to_char(1.0, '9th "Place"') AS first,
booktown-#        to_char(2.2, '9th "Place"') AS second,
booktown-#        to_char(pi(), '9th "Place"') AS third,
booktown-#        to_char(10, '99V99th "\\"Place\\""') AS shifted_up;
   first    |   second   |   third    |    shifted_up
------------+------------+------------+------------------
 1st Place  | 2nd Place  | 3rd Place  | 1000th "Place"
(1 row)
```

Note that as of PostgreSQL v7.1.x, there is a bug in the usage of the *RN* Roman Numeral conversion sequence which causes it to return invalid results unless used with the *FM* character sequence. This is scheduled for correction in 7.2, but can be worked around by using the complete *FMRN* sequence.

to_char() with timestamps

```
to_char(t, f)
```

When used with argument *t* of type `timestamp` and argument *f* of type `text` the `to_char` function formats the date and time represented by *t* to a character string returned as type `text`.

As with the numeric functionality of `to_char()`, the character string *f* describes the meta-characters which are translated by PostgreSQL into the literal values they represent. Valid meta-characters that may be used within this format string for date and time values are outlined in Table 5-15.

Table 5-15. Timestamp conversion formatting characters

Character	Description
HH, HH12	The hour of day, from 1 to 12
HH24	The hour of the day, from 0 to 23
MI	The minute, from 0 to 59
SS	The second, from 0 to 59
SSSS	The seconds past midnight, from 0 to 86,399
AM, PM, A.M., P.M.	The meridian indicator in uppercase, with optional periods
am, pm, a.m., p.m.	The meridian indicator in lowercase, with optional periods
TZ, tz	The time zone, in upper or lowercase
CC	The two-digit century (*not* the year divided by 100)
Y, YY, YYY, YYYY, Y,YYY	The year's last digit, last two digits, last three digits, or last four digits (with optional comma)
BC, AD, B.C., A.D.	Year qualifier, in uppercase
bc, ad, b.c., a.d.	Year qualifier, in lowercase
MONTH, Month, month	The full month name, padded on the right with blanks to 9 characters in length, in uppercase, init-capped, or lowercase
MON, Mon, mon	The abbreviated 3-letter month, in uppercase, init-capped, or lowercase
MM	The month number, from 1 to 12
RN, rn	The month in Roman Numerals, from I to XII, in upper or lowercase
DAY, Day, day	The full day name, padded on the right to 9 characters in length, in uppercase, init-capped, or lowercase
DY, Dy, dy	The abbreviated 3-letter day, in uppercase, init-capped, or lowercase
DDD, DD, D	The day of the year, from 1 to 366, day of the month, from 1 to 31, or day of the week, from 1 to 7 (beginning on Sunday)

Table 5-15. Timestamp conversion formatting characters (continued)

Character	Description
W	The week of the month, from 1 to 5 (from the 1st day of the month)
WW	The week of the year, from 1 to 53 (from the 1st day of the year)
IW	The ISO week of the year (from the 1st Thursday of the new year)
TH, th	The appropriate ordinal suffix for the preceding numeric value, upper or lowercase
fm	Causes extra padding to be omitted, including whitespace, and extra zeroes

The *TH* suffix and *FM* prefix must be directly adjacent to the value they are modifying. For example, to apply *FM* to the *Day* value, the complete sequence would be *FMDay* (not *FM Day*). Similarly, to attach the ordinal suffix to the *DD* day of the month, the complete sequence would be *DDTH* (not *DD TH*).

Examples

```
booktown=# SELECT to_char(now( ), 'HH:MI PM') AS the_time;
 the_time
----------
 05:04 PM
(1 row)

booktown=# SELECT to_char(now( ), 'Dy (Day), Mon (Month)')
booktown-#        AS abbreviations,
booktown-#        to_char('yesterday'::timestamp, 'FMMonth FMDDth')
booktown-#        AS yesterday,
booktown-#        to_char('yesterday'::timestamp, 'FMDDth FMMonth')
booktown-#        AS "yesterday UK";
          abbreviations          |  yesterday  | yesterday UK
---------------------------------+-------------+--------------
 Sat (Saturday ), Sep (September) | August 31st | 31st August
(1 row)

booktown=# SELECT isbn,     these must be
booktown-#        to_char(publication, 'FMMonth FMDDth, YYYY')
booktown-#        AS informal,
booktown-#        to_char(publication, 'YYYY-MM-DD') AS formal,
booktown-#        to_char(publication, 'Y,YYY "years" A.D.')
booktown-#        AS first_published
booktown-#    FROM editions LIMIT 3;
    isbn    |    informal     |   formal   | first_published
------------+-----------------+------------+------------------
 039480001X | March 1st, 1957 | 1957-03-01 | 1,957 years A.D.
 0451160916 | August 1st, 1981 | 1981-08-01 | 1,981 years A.D.
 0394800753 | March 1st, 1949 | 1949-03-01 | 1,949 years A.D.
(3 rows)
```

to_date()

```
to_date(s, f)
```

The to_date() function accepts two arguments *s* and *f*, each of type text. The argument *f* describes, using the date-specific meta-characters detailed in Table 5-15, the format of the date described by the string *s*. The result is returned as type date.

While PostgreSQL can figure out a wide variety of date formats, it cannot support every arbitrary date format. The to_date() function insures that, provided the format can be described using the meta-characters from Table 5-14, nearly any date format can be converted to a valid date value.

Example

```
booktown=# SELECT date('198025thJune')
booktown-#           AS non_standard_date_format,
booktown-#        to_date('198025thJune', 'YYYYDDthMonth')
booktown-#           AS correct_interpretation;
 non_standard_date_format | correct_interpretation
--------------------------+------------------------
 2025-08-27               | 1980-06-25
(1 row)
```

to_number()

```
to_number(s, f)
```

The to_number function accepts two arguments of the text type, *s* and *f*. The character string described by *s* should have its format described by *f*, using the same meta-characters shown in Table 5-14. The result is returned as type numeric.

Examples

```
booktown=# SELECT to_number('$2,900.00', 'L9G999D99')
booktown-#          AS monetary;
 monetary
----------
  2900.00
(1 row)

booktown=# SELECT to_number('123,456,789.00', '999G999G999D99')
booktown-#          AS formatted,
booktown-#        to_number('123456789', '999999999')
booktown-#          AS just_digits,
booktown-#        to_number('00123456789', '00999999999')
booktown-#          AS leading_zeroes;
  formatted   | just_digits | leading_zeroes
--------------+-------------+----------------
 123456789.00 |   123456789 |      123456789
(1 row)
```

to_timestamp()

```
to_timestamp(s, f)
```

The to_timestamp() function accepts two arguments *s* and *f*, each of type text. The argument *f* describes, using the meta-characters detailed in Table 5-15, the format of the date and time described by the string *s*. The result is returned as type date.

Like to_date(), this function exists primarily as a means to be able to correctly interpret the format of a non-standard date and time string.

Example

```
booktown=# SELECT timestamp('197825thJuly01:12am')
booktown-#          AS non_standard_timestamp,
booktown-#   to_timestamp('197825July01:12am',
booktown(#   'YYYYDDFMMonthHH12:MIam')
booktown-#          AS correct_interpretation;
 non_standard_timestamp | correct_interpretation
------------------------+------------------------
 2025-06-27 01:12:00-07 | 1978-07-25 01:12:00-07
(1 row)
```

 The use of the *FM* modifier can be crucial in making sure the evaluation of values following a month or day name are interpreted correctly, as these names are normally padded to nine characters in length. Note that the *FM* modifier must precede each element which you wish it to apply to, as it is not a "global" modifier.

timestamp()

```
timestamp(d)
timestamp(d, t)
```

The timestamp() function accepts either a single argument *d* of type date, or two arguments *d* and *t*, of types date and time, respectively. The arguments passed are converted to a value of type timestamp and returned. In the former case, the time is assumed to be midnight on the date specified.

Example

```
booktown=# SELECT timestamp(date('now')) AS today_at_midnight,
booktown-#        timestamp(date('now'),
booktown(#               time('now')) AS right_now;
   today_at_midnight    |       right_now
------------------------+------------------------
 2001-09-01 00:00:00-07 | 2001-09-01 18:04:16-07
(1 row)
```

Aggregate Functions

An *aggregate function* is a special kind of function that operates on *several rows* of a query at once, returning a single result. Such functions are generally only used in queries which make use of the GROUP BY clause to associate rows together by like criteria, though they may be used in queries which only contain aggregate functions in their target list. When performing the latter, the aggregate function operates on *all* selected rows from the result set.

Table 5-16 provides an overview of PostgreSQL's supported aggregate functions. To see a complete list of aggregate functions, you may use the \da command within *psql*.

Table 5-16. Aggregate functions

Function	Description
avg(*expression*)	Returns the average of the *expression* values from all rows in a group.
count(*expression*)	Returns the number of values, per each aggregated group of rows, for which *expression* is not NULL
max(*expression*)	Returns the maximum value of *expression* in the grouped rows
min(*expression*)	Returns the minimum value of *expression* in the grouped rows
stddev(*expression*)	Returns the standard deviation of the values of *expression* in the grouped rows
sum(*expression*)	Returns the sum of the values of *expression* in the grouped rows
variance(*expression*)	Returns the variance of the values of *expression* in the grouped rows

The following sections describe each aggregate function in further detail, including specific information on usage, examples, and valid input data types. In each of the functional explanations, the term *expression* refers to any valid identifier in a result set, or any valid expression operating on such an identifier.

Aggregate expressions

When calling an aggregate function, *aggregate expressions* are employed to describe an expression from the result set created by the SELECT statement. An aggregate expression is similar to an ordinary SQL expression, but may be preceded by either the ALL or the DISTINCT keyword.

The use of the DISTINCT keyword in an aggregate expression causes only grouped rows with unique values (as described by the expression) to be evaluated by the function. Any duplicate rows will be suppressed. Similar to the use of the ALL keyword in a SELECT statement, the use of ALL in an aggregate expression has no function other than to make more explicit the request for all grouped rows to be evaluated to the function. Example 5-19 demonstrates each of the aggregate expression forms.

Example 5-19: Using aggregate expressions

```
booktown=# SELECT count(location) AS set_locations,
booktown-#        count(ALL location) AS all_set_locations,
booktown-#        count(DISTINCT location) AS unique_locations,
booktown-#        count(*) AS all_rows
booktown-#        FROM subjects;
 set_locations | all_set_locations | unique_locations | all_rows
---------------+-------------------+------------------+----------
            15 |                15 |                7 |       16
(1 row)
```

There is one final form of aggregate expression, as demonstrated by the all_rows result column in Example 5-19. When the asterisk (*) symbol is supplied as the aggregate expression, it instructs the aggregate function to evaluate *all rows*, including rows with values of NULL, which are ordinarily ignored. Since the subjects table contains one row with a NULL value in the location column, the counted rows for location differ from those counted for *.

 Rows whose evaluated aggregate expression contain NULL values will not be evaluated by an aggregate function (with the exception of the count() function).

---

avg()

avg(*expression*)

The avg() function accepts an expression describing aggregated values that are either of any numeric type (numeric, bigint, smallint, real, or double precision), or of the interval time type.

The average, or mean, of the values described by *expression* in the grouped rows is returned. The resultant value is returned as a value of type numeric for expressions of type integer and double precision for expressions of type real. All other expression types cause a value of the same data type to be returned.

Examples

```
booktown=# SELECT avg(cost) AS average_cost,
booktown-#        avg(retail) AS average_price,
booktown-#        avg(retail - cost) AS average_profit
booktown-#        FROM stock;
```

```
average_cost  | average_price | average_profit
--------------+---------------+---------------
24.8235294118 | 30.0088235294 |   5.1852941176
(1 row)


booktown=# SELECT avg(cost) AS average_cost, p.name AS publisher
booktown-#        FROM (stock JOIN editions USING (isbn))
booktown-#        JOIN publishers AS p (publisher_id)
booktown-#              USING (publisher_id)
booktown-#        GROUP BY p.name;
 average_cost  |          publisher
--------------+----------------------------
26.5000000000 | Ace Books
19.0000000000 | Books of Wonder
26.5000000000 | Doubleday
25.0000000000 | HarperCollins
18.0000000000 | Henry Holt & Company, Inc.
23.0000000000 | Kids Can Press
23.0000000000 | Mojo Press
20.0000000000 | Penguin
23.0000000000 | Random House
26.5000000000 | Roc
26.0000000000 | Watson-Guptill Publications
(11 rows)
```

count()

```
count(expression)
```

The count() function returns the number of values in a set of aggregated rows where the *expression* is not NULL. The count() is not restricted as to the data type described by *expression*. It is important to understand that the count() function only counts values which are not NULL. As a result, it is important to use an *expression* whose value will not be returned NULL in order for the *expression* to be meaningful to the counted results.

You may pass the asterisk (*) character to count() in order to simply count all rows in an aggregation (including rows with NULL values).

Examples

```
booktown=# SELECT count(*) FROM editions;
 count
-------
    17
(1 row)


booktown=# SELECT count(isbn), p.name
booktown-#        FROM editions JOIN publishers AS p (publisher_id)
booktown-#                    USING (publisher_id)
booktown-#        GROUP BY p.name
booktown-#        ORDER BY count DESC;
 count |          name
```

```
-------+----------------------------
     3 | Random House
     2 | Ace Books
     2 | Doubleday
     2 | Roc
     1 | Books of Wonder
     1 | HarperCollins
     1 | Henry Holt & Company, Inc.
     1 | Kids Can Press
     1 | Mojo Press
     1 | O'Reilly & Associates
     1 | Penguin
     1 | Watson-Guptill Publications
(12 rows)
```

max()

```
max(expression)
```

The max() function returns the maximum found value described by *expression* in a set of aggregated rows. It accepts an *expression* that may represent any numeric, string, date, or time data type. The maximum is returned as a value of the same data type as the *expression*.

Examples

```
booktown=# SELECT max(cost), max(retail) FROM stock;
  max  |  max
-------+-------
 36.00 | 46.95
(1 row)
```

```
booktown=# SELECT max(retail), p.name
booktown-#        FROM (stock NATURAL JOIN editions)
booktown-#        JOIN publishers AS p (publisher_id)
booktown-#                     USING (publisher_id)
booktown-#        GROUP BY p.name
booktown-#        ORDER BY max DESC;
  max  |            name
-------+----------------------------
 46.95 | Roc
 45.95 | Ace Books
 36.95 | Doubleday
 32.95 | Random House
 28.95 | HarperCollins
 28.95 | Watson-Guptill Publications
 24.95 | Mojo Press
 24.95 | Penguin
 23.95 | Henry Holt & Company, Inc.
 23.95 | Kids Can Press
 21.95 | Books of Wonder
(11 rows)
```

min()

```
min(expression)
```

The min() function returns the minimum found value described by *expression* in a set of aggregated rows. It accepts an *expression* which may represent any numeric, string, date, or time data type. The minimum is returned as a value of the same data type as the *expression*.

Examples

```
booktown=# SELECT min(cost), min(retail) FROM stock;
  min  |  min
-------+-------
 16.00 | 16.95
(1 row)
```

```
booktown=# SELECT min(retail), p.name
booktown-#        FROM (stock NATURAL JOIN editions)
booktown-#        JOIN publishers AS p (publisher_id)
booktown-#                      USING (publisher_id)
booktown-#        GROUP BY p.name
booktown-#        ORDER BY min ASC;
  min  |           name
-------+------------------------------
 16.95 | Random House
 21.95 | Ace Books
 21.95 | Books of Wonder
 22.95 | Roc
 23.95 | Henry Holt & Company, Inc.
 23.95 | Kids Can Press
 24.95 | Mojo Press
 24.95 | Penguin
 28.95 | Doubleday
 28.95 | HarperCollins
 28.95 | Watson-Guptill Publications
(11 rows)
```

stddev()

```
stddev(expression)
```

The stddev() function accepts an expression describing values of any numeric type (numeric, bigint, smallint, real, or double precision), and returns the standard deviation of the values within the aggregated rows. The resultant value is returned as double precision for an expression describing floating point values, and numeric for all other types.

Examples

```
booktown=# SELECT stddev(retail) FROM stock;
 stddev
--------
```

```
   8.46
(1 row)

booktown=# SELECT stddev(retail), p.name
booktown-#        FROM (stock NATURAL JOIN editions)
booktown-#        JOIN publishers AS p ON (publisher_id = p.id)
booktown-#        GROUP BY p.name
booktown-#        ORDER BY stddev DESC
booktown-#        LIMIT 4;
 stddev  |     name
---------+--------------
  16.97  | Ace Books
  16.97  | Roc
   8.02  | Random House
   5.66  | Doubleday
(4 rows)
```

sum()

```
sum(expression)
```

The sum() function accepts an expression describing values of any numeric type (numeric, bigint, smallint, real, or double precision), and returns the sum of the values within the aggregated rows. The returned value is of the type numeric when operating on values of type integer and double precision when operating on values of type real. The result is returned as the same data type as the values described by *expression* for all other data types.

Examples

```
booktown=# SELECT sum(stock) FROM stock;
 sum
-----
 508
(1 row)

booktown=# SELECT sum(stock), s.subject
booktown-#        FROM ((stock NATURAL JOIN editions)
booktown(#        JOIN books ON (books.id = book_id))
booktown-#        JOIN subjects AS s
booktown-#                   ON (books.subject_id = s.id)
booktown-#        GROUP BY s.subject
booktown-#        ORDER BY sum DESC;
 sum |      subject
-----+-------------------
 189 | Horror
 166 | Science Fiction
  91 | Children's Books
  28 | Drama
  18 | Classics
  16 | Arts
(6 rows)
```

variance()

```
variance(expression)
```

The variance() function accepts an expression describing values of any numeric type (numeric, bigint, smallint, real, or double precision) and returns the variance of the values within the aggregated rows. The variance is equivalent to the stddev() squared. The resultant value is returned as double precision for an expression describing floating-point values, and numeric for all other types.

Examples

```
booktown=# SELECT variance(retail) FROM stock;
 variance
----------
    71.60
(1 row)

booktown=# SELECT variance(retail), p.name
booktown-#        FROM (stock NATURAL JOIN editions)
booktown-#        JOIN publishers AS p
booktown-#                    ON (editions.publisher_id = p.id)
booktown-#        GROUP BY p.name
booktown-#        ORDER BY variance DESC
booktown-#        LIMIT 4;
 variance |              ..ame
----------+-----------------------------
   288.00 | Ace Books
   288.00 | Roc
    64.33 | Random House
    32.00 | Doubleday
(4 rows)
```

6

PostgreSQL Clients

This chapter elaborates on the available clients for PostgreSQL. Clients exist in order to provide a user interface to the PostgreSQL server (also called the backend).

The two most accessible clients for PostgreSQL are the command-line driven *psql* and a graphical alternative, *PgAccess*. The *psql* client is installed by default, while *PgAccess* requires specification of the *--with-tcl* option during compilation of the PostgreSQL source code (as mentioned in Chapter 2, *Installing PostgreSQL*).

The psql Client: Advanced Topics

Basic information about the *psql* client is included in Chapter 4, *Using SQL with PostgreSQL*; this section documents more advanced information about the *psql* client. The topics covered include a complete list of command line options, and an explanation of each *psql* slash command. This section also contains information on how to load SQL input from external files, use the *psql* history, and substitute variables dynamically into SQL statements within *psql*.

Command Line Options

Here is the complete syntax to start *psql*:

```
psql [ options ] [ dbname [ username ] ]
```

The optional *dbname* value specifies the database to initially connect to. The optional *username* specifies the PostgreSQL user to connect as. If either value is unspecified, *psql* will default to a database and username with the same name as the operating system user starting the program.

Additionally, several run-time *options* can be set by command-line flags. By default, *psql* understands both standard Unix short options (e.g., *-c*), and GNU-style long options (e.g., *--command*). The latter are not available on all systems. In the following list, the Unix short options (which are always one letter) are shown first, followed by the equivalent long option.

-a, --echo-all

Turns on the 'echo all' option, which displays all lines as they are read by *psql*. This option can be useful for scripting, and is equivalent to issuing the command: \set ECHO all from within *psql*.

-A, --no-align

Starts *psql* in unaligned output formatting mode. If this is not specified, the output formatting mode will be set to aligned.

-c statement, --command statement

Instead of running *psql* interactively, this option executes the statement that you specify. This must be a syntactically correct SQL statement, and must be devoid of any *psql*-specific commands.

-d database, --dbname database

Explicitly specifies the database you wish *psql* to initially connect to.

-e, --echo-queries

Specifies that all queries are echoed to the screen.

-E, --echo-hidden

Displays the hidden queries generated by slash commands. You can also issue the following command from within *psql* to accomplish the same effect: \set ECHO_HIDDEN.

-f filename, --file filename

Specifies that rather than start in interactive mode, *psql* should read and execute SQL from the specified filename, and process its contents as it would if input directly. After processing the file, *psql* exits.

-F separator, --field-separator separator

Specifies that *psql* should use the specified separator character as the field (column) delimiter.

-h hostname, --host hostname

Specifies the hostname of the backend machine. This is usually not necessary when connecting to a local backend process, which uses Unix domain sockets. However, if the *postmaster* initializes its domain socket file somewhere other than the default path of */tmp*, specifying a hostname with a leading forward slash will cause *psql* to interpret the hostname value as a local directory to check for the domain socket file (e.g., -h /var/pgsql will cause *psql* to look for a domain socket file within */var/pgsql*).

-H, --html

Starts *psql* in HTML output mode.

-l, --list

Displays a list of available databases to connect to.

-o `filename`, *--output* `filename`

Redirects *psql* output to `filename`.

-p `port`, *--port* `port`

Specifies TCP/IP `port` (or numbered Unix domain socket) that *postmaster* is currently listening on. This value will be is whatever PGPORT is set to (or the default of 5432).

-P `name=value`, *--pset* `name=value`

Specifies the output formatting options using the same syntax as used with the \pset command. All option names are the same as for \pset, but with this command-line option you must use an equal sign (=) instead of a space between each formatting option name and its value.

-q, --quiet

Instructs *psql* to work in quiet mode. No *psql*-specific informative messages or informational text is displayed.

-R `separator`, *--record-separator* `separator`

Specifies `separator` as the record (row) delimiter.

-s, --single-step

Specifies that *psql* will run in "single-step" mode. While in single-step mode, you will be prompted to either continue or cancel upon executing a SQL statement.

-S, --single-line

Specifies that *psql* will run in "single-line" mode. When running in this mode, a new line acts as a semi-colon to execute a SQL statement.

-t, --tuples-only

Turns off the display of extraneous table information, such as column names and footers. To accomplish this from within *psql*, use the \t command.

-T `table_attribute`, *--table-attr* `table_attribute`

Sets an HTML attribute that you wish to be placed within the <table> output while in HTML formatting mode (e.g., width=100%). If you pass more than one `table_attribute` to this flag, they must all be contained within double quotes. You can use \pset from within *psql* to insert these attributes as well.

-U username, --username username

> Connects with the specified *username*.

-v name=value, --variable name=value

> Assigns a *value* to a variable *name*, as you would do using the \set command from within *psql*. When separating a value from a name, use an equal sign instead of a space.

-V, --version

> Displays version information.

-W, --password

> Prompts for a password before connecting to a database. This setting remains for the duration of the *psql* session.

-x, --expanded

> Activate extended row format mode. Accomplish this from within *psql* by using the \x slash command.

-X, --no-psqlrc

> Do not read or execute the startup file (~/.psqlrc).

-?, --help

> Displays brief *psql* command line argument help.

 Unstable code was introduced into version 7.0 that causes *psql* to obtain a password from the user when authentication is requested by the backend process; however, this code is not reliable and will sometimes fail, which will subsequently cause the connection attempt to fail. It is advisable to use the *-W* (*--password*) option to force a prompt if you know that such authentication will be necessary.

Slash Commands

Recall that within *psql* you have several special commands, called slash commands. These commands are *psql*-specific, and are not sent to the PostgreSQL backend. Explanations of the available *psql* slash commands follow.

Formatting commands

There are several slash commands available to format output. These include \pset, \a, \C, \f, \H, \t, \T, and \x. Except for \pset, each command controls a different formatting option. The \pset command, which is newer than the others, controls most of those same settings. The other commands exist for compatibility with older versions, and for convenience.

Most of these duplicate the effects of \pset. Each command is detailed within the description of that command and its options. For compatibility with older versions, and convenience, some of these formatting options may still have a slash command devoted entirely to them; these commands have been listed as well.

\pset *parameter* [*value*]

The general parameter setting command; this is the most important (and powerful) formatting command of the list. It encapsulates a variety of display options, and it could easily be the only formatting slash command you ever use. You may pass it various parameters to accomplish different formatting functions.

Within its syntax, *parameter* is one of the following valid parameters:

format

This parameter lets you set the output format to *aligned, unaligned, html,* or *latex.* Aligned is the default setting, for readability. Unaligned will set output to be printed all on one line, separated by the current character delimiter. The HTML and LaTeX modes output tables meant for inclusion in HTML and LaTeX documents, respectively.

border

Depending on the formatting mode, this option will make various changes to the borders used within displayed tables. For example, when outputting in HTML mode, this directly affects the border attribute of the <table> tag. This parameter takes a numeric value. Generally, the higher this number is, the larger (or more pronounced) the borders will be.

expanded

Setting this option will toggle between regular and extended format. If you have problems with data being displayed off the screen, or wrapping around in an illegible fashion, try using this option. It will tell *psql* to format all output into two columns, with the column name on the left, and data on the right.

null

This parameter allows you to set the string that is displayed to you when a null field is displayed. The string you wish to have displayed to represent a null should follow the word null. Ordinarily, that string is set to nothing. To set it back to nothing, you may set it with two apostrophes in a row (''). To set it to some other value, enclose that value in single-quotes. For example: \pset null ' ***null*** '.

`fieldsep`

This parameter accepts the delimiter to separate column values when working in the unaligned formatting mode. It is set to the pipe symbol (|) by default. You may want to use this to set the delimiter to a more commonly used delimiter, such as the tab (\t) character or comma (,). This has no effect outside of unaligned mode.

`recordsep`

This parameter specifies the record delimiter (to separate rows) when working in unaligned formatting mode. By default this is the newline character (\n).

`tuples_only`

This parameter lets you specify whether you want to see table data only (row results), or if you want to see additional characteristics about the table, such as headers and comments.

`title`

This parameter is used to attach a title to any subsequently printed titles. It will be displayed just above normal output. Use a pair of sequential apostrophes (' ') to set to an empty string.

`tableattr`

This parameter is for use with the HTML format mode; use it to define any table attributes you wish to be included upon formatting table output within the <table> tag (e.g., `width`, `cellpadding`, `cellspacing`). If you wish to define more than a single attribute, be sure to enclose them within double-quotes in a single *value*.

`pager`

This parameter toggles off and on the use of a pager for outputting table data. You may set the PAGER environment variable in your shell before starting *psql* if you wish to use a paging program other than *more* (such as *less*).

`\a`

The align command; this toggles *psql* between aligned and unaligned mode. This is equivalent to successive uses of \pset `format aligned` and \pset `format unaligned`.

`\C`

The query title command; this allows you to set a title that will be displayed at the top of any displayed result set, and is equivalent to \pset `title`.

\f

> The field delimiter command; this sets the field delimiter when using the unaligned formatting mode, and is equivalent to \pset fieldsep.

\H

> The HTML output command; this toggles between HTML output formatting and the default aligned formatting, and is equivalent to successive uses of \pset format HTML and \pset format aligned.

\t

> The table information command; this toggles the display of optional table information, and is equivalent to \pset tuples_only.

\T

> The table attribute command; this defines extra table attributes you wish to be inserted into the table tags of table data displaying while in HTML formatting mode. It is equivalent to \pset tableattr.

\x

> The toggle expanded command; this toggles expanded row formatting on and off. It is equivalent to \pset expanded.

Information display commands

The *psql* client has many commands to help you with gathering information about the database and various objects within it. Most of these commands are prefixed with \d, as this is an easy mnemonic device for *display*. Knowing how to use these commands can increase your productivity (or at least your awareness!) within the database.

\d [*relation_name*]

> The general display command; it is used to view various pieces of information about a specified relation. The relation you specify may be an index, sequence, table, or view. When issued, the command will display all of the relation's columns, types, and special attributes or defaults. When executed without a specified relation, it displays each of the relations available within the currently connected database.

\da [*aggregate_name*]

> The aggregate display command; with it, you may retrieve the list of the connected database's aggregate functions, and their accepted data types. If you specify a parameter following the slash command, it will display only the list of aggregate functions whose names begin with the *aggregate_name* pattern in a case-insensitive comparison.

\dd [*name*]

The general database object display command; it is used to display the descriptions of database objects. The object you specify may be any defined aggregate, function, operator, relation, rule, or trigger. If you do not specify a *name*, or a partial name, all objects in the database will be displayed.

\df [*function_name*]

The function display command; it is used to display information about a function defined within the database, including its arguments, and return types. You can either specify a function to display, or specify none, and list information about all functions. Like \da and \dd, a full or partial *function_name* may be supplied for a case-insensitive comparison against all functions from the beginning of each function name.

\d[istvS] [*name*]

A scoped version of the general display command; you may specify any of the options within the brackets:

i

Displays indices.

s

Displays sequences.

t

Displays tables.

v

Displays views.

S

Displays system tables.

\dl

The large object display command; this command is equivalent to the \lo_list command, which displays the list of large objects within the current database.

\do [*operator_name*]

The operator display command; this displays the list of defined operators within the current database, along with their operands (arguments), and return types. You may specify a complete or partial *operator_name* to examine, or retrieve information about all available operators.

\dp [*object_name*]

The permissions display command; this retrieves the list of all database objects (or objects at least partially matching an *object_name*, if provided) currently defined within the database, along with all their associated access permissions (public, user, and group).

`\dT` [*type_name*]

> The data type display command; this displays the list of all available data types. You may again specify a *type_name*, or partial data type name, or view all available data types in the current database.

`\l`

> The database display command; this lists all defined databases on the server, and their ownership information, and multibyte encoding type. Entering `\l+` will display any comments the databases may have (see the section titled "Documenting a Database" in Chapter 9, *Database Management* for how to comment on a database).

`\lo_list`

> The large object display command; this displays the list of all existing large objects within the current database, along with any comments that have been attached to them.

`\z` [*object_name*]

> The permissions display command, equivalent to `\dp`.

PostgreSQL and psql informative commands

Within *psql* there is a small set of informative commands that display information about PostgreSQL and *psql* itself. These are useful primarily for obtaining help with command-related questions you may have.

`\?`

> The help command; this prints out the list of slash commands documented in this chapter.

`\copyright`

> The copyright command; this displays copyright information about PostgreSQL.

`\encoding`

> The encoding command; if multibyte encoding is enabled, this can set the client encoding. If you do not supply an argument, the current encoding will be displayed on the screen.

`\help`

> The general help command; used without an argument, it will print a list of all commands for which greater help is available. Used with an argument, it will print more information (if there is data available) for the subject. Used with an asterisk (*) as the argument, it will retrieve syntax information for all documented SQL commands.

Input and output commands

The *psql* client's various input and output slash commands allow you to transfer data to and from the database in different ways. You may also specify exactly how *psql* transfers data. The commands include:

\copy *table* { FROM | TO } *file* | stdin | stdout

> The copy command; this can be used to copy from the client application (and thus, use the permissions of the user who started the client) instead of using the SQL COPY command to copy from the server. This slash command can also accept any of the standard COPY clauses. For more information on the syntax of this command, refer to the COPY entry in the command reference section at the back of this book.
>
> The differences between using \copy over COPY are important to understand and include:
>
> - Data you \copy transfers first through the client (via your connection), which may be quite a bit slower than if it were done directly through the server (i.e., the backend) process.
>
> - You have access to files on the local filesystem under whatever permissions the user account you are using has, which means you may have more (or less) accessibility to needed files than the backend process.
>
> - The terms stdin and stdout (standard input and output) have a different meaning; they refer to *psql*'s input and output stream. On the backend process they are used differently: stdin represents where the COPY was issued from, and stdout represents the query output stream.

\echo *string*

> The echo command; this sends a *string* to the standard output. This can be useful for scripting, because you can add non-database–supplied information into script output (such as comments).

\g [*file*]

> The buffer execution command; this is essentially the same as using the semicolon (;) in that it sends the current query buffer to the backend to be processed. Optionally, you can save the result set to a *file* of your choice, or have *psql* pipe it to a separate shell command by following the \g with either a filename or piped command name.

\i *file*

> The file input command; this reads input from a *file* (the name of which you supply as an argument after the \i) and causes *psql* to parse its content as if it were typed directly into the program's prompt.

\lo_export *lo_oid filename*

The large object export command; this lets you export the large object with OID *lo_oid* to *filename* on your local filesystem. This is different from the lo_export() server function in the same way the \copy and the SQL COPY commands are different.

\lo_import *filename* [*comment*]

The large object import command; this imports large objects into the database from files on your local filesystem. Optionally, you can attach a comment to the object; this is recommended, as otherwise it will be identifiable only by an OID, which you will need to remember if you wish to access it again. If you attach a comment to the object, issuing the \lo_list command displays your comment with the OID of the object, thus making it easier to find once imported.

\o [*file* | |*command*]

The output command; this redirects future output (i.e., data retrieved after this command is issued) to either a *file* of your choice or a pipe to a system *command*. If not given any arguments, the output channel will reset to standard output; use no arguments when you wish to stop sending output elsewhere. One of the most useful features of this command is the ability to pipe output to commands such as *grep*, which can then search for a pattern of your choosing, allowing you to search against database and slash command output (which will, of course, only work if *grep* is installed on your system).

\p

The buffer display command; this prints the *psql* input currently buffered. If no SQL input has been entered since the last executed statement, the last executed statement is displayed.

\qecho *string*

The query-output echo command; this sends a *string* to your chosen query output channel (which is set with the \o command), instead of stdout. This command can be useful when you need to send non-database–related information into the *psql* output.

\w *file* | |*command*

The buffer output command; this outputs the current query buffer to a specified *file*, or piped system *command*.

System commands

The following commands pertain to the general, systematic functions of *psql*. These include database re-connection, external editor invocation, setting and unsetting *psql* variables, and quitting *psql*.

\connect [*database* [*username*]]

> The database re-connection command; this connects you to another database from within *psql*. You may specify the *database* to connect to and the *username* to use (if it is not the same as the current username) and omitting this parameter will cause the current username to be used.

\edit [*file*]

> The external editor command; with this, you can either edit a *file* of your choice or (if no file is specified) the current query buffer. After you are done editing, the new buffer is input to the query buffer, and executed if terminated with a semi-colon.

> When opening a file for editing with this command, *psql* searches your environment variables for the following fields (in this order) to find out what editor to use: PSQL_EDITOR, EDITOR, and VISUAL. If none of these are present, it will attempt to launch */bin/vi*.

\q

> The quit command; this exits the program. You may also use CTRL-D in most terminal applications to quit.

\set [*name* [*value*]]

> The variable setting command; used without arguments, this displays all set variables within *psql*. Otherwise, it sets the variable *name* to *value*. If no *value* is passed, *name* is set with an empty value. If multiple values are passed, *name* is assigned the concatenation of each *value*.

\unset *variable*

> The variable unsetting command; this unsets a specified *variable* from memory. This is different from assigning a variable with an empty value, which is still technically set.

\! [*command*]

> The shell execution command; without arguments, this opens a shell which overrides the *psql* prompt until it is exited. Otherwise, it executes a specified shell *command* from within *psql*, and displays its results to stdout.

Using External Files to Enter Queries

As it is possible to use *psql* to enter queries directly from the prompt, it is possible to create queries and statements within files and let *psql* read the files and insert their content into the current buffer. This can be useful to some users.

First, enter your query into a file on your filesystem; after it is complete, open *psql*. The command to insert files into the current query buffer is \i. Example 6-1 shows how to insert a simple file-based SELECT command into the current buffer. Text from the query is displayed on-screen in the example, but this may not happen on your system by default. To see the lines of a file as it is being read, set the ECHO variable to all by typing \set ECHO all.

Example 6-1: Inserting a file into the current buffer

```
testdb=# \set ECHO all
testdb=# \i /usr/local/pgsql/query
SELECT * FROM employees WHERE firstname='Andrew';
 firstname | lastname | id
-----------+----------+-----
 Andrew    | Brookins | 100
(1 row)
```

If you find yourself doing this often for the sole purpose of using your favorite editor, using the \edit command would probably be more convenient.

The Readline and History Libraries

The *psql* client supports some of the same command-tracking features that the bash shell supports; namely, reverse-i-search, tab completion, and command history (command history is stored in */home/username/.psql_history*). These features are all available because *psql* support the readline library, which provide these functions to bash.

If the configure script finds the readline library, reverse-i-search, tab completion and command history should be automatically installed when you compile PostgreSQL. If *psql* does not support tab-completion, history, or reverse-i-search (history search), it may be because you either have the library files and/or header files installed into a non-standard directory. If this is the case, and you wish to reconfigure *psql* to use the readline and history features, your first task is to locate the library header files. (The filenames are: *libreadline.a*, *readline.h*, and *history.h*).

Once you know where the library and header files are stored on your filesystem, tell the PostgreSQL *configure* script where they are by using the following flags: *--with-includes=header_dirs*, and *--with-libs=lib_dirs*. After reconfiguration, remake the *psql* binary, and the features should become available. See the section titled "Step 3: Configuring the Source Tree" in Chapter 2 for more on the configuration process of PostgreSQL.

Variable Substitution

The *psql* client allows you to modify and create variables using the \set slash command, and delete them with the \unset slash command. Variables within *psql* work much the same way as variables within Unix and Linux shell programs, such as bash. Though the overall implementation of variables within *psql* is fairly simple, they are still useful, as you may easily insert or substitute the values of variables into slash commands and SQL commands.

When setting and using variables, be aware that *psql* uses a set of pre-defined internal variables. Setting these to non-intended values may cause unpredictable and undesirable effects within the program. For a list of these variables and their uses, see Appendix D, *Internal psql Variables.*

To set a variable, use the \set command, giving the command the name and the value of the variable you wish to set, in sequence, separated by space(s). This will either modify a previously existing variable or create a new variable if there is not one matching the variable name you supplied). As Example 6-2 shows, the variable name can be any length, and you can use any combination of letters, underscores, or numbers, and the value of the variable may be set to a string of any length.

Example 6-2: Setting a variable

```
testdb=# \set myvariable 'There are many like it, but this one is mine.'
```

Now, when you type \set without any arguments, the variable will appear in the list of variables.

Example 6-3: The variable list

```
testdb=# \set
VERSION = 'PostgreSQL 7.1.3 on i586-pc-linux-gnu, compiled by GCC 2.96'
DBNAME = 'testdb'
USER = 'postgres'
PORT = '5432'
ENCODING = 'SQL_ASCII'
PROMPT1 = '%/%R%# '
PROMPT2 = '%/%R%# '
PROMPT3 = '>> '
HISTSIZE = '500'
myvariable = 'There are many like it, but this one is mine.'
```

Once you have defined a variable, you can use what is known as *interpolation* to place it within both internal slash commands and SQL commands. This makes it possible to do things like load files into variables, and then use the loaded contents during an INSERT or SELECT, as well as more basic substitutions.

To substitute a variable value in this way, prefix the variable name with a colon (:) when you reference it from within other statements. For example, Example 6-4 demonstrates how to use a created variable during an INSERT or SELECT statement.

Example 6-4: Using interpolation during an INSERT

```
testdb=# \set manager_id 150
testdb=# INSERT INTO employees VALUES (
testdb(#     'Kevin',
testdb(#     'Murphy',
testdb(#     :manager_id
testdb(# );
testdb=# SELECT * FROM employees WHERE id = :manager_id;
 firstname | lastname | id
-----------+----------+-----
 Kevin     | Murphy   | 150
(1 row)
```

As mentioned, it is possible to insert files into variables and then use interpolation to insert their content into other commands. To read files, use backticks (`) to set a variable to the output of the *cat* command (the Unix command to display the contents of a file). Example 6-5 and Example 6-6 illustrate a basic way of doing this. In these examples, the *tabledata* file is located in the user's home directory (`~/`).

Example 6-5: Reading from a file into a variable

```
testdb=# \set data `cat tabledata`
testdb=# \echo :data
'Mike', 'Nelson', 151
```

Example 6-6: Using a variable in an INSERT

```
testdb=# INSERT INTO employees VALUES (:data);
```

After Example 6-6, you would have a new row within the employees table with the values set in the data variable.

About the psql Prompt

The *psql* client supports the complete modification of its prompt. This can be helpful for displaying various pieces of information in an obvious way (what could be more obvious than the prompt?). Prompt information is stored in the PROMPT1, PROMPT2, and PROMPT3 variables within *psql*. The program displays each of these variables at different times.

PROMPT1 contains the normal (default) prompt information while PROMPT2 contains the prompt information that is displayed on a new line during a statement or query that you have not yet terminated (because you have not ended it with either a semicolon or issued the \g command) PROMPT3 contains the prompt information displayed while entering data during an SQL COPY command. To view how your prompts are currently configured, use the \set command without arguments to view a list of defined variables. Within this list you should see entries for PROMPT1,

PROMPT2, and PROMPT3. You'll see single quotes surrounding user-configurable display strings, which define how the *psql* prompt appears. The %-prefixed characters (e.g., %m) are variables; all other characters are printed directly as shown.

Table 6-1 displays the default prompt settings for each of the prompt variables. Notice that the display in the second row, PROMPT2, assumes that a query has been continued to the next line with an open parenthesis, resulting in the (symbol preceding the hash mark (#).

Table 6-1. Default PROMPT settings

Prompt	Variable	Display
PROMPT1	'%/%R%#'	testdb=#
PROMPT2	'%/%R%# '	testdb(#
PROMPT3	'>> '	>>

Modifying the prompt

To modify the *psql* prompt, use \set to change the strings held by the three prompt variables. When defining your prompt strings, use % to substitute a variable into the string (Example 6-7 provides a list of defined substitutions you can make with the % sign). You may use \n to display a new line character. All other characters will be displayed normally. Example 6-7 modifies the PROMPT1 variable to contain an additional psql: prefix, trivially modifying the standard prompt display.

Example 6-7: Setting the prompt variables

```
testdb=# \set PROMPT1 'psql:%/%R%# '
psql:testdb=#
```

Table 6-2. Prompt substitution characters

Substitution character	Description
%~	This inserts the name of the database you are currently working in. If you are currently working in the default database, a tilde (~) will be displayed.
%#	This will insert a number sign (#) if the current user is defined as a superuser within the database. Otherwise, it will insert a greater-than sign (>).
%>	This will insert the port number the database server is currently accepting connections at.
%/	This will insert the name of the database you are currently working in.

Table 6-2. Prompt substitution characters (continued)

Substitution character	Description
%m	This will insert the hostname of the server the database is currently running on, truncated down to the string before the first dot (i.e., "yourserver.com" would become "yourserver" when inserted).
%M	This will insert the full hostname of the server the database is currently running on. If no hostname information is available, the string "localhost" will be inserted.
%n	This will insert the database username you are currently connected as.
%R	When used with PROMPT1, this will insert an equal sign (=) during normal operation; in single-line mode, it will insert a caret (^); and if your session ever becomes disconnected from the backend process, an exclamation point (!) is inserted.
	When used with PROMPT2, %R inserts a dash (–) instead of an equal sign during normal operation, and whatever you entered as the end-symbol if you started a new line during an unterminated statement (for example, if you leave a parenthesis open while entering a multiline query, this variable will display a parenthesis in the prompt).
	Nothing is inserted if this is used with the PROMPT3 variable.
%number	You may enter specific characters in prompt variables using decimal, octal, or hexadecimal numbers. To specify an octal *number*, prefix it with a 0; to specify the *number* as hexadecimal, prefix it with a 0x; otherwise *number* is interpreted as a decimal number.
%:variable	To insert the contents of a *psql variable*, use the colon (:) and the variable's identifier.
%`command`	Inserts the output of whatever command is specified with the *command* parameter.

Prompt examples

Using the \set command, you may combine the different substitution characters to form whatever prompt you would like. Example 6-8 and Example 6-9 demonstrate setting the PROMPT1 variable to an arbitrary new sequence.

Example 6-8: Customizing the prompt with database host, port, and username

```
testdb=# \set PROMPT1 '[%m:%>:%n] (%/)= '
[host:5432:postgres] (testdb)=
```

Example 6-9: Customizing the prompt with the date, database name, and username

```
testdb=# \set PROMPT1 '\n[%`date`]\n%n:%/%=# '

[Fri Aug  3 21:44:30 PDT 2001]
postgres:testdb=#
```

PgAccess: A Graphical Client

PgAccess is a graphical administration application for PostgreSQL. It is designed to be similar in function to PC database software, such as Microsoft Access.

Figure 6-1 displays the main PgAccess application window.

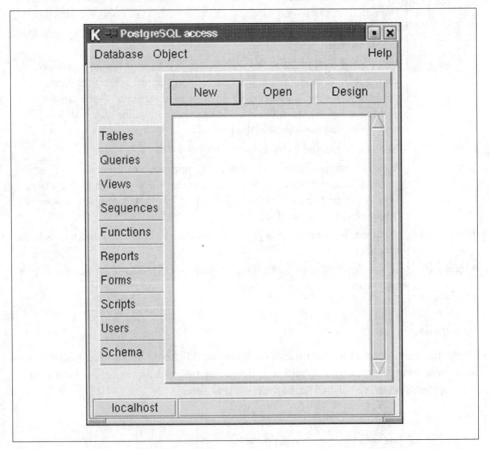

Figure 6-1. PgAccess application window

The interface allows you to view and modify various aspects of your PostgreSQL database using graphical representations of database elements, such as tables, queries, and views (among others). It can be a convenient escape from the sometimes tedious task of using the *psql* command line interface.

PgAccess was written in the Tcl/Tk scripting language; this increases its level of portability, as it can be installed and run on any system that supports the Tcl/Tk scripting language (including Linux/Unix, Windows, and MacOS). As PgAccess is a client side application, PostgreSQL is not required to be on the machine running PgAccess.

Installation and Basic Configuration

There are relatively few things you will need to do to configure PgAccess for use with PostgreSQL. Most importantly, make sure that Tcl/Tk is installed and configured properly.

To configure PostgreSQL with TCL support, you must have used the *--with-tcl* flag during source compilation. The use of the *--with-tcl* flag will configure the appropriate tcl libraries for use with PostgreSQL. This flag will install the *pgaccess* binary for you.

PgAccess will not operate unless you have configured PostgreSQL to support Tcl/Tk. Linux distributions that come with PostgreSQL, such as Red Hat and Mandrake, should have TCL support compiled in to their PostgreSQL binaries.

If you did not use the *--with-tcl* flag during your original compilation you can add TCL support to your existing PostgreSQL configuration without having to reinitialize the PostgreSQL data directories by reconfiguring PostgreSQL with the *--with-tcl* flag, and subsequently recompiling.

After the reconfiguration is complete, clean up the directory by typing: *gmake clean*, and then recompile the code by typing: *gmake*. Finally, shut down *postmaster* and type the command: *gmake install*. This will install the new binaries and libraries for the reconfigured PostgreSQL system. Once these are installed you can safely restart PostgreSQL.

If you are going to recompile PostgreSQL after it has been installed, you *must* use source from the same version of PostgreSQL that you originally compiled. If you use a different version of the source, you may lose data. As always, it is a good idea to backup your data before performing any changes to your PostgreSQL installation.

Managing Users

PgAccess provides the ability to graphically modify and manage user accounts associated with the database. Like command-line clients, it uses CREATE USER and ALTER USER to accomplish these tasks. The difference is that PgAccess provides a graphical front-end to these commands. This feature is available through the Users tab on the left side of the PgAccess window. Figure 6-2 shows this tab.

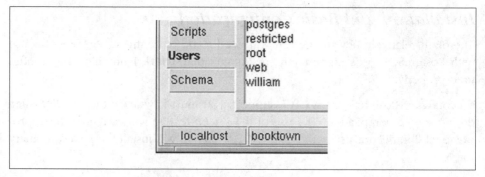

Figure 6-2. The PgAccess Users tab

Clicking on Users will display a list of all users associated with the database. Of the program's three action buttons, only New and Design perform actions from this tab.

Clicking New will allow you to create a new user within the database. As you may notice, the options in this window correlate with the options available through the use of the SQL command, CREATE USER. Use the Username field to set the new user's username, and the Password and verify password fields to set the password (if there will be one). The two check boxes set the CREATEDB and CREATEUSER permissions for the new user, if checked (remember that allowing these permissions creates the new user as a database superuser). You may use the Valid until field to set the valid-until date for the user (the same as the CREATE USER command).

Clicking the Design button allows you to modify the attributes of the selected user account as you would normally do with the SQL command, ALTER USER. As such, the options here correlate with the options available through ALTER USER, such as modifying the username, changing the password, setting the previously mentioned CREATEDB and CREATEUSER permissions, and modifying the valid-until date.

Managing Groups

As of Version 0.98.7, the most current version at the printing of this book, PgAccess does not support the management of groups. You can use the command-line interface *psql* to create and modify PostgreSQL user groups.

Creating Databases

To create a database using PgAccess, click the Database menu option at the top of the screen, then click New and type in the name you wish to give the database. This will create a database as if you had called the SQL CREATE DATABASE command from the currently logged-in database user. To use a template other than template1 for the new database or set its encoding type, you will need to either use the *createdb* program, or the CREATE DATABASE command from a command line client (see Chapter 9).

Creating Tables

It is relatively easy to create and modify the tables of a database with PgAccess through its graphical interface. Figure 6-3 shows this dialog window.

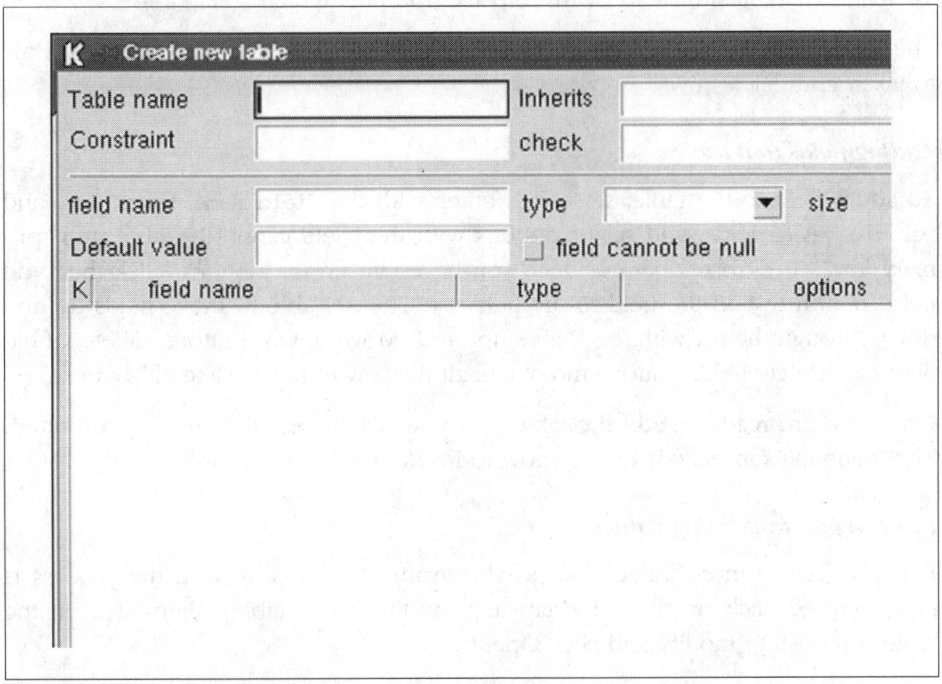

Figure 6-3. The PgAccess Create new table dialog box

To create a table, first click on the Tables tab, then click the New button to open the "Create new table" window. This window contains various fields and buttons that allow you to modify the attributes of the table you are creating. Basically, these commands are visual representations of the options found in the SQL CREATE TABLE command.

The following list names available inputs within the PgAccess Create Table Dialog:

Table name

> The name of the table you wish to create within PostgreSQL.

Inherits

> You can set table(s) from which this table will inherit attributes. A list of available tables is located in the drop-down box. Note that the list is not restricted to holding just one value; you can click the downward arrow button and choose another table to add that table to the inheritance list.

Check

> Enter any expressions you wish to have checked on INSERT and UPDATE commands.

Constraint

> Enter any constraints you wish to place upon the table.

The following subsections talk about how to add fields to a table and about how to insert and delete rows.

Adding fields to a table

To add a field to the table, set its attributes with the field name, type, size, and Default value fields, and set its options with the "field cannot be null" and "primary key" check box options. Once you have chosen the options, click the "Add field" button to add the field to the field list. You are able to move fields up and down through the list with the "Move up" and "Move down" buttons, delete a field with the "Delete field" button, and delete all fields with the "Delete all" button.

Once you are ready to add the table into your database, click the Create button. The following subsections discuss how to insert and delete of rows.

Inserting and updating values

It is possible to insert values into a table using PgAccess; in fact, the process is fairly simple. Click on the Table tab to view the list of tables, then click on the table you wish to modify and click Open.

After clicking Open, you should see a window of rows and columns that contain the various fields of your table. You can tab through these columns and rows to reach a target field, or just use your mouse to click on it. The row chosen will become highlighted and a cursor will appear showing you the location of the new data. The database will not be updated with your changes until you tab out of the field you were editing; or, alternatively, click into another field with your mouse. PgAccess displays the message: "Updating database . . ." after you complete one of these actions.

It may be useful to note that it is possible to both sort and filter the table data by making use of two fields at the top of the table window, named logically "Sort field" and "Filter conditions." It is possible to sort the table by a field or multiple fields by typing the name of the field into the "Sort field" box, optionally including "ASC" or "DESC" if you wish for the sort to be ascending or descending, respectively. You can choose to sort by multiple fields. To do this, include the names of other fields in a comma-delimited list. As an example, you could use the following to sort a list of names by the lastname field, ascending:

```
lastname ASC
```

To use the "Filter conditions" box, enter filter conditions such as the following:

```
(age < 45) and (avgsalary > 40000)
```

The process for updating table data is the same as for inserting, but you change existing rows rather than adding new ones.

Deleting values

To delete values from a table, open it in the same manner you would when attempting to insert values: click on the Tables tab, then click on the table you wish to modify and click Open. Within this window are the columns and rows of the table, filled with whatever data has been entered. You can either delete rows, or specific fields within a row. To delete a row, click on the desired row, then hit the Delete key on your keyboard. PgAccess will display a dialog box asking for confirmation of the delete, in case your choice to delete was accidental. To delete the contents of a field, or the partial contents of a field, click or tab into that field and use the Backspace key to delete characters.

Using Queries

As should be expected, you are able to design, edit, and run queries through PgAccess. Click on the Queries tab to view a list of the defined queries associated with your database. This area of the program should be familiar to Microsoft Access users, as the visual query designer and other features are very similar to their counterparts within that program.

To create a new query, click the New button. This will open the "Query builder" window. Before designing the query, you should name it with the Query name field. This name is arbitrary and serves no function within the query; it is needed only so that PgAccess has something to display for this query in the list of available queries. You may also add comments in the comment window at this point.

Manually designing a query

After naming the query, you can either design it manually or use the visual designer tool to speed up the process. To manually design the query, use the large, white box below the `Query name` field to type in the SELECT statement that will be used to query the database. You can spread this statement out over multiple lines, if you wish.

Using the visual designer

To use the visual designer tool for creation of the new query, click on the "Visual designer" button. As stated before, the interface to this tool is similar to the query designer tool in Microsoft Access. You are initially given a blank canvas to work with. Add tables to the canvas by typing the name of the table in the `Add table` field (the cursor enters text into this field by default). Alternatively, you can add tables by clicking the down-arrow button and selecting the table you wish to add from the list of available tables.

Once you've added the tables you wish to use, you can form links between them by clicking and dragging on a field, then pulling it from one table object to the other. When a link is formed it will display as a thin line that connects the two objects together. Note that you can move table objects around the canvas and the link graphic will stretch to fit whatever arrangement you desire. You may delete tables from the canvas by clicking on their labels and hitting the Delete key on your keyboard. Similarly, links may be deleted between columns by clicking on them and pressing the Delete key.

Any links between corresponding table columns will be translated into a SQL WHERE clause, specifying conditions upon which to join two table sets. A link will only represent a condition involving the equal-to operator (=). If you require a different condition, the SQL statement can be edited manually in the "Query builder" window; bear in mind that going back to the Visual Designer will cause any modified relationship to be re-created as an equal-to relationship when it is saved.

Figure 6-4 shows the PgAccess Visual Designer interface. It illustrates a fairly involved SQL query, reproduced in a more comprehensible, graphical form.

To select fields that you wish to be included in the results of the query, drag the field name down into the result zone (the cell-divided area at the bottom of the screen). You may define conditions you wish to be applied to results from the query; do this by entering a condition into the `Criteria` field. To see the SQL statement you have created with the visual design, click the "Show SQL" button. To execute your query (for testing purposes), click the "Execute SQL" button. When you are done creating the query's design, click on the "Save to query builder" button. This saves the query within the `pga_queries` table.

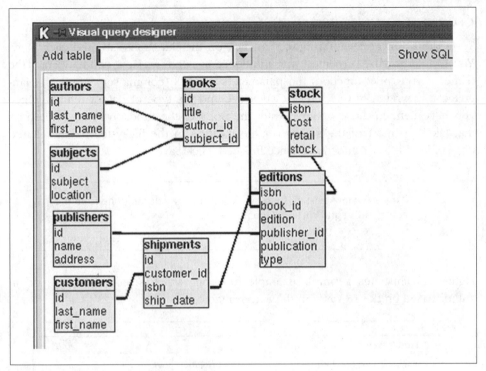

Figure 6-4. The PgAccess Visual query designer

Executing a query

To view the results of an existing query, click the Queries tab, select the desired query from the list in the main PgAccess window, and click the Open button. This displays the retrieved rows in a window similar to the window used for modifying tables, though this table is read-only. You can use the Sort field to sort the records by an expression, or the Filter conditions field to provide a filter expression.

Modifying a query

To modify an existing query, click the "Queries" tab, select it from the query list in the main PgAccess window, and click the Design button. This will display the "Query builder" window, which is the same view as if you were to create a new query. The query's name and SQL statement will be displayed in the window, as well as any comments you added onto it when it was originally designed. From here you can either edit the SQL statement directly or use the visual designer.

Remember to click the "Save query definition" button to save your modifications to an existing query.

Creating Functions

To create a function within PgAccess, click on the Functions tab, and click New. You should now be presented with the Function window. Here you may enter the name of your new function, the parameters it takes (comma-separated), the language it is written in (e.g., *SQL, C, plpgsql*), and the type of data it returns. Once you have defined those options, enter the body of the function in the white box that takes up most of the screen (or the location in the filesystem of the shared object file, if it is a *C* function). Once finished, click Save.

> You may view existing function definitions by selecting one from the function list, and clicking Open.

Figure 6-5 illustrates a simple example function, which selects the name of an author based on the id value in the authors table.

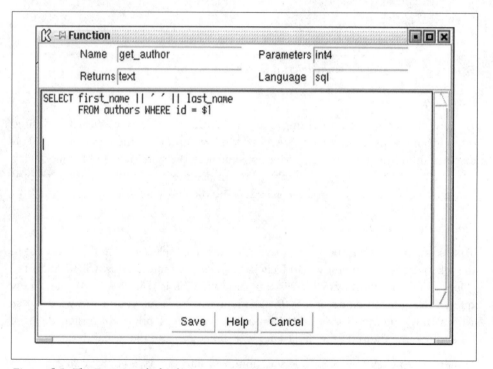

Figure 6-5. The Function dialog box

We will continue the discussion about creating functions in the next chapter.

7

Advanced Features

This chapter covers more advanced PostgreSQL subjects including optimizing table access with indices, advanced table concepts such as inheritance and constraints, the practical use of non-atomic array values, and explicit use of transactions and cursors. These sophisticated features greatly set PostgreSQL apart from many other relational database management systems.

This chapter also documents programmatic concepts such as triggers and sequences. Finally, for programmers wanting to add customized routines to the database, we document how to extend PostgreSQL through the addition of user-defined functions and operators.

Indices

Indices are database objects that can greatly increase database performance, enabling faster execution of statements involving comparative criteria. An index tracks the data on one or more columns in a table, allowing conditional clauses (such as the WHERE clause) to find their targeted rows more efficiently.

The internal workings of indices vary, and there are several implementations to choose from. This section describes the different types of indices available, and explains when you should use one type over the other.

While indices exist to enhance performance, they also contribute to system overhead. Indices must be updated as data in the column that they are applied to fluctuates. Maintaining infrequently used indices decreases performance when the amount of time spent maintaining them outweighs the time saved through using them. In general, indices should be applied only to columns that you expect to use frequently in comparative expressions.

Creating an Index

Indices are created with the CREATE INDEX SQL command. Here is the syntax for CREATE INDEX:

```
CREATE [ UNIQUE ] INDEX indexname ON table
       [ USING indextype ] ( column [ opclass ] [, ...] )
```

In this syntax, *indexname* is the name of the new index to be created, *table* is the name of the table to be indexed, and *column* is the name of a specific column to be indexed. Optionally, the *indextype* parameter may be set to specify index implementation, and the *opclass* parameter may be set to indicate what operator class should be used in sorting input values.

Operator classes are stored in PostgreSQL's pg_opclass column. Unless you are especially knowledgeable of the technical inner workings of PostgreSQL's operator classes, you shouldn't use this option.

Regarding the *column* to index, multiple names may be specified, separated by commas; doing so creates an index across *all* specified columns. Such an index will only be used by PostgreSQL when executing SQL statements that search all indexed columns in the WHERE clause through the AND keyword. Multicolumn indices are limited to a maximum of 16 columns in a default PostgreSQL installation, and may not use an index type other than B-tree.

In determining upon which columns to create an index, consider which columns will be most frequently accessed for search conditions. For example, while the books table keeps an index on its id column (the primary key), the title column is also frequently checked for in WHERE conditions. Adding a secondary index to the title column will greatly increase the performance of SQL statements making comparisons against values in that column.

Example 7-1 shows how to create such an index and uses the \d *psql* slash command to view the books table. In addition to showing the table's column types, this command also shows the indices that have been created on it.

Example 7-1: Creating an index

```
booktown=# CREATE INDEX books_title_idx
booktown-#                ON books (title);
CREATE
booktown=# \d books
          Table "books"
 Attribute  |  Type  | Modifier
```

Example 7-1: Creating an index (continued)

```
------------+---------+----------
 id         | integer | not null
 title      | text    | not null
 author_id  | integer |
 subject_id | integer |
Indices: books_id_pkey,
         books_title_idx
```

Certain types of table constraints, notably the PRIMARY KEY and UNIQUE constraints, result in the implicit creation of an index for use in enforcing the constraint. In Example 7-2 you see the creation of the Book Town authors table with the PRIMARY KEY constraint placed on its id column. This use of PRIMARY KEY causes an index called authors_pkey to be implicitly created.

Example 7-2: Implicit index creation

```
booktown=# CREATE TABLE authors (id integer PRIMARY KEY,
booktown(#                        last_name text,
booktown(#                        first_name text);
NOTICE:  CREATE TABLE/PRIMARY KEY will create implicit index 'authors_pkey' for
table 'authors'
CREATE
example=# \d authors
          Table "authors"
 Attribute  |  Type   | Modifier
------------+---------+----------
 id         | integer | not null
 last_name  | text    |
 first_name | text    |
Index: authors_pkey
```

The index created in Example 7-2 enables PostgreSQL to quickly verify that the primary key is unique for any new row inserted into the table, as well as enhances the performance of queries which use the id column as a search condition.

Unique indices

Specifying the UNIQUE keyword causes the index to disallow duplicate values within the column (or set of columns) it indexes. Creating a UNIQUE index on a table is functionally identical to creating a table with the UNIQUE constraint (see the section titled "Using Constraints" later in this chapter).

Example 7-3 creates a unique index called unique_publisher_idx on the publishers table's name column. This will disallow two publishers from having the same name in this table.

Example 7-3: Creating a unique index

```
booktown=# CREATE UNIQUE INDEX unique_publisher_idx
booktown-#                       ON publishers (name);
CREATE
booktown=# \d publishers
        Table "publishers"
 Attribute |  Type   | Modifier
-----------+---------+----------
 id        | integer | not null
 name      | text    |
 address   | text    |
Indices: publishers_pkey,
         unique_publisher_idx
```

As the NULL value does not technically match any value, duplicate instances of NULL can be inserted into a column with a unique index placed on it. This is the main practical difference between a unique index and an index implicitly created by the PRIMARY KEY constraint, which does not allow NULL values at all.

 Note that the UNIQUE clause may not be used in conjunction with the USING clause for any index type other than B-tree.

Index types

The optional USING clause can be used to specify the type of index to implement. PostgreSQL 7.1.x supports three types of indices including:

- B-tree
- R-tree
- Hash

PostgreSQL's B-tree implementation uses Lehman-Yao high-concurrency B-tree algorithms and is both the most capable, and most commonly used indexing method. For this reason, it is the default index type.

The R-tree implementation is primarily useful for spacial data type operations (i.e., operations on geometric types) and utilizes Guttman's quadratic split algorithm. The Hash implementation utilizes Litwin's linear hashing routines, which have been traditionally used for indices that involve frequent direct equal-to comparisons (e.g., with the = operator).

At the time of this writing, for PostgreSQL 7.1.x, the B-tree index implementation is by far the most capable and flexible of the available index types. At this time, it is recommended that you use the B-tree index type over the Hash implementation, even for direct = comparisons. The Hash index exists mostly for legacy reasons, though it may still be used if you are sure your system would benefit from a Hash index over a B-tree index.

As stated, the R-tree index implementation is recommended for indexing geometric types; be aware, however, that several limitations exist. For example, you cannot create a unique R-tree index, nor can you create an R-tree index on more than one column. In these cases, it makes more sense to rely on the capable B-tree index type.

The USING clause can be used with the keywords BTREE, RTREE, and HASH in order to explicitly choose the type of index you want to create. Specifying BTREE explicitly chooses the default index type.

Example 7-4 creates a table called polygons, which stores spacial data of the type polygon. An index named spacial_idx is then applied to its shape column with the R-tree implementation.

Example 7-4: Specifying an index type

```
booktown=# CREATE TABLE polygons (shape polygon);
CREATE
booktown=# CREATE INDEX spacial_idx ON polygons USING RTREE (shape);
CREATE
```

 Again, unless you have a solid conceptual understanding of why one index type might be preferable in your system over another, we advise you to use the default B-tree type.

Functional indices

A slightly modified form of the CREATE INDEX command can be used to index the results of a function on a column value, rather than the column value itself. This is called a *functional index*.

Use the following syntax to create a functional index:

```
CREATE [ UNIQUE ] INDEX indexname ON table
        [ USING indextype ] ( functionname ( column [, ...] ) [ opclass ] )
```

The only difference in this syntax is that the index is created on the results of the specified function applied to each column value. All other clauses have the same effect as the functional index.

Functional indices are useful on table columns that commonly have their values prepared through a function before being compared against values in a SQL statement. For example, the upper() function is commonly used to make case-insensitive comparisons. Creating an index using the `upper()` function enables such case-insensitive comparisons to be carried out efficiently.

Example 7-5 creates a functional index named `upper_title_idx` on the `books` table. It uses the `upper()` function on the `title` column as the basis to create the index. Then it performs an example SQL query that is more efficiently executed as a result of the newly created functional index.

Example 7-5: Creating a functional index

```
booktown=# CREATE INDEX upper_title_idx ON books
booktown-#                 (upper(title));
CREATE
booktown=# SELECT title FROM books WHERE upper(title) = 'DUNE';
 title
-------
 Dune
(1 row)
```

Destroying an Index

The SQL command to permanently destroy an existing index from a table is DROP INDEX. Here is the syntax for DROP INDEX:

```
DROP INDEX indexname [, ...]
```

In this syntax, *indexname* is the name of the index that you wish to permanently remove. Multiple indices to drop may be specified, separated by commas.

Example 7-6 drops the `upper_title_idx` index created in Example 7-5.

Example 7-6: Dropping an index

```
booktown=# DROP INDEX upper_title_idx;
DROP
```

Advanced Table Techniques

PostgreSQL provides several ways to constrain values inserted and updated within tables. One of these is the availability of table and column *constraints*.

PostgreSQL also supports an advanced object-relational table concept called *inheritance*. Inheritance allows separate tables to have an explicit parent-child relationship and, through this relationship, share columns in a hierarchical fashion.

The following sections document both types of SQL constraints, as well as the creation and application of inherited tables.

Using Constraints

Constraints are table attributes used to define rules on the type of data values allowed within specified columns. By enforcing these rules within the database, you can effectively safeguard against incorrect or inappropriate data being added to the database.

When you create a table, you can create a constraint using the CREATE TABLE command's CONSTRAINT clause. There are two types of constraints: column constraints and table constraints.

Column constraints apply only to a single column, while table constraints may apply to one or more columns. Within the CREATE TABLE command, the syntax for a column constraint follows immediately after a column definition, whereas the syntax for a table constraint exists in its own block, separated by a comma from any existing column definitions. A table constraint relies on its definition, rather than placement in the syntax, to indicate the columns affected by its restrictions.

The following sections discuss the different rules a constraint can enforce.

Column constraints

Performing the \h CREATE TABLE slash command within *psql* displays several detailed syntax diagrams for the constraints that may be placed on a table. Here is the syntax for a column constraint:

```
[ CONSTRAINT constraint_name ]
{ NOT NULL | UNIQUE | PRIMARY KEY | DEFAULT value | CHECK ( condition ) |
  REFERENCES table [ ( column ) ]
                [ MATCH FULL | MATCH PARTIAL ]
                [ ON DELETE action ]
                [ ON UPDATE action ]
                [ DEFERRABLE | NOT DEFERRABLE ]
                [ INITIALLY DEFERRED | INITIALLY IMMEDIATE ]
}
```

This syntax immediately follows the data type of the column to be constrained (and precedes any commas separating it from other columns) in the CREATE TABLE statement. It may be used with as many columns as is necessary. Notice that the CONSTRAINT keyword and constraint_name identifier are optional, and may be omitted.

There are six sets of column constraint keywords that may be applied. Some of the effects of these constraints are implicitly defined by others. The constraint keywords are as follows:

NOT NULL

Specifies that the column is not allowed to contain NULL values. Using the constraint CHECK (*column* NOT NULL) is equivalent to using the NOT NULL constraint.

UNIQUE

Specifies that the same value may not be inserted in this column twice. Note that the UNIQUE constraint allows more than one NULL value to be in a column, as NULL values technically never match another value.

PRIMARY KEY

Implies both UNIQUE and NOT NULL constraints, and causes an index to be created on the column. A table is restricted to having only one primary key constraint.

DEFAULT *value*

Causes unspecified input values to be replaced with a default value of *value*. This value must be of the same data type as the column it applies to. PostgreSQL 7.1.x does not support subselects as default values.

CHECK *condition*

Defines a *condition* that the value must satisfy for an INSERT or UPDATE operation to succeed on that row. The condition is an expression that returns a Boolean result. Used as a column constraint, only the one column being defined can be referenced by the CHECK clause.

The sixth column constraint, REFERENCES, contains the following clauses:

REFERENCES *table* [(*column*)]

Input values to the constrained column are checked against the values of the *column* column within the *table* table. If a matching value on this column is not found in the column that it references, the INSERT or UPDATE will fail. If *column* is omitted, the primary key on *table* is used, if one exists.

This column constraint is similar to the FOREIGN KEY table constraint discussed in the next section. Functionally, the REFERENCES column constraint is very similar to a FOREIGN KEY column constraint.

See Example 7-8 for an example of a table being created with a FOREIGN KEY table constraint.

MATCH FULL | MATCH PARTIAL

The MATCH clause affects what kind of NULL and non-NULL values are allowed to be mixed on insertion into a table whose foreign key references *multiple columns*. The MATCH clause is therefore only practically applicable to table constraints, though the syntax is technically valid in a column constraint as well.

MATCH FULL disallows insertion of row data whose columns contain NULL values unless all referenced columns are NULL. As of PostgreSQL 7.1.x, MATCH PARTIAL is not supported. Not specifying either clause allows NULL columns to satisfy the constraint.

Again, as column constraints may only be placed on a single column, this clause is only directly applicable to table constraints.

ON DELETE *action*

When a DELETE is executed on a referenced row in the referenced table, one of the following actions will be executed upon the constrained column, as specified by *action*:

NO ACTION

Produces an error if the reference is violated. This is the default if *action* is not specified.

RESTRICT

Identical to NO ACTION.

CASCADE

Removes all rows which reference the deleted row.

SET NULL

Assigns a NULL value to all referenced column values.

SET DEFAULT

Sets all referenced columns to their default values.

ON UPDATE action

When an UPDATE statement is performed on a referenced row in the referenced table, the same actions are available as with the ON DELETE clause. The default action is also NO ACTION.

Specifying CASCADE as the ON UPDATE action updates all of the rows that reference the updated row with the new value (rather than deleting them, as would be the case with ON DELETE CASCADE).

DEFERRABLE | NOT DEFERRABLE

DEFERRABLE gives you the option of postponing enforcement of the constraint to the end of a transaction rather than having it enforced at the end of each statement. Use the INITIALLY clause to specify the initial point at which the constraint will be enforced.

NOT DEFERRABLE means the enforcement of the constraint must always be done immediately as each statement is executed. Users do not have the option to defer enforcement to the end of a transaction when this is set. This is the default.

INITIALLY DEFERRED | INITIALLY IMMEDIATE

The constraint must be DEFERRABLE in order to specify the INITIALLY clause. INITIALLY DEFERRED causes enforcement to be postponed until the end of the transaction is reached, whereas INITIALLY IMMEDIATE causes constraint checking to be performed after each statement. INITIALLY IMMEDIATE is the default when the INITIALLY clause is not specified.

Example 7-7 shows how to create a table called employees with a variety of simple constraints.

Example 7-7: Creating a table with column constraints

```
booktown=# CREATE TABLE employees
booktown-#          (id integer PRIMARY KEY CHECK (id > 100),
booktown(#           last_name text NOT NULL,
booktown(#           first_name text);
NOTICE:  CREATE TABLE/PRIMARY KEY will create implicit index 'employees_pkey'
for table 'employees'
CREATE
```

Example 7-7 creates a column called id, of type integer which has both a PRIMARY KEY constraint and a CHECK constraint. The PRIMARY KEY constraint implies both NOT NULL and UNIQUE, as well as implicitly creates the employees_pkey index to be used on the column. The CHECK constraint verifies that the value of id is greater than 100. This means that any attempt to INSERT or UPDATE row data for the employees table with an id value of less-than or equal-to 100 will fail.

The employees table created in Example 7-7 also contains a column named last_name of type text which has a NOT NULL constraint enforced. This is a much simpler constraint; it disallows the addition of employees whose last name values are input as NULL. In other words, users must supply a last name for each employee.

 Conditions set with the CHECK clause must involve values of comparable data types.

Table constraints

Unlike column constraints, a table constraint can be defined on more than one column of a table. Here is the syntax to create a table constraint:

```
[ CONSTRAINT constraint_name ]
{ UNIQUE ( column [, ...] ) |
  PRIMARY KEY ( column [, ...] ) |
  CHECK ( condition ) |
```

```
FOREIGN KEY ( column [, ... ] )
            REFERENCES table [ ( column [, ... ] ) ]
            [ MATCH FULL | MATCH PARTIAL ]
            [ ON DELETE action ]
            [ ON UPDATE action ]
            [ DEFERRABLE | NOT DEFERRABLE ]
            [ INITIALLY DEFERRED | INITIALLY IMMEDIATE ]
```

CONSTRAINT *constraint_name* provides an optional name for the constraint. Naming a constraint is recommended, as it provides you with a meaningful name for the purpose of the constraint, rather than an automatically generated, generic name. In the future, this name also may be useful in removing constraints (e.g., when PostgreSQL's DROP CONSTRAINT clause of the ALTER TABLE command is implemented). The other clauses define four general types of table constraints:

PRIMARY KEY (*column* [, . . .])

The PRIMARY KEY table constraint is similar to the PRIMARY KEY column constraint. As a table constraint, PRIMARY KEY allows multiple columns to be defined in a parenthetical expression, separated by commas. An implicit index will be created across columns. The combination of values for each column specified must therefore amount to only unique and non-NULL values, as with the PRIMARY KEY column constraint.

UNIQUE (*column* [, . . .])

Specifies that the combination of values for the columns listed in the expression following the UNIQUE keyword may not amount to duplicate values. NULL values are allowed more than once, as NULL technically never matches any other value.

CHECK (*condition*)

Defines a *condition* that incoming row data must satisfy for an INSERT or UPDATE operation to succeed. The condition is an expression that returns a Boolean result. Used as a table constraint, more than one column can be referenced by the CHECK clause.

FOREIGN KEY (*column* [, . . .]) REFERENCES *table* [(*column* [, . . .])]

Allows multiple columns to be specified as the source for the REFERENCES clause. The syntax following the FOREIGN KEY clause and its specified columns is identical to that of the column REFERENCES constraint.

Example 7-8 creates the Book Town editions table. It creates three table constraints. A detailed explanation follows the example.

Example 7-8: Creating a table with table constraints

```
booktown=# CREATE TABLE editions
booktown-#          (isbn text,
booktown(#          book_id integer,
booktown(#          edition integer,
```

Example 7-8: Creating a table with table constraints (continued)

```
booktown(#              publisher_id integer,
booktown(#              publication date,
booktown(#              type char,
booktown(#              CONSTRAINT pkey PRIMARY KEY (isbn),
booktown(#              CONSTRAINT integrity CHECK (book_id IS NOT NULL
booktown(#                                AND edition IS NOT NULL),
booktown(#              CONSTRAINT book_exists FOREIGN KEY (book_id)
booktown(#                    REFERENCES books (id)
booktown(#                    ON DELETE CASCADE
booktown(#                    ON UPDATE CASCADE);
NOTICE:  CREATE TABLE/PRIMARY KEY will create implicit index 'pkey' for table
'editions'
NOTICE:  CREATE TABLE will create implicit trigger(s) for FOREIGN KEY check(s)
CREATE
```

The first constraint, pkey is a PRIMARY KEY constraint on the isbn column, and
behaves identically to a PRIMARY KEY column constraint (because only one column
target is supplied).

The constraint named integrity uses the CHECK clause to ensure that neither the
book_id nor edition columns ever contain NULL values.

Finally, the book_exists constraint uses the FOREIGN KEY and REFERENCES clauses to
verify that the book_id value always exists within the books table in the id column.
Furthermore, since the CASCADE keyword is supplied for both the ON DELETE and ON
UPDATE clauses, any modifications to the id column in the books table will also be
made to the corresponding rows of the editions table, and any deletions from
books will result in corresponding rows being deleted from editions.

Notice that both an implicit index named editions_pkey on the isbn column and
an implicit trigger are created from these table constraints. The implicit index is
used in the enforcement of the PRIMARY KEY constraint. The implicit trigger
enforces the FOREIGN KEY constraint.

Adding a constraint

The ALTER TABLE command is intended to allow the addition of table constraints to
existing tables. As of PostgreSQL 7.1.x, however, only the addition of CHECK and
FOREIGN KEY constraints is supported.

Here is the syntax to add a constraint with ALTER TABLE:

```
ALTER TABLE table
    ADD [ CONSTRAINT name ]
    { CHECK ( condition ) |
      FOREIGN KEY ( column [, ... ] )
              REFERENCES table [ ( column [, ... ] ) ]
              [ MATCH FULL | MATCH PARTIAL ]
              [ ON DELETE action ]
```

```
                          [ ON UPDATE action ]
                          [ DEFERRABLE | NOT DEFERRABLE ]
                          [ INITIALLY DEFERRED | INITIALLY IMMEDIATE ]
              }
```

Example 7-9 creates a new FOREIGN KEY constraint on the Book Town books table's
subject_id column. This constraint references the id column within the subjects
table, and will ensure that no values are inserted or modified on the books table's
subject_id column which cannot be found in the subjects table's id column.

Example 7-9: Adding a constraint to an existing table

```
booktown=# ALTER TABLE books
booktown-#              ADD CONSTRAINT legal_subjects
booktown-#              FOREIGN KEY (subject_id)
booktown-#              REFERENCES subjects (id);
NOTICE:  ALTER TABLE ... ADD CONSTRAINT will create implicit trigger(s) for
FOREIGN KEY check(s)
CREATE
```

Removing a constraint

As of PostgreSQL 7.1.x, constraints may not be directly removed from a table. The
only way to achieve the net effect of dropping a constraint is to create a copy of
the table which is nearly identical to the original, with any unwanted constraints
omitted. The data can then be copied from the original table to the new table, and
the tables renamed using the ALTER TABLE command so that the new copy replaces
the original table.

> Be aware of who is connected to, and accessing, any tables that you
> wish to restructure with this work-around. Data should not be
> inserted or modified at any time in the middle of the operation;
> therefore, you may need to temporarily disallow connection to the
> database if it is a highly active table, make the modifications, and
> finally, restart the system when finished.

Example 7-10 demonstrates this work-around method for removing a constraint by
effectively removing the legal_subjects FOREIGN KEY constraint from the books
table (see Example 7-9). Notice that the books_id_pkey index is removed before
the new table is created, so that the new table can be created with an index
named books_id_pkey. This is not necessary, but for the sake of consistency we
want to keep the primary key index name the same.

Example 7-10: Removing a constraint

```
booktown=# DROP INDEX books_id_pkey;
DROP
booktown=# CREATE TABLE new_books
booktown-#               (id integer CONSTRAINT books_id_pkey PRIMARY KEY,
booktown(#               title text NOT NULL,
booktown(#               author_id integer,
booktown(#               subject_id integer);
NOTICE:  CREATE TABLE/PRIMARY KEY will create implicit index 'books_id_pkey'
for table 'new_books'
CREATE
booktown=# INSERT INTO new_books SELECT * FROM books;
INSERT 0 15
booktown=# ALTER TABLE books RENAME TO old_books;
ALTER
booktown=# ALTER TABLE new_books RENAME TO books;
ALTER
```

Inheritance

PostgreSQL supports an advanced object-relational mechanism known as *inheritance*. Inheritance allows a table to *inherit* some of its column attributes from one or more other tables, creating a parent-child relationship. This causes the child table to have each of the same columns and constraints as its inherited table (or tables), as well as its own defined columns.

When performing a query on an inherited table, the query can be instructed to retrieve either all rows of a table and its descendants, or just the rows in the parent table itself. The child table, on the other hand, will never return rows from its parent.

Creating a child table

A child table is created with the CREATE TABLE SQL command by using the INHERITS clause. This clause consists of the INHERITS keyword, and the name of the table (or tables) from which to inherit.

Here is the portion of the CREATE TABLE syntax which applies to inheritance:

```
CREATE TABLE childtable definition
        INHERITS ( parenttable [, ...] )
```

In this syntax, *childtable* is the name of the new table to be created, *definition* is the complete table definition (with all the ordinary CREATE TABLE clauses), and *parenttable* is the table whose column structure is to be inherited. More than one parent table may be specified by separating table names with commas.

Example 7-11 creates a table called distinguished_authors with a single column named award of type text. Since it is instructed to inherit from the authors table by the INHERITS clause it actually is created with four columns; the first three from authors, and the fourth awards column.

Example 7-11: Creating a child table

```
booktown=# CREATE TABLE distinguished_authors (award text)
booktown-#                 INHERITS (authors);
CREATE
booktown=# \d distinguished_authors
  Table "distinguished_authors"
 Attribute  |  Type   | Modifier
------------+---------+----------
 id         | integer | not null
 last_name  | text    |
 first_name | text    |
 award      | text    |
```

As you can see, even though Example 7-11 specified only one column, the distinguished_authors table inherited all of the columns that were originally in the authors table.

Using inherited tables

The relationship between the shared columns of a parent and child table is not purely cosmetic. Inserted values on the distinguished_authors table will *also* be visible in the authors table, its parent. However, in the authors table, you will only see the three columns which were inherited. When querying a parent table, you can use the ONLY keyword to specify that rows from child tables are to be omitted from the query results.

Parent rows are never visible within a query on one of its child tables. Therefore, using the ONLY keyword on a child table would only have an effect if that child table were also inherited by *another* table, making it effectively both a parent and a child.

Example 7-12 inserts a new author named *Neil Simon* with the award of *Pulitzer Prize* into the distinguished_authors table. Notice that the first three inserted values are shared between the parent and child tables.

Example 7-12: Inserting into a child table

```
booktown=# INSERT INTO distinguished_authors
booktown-#             VALUES (nextval('author_ids'),
booktown(#             'Simon', 'Neil', 'Pulitzer Prize');
INSERT 3629421 1
```

Since the first three columns of the distinguished_authors table are inherited from the authors table, this author will also appear implicitly as a regular author in the authors table (though the data is not literally inserted into the authors table). Only the distinguished_authors table will show information about awards, however, as inheritance only works one way (descending from parent to child).

Example 7-13 executes three SELECT statements. Each of these queries chooses a different target for the FROM clause, while using the same search criteria in the WHERE clause.

Example 7-13: Selecting with inheritance

```
booktown=# SELECT * FROM distinguished_authors
booktown-#            WHERE last_name = 'Simon';
  id   | last_name | first_name |     award
-------+-----------+------------+----------------
 25043 | Simon     | Neil       | Pulitzer Prize
(1 row)

booktown=# SELECT * FROM authors WHERE last_name = 'Simon';
  id   | last_name | first_name
-------+-----------+------------
 25043 | Simon     | Neil
(1 row)

booktown=# SELECT * FROM ONLY authors WHERE last_name = 'Simon';
 id | last_name | first_name
----+-----------+------------
(0 rows)
```

Each of the three queries in Example 7-13 look for rows where the last_name column matches the string constant *Simon*. The first query selects from the distinguished_authors table, which the data was originally inserted into (in Example 7-12), and the requested row is returned.

The second query in Example 7-13 selects from the parent of distinguished_authors, which is the authors table. Again, a row is retrieved, though this row includes only the columns which are inherited by the distinguished_authors.

It is important to understand that this data was not literally inserted into both tables, but simply made visible because of the inheritance relationship. This is illustrated by the third and final query in Example 7-13, which prefixes the authors table name with the ONLY keyword. This keyword indicates that rows are not to be received from child tables, but only from the specified parent; as a result, no rows are returned by the query.

Some constraints may appear to be violated because of the nature of inherited tables. For example, a column with a UNIQUE constraint placed on it may appear to have the same value twice by including data from inherited children. Make careful use of constraints and inheritance, as a child table does not literally violate such a constraint, though it can appear to if the ONLY keyword is not used when selecting from the parent table.

Modifying inherited tables

As covered in the preceding section, adding values into child and parent tables is fairly straightforward. An insertion of values into a child table will cause values in inherited columns to appear as values in the parent table, though the data itself physically resides in the child table. Insertion of values into a parent table has no effect whatsoever on the child table.

Likewise, modifying values in a child table is self-explanatory: only the values in the child table are modified, while any values literally in the parent table are unmodified. This is because the data is not literally shared between tables, but can only be *viewed* through the hierarchy. Row retrieval on the parent table without the ONLY clause will still show both the parent rows, and the modified child rows.

The effect of modifying existing rows in a parent table is less obvious than the effect of modifying existing rows in a child table. UPDATE and DELETE statements executed on a parent table will, by default, affect not only rows in the parent table, but also any child tables that match the criteria of the statement. Example 7-14 performs an UPDATE statement on the authors table. Notice that the row data in the distinguished_authors table is actually affected by this statement.

Example 7-14: Modifying parent and child tables

```
booktown=# UPDATE authors SET first_name = 'Paul'
booktown-#                   WHERE last_name = 'Simon';
UPDATE 1
booktown=# SELECT * FROM distinguished_authors;
   id  | last_name | first_name |     award
-------+-----------+------------+----------------
 25043 | Simon     | Paul       | Pulitzer Prize
(1 row)
```

The ONLY keyword can be used with UPDATE and DELETE in a fashion similar to its use with the SELECT command in order to prevent the type of cascading modification illustrated in Example 7-14. The ONLY keyword should always precede the inherited table name in the SQL syntax.

Example 7-15 demonstrates the use of the ONLY keyword. First, the example inserts a new row for Dr. Seuss into the distinguished_authors table, along with a reference to his Pulitzer Prize. This results in the authors table appearing to have two separate entries for the same author. The old entry (that exists physically in the authors table) is then removed by use of the DELETE SQL command combined with the ONLY keyword.

Example 7-15: Modifying parent tables with ONLY

```
booktown=# INSERT INTO distinguished_authors
booktown-#              VALUES (1809, 'Geisel',
booktown(#               'Theodor Seuss', 'Pulitzer Prize');
INSERT 3629488 1
booktown=# SELECT * FROM authors
booktown-#              WHERE last_name = 'Geisel';
   id  | last_name |   first_name
------+-----------+---------------
 1809 | Geisel    | Theodor Seuss
 1809 | Geisel    | Theodor Seuss
(2 rows)

booktown=# DELETE FROM ONLY authors
booktown-#              WHERE last_name = 'Geisel';
DELETE 1
```

The end result of Example 7-15 is that the record for Dr. Seuss is added to the
distinguished_authors table, and subsequently removed from the authors table,
as follows:

```
booktown=# SELECT * FROM authors
booktown-#              WHERE last_name = 'Geisel';
   id  | last_name |   first_name
------+-----------+---------------
 1809 | Geisel    | Theodor Seuss
(1 row)

booktown=# SELECT * FROM distinguished_authors
booktown-#              WHERE last_name = 'Geisel';
   id  | last_name |   first_name  |     award
------+-----------+---------------+----------------
 1809 | Geisel    | Theodor Seuss | Pulitzer Prize
(1 row)
```

Arrays

As documented in Chapter 3, *Understanding SQL*, PostgreSQL supports non-atomic
values in individual table columns through data constructs called *arrays*. An array
itself is not a data type, but an extension of any PostgreSQL data type.

Creating an Array Column

A simple array column is created by appending a pair of square brackets to the
data type of the intended array column within a CREATE TABLE or ALTER TABLE
statement. These brackets indicate that more than a single value of the described
data type may be inserted without limit into that column.

For example, the following shows the syntax for a column named *single_array*, which is an array column of type *type*:

```
single_array type[]   -- A single array of values.
```

Additional square brackets may be added to create *multidimensional arrays*, which may store an array of array values. For example:

```
multi_array  type[][] -- A multidimensional array of values.
```

In theory, an integer value *n* could be supplied within the square brackets to produce a *fixed-length* array (one which always has *n* members, and no more). As of PostgreSQL 7.1.x, however, this restriction is not enforced, and there is no practical difference between an array created with a fixed length and one created without.

Example 7-16 creates a table named favorite_books. This table associates an integer value of an employee with a one-dimensional character string array of type text called books.

Example 7-16: Creating a table with an array column

```
booktown=# CREATE TABLE favorite_books
booktown-#              (employee_id integer, books text[]);
CREATE
```

The table created by Example 7-16 allows any number of book titles to be stored in a single array column, for each employee. The advantage of such an array of discrete text values over a single text string (which also, of course, could contain multiple titles) is that each title is kept physically separate from each other title in the array column. Since the system knows where each array value begins and ends, you can choose titles by their subscript, rather than having to manually parse them out of a long text string.

Creating a multidimensional array column is very similar. The only distinction is that another pair of square brackets follows the first pair, as shown earlier in this section. Example 7-17 creates a table called favorite_authors, with an employee_id column of type integer, and multidimensional text array of author_and_titles. This essentially creates an array of text arrays.

Example 7-17: Creating a table with a multidimensional array column

```
booktown=# CREATE TABLE favorite_authors (employee_id integer,
booktown(#                          authors_and_titles text[][]);
CREATE
```

Inserting Values into Array Columns

A special kind of syntax is used in order to insert multiple values into a single column. This syntax allows you to describe an *array constant*. As documented in Chapter 3, the syntax of an array constant (for referring to PostgreSQL array values in SQL statements) is a special arrangement of curly braces, double-quotes and commas, all bound by single-quotes. Double quotes are required only when working with an array of character strings. Therefore, the general forms of array constants are:

```
'{ "text1" [, ...] }' -- A character string array.
'{ numeric [, ...] }' -- A numeric array.
```

These syntax forms illustrate how to handle string and numeric arrays, but a column may be defined as an array of any arbitrary type (including `boolean`, `date`, and `time` types). Generally, if you would ordinarily use single-quotes to describe a value in a non-array context (such as with a string constant, or timestamp value), double-quotes should be used for that value in an array constant.

Example 7-18 inserts a pair of records into the `favorite_books` table. The first statement inserts a single favorite book for the employee with id 102, and the second statement inserts two titles for the employee with id 103.

Example 7-18 executes two SQL `INSERT` statements, which insert a pair of array constant values.

Example 7-18: Inserting array constants

```
booktown=# INSERT INTO favorite_books VALUES
booktown-#             (102, '{"The Hitchhiker\'s Guide to the Galaxy"}');
INSERT 3628399 1
booktown=# INSERT INTO favorite_books VALUES
booktown-#             (103, '{"The Hobbit", "Kitten, Squared"}');
INSERT 3628400 1
```

Notice that, in Example 7-18, curly braces are still required to insert a single value into an array. Notice also that the single-quote in the title (first `INSERT` statement) still requires a backslash preceding it, even though it is surrounded by *double-quotes*. This is because the array constant itself is parsed as if it were one long string constant, and subsequently interpreted as an array based on the context of its target column.

The insertion of values into a multidimensional array requires a pair of curly braces for each array; an array of arrays must therefore itself be bound in curly braces, while each of its member arrays should be separated by one another with commas. Example 7-19 inserts a single row containing a multidimensional array constant into the `favorite_authors` table, created in Example 7-17.

Example 7-19: Inserting values into multidimensional arrays

```
booktown=# INSERT INTO favorite_authors
booktown-#             VALUES (102,
booktown(#             '{{"J.R.R. Tolkien", "The Silmarillion"},
booktown'#               {"Charles Dickens", "Great Expectations"},
booktown'#               {"Ariel Denham", "Attic Lives"}}');
INSERT 3727961 1
```

Notice that the inserted multidimensional array in Example 7-19 contains three text arrays, which each have two members. There is no systematic relationship between these arrays, though the implied relationship from the context is that the first members of each array are authors corresponding to the second members of each array, which are the favorite titles from the associated author.

Selecting Values From Array Columns

Selecting an array column from a table will result in the entire array being returned in the same constant format described in the previous section. Example 7-20 retrieves the entire arrays for inserted rows in the books column of the favorite_books table.

Example 7-20: Selecting entire array values

```
booktown=# SELECT books FROM favorite_books;
                     books
-------------------------------------------
 {"The Hitchhiker's Guide to the Galaxy"}
 {"The Hobbit","Kitten, Squared"}
 (2 rows)
```

While it is helpful to be able to return the entire array, the ability to retrieve only a specific portion of an array is often more useful. To this end, you need to learn how to work with array subscripts and slices.

Array subscripts

The usefulness of arrays lies largely in the fact that you can use *subscripts* to specify the value that you wish to view. A subscript is an integer value surrounded by square brackets, that describes the value you want to select. This number describes the precedence of the value, from left to right in the array.

Unlike programming languages such as C, PostgreSQL begins counting array elements at 1, not 0. Example 7-21 uses the [1] subscript on the books column of the favorite_books table to select only the first of an employee's favorite titles. Notice that the query returns values without braces or double-quotes. This is because a single text value need only be returned as a single text constant, not as an array.

Example 7-21: Selecting array values with subscripts

```
booktown=# SELECT books[1] FROM favorite_books;
                    books
----------------------------------------
 The Hitchhiker's Guide to the Galaxy
 The Hobbit
(2 rows)
```

Specifying a subscript for an array element which holds no value results in a NULL value being selected. The IS NOT NULL keywords may be useful in conjunction with such selections. Example 7-22 demonstrates two queries; the first returns two rows, NULL value as well as a title. The second query only returns the title (and not the row with the NULL value as a result of its use of the WHERE clause, with the IS NOT NULL condition.

Example 7-22: Avoiding NULL values in arrays

```
booktown=# SELECT books[2] FROM favorite_books;
      books
-----------------


 Kitten, Squared
(2 rows)

booktown=# SELECT books[2] FROM favorite_books
booktown-#                 WHERE books[2] IS NOT NULL;
      books
-----------------
 Kitten, Squared
(1 row)
```

Selecting from a multidimensional array requires an additional subscript following the initial subscript. The first subscript refers to which array that you are retrieving data from, while the second subscript refers to which member of the specified array is to be retrieved. Example 7-23 demonstrates selecting the first author, and associated title for that author, from the favorite_authors table created in Example 7-19.

Example 7-23: Selecting From a Multi-Dimensional Array

```
booktown=# SELECT authors_and_titles[1][1] AS author,
booktown-#        authors_and_titles[1][2] AS title
booktown-#        FROM favorite_authors;
     author     |      title
----------------+------------------
 J.R.R. Tolkien | The Silmarillion
(1 row)
```

Array slices

PostgreSQL also supports *slices* in array selection. These are similar to array sub-scripts, but describe a *range* of values to be returned. The syntax of a slice is a pair of integers, separated by a colon (:), surrounded by square brackets. For example, [2:5] specifies the second, third, fourth, and fifth array values of a given array. The result of a slice selection is returned as an array constant that is essentially a sub-array of the entire array (though a slice may extend from the beginning to the end of an array).

Example 7-24 selects the range of the first two book titles in the books test array column from the favorite_books table. Even though the first returned row has only one title, it is still returned as an array with one member value.

Example 7-24: Selecting array values with slices

```
booktown=# SELECT books[1:2] FROM favorite_books;
                   books
-------------------------------------------
 {"The Hitchhiker's Guide to the Galaxy"}
 {"The Hobbit","Kitten, Squared"}
(2 rows)
```

Array slices can be somewhat unpredictable with multidimensional arrays as of PostgreSQL 7.1.x. It is therefore recommended to stick to exact subscript values when working with multidimensional arrays until this support is improved.

Array dimensions

It can be useful to know the number of values stored in an array. You may use the array_dims() function to accomplish this. It accepts as a parameter a single identifier, which is the name of the array column that you wish to perform the function on. The result is returned as a character string describing the array with the same syntax used in array slices. Example 7-25 calls the array_dims() function on the books column of the favorite_books table.

Example 7-25: Using array_dims()

```
booktown=# SELECT array_dims(books) FROM favorite_books;
 array_dims
------------
 [1:1]
 [1:2]
(2 rows)
```

Updating Values in Array Columns

Values in array columns may be modified in one of three ways:

Complete modification
> The entire array may be replaced with a new array constant.

Slice modification
> A slice of an array (range between two values) may be replaced with a new array constant. The constant should have the same number of values within it as the slice to be updated.

Element modification
> An individual value in the array may be replaced with a new constant of the base type of the array. Use a subscript to specify which value to replace.

Replacing an array value with a new array puts no restriction on the number of values within the new array. There need not be the same number of values in the new array as in the existing one. For instance, suppose that the employee with id 102 wishes to add another favorite book to his list in the favorite_books table. This is achieved with an UPDATE statement in Example 7-26 which completely over-writes the previous value.

Example 7-26: Completely modifying an array

```
booktown=# UPDATE favorite_books
booktown-#         SET books='{"The Hitchhiker\'s Guide to the Galaxy",
booktown'#                   "The Restaurant at the End of the Universe"}'
booktown-#         WHERE employee_id = 102;
UPDATE 1
```

The same approach used in Example 7-26 can be used to set a slice of an array by attaching a slice descriptor to the end of the target identifier (e.g., books[1:3] would refer to the first, second and third values in the books array column). More commonly, though, situations arise where a single value within an array needs to be modified, instead of the entire array, or a slice of an array.

Updating a single value in an array is done by attaching a subscript to the target identifier to indicate the specific value to be modified. Example 7-27 updates the first array value of the books column, in the favorite_books table.

Example 7-27: Modifying an array subscript

```
booktown=# SELECT books[1] FROM favorite_books;

                books
-------------------------------------------
 The Hitchhiker's Guide to the Galaxy
 The Hobbit
(2 rows)
```

Example 7-27: Modifying an array subscript (continued)

```
booktown=# UPDATE favorite_books
booktown-#        SET books[1] = 'There and Back Again: A Hobbit\'s Holiday'
booktown-#        WHERE books[1] = 'The Hobbit';
UPDATE 1
booktown=# SELECT books[1] FROM favorite_books;
```

```
                    books
-----------------------------------------
 The Hitchhiker's Guide to the Galaxy
 There and Back Again: A Hobbit's Holiday
(2 rows)
```

Automating Common Routines

As an object-relational DBMS, PostgreSQL has helped pioneer several non-standard SQL extensions. Several of these are designed to aid in the automation of commonly executed database routines.

This section covers two such extensions: sequences and triggers.

Sequences

A *sequence* in PostgreSQL is a database object that is essentially an automatically incrementing numeric value. For this reason, sequences are commonly known in other database products as *auto-increment* values. Sequences can be extremely useful in assigning non-random, unique identification numbers to tables that require such values. A sequence consists of a current numeric value, and a set of characteristics that determine how to automatically increment (or alternatively, decrement) that value upon use.

Along with its current value, a sequence also includes a minimum value, a maximum value, a starting value, and the *amount* to increment the sequence by. This increment is usually 1, but may be any whole integer.

In practice, sequences are not meant to be accessed directly. Instead, they are used through a set of functions built into PostgreSQL which either set, increment, or return the current value of the sequence.

Creating a sequence

Sequences are created with the CREATE SEQUENCE SQL command. The sequence can be specified to increment or decrement. The syntax for CREATE SEQUENCE is:

```
CREATE SEQUENCE sequencename
       [ INCREMENT increment ]
       [ MINVALUE minvalue ]
       [ MAXVALUE maxvalue ]
```

```
[ START start ]
[ CACHE cache ]
[ CYCLE ]
```

In this syntax, *sequencename* is the name of the sequence to be created. This is the only required parameter. A sequence uses the integer data type, and it therefore shares its maximum and minimum limitations of 2147483647 and –2147483647, respectively.

The optional CREATE SEQUENCE clauses are as follows:

INCREMENT *increment_val*

Sets the numeric quantity with which to modify the sequence's value to *increment_val*. This is used when the nextval() function is called on the sequence. Setting *increment_val* to a negative number results in a descending sequence. The default value is 1.

MINVALUE *minvalue*

Sets the fixed minimum value for the sequence to *minvalue*. Any attempt to lower a sequence below this value will result in an error, or in the value cycling to its maximum value (if the CYCLE keyword was used when the sequence was created).

The default value is 1 for ascending sequences, and –2147483647 for descending sequences.

MAXVALUE *maxvalue*

Sets the fixed maximum value for the sequence to *maxvalue*. Any attempt to raise a sequence above this value will result in an error, or in the value cycling to its minimum value.

The default value is 2147483647 for ascending sequences, and –1 for descending sequences.

START *start_val*

Sets the value that the sequence begins at. It may be any integer between the minimum and maximum values. The sequence defaults to start at its minimum value for ascending sequences, and its maximum value for descending sequences.

CACHE *cache*

Provides the ability for sequence values to be pre-allocated and stored in memory. This can result in faster access times to highly used sequences. The minimum and default value is 1; a higher value of *cache* results in more values being cached.

CYCLE

> Enables the sequence to continue generating new values after it has reached its maximum or minimum value. When the limit is reached, the sequence starts over at the minimum value (for ascending sequences), or at the maximum value (descending sequences).

Example 7-28 creates a simple ascending sequence named shipments_ship_id_seq that starts at a value of 0, and will be incremented by the default increment of 1 until it reaches the default maximum limit of 2147483647. By not using the CYCLE keyword, the sequence is guaranteed to always return a unique value.

Example 7-28: Creating a sequence

```
booktown=# CREATE SEQUENCE shipments_ship_id_seq
booktown-#                    MINVALUE 0;
CREATE
```

Viewing a sequence

The output from the \d command within *psql* shows whether or not a database object is a sequence, table, view or index. More specifically, the \ds command can be used to view all sequences in the currently connected database. For example:

```
booktown=# \ds
            List of relations
        Name          |  Type    |  Owner
----------------------+----------+---------
 book_ids             | sequence | manager
 shipments_ship_id_seq | sequence | manager
 subject_ids          | sequence | manager
(3 rows)
```

While not often necessary, sequences can be directly queried with SELECT statements, as if they were a table or view. When you query a sequence, you use the attributes of that sequence as columns in your select list. The attributes of a sequence are shown in Table 7-1.

Table 7-1. Sequence attributes

Attribute	Type
sequence_name	name
last_value	integer
increment_by	integer
max_value	integer
min_value	integer
cache_value	integer
log_cnt	integer

Table 7-1. Sequence attributes (continued)

Attribute	Type
is_cycled	"char"
is_called	"char"

Example 7-29 illustrates a query to the `shipments_ship_id_seq` sequence. This query selects the `last_value` attribute, which is the most currently selected value from the sequence, and the `increment_by` attribute, which is the amount the sequence is to be incremented each time the `nextval()` function is called.

Example 7-29: Viewing a sequence

```
booktown=# SELECT last_value, increment_by
booktown-#        FROM shipments_ship_id_seq;
 last_value | increment_by
------------+--------------
          0 |            1
(1 row)
```

Since the sequence in question has just been created, its `last_value` is still set to 0.

Using a sequence

Sequences are typically not queried directly, but are instead used through functions. There are three functions in PostgreSQL which apply exclusively to sequences:

`nextval('`*sequence_name*`')`

> Increments the value of the specified sequence named *sequence_name*, and returns the new value, which is of type `integer`.

`currval('`*sequence_name*`')`

> Returns the most recently returned value from `nextval('`*sequence_name*`')`. This value is associated with a PostgreSQL session, and if the `nextval()` function has not yet been called in the connected session on the specified sequence *sequence_name*, there will be no "current" value returned.

`setval('`*sequence_name*`', `*n*`)`

> Sets the current value of the specified sequence to the numeric value *n*. The value returned by the next call to `nextval()` will return *n + increment*, where *increment* is the amount that the sequence increments by each iteration.

`setval('`*sequence_name*`', `*n*`, `*b*`)`

> Also sets the current value of the specified sequence to the numeric value *n*. However, if *b* (a value of type `boolean`) is *false*, the value returned by the next call to `nextval()` will be just *n*. If *b* is *true*, the next call to `nextval()` will return *n + increment*, as it would without specifying the Boolean argument.

The most commonly used sequence function is nextval(). This is the function that actually pushes the increment of the value. It requires the name of the sequence as the argument (bound by single quotes), and returns a value of type integer.

Example 7-30 selects a couple of incremented values from the sequence named shipments_ship_id_seq.

Example 7-30: Incrementing a sequence

```
booktown=# SELECT nextval('shipments_ship_id_seq');
 nextval
---------
       1
(1 row)

booktown=# SELECT nextval('shipments_ship_id_seq');
 nextval
---------
       2
(1 row)
```

 The first call to nextval() will return the sequence's *initial* value (set by the START keyword), since it has not yet been called to increment the starting value. All subsequent calls increment the last_value column.

Sequences are commonly used as default values for tables which require unique integer identifiers. The shipments table within the booktown database, shown in Table 7-2, exemplifies this.

Table 7-2. The shipments table

Column	Type	Modifier
id	integer	NOT NULL DEFAULT nextval('shipments_ship_id_seq')
customer_id	integer	
isbn	text	
ship_date	timestamp with time zone	

The syntax to create the table in Table 7-2, with the auto-incrementing DEFAULT and PRIMARY KEY constraint, is:

```
CREATE TABLE shipments
        (id integer DEFAULT nextval('shipments_ship_id_seq') PRIMARY KEY,
         customer_id integer, isbn text, ship_date timestamp)
```

The default value for the id column in Table 7-2 is set to the nextval()'s result on the shipments_ship_id_seq sequence. Insertion of row data that does not specify a value for id will therefore choose its value from the result of this function call.

Merely placing a DEFAULT constraint on the id column does not enforce the use of that default. A user could still manually insert a value, potentially causing a conflict with future sequence values. This can be disallowed with the use of a trigger. See the section titled "Triggers" later in this chapter for more information.

After the nextval() function has been called on a sequence in a given session (a connection to PostgreSQL), the currval() function may be used on that same sequence to return the most recently returned value from the sequence. Note that this function may *only* be called on a sequence that has been called through nextval() in the active session.

Sequences' "current" values are associated with sessions in order to prevent multiple users from running into mistakes by accessing the same sequence at the same time. Two users may access the same sequence from separate sessions, but the currval() function will return only the most recently incremented value of the sequence from within *the same session* that calls currval().

Example 7-31 inserts a new row into the shipments column, without specifying the value for the id column. This causes the default value to be used, which (as noted in Table 7-2) is the result of the shipments_ship_id_seq being incremented by the nextval() function. The currval() function is then used to access the row that was just inserted.

Example 7-31: Using currval()

```
booktown=# INSERT INTO shipments (customer_id, isbn, ship_date)
booktown-#             VALUES (221, '0394800753', 'now');
INSERT 3628625 1
booktown=# SELECT * FROM shipments
booktown-#             WHERE id = currval('shipments_ship_id_seq');
  id  | customer_id |    isbn     |        ship_date
------+-------------+-------------+--------------------------
 1002 |         107 | 0394800753  | 2001-09-22 11:23:28-07
(1 row)
```

Finally, a sequence may also have its last_value attribute reset to an arbitrary numeric value (within its maximum and minimum value range) by using the setval() function. This requires the name of the sequence as a single-quote bound character string for the first argument and an integer constant representing the new value for last_value for the second argument.

There are two ways to go about this. By default, setval() assumes that the new setting is for an initialized sequence; this means that the next value returned by nextval() will actually be incremented once past the value set by setval().

Alternatively, an optional false value of type boolean may be added as the last argument to setval(), de-initializing the sequence. This modifies the sequence so that the next value returned by nextval() will be the same numeric value passed to setval() (though the sequence will of course be incremented on the next call to nextval()).

Example 7-32 sets the shipments_ship_id_seq's last_value to 1010 through each method, and selects the nextval() on the same sequence to illustrate the effective result.

Example 7-32: Setting a sequence value

```
booktown=# SELECT setval('shipments_ship_id_seq', 1010);
 setval
--------
   1010
(1 row)

booktown=# SELECT nextval('shipments_ship_id_seq');
 nextval
---------
    1011
(1 row)

booktown=# SELECT setval('shipments_ship_id_seq', 1010, false);
 setval
--------
   1010
(1 row)

booktown=# SELECT nextval('shipments_ship_id_seq');
 nextval
---------
    1010
(1 row)
```

Sequences are commonly used to ensure unique values in a column. Be sure that you understand the application of a sequence before you reset its last_value attribute.

Destroying a sequence

To destroy a sequence, or several sequences simultaneously, use the DROP
SEQUENCE SQL command. Here is the syntax for DROP SEQUENCE:

```
DROP SEQUENCE sequencename [, ...]
```

In this syntax, *sequencename* is the name of the sequence that you wish to remove.
Multiple sequence names may be specified, separated by commas.

Example 7-33 removes the shipments_ship_id_seq sequence.

Example 7-33: Removing a sequence

```
booktown=# DROP SEQUENCE shipments_ship_id_seq;
DROP
```

Before destroying a sequence, make sure that the sequence is not used by another
table, function, or any other object in the database. If this check is not performed,
then other operations that rely on the sequence will fail. The following query will
return the name of any relation which relies on a default sequence value, where
sequence_name is the name of the sequence you are interesting in finding dependencies for:

```
SELECT p.relname, a.adsrc FROM pg_class p
     JOIN pg_attrdef a ON (p.relfilenode = a.adrelid)
     WHERE a.adsrc ~ '"sequence_name"';
```

Example 7-34 uses this query to look up the name of any table with a default
value involving the shipments_ship_id_seq sequence.

Example 7-34: Checking sequence dependencies

```
booktown=# SELECT p.relname, a.adsrc FROM pg_class p JOIN pg_attrdef a
booktown-#                           ON (p.relfilenode = a.adrelid)
booktown-#          WHERE a.adsrc ~ '"shipments_ship_id_seq"';
  relname  |                 adsrc
-----------+---------------------------------------------
 shipments | nextval('"shipments_ship_id_seq"'::text)
(1 row)
```

Triggers

Often, anticipated SQL events should precede or follow a particular action. This
action might be a consistency check on a set of values to be inserted, the formatting of supplied data before it is inserted, or a modification to a separate table following the removal or modification of a set of rows. Traditionally, such actions are
handled at the programmatic level within an application connected to the
database, rather than by the database software itself.

To ease the responsibility of the application's database interaction, PostgreSQL supports a non-standard programmatic extension known as a *trigger*. A trigger defines a function which occurs before, or after, another action on a table. A trigger is implemented through C, Pl/pgSQL or any other *functional language* (with the exception of SQL) that PostgreSQL can use to define a function (see the section titled "Extending PostgreSQL" later in this chapter for more on creating functions, or Chapter 11, *PL/pgSQL* for more on PL/pgSQL).

As triggers are a PostgreSQL-specific extension, be sure not to implement a trigger-based solution when a high degree of portability to other RDBMS systems is important.

Triggers may affect any of the following SQL events on a table:

* INSERT
* UPDATE
* DELETE

Creating a trigger

In order to create a trigger, a function must first exist for it to execute. PostgreSQL supports many types of functions, including those defined by SQL, PL/pgSQL, and C. As of PostgreSQL 7.1.x, a trigger may use a function defined in any language, with the exception that the function cannot be defined as a purely SQL function.

Once a function is defined, a trigger may be defined to call that function either before or after an event on a specified table. Here is the syntax to create a trigger, followed by a description of its syntax:

```
CREATE TRIGGER name { BEFORE | AFTER } { event [ OR event ... ] }
        ON tablename
        FOR EACH { ROW | STATEMENT }
        EXECUTE PROCEDURE functionname ( arguments )
```

CREATE TRIGGER *name*

> *name* is any arbitrary name for the new trigger. A trigger may have the same name as an existing trigger in a database provided that it is defined to operate on a different table. Also, like most other non-system database objects, triggers must only have a unique name (and table to operate on) within the database they are created in.

{ BEFORE | AFTER }

The BEFORE keyword instructs the defined function to be executed before the event is attempted, which also precedes any built-in constraint checking on the values involved in the case of an INSERT or DELETE event. Alternatively, the AFTER keyword causes the function to be called only after the attempted action has finished.

{ event [OR event ...] }

event is any one of the supported SQL events; multiple events may be listed, separated by the OR keyword.

ON tablename

tablename is the name of the table which, when modified by event, initiates this trigger.

FOR EACH { ROW | STATEMENT }

The keyword following the FOR EACH clause determines how many times the function should be called when the defined event is triggered. Use the ROW keyword to specify that the function is to be executed once for *each affected row*. Conversely, if the function should be executed only once for the calling statement, the STATEMENT keyword is used.

EXECUTE PROCEDURE functionname (arguments)

functionname is the name of the existing function to be executed, with passed arguments.

Only the database object's owner, or a super user, can create a trigger on a database object.

While PostgreSQL tables support constraints to perform simple checks against static criteria, sometimes more involved procedures may be needed to validate input values. This is a typical example of where a trigger might be useful.

A trigger may be used to validate input values by preparing a validation function to be executed *before* values are inserted into a table, or before values in a table are updated. The function can then be made responsible for verifying that the values meet a complex set of restrictions, and even return an appropriate error through PostgreSQL's error logging system.

Suppose that you have written a function in a procedural language that validates attempted INSERT or UPDATE values on the shipments table, and that then performs an update on the stock table to decrement the inventory for the shipment. This function could be written in any language that PostgreSQL supports (with the noted exception of pure SQL).

Specifically, suppose that this function verifies that both the provided customer_id and isbn exist in their respective customers and editions tables. If at least one is missing, a meaningful error is returned. Otherwise, the SQL statement is allowed to execute, and on a successful INSERT statement, the stock table is automatically decremented to reflect the drop in stock from the shipment.

Example 7-35 creates a trigger to be "fired" immediately before an INSERT or UPDATE statement is processed on the shipments table. The trigger invokes the check_shipment_addition() function once per each modified row.

Example 7-35: Creating the check_shipment trigger

```
booktown=# CREATE TRIGGER check_shipment
booktown-#                 BEFORE INSERT OR UPDATE
booktown-#                 ON shipments FOR EACH ROW
booktown-#                 EXECUTE PROCEDURE check_shipment_addition();
CREATE
```

Since the check_shipment trigger is configured to execute the check_shipment_addition() function for both INSERT and UPDATE statements, the integrity of the customer_id and isbn columns are fairly robustly maintained. Its use of the ROW keyword ensures that each added or modified row will be processed by the check_shipment_addition() validation function.

No arguments are passed to the check_shipment_addition() function, as it uses internal PL/pgSQL variables to check incoming rows. See Example 11-53, in Chapter 11, for the implementation of the check_shipment_addition() function, written in PL/pgSQL.

Viewing a trigger

Triggers are stored in the pg_trigger PostgreSQL system table, and can have their characteristics queried after creation. The structure of the pg_trigger table is shown in Table 7-3.

Table 7-3. The pg_trigger table

Column	Type
tgrelid	oid
tgname	name
tgfoid	oid
tgtype	smallint
tgenabled	boolean
tgisconstraint	boolean

Table 7-3. The pg_trigger table (continued)

Column	Type
tgconstrname	name
tgconstrrelid	oid
tgdeferrable	boolean
tginitdeferred	boolean
tgnargs	smallint
tgattr	int2vector
tgargs	bytea

Most of the columns in the Table 7-3 column are unlikely to be useful in a direct query. The most immediately relevant attributes of the pg_trigger system table are tgrelid and tgname.

The tgrelid value is the trigger's relation identifier number. This value is of type oid, and corresponds to the relfilenode column in the pg_class system table. The tgname is the identifier which represents the name of the trigger, as specified in the CREATE TRIGGER command when the trigger was created.

Removing a trigger

The DROP TRIGGER command removes a trigger permanently from the database. Similar to the CREATE TRIGGER command, using this command requires you to be either the owner of the trigger, or a superuser.

Here is the syntax to remove an existing trigger:

```
DROP TRIGGER name ON table
```

Example 7-36 drops the check_shipment trigger placed on the shipments table.

Example 7-36: Dropping a trigger

```
booktown=# DROP TRIGGER check_shipment ON shipments;
DROP
```

The DROP statement indicates that the trigger was successfully dropped. Notice that you must specify not only the *name* of the trigger that you wish to remove, but also the *table* on which it is placed.

If you are unsure which table a particular trigger is placed on, you can derive this information from PostgreSQL's system tables. For example, you can perform a join between the pg_trigger system table's tgrelid column and the pg_class system table's relfilenode column, comparing the name of the trigger against the tgname column. Example 7-37 demonstrates such a query to check the assigned relation (relname) associated with the trigger named check_shipment.

Example 7-37: Selecting a trigger's assigned table

```
booktown=# SELECT relname FROM pg_class
booktown-#                INNER JOIN pg_trigger
booktown-#                ON (tgrelid = relfilenode)
booktown-#                WHERE tgname = 'check_shipment';
   relname
-----------
  shipments
(1 row)
```

 If you drop a function that a trigger is defined to use, the trigger will fail, and redefining the function with the same name will not correct the problem. Such a trigger must be recreated after its function is recreated.

Transactions and Cursors

PostgreSQL uses a multi-version approach to transactions within the database. A *transaction* is a formal term for a SQL statement's effects being synchronized with the "current" data in the database. This doesn't necessarily mean that the data is written to disk, but it becomes part of the "current" set of information stored in the database. When a statement's results have effectively been processed in the current state of the database, the transaction is considered to be *committed*.

The issue of two users attempting to commit changes to the same database object is obviously a potential concern, as their modifications may be exclusive to one another. Some database systems rely on *locking* to prevent such conflicts.

Locking is a mechanism that disallows selecting from a database object while it is being modified, and vice versa. Locking presents several obvious performance concerns. For example, data which is being updated will not be selectable until the update transaction has completed.

PostgreSQL's Multi-Version Concurrency Control (MVCC), however, allows for SQL statements to be performed within transaction-deferred *blocks*. This means that each connection to PostgreSQL essentially maintains a temporary snapshot of the database for objects modified within a transaction block, before the modifications are committed.

Without explicitly opening a transaction block, all SQL statements issued to PostgreSQL are *auto-committed*, meaning that the database is synchronized with the results of the statement immediately upon execution. When a transaction block is used, however, changes made to the database will not be visible to other users until the block is committed. This allows for several changes to various objects within a database to be made tentatively. They can then be either committed all at once, or rolled back.

Rolling back a transaction returns the state of any affected objects to the condition they were in before the transaction block began. This can be useful when recovering from a partially failed operation, in that any modifications made part-way into a process can be undone. Rolled back transactions are never actually committed; while the process appears to undo modifications to the user who performed the rollback, other users connected to the same database never know the difference.

PostgreSQL also supports *cursors*, which are flexible references to fully executed SQL queries. A cursor is able to traverse up and down a result set, and only retrieve those rows which are explicitly requested. Used properly, a cursor can aid an application in efficiently using a static result set. A cursor may only be executed within a transaction block.

The following sections cover the basic use of transactions and cursors. They show how to begin, commit, and roll back transactions, and also how to declare, move, and fetch data from a cursor.

Using Transaction Blocks

Transaction blocks are explicitly started with the BEGIN SQL command. This keyword may optionally be followed by either of the noise terms WORK or TRANSACTION, though they have no effect on the statement, or the transaction block.

Example 7-38 begins a transaction block within the booktown database.

Example 7-38: Beginning a transaction

```
booktown=# BEGIN;
BEGIN
```

Any SQL statement made after the BEGIN SQL command will appear to take effect as normal to the user making the modifications. As stated earlier, however, other users connected to the database will be oblivious to the modifications that appear to have been made from within the transaction block until it is committed.

Transaction blocks are closed with the COMMIT SQL command, which may be followed by either of the optional noise terms WORK or TRANSACTION. Example 7-39 uses the COMMIT SQL command to synchronize the database system with the result of an UPDATE statement.

Example 7-39: Committing a transaction

```
booktown=# BEGIN;
BEGIN
booktown=# UPDATE subjects SET location = NULL
```

Example 7-39: Committing a transaction (continued)

```
booktown-#                    WHERE id = 12;
UPDATE 1
booktown=# SELECT location FROM subjects WHERE id = 12;
 location
----------


(1 row)

booktown=# COMMIT;
COMMIT
```

Again, even though the SELECT statement immediately reflects the result of the UPDATE statement in Example 7-39, other users connected to the same database will not be aware of that modification until after the COMMIT statement is executed.

To roll back a transaction, the ROLLBACK SQL command is used. Again, either of the optional noise terms WORK or TRANSACTION may follow the ROLLBACK command.

Example 7-40 begins a transaction block, makes a modification to the subjects table, and verifies the modification within the block. The transaction is then rolled back, returning the table to the state it was in before the transaction began.

Example 7-40: Rolling back a transaction

```
booktown=# BEGIN;
BEGIN
booktown=# SELECT * FROM subjects WHERE id = 12;
 id | subject  | location
----+----------+----------
 12 | Religion |
(1 row)

booktown=# UPDATE subjects SET location = 'Sunset Dr'
booktown-#                    WHERE id = 12;
UPDATE 1
booktown=# SELECT * FROM subjects WHERE id = 12;
 id | subject  | location
----+----------+-----------
 12 | Religion | Sunset Dr
(1 row)

booktown=# ROLLBACK;
ROLLBACK
booktown=# SELECT * FROM subjects WHERE id = 12;
 id | subject  | location
----+----------+----------
 12 | Religion |
(1 row)
```

PostgreSQL is very strict about errors in SQL statements inside of transaction blocks. Even an innocuous parse error, such as that shown in Example 7-41, will cause the transaction to enter into the ABORT STATE. This means that no further statements may be executed until either the COMMIT or ROLLBACK command is used to end the transaction block.

Example 7-41: Recovering from the abort state

```
booktown=# BEGIN;
BEGIN
booktown=# SELECT * FROM;
ERROR:  parser: parse error at or near ";"
booktown=# SELECT * FROM books;
NOTICE:  current transaction is aborted, queries ignored until end of transaction
*ABORT STATE*
booktown=# COMMIT;
```

Using Cursors

A SQL cursor in PostgreSQL is a read-only pointer to a fully executed SELECT statement's result set. Cursors are typically used within applications that maintain a persistent connection to the PostgreSQL backend. By executing a cursor, and maintaining a reference to its returned result set, an application can more efficiently manage which rows to retrieve from a result set at different times, without having to re-execute the query with different LIMIT and OFFSET clauses.

Used within a programming Application Programming Interface (API), cursors are often used to allow multiple queries to be executed to a single database backend, which are then tracked and managed separately by the application through references to the cursor. This prevents having to store all of the results in memory within the application.

Cursors are often abstracted within a programming API (such as *libpq*++'s PgCursor class), though they can also be directly created and manipulated through standard SQL commands. For the sake of generality, this section uses *psql* to demonstrate the fundamental concepts of cursors with SQL. The four SQL commands involved with PostgreSQL cursors are DECLARE, FETCH, MOVE and CLOSE.

The DECLARE command both defines and opens a cursor, in effect defining the cursor in memory, and then populating the cursor with information about the result set returned from the executed query. The FETCH command lets you pull rows from an open cursor. The MOVE command moves the "current" location of the cursor within the result set, and the CLOSE command closes the cursor.

 If you are interested in learning how to use cursors within a particular API, consult that API's documentation.

Declaring a cursor

A cursor is both created and executed with the DECLARE SQL command. This process is also referred to as "opening" a cursor. A cursor may be declared only within an existing transaction block, so you must execute a BEGIN command prior to declaring a cursor. Here is the syntax for DECLARE:

```
DECLARE cursorname [ BINARY ] [ INSENSITIVE ] [ SCROLL ]
              CURSOR FOR query
              [ FOR { READ ONLY | UPDATE [ OF column [, ...] ] } ]
```

DECLARE *cursorname*

cursorname is the name of the cursor to create.

[BINARY]

The optional BINARY keyword causes output to be retrieved in binary format instead of standard ASCII; this can be more efficient, though it is only relevant to custom applications, as clients such as *psql* are not built to handle anything but text output.

[INSENSITIVE] [SCROLL]

The INSENSITIVE and SCROLL keywords exist for compliance with the SQL standard, though they each define PostgreSQL's default behavior and are never necessary. The INSENSITIVE SQL keyword exists to ensure that all data retrieved from the cursor remains unchanged from other cursors or connections. Since PostgreSQL requires that cursors be defined within transaction blocks, this behavior is already implied. The SCROLL SQL keyword exists to specify that multiple rows can be selected at a time from the cursor. This is the default in PostgreSQL, even if unspecified.

CURSOR FOR *query*

query is the complete query whose result set will be accessible by the cursor, when executed.

[FOR { READ ONLY | UPDATE [OF *column* [, . . .]] }]

As of PostgreSQL 7.1.x, cursors may only be defined as READ ONLY, and the FOR clause is therefore superfluous.

Example 7-42 begins a transaction block with the BEGIN keyword, and opens a cursor named all_books with SELECT * FROM books as its executed SQL statement.

Example 7-42: Declaring a cursor

```
booktown=# BEGIN;
BEGIN
booktown=# DECLARE all_books CURSOR
booktown-#         FOR SELECT * FROM books;
SELECT
```

The SELECT message returned from Example 7-42 indicates that the statement was executed successfully. This means that the rows retrieved by the query are now accessible from the all_books cursor.

Fetching from a cursor

You may retrieve rows from a cursor with the FETCH SQL command. Here is the syntax for the FETCH SQL command:

```
FETCH [ FORWARD | BACKWARD | RELATIVE ]
      [ # | ALL | NEXT | PRIOR ]
      { IN | FROM } cursor
```

In this syntax diagram, *cursor* is the name of the cursor from which to retrieve row data. A cursor always points to a "current" position in the executed statement's result set, and rows can be retrieved either ahead or behind of the current location. The FORWARD and BACKWARD keywords may be used to specify the direction, though the default is forward. The RELATIVE keyword is a noise term made available for SQL92 compliance.

 The ABSOLUTE keyword can be used, but absolute cursor positioning and fetching are not supported as of PostgreSQL 7.1.x; the cursor will still use relative positioning and provide a notice regarding the state of absolute positioning being unsupported.

Following the direction you may optionally specify a quantity. This quantity may either be a literal number of rows to be returned (in the form of an integer constant) or one of several keywords. The ALL keyword causes returns all rows from the current cursor position. The NEXT keyword (the default) returns the next single row from the current cursor position. The PRIOR keyword causes the single row preceding the current cursor position to be returned.

There is no functional difference between the IN and FROM keywords, but one of these must be specified.

Example 7-43 fetches the first four rows stored in the result set pointed to by the all_books cursor. As a direction is not specified, FORWARD is implied. It then uses a FETCH statement with the NEXT keyword to select the fifth row, and then another FETCH statement with the PRIOR keyword to again select the fourth retrieved row.

Example 7-43: Fetching rows from a cursor

```
booktown=# FETCH 4 FROM all_books;
  id  |          title          | author_id | subject_id
------+-------------------------+-----------+------------
```

Example 7-43: Fetching rows from a cursor (continued)

```
  7808 | The Shining               |  4156 |        9
  4513 | Dune                      |  1866 |       15
  4267 | 2001: A Space Odyssey     |  2001 |       15
  1608 | The Cat in the Hat        |  1809 |        2
(4 rows)
```

```
booktown=# FETCH NEXT FROM all_books;
   id  |          title             | author_id | subject_id
-------+----------------------------+-----------+------------
  1590 | Bartholomew and the Oobleck |     1809 |          2
(1 row)
```

```
booktown=# FETCH PRIOR FROM all_books;
   id  |       title       | author_id | subject_id
-------+-------------------+-----------+------------
  1608 | The Cat in the Hat |     1809 |          2
(1 row)
```

Moving a cursor

A cursor maintains a position in the result set of its referenced SELECT statement. You can use the MOVE command to move the cursor to a specified row position in that result set. Here is the syntax for the MOVE command:

```
MOVE [ FORWARD | BACKWARD | RELATIVE ]
     [ # | ALL | NEXT | PRIOR ]
     { IN | FROM } cursor
```

As you can see, the syntax is very similar to FETCH. However, the MOVE command does not retrieve any rows and only moves the current position of the specified *cursor*. The amount is specified by either an integer constant, the ALL keyword (to move as far as can be moved in the specified direction), NEXT, or PRIOR. Example 7-44 moves the cursor forward 10 rows from its current position in the result set.

Example 7-44: Moving a cursor

```
booktown=# MOVE FORWARD 10
booktown-#          IN all_books;
MOVE
```

Closing a cursor

Use the CLOSE command to explicitly close an open cursor. A cursor is also implicitly closed if the transaction block that it resides within is committed with the COMMIT command, or rolled back with the ROLLBACK command.

Here is the syntax for CLOSE, where *cursorname* is the name of the cursor intended to be closed:

```
CLOSE cursorname
```

Example 7-45 closes the all_books cursor, freeing the associated memory, and rendering the cursor's results inaccessible.

Example 7-45: Closing a cursor

```
booktown=# CLOSE all_books;
CLOSE
booktown=# COMMIT;
COMMIT
```

Extending PostgreSQL

PostgreSQL users have the option of extending the set of functions and operators available. If you have a common SQL or programmatic routine, custom functions can be an effective way to more succinctly and efficiently accomplish your tasks. Likewise, custom operators can be created to call these functions (or existing built-in functions) in order to make more efficient and legible SQL statements.

Functions and operators each exist as database objects, and are thus tied to a specific database. Creating a function while connected to the booktown database, for example, creates a function object available only to users connected to booktown.

If you intend to re-use some general functions or operators in multiple databases, you should create them in the template1 database. This will clone the function and operator objects from template1 when a new database is created.

The following sections cover the creation, use, and removal of custom functions and operators.

Creating New Functions

PostgreSQL supports a variation of the SQL99 CREATE FUNCTION command. It is not directly compatible with the standard, but it does allow for a variety of means to extend PostgreSQL by creating your own customized functions (see Chapter 5, *Operators and Functions*, for more on functions in general).

Here is the syntax for CREATE FUNCTION:

```
CREATE FUNCTION name ( [ argumenttype [, ...] ] )
                RETURNS returntype
                AS 'definition'
                LANGUAGE 'languagename'
                [ WITH ( attribute [, ...] ) ]
```

CREATE FUNCTION *name* ([*argumenttype* [, ...]])

name is the name of the new function to be created. The parenthetically grouped *argumenttype* expression defines the data types of the arguments that the function requires when called, separated by commas. Leaving this expression blank results in a function which accepts no arguments (though the parentheses are still required in both definition and usage).

RETURNS *returntype*

The *returntype* is the single data type of the value which is returned by the function.

AS '*definition*'

definition is the programmatic definition of the function itself. For procedural languages, such as PL/pgSQL, this is the literal code used to define the function. For compiled C functions, this is the absolute system path which links to the file containing the object code.

LANGUAGE '*languagename*'

languagename is the name of the language which the function is written in. The language may be any supported procedural language (such as *plpgsql*, or *plperl*, assuming it has been added to the database), *C*, or *SQL*.

[WITH (*attribute* [, ...])]

As of PostgreSQL 7.1.x, two possible values exist for *attribute*; iscachable, and isstrict:

iscachable

This attribute lets the optimizer know if it is acceptable to pre-evaluate a call to a function with arguments that have already been evaluated once. This can be useful for functions which are programmatically expensive, but not terribly dynamic (e.g., functions with which the same input arguments will invariably return the same results).

isstrict

Causes the function to always return a NULL value whenever *any* of its arguments are NULL values. The function is actually not executed in such a case, when isstrict is defined.

Functions may be *overloaded* (i.e., share the same name as an existing function) by defining them as accepting different arguments. In this way you can have a single function name that can perform several operations, depending on the number and type of the input arguments.

Creating SQL functions

The simplest kind of function to add to PostgreSQL is a pure SQL function, as it requires no external programming knowledge or experience. A SQL function is merely defined as a standard SQL statement with support for inline arguments passed as *positional parameters.*

A positional parameter is a reference used in a SQL function definition to one of the calling arguments. It is called *positional* because it is referenced by the order in which the arguments are passed to the function. The syntax of a positional parameter is a dollar sign followed by a number (e.g., $1). The number represents the ordered position in the arguments passed to the function, starting with 1.

Example 7-46 creates a function named isbn_to_title, which returns the title of a book when passed the ISBN number of the book. It accepts a single argument of type text, and returns its result as the same type.

Example 7-46: Creating a SQL function

```
booktown=# CREATE FUNCTION isbn_to_title(text) RETURNS text
booktown-#                 AS 'SELECT title FROM books
booktown'#                         JOIN editions AS e (isbn, id)
booktown'#                         USING (id)
booktown'#                         WHERE isbn = $1'
booktown-#                 LANGUAGE 'SQL';
CREATE
```

Notice the $1 in Example 7-46; when the select statement executes, the complete value of the first argument to isbn_to_title replaces this positional parameter. Notice that the positional parameter does not need to be bound by single quotes, as the quotes are part of the argument passed. Each other element of the function definition is either a standard SQL keyword or identifier.

The CREATE message indicates that the function was successfully created. Example 7-47 calls the isbn_to_title function with a single text parameter of *0929605942.* The function returns the title associated with that ISBN, as per the SQL defined in Example 7-46.

Example 7-47: Using a SQL function

```
booktown=# SELECT isbn_to_title('0929605942');
    isbn_to_title
---------------------
 The Tell-Tale Heart
(1 row)
```

Once created, any user may access the function, presuming that they have the permission to execute the SQL involved. For example, the isbn_to_title function requires read access to the editions and books tables (see Chapter 10, *User and Group Management,* for more information on user privileges).

Creating C functions

PostgreSQL is written in C and can dynamically load compiled C code for use on the fly, without recompilation of the base software. Only superusers are allowed to use CREATE FUNCTION to link to a C function, as functions can make system-level calls and potentially provide a security hole.

Documenting the entire PostgreSQL API is outside the scope of this book, but for an experienced programmer, some basic C functions can very easily be developed, compiled and linked through loadable *shared object* code.

The GNU C Compiler, *gcc*, supports a flag called *-shared*, which creates a dynamically loadable piece of object code. The most basic syntax to create such a function with *gcc* is:

```
$ gcc -shared input.c -o output.so
```

In this syntax, *input.c* is the name of the file containing the C code to be compiled, and *output.so* is the shared object file to build.

Example 7-48 is an extremely simple pair of C functions. They define two C functions called is_zero(int) and is_zero_two(int, int). The first function returns true (1) if the passed argument to it is 0; otherwise, it returns false (0). The second function returns true if at least one of the passed arguments is 0.

Example 7-48: is_zero.c, a simple C function

```c
/* is_zero.c
 * A pair of simple zero-checking functions.
 */

int is_zero(int);
int is_zero_two(int, int);

int is_zero(int incoming) {
   /* Return true only if the incoming value is 0. */
   if (incoming == 0) return 1;
   else return 0;
}

int is_zero_two(int left, int right) {
   /* Return true only if either of the values are 0. */
   if (left == 0 || right == 0) return 1;
   else return 0;
}
```

No PostgreSQL-specific headers are included in this extremely basic example. They are not required in this case because of the obvious parallels between the example C and SQL data types. For more advanced examples of the internal PostgreSQL API and data structures, check the *contrib* directory within the PostgreSQL source path.

Example 7-49 compiles the file *is_zero.c*, with the –shared flag, and outputs the shared object code to a file called *is_zero.so*. The location of that file is then passed as the *definition* of the function to the CREATE FUNCTION command, and the function type is defined as *C*.

Example 7-49: Creating a C function

```
[jworsley@cmd ~]$ gcc -shared is_zero.c -o is_zero.so
[jworsley@cmd ~]$ psql -U manager booktown
Welcome to psql, the PostgreSQL interactive terminal.

Type:  \copyright for distribution terms
       \h for help with SQL commands
       \? for help on internal slash commands
       \g or terminate with semicolon to execute query
       \q to quit


booktown=# CREATE FUNCTION is_zero(int4) RETURNS Boolean
booktown-#                   AS '/home/jworsley/is_zero.so' LANGUAGE 'C';
CREATE
```

The CREATE FUNCTION command in Example 7-49 creates a function named is_zero(), which accepts a single argument of type int4 and returns a value of type boolean. This function references the C function is_zero(int) implemented in the object code located at */home/jworsley/is_zero.so* (since C has no Boolean type, PostgreSQL must transform the integer value returned by the function to a Boolean value). In this case, 0 is translated to false, and 1 is translated to true.

By default, PostgreSQL looks for a function in the shared object code with the same name as the function being created within PostgreSQL. This works well for the is_zero(integer) function, as its name matches the compiled symbol name of the is_zero(int) function within the file *is_zero.so*. In order to avoid a C name-collision with is_zero(int), the second function in the shared object is defined as is_zero_two(int, int). To load this function into PostgreSQL with the same name (as an overloaded function, with two arguments instead of one), pass the literal C function name (also called the link symbol) as a second string constant following the location of the shared object filename.

This name should not contain parentheses or arguments, and should be separated from the filename *definition* by a comma, as in the following syntax:

```
CREATE FUNCTION name ( [ argumenttype [, ...] ] )
              RETURNS returntype
              AS 'definition', 'link_symbol'
              LANGUAGE 'C'
              [ WITH ( attribute [, ...] ) ]
```

Example 7-50 loads the same shared object code, but specifies the function symbol name as is_zero_two so that it knows which function to use for this overloaded function.

Example 7-50: Overloading a C function

```
booktown=# CREATE FUNCTION is_zero(int4, int4) RETURNS Boolean
booktown-#                  AS '/home/jworsley/is_zero.so', 'is_zero_two'
booktown-#                  LANGUAGE 'C';
CREATE
```

Like a SQL function, any user may call the C function once it has been created. As C functions can make direct modifications to the filesystem (where permissions allow) and affect other system level events, care must be taken in designing functions free from potential misuse. Example 7-51 makes several calls to the is_zero function defined in Example 7-49, and to its overloaded function, created in Example 7-50.

Example 7-51: Using a C function

```
booktown=# SELECT is_zero(0) AS zero, is_zero(1) AS one,
booktown-#        is_zero(6, 0) AS one_zero, is_zero(11,12) AS neither;
 zero | one | one_zero | neither
------+-----+----------+---------
 t    | f   | t        | f
(1 row)
```

Destroying functions

Functions may be destroyed either by their owner or by a superuser with the DROP FUNCTION SQL command. Here is the syntax for DROP FUNCTION:

```
DELETE FUNCTION name ( [ argumenttype [, ...] ] );
```

For example, Example 7-52 drops the isbn_to_title(text) function. Note that the argument types are *required* to be specified, even though the function itself is not overloaded.

Example 7-52: Dropping a function

```
booktown=# DROP FUNCTION isbn_to_title(text);
DROP
```

The DROP server message indicates that the function was successfully dropped. Like most DROP SQL commands, this action is permanent, so be sure that you wish to drop your function before you execute this command.

Creating New Operators

PostgreSQL allows the creation of custom operators in addition to custom functions. Operators are sometimes called *syntactic sugar* for functions. This is because, technically, an operator is just an alternate syntax for an existing function. For example, the addition operator (+) actually calls one of several built-in functions, including `numeric_add()`. For example:

```
booktown=# SELECT 1 + 2 AS by_operator, numeric_add(1,2) AS by_function;
 by_operator | by_function
-------------+-------------
           3 |           3
(1 row)
```

An operator definition defines what data types it operates on, and which side of the operator to expect a value of the given data type to be found on (left, right, or both). It also defines the function that is called, passing the values that are being operated on as arguments to that function.

Creating an operator

The `CREATE OPERATOR` SQL command creates a new operator. Here is the syntax for `CREATE OPERATOR`:

```
CREATE OPERATOR name ( PROCEDURE = functionname
                     [, LEFTARG = type1 ]
                     [, RIGHTARG = type2 ]
                     [, COMMUTATOR = commutatorop ]
                     [, NEGATOR = negatorop ]
                     [, RESTRICT = restrictproc ]
                     [, JOIN = joinproc ]
                     [, HASHES ]
                     [, SORT1 = leftsortop ]
                     [, SORT2 = rightsortop ] )
```

In this syntax, *name* is the name of the new operator, and *functionname* is the name of the function to be called by the operator. The remaining clauses are all optional, though at least one of the `LEFTARG` or `RIGHTARG` clauses must be applied. Note that the operator *name* may only consist of the following accepted characters:

```
+ - * / < > = ~ ! @ # % ^ & | ` ? $
```

See the reference entry on `CREATE OPERATOR` for more information on the remaining optional clauses, and further restrictions on the operator name.

Specifying only the LEFTARG data type creates an operator that operates only on a value (e.g., a constant or identifier) to its left. Conversely, specifying only the RIGHTARG data type creates an operator that operates only on a value to its right. Specifying both a LEFTARG and RIGHTARG type results in an operator that operates on a value to both the left *and* right.

The factorial operator (!) is an example of a built-in operator that affects values to its left, while the addition operator (+) is a good example of an operator that affects values both on the left and right of the operator. Note that the *functionname* must accept the appropriate number of arguments as implied by the use of the LEFTARG and RIGHTARG keywords (either one or two arguments). Furthermore, the function's accepted argument types should match the relevant operator types defined by CREATE OPERATOR for each respective value to be operated on.

Example 7-53 creates an operator named !#, which passes the value to its left to the is_zero() function (defined in Example 7-49). This means that the syntax of value !# will be effectively identical to using the functional syntax of is_zero(value).

Example 7-53: Creating a user-defined operator

```
booktown=# CREATE OPERATOR !# (PROCEDURE = is_zero,
booktown(#                     LEFTARG = integer);
CREATE
```

The CREATE message returned by Example 7-53 indicates that the operator was successfully created. As with functions, any user connected to the database will be able to use the new operator. The operator is owned by the user who creates it, meaning that no other user may remove it (unless they have superuser rights). Example 7-54 demonstrates the use of the new !# operator to check for books that are out of stock in Book Town's stock table.

Example 7-54: Using a user-defined operator

```
booktown=# SELECT * FROM stock WHERE stock !#;
    isbn    | cost  | retail | stock
------------+-------+--------+-------
 0394900014 | 23.00 | 23.95  |    0
 0451198492 | 36.00 | 46.95  |    0
 0451457994 | 17.00 | 22.95  |    0
(3 rows)
```

Overloading an operator

Operators may become overloaded in much the same way as functions. This means that an operator is created with the same name as an existing operator, but affects a different set of defined types. More than one operator may have the same name, although two operators may not share the same name if they accept the same argument definitions. As long as a function exists to accept the number and type of arguments implied by the type of operator defined, though, the operator may be overloaded.

Example 7-53 overloads the !# operator. The first CREATE OPERATOR statement creates a similar operator to the one created in Example 7-53. However, it specifies a RIGHTARG clause rather than a LEFTARG clause, resulting in a version of the operator with the same name which operates on an argument of type integer to the *right* of the operator, rather than the left. The second statement creates a third variant of the !# operator, which operates on both an argument to the left *and* right of the operator, simultaneously.

Example 7-55: Overloading a user-defined operator

```
booktown=# CREATE OPERATOR !# (PROCEDURE = is_zero,
booktown(#                     RIGHTARG = integer);
CREATE
booktown=# CREATE OPERATOR !# (PROCEDURE = is_zero,
booktown(#                     LEFTARG = integer,
booktown(#                     RIGHTARG = integer);
CREATE
```

Example 7-55 overloads the !# operator with the same is_zero() function because the function itself was overloaded in Example 7-50 in the section titled "Creating C functions," earlier in this chapter. As there are two copies of the is_zero() function—one that accepts one argument, and one that accepts two—the !# operator can be safely overloaded to accept both a single argument (on either the left or right side), as well as to accept parameters from both sides.

Once overloaded, PostgreSQL's parser can correctly interpret each defined operator in your SQL statements. Example 7-56 demonstrates three uses of the same operator, with different left and right arguments. Each use is valid, as the operator was overloaded in Example 7-55.

Example 7-56: Using an overloaded operator

```
booktown=# SELECT isbn, stock FROM stock
booktown-#                    WHERE stock !#
booktown-#                    AND !# stock
booktown-#                    AND stock !# stock;
    isbn    | stock
------------+-------
 0394900014 |     0
 0451198492 |     0
 0451457994 |     0
(3 rows)
```

Dropping an operator

An operator can be dropped with the DROP OPERATOR command. An operator may only be dropped by the user who created it, or by a PostgreSQL superuser.

 The DROP OPERATOR command applies to built-in operators as well as user-defined operators, so take care with this command if executing it as a superuser!

As operators are defined by their arguments as well as their name, DROP OPERATOR requires that you specify the left and right argument types of the operator. If there is no type for a given side, specify the NONE keyword.

Here is the syntax for DROP OPERATOR:

```
DROP OPERATOR name ( { lefttype | NONE } , { righttype | NONE } )
```

Example 7-57 drops the variant of the !# operator that affects both left and right arguments.

Example 7-57: Dropping an operator

```
booktown=# DROP OPERATOR !# (integer, integer);
DROP
```

Example 7-58 uses very similar syntax to Example 7-57, but drops the overloaded operator that affects only arguments to the right of the operator.

Example 7-58: Dropping an overloaded operator

```
booktown=# DROP OPERATOR !# (NONE, integer);
DROP
```

III

Administrating PostgreSQL

8

Authentication and Encryption

This chapter documents the fundamental concepts involved with authenticating and encrypting a client session to the PostgreSQL server. This includes how to correctly configure the *pg_hba.conf* file for a variety of authentication schemes, as well as a few common ways to encrypt your client connections.

Client Authentication

Client authentication is a central feature to PostgreSQL. Without it, you would either have to sacrifice remote connectivity, or blindly allow anyone to connect to your database and retrieve, or even modify your data. PostgreSQL has several different types of client authentication at its disposal. As the site administrator, you need to decide which one is best for your system.

As of PostgreSQL 7.1.x, host-based client access is specified in the *pg_hba.conf* file. The rights and restrictions described in this file should not be confused with a PostgreSQL user's rights to objects within the database. The *pg_hba.conf* file allows you to set the type of *host-based* authentication to be used. This authentication is performed before PostgreSQL establishes a connection to the intended database, where user rights would be relevant.

 The *pg_hba.conf* is located in the PostgreSQL data directory (e.g., */usr/local/pgsql/data*), and is installed automatically upon the execution of the *initdb* command when PostgreSQL is installed.

PostgreSQL's host-based authentication is flexible, featuring a wide variety of configurable options. You may restrict database access to specific hosts, as well as allow access to a range of IP addresses by using netmasks. Each configured host has its own *host record*, which is a single line in the *pg_hba.conf* file.

With these host records, you may specify access either to a particular database or all databases. Furthermore, you may require a user from a specified host to authenticate via the PostgreSQL users table after qualifying for a connection.

Put simply, the *pg_hba.conf* file allows you to determine *who* is allowed to connect to *which* databases from *what* machines, and to *what degree* they must prove their authenticity to gain access.

 Through remote password-based authentication, passwords may be transmitted in clear text depending on whether or not you are using encrypted sessions. Be sure that you understand how your application is communicating with PostgreSQL before allowing users to remotely connect to a PostgreSQL database.

Password Authentication

Passwords allow PostgreSQL users a way to identify themselves and prevent unauthorized individuals from connecting with a user that is not theirs. As of PostgreSQL 7.1.x, user passwords are stored in plain text in the pg_shadow system table. The structure of this table is illustrated in Table 8-1. Note that while the passwords are stored as plain text, only PostgreSQL *superusers* are allowed to view the pg_shadow table.

Table 8-1. The pg_shadow table

Column	Type
usename	name
usesysid	integer
usecreatedb	boolean
usetrace	boolean
usesuper	boolean
usecatupd	boolean
passwd	text
valuntil	abstime

The pg_shadow table is a system table, and thus is accessible from any database. It follows, therefore, that users are not assigned to a specific database. If a user exists in the pg_shadow table, that user will be able to connect to any database on the server machine if the client itself is allowed to connect.

Users typically set passwords in PostgreSQL when the user is created (with the CREATE USER command) or after the user has been created (using the ALTER USER command). Alternatively, you may manually modify a user's password by using an UPDATE statement. (For a more detailed explanation about defining passwords for users, see Chapter 10, *User and Group Management*.)

If a password is not set, a user's password defaults to NULL. If password-based authentication is enabled in the *pg_hba.conf* file, connection attempts will always fail for such a user. Conversely, if the host that establishes the connection is a *trusted* host (such as *localhost*, by default), *anyone* from the trusted host may connect as a user with a NULL password. In fact, passwords are ignored entirely for trusted hosts.

The GRANT command allows you to restrict or allow a variety of access types to tables within a database. See Chapter 10 for more on this topic.

Unless your needs for security are very minimal, you will not want to rely on password-only authentication with your PostgreSQL server. Using a password-only method to authenticate users will allow any verified user access to any database on the system, and authenticating with a password over clear text can result in unauthorized individuals acquiring user passwords. If you are likely to have your database connected to the Internet in some fashion, we strongly suggest that you read the following sections. These cover the use of the *pg_hba.conf* file and session encryption.

The pg_hba.conf file

We mentioned earlier in this section that the *pg_hba.conf* file enables client authentication between the PostgreSQL server and the client application. This file consists of a series of *entries*, which define a host and its associated permissions (e.g., the database it is allowed to connect to, the authentication method to use, and so on).

When an application requests a connection, the request will specify a PostgreSQL username and database with which it intends to connect to PostgreSQL. Optionally, a password may be provided, depending on the expected configuration for the connecting host.

PostgreSQL has its own user and password tables, which are separate from system accounts. It is not required that your PostgreSQL users match users available to the operating system.

When PostgreSQL receives a connection request it will check the *pg_hba.conf* file to verify that the machine from which the application is requesting a connection has rights to connect to the specified database. If the machine requesting access has permission to connect, PostgreSQL will check the conditions that the application must meet in order to successfully authenticate. This affects connections that are initiated locally as well as remotely.

PostgreSQL will check the authentication method via the *pg_hba.conf* for every connection request. This check is performed every time a new connection is requested from the PostgreSQL server, so there is no need to re-start PostgreSQL after you add, modify or remove an entry in the *pg_hba.conf* file. Example 8-1 is a simple example of the *pg_hba.conf* file.

Example 8-1: A simple pg_hba.conf file

```
#                      PostgreSQL HOST ACCESS CONTROL FILE
#
# Configured Hosts:

local  all                                          trust
host   all        127.0.0.1     255.255.255.255     trust
host   booktown   192.168.1.3   255.255.255.255     ident    sales
host   all        192.168.1.4   255.255.255.255     ident    audit
```

When a connection is initialized, PostgreSQL will read through the *pg_hba.conf* one entry at a time, from the top down. As soon a matching record is found, PostgreSQL will stop searching and allow or reject the connection, based on the found entry. If PostgreSQL does not find a matching entry in the *pg_hba.conf* file, the connection fails completely.

Table-level permissions still apply to a database, even if a user has permissions to connect to the database. If you can connect, but cannot select data from a table, you may want to verify that your connected user has permission to use SELECT on that table. Using the *psql* command-line application, you can check the permissions of the tables within a database by using the \z slash command. From any other interface to PostgreSQL, use the query demonstrated in Example 8-2 to see the same information provided by the \z slash command.

Example 8-2: Checking user permissions

```
testdb=# SELECT relname as "Relation", relacl as "Access permissions"
testdb=#        FROM pg_class
testdb=#        WHERE  relkind IN ('r', 'v', 'S')
testdb=#        AND relname !~ '^pg_'
testdb=#        ORDER BY relname;
 Relation |       Access permissions
----------+--------------------------------
  foo     | {"=arwR","jdrake=arwR"}
  my_list | {"=","jdrake=arwR","jworsley=r"}
(2 rows)
```

Structure of the pg_hba.conf file

The *pg_hba.conf* file contains sequential entries that define the settings PostgreSQL should use during the client authentication process for a specified host. This file is designed to be easily customizable to your system needs.

Within this file, you may associate a TCP/IP host address (or a range of addresses) with a particular database (or *all* databases), and one of several available authentication methods. You may also specify access for local connections using the term localhost, or 127.0.0.1, rather than using the system's external IP address. Several syntax rules apply to the *pg_hba.conf*.

First, you may only place one host record per line in the file. Subsequently, host records are not allowed to wrap across multiple lines. Second, each host record must contain multiple fields, which must be separated by either tabs or spaces. The number of fields in a host record is directly related to the type of host entry being defined. Example 8-3 shows two host records, the first with the fields separated by spaces, and the second with the file separated by tabs.

Example 8-3: A valid pg_hba.conf entry with spaces and tabs

```
host all 127.0.0.1 255.255.255.255 trust
host    all    127.0.0.1        255.255.255.255  trust
```

Commenting is allowed within *pg_hba.conf* by placing a hash mark (#) at the beginning of each line being commented. Example 8-4 demonstrates valid commented lines.

Example 8-4: Valid pg_hba.conf comments

```
# Book Town host entries
#
#
host all 127.0.0.1 255.255.255.255 trust
```

Regarding the actual form of each host record, there are three general *types* available in the *pg_hba.conf* (the *type* keyword is always the first word in the host record).

host

A host entry is used to specify remote hosts that are allowed to connect to the PostgreSQL server. PostgreSQL's *postmaster* backend must be running with the -*i* option (TCP/IP) in order for a host entry to work correctly.

local

A local entry is semantically the same as a host entry. However, you do not need to specify a host that is allowed to connect. The local entry is used for client connections that are initiated from the same machine that the PostgreSQL server is operating on.

hostssl

A hostssl entry is user to specify hosts (remote or local) that are allowed to connect to the PostgreSQL server using SSL. The use of SSL insures that all communication between the client and the server is encrypted. In order for this to work, both the client and the server must support SSL. The *postmaster* backend must be running with the -*l* (SSL) and -*i* (TCP/IP) options.

See Chapter 9, *Database Management* for more on how to start the *postmaster* process with the appropriate run-time options.

Example 8-5 illustrates the general syntax for each type of host record available within the *pg_hba.conf* file. Notice that the format is essentially identical for each record, with the exception that a *local* record does not require an IP address or netmask to be specified, as the connection is assumed to be from the same machine on which PostgreSQL is running.

Example 8-5: Host entry syntax

```
# A "local" record.
local    database auth_method       [ auth_option ]

# A "host" record.
host     database ip_addr  netmask  auth_method       [ auth_option ]

# A "hostssl" record.
hostssl  database ip_addr  netmask  auth_method       [ auth_option ]
```

Remember that each entry in the *pg_hba.conf* must be a single line. You cannot word wrap or use line breaks.

The following list is a description of the keywords for the *pg_hba.conf* entries mentioned previously:

database

> This is the database name that the specified host is allowed to connect to. The *database* keyword has three possible values:
>
> all
>
>> The all keyword specifies that the client connecting can connect to any database the PostgreSQL server is hosting.
>
> sameuser
>
>> The sameuser keyword specifies that the client can only connect to a database that matches the clients authenticated user name.
>
> name
>
>> A specific *name* may be specified, so that the client can only connect to the database as specified by *name*.

ip_addr, netmask

> The *ip_addr* and *netmask* fields specify either a specific IP address, or range of IP addresses, that are allowed to connect to the PostgreSQL server. Such a range can by specified by describing an IP network with an associated netmask. Otherwise, for a single IP address, the *netmask* field should be set to 255.255.255.255.
>
> If you are unsure of how to specify a netmask, view the online Linux Networking HOWTO, at *http://www.thelinuxreview.com/howto/networking*, or consult your system administrator.

auth_method

> The authentication method specifies the type of authentication the server should use for a user trying to connect to PostgreSQL. The following is a list of options available for *auth_method*:
>
> trust
>
>> The trust method allows any user from the defined host to connect to a PostgreSQL database without the use of a password, as any PostgreSQL user. You are *trusting* the host-based authentication with the use of this method, and any user on the specified host. This is a dangerous condition if the specified host is not a secure machine, or provides access to users unknown to you.
>
> reject
>
>> The reject method automatically denies access to PostgreSQL for that host or user. This can be a prudent setting for sites that you know are *never* allowed to connect to your database server.

password

> The password method specifies that a password must exist for a connect-
> ing user. The use of this method will require the connecting user to sup-
> ply a password that matches the password found in the global pg_shadow
> system table for their username. If you use the password method, the
> password will be sent in clear text.

crypt

> The crypt method is similar to the password method. When using crypt,
> the password is not sent in clear text, but through a simple form of
> encryption. The use of this method is not very secure, but is better than
> using the clear text password method.

krb4, krb5

> The krb4 and krb5 methods are used to specify Version 4 or 5 of the Ker-
> beros authentication system. The installation and configuration of Ker-
> beros is beyond the scope of this book, but if you wish to authenticate via
> Kerberos, these methods are available.

ident

> The ident method specifies that an *ident map* should be used when a
> host is requesting connections from a valid IP address listed in the
> *pg_hba.conf* file. This method requires one option.
>
> The required option may be either the special term sameuser, or a named
> map that is defined within the *pg_ident.conf* file. For more information on
> defining an ident map, see the section titled "The pg_ident.conf file."

auth_option

> The auth_option field may or may not be required, based on the type of
> authentication method that is used; as of PostgreSQL 7.1.x, only the ident
> method requires an option.

We do not suggest the use of either password or crypt without the
use of an external encryption mechanism. See the section titled
"Encrypting Sessions" in this chapter for information on installing a
central encryption mechanism for all of your PostgreSQL traffic.

Example pg_hba.conf entries

This section contains a series of examples that can be used within *pg_hba.conf*. To
begin, the host record within Example 8-6 allows a single machine with the IP
address 192.168.1.10 to connect to any database as any user, without the use of a
password. This is because it is configured with the all and trust terms, respectively.

Example 8-6: Single host entry

```
host    all    192.168.1.10    255.255.255.255  trust
```

Example 8-7 shows a host record which will reject all users from host 192.168.1.10, for any requested database. This is set by the use of the terms `all` and `reject` as the database target and authentication method, respectively.

Example 8-7: Rejection entry

```
host    all    192.168.1.10    255.255.255.255  reject
```

The host record in Example 8-8 will allow any user with the IP of 192.168.1.10, and a valid password, to connect to the database `template1`. The password will be encrypted during authentication because of the use of the term `crypt`.

Example 8-8: Single host, single database entry

```
host    template1    192.168.1.10    255.255.255.255  crypt
```

The host record in Example 8-9 allows a small subnet of computers to access any database, without the need of a password. This subnet describes any IP from 192.168.1.1 to 192.168.1.15. Again, if you are unsure of how to configure your netmask, consult your network administrator, or view the Linux Networking HOWTO at *http://www.thelinuxreview.com/howto/networking.*

Example 8-9: Small network connection entry

```
host    all    192.168.1.0    255.255.255.240  trust
```

Expanding on the use of subnets, the host record in Example 8-10 allows any machine on the 192.168.1 block to connect to the `booktown` database, without the use of a password.

Example 8-10: Larger network connection entry

```
host    booktown 192.168.1.0    255.255.255.0    trust
```

Remember, as stated earlier in this section, each host record line is read in succession from the top of the file to the bottom. The first record which matches the host attempting to connect is used. If no matching record is found, connection is completely disallowed.

The pg_ident.conf file

When specifying the `ident` term as a host record's authentication method, PostgreSQL uses the *pg_ident.conf* file to map the *identifying username* to a PostgreSQL username. The identifying username is the name provided by the connecting client's *identd* service (RFC 1413), which is required to identify the name of the system account initiating the connection. This method is similar to the `trust` method, but restricts access based on the identifying username.

As stated in the specification for the *ident* protocol, "The Identification Protocol is not intended as an authorization or access control protocol." This is only a useful method of identification for secure, controlled machines, and is *not* intended as a means for secure control from a wide array of external machines. This is because an *identd* daemon merely returns an arbitrary username describing the current system user. For example, allowing the username `jworsley` from an entire subnet of IP addresses would create a serious security hole, because anyone with a machine in that subnet could create a user named `jworsley` and become "authenticated" as a result.

The *pg_ident.conf* file should be located in the same path as the *pg_hba.conf* file. This should be the path defined by the **PGDATA** environment variable (e.g., */usr/local/pgsql/data*). Like the *pg_hba.conf*, changes to the *pg_ident.conf* file do not require PostgreSQL to be re-started.

The content of the *pg_ident.conf* associates identifying usernames with PostgreSQL usernames via definitions called ident *maps*. This is useful for users whose system usernames do not match their PostgreSQL usernames. Some rules you should keep in mind when defining and using an ident map are:

- Each ident map *member* is defined on a single line, which associates a map name with an identifying username, and a translated PostgreSQL username.

- The *pg_ident.conf* file can contain multiple map names. Each group of single lines with the same associative map name are considered a single map.

- The *pg_hba.conf* file determines the types of connections that relate to users in this file.

A single line record to define an ident map consists of 3 tokens: the name of the map, the identifying username, and the translated PostgreSQL username. This syntax is entered as follows, where each token is separated by spaces, or tabs:

```
mapname identname postgresqlname
```

`mapname`

> The map name used in the *pg_hba.conf* file to refer to the ident map.

`identname`

> The identifying username, which is generally the name of the system user attempting to establish a connection to the database. This is the name provided by the *identd* daemon, which must be running on the system attempting to connect.

postgresqlname

The database username which is allowed for the preceding identifying username. You may specify several lines with the same *identname*, but with different *postgresqlname* values, in order to allow a single system user access to several accounts, which do not all need to be on the same database.

As an example, suppose that the Book Town server has a set of system accounts named jdrake, jworsley, and auditor, used for two salespeople and an internal auditor, respectively.

You may wish to create a pair of ident maps for these two groups of users. Suppose that the sales department's workstation has an IP address of 192.168.1.3, and only needs access to the booktown database, while the audit department's workstation has an IP address of 192.168.1.4, and requires access to all databases. This scenario might result in a *pga_hba.conf,* such as the one displayed in Example 8-11.

Example 8-11: An ident configuration in pg_hba.conf

```
host    booktown    192.168.1.3    255.255.255.255    ident    sales
host    all         192.168.1.4    255.255.255.255    ident    audit
```

This host access configuration states that the sales machine may connect to the booktown database using an ident map named *sales*, and the audit workstation may connect to *any* database using an ident map named *audit*. Each of these maps must then be configured within the *pg_ident.conf* file. Example 8-12 demonstrates such a configuration.

Example 8-12: A pg_ident.conf configuration

```
# MAP    IDENT       POSTGRESQL_USERNAME
sales    jdrake      sales
sales    jworsley    sales
audit    auditor     sales
audit    auditor     postgres
```

The file shown in Example 8-12 allows either of the system users jdrake or jworsley to connect as the PostgreSQL sales user, and allows the system user named auditor to connect to PostgreSQL as either sales, or postgres.

It is possible for an identifying username to be mapped to multiple PostgreSQL usernames. This is illustrated in Example 8-12 with the auditor user.

If you wish only to use ident as a means of automatically identifying your remote username, you do not need to use the *pg_ident.conf* file. You can instead use the special term `sameuser` in the *pg_hba.conf* file, in place of a map name.

Again, this is similar to the `trusted` method, however `ident sameuser` restricts connections based on the username provided by *identd*. Providing a PostgreSQL username to connect with (e.g., with the *-U* flag to *psql*) that is different from the name sent by *identd* will result in a failure to connect.

Use of the `sameuser` map is demonstrated in Example 8-13.

Example 8-13: A sameuser configuration

```
host   booktown   192.168.1.0   255.255.255.0   ident   sameuser
```

The host record in Example 8-13 allows any machine on the 192.168.1 network block to connect to the `booktown` database, using the PostgreSQL username that matches the username provided by *identd*. The `sameuser` term causes PostgreSQL to implicitly compare the requested PostgreSQL username against the name provided by *identd*.

Authentication Failure

When authentication failure occurs, PostgreSQL will usually do its best to provide a useful error message, rather than blindly fail. The following are common error messages you may encounter, with explanations:

`FATAL 1: user "testuser" does not exist`
> The specified username was not found in the `pg_shadow` system table, meaning the user does not exist. See Chapter 10 for more on adding users.

`FATAL 1: Database "testdb" does not exist in the system catalog`
> This database cannot be found because it does not exist. Note that if you do not specify a database name to a PostgreSQL connection, it will attempt to connect to the provided username.

`No pg_hba.conf entry for host 123.123.123.1, user testuser, database testdb`
> You have succeeded in contacting the server, but the server is not accepting your connection. The server refused the connection because it cannot find an entry for `testuser` using `testdb` at their IP address (123.123.123.1) in the *pg_hba.conf* file.

`Password authentication failed for user 'testuser'`
> You have succeeded in contacting the server and it is replying back, but the connection failed password authorization. Check the password you are supplying to the server, and make sure that it is correct. Further, you can check the Kerberos or Ident software programs if you are using them for your password authentication.

You may want to check if this user has a password. If this user does not have one, and the *pg_hba.conf* file is set to check for passwords, it will still check every user for their password. For all users without a defined password, a NULL password is assigned to that user. When the user tries to log in and does not specify a password, it will compare the NULL password to the NULL input, and it will return false.

On the other hand, if the user tries to supply a password (even a blank one), it will compare that input value with the NULL password and still return false. If you are using password authentication, you must assign a password to all users. If a password is not assigned to a user in such a scheme, password authentication will always fail, and the user will not be able to log in.

Encrypting Sessions

In the digital age, privacy and data integrity have become two of the most talked about areas of computing. It seems that almost every day someone else has been cracked, or a new security hole has been found in an application you once trusted.

At the same time, the encrypting of data sessions has become veritably common place amongst computer users. Every reputable e-commerce site uses *SSL* (the Secure Sockets Layer) to protect user data while transmitting personal information such as credit cards and home addresses across the Internet.

The most common type of crack executed on a machine is not really a "crack" at all. It is usually an unsuspecting user trusting a protocol such as POP or FTP to transfer information over the Internet. By using these protocols, the user can unknowingly transmit their login and password in *clear text* (in an unencrypted form) over the Internet.

The transmission of data such as login names and passwords in clear text over the Internet means that anybody using a *sniffer* program (an application that listens to network traffic between two parties) could potentially gain access to your most personal information. In the world of databases, this scenario is no different.

If you connect remotely to PostgreSQL without the use of an encryption technology, there is a potential for misuse by crackers on the Internet. If a cracker uses a sniffer on your network, or on a network between your client and the database server that you are connecting to, they can gain complete access to the information that is stored within PostgreSQL.

We will cover three general methods of encrypting your data between PostgreSQL and client connections:

Built-in SSL

> The built-in PostgreSQL SSL support, enabled with the *--with-ssl* flag at compilation, allows *psql* (or any client written specifically to connect to PostgreSQL through SSL) to connect securely to PostgreSQL.

SSH/OpenSSH

> An *SSH* (Secure SHell) session may be used to create a *tunnel* to a remote server, provided that an SSH daemon (e.g., *sshd*) is installed and accessible by the connecting user. This requires shell access to the system running PostgreSQL for each user who wishes to connect.

Stunnel

> Stunnel is an application which creates an encrypted tunnel between a client and the PostgreSQL server. The Stunnel method requires shell access to set up, but may be configured to run on a client system for a user who does not have direct shell access to the remote server.

Built-in SSL

PostgreSQL provides the option to compile with support for SSL with the *--with-ssl* configuration parameter. This option is a good choice if you are going to be doing the majority of your work with PostgreSQL in *psql*, as it natively supports this method of connection.

Most people choose to use PostgreSQL as a backend to a variety of client applications. If this is the case, you will either need to develop your own client to understand SSL connections to PostgreSQL, or choose an external method of encrypting sessions between your client or application and the PostgreSQL server (such as with SSH, or Stunnel).

SSH/OpenSSH

OpenSSH provides an excellent method for using external encryption between a client and server. OpenSSH is a commonly implemented standard among security professionals and system administrators. It is most commonly used for terminal or file transfer applications. The SSH protocol is a *general* method of encryption, and it can be applied in a general fashion for just about any application.

Provided that you have access to a system account on the remote server, you may authenticate to that system and open a tunnel between the remote and local hosts with the *-L* flag. Such a tunnel will listen to a specified port on the local machine, encrypt incoming packet data, and forward it to the remote server in an encrypted form. The data will then be decrypted and forwarded to another specified port on the remote server.

In this fashion, you can easily create a generalized encrypted tunnel of data between the client and server. Further, the entire process is invisible to Post-greSQL, which believes it is accepting packet input from the same machine it is running on, from the user which authenticated the creation of the tunnel. Make careful note of this, as your *pg_hba.conf* will need to reflect the appropriate host.

The SSH executable is usually called *ssh*, and can be used to create a tunnel with the following syntax:

```
ssh -L localport:remotehost:remoteport username@remotehost
```

The *localport* is any arbitrary port that you wish to locally listen on. This port must be above 1024, unless you are logged in as the *root* user, which is not advis-able. This number will be the local port that your client believes it is connecting to PostgreSQL on. In actuality, the data received on this port will be forwarded to *remotehost* on its listening SSH port (usually 22), decrypted, and then forwarded again from the remote server to itself, on the specified *remoteport* number.

The phrase *username@remotehost* must be provided in order to authenticate a valid system user. Without a valid system account an SSH tunnel cannot be created. This entire process is demonstrated in Example 8-14, in which the ellipses separate a pair of terminal sessions. The first terminal connection creates the SSH tunnel, and must remain active in order for the tunnel to exist. The second terminal connec-tion actually takes advantage of the tunnel to make a connection to the local tun-nel port, which is then forwarded to the remote host, decrypted, and passed through to the PostgreSQL server.

Example 8-14: Making an SSH tunnel to PostgreSQL

```
[user@local ~]$ ssh -L 4001:remotehost:5432 user@remotehost
user@remotehost's password:
[user@remote ~]$


...


[user@local ~]$ psql -h localhost -p 4001 template1
Welcome to psql, the PostgreSQL interactive terminal.

Type:  \copyright for distribution terms
       \h for help with SQL commands
       \? for help on internal slash commands
       \g or terminate with semicolon to execute query
       \q to quit

template1=#
```

When issuing the ssh command, you may specify the *-T* flag if you don't need to be provided with a command line after creating the SSH tunnel, which is the default behavior. This will cause the terminal to appear to hang after authentication. Such a session may be terminated with CTRL-C when finished.

The only drawback to the use of an SSH tunnel is that it *requires* a system account from the user who is connecting to PostgreSQL. SSH does not provide completely transparent access to encrypted data streams until you initiate a connection and authenticate against the ssh daemon service, which is typically called *sshd*. Depending on your needs this could be a positive or negative restriction.

If you wish to set up an even more generalized encryption tunnel, read through the next section for information on Stunnel.

Configuring and Using Stunnel

While both the built-in SSL and OpenSSH encryption methods provide robust, secure connections to PostgreSQL, they each have their own idiosyncrasies and usage restrictions. Many users of PostgreSQL will therefore be interested to know that there is another dependable encryption method available for use with totally transparent remote access to the server. If you wish to encrypt database sessions transparently for any client, without needing to bind to SSH, this is possible using two easily available tools: OpenSSL and Stunnel.

If you are a Unix or Linux system administrator, you are most likely familiar with one or both of these, as they are quite useful beyond the scope of this context (in so much as encryption *in general* is useful beyond the scope of this context). If you are a system administrator who is not familiar with encryption, it is advisable that you become familiar with the subject.

OpenSSL

The OpenSSL software package is a software project developed by members of the Open Source community. It is a robust set of tools provided to help your system implement the Secure Sockets Layer (SSL), as well as other security-related protocols, such as Transport Layer Security (TLS). It also includes a cryptography library. This software package is important to anyone who is planning on using a fair amount of security on their Linux machine (not limited to PostgreSQL, though that will be our focus). Please note that because it is open-source software, you are able to download it for free, unlike commercial SSL packages that require you to purchase the software and/or licensing.

To download the newest version of OpenSSL, point your web browser to the OpenSSL web page at *http://www.openssl.org*. There should be a list of available versions along with links to download them. There are two types of versions available: major releases and beta copies. There are a couple of older listings for bug fixes. Most likely you will be interested in the newest major release, or a subsequent bug-fix.

A major release should be listed in a fashion similar to this:

```
09-Jul-2001: OpenSSL 0.9.6b is now available, a major release
```

Open the source page through the "available" link. Once there, you can download the most up-to-date version, which will logically be listed with the text "[LATEST]" printed next to it.

Download the file for the version you want, and save it into your home directory (or whichever directory you normally save files to). After it completes downloading, open a console window and *cd* into the directory in which you just saved the file. The file will be tarred and gzipped, so you will need to extract it with the following command (note that *[version]* represents the version number of the software, e.g., *0.9.6b*):

```
gzip -d openssl-[version].tar.gz
```

Then type:

```
tar xf openssl-[version].tar
```

These commands extract the OpenSSL files into a directory named *openssl-[version]* where *[version]* is whatever version number you downloaded.

If you are running the GNU version of *tar*, you can simply type *tar -xzf openssl-[version].tar.gz* instead of issuing separate *gzip* and *tar* commands.

To complete installation of OpenSSL, *cd* into the installation directory. OpenSSL is a source distribution, so a bit of compiling is in order. Before we begin to delve into compilation, there are a few requirements you need to be aware of:

- The *gmake* (or *make*) program
- Perl 5, or higher
- An ANSI C compiler

- A development environment (development libraries, and C header files)

- A supported Unix-compatible operating system

If you have all of these things, you are ready to proceed. Otherwise you will need to acquire them (e.g., download and install them) before you will be able to complete the installation of OpenSSL.

To finish installation, complete the following steps. If you have trouble, consult the *INSTALL* file (from which these steps were taken).

1. Execute the configuration script:

   ```
   $ ./config
   ```

   This step will gather information about your system and configure the OpenSSL installation scripts. It shouldn't take incredibly long, though the time will depend on the speed of your system.

2. Next, compile the OpenSSL software:

   ```
   $ make
   ```

   This is the primary *make* command. After configuration, this command begins compilation of the source code. Even on a fairly high-end machine, this process can take a bit of time.

3. After compiling, run the test:

   ```
   $ make test
   ```

   This command tests the validity of the compilation; if there are any errors, refer to the *INSTALL* file.

4. If the test is successful, you can install the OpenSSL binaries:

   ```
   $ make install
   ```

   After this step is finished, you should be done with the installation of OpenSSL. If you experience any errors, refer to the documentation (specifically the *INSTALL* and *README* files).

Stunnel

Stunnel is an SSL *wrapper*, which means it allows you to add SSL functionality to a daemon that is not normally designed to handle a secure layer. This is useful, because you can use it to create a secure connection with a PostgreSQL database, thus encrypting your database connections, thus tightening general system security, and protecting your data.

Stunnel can be found at *http://www.stunnel.org*. After opening the page in your web browser, open the download page, and click the "get the source code" link.

From here you are able to download the newest version. Save the file into your home directory, or wherever you wish to place it in your filesystem. Once you have downloaded Stunnel, open a console window and *cd* into the directory where you saved it. Then unzip and untar the file with the following commands:

```
$ gzip -d stunnel-[version].tar.gz
$ tar xf stunnel-[version].tar
```

You should now have the stunnel files extracted into a directory named *stunnel-[version]* (where *[version]* is the version number that you downloaded). Fortunately, the installation process of Stunnel is normally quicker than that of OpenSSL. Once everything is extracted, *cd* into the directory. Remember that you must have already installed OpenSSL before this point or the installation of Stunnel will *not* work. Use the following process to make and install Stunnel:

1. Run the configuration script:

    ```
    $ ./configure
    ```

    This command will gather information about your system and configure Stunnel's installation scripts.

2. Next, compile the Stunnel sources:

    ```
    $ make
    ```

    This command compiles the binary files from Stunnel's source code. The program will prompt you with some questions regarding your locality and domain name. It will use your input to help build the PEM file (which will be called *stunnel.pem*). This is the certificate with which your data is encrypted.

3. After successfully compiling Stunnel, go ahead and install it:

    ```
    $ make install
    ```

    This step will install the compiled files.

Knowing how to start Stunnel

You have two options available when deciding how to run Stunnel on your system: using *inetd*, or running the Stunnel binary as a daemon. Running it as a daemon is preferred over the former, as using *inetd* can place limitations on the software due to various issues related to SSL. These limitations include:

- Stunnel must be initialized for every connection with *inetd*
- No session cache is possible
- *inetd* requires forking (which causes extra processor overhead)

It is possible to use Stunnel to provide a secure connection for both remote and local databases. If you host a database on a computer other than the one the *psql* client is located on, it is possible to provide a secure connection from *psql* to that database. If your database is hosted on the same computer as the *psql* client, you can provide an equally secure connection between the two local programs (in case you are concerned about other users on the machine observing local connections over TCP/IP sockets).

There should be a file named *stunnel* in your Stunnel directory; this is the executable for the program. The instructions included assume you are using the executable from this directory, but you may copy it out to */usr/local/sbin*, or another preferred path. Also, you may wish to put links to this file in your start-up scripts so that it is automatically started (as one process or two, depending on how you wish to run it) when the system boots.

If you use Stunnel with *inetd*, you will not need to call it from a startup script.

Running Stunnel in daemon mode

Running Stunnel as a daemon is fairly simple, whether you are connecting to a local or remote database. To use Stunnel to connect to a local database, you must start it as a client and as a server (two different processes of the same program, each running on a different port). You then instruct *psql* to connect to the port number that the stunnel client is running on.

After *psql* has connected to the client, any data will be encrypted and then sent to the Stunnel server (located on another port, which is given to the client when you start it) where it is decrypted and sent to the actual PostgreSQL server. The client has to be told a specific port to run on, along with the port number that the server process is running on (so it knows where to connect to once it is given something to do).

The most common use of Stunnel is to send data from a local client to a remote server. The way to do this is to start the client Stunnel process locally, either by calling it during a start-up script (such as */etc/rc.d/rc.local*) or by calling it directly from the installed directory. You then must run the Stunnel process remotely on the machine on which PostgreSQL is running. As with the client, you may want to start the server automatically during system startup.

Both the client and server executions of an example Stunnel scenario are demonstrated in Example 8-15. The ellipses separate the remote server from the local client. Remember that if you do not copy the *stunnel* executable into */usr/sbin,* Stunnel will have to be run from the directory where it is located.

Example 8-15: Using Stunnel remotely

```
[user@remote ~]$ # This command starts the server on the remote machine.
[user@remote ~]$ stunnel -P/tmp/ -p ~/stunnel.pem -d 9000 -r localhost:5432


...

[user@local ~]$ # This command starts the client on the local machine.
[user@local ~]$ stunnel -P/tmp/ -c -d 5432 -r 192.168.1.2:9000
```

The remote host command (the first command) in Example 8-15 tells the server to use *~/stunnel.pem* as the certificate for encryption, and to open a Stunnel process as a daemon. The *-d 9000* parameter causes the daemon to listen for encrypted data on port 9000. The *-r localhost:5432* parameter tells the daemon process that when it receives encrypted data on its listening port (9000, in this case), it should decrypt it and send it to localhost on port 5432 (which is the PostgreSQL port number, meaning the decrypted data will be sent along to the database server on the local host).

The second command in Example 8-15 opens an instance of Stunnel on a client machine, in client mode (as dictated by the *-c* flag), listening on port 5432. The *-r 192.168.1.2:9000* parameter instructs the process that the server computer is located at 192.168.1.2, and that it is listening on port 9000 for encrypted packets.

Both modes require the *-P/tmp/* flag to provide a temporary path for the PID file, which is the file storing the system ID of the Stunnel process. You do not need to specify the PID filename, as a path is sufficient (the filename will default to something akin to *stunnel.localhost.9000.pid*), though you may specify the complete filename if you wish.

Once each of these Stunnel processes are running on their respective machines, the *psql* client may be pointed to port 5432 on the client machine. Packets sent to this port will be transparently encrypted, forwarded to port 9000 on the server machine, decrypted, and sent to PostgreSQL on port 5432. This is similar to the SSH tunnel discussed in the section titled "SSH/OpenSSH," with one notable distinction: the client Stunnel process may be created without any kind of authentication to the remote server. Thus, any user may create a secure "sender" to the database server, though it still requires that a secure "receiver" be configured to accept that incoming encrypted data.

This encryption occurs completely separately from PostgreSQL's normal authentication procedures; as far as the *postmaster* backend process is concerned, the data is coming through to it in plain text, because it is decrypted before being forwarded to the *postmaster.* Using Stunnel in conjunction with password authentication can be ideal, as it uses a password-based restriction policy, and also encrypts those passwords over the network connection.

Additionally, as mentioned, you have the option to run the two Stunnel processes locally to encrypt packets between two local TCP/IP ports. Starting both the client and server processes on the same machine is demonstrated in Example 8-16.

Example 8-16: Using Stunnel locally

```
[user@local ~]$ stunnel -P/tmp/ -p ~/stunnel-3.15/stunnel.pem -d 9000 -r 5432
[user@local ~]$ stunnel -P/tmp/ -c -d 5433 -r localhost:9000
```

The first use of *stunnel* in Example 8-16 opens the server process, and tells it to use *~/stunnel-3.15/stunnel.pem* as the certificate file. It also instructs the daemon to listen for connections on port 9000, and to send the unencrypted data from that port to port 5432. The example uses 5432 because the PostgreSQL server is running on that port.

The second use of *stunnel* in Example 8-16 opens the Stunnel client process on port 5433 (chosen arbitrarily to resemble the PostgreSQL port, in this case). That daemon is instructed to encrypt incoming data, and to forward it to the server process listening on the localhost to port 9000.

Running with inetd

If you wish to configure your system to invoke only the server-side Stunnel instance when requested, you may configure it for use with *inetd* (or *xinetd*, on newer systems), rather than in daemon mode. As has been stated previously, this can lead to negative performance effects. If you wish to use this feature in spite of this, it is fairly easy to accomplish. First, you must edit the */etc/services* file, and add an entry for the server process. Something like the following will suffice:

```
pgssl           9000/tcp # PostgreSQL stunnel wrapper
```

Depending on whether or not your system uses *inetd* or *xinetd*, you will either need to add a new service file called *pgssl* into the */etc/xinetd.d/* path, or add the service into */etc/inetd.conf.* Both of these configurations require that you enter the complete command to be executed (including any arguments to the program). The command should follow this format:

```
stunnel -P/tmp/ -p path/stunnel.pem -r port
```

In this format, *path* is the location of the certificate file (originally placed in the directory you compiled Stunnel in), and *port* is the port which PostgreSQL is listening on (usually 5432). The main syntactic difference between invoking *stunnel* through an *inetd*-style service versus as a daemon is that the *-d* flag is not passed.

An example *inetd.conf* entry (which must be placed entirely on a single line) might look as it does in Example 8-17. The location of the PEM file must of course be configured to point to your certificate file, and must be readable by the user specified in the *inetd.conf* file. Note that */usr/sbin/stunnel* is the full path to the Stunnel binary.

Example 8-17: An example inetd entry

```
pgssl stream tcp nowait root /usr/sbin/stunnel -P/tmp/ -p /root/my.pem -r 5432
```

The user specified in Example 8-17 is *root*, but you may wish to specify a more restricted user as a security concern. Any user with read access to the certificate file and execute access to the *stunnel* binary (e.g., *nobody*), may be used for non-reserved ports.

An example *xinetd* configuration entry is displayed in Example 8-18. On a machine using *xinetd*, this data would reside in */etc/xinetd.d/pgssl*. Again, be sure that the certificate pointed to by the *-p* parameter is where your certificate file is located. Additionally, as with *inetd*, you may not want to run *stunnel* as *root*.

Example 8-18: An example xinetd entry

```
# xinetd configuration for pgssl.

service pgssl
{
  disable       = no
  socket_type   = stream
  protocol      = tcp
  wait          = no
  user          = root
  server        = /usr/sbin/stunnel
  server_args   = -P/tmp/ -p /root/stunnel.pem -r 5432
}
```

After adding either an *inetd* or *xinetd* entry to your configuration, you must restart the relevant service (on Red Hat systems, this is usually done with a call to *service*):

```
[root@host ~]# service xinetd restart
Stopping xinetd:                                      [  OK  ]
Starting xinetd:                                      [  OK  ]
[root@host ~]#
```

If the *service* command is unavailable, you may usually achieve the same net effect by invoking the *killall* command with the parameters *-HUP*, and the name of the process (e.g., *killall -HUP xinetd*).

To preserve the integrity of your data encryption, be sure that your certificate file is configured to only be readable by the user which initiates the *stunnel* server process.

Wrapping up

Once these steps are completed, you should be able to make a secure connection to your PostgreSQL database with any valid PostgreSQL client. To test this with *psql*, you may use the following syntax:

```
psql -p port -h host -U username database_name
```

Enter the port number that the Stunnel client is listening on for *port*, then the host that the client is listening on for *host* (*localhost*, in this case), followed by your *username*, and the *database_name* to connect to. This should connect you to the database just as if you had opened it normally with *psql* locally.

Notice that you will need to start *postmaster* with the *-i* flag to be able to connect to it with Stunnel. The *-i* flag tells *postmaster* to enable TCP/IP connections, which are required for Stunnel to work.

9

Database Management

This chapter covers several topics associated with managing a PostgreSQL database system, including starting and stopping the PostgreSQL backend, initializing the filesystem, and the creation, removal, and maintenance of individual databases. There is also a section devoted to the topic of backing up and restoring data from a database.

Starting and Stopping PostgreSQL

In this section we cover two options provided with PostgreSQL that are used to start and stop PostgreSQL. The first is a general purpose application called *pg_ctl*, which should function identically on any machine, regardless of the system. This script is intended to be run by the system user (e.g., the user who owns the data directory) configured to execute the *postmaster* backend.

The second script provided is the *SysV*-style script, found in the *contrib/start-scripts* subdirectory within the PostgreSQL source path. The installation of the *SysV* script is discussed in Chapter 2, *Installing PostgreSQL*. By default this script is named *linux*, as it is intended for a Linux system's start-script directory, though in the installation instructions it is renamed to a script called *postgresql* in the system's service start-up directory (e.g., */etc/rc.d/init.d*).

The main functional difference between *pg_ctl* and the SysV-style service script is that *pg_ctl* is intended to be used by the user who runs the *postmaster* backend (e.g., *postgres*), whereas the service script is intended to be run by the *root* user.

The service script is not strictly Linux-specific, and should be compatible with most systems based on SysV start-up scripts. However, if you are not running Linux, you may prefer to stick with the *pg_ctl* script.

Using *pg_ctl*

The *pg_ctl* script is provided with PostgreSQL as a general control application. With it, you can start, stop, restart, or check on the status of PostgreSQL.

Here is the syntax for *pg_ctl*, from the - -*help* option:

```
pg_ctl start    [-w] [-D DATADIR] [-s] [-l FILENAME] [-o "OPTIONS"]
pg_ctl stop     [-W] [-D DATADIR] [-s] [-m SHUTDOWN-MODE]
pg_ctl restart  [-w] [-D DATADIR] [-s] [-m SHUTDOWN-MODE] [-o "OPTIONS"]
pg_ctl status   [-D DATADIR]
```

The following options may be passed to *pg_ctl*:

-w

> Causes the *pg_ctl* application to wait until the operation has finished before returning to a command line. This option may be passed to either the *start* or *restart* action; by default, the application sends the command on to the *postmaster* and exits immediately for these actions.

-W

> Causes the *pg_ctl* application *not* to wait until the operation has finished before returning to a command line. This option may only be passed to the *stop* action; by default, the application sends the stop command on to the *postmaster*, and waits for the action to finish before exiting.

-D DATADIR

> Specifies the directory that contains the default database files. This is optional, because you may have this value already set in the PGDATA environment variable. If the PGDATA environment variable is not set, the *-D* flag is required.

-s

> Suppresses any output from the *pg_ctl* application, aside from system errors. If this flag is not specified, information about the activity within the database (or specific information about startup or shutdown, depending on the action) will be displayed to the screen of the user who initiated the command.

-l FILENAME

> Specifies a file *FILENAME* to append database activity to. This option is only available with the *start* action.

-m SHUTDOWN-MODE

> Sets the *SHUTDOWN-MODE* with which to shut down the *postmaster* backend.

> *smart*
>> Makes *postmaster* wait for all clients to disconnect before shutting down.

fast

> Shuts *postmaster* down without waiting for clients to disconnect.

immediate

> Shuts *postmaster* down more abruptly than *fast* mode, bypassing normal shutdown procedures. This mode causes the database to restart in *recovery* mode the next time it starts, which verifies the integrity of the system.

This option is of course only available to the *stop* and *restart* actions.

-o "OPTIONS"

> Passes the options specified by *OPTIONS* (within double quotes) directly through to the *postmaster* (e.g., the *-i* flag to enable TCP/IP connections). See the section titled "Calling postmaster Directly" later in this chapter for a complete list of these flags.

 Many of the run-time configuration options for *postmaster* can be found in the *postgresql.conf* file, which is stored in the PostgreSQL data path (e.g., */usr/local/pgsql/data*). The options in this file are of a more technical nature, and should not be modified unless you are sure you understand their purpose.

Starting PostgreSQL with pg_ctl

To start PostgreSQL's *postmaster* backend, the *start* argument must be passed to *pg_ctl*. Remember that *pg_ctl* must be run by the *postgres* user (or whatever user you have configured to own the PostgreSQL data path).

Example 9-1 starts the *postmaster* backend, using the data path of */usr/local/pgsql/ data*. The database system starts up successfully, reports the last time the database system was shut down, and provides various debugging statements before returning the *postgres* user to a shell prompt.

Example 9-1: Starting PostgreSQL with pg_ctl

```
[postgres@booktown ~]$ pg_ctl -D /usr/local/pgsql/data start
postmaster successfully started
DEBUG:  database system was shut down at 2001-09-17 08:06:34 PDT
DEBUG:  CheckPoint record at (0, 1000524052)
DEBUG:  Redo record at (0, 1000524052); Undo record at (0, 0); Shutdown TRUE
DEBUG:  NextTransactionId: 815832; NextOid: 3628113
DEBUG:  database system is in production state

[postgres@booktown ~]$
```

Stopping PostgreSQL with pg_ctl

The PostgreSQL *postmaster* backend can be stopped in the same fashion that it is started—by passing the *stop* argument to *pg_ctl*. The application *pg_ctl* checks for the running postmaster process, and, if the stop command was executed by the user who owns the running processes (e.g., *postgres*) the server is shut down.

There are three ways in which PostgreSQL can shut down the backend: *smart*, *fast*, and *immediate*. These arguments are passed to *pg_ctl* following the *-m* flag, to indicate the desired shutdown mode.

A *smart* shutdown (the default) causes PostgreSQL to wait for all clients to first cancel their connections before shutting down. A *fast* shutdown causes Post-greSQL to simply shut down through its normal routine, without checking client status. An *immediate* shutdown bypasses the normal shutdown procedure, and will require the system to go through a *recovery* mode when restarted.

Never use *kill -9* (*kill -KILL*) on the *postmaster* process. This can result in lost or corrupted data.

Example 9-2 calls the *pg_ctl* script to stop the *postmaster* process in *fast* mode. The *postmaster* backend will not wait for any client connections to disconnect before shutting down.

Example 9-2: Stopping PostgreSQL with pg_ctl

```
[postgres@booktown ~]$ pg_ctl -D /usr/local/pgsql/data stop -m fast
Fast Shutdown request at Mon Sep 17 09:23:39 2001
DEBUG:  shutting down
waiting for postmaster to shut down.....
DEBUG:  database system is shut down
done
postmaster successfully shut down
[postgres@booktown ~]$
```

The *smart* shutdown is equivalent to a *kill -TERM* on the running postmaster process, while *fast* is equivalent to a *kill -INT*, and *imme-diate* is equivalent to a *kill -QUIT*.

Restarting PostgreSQL with pg_ctl

You may pass the *restart* argument to *pg_ctl* as shorthand for sequential *stop* and *start* calls to *pg_ctl*. This argument may also specify the *-m* flag to indicate the preferred shutdown mode.

PostgreSQL stores the most recently used start-up options in a temporary file called *postmaster.opts*, within the PostgreSQL data path (PGDATA). This file is used when *pg_ctl* is invoked with the *restart* argument to ensure that your run-time options are preserved. Avoid placing your own configurations on the *postmaster.opts* file, as it will be overwritten when *pg_ctl* is executed with the *start* argument.

Example 9-3 restarts the Book Town database server with the *postgres* user.

Example 9-3: Restarting PostgreSQL with pg_ctl

```
[postgres@booktown ~]$ pg_ctl -D /usr/local/pgsql/data restart
Smart Shutdown request at Mon Sep 17 08:33:51 2001
DEBUG:  shutting down
waiting for postmaster to shut down.....DEBUG:  database system is shut down
done
postmaster successfully shut down
postmaster successfully started
[postgres@booktown ~]$
DEBUG:  database system was shut down at 2001-09-17 08:33:53 PDT
DEBUG:  CheckPoint record at (0, 1000524116)
DEBUG:  Redo record at (0, 1000524116); Undo record at (0, 0); Shutdown TRUE
DEBUG:  NextTransactionId: 815832; NextOid: 3628113
DEBUG:  database system is in production state

[postgres@booktown ~]$
```

Checking status of PostgreSQL with pg_ctl

You may use the *status* argument to check the status of a running *postmaster* process. While not having any effect on the data itself, the data path must be known to *pg_ctl*. If the PGDATA environmental variable is not set, the *-D* flag must be passed to *pg_ctl*.

Example 9-4 checks the status of the Book Town PostgreSQL server.

Example 9-4: Checking status with pg_ctl

```
[postgres@booktown ~]$ pg_ctl -D /usr/local/pgsql/data status
pg_ctl: postmaster is running (pid: 11575)
Command line was:
/usr/local/pgsql/bin/postmaster '-D' '/usr/local/pgsql/data' '-i' '-s'
[postgres@booktown ~]$
```

A lot of typing can be saved by making sure the PGDATA variable is set. If you intend to always use the same data directory, you may set the PGDATA variable (e.g., in the */etc/profile* file, as is recommended in Chapter 2) and never have to apply the -*D* flag.

Using the SysV Script

The SysV-style script, if installed, operates similarly to the *pg_ctl* script. In fact, the SysV-style script operates as a management program that wraps around the *pg_ctl* command. The primary difference is that the SysV script is intended to be invoked by the *root* user, rather than the user who owns and runs PostgreSQL (e.g., *postgres*). The script itself handles the switching of the userids at the appropriate times.

Using the SysV script instead of manually invoking *pg_ctl* is advantageous in that it simplifies system startup and shutdown procedures. The *postgresql* script file in */etc/rc.d/init.d/* is a plain text file, and can be modified in any standard text editor. Within this file you may easily locate the startup and shutdown routines, and add or remove options to *pg_ctl* as you most commonly use them. The *pg_ctl* commands are simplified by using either the single administrative *start* or *stop* parameter with the *postgresql* script.

The instructions for installation of the *postgresql* script are covered in Chapter 2. Depending on your machine's configuration, there may be more than one method of invoking the script once it has been properly installed. Remember that the actual name of the SysV script file in the */etc/rc.d/init.d/* directory may be an arbitrary name, depending on how it was copied. The most common names given to this script are *postgresql* and *postgres*.

If your system supports the *service* command, you should be able to use it as a wrapper to the installed PostgreSQL script with the following syntax:

```
service postgresql { start | stop | restart | status }
```

The *service* command accepts only the parameters described in the preceding syntax. No other options are accepted. You can modify the way any of these general modes run by editing the script (e.g., */etc/rc.d/init.d/postgresql*) manually. Example 9-5 uses the *service* command to start PostgreSQL.

Example 9-5: Starting PostgreSQL with service command

```
[root@booktown ~]# service postgresql start
Starting PostgreSQL: ok
[root@booktown ~]#
```

Alternatively, if the *service* command does not exist on your system, the *postgresql* script can be manually invoked with its complete system path:

```
/etc/rc.d/init.d/postgresql { start | stop | restart | status }
```

Example 9-6 checks the status of PostgreSQL's backend process by directly calling the *postgresql* script using the complete path. This assumes that your system has its SysV start-up scripts installed in the */etc/rc.d/init.d/* directory.

Example 9-6: Checking status with postgresql script

```
[root@booktown ~]# /etc/rc.d/init.d/postgresql status
pg_ctl: postmaster is running (pid: 13238)
Command line was:
/usr/local/pgsql/bin/postmaster '-D' '/usr/local/pgsql/data'
[root@booktown ~]#
```

As you can see from the output of Example 9-6, the SysV script is just a convenient wrapper to the *pg_ctl* command discussed in the previous section.

Calling postmaster Directly

The *postmaster* program is the multi-user PostgreSQL database server backend itself. This is the process that your PostgreSQL clients actually connect to, where a connection to a *postgres* backend is negotiated.

This binary is typically not called manually, but is indirectly executed through either the *pg_ctl* or SysV script discussed earlier in this section. However, these scripts at some point call the *postmaster* binary directly, and it can be helpful in configuring your PostgreSQL system to know what the *postmaster* is, and what it does.

The *postmaster* can only access one database cluster at a time, though you may have several concurrent *postmaster* applications running on different ports with a different database cluster for each.

Here is the syntax for the *postmaster* program:

```
postmaster [ -A { 0 | 1 } ] [ -B buffers ] [ -c name=value ] [ -d debug_level ]
           [ -D datadir ] [ -F ] [ -h hostname ] [ -i ] [ -k directory ] [ -l ]
           [ -N max_connections ] [ -o options ] [ -p port ] [ -S ] [ -n | -s ]
```

The following are each of the parameters available to the *postmaster* program, as of PostgreSQL 7.1.x:

-A { 0 | 1 }

The run-time assertion check flag. This enables debugging, if this option was enabled during compilation of PostgreSQL. This flag should only be used by knowledgeable developers working on PostgreSQL itself.

-B buffers

The number of shared-memory disk buffers that *postmaster* will allocate for use by the backend. By default, this is 64.

The value passed to *-B* must be at least twice the number supplied for the *-N* parameter.

-c name=value

An arbitrary run-time configuration, setting *name* to *value*. Any configuration settings found in the *postgresql.conf* file (within the database cluster's data directory) may be over-ridden with this option.

-d debug_level

The debug level, which determines the amount of debugging output that will be logged by the backend. The default is 0. The higher the number, the more output will be generated. Values as high as 4 are reasonable for normal use, though a value of 4 will quickly take up disk space if you are logging the debug output.

Unless the standard output and standard error streams from *postmaster* are redirected to a file (e.g., from the shell, or with the *-l* option to *pg_ctl*) all debugging information will be displayed to the controlling terminal session of the *postmaster* process.

-D datadir

The data directory of the intended database cluster. If this is not supplied, *postmaster* will use either the value of the PGDATA environment variable, or the */data* path off of the path defined in the POSTGRESHOME environment variable. If neither environment variable is set, the default compile-time directory is used (e.g., */usr/local/pgsql/data*).

-F

The fsync-disabling option. Using this increases performance, at the risk of data corruption, in the event that the operating system or physical hardware crashes unexpectedly. Be sure you know what you are doing before you use this flag!

-h host

 The host address to listen on; by default, PostgreSQL's backends will listen on all configured addresses, including *localhost*.

-i

 The TCP/IP client-connection flag, which allows connections via TCP/IP. If this option is not specified, the backend will accept only local domain socket connections.

-k directory

 The directory for the UNIX domain socket, which *postmaster* will listen on for local connections. This defaults to */tmp/*.

-l

 The SSL flag. Use this to enable SSL connections. The *-i* parameter must also be given.

 You must have compiled PostgreSQL with SSL enabled to use the *-I* option.

-N max_connections

 The maximum number of concurrent backend processes that *postmaster* can start. By default, this value is set to 32. The maximum allowed number for this value is 1024. Make sure that your allocated *buffers* are configured for the maximum number of concurrent backends (the *-B* parameter, which must be at least twice the *max_connections* value).

-o options

 Any *options* that *postmaster* should send to the *postgres* backends when they are first started. These options are listed in Appendix B, *Backend Options for postgres*. Surround the *options* string with quotes, if more than one option is passed.

-p port

 The TCP/IP *port* number (or socket file extension) that this instance of *postmaster* should listen for connections on. If this is left unspecified, the default is taken from the PGPORT environment variable, or the compile-time default (usually 5432).

-S

 The *silent mode* flag. This will cause PostgreSQL to disassociate from the user's terminal session, start its own process group, and redirect its standard output and standard error to */dev/null*.

Using the *-S* switch makes it very difficult to troubleshoot problems, since all tracing and logging output that would normally be generated by the postmaster and its child backend processes will be discarded.

The *postmaster* also accepts the following two debugging options, for interested developers:

-n

The *-n* flag stops *postmaster* from re-initializing shared data structures. A debugging tool can then be used to gain information about the memory's state at the time of the crash.

-s

The *-s* flag causes *postmaster* to use the *SIGSTOP* signal to stop backend processes, without terminating the processes. Using this signal will keep the backend processes in memory instead of terminating them, which allows a developer to collect a core dump from each backend process manually. Each core dump can then be individually examined for debugging information.

Initializing the Filesystem

Before you can create a database in a database cluster, the filesystem must first be initialized. There are two ways to initialize the filesystem for use with PostgreSQL; you may either use the *initdb* application to create an entirely new database cluster (as was used to prepare your initial database system, in Chapter 2), or you may use the *initlocation* application to prepare a secondary data directory.

A database cluster represents several associated databases. A single instance of the *postmaster* process can only access one database cluster at a time. Alternatively, through *initlocation*, you can create databases that are part of an existing cluster that just happen to be stored in another data directory.

The following sections cover these two applications.

Initializing a Database Cluster

Use the *initdb* program to create and initialize a new database cluster within your filesystem. Again, a database cluster is the framework upon which PostgreSQL databases are created. You should already have one cluster in the data directory which was initialized in Chapter 2.

You may use *initdb* to initialize a new data directory for a database cluster, and instruct *postmaster* to start up using that data cluster instead of the default.

Alternatively, you may have two *postmaster* processes running at the same time with different database clusters, provided that they are configured to listen on different ports.

After you use *initdb* to create a new database cluster, that new cluster's filesystem will be owned by whatever operating system user you were logged in as when issuing the command.

 Do not run the *initdb* program while logged in as the *root* user! The cluster needs to be created and *owned* by whichever normal user is going to become the new cluster's database superuser.

You can also use *initdb* to correct a corrupted *template1* database by executing *initb* with the *-t* (or *--template*) parameter. This will re-generate the template1 database from scratch.

Here is the syntax for *initdb*:

```
initdb [ -D dbdir | --pgdatadbdir ]
       [ -i sysid | --sysid sysid ]
       [ -W | --pwprompt ]
       [ -E encoding | --encoding=encoding ]
       [ -L libdir | --pglib=libdir ]
       [ -n | --noclean ]
       [ -d | --debug ]
       [ -t | --template ]
```

The following are the valid options for *initdb*:

[-D dbdir | --pgdata=dbdir]

The directory that you wish to initialize a new database cluster within. If you do not specify a directory name, the command will look at the PGDATA environment variable.

[-i sysid | --sysid=sysid]

The system ID of the database superuser to be created. If unspecified, the ID will be the operating system ID of the system user who runs the *initdb* program.

[-W | --pwprompt]

Prompt for a password upon connection.

[-E encoding | --encoding=encoding]

The name of the multi-byte encoding type of the template database within this cluster. Whatever type you set here will become the default type for any databases you later create using this cluster. This is only relevant if you have enabled multi-byte encoding in PostgreSQL.

[-l `libdir` *| --pglib=*`libdir` *]*

The location of the PostgreSQL library files used by *initdb* when creating a database cluster. It is rarely necessary to use this parameter. The location of the libraries is usually known by the *initdb* program, and if it isn't known, *initdb* will prompt you for the location.

[-t | --template]

The *template* switch, which causes *initdb* to re-initialize only the `template1` database within an already existing database cluster. This can help during PostgreSQL version updates, or if your `template1` database ever becomes corrupted, or is lost.

[-n | --noclean]

The *noclean* switch, which specifies that *initdb* should *not* clean up its files in the event that it is unable to complete cluster creation due to an error. This parameter is only useful for debugging purposes.

[-d | --debug]

The debug switch, which causes debugging information from the creation of the catalog tables to be displayed.

If the command completes successfully, *initdb* will have created a database cluster in the specified data directory; this cluster can then be used by the backend to store its databases.

Example 9-7 initializes a new database cluster in the */usr/local/pgsql/booktown* directory.

Example 9-7: Initializing a new database cluster

```
[postgres@booktown ~]$ initdb /usr/local/pgsql/booktown
This database system will be initialized with username "postgres".
This user will own all the data files and must also own the server process.

Creating directory /usr/local/pgsql/booktown
Creating directory /usr/local/pgsql/booktown/base
Creating directory /usr/local/pgsql/booktown/global
Creating directory /usr/local/pgsql/booktown/pg_xlog
Creating template1 database in /usr/local/pgsql/booktown/base/1
DEBUG:   database system was shut down at 2001-08-27 16:51:07 PDT
DEBUG:   CheckPoint record at (0, 8)
DEBUG:   Redo record at (0, 8); Undo record at (0, 8); Shutdown TRUE
DEBUG:   NextTransactionId: 514; NextOid: 16384
DEBUG:   database system is in production state
Creating global relations in /usr/local/pgsql/booktown/global
DEBUG:   database system was shut down at 2001-08-27 16:51:14 PDT
DEBUG:   CheckPoint record at (0, 108)
DEBUG:   Redo record at (0, 108); Undo record at (0, 0); Shutdown TRUE
DEBUG:   NextTransactionId: 514; NextOid: 17199
DEBUG:   database system is in production state
```

Example 9-7: Initializing a new database cluster (continued)

```
Initializing pg_shadow.
Enabling unlimited row width for system tables.
Creating system views.
Loading pg_description.
Setting lastsysoid.
Vacuuming database.
Copying template1 to template0.

Success. You can now start the database server using:

    /usr/local/pgsql/bin/postmaster -D /usr/local/pgsql/booktown
or
    /usr/local/pgsql/bin/pg_ctl -D /usr/local/pgsql/booktown -l logfile start
```

Initializing a Secondary Database Location

If you are not interested in creating a new database cluster, but simply wish to store a particular database in a different data directory, use *initlocation*. The *initlocation* program creates the directories needed for a secondary database storage area. For more information on how to create a database in a secondary data storage area, refer to the section titled "Creating and Removing a Database" later in this chapter. Here is the syntax for *initlocation*:

```
    initlocation directory
```

In this syntax, *directory* is the path for the new secondary database location. This command should be run as the user which runs the *postmaster*, so that it will have the necessary rights in the created path.

Example 9-8 demonstrates how to initialize a secondary database storage area in the */usr/local/pgsql/booktown2* directory:

Example 9-8: Initializing a secondary database location

```
[postgres@booktown ~]$ initlocation /usr/local/pgsql/booktown2
```

Creating and Removing a Database

PostgreSQL installs two default *template* databases. Upon creation, a new database is *cloned* from one of these templates. They are template0, and template1. Of these, you may only connect to template1. This is because the template0 database exists as an empty template, while template1 may be modified to include commonly used languages, functions, and even database objects, such as tables, views, or sequences. Neither of the template databases may be removed from the system.

The following sections cover creating and removing databases from PostgreSQL.

Creating a Database

PostgreSQL provides two methods for creating a new database: the CREATE
DATABASE SQL command, and the *createdb* command-line executable. To use either
of these methods requires that you have the necessary rights. You do not have to
be a PostgreSQL superuser to create a database, but you must have the usecreatedb right set in the pg_shadow table.

If you are unsure of whether or not this right has been granted to your user, check
through a query to the pg_user view (which in turn queries the pg_shadow table;
only superusers may query the pg_shadow directly). The usecreatedb column in the
pg_shadow table contains a boolean value, which reflects if this right has been
granted. Example 9-9 illustrates an example query to the pg_user view to check for
usecreatedb rights for the guest user.

Example 9-9: Checking usecreatedb rights

```
template1=> SELECT usecreatedb FROM pg_user WHERE usename='guest';
 usecreatedb
-------------
 f
(1 row)
```

Using CREATE DATABASE

The syntax for the CREATE DATABASE SQL command is as follows:

```
CREATE DATABASE dbname
         [ WITH [ LOCATION = 'dbpath' ]
                [ TEMPLATE = template ]
                [ ENCODING = encoding ] ]
```

In this syntax, *dbname* is the name of the new database to be created. All database
names must begin with an alphabetical character, and are limited to 31 characters
in length. PostgreSQL allows any number of databases to be created in a given
data directory (assuming there is available disk space).

By appending the optional WITH keyword, up to three more optional attributes
may be specified:

LOCATION = 'dbpath'

The *dbpath* value describes an *environment variable*, initialized in the shell
environment of the user which runs the PostgreSQL backend. For example,
you might put the following line in */home/postgres/.bash_profile*:

```
export PGDATA2="/usr/local/pgsql/data2"
```

Thus, enabling the use of PGDATA2 as a variable (once PostgreSQL has been
restarted with the environment variable set in memory), and a valid value for
dbpath. This is a general security precaution to prevent users from writing to

an inappropriate location in the filesystem.

If the LOCATION keyword is omitted, PostgreSQL will create the database in the default data directory (e.g., */usr/local/pgsql/data*).

TEMPLATE = *template*

The *template* identifier refers to a database to "clone" in creating the new database. Any database objects within that database will be duplicated in the creation of the database *dbname*.

If unspecified, PostgreSQL will implicitly choose template1 as the database to duplicate objects from. If you wish for a completely fresh database to be created, you may specify template0 to avoid copying the objects with which you may have populated template1.

ENCODING = *encoding*

The *encoding* value can be either a string constant describing the encoding type (e.g., *SQL_ASCII*, *LATIN1*, etc), or its equivalent PostgreSQL numeric constant. The available PostgreSQL multibyte encoding formats, and their numeric constant values, are listed in Appendix A, *Multibyte Encoding Types*.

If the ENCODING keyword is unspecified, PostgreSQL will create a database using its default encoding. This is usually *SQL_ASCII*, though it may have been set to a different default during the initial configuration of PostgreSQL (see Chapter 2 for more on default encoding).

The value of *dbpath* passed to the LOCATION keyword must be set to the name of an environment variable. This variable may not literally describe a system path (e.g., */usr/local/pgsql/data2*) unless the *CPPFLAGS=-DALLOW_ABSOLUTE_DBPATHS* argument was passed to the *gmake* command when PostgreSQL was originally compiled and installed.

You must connect to a database prior to issuing the CREATE DATABASE command. If you have not yet created a database, you may "bootstrap" your way into creating one through the use of the default template1 database. By connecting to this database, you may create new databases which can then be connected to directly.

Once a database is created, the creator automatically becomes it's owner, or *DBA* (database administrator). This user will *own* each object within the database, and therefore be able to grant rights on those objects to other users. Be sure to create your databases with the user that you'll use to actively maintain the database with.

Example 9-10 demonstrates connecting to the template1 database as the Book Town managerial user named manager, and creating Book Town's example database, booktown. This example uses *psql*, but the same SQL syntax will work with any valid PostgreSQL client.

Example 9-10: Creating a database

```
[jworsley@booktown ~]$ psql -U manager template1
Welcome to psql, the PostgreSQL interactive terminal.

Type:  \copyright for distribution terms
       \h for help with SQL commands
       \? for help on internal slash commands
       \g or terminate with semicolon to execute query
       \q to quit

template1=# CREATE DATABASE booktown;
CREATE DATABASE
```

The returned message CREATE DATABASE indicates that the database was created successfully. Other server messages returned may include the following:

ERROR: CREATE DATABASE: permission denied

This message indicates that the user attempting to create the database does not have the rights to create a database. This right (or lack thereof) is indicated by the usecreatedb column in the pg_shadow table, described earlier in this chapter. See Chapter 10, *User and Group Management* for more information on enabling this right.

ERROR: CREATE DATABASE: database "booktown" already exists

This message indicates that a database with the specified *dbname* (in this example, booktown) already exists. You may not have two databases with the same name (even in different physical locations on the filesystem).

 If another user is accessing a database that you wish to use as a template, you must wait until the user is no longer accessing it in order to do so.

Using createdb

PostgreSQL also provides a command-line wrapper to the CREATE DATABASE command, in an application called *createdb*. The only alternate functionality to *createdb* over its SQL counterpart is that it may be run directly from the command line, and it allows a comment to be added into the database, all in one command. In SQL, this would require at least two statements: the CREATE DATABASE statement, and a COMMENT statement.

The syntax for the *createdb* application is as follows:

```
createdb [ options ] dbname [ description ]
```

In this syntax, *dbname* is the name of the database to be created, *options* consists of any of the listed optional flags, and *description* is the comment to be added with an implicit COMMENT command (see the section titled "Documenting a Database" for more on database comments).

The *options* arguments may be provided either as single-dashed flags, each followed by a space and an argument (e.g., *-D PATH*), or the GNU-style, double-dashed counterpart, each followed by an equals sign (=) and an argument, if necessary (e.g., *--location=PATH*). Single-dashed flags will always consist of a single letter, while double-dashed flags will be more verbose (usually an entire word).

The following are the options available to *createdb*:

-D PATH, --location=PATH

Equivalent to the LOCATION keyword used with the CREATE DATABASE command. PATH should be the environment variable (set for the user running the PostgreSQL backend) which is set to the system path where the new database files were created.

-T TEMPLATE, --template=TEMPLATE

Equivalent to the TEMPLATE keyword used with the CREATE DATABASE command. TEMPLATE should be the identifier describing the database (e.g., template0) to use as the basis from which to create the new database, duplicating all objects.

-E ENCODING, --encoding=ENCODING

Equivalent to the ENCODING keyword used with the CREATE DATABASE command. ENCODING describes a valid encoding string constant, as explained in Appendix A. A numeric constant cannot be passed through *createdb*, even though one can be passed through CREATE DATABASE. This is because ENCODING is always passed to *createdb* as a string constant.

-h HOSTNAME, --host=HOSTNAME

The HOSTNAME that will be connected to, to create the database. Defaults to *localhost*, or the host defined by the PGHOST environment variable.

-p PORT, --port=PORT

Specifies that the database connection is made on port PORT, rather than the default port (usually 5432, though it may have been configured differently when PostgreSQL was compiled, by the *--with-pgport* flag).

-U USERNAME, --username=USERNAME

Specifies that the username USERNAME is the user who connects to PostgreSQL (rather than the name of the system user executing *createdb*) to create the database.

-W, --password

Accepts no parameters, and causes a password prompt, which happens auto-matically if the *pg_hba.conf* file is configured not to *trust* the requesting host.

-e, --echo

Accepts no parameters, and causes the CREATE DATABASE statement sent to PostgreSQL to be displayed to the screen as it is executed by *createdb*.

-q, --quiet

Accepts no parameters, and causes no output to be sent to *stdout* (though errors will still be sent to *stderr*).

The success and failure messages for *createdb* are identical to those created by CREATE DATABASE, though you may also receive connection errors similar to those received from *psql* if invalid host or user information is provided. See the section titled "Using CREATE DATABASE" earlier in this chapter for more information on these messages.

Example 9-11 shows the use of the *createdb* application, creating the new database *example* as the manager user, in the directory described by the PGDATA2 variable. Notice that both forms of options may be simultaneously supplied (sin-gle-dashed, and GNU-style).

Example 9-11: Using the createdb application

```
[jworsley@booktown ~]$ createdb --location=PGDATA2 -U manager example
CREATE DATABASE
```

Removing a Database

Similar to its approach in creating databases, PostgreSQL offers two methods to remove a database permanently from your system: the DROP DATABASE SQL com-mand, and the *dropdb* command-line executable. The use of these methods requires the usecreatedb right to be set in the pg_shadow table for the user initiat-ing the command.

Upon dropping a database, all tables, data, and other objects in that database are destroyed. The system files associated with the database *are also physically removed.* PostgreSQL will not prompt you to verify the *permanent* deletion of the database. This action cannot be undone, nor can it be executed within a transaction block.

Using DROP DATABASE

The syntax for the DROP DATABASE SQL command is as follows:

```
DROP DATABASE dbname
```

In this syntax, *dbname* represents the name of the database to be removed from the system. Note that no user may be connected to the database that you are trying to remove, or the command will fail. Example 9-12 demonstrates dropping a database called example.

Example 9-12: Using DROP DATABASE

```
template1=# DROP DATABASE example;
DROP DATABASE
```

The DROP DATABASE server message indicates that the database was successfully removed, and its associated system files deleted. Other messages you may receive from the command follow:

ERROR: DROP DATABASE: cannot be executed on the currently open database
> This message indicates that you are connected to the database you are trying to remove. A database cannot be removed from the system while you are actively connected to it.

ERROR: DROP DATABASE: database "example" is being accessed by other users
> This message indicates that another user is connected to the database you are attempting to remove. You must wait until all users are disconnected before being able to successfully remove a database.

ERROR: DROP DATABASE: database "example" does not exist
> This message indicates that there is no database with the specified *dbname* (in this case, example).

Using dropdb

Similar to the *createdb* script, there is another command-line wrapper called *dropdb* that executes the DROP DATABASE SQL command. The only functionality that *dropdb* provides, as compared to the DROP DATABASE command, is that you execute it from a shell, and you can use the interactive flag to have it prompt you for confirmation.

The syntax for the *dropdb* script is as follows:

```
dropdb [ options ] dbname
```

In this syntax, *dbname* is the name of the database to be permanently removed from PostgreSQL, and *options* describe each of the options available to the application. Most of these options exist to describe the PostgreSQL connection options, and to mimic the options described in the section titled "Using createdb" earlier in this chapter. The notable exception is the *-i*, or *--interactive*, flag.

Here is the complete list of options for *dropdb*:

-h HOSTNAME, --host=HOSTNAME

> The HOSTNAME that will be connected to, to drop the database. Defaults to *localhost*, or a host defined by the PGHOST environment variable.

-p PORT, --port=PORT

> Specifies that the database connection is made on port PORT, rather than the default port (usually 5432, though it may have been configured differently when PostgreSQL was compiled, by the *--with-pgport* flag).

-U USERNAME, --username=USERNAME

> Specifies that the username USERNAME is the user who connects to PostgreSQL (rather than the name of the system user executing *dropdb*) to drop the database.

-W, --password

> Accepts no parameters, and causes a password prompt, which happens automatically if the *pg_hba.conf* file is configured not to *trust* the requesting host.

-i, --interactive

> Accepts no parameters, and causes the user to be prompted to confirm the removal of the database before actually destroying the data.

-e, --echo

> Accepts no parameters, and causes the DROP DATABASE statement sent to PostgreSQL to be displayed to the screen as it is executed by *dropdb*.

-q, --quiet

> Accepts no parameters, and causes no output to be sent to *stdout* (though errors will still be sent to *stderr*).

It is prudent to always execute the *dropdb* command with the *-i* flag, as it requires a confirmation before anything is actually removed from PostgreSQL. Example 9-13 demonstrates the removal of a database named example with the *-i* interactive flag, as the manager user.

Example 9-13: Using the dropdb command

```
[jworsley@booktown ~]$ dropdb -U manager -i example
Database "example" will be permanently deleted.
Are you sure? (y/n) y
DROP DATABASE
```

Maintaining a Database

Database maintenance is a broad subject. This section covers the physical maintenance of the system (pertaining to its disk usage), analytical maintenance (to
increase performance), and database object documentation (to add to the maintainability and clarity of the schema).

The primary tool for physical and analytical database maintenance in PostgreSQL
is the VACUUM SQL command, and its accompanying command-line script, *vacuumdb*. They each perform the same two general functions:

- Remove any leftover data from rollbacks and other processes that can leave
  temporary data

- Analyze activity in the database to assist PostgreSQL in designing efficient
  queries

It is good practice to perform a VACUUM nightly on a production database. While it
can be run at the same time data is accessed, doing so will decrease the response
time of the server. As such, it is generally preferable to schedule it at a time when
you do not expect a great deal of database activity.

Any time an exceptionally large number of records are added or deleted, it is prudent to perform a VACUUM to analyze the database, which automatically updates the
PostgreSQL query optimizer of major changes to the tables. By doing this you
allow PostgreSQL to have a more up-to-date profile of the data within the
database, providing a better set of information with which to plan the most efficient queries. All of these actions should result in a faster, more efficient response
from the database.

The VACUUM command locks tables in *access exclusive mode.* This
means that any query involving a table being vacuumed will pause
and wait until the vacuum of the affected table is complete before
continuing.

Using VACUUM

The syntax for the VACUUM SQL command is as follows:

```
VACUUM [ VERBOSE ] [ ANALYZE ] [ table ]
VACUUM [ VERBOSE ] ANALYZE [ table [ ( column [, ...] ) ] ]
```

Used without any of the optional keywords or identifiers, a VACUUM statement will
clean up each table in the presently connected database, one at a time, deleting
temporary data and recovering disk space. This use of VACUUM is primarily to

maximize free disk space.

An optional `table` identifier may be specified if you want the VACUUM to clean a single table in the connected database, rather than all tables. It will also update statistics in the system catalogs pertaining to the number of records and amount of data stored in each table. Example 9-14 shows the use of a VACUUM statement in the booktown database, on the books table.

Example 9-14: Using VACUUM on a table

```
booktown=# VACUUM books;
VACUUM
```

The VACUUM message returned in Example 9-14 indicates that the process finished successfully. If a specified table cannot be found, you will instead receive the following notice:

```
NOTICE:  Vacuum: table not found
```

With the use of the optional ANALYZE keyword, PostgreSQL examines the allocation of data in each column for each table (or the specified table, if provided), and uses the information to prepare the query optimizer for better planning. With the use of the ANALYZE keyword, you also have the option to analyze only specified columns. Example 9-15 shows the use of the VACUUM ANALYZE command on the entire booktown database.

Example 9-15: Using VACUUM ANALYZE on a database

```
booktown=# VACUUM ANALYZE;
VACUUM
```

Finally, the optional VERBOSE keyword may be applied if you are interested in seeing a detailed internal report of the findings of the VACUUM statement. This is most likely not of interest to anyone not actively developing the PostgreSQL engine, or related software.

Using vacuumdb

As with many of the database management SQL commands, the VACUUM command has a command-line executable wrapper called *vacuumdb*. The *vacuumdb* script provides one significant added function to the normal use of the VACUUM SQL statement, in that you can instruct it to perform a VACUUM on each PostgreSQL database on your system.

Additionally, since it accepts connection parameters on how to connect to PostgreSQL, you may use *vacuumdb* remotely (i.e., without having to first connect to the machine via a terminal client, and then executing *vacuumdb* or *psql* from the remote machine). This is provided that your authentication scheme in

PostgreSQL's *pg_hba.conf* file is configured for outside access (see Chapter 8, *Authentication and Encryption* for more information on this).

Here is the syntax for *vacuumdb*:

```
vacuumdb [ options ] [ dbname ]
```

Like the *createdb* and *dropdb* scripts, *vacuumdb* accepts both single-dashed and GNU-style double-dashed arguments from the command line. The only required option is the *dbname* (unless you specify *--all*), which describes the database to be cleaned and analyzed. The *options* parameters describe which mode the VACUUM command should be invoked in. The following are the available options for the *vacuumdb* script:

-h HOSTNAME, --host=HOSTNAME
> Specifies that you are connected to *HOSTNAME*, rather than the localhost. Use this option when vacuuming a remote database.

-p PORT, --port=PORT
> Specifies that the database connection is made on port *PORT*, rather than the default port (usually 5432, though it may have been configured differently when PostgreSQL was compiled, by the *--with-pgport* flag).

-U USERNAME, --username=USERNAME
> Specifies that the username *USERNAME* is the user who connects to PostgreSQL (rather than the name of the system user executing *vacuumdb*).

-W, --password
> Accepts no parameters, and causes a password prompt, which occurs automatically if the *pg_hba.conf* file on the target server is configured not to *trust* the requesting host.

-d DBNAME, --dbname=DBNAME
> Explicitly specifies the name of the database to perform the VACUUM statement on. This option is mutually exclusive to the *--all* option.

-a, --all
> Applies the VACUUM command, with specified options, to all databases in the system catalog.

-z, --analyze
> Equivalent to the ANALYZE keyword for the VACUUM SQL command. Updates stored statistics about the data allocation between columns, which are used by the query optimizer to help guide internal query planning.

-t 'TABLE [(column [, ...])]', --table='TABLE [(column [, ...])]'
> Targets a specific table *TABLE* (or specific *columns* within that table) to be affected. The *--analyze* option is required to target specific columns.

-v, --verbose

> Equivalent to the VERBOSE keyword for the VACUUM SQL command. Causes a detailed internal report of the processing performed to be displayed.

-e, --echo

> Accepts no parameters, and causes the query sent to PostgreSQL to be displayed to the screen as it is executed by *vacuumdb*.

-q, --quiet

> Accepts no parameters, and causes no output to be sent to *stdout* (though any errors will still be sent to *stderr*).

Example 9-16 demonstrates the use of the *vacuumdb* script from the Book Town server. The *-U* flag specifies that the connection should use the manager user to connect, while the *--all* flag causes all databases in the system catalog to be affected in sequence.

Example 9-16: Using vacuumdb on all databases

```
[jworsley@booktown ~]$ vacuumdb -U manager --all
Vacuuming postgres
VACUUM
Vacuuming booktown
VACUUM
Vacuuming template1
VACUUM
```

As mentioned, because of the connectivity options available to the *vacuumdb* script, it can be easily executed from a remote server. Example 9-17 shows a similar process to the command used in Example 9-16, but with the addition of the *-h* flag to specify a remote server named *booktown.commandprompt.com*. Example 9-17 also targets the booktown database specifically, rather than all databases.

Example 9-17: Using vacuumdb on a remote database

```
[jworsley@cmd ~]$ vacuumdb -h booktown.commandprompt.com -U manager booktown
VACUUM
```

Documenting a Database

Using COMMENT

PostgreSQL offers a non-standard SQL command called COMMENT, which allows for documentation of any database object. By using COMMENT on a table, function, operator, or other database object, you can provide a description that is stored in the pg_description system table. Descriptions can be easily retrieved through a set of extended *psql* slash commands.

Many standard objects in the database have default descriptions, which can be perused (along with user-added descriptions) with the *psql* \dd slash command.

Here is the syntax for COMMENT:

```
COMMENT ON [ [ DATABASE | INDEX | RULE | SEQUENCE | TABLE | TYPE | VIEW ]
    { object_name |
      COLUMN table_name.column_name |
      AGGREGATE aggregate_name aggregate_type |
      FUNCTION function_name ( argument_type [, ...] ) |
      OPERATOR operator_name ( leftoperand_type , rightoperand_type ) |
      TRIGGER trigger_name ON table_name }
] IS 'description'
```

In this syntax, *object_name* is the name of the database object that you wish to add a comment or *description* to. The keywords for the major database objects are optional, but if you intend to place a comment on a column, function, aggregate function, operator, or trigger, you must specify the preceding keyword so that PostgreSQL knows what kind of syntax to expect, and where to look for the object name specified.

Note that any comment added to a database is tied to both the database in which it is added, and the *user* who added it. You can only see those comments that you create.

The *description* string constant following the IS keyword is the literal comment to be placed in the database. Example 9-18 demonstrates placing a simple description on the id column of the booktown database.

Example 9-18: Commenting the books table

```
booktown=# COMMENT ON COLUMN books.id
booktown-#          IS 'An Internal Book Town Identifier';
COMMENT
```

The COMMENT server message returned in Example 9-18 indicates that the comment was successfully placed on the column.

Retrieving comments

You may retrieve comments from the database easily by using the *psql* slash-plus commands. These are as follows:

\d+

Displays the same information as the standard \d command (displaying all tables, views, sequences, and indices in the currently connected database), but adds a column for the comments as well.

\l+

Displays comments on all databases.

\df+ [*pattern*]

Displays descriptions for each function in the currently connected database (as well as the language and source of the function). You may wish to view this slash command in expanded mode for readability by first initiating the \x slash command (see Chapter 6, *PostgreSQL Clients* for more about this). You can optionally supply a regular expression *pattern* to compare against existing function names, allowing you to limit the number of functions displayed.

\dt+

Displays comments on all tables in the currently connected database.

\di+

Displays comments on all indices in the currently connected database.

\ds+

Displays comments on all sequences in the currently connected database.

\dv+

Displays comments on all views in the currently connected database.

\dS+

Displays comments on system tables. Note that comments placed on system tables are still tied to a particular database, even though they are accessible from all databases, and will therefore not be visible when performing a \dS+ slash command from another database connection.

\dd

Displays all descriptions for all database objects.

Example 9-19 demonstrates the retrieval of the comment that was placed on the books table in Example 9-18 with the use of the *psql* \d+ command.

Example 9-19: Retrieving a comment

```
booktown=# \d+ books
                          Table "books"
 Attribute  |  Type   | Modifier  |           Description
------------+---------+-----------+----------------------------------
 id         | integer | not null  | An Internal Book Town Identifier
 title      | text    | not null  |
 author_id  | integer |           |
 subject_id | integer |           |
Index: books_id_pkey
```

The COMMENT SQL command provides a very simple way of internally documenting your objects, from tables to functions. This can be of great help when working with large or complicated database schema. Even the best of naming conventions do not always result in database objects whose applications are self-evident; this is especially the case when working with multiple developers.

Backing Up and Restoring Data

The concept of backup and restoration of data is a vital one to any database administrator. No system is immune from hard drive crashes, careless users, or any number of potential catastrophes that can endanger data stored within PostgreSQL.

This section covers two general methods for backing up your data. The first approach uses the *pg_dump* application distributed with PostgreSQL to create a set of SQL instructions with which a database can be fully restored. The second method consists of backing up the filesystem itself.

Using pg_dump

The *pg_dump* (which is short for "PostgreSQL dump") application is run from a command line, and creates a list of SQL commands. These commands, executed in the order provided, re-create the database from scratch.

Here is the syntax for *pg_dump*:

```
pg_dump [ options ] dbname
```

In this syntax, *dbname* is the name of the database that you want to "dump" SQL instructions for. The available *options* are similar in format to those of the other database management utilities included with PostgreSQL, such as *createdb*. The most common flag specified in the *options* to *pg_dump* is the *-f* flag, which specifies the file to store the dumped SQL statements within.

If the *-f* flag is not specified to *pg_dump*, the dumped SQL will be written to *stdout* rather than stored in a file.

The complete list of *pg_dump* options follow:

-a, --data-only

Forces only COPY or INSERT SQL statements to be dumped (depending on whether or not the *-d* flag is used). This results in a backup of data, and not database objects (or *schema*). If the *-d* flag is *not* passed along with this flag, the dumped COPY commands are used to copy all data from *stdin* (i.e., the rows are stored literally within the dumped file as COPY commands from *stdin*). Otherwise, each row is represented as sequential INSERT statements.

-b, --blobs

Causes any large objects to be dumped as well as normal data. This option also requires that the *-F* flag be provided with either the *t* or *c* format. By default, large object data is not dumped.

-c, --clean

Specifies that SQL statements to drop all existing objects will precede the SQL statements to create those objects. This option is useful in re-initializing an existing database, rather than dropping it and recreating it from scratch.

-C, --create

Specifies that the SQL statement to create the database (CREATE DATABASE) should be included in the dump.

-d, --inserts

Causes INSERT statements to be dumped for each row of data, rather than the default COPY statements. This can be safer, as a single corrupted row will cause a COPY statement to fail, though it is a much slower process to add a single row at a time during restoration.

-D, --attribute-inserts

Like the *-d* flag, causes INSERT statements to be dumped; however, with this flag, each INSERT statement is created with an explicit column target list in parentheses, immediately preceding the VALUES.

-f FILENAME, --file=FILENAME

Directs the output of *pg_dump* to a file named *FILENAME*, rather than to *stdout*. The user executing *pg_dump* must have system permissions to write to this file.

-F { c | t | p }, --format { c | t | p }

Determines the file format of the output:

c (*gzip* compressed)

A format of *c* creates a *gzip*-compressed *tar* file (i.e., a *.tar.gz* file).

t (*tar*)

A value of *t* creates a *tar* file (i.e., a *.tar* file).

p (plain text)

The default value of *p* causes plain text output.

Note that *pg_restore* is typically used to handle files created with the *c* or *t* (*gzip*-compressed or *tar*) formats.

-h HOSTNAME, --host=HOSTNAME

Specifies that *HOSTNAME* should be connected to, rather than the localhost. Use this when the target database is on another server.

-i, --ignore-version

Overrides the check between the version of *pg_dump* and the version of Post-greSQL running. This option is not recommended unless there is no other alternative, as it most likely will produce errors due to changes in the system catalogs between versions. Normally, you should use the version of *pg_dump* matching the database that you are backing up.

-n, --no-quotes

Suppresses any double-quotes surrounding identifiers unless there are some normally illegal characters in the identifier (e.g., spaces, uppercase letters).

-N, --quotes

Explicitly indicates that double-quotes should be used around all identifiers. This has been the default behavior of *pg_dump* since PostgreSQL 6.4.

-o, --oid

Causes OIDs (object identifiers) for each row of data to be dumped as well. This can be vital if any of your applications based around the data in Post-greSQL use OIDs in any kind of meaningful or associative way.

-O, --no-owner

Causes ownership to not be taken into account in the dump. A restore with suppressed ownership will cause all re-created objects to belong to the user performing the restore.

-p PORT, --port=PORT

Specifies that the database connection should be made on port *PORT*, rather than the default port (usually 5432, though it may have been configured differently when PostgreSQL was compiled, by the *--with-pgport* flag).

-R, --no-reconnect

Suppresses any \connect statements, which are usually used to enforce currently reflected ownerships when a backup is restored. This is similar in practice to the *-O* flag, but also precludes the ability to use the *-C* flag, as a reconnect is required after creation of a new database.

-s, --schema-only

Causes only the *schema-related* (database objects such as tables, sequences, indices and views) SQL statements to be dumped, ignoring re-creation of the data. This can be useful in moving a general database structure from a development machine to a production machine.

-t TABLE, --table=TABLE

Causes only *TABLE* to be dumped from the specified database, rather than all tables.

-u, - -password

> Provides a prompt for a username and password. As of PostgreSQL 7.1.x, this is the only method to provide an alternate username. If the user's password is unset (NULL), you may simply press enter when prompted for it.

-v, - -verbose

> Causes verbose output from the *pg_dump* functions being performed to be displayed to *stderr* (not *stdout*).

-x, - -no-acl

> Suppresses any GRANT or REVOKE statements, which are usually used to preserve the rights set at the time of the dump. Use this flag if you do not wish to enforce any existing rights or restrictions when re-creating a database from this dump.

-Z, - -compress { 0 - 9 }

> Sets the degree of compression (0 for the least compression, 9 for the most) when used with the *-F c* argument.

Any system user may run *pg_dump* by default, but the user with which you connect to PostgreSQL must have SELECT rights for every object in the database being dumped. Example 9-20 demonstrates the use of *pg_dump* on the booktown database, with the manager PostgreSQL user. The *-C* flag passed causes the CREATE DATABASE command to be included in the SQL dump as well. This command is not always included, as you may prefer to create the database beforehand with non-standard options.

Example 9-20: Using pg_dump

```
[jworsley@booktown ~]$ pg_dump -u -C -f booktown.sql booktown
Username: manager
Password:

[jworsley@booktown ~]$ ls -l booktown.sql
-rw-rw-r--   1 jworsley jworsley   46542 Sep 13 16:42 booktown.sql
```

Note that since *pg_dump* provides the standard connection options for specifying a host connection (e.g., the *-h*, *-u* and *-p* flags), it can be used to perform remote backups from any host allowed to make a remote connection (according to the *pg_hba.conf* file: see Chapter 8 for more on this subject).

Example 9-21 shows a user on a remote server specifying a connection to the *booktown.commandprompt.com* server, in order to create a backup file in *compressed* format (with the *-F c* flag) called *booktown.sql.tar.gz*.

Example 9-21: Using pg_dump remotely

```
[jworsley@cmd ~]$ pg_dump -u -h booktown.commandprompt.com \
>                        -F c -f booktown.sql.tar.gz booktown
Username: manager
Password:

[jworsley@cmd ~]$ ls -l booktown.sql.tar.gz
-rw-rw-r--   1 jworsley jworsley   45909 Sep 13 17:12 booktown.sql.tar.gz
```

If you wish to use large objects in your dumped file, it is necessary that you use either the *tar* (*t*) or *gzip*-compressed (*c*) format, since the plain-text format cannot include large objects. Otherwise, normal plain-text formatted dumps are suitable for most users.

Creating a dump in *tar* format can often result in a backup file more than twice the size of its plain-text counterpart, even without large objects. This is because the *tar* format involves a hierarchy TOC (table of contents) of *.dat* files. This hierarchy represents the needed information on using the tar format with the corresponding *pg_restore* command; thus, more disk space is taken up by the extra instructions. Since *tar* is not a compression utility, the *gzip*-compressed (*c*) format exists as well to compress the tarred file into *gzipped* format automatically.

Using pg_dumpall

PostgreSQL supplies a supplementary wrapper command to the *pg_dump* application called *pg_dumpall*. The primary use of this application is to allow the entire cluster of PostgreSQL databases on a system to be dumped at once, rather than having to perform a *pg_dump* for each database, one at a time.

Here is the syntax for *pg_dumpall*, displayed from the *--help* flag:

```
pg_dumpall [ -c ] [ -h HOSTNAME ] [ -p PORT ] [ -g ]
```

The *pg_dumpall* command accepts the same connection parameters available to *pg_dump*. The following are the *pg_dumpall*-specific parameters:

-c   Specifies that SQL statements to drop existing global objects will precede the SQL statements to create those objects.

-h HOSTNAME, --host=HOSTNAME
Specifies that HOSTNAME should be connected to, rather than the localhost, or the host defined by the PGHOST environment variable. Use this when the target database is on another server.

-p PORT, --port=PORT
Specifies that the database connection should be made on port PORT, rather than the default port (usually 5432).

-g, --globals-only

Specifies that only global objects will be dumped. This is primarily useful for recreating just users and groups, or for duplicating them on another machine (by taking the dump to another machine, and executing it). The *-g* flag implicitly causes all users to be deleted from the pg_shadow table prior to the CREATE statements. Exercise caution with the output from this command!

 Do not pass the *-?* flag to *pg_dumpall*, as it will result in passing that flag to *pg_dump* for each database, which may result in quite a few more help screens than you would expect. If you wish to view *pg_dumpall*'s help, use the *--help* flag.

Note that as of PostgreSQL 7.1.x, the use of the *pg_dumpall* script does have some practical limitations over the normal use of *pg_dump*. For example, the *-u* flag cannot be used to provide a different username and password, and the *-F* flag may not be used to specify a format other than plain text (your backups will be stored as plain text, regardless of chosen format). This means that the *-b* flag cannot be used with *pg_dumpall* either, as it requires a format other than plain-text.

While the *-f* flag can be used to pass a filename through to *pg_dump*, doing so does not create a complete dump, as *pg_dumpall*'s global data is still sent to *stdout*. To solve the problem of not having the *-f* flag available to *pg_dumpall*, the shell re-direction operator (>) can be used to redirect the output of *pg_dumpall* to a file.

A simple workaround to the lack of the *-u* flag is to set the PGUSER environment variable. You can also set the PGPASSWORD environment variable in this fashion if you are connecting to a system which requires password authentication, and you do not wish to provide a password for *each* database that it connects to and dumps.

Example 9-22 demonstrates a simple bash-shell shorthand for a temporary environment variable (PGUSER) when invoking any PostgreSQL client. While not usually necessary, it can be a handy trick to know for exceptions such as the *pg_dumpall* script. Example 9-22 uses this technique to create one dump file for all databases.

Example 9-22: Using pg_dumpall

```
[jworsley@booktown ~]$ PGUSER=postgres pg_dumpall > all.sql
```

The first part of the shell statement demonstrated in Example 9-22 sets a temporary environment variable named PGUSER to the value of *postgres*. This variable is set for the duration of the *pg_dumpall* command, and expires when the command has finished.

The *pg_dumpall* command generally requires that the user executing the script be a PostgreSQL superuser. This is because the *pg_dumpall* command requires access to the PostgreSQL system catalogs, as it dumps global objects as well as database objects.

You can also run the *pg_dumpall* command remotely, though be sure to set any environment variables as needed. These will depend greatly on the remote host configuration in the *pg_hba.conf* file.

You should use the *pg_dumpall* command if it is especially inconvenient to backup all your existing databases individually, or if you have any kind of complex user and group system in place. If you are inhibited by the limitations of *pg_dumpall* for data output (particularly if your database makes use of large objects), the simplest solution is to use *pg_dumpall* with the *-g* flag to keep a backup of all user and group data, and to subsequently use *pg_dump* for each database which needs to be backed up, individually.

Restoring a Database

Data from a SQL dump can be restored to a database in one of two ways. If the dump created by *pg_dump* as a simple, plain-text file, it may be passed through to *psql* directly as an input file. Alternatively, if another output format was chosen (e.g., the *tar* or *compressed tar* format), the *pg_restore* command must be used.

A database may either be restored from scratch, to an empty database, or to a non-existent database; how you go about restoring a database depends largely on how it was dumped (e.g., if only data were dumped, or if the commands to create the database were included).

Using psql for plain text dumps

A plain text output file from *pg_dump* may be passed through to *psql* as an input file. This executes sequentially each of the dumped SQL instructions. Depending on how the dump was created, and for what purpose, there are a variety of ways to invoke *psql* with the dump.

If your dump was created with the *-C* flag, the SQL statement to create the database is included in the dump file itself. This means that, most likely, the database was either dropped, or has not yet been created on the system on which it is being restored. If the database already exists, it may need to be dropped, *but only do this if you are sure the dump is up to date.*

On the other hand, if the *-C* flag was *not* used, you may need to first create the database before connecting to it and restoring its attributes and data. Remember also that you need to specify the usual connection parameters to *psql* in order to operate as a user with the rights to create a database.

Example 9-23 demonstrates recreating the `booktown` database with the *booktown.sql* file created in Example 9-20, in the section titled "Using pg_dump" earlier in this chapter. Since the *-C* flag was used in this example, there is no need to create the database first; it can be created by bootstrapping through the `template1` database.

Example 9-23: Recreating the booktown database

```
[jworsley@booktown ~]$ psql -U manager -f booktown.sql template1
CREATE DATABASE
You are now connected to database booktown as user postgres.
COMMENT
CREATE
CREATE
CHANGE

[...]
```

As each dumped command in the *booktown.sql* file is processed by PostgreSQL, the resulting server messages (e.g., CREATE, CHANGE) will be displayed to *stderr*.

  Since *psql* can be used remotely, this same technique may be used across a network, provided the correct connection parameters are used from an authorized host.

Using pg_restore for tarred and compressed dumps

For files created by *pg_dump* with a file format other than plain text, the *pg_restore* command exists to seamlessly restore the dumped database from the tar, or compressed tar file.

Here is the syntax for the *pg_restore* command:

```
pg_restore [ options ] [ file ]
```

In this syntax, if *file* is not specified, *pg_restore* will wait for data from *stdin*. This means that you may effectively use the < shell redirection character with the same results. Notice especially in the *options* the *-d* flag. If left unspecified, *pg_restore* will simply display the database restoration statements to *stdout* (and thus, to the screen) rather than actually restoring a database.

If you are using the -C flag to create a database from scratch, you must still supply the -d flag (with the name of an existing database to connect to first, e.g., template1) from which to initialize a connection and create the new database. In such a case, it is not important to which database you initially connect, as it is only a temporary connection until the new database is created.

Many of the options for *pg_restore* directly mirror those available in *pg_dump*. In some cases, the same option must be supplied in both *pg_dump* and *pg_restore* in order for the desired functionality to be achieved. For example, this is the case with the -C flag. If used with *pg_dump*, but not *pg_restore*, the CREATE DATABASE command will be ignored by *pg_restore*, even though the command is present in the dump file.

The following are more detailed explanations of each option:

-a, --data-only

Causes any reference to creation of database schema objects to be ignored, restoring only data records (those with COPY or INSERT statements).

-c, --clean

Causes any DROP SQL statements to be executed before creating database objects. Without the -c flag, these statements are ignored, even if they are present in the dump file.

-C, --create

Causes the CREATE DATABASE SQL statement (if found in the dump file) to be executed. Without the -C flag, the statement is ignored.

-d NAME, --dbname=NAME

Specifies the database called NAME to be connected to for the restoration. If the -C flag is used to create a new database, the -d flag should be pointed to template1. If this parameter is not specified, the commands to restore the database will instead be displayed to *stdout* rather than sent to PostgreSQL.

-f FILENAME, --file=FILENAME

Indicates that FILENAME is the target for the database restoration SQL commands, rather than a the *postmaster* backend (with the -d flag), or *stdout* (the default).

-F { c | t }, --format={ c | t }

Specifies the format of the input file, FILENAME. A value of c indicates that it is a compressed and tarred dump, while t indicates that it is only tarred. Note that this option is usually not necessary, as *pg_restore* can judge what kind of file it is dealing with through its header data.

-h HOSTNAME, --host=HOSTNAME

Specifies that you should connect to HOSTNAME, rather than the localhost.

-i, --index

Specifies that *only* indices be recreated. Note that due to a bug, the *-i* flag may not work, though the *--index* flag should (as of PostgreSQL 7.1.x).

-l, --list

Specifies that only the table of contents of database objects should be output in a comma-delimited, PostgreSQL specific TOC (table of contents) format. This output can be redirected to a file (either with shell redirection via the < character, or with the *-f* flag) and later used with the *-L* flag to control what database objects are restored.

-L FILENAME, --use-list=FILENAME

Indicates use of the PostgreSQL TOC file FILENAME to determine which objects should be restored by *pg_restore*. This file is generated using the *-l* flag. After generating the file, delete lines for objects you do now wish to restore, or preface those lines with a semicolon (;). When *-L* is used, *pg_restore* only restores those objects listed in the specified TOC file.

-N, --orig-order

Causes the restore to occur in the same order that the *pg_dump* originally dumped the objects in (through the use of the extra TOC information in a *tar* or *gzip*-compressed format). This is not the same as the literal order in which the statements are placed in the dump file itself, which is the default restore order. This option excludes the use of the *-o* or *-r* options.

If, during a restoration, database objects are created in an incorrect order (e.g., an object which relies on another existing object is created before the object it relies on), you can re-initialize a database and try this flag to override the order which was originally chosen by *pg_dump*.

-o, --oid-order

Causes the restore to occur strictly in the order of OIDs, ascending; this option excludes the use of the *-N* or *-r* options.

-O, --no-owner

Forces *pg_restore* to ignore any \connect statements which would be used to enforce ownership.

-p PORT, --port=PORT

Specifies that the database connection should be made on port PORT, rather than the default port (usually 5432, though it may have been configured differently when PostgreSQL was compiled, by the *--with-pgport* flag).

-P, --function

Specifies that *only* functions are to be recreated. Like the *-i* flag, due to a bug, the *-P* flag may not work, though the *--function* flag should, as of PostgreSQL 7.1.x.

-r, --rearrange

Causes the restore to occur in the order chosen by *pg_dump* at the time of the dump file's creation. Most of the objects are created in OID order with this option, though statements creating rules and indices are placed towards the end of the file. This option is the default.

-R, --no-reconnect

Forces *pg_restore* to ignore *all* \connect statements (not just those intended to enforce ownership). This cannot be used with the *-C* flag, which requires at least one reconnection after the creation of a new database.

-s, --schema-only

Causes only the creation of database schema objects, such as tables, views, sequences, and indices. No rows will be copied or inserted into the tables, and sequences will initialize to their default values. This can be used, for example, to create an empty production database that matches the structure of a development database.

-S NAME, --superuser=NAME

Specifies the superuser with username NAME to be used in disabling triggers (if necessary, to recreate a trigger), as well as to set ownership of schema elements.

-t NAME, --table[=NAME]

Causes only the table NAME to be restored, rather than all database objects. Specifying just *--table* causes only tables to be restored.

-T NAME, --trigger[=NAME]

Causes only the trigger NAME to be restored, rather than all database objects. Specifying just *--trigger* causes only triggers to be restored.

-u, --password

Causes *pg_restore* to provide a prompt for a username and password.

-v, --verbose

Causes verbose output of each action as it is performed. This output is sent to *stderr*, rather than *stdout*.

-x, --no-acl

Suppresses any SQL GRANT or REVOKE statement in the dump being restored.

Example 9-24 demonstrates a restoration of the booktown database on a separate machine from which the original was made. It uses the *booktown.sql.tar* file created in Example 9-21, in the section titled "Using pg_dump," earlier in this chapter, as the source for the restoration.

Example 9-24: Restore with pg_restore

```
[jworsley@cmd ~]$ pg_restore -v -C -O -d template1 booktown.sql.tar
Connecting to database for restore
Creating DATABASE booktown
Connecting to new DB 'booktown' as postgres
Connecting to booktown as postgres
Creating COMMENT DATABASE "booktown"
Creating TABLE inventory

[...]
```

You can see upon examining the *pg_restore* command in Example 9-24 that it uses the *-v* flag for verbose output as it operates, the *-C* flag to create the database (as this is a new database on this machine), and the *-O* flag to ignore ownership from the original database (as the users on another machine are not guaranteed to exist locally). Notice also the *-d* flag is used to connect to the template1 database before creating, and connecting to, the booktown database.

Note that the use of the *-O* flag can be dangerous if ownership is an important part of the recreation of a database. It can play a helpful role in moving from a development environment to a production environment (e.g., if test or development account names were associated with various database objects). However, if a database is being restored on an existing machine (e.g., from a nightly backup), it is not recommended that the *-O* flag be used.

Remember that *pg_restore* exists only for files that are output in either *tar* format (*t*), or compressed *tar* format (*c*). Plain text SQL dumps may be processed with *psql*, as documented in the section titled "Using psql for plain text dumps," earlier in this chapter.

When to Backup and Restore Data

An important consideration to the use of the *pg_dump*, *pg_dumpall*, and *pg_restore* commands is *when* to use them, and when not to. Fortunately, in respect to each of these procedures, PostgreSQL is quite accommodating.

When to backup

With regards to backing up data with either *pg_dump* or *pg_dumpall*, there are few considerations necessary for when they may be performed. PostgreSQL has supported *hot backup* procedures since Version 6.5—these allow you to request data without blocking the normal activity of other concurrent users. It is called a hot backup because it is performed while the system is running, uninterrupted.

Therefore, the only potential considerations for backing up PostgreSQL center around performance. An exceptionally large database may take a while to dump all of its contents. The use of large objects may also be a factor if you intend to back up large object data with *pg_dump*'s *-b* flag (thus, adding to the amount of data needing to be output).

If you have a large database that takes a substantial amount of time to complete a dump, it is recommended that you schedule the *pg_dump* execution for a time when the database is not heavily used. Even though a dump does not block users from requesting and completing transactions, it can still slow down the general performance of such a system during heavy, or even medium usage.

When to restore

With respect to restoration there are several more considerations to be taken into account than when merely backing up data. Specifically, these apply to how "deep" a restoration must go; restoring just the data is a very different operation from totally recreating the database from scratch, and the restrictions involved scale with the depth of the operation.

The least restrictive kind of restoration is one which restores data *only*. This can be executed while users are actively connected to the database. It may even be executed while connected users are in the middle of transactions. This is possible through PostgreSQL's multiversion control. Such a restore can be performed on the fly, without having to restart the database system. Once modifications are synchronized with the database, the changes are immediately available to connected users.

A restoration involving dropping and recreating database schema (e.g., tables, views, etc.) may also be performed while the system is running. This method is not as seamless as a data-only restoration, because database objects will briefly be removed from the system, which may cause temporary problems to applications relying on certain objects to exist. The exact nature of such a restriction is dependent on the nature of the application accessing the database.

The most restrictive kind of restoration is one which involves dropping the database itself. If such a restoration is scheduled, it *must* be done at a time when no other user is connected to that database. The DROP DATABASE command will fail if any user is actively connected at the time it is executed.

It may in fact be necessary to shut down and restart PostgreSQL with TCP/IP connections disabled if a highly-used database is intended to be dropped and recreated from scratch; this will prevent any external machine from connecting to the database server until the work is completed.

Backing Up the Filesystem

While PostgreSQL abstracts the literal data files from its users, all of the data within PostgreSQL databases can be found in normal system files. These files are constantly in a state of flux when the database is running, as not all changes made in PostgreSQL are immediately written to disk. These files are stored within the PostgreSQL directory (e.g., */usr/local/pgsql/data*, or whatever path is specified by the PGDATA environment variable).

Rather than creating a set of SQL instructions to re-create a database, you may instead opt to stop the PostgreSQL server (in order to ensure that all changes are synchronized with the hard disk) and create a backup of that area of the filesystem. Typically this is done with the *tar* utility, and optionally compressed with a compression utility such as *gzip*.

Example 9-25 demonstrates the backing up of a filesystem in which PostgreSQL keeps its data, as performed by the user who owns the data files (which is the same user that runs PostgreSQL's backend). In this case, the path is */usr/local/ pgsql/data*, and the system user is *postgres*.

Example 9-25: Backing up the PostgreSQL filesystem

```
[postgres@booktown ~]$ cd /usr/local/pgsql
[postgres@booktown pgsql]$ pg_ctl stop
Smart Shutdown request at Fri Sep 14 14:54:15 2001
DEBUG:  shutting down
waiting for postmaster to shut down......DEBUG:  database system is shut down
done
postmaster successfully shut down
[postgres@booktown pgsql]$ tar czf pgsql.bak.tar.gz data/
[postgres@booktown pgsql]$ ls -l *.tar.gz
-rw-rw-r--    1 postgres postgres 66124795 Sep 14 14:36 pgsql.bak.tar.gz
```

Notice that the *pg_ctl* command is called before the *tar* process, to stop the PostgreSQL backend (if installed, the SysV script may be invoked with the *service* command to the same end). As stated, this is to ensure that the most recent changes to the database have been synchronized with the hard disk, as well as to verify that none of the data files are modified while backed up.

The primary advantage to backing up your data in this fashion is that you have a *literal* backup of PostgreSQL's data files. In order to restore a crashed database from this kind of file, it needs to be decompressed in the appropriate location, and for the backend to be re-started. There is no need for negotiation of options, ownership, or potential conflicts between the *pg_dump* output and restoring it to a live PostgreSQL server through sequential SQL statements.

However, while this method is easier to implement, it presents several limitations. First, the database must be shut down completely to backup or restore the data, eliminating the primary advantage of a hot backup-capable DBMS, which is limited downtime. Further, it is not possible to backup only specific databases, or tables. The entire data directory must be backed up for a complete restoration of the filesystem. This is because there are many files associated with a particular database, and it is not obvious which files correlate to which databases.

Finally, because more than abstract information is represented on disk by a live database, a much greater amount of disk space is required to backup even a compressed copy of the entire data directory.

10

User and Group Management

As in most database systems, *users* and *groups* handle an important role within PostgreSQL. Used correctly, users and groups can allow for fine-grained, versatile access control to your database objects.

PostgreSQL stores both user and group data within its own system catalogs. These are different from the users and groups defined within the operating system on which the software is installed. Any connection to PostgreSQL must be made with a specific user, and any user may belong to one or more defined groups.

Users control the allocation of rights and track who is allowed to perform actions on the system (and which actions they may perform). Groups exist as a means to simplify the allocation of these rights. Both users and groups exist as global database objects, which means they are not tied to any particular database.

This chapter addresses the management and practical application of PostgreSQL users and groups.

Managing Users

In order to establish a connection to PostgreSQL, you must supply a basic form of identification. This is called a *username*, as it identifies the *user* who the system will recognize as connected to a database. Users within PostgreSQL are not necessarily related to users of the operating system (which are sometimes called system *accounts*), though you may choose to name your PostgreSQL users after the system accounts that will be accessing them.

Each user has an internal system ID to PostgreSQL (called a *sysid*), as well as a password, though the password is not necessarily required to connect (depending on the configuration of the *pg_hba.conf* (see Chapter 8, *Authentication and*

Encryption, for more on this subject). The user's system ID is used to associate objects in a database with their *owner* (the user who is allowed to grant and revoke rights on an object).

As well as being used to associate database objects with their owner, users may also have *global* rights assigned to them when they are created. These rights determine whether or not a user is allowed to create and destroy databases, and whether or not the user is a *superuser* (a user who is allowed all rights, in all databases, including the right to create users). The assignment of these rights may be modified at any time by an existing superuser.

PostgreSQL installs a single superuser by default named *postgres*. All other users must be added by this user, or by another subsequently added superuser.

Viewing Users

All user information is stored in a PostgreSQL system table called `pg_shadow`, shown in Table 10-1. This table is only selectable by superusers, though a limited view of this table called `pg_user` is accessible to normal users.

Table 10-1. The pg_shadow table

Column	Type
usename	name
usesysid	integer
usecreatedb	boolean
usetrace	boolean
usesuper	boolean
usecatupd	boolean
passwd	text
valuntil	abstime

The primary difference between the selectable data in `pg_user` and `pg_shadow` is that the actual value of the `passwd` column is not shown (it is replaced with a string of asterisks). This is a security measure to ensure that normal users are not able to determine one another's passwords.

The `usename` column stores the name of the system user, which is a unique character string (no two users may have the same name, as users are global database objects). Similarly, the `usesysid` column stores a unique integer value associated with the user. The `usecreatedb` and `usesuper` each correspond to the pair of privileges which can be set upon creation of a user, as documented in the section titled "Creating Users."

Creating Users

PostgreSQL provides two methods by which database users may be created. Each requires authentication as a superuser, for only superusers can create new users.

The first method is through the use of the SQL command CREATE USER, which may be executed by any properly authenticated PostgreSQL client (e.g., *psql*). The second is a command-line wrapper called *createuser*, which may be more convenient for a system administrator, as it can be executed in a single command without the need to interact with a PostgreSQL client.

The following sections document each of these methods.

Creating a user with the CREATE USER SQL command

The CREATE USER command requires only one parameter: the name of the new user. There are also a variety of options that may be set, including a password, explicit system ID, group, and a set of rights that may be explicitly allocated. Here is the complete syntax for CREATE USER:

```
CREATE USER username
    [ WITH [ SYSID uid ]
           [ PASSWORD 'password' ] ]
    [ CREATEDB   | NOCREATEDB ]
    [ CREATEUSER | NOCREATEUSER ]
    [ IN GROUP groupname [, ...] ]
    [ VALID UNTIL 'abstime' ]
```

In this syntax, *username* is the name of the new user to be created. You cannot have two users with the same name. By specifying the WITH keyword, either or both of the SYSID and PASSWORD keywords may be applied.

Every other optional keyword may follow in the order displayed (not requiring the use of the WITH keyword). The following is a detailed explanation of each optional keyword and its meaning:

SYSID *uid*
> Specifies that the system ID is to be set to the value of *uid*. If omitted, a reasonable, unique numeric default is chosen.

PASSWORD '*password*'
> Sets the new user's password to *password*. If unspecified, the password defaults to NULL.

CREATEDB | NOCREATEDB
> Specifying the CREATEDB keyword grants the new user the right to create new databases, as well as the right to destroy databases which they own. Specifying NOCREATEDB explicitly enforces the default, which is the lack of this right.

CREATEUSER | NOCREATEUSER

Grants the right to create new users, which implicitly creates a superuser. Notice that a user with the rights to create other users will therefore have *all rights*, in all databases (including the rights to create a database, even if NOCRE- ATEDB was specified). NOCREATEUSER explicitly enforces the default, which is the lack of this right.

IN GROUP *groupname* [, . . .]

Adds the new user to the group named *groupname*. Multiple group names may be specified by separating them with commas. The group(s) must exist in order for the statement to succeed.

VALID UNTIL '*abstime*'

Sets the user's password to expire at *abstime*, which must be of a recognizable timestamp format. After that date, the password must be reset, and the expira- tion moved forward.

VALID UNTIL '*infinity*'

Sets the user's password to be valid indefinitely.

By not specifying either CREATEDB or CREATEUSER, users are implicitly "normal" with no special rights. They may not create databases or other users, nor may they destroy databases or users. Such users may connect to databases in PostgreSQL, but they can only perform the statements which they have been granted access to (see the section titled "Granting Privileges" for more on granting rights).

Example 10-1 creates a normal user named salesuser. It also sets a password of *NOrm4!* by the use of the WITH PASSWORD clause. By omitting the VALID UNTIL clause, this password will never expire.

Example 10-1: Creating a normal user

```
template1=# CREATE USER salesuser
template1-#              WITH PASSWORD 'NOrm4!';
CREATE USER
```

The CREATE USER server message returned in Example 10-1 indicates that the user was added successfully. Other messages you may receive from this command are as follows:

ERROR: CREATE USER: permission denied

This message is returned if the user issuing the CREATE USER command is not a superuser. Only superusers may create new users.

ERROR: CREATE USER: user name "salesuser" already exists

This message indicates that a user with the name salesuser already exists.

If you wish to create a user who has the ability to create databases within Post- greSQL but not create or destroy PostgreSQL users, you may specify the CREATEDB keyword rather than CREATEUSER. This allows the named user to arbitrarily create databases, as well as drop any databases which they own. See Chapter 9, *Database Management*, for more on this the topic of creating and destroying databases.

Example 10-2 illustrates the creation of a user named dbuser who has the right to create new databases. This is achieved by specifying the CREATEDB keyword after the username. Notice also the use of the WITH PASSWORD and VALID UNTIL keywords. These set the password for dbuser to *DbuS3r*, which will be valid until November 11th, 2002.

Example 10-2: Creating a user with CREATEDB rights

```
template1=# CREATE USER dbuser CREATEDB
template1-#          WITH PASSWORD 'DbuS3r'
template1-#          VALID UNTIL '2002-11-11';
CREATE USER
```

Resetting an expired user's password does not modify the VALID UNTIL value. In order to re-active a user's access whose password has expired, both the WITH PASSWORD and VALID UNTIL keywords must be provided to the ALTER USER command. See the section titled "Altering Users" for more on this command.

VALID UNTIL settings are only relevant to systems which are not trusted; sites which are trusted do not require passwords. See Chapter 8 for more on host-based authentication.

You may wish to create an alternate superuser from the *postgres* user, though caution should be exercised in creating superusers. These users are granted *every right* within PostgreSQL, including creating users, removing users, and destroying databases. Example 10-3 demonstrates the creation of a PostgreSQL superuser named manager from the *psql* prompt.

Example 10-3: Creating a superuser

```
template1=# CREATE USER manager CREATEUSER;
CREATE USER
```

Creating a user with the createuser script

The *createuser* script is executed directly from the command line, and can operate in one of two ways. If issued without any arguments, it will interactively prompt you for the username and each of the rights, and attempt to make a local connection to PostgreSQL. Alternatively, you may choose to specify the options and the username to be created on the command line.

As with other command-line applications for PostgreSQL, arguments may be supplied either in their short form (with a single dash, and character), or in their long form (with two dashes, and the full name of the argument).

Here is the syntax for *createuser*:

```
createuser [ options ] [ username ]
```

The *username* in the syntax represents the name of the user you wish to create. Replace *options* with one or more of the following flags:

-d, --createdb
> Equivalent to the CREATEDB keyword of the CREATE USER SQL command. Allows the new user to create databases.

-D, --no-createdb
> Equivalent to the NOCREATEDB keyword of the CREATE USER SQL command. Explicitly indicates that the new user may not create databases. This is the default.

-a, --adduser
> Equivalent to the CREATEUSER keyword of the CREATE USER SQL command. Allows the new user to create users, and raises the status of the user to a superuser (enabling *all* rights within PostgreSQL).

-A, --no-adduser
> Equivalent to the NOCREATEUSER keyword of the CREATE USER SQL command. Explicitly indicates that the new user is not a superuser. This is the default.

-i SYSID, --sysid=SYSID
> Sets the new users system ID to *SYSID*.

-P, --pwprompt
> Results in a password prompt allowing you to set the password of the new user *username*.

-h HOSTNAME, --host=HOSTNAME
> Specifies that *HOSTNAME* will be connected to, rather than the localhost, or the host defined by the PGHOST environment variable.

-p PORT, --port=PORT
> Specifies that the database connection will be made on port *PORT*, rather than the default port (usually 5432).

-U USERNAME, --username=USERNAME
> Specifies that *USERNAME* will be the user who connects to PostgreSQL (The default is to connect using the name of the system user executing the *createuser* script).

-W, --password

Results in a password prompt for the connecting user, which happens automatically if the *pg_hba.conf* file is configured not to *trust* the requesting host.

-e, --echo

Causes the CREATE USER command sent to PostgreSQL to be displayed to the screen as it is executed by *createuser.*

-q, --quiet

Prevents output from being sent to *stdout* (though errors will still be sent to *stderr*).

If any of the *-d, -D, -a, -A,* or *username* arguments are omitted, *createuser* will prompt you for each missing argument. This is because PostgreSQL will not make any assumptions about the rights intended for the new user, nor about the new user's name. Example 10-4 creates a user named newuser, who has neither the right to create a database, nor create users.

Example 10-4: Creating a user with createuser

```
[jworsley@booktown ~]$ createuser -U manager -D -A newuser
CREATE USER
```

Notice also the *-U manager* flag passed to the *createuser* script. This indicates that the user with which to connect to PostgreSQL is manager, not jworsley as the script would otherwise assume, based on the name of the system account invoking the script.

If you prefer to be interactively prompted for each setting, (instead of having to remember the meaning of each flag or check the reference each time) you may simply omit the flags you are uncertain of. The *createuser* script will then prompt you for the basic *createuser* options. These options include the PostgreSQL username, whether the user may create databases, and whether or not the user may add new users to PostgreSQL.

Example 10-5 demonstrates using the *createuser* script in interactive mode. The net effect of this example is the same as the single line executed in Example 10-4.

Example 10-5: Interactively creating a user with createuser

```
[jworsley@booktown ~]$ createuser
Enter name of user to add: newuser
Shall the new user be allowed to create databases? (y/n) n
Shall the new user be allowed to create more new users? (y/n) n
CREATE USER
```

Altering Users

Existing users may only be modified by PostgreSQL superusers. Possible modifications include each of the options available at the creation of the user (e.g., password, password expiration date, global rights), except for the system ID of an existing user, which may not be modified. Modification of existing users is achieved through the use of the ALTER USER SQL statement.

Here is the syntax for ALTER USER:

```
ALTER USER username
          [ WITH PASSWORD 'password' ]
          [ CREATEDB | NOCREATEDB ]
          [ CREATEUSER | NOCREATEUSER ]
          [ VALID UNTIL 'abstime' ]
```

The required *username* argument specifies which user is to be modified. Any of the following parameters may additionally be specified:

WITH PASSWORD '*password*'

> Sets *username*'s password to *password*.

CREATEDB | NOCREATEDB

> Grants or revokes from *username* the right to create databases.

CREATEUSER | NOCREATEUSER

> Grants or revokes from *username* the status of superuser, which enables *all* possible right within PostgreSQL (most notably the ability to create and destroy users and superusers).

VALID UNTIL '*abstime*'

> Sets *username*'s password to expire at *abstime*, which must be of some valid timestamp format. This value is only relevant for systems requiring password authentication, and is otherwise ignored (e.g., for trusted sites).

A common function of ALTER USER is to reset the password (and potentially the expiration date) of a user. If a PostgreSQL user had an expiration date set when their user was originally added, and that date has passed, and the user requires password-based authentication, a superuser will have to reset both the password *and* the expiration date to re-activate a user's ability to connect. If you want to cause a user's password to never expire, set it to the special timestamp *infinity*.

Example 10-6 modifies a user named salesuser. The user's password is set to *n3Wp4s4* by the WITH PASSWORD clause, and set to expire on January 1st, 2003 by the VALID UNTIL clause.

Example 10-6: Resetting a password

```
template1=# ALTER USER salesuser
template1-#           WITH PASSWORD 'n3WP4s4'
template1-#           VALID UNTIL '2003-01-01';
ALTER USER
```

At times you may wish to grant a user additional rights beyond those originally granted to them. The use of the CREATEUSER keyword in Example 10-7 modifies the user salesuser to have all rights in PostgreSQL, making the user into a superuser. Note that this makes the CREATEDB right moot, as superusers can create databases implicitly.

Example 10-7: Adding superuser rights

```
template1=# ALTER USER salesuser
template1-#           CREATEUSER;
ALTER USER
```

Conversely, there may be times when a user no longer deserves rights that have been granted in the past. These rights may be just as easily removed by a superuser with the NOCREATEDB and NOCREATEUSER keywords.

Example 10-8: Removing superuser rights

```
template1=# ALTER USER salesuser
template1-#           NOCREATEDB NOCREATEUSER;
ALTER USER
```

As any superuser may revoke rights from another superuser, or even remove another superuser, it is wise to be *extremely careful* when granting the CREATEUSER right.

Removing Users

PostgreSQL users may at any time be removed from the system by authenticated superusers. The only restriction is that a user may not be removed if any databases exist which are owned by that user. If a user owns a database, that database must be dropped before the user can be removed from the system.

As with the creation of PostgreSQL users, there are two methods by which users may be removed. These are the DROP USER SQL command, and the *dropuser* command-line executable.

Removing users with the DROP USER SQL command

A superuser may remove a user by issuing the DROP USER command from a valid PostgreSQL client. The *psql* program is most commonly used to achieve this task.

Here is the syntax for DROP USER:

```
DROP USER username
```

In this syntax, *username* is the name of the user that you intend to permanently remove from the system. Example 10-9 shows the use of the *psql* client to connect to PostgreSQL as the manager user in order to remove the salesuser database user.

Example 10-9: Removing a user with DROP USER

```
[jworsley@booktown ~]$ psql -U manager template1
Welcome to psql, the PostgreSQL interactive terminal.

Type:  \copyright for distribution terms
       \h for help with SQL commands
       \? for help on internal slash commands
       \g or terminate with semicolon to execute query
       \q to quit

template1=# DROP USER salesuser;
DROP USER
```

The DROP USER server message indicates that the user was successfully removed from the system. Other messages that you might receive from this command include:

ERROR: DROP USER: permission denied
> Indicates that the user initiating the command does not have the right to drop a user. Only superusers may drop existing database users.

ERROR: DROP USER: user "salesuser" does not exist
> Indicates that there is no such user with the name salesuser.

Removing users with the dropuser operating system command

The *dropuser* command operates much like the *createuser* script. It offers the same connection options, ensuring that it can be used remotely as well as locally, and requires only the username of the user to be removed from the system.

Here is the syntax for *dropuser*:

```
dropuser [ options ] [ username ]
```

Each of the connectivity options is identical to those for *createuser*, described in the section titled "Creating a user with the createuser script," earlier in this chapter. Example 10-10 demonstrates the same net effect as the SQL statement in Example 10-9 by removing the user named salesuser as the manager user with *dropuser*.

Example 10-10: Removing a user with dropuser

```
[jworsley@booktown ~]$ dropuser -U manager salesuser
DROP USER
```

The output from *dropuser* is the same as the output for the SQL DROP USER command. If you omit the username that you wish to remove when you execute the script *dropuser*, you will be prompted interactively for the name of the user to be removed from the system.

Managing Groups

Groups serve to simplify the assignment of rights. Ordinary privileges must be granted to a single user, one at a time. This can be tedious if several users need to be assigned the same access to a variety of database objects.

Groups are created to avoid this problem. A group simply requires a name, and can be created empty (without users). Once created, users who are intended to share common access privileges are added into the group together, and are henceforth associated by their membership in that group. Rights on database objects are then granted to the *group*, rather than to each *member* of the group. For a system with many users and databases, groups make managing rights less of an administrative chore.

Users may belong to any number of groups, or no groups at all.

Creating and Removing Groups

Before you get started managing groups, you should first understand how to create and remove them from the system. Each of these procedures requires superuser privileges. See the section titled "Managing Users" earlier in this chapter for more about superusers.

Creating a group

Any superuser may create a new group in PostgreSQL with the CREATE GROUP command. Here is the syntax for CREATE GROUP:

```
CREATE GROUP groupname [ WITH
                       [ SYSID groupid ]
                       [ USER  username [, ...] ] ]
```

In this syntax, *groupname* is the name of the group that you wish to create. A group's name must start with an alphabetical character, and may not exceed 31 characters in length. Providing the WITH keyword allows for either of the optional attributes to be specified. If you wish to specify the system ID to use for the new group, use the SYSID keyword to specify the *groupid* value. Use the USER keyword to include one or more users in the group at creation time. Separate usernames by commas.

Additionally, the PostgreSQL user and group tables operate separately from each other. This separation does allow a user's usesysid and a group's grosysid to be identical within the PostgreSQL system.

As an example, Example 10-11 creates the sales group, and adds two users to it upon its creation. These users are allen, and vincent (presumably, members of Book Town's sales department).

Example 10-11: Creating a group

```
booktown=# CREATE GROUP sales
booktown-#                    WITH USER allen, vincent;
CREATE GROUP
```

The CREATE GROUP server message indicates that the group was created successfully. You may verify the creation of a group, as well as view all existing groups, with a query on the pg_group system table. Example 10-12 executes such a query.

Example 10-12: Verifying a group

```
booktown=# SELECT * FROM pg_group;
   groname   | grosysid |   grolist
-------------+----------+-------------
 sales       |        1 | {7017,7016}
 accounting  |        2 |
 marketing   |        3 |
(3 rows)
```

Notice that the grolist column is an array, containing the PostgreSQL user ID of each user in the group. These are the same user IDs which can be seen in the pg_user view. For example:

```
booktown=# SELECT usename FROM pg_user
booktown-#                 WHERE usesysid = 7017 OR usesysid = 7016;
 usename
---------
 allen
 vincent
(2 rows)
```

Removing a group

Any superuser may also remove a group with the DROP GROUP SQL command. You should exercise caution with this command, as it is irreversible, and you will not be prompted to verify the removal of the group (even if there are users still in the group). Unlike DROP DATABASE, DROP GROUP may be performed within a transaction block.

Here is the syntax for DROP GROUP:

```
DROP GROUP groupname
```

The *groupname* is the name of the group to be permanently removed. Example 10-13 removes an outdated marketing group from the Book Town database.

Example 10-13: Removing a group

```
booktown=# DROP GROUP marketing;
DROP GROUP
```

The DROP GROUP server message returned from Example 10-13 indicates that the group was successfully destroyed. Note that removing a group does not remove permissions placed on it, but rather "disembodies" them. Any permissions placed on a database object which have rights assigned to a dropped group will appear to be assigned to a group *system ID*, rather than to a group.

Inadvertently dropped groups can be restored to their previous functionality by creating a new group with the same system ID as the dropped group. This involves the SYSID keyword, as documented in the section titled "Creating a group." If you assign group permissions to a table and then drop the group, the group permissions on the table will be retained. However, you will need to add the appropriate users to the newly recreated group for the table permissions to be effective for members of that group.

Associating Users with Groups

Users are both added and removed from groups in PostgreSQL through the ALTER GROUP SQL command. Here is the syntax for the ALTER GROUP command:

```
ALTER GROUP groupname { ADD | DROP } USER username [, ... ]
```

The *groupname* is the name of the group to be modified, while the *username* is the name of the user to be added or removed, depending on whether the ADD or DROP keyword is used.

Adding a user to a group

Suppose that Booktown hires two new sales associates, David and Ben, and gives them usernames david and ben, respectively. Example 10-14 uses the ALTER GROUP command adds these new users to the sales group.

Example 10-14: Adding a user to a group

```
booktown=# ALTER GROUP sales ADD USER david, ben;
ALTER GROUP
```

The ALTER GROUP server message returned in Example 10-14 indicates that the users david and ben were successfully added to the sales group. Example 10-15 demonstrates another query to the pg_group table to verify the addition of those new users to the group. Note that there are now four system IDs in the grolist column for the sales group.

Example 10-15: Verifying user addition

```
booktown=# SELECT * FROM pg_group WHERE groname = 'sales';
 groname | grosysid |         grolist
---------+----------+-----------------------
 sales   |        1 | {7019,7018,7017,7016}
(1 row)
```

Removing a user from a group

Suppose that some time later David is transferred from sales to accounting. In order to maintain the correct group association, and to make sure that David does not have any rights granted exclusively to the sales group, his user (david) should be removed from that group; Example 10-16 achieves this.

Example 10-16: Removing a user from a group

```
booktown=# ALTER GROUP sales DROP USER david;
ALTER GROUP
```

The ALTER GROUP message returned from Example 10-16 indicates that the david user was successfully removed from the sales group.

To complete his transition to the accounting department, David must then have his user added to the accounting group. The following statements use similar syntax as the statements in Example 10-14 and Example 10-15. The net effect is that the david user is added into the accounting group. This means that any special rights granted to this group will be implicitly granted to david for as long as he is a member of the group.

```
booktown=# ALTER GROUP accounting ADD USER david;
ALTER GROUP
booktown=# SELECT * FROM pg_group;
```

```
  groname   | grosysid |     grolist
------------+----------+------------------
  sales     |        1 | {7016,7017,7019}
  accounting |        2 | {7018}
(2 rows)
```

Granting Privileges

PostgreSQL maintains a tightly controlled set of access control lists or *ACLs*. This information describes which users are allowed to select from, update, and otherwise modify objects within a database. A set of access privileges and restrictions exist for each applicable database object in PostgreSQL (e.g., tables, views, and sequences). Superusers and owners of database objects maintain these ACLs through a pair of SQL commands: GRANT and REVOKE.

As stated in Chapter 9, when a user first creates a database, they are implicitly the owner of that database. Similarly, whenever someone creates that database object, it is owned by that individual who issued the related CREATE SQL command.

Aside from PostgreSQL superusers (who may manipulate any database object in any way), only the owners of database objects are allowed to grant and revoke privileges on the objects which they own. Though any user may connect to a database, if they wish access to objects within that database they must have those privileges explicitly granted to them.

Understanding Access Control

As mentioned earlier in this section, access control lists apply to three types of database objects: tables, lists, and sequences. For these objects, there are four general privileges which may be granted to, or revoked from, a user or group. The ability to revoke rights exists only to undo the function of having granted them. Users and groups have no rights to begin with.

From the *psql* client, you can view ACL permission summaries by using the \z slash command. This command displays all access permissions in the currently connected database. To see permissions on a specific object, specify that object's name as a parameter to the \z command. You can use a regular expression in place of a name to see privileges on a group of objects.

Table 10-2 lists each of the Access Control privileges available within PostgreSQL. Each privilege also has an associated symbol, which appears as a single alphabetical character. These symbols are shorthand for the described privilege, and are used by the *psql* \z slash command when displaying summaries of access permissions.

Table 10-2. PostgreSQL ACL privileges

Keyword	Symbol	Description
SELECT	*r*	Allows a user to retrieve data from a table, view or sequence (though the nextval() function may not be called with only SELECT rights). Also known as "read" rights.
INSERT	*a*	Allows a user to insert new rows into a table. Also known as "append" rights.
UPDATE, DELETE	*w*	Allows a user to modify or remove rows of data from a table. If either the UPDATE or DELETE right is granted, the other is implicitly granted as well. Also known as "write" rights.
RULE	*R*	Allows a user to create a rewrite rule on a table or view.
ALL	*arwR*	Represents a shorthand way to grant or revoke all rights at once. ALL is not a right in and of itself. Granting ALL results in the granting of SELECT, INSERT, UPDATE, DELETE, and RULE.

Granting Privileges with GRANT

To assign a privilege to a user or group, use SQL's GRANT command. Here is the syntax for GRANT:

```
GRANT privilege [, ...] ON object [, ...]
      TO { PUBLIC | username | GROUP groupname }
```

In this syntax, *privilege* is any of the privileges listed in Table 10-2, *object* is the name of the database object (table, view or sequence) that a privilege is being granted on, and the token following the TO keyword describes who the privilege is being granted to. Multiple privileges and objects may be listed, separated from one another by commas.

Only one of the terms following TO may be used in a single GRANT statement. Granting rights with the PUBLIC keyword indiscriminately grants the intended privilege to the special "public" target. PUBLIC privileges are shared by all users. Specifying a *username* grants the privilege to specific user. Likewise, specifying a *groupname* grants the privilege to a specific group.

Suppose, for example, that the manager user needs all rights to the customers, books, editions and publishers tables. Example 10-17 gives the manager user those rights, using a single GRANT statement.

Example 10-17: Granting user privileges

```
booktown=# GRANT ALL ON customers, books, editions, publishers
booktown-#             TO manager;
CHANGE
```

The use of the ALL keyword in Example 10-17 grants all possible ACL rights (SELECT, UPDATE, etc.) for the specified objects to the user manager. The CHANGE message from the server indicates that the privileges were correctly modified. Remember that you can use the \z command in *psql* in order to verify permissions on a database object.

```
booktown=# \z publishers
Access permissions for database "booktown"
  Relation  |  Access permissions
------------+----------------------
 publishers | {"=","manager=arwR"}
(1 row)
```

As another example, let's look at the use of the GROUP keyword to grant privileges to members of a group *groupname*. For instance, the entire sales department at the Book Town should be given permission to view the customers table, but not to modify it. Example 10-18 grants SELECT access on the customers table to any member of the sales group.

Example 10-18: Granting group privileges

```
booktown=# GRANT SELECT ON customers TO GROUP sales;
CHANGE
booktown=# \z customers
 Access permissions for database "booktown"
 Relation  |          Access permissions
-----------+------------------------------------
 customers | {"=","manager=arwR","group sales=r"}
(1 row)
```

Restricting Rights with REVOKE

By default, a normal user has no privileges on any database object that they do not own. To explicitly revoke a right after it has been granted, the object's owner (or a superuser) can issue the REVOKE command. This command is very similar in form to the GRANT command.

Here is the syntax for REVOKE:

```
REVOKE privilege [, ...] ON object [, ...]
       FROM { PUBLIC | username | GROUP groupname }
```

The structure of the REVOKE command syntax is identical to that of the GRANT command, with the exception that the SQL command itself is REVOKE rather than GRANT, and the keyword FROM is used, rather than the TO keyword.

Revoking privileges from PUBLIC only affects the special "public" group, which includes all users. Revoking rights from PUBLIC will not affect any users who have been explicitly granted those privileges.

Suppose the UPDATE rights on the books table have been granted to the user david. When David is transferred to another department, and no longer needs the ability to modify book information, you should revoke David's UPDATE privilege on the books table.

Example 10-19 uses the \z slash command in *psql* to check the permissions on the books table, revealing that david has write-access privileges to that table. A REVOKE statement then explicitly revokes the UPDATE and DELETE privileges on the books table from the user david. Finally, at the end of the example another \z slash command is executed to verify the removal of the privilege.

Example 10-19: Revoking rights

```
booktown=# \z books
Access permissions for database "booktown"
 Relation |        Access permissions
----------+-------------------------------------
 books    | {"=","manager=arwR","david=w"}
(1 row)

booktown=# REVOKE UPDATE, DELETE ON books
booktown-#          FROM david;
CHANGE
booktown=# \z books
Access permissions for database "booktown"
 Relation |  Access permissions
----------+----------------------
 books    | {"=","manager=arwR"}
(1 row)
```

Using Views for Access Control

While you cannot control read-access to specified columns or rows of a table, you can achieve this indirectly through the careful use of views. By creating a view on a table, and forcing users to access the table through that view, you can allow only desired columns or rows to be selected.

You limit columns by specifying a column list in the view's SELECT statement when you create the view. The view will then return only the columns you specify. You limit rows by writing a WHERE clause in the view's SELECT statement. The view will then return only those rows that match the WHERE clause (see Chapter 4, *Using*

SQL with PostgreSQL, for more about creating views).

As ACL privileges may be applied to views as well as tables, you may then grant SELECT rights to the limited view, but not the table itself. Users will then be able to select from the view even though they don't have access to the underlying table.

For instance, the Book Town store has a stock table correlating a book's ISBN number to its purchase cost, retail price, and the current available stock. The table structure is shown in Table 10-3.

Table 10-3. The stock table

Column	Type	Modifier
isbn	text	NOT NULL
cost	numeric(5,2)	
retail	numeric(5,2)	
stock	integer	

Suppose that the manager of Book Town doesn't want the salespeople to have access to the purchase cost of each book. This information can be restricted by generating a view which retrieves data from only the isbn, retail and stock columns. Example 10-20 creates such a view, grants rights to the sales group, and verifies the rights with the \z *psql* slash command.

Example 10-20: Controlling SELECT privileges with a view

```
booktown=# CREATE VIEW stock_view
booktown-#               AS SELECT isbn, retail, stock
booktown-#                  FROM stock;
CREATE
booktown=# GRANT SELECT ON stock_view TO GROUP sales;
CHANGE
booktown=# \z stock
       Access permissions for database "booktown"
   Relation    |            Access permissions
---------------+---------------------------------------------
  stock        |
  stock_backup |
  stock_view   | {"=","manager=arwR","group sales=r"}
(3 rows)
```

Example 10-21 demonstrates the addition of a new user, barbara. It grants SELECT rights on the stock_view. Since the barbara user does not have any implicit rights on the stock table, it is inaccessible; this is the case, even though the view on that table *is* accessible as a result of the GRANT statement.

Example 10-21: Controlling SELECT

```
booktown=# CREATE USER barbara;
CREATE USER
booktown=# GRANT USER barbara SELECT ON stock_view;
booktown=# \c - barbara
You are now connected as new user barbara.
booktown=> SELECT * FROM stock;
ERROR:  stock: Permission denied.
booktown=> SELECT * FROM stock_view;
    isbn    | retail | stock
------------+--------+-------
 0385121679 |  36.95 |    65
 039480001X |  32.95 |    31
 0394900014 |  23.95 |     0
 044100590X |  45.95 |    89
 0441172717 |  21.95 |    77
 0451160916 |  28.95 |    22
 0451198492 |  46.95 |     0
 0451457994 |  22.95 |     0
 0590445065 |  23.95 |    10
 0679803335 |  24.95 |    18
 0694003611 |  28.95 |    50
 0760720002 |  23.95 |    28
 0823015505 |  28.95 |    16
 0929605942 |  21.95 |    25
 1885418035 |  24.95 |    77
 0394800753 |  16.95 |     4
(16 rows)
```

Notice that when connected as the `barbara` user, the `SELECT` statement from the `stock_view` is successful, while the `stock` table presents a `Permission denied` error.

IV

PostgreSQL Programming

11

PL/pgSQL

PL/pgSQL is a loadable, *procedural language,* similar to the Oracle procedural language, PL/SQL. A procedural language is a programming language used to specify a sequence of steps that are followed to produce an intended programmatic result.

You can use PL/pgSQL to group sequences of SQL and programmatic statements together within a database server, reducing network and communications overhead incurred by client applications having to constantly request data from the database and perform logic operations upon that data from a remote location.

You have access to all PostgreSQL data types, operators, and functions within PL/pgSQL code. The "SQL" in PL/pgSQL is indicative of the fact that you are allowed to directly use the SQL language from within PL/pgSQL code. The use of SQL within PL/pgSQL code can increase the power, flexibility, and performance of your programs. If multiple SQL statements are executed from a PL/pgSQL code block, the statements are processed at one time, instead of the normal behavior of processing a single statement at a time.

Another important aspect of using PL/pgSQL is its portability; its functions are compatible with all platforms that can operate the PostgreSQL database system.

The following sections describe how to make PL/pgSQL available as a procedural language in your database.

Adding PL/pgSQL to Your Database

Programming languages are made available to databases by being created as a database object. You will therefore need to add the PL/pgSQL language to your database before you can use it (it is installed with PostgreSQL by default). The following steps demonstrate how to add PL/pgSQL to an existing database.

Adding PL/pgSQL to Your Database

To add PL/pgSQL to your PostgreSQL database, you can either use the *createlang* application from the command line, or the CREATE LANGUAGE SQL command from within a database client such as *psql*. The use of the CREATE LANGUAGE command first requires the creation of the PL/pgSQL *call handler*, which is the function that actually processes and interprets the PL/pgSQL code.

Though the *createlang* utility is simpler to use, as it abstracts the creation of the call handler and the language away from the user, the following sections document both methods.

 Installing PL/pgSQL in the template1 database causes all subsequent databases that are created with template1 as their template (which is the default) to also have PL/pgSQL installed.

Using psql to add PL/pgSQL

CREATE LANGUAGE is the SQL command which adds procedural languages to the currently connected database. Before it can be used, however, the CREATE FUNCTION command must first be used to create the procedural call handler.

Here is the syntax to create a PL/pgSQL call handler with CREATE FUNCTION:

```
CREATE FUNCTION plpgsql_call_handler()
        RETURNS OPAQUE AS '/postgres_library_path/plpgsql.so' LANGUAGE 'C'
```

In this syntax, *postgres_library_path* is the absolute system path to the installed PostgreSQL library files. This path, by default, is */usr/local/pgsql/lib*. Example 11-1 uses the CREATE FUNCTION command to create the PL/pgSQL call handler, assuming the *plpgsql.so* file is in the default location.

Example 11-1: Creating the PL/pgSQL call handler

```
booktown=# CREATE FUNCTION plpgsql_call_handler ()
booktown-#               RETURNS OPAQUE
booktown-#               AS '/usr/local/pgsql/lib/plpgsql.so'
booktown-#               LANGUAGE 'C';
CREATE
```

Example 11-1 only creates the function handler; the language itself must also be added with the CREATE LANGUAGE command. Here is the syntax to add PL/pgSQL to a database:

```
CREATE LANGUAGE 'plpgsql' HANDLER plpgsql_call_handler
              LANCOMPILER 'PL/pgSQL'
```

In this syntax, *plpgsql* is the name of the language to be created, the plpgsql_call_handler is the name of the call handler function (e.g., the one created in Example 11-1), and the *PL/pgSQL* string constant following the LANCOMPILER keyword is an arbitrary descriptive note.

Example 11-2 adds PL/pgSQL to the booktown database with the CREATE LANGUAGE command.

Example 11-2: Adding PL/pgSQL with CREATE LANGUAGE

```
booktown=# CREATE LANGUAGE 'plpgsql' HANDLER plpgsql_call_handler
booktown=#                            LANCOMPILER 'PL/pgSQL';
CREATE
```

The name following the HANDLER keyword should be the same name which is used to create the call handler. Since Example 11-1 created a call handler named plpgsql_call_handler, Example 11-2 uses the same name.

The string following the LANCOMPILER keyword is an outdated legacy clause, and its value is not consequential. Even so, as of PostgreSQL 7.1.x, it is a required clause. It is commonly used as a comment space to describe the language.

Using createlang to add PL/pgSQL

To execute *createlang* you will first need to be at the command prompt. If the operating system username you are currently logged into is the same as that of a database superuser account on the target database, you can call *createlang* with the command shown in Example 11-3 (you will be asked for a password if the database requires one). Otherwise, to pass the username of a database superuser to *createlang*, use the *-U* flag as shown in Example 11-4.

Example 11-3: Using createlang as a database superuser

```
$ cd /usr/local/pgsql/bin
booktown=# createlang plpgsql booktown
```

Example 11-4: Explicitly passing a superuser account name to createlang

```
$ cd /usr/local/pgsql/bin
$ createlang plpgsql -U manager booktown
```

The *createlang* program will return you to a shell prompt without any output upon successful execution.

Language Structure

The structure of PL/pgSQL is fairly simple, mainly due to the fact that each portion of code is designed to exist as a function. While it may not look immediately similar to other languages, PL/pgSQL's structure is similar to other programming languages such as C, in which each portion of code acts (and is created) as a function, all variables must be declared before being used, and code segments accept arguments when called and return arguments at their end.

Regarding its syntax, PL/pgSQL functions are case insensitive. You can use mixed, upper-, or lowercase for keywords and identifiers. Additionally, you will notice the use of pairs of apostrophes (single quotes) in many places within this chapter. These are required whenever a single apostrophe would ordinarily be used. The pair of apostrophes is a means to escape an apostrophe within the function definition to PostgreSQL, since a function definition is actually a large string constant within a CREATE FUNCTION statement.

This section will discuss the block organization of PL/pgSQL code, how to use comments, how PL/pgSQL expressions are organized, and the usage of statements.

Code Blocks

PL/pgSQL code is organized in blocks of code. This method of organization is known as *block structured code.* Code blocks are entered within a SQL CREATE FUNCTION call that creates the PL/pgSQL function in the PostgreSQL database. This CREATE FUNCTION command names the new function, states its argument types, and states the return type. The function's main code block then starts with a declaration section.

All variables are declared and optionally initialized to a default value in the declaration section of a code block. A variable declaration specifies the variable's name and type. The declaration section is denoted by the DECLARE keyword. Each variable declaration is ended with a semicolon.

After declaring variables, the main body of the code block is started with the BEGIN keyword. The code block's statements should appear after the BEGIN keyword.

The END keyword designates the end of the code block. The main block of a PL/pgSQL function should return a value of its specified return type and end any sub-blocks (code blocks started within another code block) before its END keyword is reached.

Example 11-5 shows the structure of a PL/pgSQL code block.

Example 11-5: Structure of a PL/pgSQL code block

```
CREATE FUNCTION identifier (arguments) RETURNS type AS '
  DECLARE
    declaration;
    [...]
  BEGIN
    statement;
    [...]
  END;
' LANGUAGE 'plpgsql';
```

A block of PL/pgSQL code can contain an unlimited amount of *sub-blocks*, which are code blocks nested within other code blocks. Sub-blocks are read and interpreted in the same manner as normal blocks; hence, they may also contain subblocks of their own.

Sub-blocks can be useful for the organization of code within a large PL/pgSQL function. All sub-blocks must follow normal block structure, meaning they must start with the DECLARE keyword, followed by the BEGIN keyword and a body of statements, then end with the END keyword.

Comments

There are two methods of commenting in PL/pgSQL, both similar to the comment structure of other programming languages. The two methods are single-line comments, and block comments (multiple line comments).

Comment syntax

The first method of commenting is single line commenting. Single line comments begin with two dashes (--) and have no end-character. The parser interprets all characters on the same line after the two dashes as part of the comment. Example 11-6 demonstrates the use of single line comments.

Example 11-6: Using single-line comments

```
-- This will be interpreted as a single-line comment.
```

The second type of comment is the multiline or *block* comment, which should be familiar to most anyone who has worked with programming languages before. Block comments begin with the forward slash and asterisk characters (/*) and end with the asterisk and forward slash characters (*/). Block comments can span multiple lines, and any text between the opening /* and closing */ is considered a comment. Example 11-7 shows the correct usage of a block comment.

Example 11-7: Using block comments

```
/*
 *  This is a
 *  block comment.
 */
```

While single-line comments can be nested within block comments, block comments cannot be nested within other block comments.

Good commenting style

In any programming language, it is helpful to write useful comments. A comment is considered useful if it can express to the user why a certain section of code was designed a certain way, or why syntax was used in an abnormal or creative manner. Comments that restate what is happening programmatically can be helpful at times, but you must remain aware of what is happening in your program and be sure to express *why* certain things are being done (instead of just *how*).

In our PL/pgSQL code examples we will use comments to explain how and why we do certain things within a particular section of code. This is to help you, as a new PL/pgSQL user, learn more about the language and its uses.

Statements and Expressions

PL/pgSQL code is composed of statements and expressions (as most programming languages are). Most of your code will be made of statements, and you will probably find yourself using expressions often, as they are essential to certain types of data manipulation. The concept of statements and expressions is generally applicable to all programming languages in alike (or at least very similar) ways, and if you have worked with programming languages before, you may already have a general understanding of them.

Statements

A statement performs an action within PL/pgSQL code, such as assignment of a value to a variable or the execution of a query. The organization of statements within a PL/pgSQL code block controls the order in which operations are executed within that code block. The bulk of your statements will be placed in the main operation section of a code block, which is located after the BEGIN keyword and before the END keyword. Some declarative statements should appear in the declaration section (after the DECLARE keyword), but these should only declare and/or initialize the variables that will be referenced within the code block.

Every statement should end with a semicolon character (;). This is similar to SQL, which also requires each statement to be ended with a semicolon. Types of statements (and their uses) are discussed throughout the rest of this chapter, as most everything you will do within PL/pgSQL will be done with statements.

Expressions

Expressions are calculations or operations that return their results as one of PostgreSQL's base data types. An example expression is x := a + b, which adds the variables a and b, then assigns the result to the variable x. Example 11-8 shows a simple PL/pgSQL function that assigns the returned result of a multiplication expression to the variable x, and Example 11-9 shows the output when selecting the function in *psql*.

Example 11-8: Using expressions

```
CREATE FUNCTION a_function () RETURNS int4 AS '
DECLARE
    an_integer int4;
BEGIN
    an_integer := 10 * 10;
    return an_integer;
END;
' LANGUAGE 'plpgsql';
```

Example 11-9: Output of a_function()

```
booktown=# SELECT a_function() AS output;
 output
--------
    100
(1 row)
```

With the exception of *dynamic queries* (SQL queries run with the EXECUTE keyword), all PL/pgSQL expressions in a function are only prepared once during the lifetime of the PostgreSQL backend process. Since expressions are only prepared once, constant values (not constant variables, but values such as the *now* and *current* timestamp values) used in PL/pgSQL expressions are only prepared once, causing code with constant values that require run-time interpretation to break. Example 11-10 shows how to force PL/pgSQL to evaluate constant timestamp values at a function's run-time, instead of once per creation.

The add_shipment function in Example 11-10 is a fairly advanced function that uses techniques and aspects of the language covered later in this chapter. Essentially, add_shipment accepts a customer ID number and book ISBN, calculates the next shipment ID by adding one to the current highest shipment ID, then inserts the values with a *now* timestamp into the shipments table.

If we had used *now* directly in the INSERT INTO statement, the *now* string would have been cast into a timestamp at the time the function was created, and the timestamp created would be used in all future calls of the function.

Example 11-10: Using timestamp values correctly

```
CREATE FUNCTION add_shipment (integer, text) RETURNS timestamp AS '
  DECLARE

      -- Declare aliases for function arguments.
      customer_id ALIAS FOR $1;
      isbn ALIAS FOR $2;

      -- Declare a variable to hold the shipment ID number and
      -- the current time.
      shipment_id integer;
      right_now timestamp;

  BEGIN

      -- Set the current time variable to the string ''now''.
      right_now := ''now'';

      -- Order the existing shipments by their ID numbers, beginning
      -- with the highest number, then insert the first ID number into
      -- the shipment_id variable.
      SELECT INTO shipment_id id FROM shipments ORDER BY id DESC;

      -- Add one to the shipment_id variable.
      shipment_id := shipment_id + 1;

      -- Insert a shipment record into the shipments table.  The
      -- right_now variable will be typecast to a timestamp at
      -- run-time, causing constant value now to be interpreted as
      -- the timestamp each time the function is run.
      INSERT INTO shipments VALUES ( shipment_id, customer_id, isbn, right_now );

      -- Return a timestamp using the constant value now.
      RETURN right_now;
  END;
' LANGUAGE 'plpgsql';
```

Using Variables

Variables are used within PL/pgSQL code to store modifiable data of an explicitly stated type. All variables that you will be using within a code block must be declared under the DECLARE keyword. If a variable is not initialized to a default value when it is declared, its value will default to the SQL NULL type.

As you will read later on in the section titled "Controlling Program Flow," there is a type of statement known as the FOR loop that initializes a variable used for iteration. The FOR loop's iteration variable does not have to be pre-declared in the DECLARE section for the block the loop is located within; hence, the FOR loop is the only exception to the rule that all PL/pgSQL variables must be declared at the beginning of the block they are located within.

Data Types

Variables in PL/pgSQL can be represented by any of SQL's standard data types, such as an integer or char. In addition to SQL data types, PL/pgSQL also provides the additional RECORD data type, which is designed to allow you to store row information without specifying the columns that will be supplied when data is inserted into the variable. More information on using RECORD data types is provided later in this chapter. For further information on standard SQL data types, see the section titled "Data Types" in Chapter 3; the following is a brief list of commonly used data types in PL/pgSQL:

- boolean
- text
- char
- integer
- double precision
- date
- time

Declaration

For variables to be available to the code within a PL/pgSQL code block, they must be declared in the declarations section of the block, which is denoted by the DECLARE keyword at the beginning of the block. Variables declared in a block will be available to all sub-blocks within it, but remember that (as mentioned in the section titled "Language Structure" earlier in this chapter) variables declared within a sub-block are destroyed when that sub-block ends, and are not available for use by their parent blocks. The format for declaring a variable is shown in Example 11-11.

Example 11-11: Declaring a PL/pgSQL variable

```
variable_name data_type [ := value ];
```

As you can see by Example 11-11, you declare a variable by providing its name and type (in that order), then end the declaration with a semicolon.

Example 11-12 shows the declaration of a variable of the `integer` data type, a variable of the `varchar` data type (the value in parentheses denotes that this variable type holds ten characters), and a variable of the `float` data type.

Example 11-12: Variable Declarations

```
CREATE FUNCTION identifier (arguments) RETURNS type AS '
  DECLARE

      -- Declare an integer.
    subject_id integer;

      -- Declare a variable length character.
    book_title varchar(10);

      -- Declare a floating point number.
    book_price float;

  BEGIN
    statements
  END;
' LANGUAGE 'plpgsql';
```

You may also specify additional options for a variable. Adding the CONSTANT keyword indicates that a variable will be created as a constant. Constants are discussed later in this section.

The NOT NULL keywords indicate that a variable cannot be set as NULL. A variable declared as NOT NULL will cause a run-time error if it is set to NULL within the code block. Due to the fact that all variables are set to NULL when declared without a default value, a default value must be provided for any variable that is declared as NOT NULL.

The DEFAULT keyword allows you to provide a default value for a variable. Alternatively, you can use the := operator without specifying the DEFAULT keyword, to the same effect.

The following illustrates the use of these options within a variable declaration:

```
variable_name [ CONSTANT ] data_type [ NOT NULL ] [ { DEFAULT | := } value ];
```

Example 11-13 shows the declaration of a constant variable with the default value of 5, the declaration of a variable with the value of 10 which cannot be set to NULL, and the declaration of a character with the default value of one *a*.

Example 11-13: Using variable declaration options

```
CREATE FUNCTION example_function () RETURNS text AS '
  DECLARE

      -- Declare a constant integer with a
      -- default value of 5.
      five CONSTANT integer := 5;

      -- Declare an integer with a default
      -- value of 100 that cannot be NULL.
      ten integer NOT NULL := 10;

      -- Declare a character with
      -- a default value of "a".
      letter char DEFAULT ''a'';

  BEGIN
      -- This just returns the letter, and
      -- ends the function.
      return letter;
  END;
' LANGUAGE 'plpgsql';
```

The **RENAME** keyword covered in online documentation for PL/pgSQL, which is intended to rename existing variables to new names, does not work at all in PL/pgSQL (as of PostgreSQL 7.1.x). The use of this keyword on an existing variable indiscriminately causes a parsing error. It is therefore not recommended, nor documented in this chapter.

Assignment

Variable assignment is done with PL/pgSQL's assignment operator (:=), in the form of *left_variable* := *right_variable*, in which the value of the right variable is assigned to the left variable. Also valid is *left_variable* := *expression*, which assigns the left-hand variable the value of the expression on the right side of the assignment operator.

Variables can be assigned default values within the declaration section of a PL/pgSQL code block. This is known as *default value assignment*, and is done by using the assignment operator (:=) on the same line as the variable's declaration. This topic is discussed in more detail later in this section, but Example 11-14 provides a quick demonstration.

Example 11-14: Default value assignment

```
CREATE FUNCTION identifier (arguments) RETURNS type AS '
  DECLARE
    an_integer int4 := 10;
  BEGIN
    statement;
    [...]
  END;
' LANGUAGE 'plpgsql';
```

It is also possible to use a SELECT INTO statement to assign variables the results of
queries. This use of SELECT INTO is different from the SQL command SELECT INTO,
which assigns the results of a query to a new table.

> To assign the results of a query to a new table within PL/pgSQL, use
> the alternative SQL syntax CREATE TABLE AS SELECT.

SELECT INTO is primarily used to assign row and record information to variables
declared as %ROWTYPE or RECORD types. To use SELECT INTO with a normal variable,
the variable in question must be the same type as the column you reference in the
SQL SELECT statement provided. The syntax of SELECT INTO statement is shown in
the following syntax:

```
CREATE FUNCTION identifier (arguments) RETURNS type AS '
  DECLARE
    statement;
  BEGIN
    SELECT INTO target_variable [, ...] target_column [, ...] select_clauses;
  END;
' LANGUAGE 'plpgsql';
```

In this syntax, *target_variable* is the name of a variable that is being populated
with values, and *select_clauses* consists of any supported SQL SELECT clauses that
would ordinarily follow the target column list in a SELECT statement.

Example 11-15 shows a simple function that demonstrates the use of a SELECT
INTO statement. The ALIAS keyword is described in the section titled "Argument
Variables," later in this chapter. See the section titled "Controlling Program Flow"
for examples of using SELECT INTO with RECORD and %ROWTYPE variables.

Example 11-15: Using the SELECT INTO statement

```
CREATE FUNCTION get_customer_id (text,text) RETURNS integer AS '
  DECLARE

    -- Declare aliases for user input.
```

Example 11-15: Using the SELECT INTO statement (continued)

```
    l_name ALIAS FOR $1;
    f_name ALIAS FOR $2;

    -- Declare a variable to hold the customer ID number.
    customer_id integer;

  BEGIN

    -- Retrieve the customer ID number of the customer whose first and last
    --  name match the values supplied as function arguments.
    SELECT INTO customer_id id FROM customers
      WHERE last_name = l_name AND first_name = f_name;

    -- Return the ID number.
    RETURN customer_id;
  END;
' LANGUAGE 'plpgsql';
```

Example 11-16 shows the results of the get_customer_id() function when passed the arguments *Jackson* and *Annie*. The number returned is the correct ID number for Annie Jackson in the customers table.

Example 11-16: Result of the get_customer_id() function

```
booktown=# SELECT get_customer_id('Jackson','Annie');
 get_customer_id
-----------------
 107
(1 row)
```

If you wish to assign multiple column values to multiple variables, you may do so by using two comma-delimited groups of variable names and column names, separated from one another by white space. Example 11-17 creates essentially an inverse function to the get_customer_id() function created in Example 11-15.

Example 11-17: Using SELECT INTO with multiple columns

```
CREATE FUNCTION get_customer_name (integer) RETURNS text AS '
  DECLARE

    -- Declare aliases for user input.
    customer_id ALIAS FOR $1;

    -- Declare variables to hold the customer name.
    customer_fname text;
    customer_lname text;

  BEGIN

    -- Retrieve the customer first and last name for the customer
    -- whose ID matches the value supplied as a function argument.
```

Example 11-17: Using SELECT INTO with multiple columns (continued)

```
        SELECT INTO customer_fname, customer_lname
                  first_name, last_name
                  FROM customers WHERE id = customer_id;

        -- Return the name.
        RETURN customer_fname || '' '' || customer_lname;

    END;
' LANGUAGE 'plpgsql';
```

Example 11-18 shows the results of the get_customer_name() function, when passed an argument of 107.

Example 11-18: Result of the get_customer_name() function

```
booktown=# SELECT get_customer_name(107);
 get_customer_name
-------------------
 Annie Jackson
 (1 row)
```

Use the special FOUND Boolean variable directly after a SELECT INTO statement to check whether or not the statement successfully inserted a value into the specified variable. You can also use ISNULL or IS NULL to find out if the specified variable is NULL after being selected into (in most situations, this would mean the SELECT INTO statement failed).

FOUND, IS NULL, and ISNULL should be used within a conditional (IF/THEN) statement. PL/pgSQL's conditional statements are detailed in the "Controlling Program Flow" section of this chapter. Example 11-19 is a basic demonstration of how the FOUND Boolean could be used with the get_customer_id() function.

Example 11-19: Using the FOUND boolean in get_customer_id()

```
    [...]
        SELECT INTO customer_id id FROM customers
              WHERE last_name = l_name AND first_name = f_name;

        -- If a match could not be found, return -1 (another function calling
        -- this function could then be made to interpret a -1 as an error.
        IF NOT FOUND THEN
          return -1;
        END IF;
    [...]
```

Example 11-20 shows that get_customer_id() now returns a –1 value when passed the name of a non-existent customer.

Example 11-20: Result of the new get_customer_id() function

```
booktown=# SELECT get_customer_id('Schmoe','Joe');
 get_customer_id
-----------------
 -1
(1 row)
```

Argument Variables

PL/pgSQL functions can accept argument variables of different types. Function arguments allow you to pass information from the user into the function that the function may require. Arguments greatly extend the possible uses of PL/pgSQL functions. User input generally provides a function with the data it will either operate on or use for operation. Users pass arguments to functions when the function is called by including them within parentheses, separated by commas.

Arguments must follow the argument list defined when the function is first created. Example 11-21 shows a pair of example function calls from *psql*.

Example 11-21: Function call examples

```
booktown=# SELECT get_author('John');
 get_author
--------------
 John Worsley
(1 row)

booktown=# SELECT get_author(1111);
 get_author
--------------
 Ariel Denham
(1 row)
```

> The get_author(text) and get_author(integer) functions are discussed later in this chapter.

Each function argument that is received by a function is incrementally assigned to an identifier that begins with the dollar sign ($) and is labeled with the argument number. The identifier $1 is used for the first argument, $2 is used for the second argument, and so forth. The maximum number of function arguments that can be processed is sixteen, so the argument identifiers can range from $1 to $16. Example 11-22 shows a function that doubles an integer argument variable that is passed to it.

Example 11-22: Directly using argument variables

```
CREATE FUNCTION double_price (float) RETURNS float AS '
  DECLARE
  BEGIN

      -- Return the argument variable multiplied by two.
      return $1 * 2;

  END;
' LANGUAGE 'plpgsql';
```

Referencing arguments with the dollar sign and the argument's order number can become confusing in functions that accept a large number of arguments. To help in functions where the ability to better distinguish argument variables from one another is needed (or just when you wish to use a more meaningful name for an argument variable), PL/pgSQL allows you to create variable *aliases.*

Aliases are created with the ALIAS keyword and give you the ability to designate an alternate identifier to use when referencing argument variables. All aliases must be declared in the declaration section of a block before they can be used (just like normal variables). Example 11-23 shows the syntax of the ALIAS keyword.

Example 11-23: Syntax of the ALIAS keyword

```
CREATE FUNCTION function_identifier (arguments) RETURNS type AS '
  DECLARE
    identifier ALIAS FOR $1;
    identifier ALIAS FOR $2;
  BEGIN
    [...]
  END;
' LANGUAGE 'plpgsql';
```

Example 11-24 creates a simple function to demonstrate the use of aliases in a PL/pgSQL function. The `triple_price()` function accepts a floating point number as the price and returns that number multiplied by three.

Example 11-24: Using PL/pgSQL aliases

```
CREATE FUNCTION triple_price (float) RETURNS float AS '
  DECLARE
      -- Declare input_price as an alias for the argument variable
      -- normally referenced with the $1 identifier.
      input_price ALIAS FOR $1;

  BEGIN
      -- Return the input price multiplied by three.
      RETURN input_price * 3;
  END;
' LANGUAGE 'plpgsql';
```

Now, if we use the `triple_price` function within a SQL SELECT statement in a client such as *psql*, we receive the results shown in Example 11-25.

Example 11-25: Result of the triple_price( ) function

```
booktown=# SELECT triple_price(12.50);
 triple_price
--------------
         37.5
(1 row)
```

Returning Variables

PL/pgSQL functions must return a value that matches the data type specified as their return type in the CREATE FUNCTION command that created them. Values are returned with a RETURN statement. A RETURN statement is typically located at the end of a function, but will also often be located within an IF statement or other statement that directs the flow of the function. If a function's RETURN statement is located within one of these control statements, you should still include a return statement at the end of the function (even if the function is designed to never reach that last RETURN statement). The syntax of a RETURN statement is shown in Example 11-26.

Example 11-26: Syntax of the RETURN statement

```
CREATE FUNCTION function_identifier (arguments) RETURNS type AS '
  DECLARE
    declaration;
    [...]
  BEGIN
    statement;
    [...]
    RETURN { variable_name | value }
  END;
' LANGUAGE 'plpgsql';
```

For a demonstration of the RETURN statement, examine any PL/pgSQL function example within this chapter.

Attributes

PL/pgSQL provides variable *attributes* to assist you in working with database objects. These attributes are %TYPE and %ROWTYPE. Use attributes to declare a variable to match the type of a database object (using the %TYPE attribute) or to match the row structure of a row (with the %ROWTYPE attribute). A variable should be declared using an attribute when it will be used within the code block to hold values taken from a database object. Knowledge of the database object's type is not required when using attributes to declare variables. If an object's type changes in the future, your variable's type will automatically change to that data type without any extra code.

The %TYPE attribute

The %TYPE attribute is used to declare a variable with the data type of a referenced database object (most commonly a table column). The format for declaring a variable in this manner is shown in Example 11-27.

Example 11-27: Declaring a variable using %TYPE

```
variable_name table_name.column_name%TYPE
```

Example 11-28 shows the code for a function that uses %TYPE to store the last name of an author. This function uses string concatenation with the concatenation operator (||), which is documented in a later section. The use of the SELECT INTO statement was discussed earlier in this chapter.

Focus on the use of the %TYPE attribute in Example 11-28. Essentially, a variable is declared as being the same type as a column within the authors table. SELECT is then used to find a row with a first_name field that matches the name the user passed to the function. The SELECT statement retrieves the value of that row's last_name column and inserts it into the l_name variable. An example of the user's input to the function is shown right after Example 11-28, in Example 11-29, and more examples of user input can be found later in this chapter.

Example 11-28: Using the %TYPE attribute

```
CREATE FUNCTION get_author (text) RETURNS text AS '
  DECLARE
        -- Declare an alias for the function argument,
        -- which should be the first name of an author.
        f_name ALIAS FOR $1;

        -- Declare a variable with the same type as
        -- the last_name field of the authors table.
        l_name authors.last_name%TYPE;

  BEGIN
        -- Retrieve the last name of an author from the
        -- authors table whose first name matches the
        -- argument received by the function, and
        -- insert it into the l_name variable.
        SELECT INTO l_name last_name FROM authors WHERE first_name = f_name;

        -- Return the first name and last name, separated
        -- by a space.
        return f_name || '' '' || l_name;
  END;
' LANGUAGE 'plpgsql';
```

Example 11-29 shows the results of using the get_author() function.

Example 11-29: Results of the get_author() function

```
booktown=# SELECT get_author('Andrew');
   get_author
-----------------
 Andrew Brookins
(1 row)
```

The %ROWTYPE attribute

%ROWTYPE is used to declare a PL/pgSQL record variable with the same structure as the rows in a table you specify. It is similar to the RECORD data type, but a variable declared with %ROWTYPE will have the exact structure of a table's row, whereas a RECORD variable is not structured and will accept a row from any table.

Example 11-30 overloads the get_author() function that was created in Example 11-28 to accomplish a similar goal. Notice, though, that this new version of get_author() accepts an argument of type integer rather than text, and checks for the author by comparing their id against the passed integer argument.

Notice also that this function is implemented using a variable declared with %ROW-TYPE. The use of %ROWTYPE to accomplish a simple task such as this may make it seem overly complicated, but as you learn more about PL/pgSQL, the importance of %ROWTYPE will become more apparent.

The use of the dot (.) within the found_author variable in Example 11-30 references a named field value in found_author.

Example 11-30: Using the %ROWTYPE attribute

```
CREATE FUNCTION get_author (integer) RETURNS text AS '
  DECLARE

      -- Declare an alias for the function argument,
      -- which should be the id of the author.
      author_id ALIAS FOR $1;

      -- Declare a variable that uses the structure of
      -- the authors table.
      found_author authors%ROWTYPE;

  BEGIN

      -- Retrieve a row of author information for
      -- the author whose id number matches
      -- the argument received by the function.
      SELECT INTO found_author * FROM authors WHERE id = author_id;

      -- Return the first name and last name, separated by a space.
```

Example 11-30: Using the %ROWTYPE attribute (continued)

```
      RETURN found_author.first_name || '' '' || found_author.last_name;

   END;
' LANGUAGE 'plpgsql';
```

Observe the use of the asterisk (*) for the column list in Example 11-30. Since found_author is declared with the %ROWTYPE attribute on the authors table, it is created with the same data structure as the authors table. The asterisk can therefore be used to populate the found_author variable with each column value selected from the SELECT INTO statement in Example 11-15.

Example 11-31: Results of the new get_author( ) function

```
booktown=# SELECT get_author(1212);
   get_author
--------------
   John Worsley
(1 row)
```

Concatenation

Concatenation is the process of combining two (or more) strings together to produce another string. It is a standard operation built into PostgreSQL, and may therefore be used directly on variables within a PL/pgSQL function. When working with several variables containing character data, it is an irreplaceable formatting tool.

Concatenation can only be used with character strings. Strings are concatenated by placing the concatenation operator (||) between two or more character strings (string literal or a character string variable) that you wish to be combined. This can be used to combine two strings together to form a compound word, and to combine multiple strings together to form complex character string combinations.

Concatenation can only be used in situations where your function requires a string value, such as when a string must be returned (as shown in Example 11-32), or when you are assigning a new value to a string variable (as shown in Example 11-33).

Example 11-32: Returning a concatenated string

```
CREATE FUNCTION compound_word(text, text) RETURNS text AS '
   DECLARE

      -- Define aliases for function arguments.
      word1 ALIAS FOR $1;
      word2 ALIAS FOR $2;

   BEGIN
```

Example 11-32: Returning a concatenated string (continued)

```
        -- Return the resulting joined words.
    RETURN word1 || word2;

  END;

' LANGUAGE 'plpgsql';
```

When the words break and fast are passed as arguments to the compound_word( ) function, the function returns *breakfast* as the concatenated string:

```
booktown=# SELECT compound_word('break', 'fast');
 compound_word
---------------
 breakfast
(1 row)
```

Example 11-33: Assigning a concatenated value to a string

```
CREATE FUNCTION title_and_author (text, text) RETURNS text AS '
    DECLARE

        -- Declare aliases for the two function arguments.
        title ALIAS for $1;
        author ALIAS for $2;

        -- Declare a text variable to hold the string result
        -- of the concatenation.
        result text;

    BEGIN

        -- Combine the title variable and the author
        -- variable together, placing a comma and the
        -- word by between them.
        result := title || '', by '' || author;

        -- Return the resulting string.
        return result;

    END;
' language 'plpgsql';
```

If you pass the strings *Practical PostgreSQL* and *Command Prompt, Inc.* to the function created in Example 11-33, the function returns *Practical PostgreSQL, by Command Prompt, Inc.*:

```
booktown=# SELECT title_and_author('Practical PostgreSQL','Command Prompt, Inc.');
              title_and_author
-------------------------------------------------
 Practical PostgreSQL, by Command Prompt, Inc.
(1 row)
```

Controlling Program Flow

Most programming languages in existence provide ways of controlling the flow of programs they are used to create. PL/pgSQL is no different. Technically, by defining the structure of statements within a PL/pgSQL function, you are controlling its "flow," in that you are controlling the manner in which it operates and the order its operations are executed. However, there are more extensive ways in which you can control the flow of a PL/pgSQL, such as conditional statements and the use of loops.

Conditional Statements

A conditional statement specifies an action (or set of actions) that should be executed instead of continuing execution of the function, based on the result of logical condition specified within the statement. That definition of conditional statements may make them sound a bit complex, but they are actually fairly simple. Essentially, a conditional statement informs the parser that if a given condition is true, a specified action should be taken.

The IF/THEN statement

The IF/THEN statement allows you to specify a statement (or block of statements) that should be executed if a given condition evaluates true. The syntax of the IF/THEN statement is shown in Example 11-34.

Example 11-34: Syntax of an IF/THEN statement

```
CREATE FUNCTION identifier (arguments) RETURNS type AS '
  DECLARE
    declarations
  BEGIN

    IF condition THEN
      statement;
      [...]
    END IF;

  END;
' LANGUAGE 'plpgsql';
```

In Example 11-35, a function is created that checks the stock of a book when given its book ID and edition number. The book ID is an internally recorded and tracked number listed in a few of the database's tables; thus, this function is designed to be used by other functions, as most users won't directly know the book ID number. The stock_amount function first retrieves the book's ISBN number with a SELECT INTO statement.

If the SELECT INTO statement could not retrieve an ISBN number for the book with the provided book ID number and edition number the stock amount function returns a value of –1, which should be interpreted as an error by the function that called it. The function's flow continues on if there was an ISBN number found for the book, and another SELECT INTO statement is used to retrieve the amount of stock remaining for the book in question. The stock amount is then returned and the function ends.

Example 11-35: Using the IF/THEN statement

```
CREATE FUNCTION stock_amount (integer, integer) RETURNS integer AS '
    DECLARE

        -- Declare aliases for function arguments.
        b_id ALIAS FOR $1;
        b_edition ALIAS FOR $2;

        -- Declare variable to store the ISBN number.
        b_isbn text;

        -- Declare variable to store the stock amount.
        stock_amount integer;

    BEGIN

        -- This SELECT INTO statement retrieves the ISBN number of the row in
        -- the editions table that had both the book ID number and edition number
        -- that were provided as function arguments.

        SELECT INTO b_isbn isbn FROM editions WHERE
                book_id = b_id AND edition = b_edition;

        -- Check to see if the ISBN number retrieved is NULL.  This will
        -- happen if there is not an existing book with both the ID number
        -- and edition number specified in the function arguments. If the
        -- ISBN is null, the function returns a value of -1 and ends.

        IF b_isbn IS NULL THEN
          RETURN -1;
        END IF;

        -- Retrieve the amount of books available from the stock table
        -- and record the number in the stock_amount variable.
        SELECT INTO stock_amount stock FROM stock WHERE isbn = b_isbn;

        -- Return the amount of books available.
        RETURN stock_amount;

    END;
' LANGUAGE 'plpgsql';
```

Example 11-36 shows the result of the stock_amount function when it is called for
the book ID value 7808 and edition number 1.

Example 11-36: Results of the stock_amount( ) function

```
booktown=# SELECT stock_amount(7808,1);
 stock_amount
--------------
           22
(1 row)
```

The IF/THEN/ELSE statement

The IF/THEN/ELSE statement allows you to specify a block of statements that
should be executed if a condition evaluates to true, and also a block of statements
that should be executed if the condition evaluates to false. The syntax of the IF/
THEN/ELSE statement is shown in Example 11-37.

Example 11-37: Syntax of an IF/THEN/ELSE statement

```
CREATE FUNCTION identifier (arguments) RETURNS type AS '
  DECLARE
    declarations
  BEGIN

    IF condition THEN
      statement;
      [...]
    ELSE
      statement;
      [...]
    END IF;

  END;
' LANGUAGE 'plpgsql';
```

In Example 11-38, essentially the same steps that were taken in Example 11-35 are
taken again to retrieve the ISBN number, store it, then use it to retrieve the quantity in stock for the book in question.

Once the in-stock number is retrieved, an IF/THEN/ELSE statement is used to
decide whether or not the number is above zero. If it is above zero the function
returns a TRUE value, indicating that the title is in stock. If the in-stock is below
zero, the function returns a FALSE value, indicating the title is out of stock. Again,
this is a function designed to be used by another function, so only values are
returned. Returned values must be interpreted by the function that called the
in_stock( ) function.

Example 11-38: Using the IF/THEN/ELSE statement

```
CREATE FUNCTION in_stock (integer,integer) RETURNS boolean AS '
  DECLARE

    -- Declare aliases for function arguments.
    b_id ALIAS FOR $1;
    b_edition ALIAS FOR $2;

    -- Declare a text variable to hold the ISBN of the book
    -- once found.
    b_isbn text;

    -- Declare an integer variable to hold the amount of stock.
    stock_amount integer;

  BEGIN

    -- This SELECT INTO statement retrieves the ISBN number of
    -- the row in the editions table that had both the book ID
    -- number and edition number that were provided as function
    -- arguments.
    SELECT INTO b_isbn isbn FROM editions WHERE
      book_id = b_id AND edition = b_edition;

    -- Check to see if the ISBN number retrieved  is NULL.  This
    -- will happen if there is not an existing book with both the
    -- ID number and edition number specified in the function
    -- arguments. If the ISBN is null, the function returns a
    -- FALSE value and ends.
    IF b_isbn IS NULL THEN
      RETURN FALSE;
    END IF;

    -- Retrieve the amount of books available from the stock
    -- table and record the number in the stock_amount variable.
    SELECT INTO stock_amount stock FROM stock WHERE isbn = b_isbn;

    -- Use an IF/THEN/ELSE check to see if the amount of books
    -- available is less than or equal to 0.  If so, return FALSE.
    -- If not, return TRUE.
    IF stock_amount <= 0 THEN
      RETURN FALSE;
    ELSE
      RETURN TRUE;
    END IF;

  END;
' LANGUAGE 'plpgsql';
```

Example 11-39 shows the result of the `check_stock()` function when it is called with the book ID value 4513 and edition number 2. A value of true is returned, indicating that the title is in stock.

Example 11-39: Results of the in_stock( ) function

```
booktown=# SELECT in_stock(4513,2);
 in_stock
----------
 t
(1 row)
```

Example 11-39 shows that a TRUE value was returned, indicating that the title is in stock.

The IF/THEN/ELSE/IF statement

The IF/THEN/ELSE/IF statement is a mechanism for linking several IF statements together in a series. First, one condition is checked. If the first condition evaluates to FALSE, another condition is checked, and so forth. A final ELSE can provide for the case when no condition evaluates to TRUE. The syntax for the IF/THEN/ELSE/IF statement follows:

```
CREATE FUNCTION identifier (arguments) RETURNS type AS '
  DECLARE
    declarations
  BEGIN
    IF condition THEN
      statement;
      [...]
    ELSE IF condition
      statement;
      [...]
    END IF;
  END;
' LANGUAGE 'plpgsql';
```

This syntax shows the creation of a function that demonstrates the use of the IF/THEN/ELSE/IF statement. The books_by_subject() function first uses the provided argument, which should be a book subject, to retrieve the subject ID number of the subject in question. The first IF statement then checks to see if the argument received is the value all.

If the argument variable's value is all, the IF/THEN statement executes extract_all_titles() and assigns the returned list of books and subjects (returned as a text variable) to the found_text variable.

If all was not sent to the function as a parameter, an ELSE IF statement is used to check whether or not the subject ID number that was retrieved is zero or higher. If the value of sub_id *is* zero or higher, the function executes the statements in the body of the ELSE IF statement, which first use extract_title() to retrieve a list of the titles of all existing books classified under the user's provided subject, and returns the name of the subject with the acquired list of books.

Another ELSE IF statement is then nested within the previous ELSE IF statement, and is executed if the subject ID number has been set to NULL. If sub_id is null, the subject title passed to the function was not found in the booktown database when it was retrieved by the SELECT INTO statement at the function's beginning. In that case, the function returns the string *subject not found.*

 The two functions used within Example 11-38 are created later in this section as examples of using loops to control program flow.

Example 11-40: Using the IF/THEN/ELSE/IF statement

```
CREATE FUNCTION books_by_subject (text) RETURNS text AS '
  DECLARE

      -- Declare an alias for user input, which should be either all
      -- or the name of a subject.
    sub_title ALIAS FOR $1;

      -- Declare an integer to store the subject ID in, and a text
      -- variable to store the list of found books.  The text variable
      --  is set to a blank string.
    sub_id integer;
    found_text text :='''';

  BEGIN

      -- Retrieve the subject ID number for the book matching the
      -- title supplied by the user.
    SELECT INTO sub_id id FROM subjects WHERE subject = sub_title;

      -- Check to see if the function was given all as the the subject
      -- name.  If so, execute the SELECT INTO statement and return
      -- the found_text variable.
    IF sub_title = ''all'' THEN
      found_text extract_all_titles();
      RETURN found_text;

        -- If the function was NOT sent all as the name of the subject,
        -- check to see the subject ID number turned out to be within
        -- the valid range of subjects. If it did, execute the
        -- extract_title() function with the subject ID number as its
        -- argument, then assign the result to the found_text variable.
    ELSE IF sub_id  >= 0 THEN
        found_text := extract_title(sub_id);
        RETURN  ''\n'' || sub_title || '':\n'' || found_text;

          -- If the subject ID number was NULL, return a message telling
          -- the user that the subject specified could not be found.
```

Example 11-40: Using the IF/THEN/ELSE/IF statement (continued)

```
                ELSE IF sub_id IS NULL THEN
                    RETURN ''Subject not found.'';
                END IF;
            END IF;
        END IF;
        RETURN ''An error occurred. .'';
    END;
' LANGUAGE 'plpgsql';
```

Example 11-41 first shows the result of the `books_by_subject` function when it is called with `all` as the argument (an indication that the user wishes to view the books within all defined subjects). The example then shows the results received when *Computers* is passed as the function's argument (an indication that the user wishes to view only books categorized as computer-related books).

Example 11-41: Results of the books_by_subject() function

```
booktown=# SELECT books_by_subject('all');
books_by_subject

Arts:
Dynamic Anatomy

Business:

Children's Books:
The Cat in the Hat
Bartholomew and the Oobleck
Franklin in the Dark
Goodnight Moon
[...]
Science:

Science Fiction:
Dune
2001: A Space Odyssey

(1 row)

booktown=# SELECT books_by_subject('Computers');
                    books_by_subject
-------------------------------------------------------------

Computers:
Learning Python
Perl Cookbook
Practical PostgreSQL
Programming Python

(1 row)
```

Loops

Loops, like conditional statements, are another method of controlling the flow of functions. Loops use *iteration* in a number of different ways to accomplish tasks, and through the use of iteration you can greatly expand the functionality of a PL/pgSQL function.

PL/pgSQL implements three iterative loops: the basic loop, the slightly more advanced WHILE loop, and the FOR loop. Of the three, you will most likely be using the FOR loop most often, as it can be applied to a multitude of different programmatic situations, though the other loops are also useful.

The basic loop

Use the LOOP keyword to begin a basic, unconditional loop within a function. An unconditional loop will execute the statements within its body until an EXIT statement is reached. To form an EXIT statement, the EXIT keyword can be accompanied by WHEN, followed by an expression to specify when the loop should exit. Th expression should be a Boolean expression, such as one that checks to see whether a variable has reached a specified value. Following is the syntax (without the ELSE keyword) for an unconditional loop:

```
LOOP
  statement;
  [...]
END LOOP;
```

An unconditional loop statement will continue to loop until it reaches an EXIT statement. EXIT statements explicitly terminate unconditional loops. When terminating a loop with EXIT, you may optionally specify a *label* and/or a condition on which the loop should exit.

A label is an arbitrary identifier, prefixed with a pair of less-than symbols (<<) and suffixed with a pair of greater-than symbols (>>). In the case of a loop, it may be placed directly before the loop block begins to identify that loop block with a chosen label. Here is an example of a defined loop with label syntax:

```
<<label_name>>
LOOP
  [ ... ]
END LOOP;
```

By providing a label, you can specify which loop to exit when you have several loops nested inside each other (the use of labels in EXIT will only work if you have specified a label for the loop you are attempting to terminate).

By providing a condition in an EXIT statement you specify that the loop should be terminated when the condition is true.

Here is the syntax for an EXIT statement, within a LOOP:

```
[ <<label>> ]
LOOP
    statement;
    [...]
    EXIT [ label ] [ WHEN condition ];
END LOOP;
```

Example 11-42 shows a demonstration of an unconditional loop and an EXIT statement that ends it based on a condition. The square_integer_loop() function squares an integer (multiplies the number by itself) until it reaches a value higher than ten thousand. The function then returns the resulting value.

Example 11-42: Using the basic loop

```
CREATE FUNCTION square_integer_loop (integer) RETURNS integer AS '
  DECLARE

      -- Declare aliases for function argument.
      num1 ALIAS FOR $1;

      -- Declare an integer to hold the result.
      result integer;

  BEGIN

    -- Assign the user input number to the result variable.
    result := num1;

    LOOP
      result := result * result;
      EXIT WHEN result >= 10000;
    END LOOP;

    RETURN result;
  END;
' LANGUAGE 'plpgsql';
```

Example 11-43 shows the result of invoking square_integer_loop() and passing the value 3 as an argument.

Example 11-43: Result of the square_integer_loop() function

```
booktown=# SELECT square_integer_loop(3);
 square_integer_loop
---------------------
                6561
(1 row)
```

The WHILE loop

The WHILE loop is used to loop through a block of statements until a specified condition becomes false. Each time a WHILE loop is entered, its condition will be evaluated before the statement block is executed.

If the condition is evaluated as TRUE, the statements will then be executed. If the condition is never evaluated as false, the statement block will repeatedly execute until the client process that it originated from is terminated. The syntax of the WHILE loop is shown here:

```
[ <<label>> ]
WHILE condition LOOP
  statement;
  [...]
END LOOP;
```

In Example 11-44, the add_two_loop() function demonstrates the use of a WHILE loop designed to add one to a number until the number reaches a specified value. The starting number and ending number are both supplied by the user as function arguments. The != symbol in Example 11-44 is the inequality operator. That inequality operator indicates that the WHILE loop will run while the result variable *is not equal to* the high_number variable. In other words, the WHILE loop in Example 11-44 will run until result is equal to high_number.

Example 11-44: Using the WHILE loop

```
CREATE FUNCTION add_two_loop (integer, integer) RETURNS integer AS '
  DECLARE

      -- Declare aliases for function arguments.
    low_number ALIAS FOR $1;
    high_number ALIAS FOR $2;

      -- Declare a variable to hold the result.
    result integer = 0;

  BEGIN

      -- Add one to the variable result until the value of result is
      -- equal to high_number.
    WHILE result != high_number LOOP
      result := result + 1;
    END LOOP;

    RETURN result;
  END;
' LANGUAGE 'plpgsql';
```

The FOR loop

The FOR loop is arguably the most important loop implemented in PL/pgSQL. Use the FOR loop to iterate a statement block over a range of integers that you specify. The structure of a FOR loop in PL/pgSQL is similar to FOR loops in other procedural languages, such as C.

In a PL/pgSQL FOR loop an integer variable is stated first, to track the iteration of the loop, then the integer range is given, and finally a statement block is provided. The integer variable created to track the loop's iteration is destroyed once the loop exits; it does not have to be declared in the declaration section of the block. The following shows the syntax of the FOR loop:

```
[ <<label>> ]
FOR identifier IN [ REVERSE ] expression1 .. expression2  LOOP
    statement;
    [...]
END LOOP;
```

The FOR loop will perform a single iteration for each incremented value of *identifier* which is in the range of values between, and including, *expression1* and *expression2*. The *identifier* value will be initialized to the value of *expression1*, and incremented by one each iteration. If REVERSE is specified, *identifier* will be decremented rather than incremented.

The identifier used to track iteration does not need to be declared outside of the FOR block, unless you wish to be able to access its value after the loop has finished.

The FOR loop can also be used to cycle through the the results of a query. The second FOR loop in Example 11-45 demonstrates using a FOR loop to work with RECORD and %ROWTYPE variables. The syntax of a FOR loop that iterates through RECORD and %ROWTYPE variables is shown in the following syntax:

```
[ <<label>> ]
FOR { record_variable | %rowtype_variable } IN select_statement LOOP
    statement;
    [...]
END LOOP;
```

In Example 11-45, the extract_all_titles() function is used to extract a list of all book titles that exist in the database, organized by subject. When a subject has no book titles, a blank line is displayed. The list is returned as a text variable. A FOR loop is utilized within the extract_all_titles() function to cycle through the available subjects by number.

Another FOR loop is nested within the original loop to cycle through the available books and retrieve all books with subject_id values that match the original loop's iteration variable, which represents the current subject ID number the function is scanning for. In Example 11-45, the iteration variable i is initialized to zero because the first subject ID number in our subjects table is 0.

Example 11-45: Using the FOR loop

```
CREATE FUNCTION extract_all_titles2 () RETURNS text AS '
  DECLARE

    -- Declare a variable for the subject ID number.

    sub_id integer;

    -- Declare a variable to hold the list of titles.

    text_output text = '' '';

    -- Declare a variable to hold the subject title.

    sub_title text;

    -- Declare a variable to hold records from the  books table.

    row_data books%ROWTYPE;

  BEGIN

    -- Outer FOR loop: loop through the body of this loop until the
    -- variable i equals 15.  Start the looping at 0.  Essentially,
    --loop the following statements 16 times (once for each subject).

    FOR i IN 0..15 LOOP

      -- Retrieve the subject name of the subject with an ID number
      -- that matches the variable i.

      SELECT INTO sub_title subject FROM subjects WHERE id = i;

      -- Insert the subject name, a colon, and a new line into the
      -- text_output variable.

      text_output = text_output || ''\n'' || sub_title || '':\n'';

      -- Loop through all records in the books table with a subject ID
      -- that matches the variable i.

      FOR row_data IN SELECT * FROM books
        WHERE subject_id = i  LOOP

        -- Insert the title of a matching book into the text_output
        -- variable, followed by a newline.
```

Example 11-45: Using the FOR loop (continued)

```
                text_output := text_output || row_data.title || ''\n'';

        END LOOP;
    END LOOP;

        -- Return the list.
    RETURN text_output;
    END;
 ' LANGUAGE 'plpgsql';
```

Example 11-46 shows the code of another function that uses a FOR loop to iterate through the results of a SQL query. With each iteration of the loop the FOR loop in Example 11-46 places the contents of a result row from a query against the books table into the row_data variable, and then inserts the value of the row's title field into the text_output variable.

The loop ends when the last record in books is reached. By the end of the loop, text_output will contain a list of all book titles that match the subject ID number passed to the function. The text_output variable is returned at the end of the function.

Example 11-46: Using the FOR loop with %ROWTYPE

```
    CREATE FUNCTION extract_title (integer) RETURNS text AS '
    DECLARE

        -- Declare an alias for function argument.
        sub_id ALIAS FOR $1;

        -- Declare a variable to hold book titles and set its default
        --    value to a new line.
        text_output text :=''\n'';

        -- Declare a variable to hold rows from the books table.
        row_data books%ROWTYPE;

    BEGIN

        -- Iterate through the results of a query.
        FOR row_data IN SELECT * FROM books
        WHERE subject_id = sub_id ORDER BY title  LOOP

            -- Insert the title of a matching book into the text_output variable.
            text_output := text_output || row_data.title || ''\n'';
        END LOOP;

        -- Return the list of books.
        RETURN text_output;
    END;
 ' LANGUAGE 'plpgsql';
```

Example 11-47 shows the results of the `extract_title()` function when 2, which represents "Children's Books" in the subject table, is passed as an argument.

Example 11-47: Result of the extract_title() function

```
booktown=# SELECT extract_title(2);
                         extract_title
---------------------------------------------------------------------

Bartholomew and the Oobleck
Franklin in the Dark
Goodnight Moon
The Cat in the Hat

(1 row)
```

The `row_data` variable is declared as a `%ROWTYPE` of the `books` table because it will only be used to hold records from the `books` table. We could have declared `row_data` as a `RECORD` to accomplish the same result, but the `RECORD` type should be used when you are going to be using the variable for more than just the rows of one specific table:

```
row_data RECORD;
```

The `extract_title()` function will return the same results whether row data is declared as `RECORD`, or is declared using `%ROWTYPE`.

Handling Errors and Exceptions

`RAISE` statements raise errors and exceptions during a PL/pgSQL function's operation. A `RAISE` statement sends specified information to the PostgreSQL `elog` mechanism (the standard PostgreSQL error logging utility, which typically logs data either to */var/log/messages*, or to *$PGDATA/serverlog*, as well as displaying to *stderr*).

A `RAISE` statement is also given the level of error it should raise, and the string it should send to PostgreSQL. Additionally, you can list variables and expressions whose values you wish to have placed into the string. Use percent signs (`%`) to mark the locations in the string at which you want those values inserted. The syntax of the `RAISE` statement is as follows:

```
RAISE level ''message string'' [, identifier [...] ];
```

Table 11-1 lists the three possible values for the `RAISE` statement's level and their meanings.

Table 11-1. Possible level values

Value	Explanation
DEBUG	DEBUG level statements send the specified text as a DEBUG: message to the PostgreSQL log and the client program if the client is connected to a database cluster running in debug mode. DEBUG level RAISE statements will be ignored by a database running in production mode.
NOTICE	NOTICE level statements send the specified text as a NOTICE: message to the PostgreSQL log and the client program in any PostgreSQL operation mode.
EXCEPTION	EXCEPTION level statements send the specified text as an ERROR: message to the client program and the PostgreSQL database log. The EXCEPTION level also causes the current transaction to be aborted.

In Example 11-48, the first RAISE statement raises a debug level message. The second and third RAISE statements send a notice to the user. Notice the use of the percent-sign (%) in the third RAISE statement to mark the location in the string at which the value of an integer is to be inserted. Finally, the fourth RAISE statement displays an error and throws an exception, causing the function to end and the transaction to be aborted.

Example 11-48: Using the RAISE statement

```
CREATE FUNCTION raise_test () RETURNS integer AS '
  DECLARE

    -- Declare an integer variable for testing.
    an_integer integer = 1;

  BEGIN

    -- Raise a debug level message.
    RAISE DEBUG ''The raise_test() function began.'';

    an_integer = an_integer + 1;

    -- Raise a notice stating that the an_integer variable was changed,
    -- then raise another notice stating its new value.
    RAISE NOTICE ''Variable an_integer was changed.'';
    RAISE NOTICE ''Variable an_integer's value is now %.'',an_integer;

    -- Raise an exception.
```

Example 11-48: Using the RAISE statement (continued)

```
    RAISE EXCEPTION ''Variable % changed.  Transaction aborted.'',an_integer;

    RETURN 1;
  END;
' LANGUAGE 'plpgsql';
```

Example 11-49 shows the results of the raise_test() function when called from our booktown database. The DEBUG output does not show, because our database is not running in debug mode.

Example 11-49: Results of the raise_test() function

```
booktown=# SELECT raise_test();
NOTICE:  Variable an_integer was changed.
NOTICE:  Variable an_integer's value is now 2.
ERROR:  Variable 2 changed.  Aborting transaction.
```

Calling Functions

The normal syntax to call another PL/pgSQL function from within PL/pgSQL is to either reference the function in a SQL SELECT statement, or during the assignment of a variable. For example:

```
SELECT function_identifier(arguments);
variable_identifier := function_identifier(arguments);
```

The use of assignments and SELECT statements to execute functions is standard in PL/pgSQL because all functions in a PostgreSQL database *must* return a value of some type. Use the PERFORM keyword to call a function and ignore its return data. Example 11-50 shows the syntax of the PERFORM keyword.

Example 11-50: Syntax of the PERFORM keyword

```
PERFORM function_identifier(arguments);
```

Example 11-51 demonstrates the use of PERFORM to invoke a PL/pgSQL function, and shows how to call another PL/pgSQL function through assignment (via a SELECT INTO statement). The ship_item function is a useful wrapper to the add_shipment function. It accepts basic information, makes sure the customer and book both exist, and then sends the information to add_shipment.

Example 11-51: Using the PERFORM keyword

```
CREATE FUNCTION ship_item (text,text,text) RETURNS integer AS '
  DECLARE

    -- Declare function argument aliases.
    l_name ALIAS FOR $1;
    f_name ALIAS FOR $2;
```

Example 11-51: Using the PERFORM keyword (continued)

```
        book_isbn ALIAS FOR $3;

          -- Declare a variable to hold the book ID number.  This variable
          -- is necessary to check for the existence of the provided ISBN.
        book_id integer;

          -- Declare a variable to hold the customer ID number.  This variable
          -- is necessary to check for the existence of the customer.
        customer_id integer;

    BEGIN

          -- Retrieve the customer ID number with a previously created
          -- function.
        SELECT INTO customer_id get_customer_id(l_name,f_name);

          -- If the customer does not exist, return -1 and exit.  The
          -- get_customer_id function returns a -1 if the customer is not found.
        IF customer_id = -1 THEN
          RETURN -1;
        END IF;

          -- Retrieve the ID number of the book with the specified ISBN.
        SELECT INTO book_id book_id FROM editions WHERE isbn = book_isbn;

          -- If the book does not exist in the system, return a -1.
        IF NOT FOUND THEN
          RETURN -1;
        END IF;

          -- If the book and customer both exist, add the shipment.
        PERFORM add_shipment(customer_id,book_isbn);

          -- Return 1 to indicate the function was successful.
        RETURN 1;
    END;
  ' LANGUAGE 'plpgsql';
```

PL/pgSQL and Triggers

Trigger functions can be created with PL/pgSQL and referenced within a PostgreSQL *trigger* definition. The term "trigger function" is simply a way of referring
to a function that is intended to be invoked by a trigger. Triggers define operations
that are performed when a specific event occurs within the database. A PL/pgSQL
trigger function can be referenced by a trigger as the operation to be performed
when the trigger's event occurs.

The definition of a trigger and the definition of its associated trigger function are
two different things. A trigger is defined with the SQL CREATE TRIGGER command,

whereas trigger functions are defined using the SQL CREATE FUNCTION command. Trigger definitions are explained in detail in Chapter 7, *Advanced Features*.

A trigger function should be defined as accepting no arguments, and returns a value of the special opaque data type. The CREATE FUNCTION syntax for defining a PL/pgSQL trigger function is shown in Example 11-52.

Example 11-52: Creating trigger functions

```
CREATE FUNCTION function_identifier () RETURNS opaque AS '
  DECLARE
    declarations;
    [...]
  BEGIN
    statements;
    [...]
  END;
' LANGUAGE 'plpgsql';
```

Trigger functions have access to a variety of special variables that exist to provide information about the calling trigger, and to allow the trigger function to manipulate table data. Each special trigger function variable is listed in Table 11-2.

Table 11-2. Trigger function variables

Name	Data type	Description
NEW	RECORD	Contains the new database row created after INSERT and UPDATE operations run by ROW level triggers. Use this variable to make modifications to the new row.
OLD	RECORD	Contains the old database row left after UPDATE AND DELETE operations performed by ROW level triggers.
TG_NAME	name	Contains the name of the fired trigger.
TG_WHEN	text	Contains either a BEFORE or AFTER string, depending on whether the trigger was defined as running after or before its specified event.
TG_LEVEL	text	Contains either a ROW or STATEMENT string, depending on the defined level of the trigger.
TG_OP	text	Contains an INSERT, UPDATE, or DELETE string that indicates the operation the trigger is invoked on.
TG_RELID	oid	Contains the object ID of the table that invoked the trigger.
TG_RELNAME	name	Contains the name of the table which invoked the trigger.
TG_NARGS	integer	Contains the number of arguments the trigger's definition specifies the trigger function as having.
TG_ARGV[]	array of text	Contains the arguments specified by the CREATE TRIGGER statement. The array index begins at zero.

Example 11-53 illustrates the definition of a PL/pgSQL trigger function and demonstrates the usage of the previously listed special variables. The `check_shipment_addition` trigger function is called after an INSERT or UPDATE operation is performed upon the `shipments` table.

The `check_shipment_addition()` function checks to make sure each added shipment contains a valid customer ID number and a valid ISBN for the book specified. It then subtracts one from the total amount of stock in the `stock` table for the specified book if the calling SQL operation is an INSERT statement (but *not* an UPDATE statement).

Example 11-53: The check_shipment_addition() PL/pgSQL trigger function

```
CREATE FUNCTION check_shipment_addition () RETURNS opaque AS '
  DECLARE
    -- Declare a variable to hold the customer ID.
    id_number integer;

    -- Declare a variable to hold the ISBN.
    book_isbn text;
  BEGIN
    -- If there is an ID number that matches the customer ID in
    -- the new table, retrieve it from the customers table.
    SELECT INTO id_number id FROM customers WHERE id = NEW.customer_id;

    -- If there was no matching ID number, raise an exception.
    IF NOT FOUND THEN
      RAISE EXCEPTION ''Invalid customer ID number.'';
    END IF;

    -- If there is an ISBN that matches the ISBN specified in the
    -- new table, retrieve it from the editions table.
    SELECT INTO book_isbn isbn FROM editions WHERE isbn = NEW.isbn;

    -- If there is no matching ISBN, raise an exception.
    IF NOT FOUND THEN
      RAISE EXCEPTION ''Invalid ISBN.'';
    END IF;

    -- If the previous checks succeeded, update the stock amount
    -- for INSERT commands.
    IF TG_OP = ''INSERT'' THEN
      UPDATE stock SET stock = stock -1 WHERE isbn = NEW.isbn;
    END IF;

    RETURN NEW;
  END;
' LANGUAGE 'plpgsql';
```

Once the `check_shipment_addition()` function has been created, a trigger may be set on the `shipments` table to call it. Example 11-54 shows the syntax to create the `check_shipment` trigger in the `booktown` database from within *psql*.

Example 11-54: The check_shipment trigger

```
booktown=# CREATE TRIGGER check_shipment
booktown-#               BEFORE INSERT OR UPDATE
booktown-#               ON shipments FOR EACH ROW
booktown-#               EXECUTE PROCEDURE check_shipment_addition();
CREATE
```

Note that the check_shipment_addition trigger function *must* be defined within the booktown database before its associated trigger is defined. Always define trigger functions before defining the triggers that reference them.

See Chapter 7 for more in-depth information on triggers.

12

JDBC

This chapter covers *JDBC* (Java DataBase Connectivity), which is a set of classes and methods available for the Java programming language. The use of JDBC with Java is a simple, generic, and portable way of interacting with different types of databases. For this chapter, some existing knowledge of how to program in Java is assumed.

The JDBC interfaces, defined by Sun, cover all of the interactions you can have with a standard SQL database. The vendor (in this case, PostgreSQL) supplies concrete implementations that implement these interfaces. These concrete implementations handle the vendor-specific interactions with the database: connecting, logging in, using stored procedures, and so forth. These interfaces are designed this way so that a program using JDBC can connect to any JDBC-compliant database, without your having to rewrite the code. However, there are some caveats.

One issue is that JDBC does not do any client-side SQL parsing or syntax checking. SQL statements are passed off transparently to the database, whether or not they are valid. Therefore, if the SQL is valid on one vendor's database, but invalid on another vendor's database the implementation won't know until the actual connection is made and the SQL is sent across. Sun is attempting to deal with this problem, and there may be some provisions made to correct this, either in later versions of JDBC or in a different standard.

Another issue is that each vendor has additional helper classes specific to that vendor. For instance, PostgreSQL has extensions for geometric data types. Other vendors won't support these extensions; they are specific to PostgreSQL. If you use such vendor-specific classes, your program will not work with another JDBC database, despite using the JDBC "standard."

One advantage of the PostgreSQL JDBC driver is that it is a "Type 4" driver. This means that it is written in Pure Java, so it can be taken anywhere, and used anywhere as long as the platform it is used on has TCP/IP capabilities, because the driver only connects via TCP/IP.

Building the PostgreSQL JDBC Driver

This section assumes that you already have a PostgreSQL database set up and ready to go. Make sure that you have it set to accept incoming TCP/IP connections. This can be configured when running the *postmaster* command. For more information on database start-up options, see Chapter 9, *Database Management*.

Before you can use JDBC, you must build the PostgreSQL JDBC drivers. To do this, you must have the Java source code that is used to build the driver. This source is included both in the complete PostgreSQL package, and in the *opt* package. These can be downloaded from the PostgreSQL site; for more information about downloading and installing these, see Chapter 2, *Installing PostgreSQL*.

You also need Ant. Ant is a standard build system for Java products, somewhat similar to *gmake*, and is created by Apache's Jakarta project. It is required to build the PostgreSQL JDBC driver. For more information on Ant, see: *http://jakarta.apache.org/ant/index.html*. Make sure that Ant's *bin* directory is in your path.

First you need to configure the makefile system to recognize that you are using Java. If you did not originally build PostgreSQL with Java support, move into the top level of the PostgreSQL source tree, and type *./configure with-java*, along with any other configure options you originally used. This will regenerate makefiles and, if necessary, will add support for Java.

Next you must actually build the driver and implementations. Change to the *src/interfaces/jdbc* directory and issue the *gmake* command. This will build two jar files: *postgresql.jar*, containing the `Driver` class and other concrete implementations, and *postgresql-examples.jar*, containing compiled example classes.

Using the PostgreSQL Driver

This section describes the process for using the built-in PostgreSQL JDBC driver. First, add the path to your *postgresql.jar* file into your CLASSPATH setting. This can be done either by setting your CLASSPATH environment variable, or by passing the path as an argument on the command line to your Java executable each time a Java application is executed. For more information, see your JVM vendor's instructions for setting your classpath.

Next, when coding a Java application, you need to ensure that the Driver gets registered within your code. When the Driver class passes through the Java class loader, it registers itself with the DriverManager class so that JDBC will know what Driver to use when connecting to a specific type of database. For instance, when you connect to a PostgreSQL database, you would obviously use the PostgreSQL driver class.

To make sure that the Driver class passes through the class loader, you can do a lookup by class name, as shown in the Java code snippet in Example 12-1.

Example 12-1: Class name lookup

```
try {
  Class.forName("org.postgresql.Driver");
} catch (ClassNotFoundException cnfe) {
  System.err.println("Couldn't find driver class:");
  cnfe.printStackTrace();
}
```

Class.forName is a method that finds a class by name. In this case, you look for the Driver. This causes the class loader to search through the CLASSPATH and find a class by that name. If it finds it, the class loader will then read in the binary description of the class. If it does not find it, it will throw a ClassNotFoundException, in which case you can print out an error message to that effect. If you reach this state, you either haven't built the driver correctly, or the *.jar* file is not in your classpath.

Once you have registered the Driver class, you need to request a connection to a PostgreSQL database. To do this, you use a class called DriverManager. The DriverManager class is responsible for handling JDBC URLs, finding an appropriate driver, and then using that driver to provide a connection to the database.

JDBC URLs are of the following format, in three colon-delimited parts:

```
jdbc:[drivertype]:[database]
```

The first part, jdbc, is a constant. It represents that you are connecting to a JDBC data source. The second part, *[drivertype]*, represents the kind of database you want to connect to. Use *postgresql* to connect to a PostgreSQL database. The third part is passed off to the driver, which finds the actual database. It takes on one of the following formats:

```
databasename
//hostname/databasename
//hostname:portnumber/databasename
```

In the first case, the PostgreSQL database is running on the local machine, on the default port number. The *databasename* is the literal name of the database you wish to connect to. The second case is used for when you want to specify a hostname and a database. This also uses the default port number. The third case allows you to specify a port number as well. Even if you use the first type of URL, the JDBC connection will always be made via TCP/IP.

For the purposes of the examples from now on, this chapter will use the URL: *jdbc:postgresql://localhost/booktown,* meaning you are connecting to host *localhost* and database booktown. With that in mind, try to make a connection, using all you have learned so far. Example 12-2 shows a simple Java program that opens a JDBC connection to the booktown database.

Example 12-2: A simple JDBC connection

```
import java.sql.DriverManager;
import java.sql.Connection;
import java.sql.SQLException;

public class Example1 {
  public static void main(String[] argv) {
  System.out.println("Checking if Driver is registered with DriverManager.");

  try {
    Class.forName("org.postgresql.Driver");
  } catch (ClassNotFoundException cnfe) {
    System.out.println("Couldn't find the driver!");
    System.out.println("Let's print a stack trace, and exit.");
    cnfe.printStackTrace();
    System.exit(1);
  }

  System.out.println("Registered the driver ok, so let's make a connection.");

  Connection c = null;

  try {
    // The second and third arguments are the username and password,
    // respectively. They should be whatever is necessary to connect
    // to the database.
    c = DriverManager.getConnection("jdbc:postgresql://localhost/booktown",
                                    "username", "password");
  } catch (SQLException se) {
    System.out.println("Couldn't connect: print out a stack trace and exit.");
    se.printStackTrace();
    System.exit(1);
  }

  if (c != null)
    System.out.println("Hooray! We connected to the database!");
  else
    System.out.println("We should never get here.");
  }
}
```

At this point you should be able to use this Connection object to do anything you want with the PostgreSQL database.

Notice the first three lines of Example 12-2. These three import statements make available the required classes to register with the DriverManager object, to create a Connection object, and to use SQLException objects. In general, to make available a JDBC class, the syntax is as follows, where classname is the name of the class you wish to be able to instantiate, and access:

```
import java.sql.classname
```

If you are unsure of what classes to import, you may use the following line to make all of the JDBC classes available to your program:

```
import java.sql.*
```

Understand that importing the entire set of JDBC classes can introduce a great deal of extra overhead. For maximum efficiency, you should only import those classes that you know your application requires.

Using JDBC

This section will be a brief introduction to JDBC, addressing the basics of JDBC, issues, caveats, and so forth. For more detailed information, visit the JDBC website (*http://java.sun.com/products/jdbc/*), which has many good resources and will always provide the most up to date information. Also, the API documentation included with your JDK has detailed information on specific classes, methods, and fields. Look for the java.sql package.

JDBC has classes to represent most of the basic pieces of a program's interaction with SQL. The classes are: Connection, Statement, ResultSet, Blob, and Clob, and they all map directly to some concept in SQL. JDBC also has helper classes, such as ResultSetMetaData and DatabaseMetaData, that represent meta-information. These are useful for when you'd like to get information about the capabilities of the database. They are also useful for getting the types of results returned by a query, either for debugging, or because you don't know about the data you are dealing with.

PostgreSQL's JDBC interface also provides classes to map to PostgreSQL's non-standard extensions to JDBC's SQL support. These non-standard extensions include: Fastpath, geometric types, native large objects, and a class that aids serialization of Java objects into the database.

Basic JDBC Usage

Example 12-2 used a Connection object, representing a physical connection to the database. You can use this Connection object to create Statement objects. Statement objects are JDBC's way of getting SQL statements to the database.

There are three main types of Statement objects: the base class Statement, the PreparedStatement, and the CallableStatement.

To create a Statement object, use the createStatement method as shown in Example 12-3:

Example 12-3: A JDBC statement object

```
Statement s = c.createStatement();
```

Example 12-3 creates a Statement object named s, from the Connection object c. You can now use this Statement object to execute queries and updates on the database.

There are two main methods in the Statement class that are important. The first is executeQuery. This method takes one argument, the SQL statement to be executed, and returns an object of type ResultSet, which is discussed later. This method is used for executing queries which will return a set of data back, for instance, a SELECT statement. The ResultSet object returned represents the data resulting from the query.

Example 12-4 retrieves some data from the booktown database:

Example 12-4: A simple JDBC select

```
Statement s = null;
try {
  s = c.createStatement();
} catch (SQLException se) {
  System.out.println("We got an exception while creating a statement:" +
                     "that probably means we're no longer connected.");
  se.printStackTrace();
  System.exit(1);
}
ResultSet rs = null;
try {
  rs = s.executeQuery("SELECT * FROM books");
} catch (SQLException se) {
  System.out.println("We got an exception while executing our query:" +
                     "that probably means our SQL is invalid");
  se.printStackTrace();
  System.exit(1);
}

int index = 0;
```

Example 12-4: A simple JDBC select (continued)

```
try {
  while (rs.next()) {
      System.out.println("Here's the result of row " + index++ + ":");
      System.out.println(rs.getString(1));
  }
} catch (SQLException se) {
  System.out.println("We got an exception while getting a result:this " +
                      "shouldn't happen: we've done something really bad.");
  se.printStackTrace();
  System.exit(1);
}
```

Example 12-4 creates a `Statement` object, and then uses that `Statement` object's `executeQuery` method to execute the query `SELECT * FROM books`. You get back a `ResultSet`, and use that `ResultSet` to print out some of the information you got back.

The `ResultSet` object is our primary interface for fetching information from the database. It has two main features. It can step through the set of rows returned, and it can return the value for a specific column in that row. It works in a similar fashion to a standard Java Enumeration: it starts before the first element, and you use the `next` method to step through the rest of the elements.

`next` returns true if the `ResultSet` was able to step to the next results; that is to say, there are results to be read. The `while` loop in Example 12-4 will print out the first column of each of the rows returned. If no rows were returned, `next` will return false initially, representing this fact, and therefore nothing will be printed.

`ResultSet` can return values of all sorts of different types; Example 12-4 treats the first column as if it were a `String`. Fortunately, all standard SQL data types can be represented as `String`, so regardless of the type of the first column, you will be able to fetch the value of the first column and print it out. There are many other methods available on `ResultSet`, including methods for fetching all of the various SQL data types and converting them to native Java types. Consult the API documentation on `ResultSet` for more information.

The other important method is `executeUpdate`. This method, again, takes one argument, which is the SQL statement to be executed. The difference between `executeQuery` and `executeUpdate` is that `executeUpdate` is for executing statements that change data in the database. For example, use `executeUpdate` to execute a `CREATE` an `INSERT` or an `UPDATE` statement. `executeUpdate` returns an int, and the value of that `int` corresponds to the number of records that were modified.

Example 12-5 uses the `executeUpdate` method to insert a new row into the `books` table.

Example 12-5: A simple JDBC insert

```
Statement s = null;
try {
  s = c.createStatement();
} catch (SQLException se) {
  System.out.println("We got an exception while creating a statement:" +
                     "that probably means we're no longer connected.");
  se.printStackTrace();
  System.exit(1);
}

int m = 0;

try {
  m = s.executeUpdate("INSERT INTO books VALUES " +
                      "(41472, 'Practical PostgreSQL', 1212, 4)");
} catch (SQLException se) {
  System.out.println("We got an exception while executing our query:" +
                     "that probably means our SQL is invalid");
  se.printStackTrace();
  System.exit(1);
}

System.out.println("Successfully modified " + m + " rows.\n");
```

Using Advanced JDBC Features

As mentioned earlier, besides the basic `Statement` object, there are two additional types of statements available in JDBC: `PreparedStatements` and `CallableStatements`. These two types are described later in this section.

In addition to these statements, this section also describes the use of the `ResultSetMetaData` and `DatabaseMetaData` objects. You can use these last two objects to interrogate JDBC for information about a given set of query results, or for information about your database. The ability to get such information at run-time enables you to dynamically execute any SQL statement, even one that is unknown when you write your program.

CallableStatement

Callable statements are implemented by the `CallableStatement` object. A `CallableStatement` is a way to execute stored procedures in a JDBC-compatible database. The best reference for this is Sun's Javasoft web site (*http://java.sun.com/products/jdbc/*), because callable statements represent a changing and evolving standard, and their application will depend greatly on your version of Java, and JDBC.

PreparedStatement

A PreparedStatement, in contrast to a CallableStatement, is used for SQL statements that are executed multiple times with different values. For instance, you
might want to insert several values into a table, one after another. The advantage
of the PreparedStatement is that it is pre-compiled, reducing the overhead of parsing SQL statements on every execution. Example 12-6 is an example of how a
PreparedStatement might be used.

Example 12-6: A JDBC prepared statement

```
PreparedStatement ps = null;

try {
  ps = c.prepareStatement("INSERT INTO authors VALUES (?, ?, ?)");
  ps.setInt(1, 495);
  ps.setString(2, "Light-Williams");
  ps.setString(3, "Corwin");
} catch (SQLException se) {
  System.out.println("We got an exception while preparing a statement:" +
                     "Probably bad SQL.");
  se.printStackTrace();
  System.exit(1);
}

try {
  ps.executeUpdate();
} catch (SQLException se) {
  System.out.println("We got an exception while executing an update:" +
                     "possibly bad SQL, or check the connection.");
  se.printStackTrace();
  System.exit(1);
}
```

You can see that Example 12-6 prepares a statement in a similar fashion as before,
except it uses a question mark (?) character in place of each value that you want
to supply. Use the appropriate PreparedStatement set method (e.g., setInt, set-
String) to set each value. The specific set method that you use for a column
depends on the data type of the column.

The PreparedStatement approach is useful because it avoids manual conversion of
Java types to SQL types. For instance, the you do not have to worry about quoting
or escaping when going to a text type.

Notice that the first parameter passed to a set method indicates the specific place-
holder parameter (the question marks) that you are setting. A value of 1 corresponds to the first question mark, a value of 2 corresponds to the second, and so
on.

The other strength of the PreparedStatement is that you can use it over and over
again with new parameter values, rather than having to create a new Statement

object for each new set of parameters. This approach is obviously more efficient, as only one object is created.

Use the set methods each time to specify new parameter values.

ResultSetMetaData

You can interrogate JDBC for detailed information about a query's result set using a `ResultSetMetaData` object. `ResultSetMetaData` is a class that is used to find information about the `ResultSet` returned from a `executeQuery` call. It contains information about the number of columns, the types of data they contain, the names of the columns, and so on.

Two of the most common methods in the `ResultSetMetaData` are `getColumnName` and `getColumnTypeName`. These retrieve the name of a column, and the name of its associated data type, respectively, each in the form of a `String`.

The `getColumnType` method is *not* the same as the `getColumnType-Name`. `getColumnType` returns an `int` corresponding to a data type's internal JDBC identification code, whereas `getColumnTypeName` returns the name as a `String`.

Example 12-7 is an example of using the `ResultSetMetaData` to get the name and data type of the first column in a `ResultSet` called `rs`. This code could logically follow the acquisition of the `ResultSet` named `rs` in Example 12-4.

Overall, the `PreparedStatement` mechanism is considerably more robust than the `Statement` class.

Example 12-7: JDBC ResultSetMetaData

```
ResultSetMetaData rsmd = null;
try {
  rsmd = rs.getMetaData();
} catch (SQLException se) {
  System.out.println("We got an exception while getting the metadata:" +
                     "check the connection.");
  se.printStackTrace();
  System.exit(1);
}

String columnName = null,
       columnType = null;
try {
  columnName = rsmd.getColumnName(1);
  columnType = rsmd.getColumnTypeName(1);
} catch (SQLException se) {
```

Example 12-7: JDBC ResultSetMetaData (continued)

```
    System.out.println("We got an exception while getting the column name:" +
                        "check the connection.");
    se.printStackTrace();
    System.exit(1);
}
```

```
System.out.print("The name of the first column is: '");
System.out.print(columnName);
System.out.println("'");
System.out.print("The data type of the first column is: ");
System.out.println(columnType);
```

There are many other useful methods in the ResultSetMetaData class, all of which
are well documented in the JDK API documentation.

DatabaseMetaData

Finally, DatabaseMetaData is a class that can be used to fetch information about the
database you are using. Use it to answer questions such as:

* What kind of catalogs are in the database?

* What brand of database am I working with?

* What username am I?

Example 12-8 uses DatabaseMetaData to query the JDBC driver for the username
used to establish the connection, and the database URL.

Example 12-8: JDBC DatabaseMetaData

```
DatabaseMetaData dbmd = null;

try {
    dbmd = c.getMetaData();
} catch (SQLException se) {
    System.out.println("We got an exception while getting the metadata:" +
                        " check the connection.");
    se.printStackTrace();
    System.exit(1);
}

String username = null;
try {
    username = dbmd.getUserName();
} catch (SQLException se) {
    System.out.println("We got an exception while getting the username:" +
                        "check the connection.");
    se.printStackTrace();
    System.exit(1);
}
```

Example 12-8: JDBC DatabaseMetaData (continued)

```
String url = null;
try {
  url = dbmd.getURL();
} catch (SQLException se) {
  System.out.println("We got an exception while getting the URL:" +
                     "check the connection.");
  se.printStackTrace();
  System.exit(1);
}

System.out.println("You are connected to '" + url +
                   "' with user name '" + username + "'");
```

Once again, the best source for the most current information about DatabaseMeta-Data's many other methods is in the JDK API documentation.

Issues Specific to PostgreSQL and JDBC

This section will detail three common issues with JDBC, just to save you the trouble of puzzling through them yourself. The first is fairly simple. ResultSets returned from an executeQuery call always start out with the row pointer set to to the point before the first row returned by the query. This means that you must advance to the first row returned before trying to fetch information from a Result-Set by calling the next method. Example 12-9 illustrates this. Notice that you'll get an exception from the first invocation of getString, because there is no current row. After a call to next, the getString function successfully returns a value from the first row in the set.

Example 12-9: JDBC first row fetch

```
ResultSet newSet = null;

try {
  newSet = s.executeQuery("SELECT * FROM book");
} catch (SQLException se) {
  System.out.println("We got an exception while executing our query:" +
                     "This probably means that our SQL is invalid.");
  se.printStackTrace();
  System.exit(1);
}

try {
  String value = newSet.getString(1); // BAD: we haven't called next() yet
} catch (Exception e) {
  System.out.println("We'll get an exception here, because we haven't" +
                     " stepped to the first row of the ResultSet yet.");
  e.printStackTrace();
}
```

Example 12-9: JDBC first row fetch (continued)

```
try {
  newSet.next();
  String value = newSet.getString(1);
} catch (SQLException se) {
  System.out.println("We'll only get an exception here if we've lost" +
                     "our connection, which isn't our fault.");
  se.printStackTrace();
  System.exit(1);
}
```

The next issue is also related to ResultSets, but it's far simpler than the first. You cannot get the number of rows returned from an executed statement without first stepping through the ResultSet using next, and incrementing a counter. In other words, there is no simple ResultSet method to return the number of rows retrieved. This is due to the fact that JDBC doesn't necessarily fetch any rows from PostgreSQL (or, for that matter, know whether or not there is a next row) until after you call the next method.

The last issue is more of a caveat. In a multithreaded environment, it's good to ensure that each thread uses its own Statement and ResultSet objects. That's because there is some state maintained in these objects, and using them from different threads will corrupt that state.

13

LXP

LXP (or *mod_lxp*) is an Application Server designed as an Apache Module. LXP is used to broker and dynamically format HTML content through a process called *server-side inclusion*. This involves assembling HTML output from a variety of sources, which can include HTML source files, XML files, or even data within a PostgreSQL database.

LXP's content inclusion is performed entirely on the server, ensuring the same output regardless of the web browser. LXP is intended to behave more intuitively, seamlessly, and comprehensively than other available content inclusion methods via its unique mark-up based approach and native PostgreSQL connectivity.

LXP uses a unique form of *programmatic mark-up tags*, which are interpreted entirely on the server and translated into standard HTML output before being sent to the client. While the effects of these tags are programmatic in nature, they differ from a "scripting language" such as PHP or Perl, by relying for their implementation on the same structural concepts as those behind HTML and XML for their implementation.

One of the goals of LXP is to provide dynamic, conditional capabilities that do not violate the syntax and methodology of a mark-up–based document. An LXP document should be readable to anyone fluent in HTML, though the meaning of the extra tags may not be immediately obvious. Simultaneously, experienced programmers can take advantage of the more advanced features within the content model of *LXP*.

Why Use LXP?

LXP provides a simple way to build powerful web sites without using a "programming" language. If you can use mark-up, you can use LXP to help provide dynamically manageable content.

Additionally, LXP's integration with PostgreSQL allows for a deeper degree of content in your web sites. Traditionally, if you wanted to perform logic on result sets from a database, you would have to use PHP, Perl, or compiled C or C++. With LXP, use of such languages is no longer required.

Using LXP allows you to utilize the power of PostgreSQL's features—including user-defined functions, triggers, and procedural languages (such as PL/pgSQL)—to provide the logic for your data. With LXP, there is no longer a need to use complicated programming languages for the majority of your simple tasks. Even mathematical operations, date and time evaluations, and involved string formatting can be performed with LXP, via the connection to PostgreSQL.

While this simplicity is one of LXP's strengths, we understand that sometimes a more comprehensive solution is required (or simply preferred) for the design of a given function. For this reason, if you need the power of a comprehensive programming language in part of your web site, you can use either of LXP's *Apache* or *URI* methods to embed any available document type within LXP-managed output.

Core Features

LXP provides a core set of features that include external file inclusion, XML parsing, and a direct SQL interface to PostgreSQL. As of Version 0.8, SQL execution is performed with either a dynamic or persistent connection to the PostgreSQL RDBMS.

LXP also supports a few more advanced techniques commonly found in programming languages, such as variable setting, insertion and substitution, arrays, branching logic, loop iteration, and a basic search-and-replace variable formatting interface.

Content Inclusion and Management

The essential concept of content inclusion is that other files, or sources of data, can be *included* (e.g., inserted or embedded) within a requested document's HTML output. Instructing an LXP document to include another file means that the output from that included file will appear inline, as if it had been part of the originally requested document itself. This can aid both the efficiency and maintainability of a large, dynamic web site.

LXP can natively include a variety of external files, from plain HTML, to XML, to token-delimited flat files. However, one of the strongest features of LXP's content inclusion capability is that LXP can embed *any* content type that your Apache web server has been configured to handle.

Earlier incarnations of LXP had somewhat rigid support for the inclusion of PHP scripts. As of Version 0.8, however, LXP can include any available content type via Apache subrequests. This allows you to embed server-side documents written in languages including, but not limited to, *PHP, Perl,* and any executable CGI application. Any CGI arguments or LXP variables available to LXP are passed on to the included document as if it had been called directly with those variables through an HTTP request.

LXP also utilizes *expat*, a nonvalidating XML parsing library. While *expat* doesn't validate your XML based on a DTD, the XML to be parsed *must at least* be *well-formed* (e.g., no invalid characters, mismatched tags, etc.).

The XML parser implementation was written into LXP with support for easy RSS/ RDF formats in particular (*Rich Site Summary* and *Resource Description Framework*, respectively). These file formats are available on popular web sites to provide a short summary of the information supplied on their site to other hosts that link to their content (e.g., the headlines from a news site, along with URL information).

LXP's XML method is evolving into a more generalized tool, but it can presently be used to a limited extent with any well-formed XML.

Direct SQL Methods and PostgreSQL Connectivity

LXP provides both dynamic and persistent PostgreSQL database connectivity, allowing for versatile execution of SQL statements. The *SQL inclusion method* allows the execution of a query from within an LXP document. Once a query is executed, its results are passed to the LXP parser for inline formatting. These values can either be displayed immediately, or set as variables for use later in the document.

The persistent connections, inline formatting, and direct SQL query tags lend LXP unparalleled ease of use in the arrangement of content from a database. An example use of the LXP database connectivity can be found in the *Fingerless* LXP package, a simple and flexible weblog implementation.

Fingerless

Fingerless, first introduced in LXP 0.7, is an LXP-based weblog system, similar to those seen on sites such as *Slashdot.org* and *Kuro5hin.org*.

As of the 0.8 release, the Fingerless implementation has been re-factored into an external package utilizing general LXP tags and persistent SQL connectivity. As such, this documentation will not cover the now deprecated Fingerless builtin methods, which will be removed from the LXP core in the next major release. For an example of a web site running Fingerless, however, visit: *http://www.thelinuxreview.com*.

Installing and Configuring LXP

To install LXP, you must have the Apache web server installed and configured to support *mod_so*. This is the Apache Shared Object module. If you have not built Apache with this module, you will need to reconfigure it, making sure to include the *--enable-module=so* configuration option before compiling.

 If you choose to manually compile Apache, be sure that you remove any existing Apache RPMs first. You can usually identify these with the *rpm -qa |grep apache* command.

If Apache is installed, and the Shared Object module is enabled, you may insert the CD included with this book, mount it, and proceed with the installation. You will need to be logged in as *root* in order to successfully install LXP, since it requires access to system-level files and directories.

Installing LXP

There are two ways to install LXP as of Version 0.8; you may use the *lxpinstall.sh* script, found in the *lxp* directory on the CD, or you may install it manually. The *lxpinstall.sh* script is intended to both install the required LXP files and to configure your *httpd.conf* file to load and enable the LXP module.

If you encounter any errors during the installation from *lxpinstall.sh*, see the following section about manual configuration.

Using lxpinstall.sh

The *lxpinstall.sh* script is extremely straightforward. On a fresh system, the only option you should be prompted to respond to is at the end of the script, when it asks you whether or not to automatically restart Apache (as must be done, to enable LXP). You may run it again afterward in case something goes wrong, though it will prompt you whether or not certain files should be overwritten.

Example 13-1 changes to the *lxp* directory on the CD (mounted in */mnt/cdrom*, in this case), and runs the *lxpinstall.sh* file.

Example 13-1: Installing LXP with lxpinstall.sh

```
[root@host root]# cd /mnt/cdrom/lxp
[root@host lxp]# ./lxpinstall.sh
================================================================
Thank you for installing Command Prompt LXP, 0.8.0.
Copyright (c) 1999-2001, Command Prompt, Inc.
See the LICENSE file for licensing restrictions.
================================================================
[cmd] Checking for PostgreSQL libs (this may take a moment) ...
[cmd] Found PostgreSQL libpq library.
[cmd] Using apxs: '/usr/local/apache/bin/apxs'
[cmd] Using '/usr/local/apache/libexec/' for shared object file


================================================================
[cmd] Installing 'liblxp.so'
[activating module 'lxp' in /usr/local/apache/conf/httpd.conf]
cp lib/liblxp.so /usr/local/apache/libexec/liblxp.so
chmod 755 /usr/local/apache/libexec/liblxp.so
cp /usr/local/apache/conf/httpd.conf /usr/local/apache/conf/httpd.conf.bak
cp /usr/local/apache/conf/httpd.conf.new /usr/local/apache/conf/httpd.conf
rm /usr/local/apache/conf/httpd.conf.new


================================================================
[cmd] Using '/usr/local/apache/conf/httpd.conf' for configuration
[cmd] Backing up original configuration file...
/usr/local/apache/conf/httpd.conf -> /usr/local/apache/conf/httpd.conf.lxp_backup
[cmd] Backing up original configuration file...
/usr/local/apache/conf/srm.conf -> /usr/local/apache/conf/srm.conf.lxp_backup
[cmd] Adding LXP directives to httpd.conf...


================================================================
[cmd] Installing 'lxp.conf' into /usr/local/cmd/etc ...
conf/lxp.conf-dist -> /usr/local/cmd/etc/lxp.conf


================================================================
[cmd] Re-start Apache with '/usr/local/apache/bin/apachectl'? (y/n) y
/usr/local/apache/bin/apachectl stop: httpd stopped
/usr/local/apache/bin/apachectl start: httpd started
[cmd] Command Prompt LXP 0.8.0 successfully installed.
```

In case there is a problem with your *httpd.conf* reconfiguration, remember that LXP creates a backup of your original configuration called *httpd.conf.lxp_backup* in the same directory as your *httpd.conf* before making any modifications.

You may receive the following error when running the *lxpinstall.sh* script:

```
[cmd] ERROR: LXP requires Apache be configured with Shared Object support,
[cmd] but we couldn't find Apache's apxs script.
[cmd] Please make sure it is in your path, if you know mod_so is enabled.
[cmd] exit error 1
```

This error indicates that *apxs*, the Apache Extension tool, could not be found on your system. It is typically found in */usr/local/apache/bin*, though it may be missing if your Apache web server was not built with *mod_so* support enabled, or if you have not installed the *apache-devel* RPM for your system. If you know it is installed, be sure that the directory it resides within is in your PATH environment variable.

Alternatively, you may get an error message similar to the following:

```
[cmd] ERROR: apxs couldn't find your configuration file
[cmd] (Tried /usr/local/apache/conf/httpd.conf)
[cmd] exit error 3
```

If you are not using a configuration file with a standard name (i.e., *httpd.conf*), you will need to manually configure it. See the next section instructions.

Manual installation

This section describes how to manually install LXP if the *lxpinstall.sh* script does not work for you. If you've already installed LXP successfully through this script, you may skip this section.

There are three steps to manually installing LXP:

- Installing the LXP shared-object file
- Installing the LXP configuration file
- Configuring Apache's *httpd.conf* file

The *liblxp.so* file (located in the */lxp/lib* directory on the CD) must be copied to the directory that your Apache web server is configured to load external modules from. This is typically */usr/local/apache/libexec* for manual installations of Apache, and */etc/httpd/modules* for RPM installations. Note that this directory varies wildly, and may be different in your distribution. You should be able to install into this directory through the use of *apxs*, however, with the following syntax:

```
apxs -i -n module -a shared_object
```

Example 13-2 demonstrates using the *apxs* script to install and configure the *liblxp.so* file directly into Apache's module directory.

Example 13-2: Manually installing liblxp.so

```
[root@host lib]# apxs -i -n "lxp" -a lib/liblxp.so
cp lib/liblxp.so /usr/local/apache/libexec/liblxp.so
chmod 755 /usr/local/apache/libexec/liblxp.so
[activating module 'lxp' in /usr/local/apache/conf/httpd.conf]
[root@host lib]#
```

If you do not have PostgreSQL installed, the *libpq.so.2.2* file (also located in the */lxp/lib* directory on the CD) should be copied to the */usr/local/cmd/lib* directory. A symbolic link named *libpq.so.2* should also be created to point to this file. If you have not run *lxpinstall.sh*, you may need to create this directory. Example 13-3 demonstrates this process.

Example 13-3: Manually installing libpq.so.2.2

```
[root@host lib]# mkdir -p /usr/local/cmd/lib
[root@host lib]# cp -iv libpq.so.2.2 /usr/local/cmd/lib/
libpq.so.2.2 -> /usr/local/cmd/lib/libpq.so.2.2
[root@host lib]# ln -s /usr/local/cmd/lib/libpq.so.2.2 /usr/local/cmd/lib/libpq.so.2
[root@host lib]#
```

Next, the *lxp.conf* file must be installed in the */usr/local/cmd/etc* directory. This is the configuration file for LXP 0.8, discussed in detail in the next section. The distributed configuration file is found in the *lxp/conf* directory on the CD, and is named *lxp.conf-dist*. Copy this file to */usr/local/cmd/etc* from the *lxp/conf* directory on the CD, as shown in Example 13-4. If you have not run *lxpinstall.sh* at all, you may need to create this directory. Be sure to rename it from *lxp.conf-dist* to *lxp.conf*!

Example 13-4: Manually installing lxp.conf

```
[root@host lxp]# mkdir -p /usr/local/cmd/etc
[root@host lxp]# cp -v conf/lxp.conf-dist /usr/local/cmd/etc/lxp.conf
conf/lxp.conf-dist -> /usr/local/cmd/etc/lxp.conf
[root@host lxp]#
```

Finally, Apache's *httpd.conf* file must be configured for the LXP content type.

In some circumstances, *httpd.conf* may have been renamed to something else (such as *httpsd.conf*, in the case of ApacheSSL).

There are two lines that must be added to the *httpd.conf* file for LXP to be correctly configured. These modifications are shown in Example 13-5.

Example 13-5: Configuring httpd.conf for LXP

```
DirectoryIndex index.html index.lxp
AddType application/x-httpd-lxp .lxp
```

A line similar to the first line in Example 13-5 should already exist in your *httpd.conf* file. You must add `index.lxp` as a value to this directive if you wish for Apache to automatically look for an LXP index in a directory request.

The second line must be added from scratch. This `AddType` directive should be entered exactly as it is shown in Example 13-5. This line enables the LXP module to process files ending in *.lxp*.

It is generally not important where you put these last two directives within the *httpd.conf* file, though you may wish to place them with similarly named directives that already exist, to keep the configuration file organized.

Once you have finished, you must restart Apache for the changes to take effect. This is typically done with either the *apachectl* command, or the *httpd* service script.

Nuts and Bolts: Configuring lxp.conf

After installing LXP, you will find the *lxp.conf* file in the */usr/local/cmd/etc* directory. This file defines the database settings with which LXP connects to the Post-greSQL database for persistent connections. The file also contains a pair of debugging options.

The *lxp.conf* file is a simple configuration file using common conventions. The format of this file can consist of *comments*, *directives*, and associated *values* for each directive.

Comments are always prefixed with a hash mark (#). They can be at the beginning of a line, or follow a directive and value. They are totally ignored by LXP when the configuration is loaded, and are only useful for remembering notes on why directives are set and what possible options there may be. You can add your own comments without harming the functionality of LXP as long as you remember to precede the comment with a hash mark (#).

Directives have a very basic affect upon the functionality of LXP. They typically start at the beginning of a line, have a name (without spaces), and are followed by their associated value. The directive name defines a behavior to affect, while the value sets how to affect that behavior. Some directives accept multiple values, which are separated by either tabs or spaces. Here is example syntax:

```
# Here's an example directive.

MyDirective     SomeValue       # MyDirective defines some arbitrary value.
```

You may never need to make serious alterations in your *lxp.conf* file, but it's a good idea to know what it is, and what it does, in case you ever need to change one of these basic behaviors. As of LXP 0.8, the *lxp.conf* file is broken up into two sections; general settings and database settings.

General settings

The first two directives under the General settings section are `Debug` and `MaxIncludeDepth`:

```
######################
# General LXP settings.
######################

Debug             No  # (Yes|No)
MaxIncludeDepth   15  # (Number)
```

Setting the `Debug` directive to `Yes` adds a debugging-header to the top of all LXP documents. This can be useful for tracking down unexplained behavior of LXP files and included scripts. The debug header includes the name of the LXP document requested, any cookies found for the given domain, any GET/POST variables that are passed, and *maximum depth inclusion*.

The maximum depth inclusion is the highest number of includes LXP will traverse down before stopping and displaying an error. This is used to prevent accidental infinite includes (e.g., *a.lxp* includes *b.lxp*, which includes *a.lxp*). Set this value with the `MaxIncludeDepth` directive. The default value is 15.

> The value assigned to `MaxIncludeDepth` does not limit the total number of files that can be included within a document. It describes only the *deepest* level LXP can go in *sub-inclusions* (e.g., *a.lxp* includes *b.lxp*, which includes *c.lxp*, which includes *d.lxp*, etc).

Database settings

The next six directives pertain to database connectivity with PostgreSQL. Most of the default options are usable on most systems, but you may wish to modify these if you have special needs for your PostgreSQL installation:

```
#############################################
# PostgreSQL persistent connectivity options.
#############################################

UseDb    No         # (Yes|No) Set to Yes if you wish to connect to the database.

DbName   template1  # The database to use. By default, "template1".
```

```
DbHost  localhost # The database host to use. By default, "localhost".
DbPort  5432      # The port to connect to PostgreSQL on.
DbUser  postgres  # The username to connect with. By default, "postgres".
DbPass            # The password to connect with. By default, empty
```

If you wish to enable LXP's persistent connections to a database, set `UseDb` to `Yes`. If set to `No`, you will still be able to use the Direct SQL Interface to dynamically open up connections (see the section titled "Including SQL Content"), but you will incur the cost of a new PostgreSQL backend connection for *each* connection request.

The remaining options—`DbName`, `DbHost`, `DbPort`, `DbUser`, and `DbPass`—should be familiar to anyone with experience connecting to PostgreSQL. The defaults will usually work fine, but you might wish to change them if you have special needs (for example, if you wish to store your data on a separate database server, you would change `DbHost` to point to the appropriate machine).

When utilizing the persistent connections between Apache and LXP's PostgreSQL database, it is important to recognize that there will be a separate *postmaster* binary running for each *httpd* process. Be sure that your system is configured to be capable of loading as many PostgreSQL *postmaster* backends as Apache requires (i.e., the number defined by the `MaxClients` directive in Apache's *httpd.conf*) file.

Understanding LXP Mark-Up

While LXP performs programmatic tasks, one of the aims of LXP is to achieve these tasks without having to change the general syntax that one uses when putting together HTML (or XHTML) mark-up. On the server, an LXP document appears to be a normal HTML file with some unfamiliar *tags*.

Here is an introductory example of a simple LXP document:

```
<lxp>
  <dock type="init">
    <include src="parts/init.lxp" />
  </dock>
  <include src="parts/head.html" />

  <h1>Welcome</h1>

  <hr width="400">

  <if lxp.authenticated='t'>
    Welcome to my webpage, <putcookie name="user" />
  </if>
  <else>
```

```
      <strong>Please login.</strong>
      <include src="parts/login.lxp" />
   </else>

   <include src="parts/foot.html" />
</lxp>
```

LXP Tags

A tag (formally called an *element*) is defined as a structure in a document beginning with a less-than symbol (<) and ending with a greater-than symbol (>). Tags always begin with a name, which defines the nature of the tag, and can optionally have a set of space-delimited *attributes*. Attributes are always described in the form of a *name=value* pair, where *name* is an attribute name unique to that tag, and *value* is some arbitrary value assigned to that attribute.

All of LXP's tags follow the same general structure of any mark-up language. Tags begin a *region* (or *block*) with an *opening* tag (e.g., <tag>), and close each region with an associated slash-prefixed *closing* tag (e.g., </tag>.

As with HTML and XML, some tags do not require closing. These are called *empty element* tags, and do not define a region, but perform a one-time operation. Empty element tags are typically characterized by a trailing forward slash at the end of the tag (e.g., <tag />.

LXP's parser does not syntactically require trailing-slashes in empty element tags, though omitting them can cause unpredictable behavior in some circumstances. For example, nesting the <include> tag can cause some confusion to branching logic if trailing slashes are omitted. This is because the <include> tag may be either an empty-element tag (as in the case of an external document inclusion), or an opening tag requiring a closing tag (as in the case of the direct SQL inclusion).

 It is a good idea to be in the habit of using trailing slashes in empty-element tags. In HTML, some tags do not formally require a trailing slash (e.g., <br> versus XHTML's <br />). With the rise of XHTML and XML, however, requirements for mark-up–based documents are becoming more strict.

Both opening and empty-element tags have names, and may also contain some number of attributes. While the name describes the intent of a tag, the attributes typically define the *details* of the operation to be performed, and vary in their meaning from tag to tag. A closing tag should only have a name, immediately following its initial forward slash (e.g., </tag>).

LXP tag and attribute names are generally case-insensitive, though there are times when an attribute name refers literally to a variable's name (such as in the <if> tag). In these instances, case can matter, depending on the case conventions you use with your variables. The examples in this document prefer lowercase, following the lead of the XHTML standard (which defines element names and attributes as all lowercase).

Example 13-6 shows a simple LXP mark-up region with one opening tag, one closing tag, and two empty-element tags within their defined region.

Example 13-6: A Simple LXP mark-up region

```
<lxp>
  <setvar example="test" />
  <putvar name="example" />
</lxp>
```

LXP aims for simplicity and seamlessness in application development, and this basic structural aspect of LXP is an example of this ethic.

LXP Regions

Arguably the most important LXP tag is the <lxp> tag itself, which enables an *LXP region*. This is similar to a <script> tag, or the PHP short tag, in that it instructs the LXP module to begin looking for LXP content.

Unlike PHP, however, while parsing an LXP region the module will simply ignore any tags that it does not recognize as an LXP tag. The <lxp> tag simply enables the ability to use LXP tags in a given region without impairing your ability to write normal HTML mark-up (though the effect of LXP tags can control which parts of the HTML are displayed).

It should follow from this discussion that </lxp> closes an LXP region and disables the ability to use LXP tags until the next <lxp> tag is opened.

An LXP document does not automatically look for LXP tags. A document will be rendered faster if LXP regions are limited to areas requiring LXP capabilities, as it is more involved to parse an LXP region for dynamic content than it is to process a plain HTML region.

LXP Variables and Objects

A *variable* is a modifiable value in memory that is accessed through an associated name. This name is used to identify, and subsequently utilize in some fashion, the value that it represents. The specific use varies based on the LXP tag employed.

LXP also implements a special type of data structure called an *object*. An LXP object is typically used to identify several associated variable values through a common name. The particular value you wish to address in an LXP object is identified either by a trailing subscript (a numeric or text value, in square brackets, such as `example[0]`) or a dot-notated trailing identifier (such as `for.count`).

The concept of an LXP object is similar to the programmatic concept of arrays and objects in traditional programming languages, though LXP objects are generally much simpler in their nature. In practice, the only difference between variables and objects is syntactic, having to do with how values are identified. Variables are identified with a plain name (e.g., `my_value`), while objects are identified by a name and a secondary identifier (e.g., `my_value[0]`, `my_value[1]`, `my_value.size`).

From a programmer's perspective, variables and objects are considered *global*, meaning that once set, they are available anywhere in a document. Included documents will also have access to the variables which are set in memory.

Naming Conventions

The valid characters with which you may define an LXP variable's name are:

- Any letter (*a–z, A–Z*)
- Any digit (*0–9*)
- The underscore (_)

The valid characters with which you define a complete LXP object's name are:

- Any letter (*a–z, A–Z*)
- Any digit (*0–9*)
- The underscore (_)
- The period (.)
- Square brackets (*[]*)

Note that while numbers are the most common form of subscript (since they are used implicitly by CGI arrays; see the section titled "CGI Arrays"), any legal characters may be used within square brackets following an object's name (e.g., `pseudo_array[example]`).

When parsing the attributes of an LXP tag, some special character symbols may be used to *substitute* the value of a variable directly into either the attribute's name or value (see the section titled "Tag Parsing" for more about this technique). These characters are: the dollar sign ($) for variables, and the at sign (@) for objects.

It *must* be understood that while special character symbols are sometimes used to substitute variable values into a tag's attributes, these character symbols are *not* part of a variable's name and should *not* be used in contexts where a literal variable or object name is expected.

Using Variables and Objects

Variable values can be displayed anywhere in the body of an LXP region through the <putvar> tag. Here is the syntax for <putvar>, where variablename is the name of the variable whose value is to be displayed:

```
<putvar name="variablename" />
```

Variable values may also be set and reset via the <setvar> and <setvars> tags. Here is the syntax for these tags:

```
<setvar variablename="variablevalue" />
<setvars variable1="value1"
         variable2="value2"
         [...]
         />
```

Like variables, the values referenced by objects can also be displayed and set by the <putvar> and <setvar> tags.

 Remember that the use of either a dot (period) or square brackets in setting a name with <setvar> implies that you are setting a variable value to an *object*, rather than a plain variable. Such a value can therefore only be substituted later with the at sign, rather than the dollar sign.

CGI Arguments

Like many web-based programming languages, LXP keeps an internal list of CGI *arguments* that have been passed to it. These arguments are implicitly treated by LXP as variables.

For the purpose of this chapter, the terms "argument" and "variable" will be nearly synonymous. In context, the term "argument" applies specifically to form-passed variables, while "variable" applies to any variable set in memory (either passed by a form, or set by the developer).

Arguments are each passed from forms with a *name* and a *value*. For each argument passed to an LXP document (e.g., via an HTML form), a single variable is created with the passed argument used as the variable's name.

If two arguments have the same name, the last value passed by the form is used (with the exception of array values; see the section titled "CGI Arrays").

CGI Arrays

Objects are useful when handling CGI *arrays*. Ordinarily, if more than one argument value is passed to an LXP document with the same argument name, the value of the last passed argument is used, and any preceding values are ignored. However, by passing a CGI argument with a name ending in empty square brackets (e.g., `<select name="test[]">`), an LXP object will automatically have an array of values assigned to an object bearing the name preceding the square brackets.

In other words, any argument passed from a CGI form whose name ends in square brackets (e.g., `test[]`) will be implicitly treated by LXP as an array of values. When such an argument is passed to LXP by a submitted form, each separate value found for it is automatically set as a separate variable value in memory, with an incrementing numeric value between the brackets following the object's name.

For example, if an HTML form passes an argument named `test[]` that has three values set to its name, three variable values will be set for a `test` object. These values may be referenced as `test[0]`, `test[1]`, and `test[2]`, respectively.

Direct SQL objects

During a direct SQL query's execution, a special object called `this` is used to reference column values in the result set. Each column selected from the result set can be referenced as `this.column_name` where *column_name* is the name of the column.

Additionally, an object called `sql` is created with meta-information about the query. These pieces of information include the number of the current row being accessed (`sql.row`), the offset of the current row being accessed (`sql.offset`), the number of rows last selected by a SQL query (`sql.numrows`), and the number of columns last selected by a SQL query (`sql.numcols`, or `sql.numfields`).

Global LXP objects

Two special objects named `lxp` and `env` are pre-defined system objects that can supply information about the LXP system and environment variables.

Any environment variable set by Apache's CGI configuration (e.g., `REMOTE_ADDR`) can be accessed by referencing the name of the variable as a dot-notated identifier through the `env` object. For example, the `env.REMOTE_ADDR` variable value identifies the address of the remote client accessing the current document (if that feature is enabled in Apache).

The `lxp` object is reserved for system purposes. As of Version 0.8, only three values are defined. The most useful of these is the `lxp.self` value, which describes the URI which Apache received for the current LXP request (e.g., */app/index.lxp*).

Additionally, the `lxp.version` variable value contains the current version of the LXP software being used, and the `lxp.copyright` variable value contains the copyright on the software.

Users submitting data to an LXP document are not able to pass variables beginning with `lxp.` via a `GET` or `POST` request. Thus, any variable beginning with `lxp.` is a *protected* variable, and can only be set by an LXP document through the `<setvar>` tag. This can be useful in maintaining the integrity of sensitive variables, such as the results of password-based authentication.

Using Cookies with LXP

LXP has the ability to both set and retrieve cookie values. The LXP tag to set a cookie is `<setcookie>`, and the LXP tag to display a cookie value is `<putcookie>`.

Setting Cookies

The setting of a cookie must happen *before* any content is sent from the Apache server. This is because the cookie is included in the headers that precede the actual output of the requested document.

A special construct exists for this type of scenario, called the *initialization dock*, which is defined with `<dock type="init">`. This tag must be the first LXP tag following the `<lxp>` tag in your document. Within it, you may use the `<setcookie>` tag. Here is the syntax for opening an initialization dock:

```
<lxp>
  <dock type="init">
```

Once the dock is open, you may set cookies with the following syntax:

```
<setcookie name="cookie_name" value="cookie_value"
        domain="cookie_domain" path="cookie_path"
        expires="cookie_expiration" />
```

When the dock is closed with `</dock>`, the cookies will be set, and content following the closing dock tag will be sent to the client.

Only the `name` and `value` attributes are required to set a cookie. Supplying an empty value has the effect of deleting the cookie.

Setting an explicit domain is helpful in specifying the detail of a domain the cookie should be accepted for (e.g., *www.thelinuxreview.com*, versus *.thelinuxreview.com* for all subdomains). Similarly, the `path` attribute specifies a URI path to maintain the cookie for (e.g., `path="/app/"`).

If the `expires` attribute is omitted, the cookie is set as a *session* cookie, and it will expire when the browser is closed. Otherwise, the value represents either the number of hours in which the cookie should expire, or the complete *epoch* value (the number of seconds since 1970 to the moment the cookie should expire). If the value is larger than one million, it is implied that it is describing the latter.

Note that, unlike some web languages, LXP documents will be immediately aware of any cookies that you have set within the same request that sets the cookie. This awareness is handled through logic internal to LXP, and included documents of other types (such as PHP) will not be aware of a cookie that has been set until a request following the one which sets the cookie is submitted. This is due to the client-side nature of cookies.

 An initialization dock is also a good region in which to perform any general initialization for a document, as no comments or newlines in an initialization dock will be sent to the browser. You can include an external LXP file from within the dock.

Accessing Cookie Values

Unlike some other web-languages, such as PHP, cookies are not implicitly treated as variables. Instead, LXP maintains a separate list of cookies in addition to its list of variables. This is done to ensure that methods that should apply to cookies always do, and to prevent the collision of variable names and cookie names.

Therefore, to display a cookie, use the `<putcookie>` tag, as shown in Example 13-7.

Example 13-7: Displaying a cookie value

```
<lxp>
  Your cookie "user" is set to: <putcookie name="user" />
</lxp>
```

If you wish to substitute the value of a cookie into an LXP attribute, you might think you could do so with the same dollar sign notation used to substitute variable values. However, this introduces a point of ambiguity between cookie values and variable values. Therefore, cookie values may be accessed through the special cookies LXP object.

Example 13-8: Substituting cookie values

```
<lxp>
  <setvar welcome_msg="Welcome, @cookies.user!" />

  <if cookies.user>
    <putvar name="welcome_msg" />
  </if>
</lxp>
```

As of LXP 0.8, for backwards compatibility, if a variable is not found with a specified substitution name (e.g., $my_cookie), LXP will search the list of cookies for a cookie with that name. This behavior is scheduled to either be removed (or be made configurable) in future versions of LXP, however.

Tag Parsing

When a tag is parsed, its attributes are read in one of two ways—literally, or interpretively. Similar to existing conventions in a variety of languages, defining a value in single-quotes (e.g., name='value') causes the contents of the value to be parsed literally, regardless of the characters between quotes. Using double-quotes causes its contents to be parsed interpretively, meaning that some characters will be treated in special ways.

Specifically, these special characters are the dollar sign ($), the at sign (@), and the ampersand (&). These characters correspond to variable substitution, object variable value substitution, and entity substitution, respectively.

Value substitution is the process by which a variable, cookie, object, or entity's *value* is substituted for its syntactically referenced *name*. This occurs at the name's original location in any arbitrary string of characters.

Variable Substitution

What may be confusing to experienced programmers at first is that LXP supports the familiar dollar sign notation to substitute a named variable (e.g., $myvariable) with its associated value in a mixed character string.

When using LXP, it is important to understand the contexts in which variables are substituted (and the context in which they are not). Subsequently, it is also important to understand when to use variable substitution and when not to.

The first rule is that variables will *never* be substituted outside of an LXP tag. Example 13-9 attempts incorrectly to place the value of a variable named variable within an LXP document.

Example 13-9: Invalid variable substitution

```
<lxp>
  Here is my variable: $variable <!-- Wrong -->
</lxp>
```

Instead, suppose that the URL *http://localhost/test.lxp?setbar=foo* is opened in a browser, and that *test.lxp* contains the LXP mark-up shown in Example 13-10.

Example 13-10: Valid variable substitution

```
<lxp>
  <setvar bar="$setbar" /> <!-- sets bar's value to setbar's value -->
  <putvar name="bar" />    <!-- output the value of bar -->
<lxp>
```

The mark-up in Example 13-10 opens an LXP region and uses the <setvar> tag to assign the *value* of the variable named setbar to a new variable named bar. Variable substitution is correctly used in this case, because it occurs within an LXP tag.

Since the previously mentioned URL assigned a value of foo to setbar, this means that the new variable bar will be assigned a value of foo.

The use of the <putvar> tag introduces the second rule to watch out for in LXP. Some tags (such as the <putvar> tag) expect to receive a literal variable name in order to perform their job. Remember that dollar signs and at signs are not actually part of variable names; they are only used to substitute values in place of names.

You might be inclined to think that the syntax of the <putvar> tag in Example 13-10 should have read like this:

```
<putvar name="$bar" /> <!-- output the value of bar -->
```

This would actually result, however, in the value of the variable bar being substituted into the value of the name attribute. Since the value of the bar variable is foo, LXP would attempt to insert a variable with the *name* of foo.

The simplest way to know whether or not to use substitution characters is to remain aware of what the purpose of the tag is. If an attribute should be replaced with a variable's *value*, use the $ symbol to substitute it. If an attribute is literally specifying a variable by name, as with the <putvar> tag, do not substitute it.

A literal dollar sign ($) may be used within double quotes by placing two of them immediately one after the other, sequentially (e.g., <setvar price="$$99.95" />).

When using substitution, if a variable with the specified name is not found, LXP will check for a cookie with the specified name. If one is found, its value will be substituted.

Object Variable Value Substitution

The substitution of a variable value from an object is very similar to normal variable substitution. However, instead of using the dollar sign ($) to substitute a value, you use the at sign (@). Syntactically, the only difference between referencing a variable value with @ instead of $ is that dots (.) and square brackets ([]) are allowed as part of the object name.

A literal at sign (@) can be placed inside of an attribute's value by typing the character twice consecutively (e.g., <setvar email="jlx@@commandprompt.com" />).

Entity substitution

LXP automatically converts any recognized entity within an LXP tag's attribute value into its literally interpreted character symbol. As of Version 0.8, LXP's recognized entities consist of the five pre-defined XML entities:

- Ampersand (&)
- Less-than symbol (<)
- Greater-than symbol (>)
- Apostrophe (')
- Double-quote (")

It's useful to know about entity substitution, as sometimes both apostrophes and quotes may be needed within the value of an LXP tag attribute, making it otherwise impossible to insert them without the use of these entities. LXP's developers considered programmatic back-slash escape sequences as a means to solve this (as is common in other programming languages), but LXP's ability to natively handle entities both preserves the mark-up mentality and adds a new level of sophistication to the language.

Example 13-11 provides an example of entity substitution within the LXP
<include> tag.

Example 13-11: Using entity substitution

```
<lxp>
  <setvar field="field_two" />
  <include sql="SELECT field_one, $field FROM &quot;CAPITALIZED_TABLE&quot;"
          method="SQL">
    <strong>Column One:</strong> <field name="field_one" /><br>
    <strong>Column Two:</strong> <field name="field_two" /><br>
  </include>
</lxp>
```

Example 13-11 demonstrates the use of entities inside of a direct SQL query in
order to place quotes within quotes. This is frequently required to make identifiers
case-sensitive within PostgreSQL, as identifiers are otherwise folded to lowercase.

When parsed, the " is changed into its literal counter-part, making the actual
executed query as follows:

```
SELECT field_one, field_two FROM "CAPITALIZED_TABLE"
```

See the section titled "Including SQL Content" for an explanation of what exactly
this example's LXP markup would achieve.

Using <varparser>

LXP supports a simple search-and-replace mechanism for variable values with its
<varparser> tag. This tag takes two attributes—find and replace. When you use
the <varparser> tag, a region is opened within which any variable value that is
substituted will be filtered through the defined search-and-replace rule.

The <varparser> is primarily useful for stripping or escaping unwanted characters.
For example, in preparation to execute a SQL statement, single-quotes (') must be
prefixed by a backslash, as a single-quote delimits string constants to PostgreSQL.
Example 13-12 demonstrates the escaping of single-quotes in a variable called txt.

Example 13-12: Using <varparser> to prepare SQL

```
<lxp>
  <varparser find="'" replace="\'">
    <include sql="SELECT * FROM table WHERE txtfield = '$txt'">
      <field /><br />
    </include>
  </varparser>
</lxp>
```

In Example 13-12, the <varparser find="'" replace="\'"> tag instructs LXP to
replace any single-quote with a back-referenced \' sequence within any *substituted* variable value.

Note that this search-and-replace occurs *only* for *substituted variable values*. As such, the literally typed apostrophes in the sql attribute of the <include> tag are left unchanged; only the contents of variable values being *substituted* within that attribute (e.g., the txt variable's value, in Example 13-12) are modified upon their substitution.

The closing </varparser> tag puts LXP back into normal variable substitution mode.

 You can configure several simultaneous search-and-replace rules by nesting several <varparser> tags within one another.

Branching Logic

A simple method of conditionally rendering content lies in LXP's native support for a small set of branching logic tags. These allow you to either display or hide regions of markup by performing equivalence checks on variables or cookies. LXP's basic branching logic tags include:

- <if>
- <ifnot>
- <ifcookie>
- <ifnotcookie>
- <else>
- <elseif>
- <elseifnot>

The <if> and <ifnot> tags operate on LXP variables (or object variable values), whereas the <ifcookie> and <ifnotcookie> tags operate on stored cookies for the current domain. In other words, the logical functions of <if> and <ifcookie> are the same; only the sources for logical evaluation differ.

The <else> tag is more generalized, and implements subsequent, inverted logic evaluations on any of the previously mentioned tags. The <elseif> and <elseifnot> tags are actually just shortcut tags with the same result as nesting an <if> or <ifnot> tag within an <else> region.

The <if> and <ifnot> Tags

When used without any accompanying attributes, the <if> and <ifnot> tags perform no useful function. However, with meaningful attributes, these tags can be used to quickly and simply flag regions of mark-up for display under specific circumstances.

Using <if>

The <if> tag examines its defined attributes through equivalence comparisons to variables whose names match the attribute names. If the specified attribute's value matches the variable's value exactly, the region of mark-up between that <if> and its associated </if> closing tag will be processed by LXP. Otherwise, that region (between <if> and </if>) will be completely ignored (including any LXP mark-up) up to its closing tag.

You may include in the <if> tag either an attribute name, a complete attribute pair, or a series of attribute pairs, depending on the intended logical assessment you wish to make.

Providing only an attribute name (e.g., <if test>) causes LXP to check only for the existence of *any* characters assigned to the variable value with that name. In this case, if the variable is set to an empty value (or not set at all), the <if> match fails, and its defined region is *muted* (not displayed). Otherwise, if a value is found, the region is processed as it would be normally.

Providing one or more attribute pairs results in each attribute value being compared to the variable with the specified attribute name. When more than one attribute is specified in the tag, *each* condition must match exactly for the <if> conditions to be considered a match as a whole, and for the region to be processed.

Example 13-13 uses the <if> tag to check for the existence of any variable value named name, and compares the variable named access to the value of 1.

Example 13-13: Using the <if> tag

```
<lxp>
  <if name access="1">
    <strong>Success!</strong><br />
    A <em>name</em> is set, and <em>access</em> is set to 1.<br />
  </if>
</lxp>
```

Using *<ifnot>*

The <ifnot> tag logically performs the opposite of the <if> tag in every respect. For example, when multiple attributes are passed, each equivalence comparison must *fail* for the <ifnot> region to be processed.

Example 13-14 uses the <ifnot> tag to test for the lack of a variable called error, as well as to check that a variable named access is not set to the value of 0.

Example 13-14: Using the <ifnot> tag

```
<lxp>
  <ifnot error access="0">
    <strong>Success!</strong><br />
    An <em>error</em> is not set, and <em>access</em> is not set to 0.<br />
  </ifnot>
</lxp>
```

You may not define two attributes with the same name in a single LXP tag (e.g., <ifnot access="0" access="2"> is not valid). Therefore, two logical assessments on one variable requires the use of two logic tags.

Nesting logic

The term *nesting* refers to placing tags within regions marked-up by other tags. You may safely nest logical tags as much as you like, provided you carefully keep track of where they open and close.

In some cases, you may have to nest logic tags in order to perform multiple checks on a single variable. This is because you can only place a variable's name inside of a logic tag once.

Example 13-15 nests several logic tags within one top-level <if> tag.

Example 13-15: Using nested logic

```
<lxp>
  <if answer>
    <strong>You have supplied an answer!</strong><br />

    <if answer="12">
      Your answer is correct!<br />
    </if>

    <ifnot answer="12">
      Your answer of <putvar name="answer">, though, is incorrect.<br />
    </ifnot>
```

Example 13-15: Using nested logic (continued)

```
      <if answer="12" cheatcode>
        You appear to be cheating, however.
      </if>
    </if>
  </lxp>
```

In Example 13-15, the first `<if>` tag checks to see if an argument titled answer is set at all. If it is not, the entire region it encapsulates is muted.

The second `<if>` tag evaluates the passed answer argument to see if it is equal to 12. If it is, that `<if>` tag's region is processed. Otherwise, that region will be muted.

The `<ifnot>` tag then checks to see if the passed argument named answer is *not* equal to 12. If it is not, the region that the `<ifnot>` encapsulates will be processed.

Lastly, the final `<if>` tag in Example 13-15 checks to see if the passed value for answer is equal to 12, and for the existence of a passed argument called cheatcode. If the variable answer is found to equal 12, and the variable cheatcode is found at all, the region encapsulated by the last `<if>` tag will be processed (meaning, in this case, that it is merely displayed).

Using *<ifcookie> and <ifnotcookie>*

The `<ifcookie>` and `<ifnotcookie>` tags behave identically to the `<if>` and `<ifnot>` tags, with the notable exception being that they derive the source of their logical evaluations from the cookies stored in the browser for the domain being accessed by the web browser, rather than from stored variables.

Example 13-16 welcomes a user with a personalized message if they have a cookie stored in their browser named username.

Example 13-16: Using ifcookie and ifnotcookie

```
  <lxp>
    <ifcookie username>
      Welcome back, <putcookie name="username">.<br />
    </ifcookie>
    <ifnotcookie username>
      <include src="login.php" />
    </ifnotcookie>
  </lxp>
```

In Example 13-16, if the username cookie doesn't exist, the user will see a login screen provided by a PHP document. This document is rendered through an Apache sub-request inclusion (see the section titled "Including External Content Types").

The <else>, <elseif>, and <elseifnot> Tags

The <else>, <elseif>, and <elseifnot> tags aid in the creation of more involved conditional logic than a single <if> or <ifnot> statement.

The <else> tag marks a region to be displayed only if the last logical evaluation (at the same logical *depth*, if working with nested logic tags) was false. If the last logical evaluation was true, the <else> region will be muted.

Example 13-17 creates a simple <if> condition to check for the existence of a variable called answer. If it is not found, the region marked up by the <else> and </else> tags will be displayed; otherwise, that region will be muted.

Example 13-17: Using the <else> tag

```
<lxp>
  <if answer>
    Thank you for supplying an answer.
  </if>
  <else>
    You have not yet supplied an answer.<br />
    <include src="forms/question.lxp" />
  </else>
</lxp>
```

As mentioned earlier in this section, the <elseif> and <elseifnot> tags are just shortcuts. They behave exactly as the <if> and <ifnot> tags do, respectively, if they were nested within an <else> region. For example, the following two blocks of markup are functionally identical:

```
<if condition1="true">
  Condition 1 is True.
</if>
<else>
  <if condition2="true">
    Condition 2 is true.
  </if>
</else>
```

...

```
<if condition1="true">
  Condition 1 is True.
</if>
<elseif condition2="true">
  Condition 2 is true.
</elseif>
```

Using <else> tags streamlines both the maintainability and efficiency of the conditional logic. By using <else>, you can rely on LXP to keep track of whether or not the last condition was or was not met, and not have to re-evaluate the same conditions with the opposite logic tag.

Example 13-18 re-implements the same logic that was used in Example 13-15 earlier in this section, but improves it with the use of the <else> tag.

Example 13-18: Using nested logic with <else> tags

```
<lxp>
  <if answer>
    <strong>You have supplied an answer!</strong><br />

    <if answer="12">
      Your answer is correct!<br />
      <if cheatcode>
        You appear to be cheating, however.
      </if>
      <else>
        Congratulations for not cheating!
      </else>
    </if>
    <else>
      Your answer of <putvar name="answer">, though, is incorrect.<br />
    </else>

  </if>
  <else>
    You have not yet supplied an answer.<br />
    <include src="forms/question.lxp" />
  </else>
</lxp>
```

Loop Iteration

If you have an LXP region that you wish to iterate more than once, the <for> tag exists for this purpose. It requires at least a start attribute, and either an end or endbefore attribute. Each attribute should be given a numeric value.

The start attribute defines a whole integer value to begin the loop iteration with. That value initializes an iteration count, which will be incremented by 1 for each iteration of the loop. If the end attribute is defined, the loop will stop iterating after the iteration count has looped *through* the number specified by end. Alternatively, if the endbefore attribute is defined, the loop will stop one iteration earlier. Using end and endbefore is respectively equivalent to using the <= and < operators in a programming language such as PHP or C.

While iterating, a special LXP object called for maintains a value called count, which stores the value of the current loop's iteration count. Example 13-19 demonstrates a simple for loop that will iterate from 1 to 5.

Example 13-19: A simple <for> loop

```
<lxp>
  <for start="1" end="5">
    Iterating loop: <putvar name="for.count" /><br />
  </for>
</lxp>
```

Here is the output from this loop, when processed by LXP:

```
Iterating loop: 1<br />

Iterating loop: 2<br />

Iterating loop: 3<br />

Iterating loop: 4<br />

Iterating loop: 5<br />
```

The <for> loop iterator can be invaluable when dealing with arrays of values that you need to return by using LXP. As mentioned earlier in this chapter, if a variable is defined with trailing square-brackets ([]), it will be implicitly given an offset by LXP for each value found with that name. LXP will also create an object variable of the same name, but without square-brackets, with two attributes: size and last. The size value (e.g., my_array.size) stores the number of elements in the implicitly defined array, while the last value (e.g. my_array.last) stores the offset of the last value.

Example 13-20 demonstrates the handling of a passed variable called my_array[].

Example 13-20: Handling array results with <for>

```
<lxp>
  <for start="0" end="@my_array.last">
    Here is the value of my_array, at offset <putvar name="for.count" />:
    <putvar name="my_array[@for.count]" />
    <br />
  </for>
</lxp>
```

Notice that the at sign (@) for the my_array object is only used where its *variable value* is desired, rather than its name. Thus, it is omitted in the <putvar> tag, since the name attribute expects a literal variable name, and not the variable's value.

If you manually assign index offsets to variables in a form (e.g., my_array[0], my_array[1]) rather than creating an implied array (e.g., my_array[]), LXP will not set the size and last values for such an array of values.

Content Inclusion

The heart of LXP's content management is its content inclusion workhorse: the
<include> tag. The <include> tag can operate in one of many ways, depending
either on the explicit value of the method attribute with which it is initiated, or the
implicit context determined by its attributes.

The <include> tag can be used, in its simplest form, to simply include a flat HTML
file, such as a standard header, sidebar, and footer. In its more advanced incarnations, the <include> tag can be used to parse token-delimited files by using arbitrary tokens, parse basic XML documents, embed PHP output inline within the LXP
document, make direct SQL queries, and, of course, include other LXP documents.

Table 13-1 lists each of the LXP inclusion methods available to the <include> tag.
The method in the first column is value that you supply to the <include> tag's
method attribute. The alias in the second column describes any alternative names
that you can use to invoke the same method. The "Implied by" column shows any
attribute values which would imply a method (bypassing the need for an explicit
method attribute), and the "Description" column gives a brief description of the
method itself.

Table 13-1. LXP inclusion methods

Method	Aliases	Implied by	Description
LXP		*.lxp* extension ending src attribute	Processes the source file through *mod_lxp*
flat		Unrecognized extension in src attribute, and no sql or query attribute	Displays a file's literal contents
parsed			Parses a token-delimited file, and breaks it up into accessible <field> values
XML	RSS, RDF	*.xml, .rdf* or *.rss* extension at the end of the src attribute	Parses a well-formed XML file, and breaks it up into accessible <field> values
local	Apache	*.php, .php3,* or *.phtml* extension at the end of the src attribute	Displays output of an Apache subrequest with a src attribute of a system filename
URI			Displays output of an Apache subrequest with a src attribute of an HTTP URI
SQL		Existence of sql or query attribute	Executes a SQL statement, making query results accessible both as variables, and with the <field> tag

The source of content inclusion is invariably defined in the src attribute of the <include> tag. In most cases this is a system filename, though it may describe a database source or Apache URI request, depending on the method. When you include a file described by a relative path (one that is not explicitly defined from the root of the filesystem), LXP will use the working directory of the LXP document which is performing the inclusion.

> To prevent accidental infinite recursion (e.g., including a file that includes itself), LXP documents may only include to the depth specified in the *lxp.conf* file's MaxIncludeDepth directive (see the section titled "Nuts and Bolts: Configuring lxp.conf"). The default maximum include depth is 15.

Including LXP Files

Any LXP file can be included within another LXP file, if the Apache server has read access to the document specified in the src attribute. Any variables set in the including LXP document will be both accessible, and modifiable, by the included LXP document.

To include an LXP file, open an LXP region, and use the following syntax where *lxpfile* is the name of the LXP file you wish to include:

```
<include src="lxpfile" />
```

> When an LXP file is included, it is parsed as if it had been directly called. Therefore, you must still use the <lxp> tag to open an LXP region in the included LXP document before you are able to use LXP tags within it.

Since the output of the included LXP document is embedded in place of the <include> tag itself, no closing tag is necessary with this inclusion method. In this case, the <include> tag should be an empty-element tag (i.e., with a trailing slash). If the LXP file you are including does not have an extension ending in *.lxp*, you may force it to be parsed by the LXP module by using the method="lxp" attribute.

Suppose that you have an LXP application that provides different content depending on the virtual host accessing the site. Each virtual host's DocumentRoot could store just a single *index.lxp* file, configured to include the root LXP application from another directory. Example 13-21 demonstrates such a simple top-level file, which sets two protected LXP variables, and includes the root LXP file.

Example 13-21: Including an LXP document

```
<lxp>
  <setvar lxp.virtual_host="0" />
  <setvar lxp.access_level="1" />
  <include src="../application/index.lxp" />
</lxp>
```

Including Flat Files

Flat file is a term used to refer to a plain-text document. A flat file is a non-parsed document (such as a simple HTML document, or text file), as far as the server is concerned.

As with the inclusion of LXP documents, the *flat file* inclusion method does not require a closing tag, and should therefore be used as an empty-element tag with a trailing slash. To include a flat file, open an LXP region, and use the following syntax where `flatfile` is the name of the file you wish to include:

```
<include src="flatfile" />
```

If the flat file you are including has a recognized file extension, you may force it to be displayed literally by using the `method="flat"` attribute. Example 13-22 demonstrates an LXP document which includes three HTML files, from a relative directory called *parts*, to be used as a header, sidebar, and footer. Since their extensions do not imply any more complex method, the files are included as-is in the main document.

Example 13-22: Including flat files

```
<lxp>
  <include src="parts/header.html" />
  <include src="parts/leftbar.html" />
    Welcome to my home page.<br />
  <include src="parts/footer.html />
</lxp>
```

As you can see, this sort of inclusion can make web sites with consistent themes far easier to maintain by modularizing components in a manner similar to what is done when using server-side-includes or PHP's `readfile()` function. In addition, flat file inclusion allows you to achieve this modularity without having to leave the simplicity and elegance of mark-up design. This is certainly not the full extent of the *<include>* tag's power, as you will find out in subsequent sections.

Including Token-Delimited Files

A common function of many dynamic web sites is to post the contents of token-delimited files (such as Linux Today's *headlines* file) on their web site in some kind of programmatically filtered format. These filters generally are implemented differently from page to page, and site to site, and rely on somewhat involved algorithms to pull apart the data and put it back together again into a useful format.

The LXP approach to displaying such files is with the use of the `<include>` tag, by specifying the `method="parsed"` attribute. This use of the `<include>` tag breaks up the parsed *fields* into sequential values, accessible via the general-purpose LXP `<field>` tag.

Blocks are delimited from one another by the value supplied to the `delimiter` attribute. Within a block, *fields* are separated from one another by each newline (symbolically, \n, a literal line-wrap) found within the block. You may optionally specify a different field delimiter value using the `separator` attribute.

The parsed method for the `<include>` tag requires a closing `</include>` tag, because for each block that LXP reads from the file, it loops back to the beginning of the `<include>` tag and re-iterates the mark-up until the last block is processed.

If you wish to limit the number of blocks to be displayed, the last block number can be specified with the `lastblock` attribute. Additionally, the `firstblock` attribute can be used to skip any leading blocks (e.g., an introductory statement that might be embedded at the top of the text file preceding the first delimiter).

Here is an example of such a token-delimited file, from *www.linuxtoday.com*:

```
Welcome to lthead.txt.  Fields are delimited by two ampersands.
The first field is the headline.  The second field is the URL to the story.
The third field is the date the story was posted.
Have Fun! (webmaster@linuxtoday.com)
&&
LinuxProgramming: python-dev summary 2001-06-21 - 2001-07-05
http://linuxtoday.com/news_story.php3?ltsn=2001-07-05-019-21-OS-SW
Jul 5, 2001, 21:30:38
&&
Chicago Sun-Times: Test drive Linux using friendly tryout software
http://linuxtoday.com/news_story.php3?ltsn=2001-07-05-018-21-PS-CY
Jul 5, 2001, 21:00:48
&&
[...]
```

Example 13-23 opens the file */home/web/headlines/lthead.txt*, and parses it into blocks using the `&&` character sequence as the block delimiter.

Example 13-23: Including a token-delimited file

```
<lxp>
  <include src="/home/web/headlines/lthead.txt" delimiter="&&"
          firstblock="2" lastblock="4" method="parsed">
    <table border="0" cellspacing="1"><tr>
      <td bgcolor="#ffffff" width="100%">
        <div class="content">
        - <field />
        </div>
      </td>
    </tr><tr>
      <td bgcolor="#e0e0e8" width="100%">
        <strong>
        <field type="url" link="Read More..." target="_blank" />
        </strong><br />
      </td>
    </tr></table>
  </include>
</lxp>
```

When an inclusion such as the one in Example 13-23 is processed, the `<field>` tags are replaced with the field values found within the parsed blocks. Fields are assigned to `<field>` tags in the order in which they are found.

As you can see in Example 13-23, you may also specify an alternate `type` attribute for an LXP `<field>`. Valid types in a parsed inclusion are `hidden` (this hides the field if there is a value that you wish to skip over, and not display) and `url`.

The `hidden` type is used for a field which you wish to merely skip over. Since token-delimited files have no identifying name for each block, each field must be processed in the order that is encountered by LXP in the source file. Therefore, a field can be assigned a `type="hidden"` attribute in order to skip it rather than display it, allowing you to display fields that are past it in the file.

The `url` type is useful in this context when you know that a particular field will be a URL, as it creates a hyperlink to that URL (with an HTML `<a>` tag), rather than just displaying the URL itself. You can set the text of the generated hyperlink to appear as an arbitrary value, other than just the URL itself (such as the `Read More...` value used in Example 13-23), by specifying the value of the `link` attribute within the `<field>` tag.

Here is example output of what you would see from LXP, after parsing the markup from Example 13-23:

```
<table border="0" cellspacing="1"><tr>
  <td bgcolor="#ffffff" width="100%">
    <div class="content">
    - LinuxProgramming: python-dev summary 2001-06-21 - 2001-07-05
    </div>
  </td>
```

```
  </tr><tr>
    <td bgcolor="#e0e0e8" width="100%">
      <strong>
      <a href="http://linuxtoday.com/news_story.php3?ltsn=2001-07-05-019-21-OS-SW"
target="_blank">Read More...</a>
      </strong><br />
    </td>
  </tr></table>

  <table border="0" cellspacing="1"><tr>
    <td bgcolor="#ffffff" width="100%">
      <div class="content">
        - Chicago Sun-Times: Test drive Linux using friendly tryout software
      </div>
    </td>
  </tr><tr>
    <td bgcolor="#e0e0e8" width="100%">
      <strong>
      <a href="http://linuxtoday.com/news_story.php3?ltsn=2001-07-05-018-21-PS-CY"
target="_blank">Read More...</a>
      </strong><br />
    </td>
  </tr></table>

  [...]
```

 When using an LXP `<field type="url">` tag, you can pass non-LXP attributes such as `class`, or `target`, and they will be placed in the generated `<a>` tag.

Including XML, RSS and RDF Files

To include an external well-formed XML document, the approach is very similar to the `parsed` method. The `method` attribute may be set to either XML, RSS, or RDF to explicitly set the method to XML parsing. Including a `src` attribute that ends in any of the *.xml*, *.rss*, or *.rdf* extensions will implicitly invoke this method as well.

The `delimiter` attribute in this context sets the name of the element (tag) within which to look for element fields to parse. For example, most of the relevant fields in an RDF file are contained directly within the `<item>` element; for this reason, `item` is the default delimiter element. For each delimiting element found, the entire `<include>` region will be looped through once.

Like the `parsed` method, the XML method uses the generalized `<field>` tag to display the contents of a field value. In this context, a field value refers to the character data within a named element (tag) inside the delimiting element. Field values will be displayed in the order in which they appear in the XML file unless a `name` attribute is set within the `<field>` tag, assigning the name of the element field to output. For example, a `name="title"` attribute refers to the character data within `<title>` and `</title>` in the source XML document.

As an example, suppose that you have an XML source document called *languages.xml* that describes languages related to PostgreSQL, with the following structure:

```
<?xml version="1.0" encoding="utf-8"?>
<languages>
  <language>
    <name>C</name>
    <notes>Built-in language.</notes>
  </language>
  <language>
    <name>LXP</name>
    <notes>Web-based content language.</notes>
  </language>
  <language>
    <name>PL/pgSQL</name>
    <notes>PostgreSQL procedural language.</notes>
  </language>
</languages>
```

In this scheme, notice that each language is described within the `<language>` element. To parse such an XML file in the same manner as the RDF example described earlier, set the `delimiter` attribute of the `<include>` tag to `language` and the `src` attribute to `languages.xml`. This is demonstrated in Example 13-24.

Example 13-24: Including an XML file

```
<lxp>
  <include src="languages.xml" delimiter="language" method="xml">
    Language Name: <field name="name" /><br />
    Language Notes: <field name="notes" /><br />
    <hr />
  </include>
</lxp>
```

When processed, the output of Example 13-24 would look like this:

```
Language Name: C<br />
Language Notes: Built-in language.<br />
<hr />

Language Name: LXP<br />
Language Notes: Web-based content language.<br />
<hr />

Language Name: PL/pgSQL<br />
Language Notes: PostgreSQL procedural language.<br />
<hr />
```

Example 13-25 demonstrates the display of a simple RDF XML document. This example differs from Example 13-24 in that it addresses, specifically, an RDF document. As a result, the `delimiter` attribute can be omitted, since the default value of *item* is appropriate for the RDF schema.

Example 13-25: Including an RDF file

```
<lxp>
  <include src="/home/web/ports/headlines/slashdot.rdf" lastblock="5">
  <table border="0" cellspacing="1"><tr>
    <td bgcolor="#ffffff" width="100%">
      <div class="content">- <field name="title"></div>
    </td>
  </tr><tr>
    <td bgcolor="#e0e0e8" width="100%">
      <strong>
        <field name="link" type="url" link="Read More..." target="_blank">
      </strong><br />
    </td>
  </tr></table>
  </include>
</lxp>
```

Notice also the use of the `lastblock` attribute in Example 13-25, which was also described in the section titled "Including Token-Delimited Files" earlier in this chapter. Both the `firstblock` and `lastblock` attributes can also be used with XML, RDF, and RSS files to limit and offset which blocks of data are displayed.

Remember that any XML document you attempt to include through LXP *must* be well-formed, or the parser will fail. XML parse errors should appear in the Apache error log, prefixed with `[lxp] XML Parse Error`.

Including External Content Types

To include an external content-type configured within Apache, the `<include>` tag can be invoked with either the URI or local method. Each performs a subrequest to Apache, meaning that the inclusion is processed as if it is a direct request to Apache, with the output embedded at the location of the `<include>` tag in the LXP document.

The difference between these two methods is that the URI method accepts a `src` attribute of the form that Apache would literally accept from a web browser, prefixed with a forward-slash, and beginning at the document root directory of the configured host (e.g., */example.php*). Alternatively, the local method tells Apache where the file is located in the local filesystem (e.g., */home/web/example.php*).

Example 13-26 shows an LXP file which includes a PHP script in two ways. Note that each of these methods goes through Apache, and will thus be reliant on Apache to be properly configured for the requested content type, and especially in the case of the local method, have the necessary rights on the directory containing the included script.

Example 13-26: Including other content types

```
<lxp>
   An example PHP script:<br />
   <include src="/example.php" method="URI" />
   <hr />
   The same PHP script, using the local method:<br />
   <include src="/home/web/default/example.php" method="local" />
</lxp>
```

Omitting the method attribute when including a document (specified by the a src attribute) with a name ending with any of the common PHP extensions (*.php*, *.php3*, and *.phtml*) results in the method being implied as local. As of LXP 0.8, however, there is no way to imply the URI method. You must therefore specify method="URI" to use the URI method.

Including SQL Content

The *SQL* method in LXP offers a great amount of power through direct connectivity to PostgreSQL. It allows for the embedding of 100% dynamic, database results directly within a web page without the need to call out to a programming language, create explicit connection or statement programming objects, or even to parse and format the results.

To use the *SQL* method, you may either explicitly use the <include> tag with a method attribute of SQL, or implicitly define the <include> tag as using the *SQL* method by setting the value of the sql attribute to the SQL statement you wish to execute. In the following example, the SQL method is implied as a result of specifying a value for the sql attribute:

```
<include sql="SELECT * FROM pg_database">
```

Like each of the parsing methods, the <include> tag loops between its opening <include> and closing </include> tags for each row returned from a successfully executed SQL query.

Setting the database source

When using the *SQL* inclusion method, the src attribute is used within the <include> tag to define the database source to connect to. If this attribute is omitted, LXP will attempt to connect to its persistent database connection, if one exists.

While there exists a single persistent database connection for each Apache *httpd* process, the LXP module actually maintains the connection—not Apache.

The format of this connection string will be familiar to anyone who has connected to PostgreSQL through C or PHP. It is a single, character string, within which there are several sub-attributes describing the data source. Available sub-attributes are shown in Table 13-2.

Table 13-2. Database connection attributes

Attribute	Description
dbname	The database to connect with (defaults to the same name as the connecting user)
host	The hostname to connect to
user	The username to connect with (defaults to the user running Apache)
password	The password to use, if authentication is required
port	The port to connect to (Defaults to 5432)

Within the src attribute's value, attribute pairs are separated by whitespace, and an equal sign separates each attribute from its value. The order in which the database attributes appear is not important.

Example 13-27 shows the execution of a SQL query, which uses a connection to a database called example, on a host named db_server, with the username john.

Example 13-27: Connecting to a non-default database

```
<lxp>
  <include sql="SELECT * FROM users ORDER BY username ASC"
           src="dbname=example host=db_server user=john">
    User: <field /><br />
  </include>
</lxp>
```

For LXP 0.8, if you wish to nest a SQL include within another SQL include, the nested include *must* have an explicit src attribute defined, even if it is connecting to the default database connection. This restriction is corrected with LXP 0.8.1.

Accessing column values

Column values can be accessed in one of two ways while iterating through a SQL inclusion region; either through the general <field> tag, or through the this object, which is populated with a value for each column upon each row iteration.

Like the XML inclusion, a name attribute can be applied to a <field> tag in order to specify which column is to be displayed. Otherwise, the column values are displayed in the order they were targeted by the query, from left to right, with each successive use of the <field> tag.

Alternatively, the values of each column can be accessed by a variable named this.*column*, where *column* is the name of the column to be identified. For example, the following two tags would output the same value within an included SQL region:

```
<field name="id" />
<putvar name="this.id" />
```

The main reason for the existence of the this object is so that branching logic, and variable substitution, can be performed using the values of the returned SQL result set. Example 13-28 executes a SQL query, and formats its output conditionally through the use of branching logic.

Example 13-28: Including SQL content

```
<lxp>
  <include sql="SELECT datname, datdba AS user_id FROM pg_database">
    <if this.user_id="$userid">
      <strong><field /></strong><br />
      <setvar owned_databases="$owned_databases @this.datname" />
    </if>
    <else>
      <field /><br />
    </else>
  </include>
</lxp>
```

Accessing SQL meta-data

When executing a SQL query, some special variable values containing data about the current result set are assigned to an LXP object called sql. These are:

- sql.numrows
- sql.numcols
- sql.numfields (alias to sql.numcols)

- `sql.row`

- `sql.offset`

The `sql.numrows` variable value contains the number of rows retrieved by the query. The `sql.numcols` (and its `sql.numfields` alias) variable value contains the number of columns in each row. When looping between `<include>` and `</include>`, the `sql.row` variable value contains the numeric index of the current row, counting from 1, while the `sql.offset` variable value contains the numeric index of the current row counting from 0.

Example 13-29 uses the the `sql.row` variable to display the current row index within the looped `<include>` region. In addition, the `sql.numrows` variable is used after the query results are displayed to show how many rows were retrieved.

Example 13-29: Using SQL object variable values

```
<lxp>
  <include sql="SELECT * FROM pg_user ORDER BY usename LIMIT 5">
    User #<putvar name="sql.row" />: <putvar name="this.usename" /><br />
  </include>
  <br />
  Selected <putvar name="sql.numrows" /> rows.
</lxp>
```

The output of Example 13-29 would look like this:

```
    User #1: allen<br />

    User #2: barbara<br />

    User #3: ben<br />

    User #4: corwin<br />

    User #5: david<br />

<br />
Selected 5 rows.
```

Setting SQL object variables

If you prefer to execute a SQL query only as a means to have access to the result set returned (bypassing the automatic looping iteration of the `<include>` tag), you may supply the `setvars` attribute with the name of an LXP object to be populated with the query results, and immediately close the region with a closing `</include>` tag.

For result sets with a single row returned, this approach sets a variable named *object.column* for each column in the row, where *object* is the name specified by the `setvars` attribute, and *column* is the name of a column returned by the query.

For result sets with more than a single row, square-brackets containing an offset describing the row number are appended to the column name (e.g., object.col-umn[0], object.column[1], etc.).

Example 13-30 executes a query on the pg_user table, to retrieve three columns about a particular user.

Example 13-30: Selecting SQL results into an LXP object

```
<lxp>
   <include sql="SELECT usename, usesuper, usecreatedb
                        FROM pg_user
                        WHERE usesysid = $userid"
           setvars="userinfo"></include>

   <if sql.numrows="1">
     User name: <putvar name="userinfo.usename"><br />
     <if userinfo.usecreatedb='t'>
       <strong>This user can create databases.</strong><br />
     </if>
     <if userinfo.usesuper='t'>
       <strong>This user is a superuser.</strong><br />
     </if>
   </if>
   <else>
     Error: No user was found.
   </else>
</lxp>
```

Displaying Foreign Tags with <xtag>

There may be times when you wish to use an LXP variable value within the contents of an HTML tag. For example, you may have a graphic with a dynamically assigned width. Since LXP only performs variable value substitution within LXP tags, you cannot substitute an LXP variable within an HTML tag as you would with an LXP tag. In other words, the $width variable reference in the following example will not work:

```
<lxp>
   <!-- WRONG: LXP variable will not be substituted in non-LXP tag -->
   <img src="/images/spacer.gif" width="$width" />
</lxp>
```

You might think an obvious solution would be to place the LXP <putvar> tag inside of the HTML tag. There is a problem with this approach, however. Specifically, such syntax breaks the integrity of the mark-up of the document. For a mark-up language to be *well formed*, tags must not be nested within the actual contents of another tag as shown in this example:

```
<lxp>
  <!-- Not recommended: Tags should not be nested in one another -->
  <img src="/images/spacer.gif" width="<putvar name="width" />">
</lxp>
```

Note that nesting LXP tags within non-LXP tags can work in some circumstances, though it is not recommended. The LXP well-formedness requirements will probably grow more stringent in the future, and this kind of nesting is an easy way to make your LXP mark-up both lose its readability, as well as its mark-up integrity.

The LXP solution to this problem is the <xtag> element. The <xtag> is used as a wrapper to display any foreign (non-LXP) tag. It has one required attribute, which is xname. This attribute determines what tag will be output in place of <xtag> when the <xtag> is processed by LXP. For example, <xtag xname="a"> will be displayed as <a>.

Optionally, the xappend attribute may be used to append an arbitrary character string to the end of the generated tag. For example, using xappend=" checked" for an HTML checkbox input tag will create an <input type="checkbox" checked> tag.

Any other attributes will be passed through to the wrapped tag, directly. This is the key to the usefulness of the <xtag>, because variable values may be substituted within an <xtag>, and are then directly embedded within the resulting foreign tag. As an example, the correct way to wrap an HTML <img> tag in LXP is shown in Example 13-31.

Example 13-31: Using <xtag> for empty elements

```
<lxp>
  <xtag xname="img" src="images/spacer.gif" width="$width" />
</lxp>
```

Here is the displayed output from this document, once processed by LXP, assuming that the width variable has a value of 10:

```
<img src="images/spacer/gif" width="10" />
```

Notice the trailing slash used in the <xtag> element within Example 13-31. An <xtag> may be an opening, closing, or empty-element tag, depending on what tag you ultimately wish to display. A vital nuance to the nature of <xtag> is that LXP *keeps track* of what opening <xtag> elements have been left open, and chooses the appropriate tag name to use when it reaches a closing </xtag>.

If you are wrapping a foreign tag that does not close (e.g., the HTML <img> tag), you *must* adhere to document strictness and make that <xtag> an empty-element tag with a trailing slash. If you do not, LXP will name the next closing </xtag> with the xname assigned to the last opening <xtag> (e.g., img), which in this case will result in mismatched tag output. Consider the following mark-up:

```
<lxp>
  <xtag xname="table" width="$table_width">
    <tr>
      <-- WRONG: The following empty-element requires trailing slash -->
      <td><xtag xname="img" src="images/spacer.gif" width="$width"></td>
    </tr>
  </xtag>
</lxp>
```

This code uses three <xtag> elements; one opening and one closing (correspond-
ing to a wrapped <table> element), and one opening <xtag> used to wrap an
<img> tag. Since the <img> tag does not have a closing tag in HTML, this <xtag>
should instead be an empty-element tag, but it will not be read that way by LXP
(notice the lack of a trailing slash). The problem with this mark-up is that since
LXP keeps track of open <xtag> elements, when it reaches the first closing</xtag>,
it expects to close not the intended <table> tag, but the <img> tag.

Assuming the table_width variable has a value of 100, and the width variable has
a value of 10, the incorrect output looks like this:

```
<table width="100">
  <tr>
    <-- WRONG: The following empty-element requires trailing slash -->
    <td><img src="images/spacer.gif" width="10"></td>
  </tr>
</img>
```

Example 13-32 shows the correct way to mix various <xtag> elements.

Example 13-32: Using nested <xtag> elements

```
<lxp>
  <xtag xname="table" width="$table_width">
    <tr>
      <-- RIGHT: Empty-element has required trailing slash -->
      <td><xtag xname="img" src="images/spacer.gif" width="$width" /></td>
    </tr>
  </xtag>
</lxp>
```

Since the second <xtag> element in Example 13-32 uses a trailing slash, as is
required when you wrap a tag that does not explicitly close, LXP does not antici-
pate a closing tag for the <img> tag, and the output looks (correctly) like this:

```
<table width="100">
  <tr>
    <-- RIGHT: Empty-element has required trailing slash -->
    <td><img src="images/spacer.gif" width="10" /></td>
  </tr>
</table>
```

V

Command Reference

14

PostgreSQL Command Reference

This command reference covers each of the major SQL commands supported by PostgreSQL. It contains both standard SQL commands (e.g., INSERT, SELECT) and PostgreSQL-specific commands (e.g., CREATE OPERATOR, CREATE TYPE).

Each reference entry is broken up into three sections: a *synopsis*, a *description*, and an *examples* section. The synopsis contains a syntax diagram, parameter explanation, and a list of possible results from executing the command. The description briefly summarizes the general use of the command. The examples section contains at least one functional example of using the command.

ABORT — Rolls back changes made during a transaction block.

Synopsis

```
ABORT [ WORK | TRANSACTION ]
```

Parameters

WORK | TRANSACTION

A pair of optional noise keywords. They can be ignored, or used to make your SQL more readable.

Results

ROLLBACK

The message returned when an ABORT completes successfully.

NOTICE: ROLLBACK: no transaction in progress

The notice returned if the database server is unable to find any transaction in progress.

Examples

The following example demonstrates the use of ABORT to undo an accidental DELETE command:

```
booktown=# BEGIN WORK;
BEGIN
booktown=# DELETE FROM publishers WHERE id < 100;
DELETE 6
booktown=# ABORT WORK;
ROLLBACK
```

ALTER GROUP — Modifies the structure of a user group.

Synopsis

```
ALTER GROUP name ADD USER
            username [, ... ]
ALTER GROUP name DROP USER
            username [, ... ]
```

Parameters

name

The name of an existing group to alter.

username

The names of existing users you wish to add or remove from the specified group. Multiple names are delimited by commas.

Results

ALTER GROUP

The message returned when an ALTER GROUP modification is successful.

Description

Database superusers can use the ALTER GROUP command to add and remove specified users from a group. As groups can be allocated privileges, adding members to a group grants those privileges by proxy. Users must exist before they can be added to a group. Dropping a user from a group does not drop a user from the system.

Use CREATE GROUP to create a new group and DROP GROUP to remove a group. Use GRANT and REVOKE to manage privileges on a group.

Examples

The following example adds the PostgreSQL database users jessica and william to the sales group:

```
booktown=# ALTER GROUP sales ADD USER jessica, william;
ALTER
```

The next example removes the user jessica from the sales group:

```
booktown=# ALTER GROUP sales DROP USER jessica;
ALTER
```

ALTER TABLE — Modifies table and column attributes.

Synopsis

```
ALTER TABLE table [ * ]
      ADD [ COLUMN ] column type
ALTER TABLE table [ * ]
      ALTER [ COLUMN ] column { SET DEFAULT defaultvalue | DROP DEFAULT }
ALTER TABLE table [ * ]
      RENAME [ COLUMN ] column TO newcolumn
ALTER TABLE table
      RENAME TO newtable
ALTER TABLE table
      ADD CONSTRAINT newconstraint definition
ALTER TABLE table
      OWNER TO newowner
```

Parameters

table

The name of the (existing) table you intend to modify.

column

The name of a new column, or existing column that you intend to modify.

type

The data type of a new column being created. (This is used only during the creation of a new column.)

defaultvalue

A new default value for the specified column.

newcolumn

A new name for *column*.

newtable

A new name for *table*.

newconstraint definition

The name and definition of a new table constraint to be added to an existing table. See Chapter 7, *Advanced Features*, for more details on how to define a table constraint.

newowner

The new owner of *table* (when transferring ownership).

Results

ALTER

The message returned when a column or table modification is completed successfully.

ERROR

The message returned if the table or column modifications cannot be completed, along with an explanation of what failed, if possible.

Description

The ALTER TABLE command is used to modify the structure of tables existing within a database in various ways. To rename a column or table, use the RENAME keyword. Renaming in this manner will not alter any of the data in either a column or a table. If you wish to add a new table constraint to a table, use the ADD CONSTRAINT clause with the same constraint syntax used with CREATE TABLE for a table constraint (see the reference entry titled "CREATE TABLE").

As of the most current version of PostgreSQL available at this printing (7.1.x), the only constraints that can be added to a table through the ADD CONSTRAINT clause are the CHECK and FOREIGN KEY constraints. To implicitly add a UNIQUE constraint, a workaround is to create a UNIQUE index, using the CREATE INDEX command (see the reference entry titled "CREATE INDEX"). To add any other constraints, you will have to recreate and reload data into the table in question.

To add a new column to a table, use ADD COLUMN with the same column syntax used in CREATE TABLE (see the reference entry titled "CREATE TABLE"). To modify or delete a column's default setting, use ALTER COLUMN with either the SET DEFAULT or DROP DEFAULT clause. (Remember that defaults are only applicable to newly added rows, and will not affect existing rows.)

As of PostgreSQL 7.1.x, you are not able to set the default value or constraint settings for a column at the same time as when it is added with the ADD COLUMN clause. You can, however, use the SET DEFAULT clause of ALTER TABLE to set the default values *after* the column is created. If you do this after the table has been in use for any period of time, be sure to use the UPDATE command to update the column's data in any existing rows to the new default.

 You must be the owner of a table, or a superuser, in order to modify it.

Examples

The following example adds a text column named address to the employees table:

```
booktown=# ALTER TABLE employees ADD COLUMN address text;
ALTER
```

Next, the newly added address column is renamed to mailing_address:

```
booktown=# ALTER TABLE employees RENAME COLUMN address TO mailing_address;
ALTER
```

The following example renames the employees table to personnel:

```
booktown=# ALTER TABLE employees RENAME TO personnel;
ALTER
```

The following example then changes the owner of the personnel table to the Post-greSQL user jonathan:

```
booktown=# ALTER TABLE personnel OWNER TO jonathan;
ALTER
```

Finally, the following syntax adds a FOREIGN KEY constraint to the schedules table named valid_employee, which verifies the employee id column in the personnel table:

```
booktown=# ALTER TABLE schedules ADD CONSTRAINT valid_employee
booktown-#                         FOREIGN KEY (employee_id)
booktown-#                         REFERENCES personnel (id) MATCH FULL;
NOTICE:  ALTER TABLE ... ADD CONSTRAINT will create implicit trigger(s) for
FOREIGN KEY check(s)
CREATE
```

ALTER USER — Modifies user properties and permissions.

Synopsis

```
ALTER USER username
    [ WITH PASSWORD 'password' ]
    [ CREATEDB | NOCREATEDB ] [ CREATEUSER | NOCREATEUSER ]
    [ VALID UNTIL 'abstime' ]
```

Parameters & Keywords

username

The name of the PostgreSQL database user to be modified.

password

An optional new password to assign to the modified PostgreSQL user.

CREATEDB | NOCREATEDB

> The privilege to create new databases. Use CREATEDB, to give the user permission to create databases. Use NOCREATEDB to explicitly deny that permission (which is the default).

CREATEUSER | NOCREATEUSER

> The superuser privilege. The use of CREATEUSER allows access to both the CREATE USER and DROP USER commands, as well as makes the user a *superuser* (with universal rights across all databases). NOCREATEUSER is the default.

> Specifying that a PostgreSQL user is able to create other users *also* automatically classifies the user as a superuser in the database; this can be a security risk if unintentional. A superuser can override all other access restrictions.

abstime

> The timestamp that defines when a user's password expires. When the date and time defined by *abstime* is reached, the user's defined password will become invalid. If unset, the password never expires.

Results

ALTER USER

> The message returned when the ALTER USER command is successful.

ERROR: ALTER USER: user "*username*" does not exist

> The error returned if *username* does not exist in the pg_shadow users table.

Description

Use the ALTER USER to change the attributes and permissions of a PostgreSQL database user.

Only a database superuser can change privileges and password expiration values with ALTER USER. Ordinary users are only permitted to change their own password.

To create and remove PostgreSQL database users, use the CREATE USER command and the DROP USER command, respectively.

Examples

The following example changes the password for user mark:

```
booktown=# ALTER USER mark WITH PASSWORD 'ml0215em';
ALTER USER
```

The next example demonstrates changing the password expiration date for the user mark:

```
booktown=# ALTER USER mark VALID UNTIL 'Dec 24 2012';
ALTER USER
```

BEGIN — Starts a chained-mode transaction block.

Synopsis

```
BEGIN [ WORK | TRANSACTION ]
```

Parameters

WORK | TRANSACTION

A pair of optional noise keywords. They can be ignored, or used to make your SQL more readable.

Results

BEGIN

The message returned when a transaction begins.

NOTICE: BEGIN: already a transaction in progress

The notice returned if a transaction is already in progress within your PostgreSQL session. You cannot nest multiple transactions. The transaction you have in progress is not altered when this happens.

Description

PostgreSQL executes transactions in *unchained mode* by default. Also called *auto-commit*, this mode encapsulates each user statement in an implicit transaction, and automatically finalizes the transaction by either committing the modification, or performing a rollback, depending on whether or not the execution was successful.

Using BEGIN specifies that you want to enter a transaction block using chained mode, in which statements will be queued by the database, and then sent in a single transaction when the database receives a COMMIT command. Alternatively, the queued statements can be discarded by a ROLLBACK, or by an unexpected disconnection.

Chained mode can be useful when you are working with multiple related tables, and also to increase database performance in general. Executing statements in chained mode uses less CPU and disk resources, as there is only one commit needed per block of statements executed.

When a transaction is committed, the database will attempt to run all updates that have been specified within it. If there are were no errors, the updates will be performed; otherwise the transaction block will be aborted.

Examples

The following example begins a transaction block, creates a table, and commits it:

```
booktown=# BEGIN WORK;
BEGIN
booktown=# CREATE TABLE test (id integer, name text);
CREATE
booktown=# COMMIT WORK;
COMMIT
```

CLOSE — Closes a previously defined cursor object.

Synopsis

```
CLOSE cursor
```

Parameters

cursor

The name of a currently open cursor that you wish to close.

Results

CLOSE

The message returned when the cursor is successfully closed.

NOTICE: PerformPortalClose: portal "cursor" not found

The notice returned if the specified cursor is either not declared, or not open.

Description

The CLOSE command closes an open cursor and frees the resources it was using. Cursors should always be closed after they are no longer needed. Once a cursor is closed, further operations are not allowed on it.

 Executing a COMMIT or ROLLBACK terminates the current transaction, closing all open cursors.

Examples

The following example opens a transaction, declares the cur_publishers cursor, and closes it:

```
booktown=# BEGIN;
BEGIN
booktown=# DECLARE cur_publishers CURSOR FOR SELECT * FROM publishers;
SELECT
booktown=# CLOSE cur_publishers;
CLOSE
```

CLUSTER — Provides the backend server with clustering information about a table.

Synopsis

```
CLUSTER indexname ON tablename
```

Parameters

indexname

The name of the index to use in clustering.

tablename

The name of the table you wish to cluster.

Results

CLUSTER

The message returned when a table is successfully clustered.

ERROR: CLUSTER: "*indexname*" is not an index for table "*tablename*"

The error returned if you attempt to cluster an index *indexname* which is not placed on the specified table (*tablename*).

ERROR: Index "*indexname*" does not exist

The error returned if the specified index (*indexname*) cannot be found in the connected database.

ERROR: Relation "*tablename*" does not exist

The error returned if the specified table (*tablename*) cannot be found in the connected database.

ERROR: Relation "*child_table*" inherits from "*tablename*"

The error returned if the specified table (*tablename*) is inherited by another table (*child_table*).

Description

Use the CLUSTER command to cluster a table on a specific index. The table (identified by the *tablename* parameter) must already, exist and the index (identified by the *indexname* parameter) must exist, and be placed on the table.

During clustering, a table is reordered for performance in an arrangement based on the specified index. A cluster is a one-time operation upon a table; to recluster a table, you must execute the command again.

When a cluster is created, the rows of the table are actually copied to a temporary table according to an order derived from the specified index. That temporary table is then renamed to the original table name. Because of this, all permissions and other indices are lost when clustering is performed.

Examples

The following example clusters the subjects table on the basis of its sub-jects_pkey index:

```
booktown=# CLUSTER subjects_pkey ON subjects;
CLUSTER
```

COMMENT — Adds a comment to an object within the database.

Synopsis

```
COMMENT ON
[
    [ DATABASE | INDEX | RULE | SEQUENCE | TABLE | TYPE | VIEW ] object_name |
    COLUMN table_name.column_name |
    FUNCTION func_name ( argument [, ...] ) |
    AGGREGATE aggr_func aggr_type |
    OPERATOR operator ( left_type , right_type ) |
    TRIGGER trigger_name ON table_name
] IS 'text'
```

Parameters

DATABASE | INDEX | RULE | SEQUENCE | TABLE | TYPE | VIEW

The type of database object that you are adding a comment to.

object_name

The name of the object (database, index, rule, sequence, table, type, or view) to which you are adding a comment.

COLUMN *table_name.column_name*

The complete column name (within the table *table_name*) you are adding a comment to.

FUNCTION *func_name* (*argument* [, ...])

The name of the function on which you are commenting, specified also by the *argument* data types that it accepts.

AGGREGATE *aggr_func aggr_type*

The aggregate function name (and associated data type *aggr_type*, which it accepts) to which you are adding a comment.

OPERATOR *operator* (*left_type, right_type*)

The name of the operator on which you are commenting (*operator*), further described by the data type it operates on to the left, and the data type it oper-ates on to the right, separated by a comma, enclosed within parentheses. If either side is inapplicable, the NONE keyword may be used.

TRIGGER *trigger_name ON table_name*

> The name of the trigger on which you are placing a comment, and the name of the table upon which the trigger is placed.

text

> The actual text of the comment to add.

Results

COMMENT

> The message returned when an object is successfully commented.

Description

COMMENT is a PostgreSQL-specific command that allows you to add comments to most objects within a database, including a database itself. Comments can be retrieved by using the following commands from within the *psql* client:

\l+

> Displays all databases available, with comments.

\dd

> Displays *all* database objects, with comments.

\d+

> Displays all database objects in the connected database, with comments.

\dt+

> Displays all tables in the connected database, with comments.

\di+

> Displays all indices in the connected database, with comments.

\ds+

> Displays all sequences in the connected database, with comments.

\dv+

> Displays all views in the connected database, with comments.

\df+

> Displays all functions in the connected database, with comments.

\da+

> Displays all aggregate functions in the connected database, with comments.

\do+

> Displays all operators in the connected database, with comments.

\dT+

> Displays all data types in the connected database, with comments.

You can remove a comment by setting its *text* to NULL.

A comment that has been made on an object will be removed when that object is removed from the system.

Examples

The following example adds a comment to the customers table:

```
booktown=# COMMENT ON TABLE customers IS 'For customer names.';
COMMENT
```

The next example deletes the previously added comment from the customer table:

```
booktown=# COMMENT ON TABLE customers IS NULL;
```

COMMIT — Ends the current transaction block and finalizes changes made within it.

Synopsis

```
COMMIT [ WORK | TRANSACTION ]
```

Parameters

WORK | TRANSACTION

A pair of optional noise keywords. They can be ignored, or used to make your SQL more readable.

Results

COMMIT

The message returned when the current transaction is successfully committed.

NOTICE: COMMIT: no transaction in progress

The notice returned if there is no current transaction for the COMMIT command to actually commit.

Description

Use the COMMIT command to finalize the current transaction. Once a COMMIT is performed, any modifications made by the transaction are saved into the database.

If something unintended happens during a transaction block, you can use the ROLLBACK command to abort the current transaction. This undoes the effect of any SQL executed after the last BEGIN statement.

Examples

The following example begins a transaction, modifies data, and then commits the modifications:

```
booktown=# BEGIN WORK;
BEGIN
booktown=# INSERT INTO employees VALUES (106, 'Hall', 'Timothy');
INSERT 3574402 1
booktown=# COMMIT WORK;
COMMIT
```

COPY — Copies data between files and tables.

Synopsis

```
COPY [ BINARY ] table [ WITH OIDS ]
    FROM { 'filename' | stdin }
    [ [ USING ] DELIMITERS 'delimiter' ]
    [ WITH NULL AS 'null_string' ]
COPY [ BINARY ] table [ WITH OIDS ]
    TO { 'filename' | stdout }
    [ [ USING ] DELIMITERS 'delimiter' ]
    [ WITH NULL AS 'null_string' ]
```

Parameters

BINARY

The BINARY mode keyword. This specifies that you wish for COPY to store and read data in PostgreSQL's own binary format (rather than text). When using binary format, the WITH NULL and DELIMITERS keywords are not applicable.

table

The name of an existing table to either copy data from, or to.

FROM

The FROM keyword, which indicates that the COPY operation will copy data *from* either a file or *stdin* into *table*.

TO The TO keyword, which indicates that the COPY operation will copy data *to* either a file or stdout, from the data in *table*.

WITH OIDS

The optional oid specifier. This indicates that the copy operation is to either select or insert the unique object ID (oid) of each row, depending on whether or not it is a COPY FROM or COPY TO.

filename

The *absolute* path to the file chosen for input or output (i.e., */usr/local/pgsql/data/employeetable*). You must specify an absolute path.

stdin

> The *standard input* option. When used in place of a filename, this indicates that data will be accepted from the client application, rather than a file. If you are using *psql* to enter data, you will be prompted to type in text if you initiate a COPY FROM on stdin.

stdout

> The *standard output* option. When used in place of a filename, this indicates that output will be sent directly to the client, rather than to a file (e.g., to *psql*).

delimiter

> The character symbol that separates column values in a row. On a COPY FROM, PostgreSQL will expect this character to delimit columns. On a COPY TO, PostgreSQL will delimit each column value by this character in its output. If omitted, the default delimiter is used, which is a tab (\t).

> The delimiter you choose must only be one character; if you enter something longer than one character, only the first character of what you enter will be used as the delimiter.

null_string

> The character sequence used to identify a NULL value. By default, \N is used, but you can change it to something more suited to your needs. Recognize that when data is copied into the database, any strings that match your specified NULL string will be interpreted as NULL values, so make sure to use the same string when you copy data in to the database as you used when you copied the data out to begin with, and try to choose a sequence that should never have a valid, non-NULL counterpart.

Results

COPY

> The message returned when a COPY procedure finishes successfully.

ERROR

> The error returned if a COPY procedure fails, accompanied by a reason for failure.

Description

Use the COPY command to transfer data between tables in a PostgreSQL database and files within a filesystem. There are two ways to use it: COPY TO and COPY FROM.

Use COPY TO when you want to output the entire contents of a table in your database to a file, or to standard output (*stdout*, i.e., the client connected to the database). Use COPY FROM when you wish to import data from a standard file, or standard input (*stdin*, from the client).

The SQL COPY command should not be confused with the *psql* \copy command. \copy performs a COPY FROM stdin or COPY TO stdout, storing the acquired data in a *psql*-accessible file. This means the file access rights are controlled by the client (frontend), instead of the *postmaster* (backend).

See the section titled "Adding Data with INSERT and COPY" in Chapter 4, *Using SQL with PostgreSQL*, for more on the nuances of this command.

You can either use normal text for transferring data, or you can use binary format (when specified with the BINARY keyword). Using binary format will speed up COPY commands significantly; however, binary formatting decreases the portability of your application due to low-level byte ordering differences.

Restrictions and limitations

There are a few restrictions to the COPY command. In order for COPY to read from the tables specified, your PostgreSQL user must have SELECT access granted on them. If you are directing COPY to insert values into a table, your PostgreSQL user must also have INSERT or UPDATE access.

Likewise, if you are copying files to or from a system file, the user running the PostgreSQL backend (the *postmaster*) must have the necessary filesystem permissions on the specified file. To sidestep this restriction, the \copy command exists within *psql* (see Chapter 6, *PostgreSQL Clients*, for more on this).

Using the COPY TO command will check constraints, and any triggers you may have set up, but it will not invoke rules or act on column defaults.

COPY will stop operation upon reaching the first error. This should not lead to problems in the event of a COPY FROM, but the target relation will be partially modified in a COPY TO. The VACUUM command should be used to clean up after a failed COPY command.

File formatting

If you are a developer interested in the technical format of PostgreSQL's binary output, see Appendix C, *Binary COPY Format*. If you choose to use normal text formatting instead of binary, the file COPY creates will be formatted as such: each row will appear on a single line, with column values separated by the *delimiter* character. Any embedded characters located in the file have a preceding backslash (\), and column values are output as plain text strings.

If WITH OIDS is specified, the oid will be placed at the beginning of the line. If you create an output file using the WITH OIDS clause, and wish to import that data back into PostgreSQL (or on another PostgreSQL machine), remember to again specify the WITH OIDS clause. Otherwise, it will be interpreted as a normal column.

When COPY sends its results to standard output (*stdout*), it will end the transfer with the following format: a backslash (\), a period (.), and a newline to mark the end of the file. If an EOF (end of file) is reached before the normal end-format, it will automatically terminate.

Due to the backslash character having multiple definitions, you'll need to use an escape sequence to represent an actual backslash character. Do this by typing two consecutive backslashes (\\). The other characters that require this method to display correctly are as follows: the tab character is represented as a backslash and a tab, and a newline is represented by a backslash and a newline.

Remember to pre-format any non-PostgreSQL text data that you are loading into the database by changing backslashes to double-backslashes.

Examples

The example below copies the employees table to the emp_table file, using a pipe (|) as the field delimiter:

```
booktown=# COPY employees TO '/tmp/employee_data' USING DELIMITERS '|';
COPY
```

The following example copies data from a system file into the publishers table:

```
booktown=# COPY publishers FROM '/tmp/publisher_data';
COPY
```

CREATE AGGREGATE — Defines a new aggregate function within the database.

Synopsis

```
CREATE AGGREGATE name ( BASETYPE = input_type
    [ , SFUNC = sfunc, STYPE = state_type ]
    [ , FINALFUNC = ffunc ]
    [ , INITCOND = initial_condition ] )
```

Parameters

name

The name of the aggregate function you are creating.

input_type

The input data type on which the new function will operate. If the aggregate function ignores input values (as the count() function does), you can use the ANY string constant as the data type.

sfunc

The name of the function you wish to be called to handle all non-NULL input data values. These functions usually follow the same format, having two arguments. The first argument is of the *state_type* data type, and the second of the *input_type* data type. If the aggregate does not examine input values, it will take only one argument of type *state_type*. Either way, the function must return a value of type *state_type*.

state_type

The data type for the state value of the aggregate.

ffunc

The name of the final function called upon to compute the aggregate's result after all input has been examined. This function is required to accept a single argument of type *state_type*.

The output data type of the aggregate function is defined as the return type of *this* function. If you do not specify *ffunc*, the ending state value is used as the aggregate's result, and the output data type is determined by *state_type*.

initial_condition

The initial value of the aggregate function's state value. This is a literal constant of the the same data type as *state_type*. The state value will be initialized to NULL if *initial_condition* is not specified.

Results

CREATE

The message returned when an aggregate is created successfully.

ERROR: AggregateCreate: function "*sfunc(state_type, input)*" does not exist
The error returned if the specified state function *sfunc*, accepting arguments of types *state_type* and *input*, does not exist.

ERROR: AggregateCreate: function "*sfunc(state_type)*" does not exist
The error returned if the specified *sfunc*, accepting one argument of type *state_type*, does not exist. This error should only be displayed if the *input_type* is set to *ANY*.

Description

Use the CREATE AGGREGATE command to define new aggregate functions in PostgreSQL. Some commonly used aggregate functions are already included with PostgreSQL, such as min( ), avg( ), and max( ). See Chapter 5, *Operators and Functions*, for more on PostgreSQL's built-in functions.

Aggregate functions are characterized primarily by their input data type. It is possible for two or more aggregate functions to exist with the same name, as long as they accept different data types. This is called function overloading.

In order to avoid confusion, do not try to create normal functions with the same name and input type as an aggregate. If you do, aggregate functions will receive precedence.

An aggregate function is comprised of either one or two normal functions. The required function is the state transition function (the *sfunc*), and the optional function is the finalization function (*ffunc*).

PostgreSQL uses a temporary *stype* variable that is updated by the state transition function for every input row it receives. If you have defined a finalization function for your aggregate, it will be called to calculate the output value after all data has been processed; otherwise, the ending state value is returned without further processing.

Aggregate functions can also set an initial value for the internal state value; this is known as an *initial condition*, and is specified with the INITCOND keyword. PostgreSQL stores this value in the database as a value of type text, but it must represent a constant of the same data type as the state value defined by the STYPE keyword. This value will be initialized to NULL if nothing is supplied.

If the state transition function was created with the isstrict attribute (see the reference entry titled "CREATE FUNCTION"), it cannot be called with NULL parameters. Transition functions declared in this manner cause aggregate execution to behave differently then normal; specifically, all NULL input parameters are ignored, and the function is not called. The previous state value is retained, and the aggregate function continues to process input values.

Furthermore, if the initial state value is set to NULL, it will be replaced by the first non-NULL parameter value, and the transition function is called with the second non-NULL parameter value. This can be useful for creating aggregates such as max(). Note that this behavior will only occur when *state_type* is the same as *input_type*. If these types are different, you must either provide a non-NULL initial condition, or use a non-strict transition function.

When the state transition function is not declared as strict, it will be called unconditionally for each input value. This causes it to handle NULL values and NULL transition values by itself, which allows the aggregate author to have more control over the aggregate's handling of NULL input.

If the finalization function of an aggregate is declared strict, it will not be called if the ending state value is a NULL value; instead, it will output a NULL result automatically.

Examples

The following example defines an aggregate function named sum(), for use with the text data type. This aggregate calls the textcat(text,text) function built into PostgreSQL to return a concatenated "sum" of all the text found in its input values:

```
booktown=# CREATE AGGREGATE sum ( BASETYPE = text,
booktown(#                        SFUNC = textcat,
booktown(#                        STYPE = text,
booktown(#                        INITCOND = '' );
CREATE
booktown=# SELECT sum(title || ' ') FROM books WHERE title ~ '^L';
               sum
-------------------------------
 Little Women Learning Python
(1 row)
```

CREATE DATABASE — Creates a new database in PostgreSQL.

Synopsis

```
CREATE DATABASE name
  [ WITH [ LOCATION = { 'dbpath' | DEFAULT } ]
         [ TEMPLATE = template | DEFAULT ]
         [ ENCODING = encoding_name | encoding_number | DEFAULT ] ]
```

Parameters

name

The name of the database you are creating.

dbpath

The directory in which to save the database. You may use the DEFAULT keyword to save the database in the default data directory, as specified by the PGDATA environment variable (or -*D* flag, passed to the *postmaster*).

Note that the *dbpath* value must normally be the name of system-level *environment variable*, which is set within the PostgreSQL user's environment to a value describing an initialized database directory. However, if PostgreSQL was compiled by the *gmake* command with the *CPPFLAGS=-DALLOW_ABSOLUTE_DBPATHS* argument passed to it, you can also specify a complete, absolute directory path.

template

The name of the template you wish to base the new database off of. Use the DEFAULT keyword to specify the default template (usually template1).

encoding_name | encoding_num

The multibyte encoding method to use for the database. This can be entered as a string literal, or an encoding type's corresponding integer encoding number. See Appendix A, *Multibyte Encoding Types*, for a list of PostgreSQL's multibyte encoding types.

You may use the DEFAULT keyword to explicitly specify the default encoding method (this is already the default).

Results

CREATE DATABASE

The message returned when a new database is created successfully.

ERROR: user '*username*' is not allowed to create/drop databases

The error returned if your PostgreSQL user does not have the createdb privilege necessary to create a database. A database administrator can add permissions to a PostgreSQL user by using the ALTER USER command.

ERROR: Absolute paths are not allowed as database locations

The error returned if *dbpath* is specified as an absolute system path, and PostgreSQL was not compiled with the *CPPFLAGS=-DALLOW_ABSO-LUTE_DBPATHS* argument to *gmake*.

ERROR: Relative paths are not allowed as database locations

The error returned if *dbpath* is specified as a relative system path, which is never allowed, as of PostgreSQL 7.1.x. You must set *dbpath* to the name of the *postmaster*'s configured *environment variable* describing the location of your intended database location.

ERROR: *createdb*: database "*name*" already exists

The error returned if a database named *name* already exists within the system catalog.

ERROR: database path may not contain single quotes

The error returned if you use single quotes (') within the *dbpath* parameter (the location to save the database). Such single quotes are not compatible with the system's directory creation program.

ERROR: CREATE DATABASE: unable to create database directory '/path'

The error returned if it is not possible to save the database files in the path you specified. This can be due to a full disk, insufficient permissions on the specified directory, or the directory not having been initialized by either *initdb* or *initlocation*.

The username under which PostgreSQL's *postmaster* is running must have access to the path specified as the database location.

ERROR: CREATE DATABASE: May not be called in a transaction block

The error returned if you attempt to use CREATE DATABASE during an explicit transaction block. You cannot use CREATE DATABASE within an open transaction block.

Description

Use CREATE DATABASE to create a new database on the system. When you create a new database, the PostgreSQL user you are logged in as will automatically become the owner of the new database, so be sure you are logged in correctly before using this command.

If absolutely necessary, you can change the owner of a database by performing an UPDATE on the pg_database system table's datdba column to be a different user's PostgreSQL system ID.

The *dbpath* usually describes an environment variable, which contains the location of the path to create the database in. This environment variable must exist in the environment of the user running the *postmaster*. In this manner, administrators have more control over where on the filesystem databases can be created. See Chapter 9, *Database Management*, for more information on this.

The directory you choose to store the database in must be prepared with the *init-location* (or *initdb*) command beforehand. See Chapter 9 for more on these commands.

If PostgreSQL has been compiled with *ALLOW_ABSOLUTE_DBPATHS* (by passing *CPPFLAGS=-DALLOW_ABSOLUTE_DBPATHS* to *gmake* after configuration), absolute pathnames are allowed. They are not allowed by default, due to security and data integrity issues that can arise from using database locations specified as absolute paths.

To create a new database, PostgreSQL clones a database template (template1, by default). If you wish to use a different database template, specify it with the TEMPLATE clause. To create a completely new database (with no cloned template objects), pass template0 as the name of the template to clone from.

Examples

The following example creates a database with the name of booktown:

```
template1=# CREATE DATABASE booktown;
CREATE DATABASE
```

This next example specifies the creation of a database with a different data directory location for the new database:

```
template1=# CREATE DATABASE booktown WITH LOCATION = '/usr/local/pgsql/booktown';
CREATE DATABASE
```

CREATE FUNCTION — Defines a new function within the database.

Synopsis

```
CREATE FUNCTION name ( [ argtype [, ...] ] )
       RETURNS returntype
       AS 'definition'
       LANGUAGE 'langname'
       [ WITH ( attribute [, ...] ) ]
CREATE FUNCTION name ( [ argtype [, ...] ] )
       RETURNS returntype
       AS 'obj_file' [, 'link_symbol' ]
       LANGUAGE 'langname'
       [ WITH ( attribute [, ...] ) ]
```

Parameters

name

The name of the new function being created.

argtype

The data type of the argument, or arguments, to be accepted by the new function. There are three general input types you may use: base types, complex types, or the special opaque type. The opaque type explicitly allows the function to accept arguments of invalid SQL types. The opaque type is generally used by internal functions, or functions written in internal language such as C, or PL/pgSQL, where the return type is not provided as a standard SQL data type.

returntype

The data type of the value or values returned by the new function. This may be set as a base type, complex type, setof type (a normal data type, prefixed by setof), or the opaque type.

Using the setof modifier determines that the function will return multiple rows worth of data (by default, a function returns only one row). For example, a return type defined as setof integer creates a function that can return more than a single row of integer values.

attribute

An optional function attribute. Valid attributes, as of PostgreSQL 7.1.x, are isstrict and iscacheable.

definition

The definition of the function to create. This is entered as a string, bound by quotes, though its contents vary widely between languages. The exact content of this string may be an internal function name, a SQL statement, or procedural code in a language such as PL/pgSQL.

`obj_file [, link_symbol]`

> The file that contains the dynamically loadable object code, and the function name in the C source. The `link_symbol` is only required if the source C function has a name that is different from the intended SQL function name.

`langname`

> The name of the language the new function is written in. Possible values for this parameter are *C, SQL, internal,* or the name of a procedural language created using the CREATE LANGUAGE command (e.g., *plpgsql*). See the reference entry titled "CREATE LANGUAGE" for further details.

Results

CREATE

> The message returned when a function is created successfully.

Description

Use the CREATE FUNCTION command to create a new function in the connected database. Ownership of the function is set to the PostgreSQL user that created it.

Function attributes

`iscachable`

> The `iscacheable` attribute specifies that the function will always return the same result when passed the same argument values (i.e., calculated results are cached). Such a function does not perform a database lookup or use information not directly present in the parameter list. This option is used by the optimizer to determine whether it is safe to pre-evaluate the result of a function call based on past calls, rather than re-executing the function on cached values for previously passed arguments.

`isstrict`

> The `isstrict` attribute specifies that the function is strict in its handling of NULL values. This means that whenever the function is passed a NULL argument, it will not operate, and will simply return a NULL value.

Function overloading

PostgreSQL allows *function overloading*. Users of object-oriented programming languages may be familiar with this term. In PostgreSQL, the term means to create multiple functions with the same name, provided each of them has a unique set of argument types.

Overloading is useful for creating what seems to be a single function that can handle a large variety of different input types; to the user, the series of functions you have created become a single, seamless, versatile tool.

Differing from PostgreSQL's ability to overload functions based on argument types, two compiled C functions in one object file are unable to share the same name. To avoid this problem, you can arbitrarily rename the second C function that you wish to overload within PostgreSQL to a unique function name in your C source, compile the object code, and then explicitly define the *link_symbol* parameter as that arbitrary name when creating the overloaded C function.

Examples

The following example creates a simple SQL function that returns a book title based on the ID number passed to the function:

```
booktown=# CREATE FUNCTION title(integer) RETURNS text
booktown-#        AS 'SELECT title from books where id = $1'
booktown-#        LANGUAGE 'sql';
CREATE
```

The `title()` function can now be used within the `booktown` database to retrieve rows with ID numbers matching the number passed as an argument:

```
booktown=# SELECT title(41472) AS book_title;
     book_title
----------------------
 Practical PostgreSQL
(1 row)
```

CREATE GROUP — Creates a new PostgreSQL group within the database.

Synopsis

```
CREATE GROUP name
       [ WITH [ SYSID gid ]
              [ USER  username [, ...] ] ]
```

Parameters

name

The name of the new group to create.

gid

The group ID to use for the new group. If you do not explicitly specify the group ID, it will automatically be calculated as one higher than the highest group ID currently in use.

username

The user (or comma-delimited list of users) that you wish to automatically include in the group you are creating. The users listed in this parameter must already exist within the database.

Results

CREATE GROUP

The message returned when a PostgreSQL group is created successfully.

ERROR: CREATE GROUP: group name "*name*" already exists

The error returned if a PostgreSQL group named *name* currently exists in the system.

ERROR: CREATE GROUP: permission denied

The error returned if a non-superuser attempts to create a group.

ERROR: CREATE GROUP: user "*username*" does not exist

The error returned if the *username* in the WITH USER clause does not currently exist.

Description

A database superuser can use CREATE GROUP to create a new group in PostgreSQL. A group is a system-wide database object that can be assigned privileges (with the GRANT command), and have users added to it as members. Members of a group are assigned its privileges by proxy.

To modify a group (and the list of users that it is composed of it), use the ALTER GROUP command. If you wish to remove a group entirely, use the DROP GROUP command.

Examples

The following example creates an empty group named management:

```
booktown=# CREATE GROUP management;
CREATE GROUP
```

The next example creates a group called accounting, and *automatically* adds two users to it by specifying their usernames following the WITH USER clause:

```
booktown=# CREATE GROUP accounting WITH USER vincent, allen;
CREATE GROUP
```

CREATE INDEX — Places an index on a table.

Synopsis

```
CREATE [ UNIQUE ] INDEX index_name ON table
       [ USING method ] ( column [ op_class ] [, ...] )
CREATE [ UNIQUE ] INDEX index_name ON table
       [ USING method ] ( func_name ( column [, ... ] ) [ op_class ] )
```

Parameters

UNIQUE

> The optional UNIQUE keyword. When used, this causes the database to check for, and prevent, duplicate values within the column (or combined columns) it is placed upon. This check will occur both when the index is created and each time data is added to the table. PostgreSQL will then generate an error whenever an INSERT or UPDATE request is made that would place duplicate data within the index, and the command will fail.

index_name

> The name for the new index.

table

> The name of the table you are placing the index on.

method

> The type of indexing method you wish to use for the index. There are three methods available to choose from, the default being btree:

> btree

>> The PostgreSQL implementation of Lehman-Yao high-concurrency B-trees.

> rtree

>> The PostgreSQL implementation of standard R-trees using Guttman's quadratic split algorithm.

> hash

>> The PostgreSQL implementation of Litwin's linear hashing.

column

> The name of the column (or comma-delimited list of columns) on which to place the index.

op_class

> The optionally specified associated operator class. For most users, this should not be specified.

func_name

> The name of a function you wish CREATE INDEX to use on the specified columns (rather than indexing the data values literally in those columns). The specified function must return a valid value that can be indexed (e.g., not a set of values).

Results

CREATE

The message returned when an index is created successfully.

ERROR: Cannot create index: '*index_name*' already exists

The error returned if an index with the name you specified already exists.

ERROR: DefineIndex: attribute "*column*" not found

The error returned if the specified *column* does not exist in the specified *table* to index.

ERROR: DefineIndex: relation "*table*" not found

The error returned if the specified *table* does not exist in the connected database.

Description

Use CREATE INDEX to build an optimization index on a specified table, based on one or more of its columns. Remember that while indices are designed to improve the performance and effectiveness of your database, using them on tables whose cost of index maintenance outweighs the practical benefit actually *decreases* overall performance.

Column index

You may create an index specifying a list of one or more table columns. This is the "traditional" index type. It may be used by queries that directly reference the indexed columns in a WHERE clause. Note that R-tree and Hash indices may only index one column, though B-tree indices can index up to sixteen columns.

Functional index

An alternate type of index is one called a *functional index*. A functional index is an index based on the returned value of a function applied to one or more columns. Such an index is useful for queries that use the same function in a WHERE clause frequently.

For example, if you have a query that always references upper(last_name) in its WHERE clause, you could optimized that query by creating a functional index on upper(last_name).

Operators and operator classes

The PostgreSQL query optimizer will use different indices for different operators used in a comparison. It will choose which type of index to used based on the pre-defined list shown in Table 14-1.

Table 14-1. Operator/index correspondence

Index	Operator
B-tree	<, <=, >=, >
R-tree	<<, &<, &>, >>, @, ~=, &&
Hash	=

You can optionally specify an *operator class* for each column on which an index is placed. This is done by setting the optional op_class parameter to the class of operator you intend to use. This option only exists because, in some circumstances, there can be more than one meaningful way to order data. The default indexing method is generally sufficient for most users, however, and this option is best left unused unless you are creating your own custom types and operators.

Examples

The following example creates a unique index on the id column of the employees table:

```
booktown=# CREATE UNIQUE INDEX employee_id_idx
booktown-#              ON employees (id);
CREATE
```

The next example creates a functional index on the last_name column of the employees table, using the upper() function:

```
booktown=# CREATE INDEX employee_upper_name_idx
booktown-#          ON employees (upper(last_name));
CREATE
```

CREATE LANGUAGE — Defines a new language to be used by functions.

Synopsis

```
CREATE [ TRUSTED ] [ PROCEDURAL ] LANGUAGE 'langname'
    HANDLER call_handler
    LANCOMPILER 'comment'
```

Parameters

TRUSTED

The TRUSTED keyword indicates that the PostgreSQL lets unprivileged users bypass user and permission-related access restrictions on the language. If this parameter is not specified during creation of the language, only database superusers will be able to use the language to create new functions.

PROCEDURAL

> The optional PROCEDURAL noise term. This may be used to increase readability of your CREATE LANGUAGE statements, but has no effect.

langname

> The name of the new procedural language to define. This name is case insensitive. A procedural language will not (and cannot) override an existing, built-in PostgreSQL language.

HANDLER *call_handler*

> The name of the already-defined function that will be called to execute the PL procedures.

comment

> A string that is inserted into the lancompiler column of the pg_language system table. The LANCOMPILER clause is a legacy clause with no practical effect, and may be removed in a future PostgreSQL release. However, as of version 7.1.x, this is still a required clause.

Results

CREATE

> The message returned when a new language is successfully created.

ERROR: PL handler function *call_handler()* doesn't exist

> The error returned if the function you specified as the call handler with *call_handler* parameter cannot be found.

Description

Use the CREATE LANGUAGE command to load a new procedural language into the connected database. This command can be used with languages that you specified using --*with-langname* when you first installed PostgreSQL, or one you have created yourself. For instance, to correctly add the pltcl language into PostgreSQL, you should have used the tag --*with-tcl* when you configured PostgreSQL to make its call handler available.

After this command has been issued, you should be able to define functions using the newly added language. Note that the user who executes the CREATE LANGUAGE command must be a superuser.

As of PostgreSQL 7.1.x (the most current version at the printing of this book), once a procedural languages is defined, the definition cannot be modified. To change the definition of your procedural language, you will need to drop it from the database with the DROP LANGUAGE command and recreate it.

If you use CREATE LANGUAGE to create a language in the template1 database, all subsequent databases that are created from the template1 (the default template) will support that language.

In order for a procedural language to be used by PostgreSQL, a call handler must be written for it. That call handler must be compiled into a binary form; it is therefore required that the language used to write a handler be one that compiles into a binary format, such as C or C++.

The call handler must be created within PostgreSQL as a function that does not accept arguments and has a return type of opaque. By defining the handler function in this manner, you enable PostgreSQL to prevent the function (and thus, the language) from ever being used in an arbitrary SQL statement.

Examples

A handler must already exist for the language in question when you use the CREATE LANGUAGE command. The first step in registering a procedural language is to create a function that specifies the location of object code for the call handler. The following example creates an example call handler, whose object code is located at */usr/local/pgsql/lib/libexample.so*:

```
booktown=# CREATE FUNCTION example_call_handler ( ) RETURNS opaque
booktown-#            AS '/usr/local/pgsql/lib/libexample.so'
booktown-#            LANGUAGE 'C';
CREATE
```

You do not need to define the call handler function if it has already been created by the programmer. For illustrative purposes, we are assuming that the programmer has not defined a function that refers to the call handler.

The second step is to use CREATE LANGUAGE to load the existing language into the connected database. The following example creates a language called plexample, which uses the call handler created in the preceding example:

```
booktown=# CREATE PROCEDURAL LANGUAGE 'plexample'
booktown-#            HANDLER example_call_handler
booktown-#            LANCOMPILER 'My Example';
CREATE
```

CREATE OPERATOR — Defines a new operator within the database.

Synopsis

```
CREATE OPERATOR name ( PROCEDURE = func_name
    [, LEFTARG = type1 ] [, RIGHTARG = type2 ]
    [, COMMUTATOR = com_op ] [, NEGATOR = neg_op ]
    [, RESTRICT = res_proc ] [, JOIN = join_proc ]
    [, HASHES ] [, SORT1 = left_sort_op ] [, SORT2 = right_sort_op ] )
```

Parameters

name

The character sequence of the new operator. Read further for a list of valid characters to use in names and symbols.

func_name

The function that implements the new operator.

type1

The type of the left-hand argument. Do not use this option with a unary operator that always appears to the left of the value on which it operates.

type2

The data type of the right-hand argument. Do not use this option with a unary operator that always appears to the right of the value on which it operates.

com_op

The commutator operator for the new operator. A commutator is another existing operator which executes the commutation (order reversal) of the procedure defined for the new operator, e.g., with the left argument treated as the right argument, and the right argument treated as the left argument.

neg_op

The negator operator for the new operator. A negator is another existing operator which executes the literal inversion of the procedure define for the new operator. A negator should only be defined if the result of applying the NOT keyword to the new operator always results in the same output that the negator would return on the same condition.

res_proc

The name of the restriction selectivity estimator function for the new operator. This function must already exist, must accept arguments of the same data types as defined for this new operator, and return a floating point value.

join_proc

The name of the join selectivity estimator function for the new operator. This function must already exist, and must be defined to accept arguments of the same data types as defined for this new operator, and return a floating point value.

HASHES

The HASHES keyword, which indicates that the new operator can support a hash join.

left_sort_op

The operator that sorts left-hand values, if the new operator can support a merge join.

right_sort_op

The operator that sorts right-hand values, if the new operator can support a merge join.

Results

CREATE

The message returned when a new operator is created successfully.

Description

Use the CREATE OPERATOR command to define a new operator. The PostgreSQL user that creates the operator becomes the operator owner when creation is successful.

The operator *name* is a character sequence up to 31 characters in length. Characters in the operator name must be within the following list of accepted characters:

```
+ - * / < > = ~ ! @ # % ^ & | ` ? $
```

There are some restrictions on allowed character sequences for the name:

- The dollar sign ($) is only allowed within an operator name consisting of multiple characters. It cannot be specified as single-character operator name.

- The double-dash (--) and the forward slash and star (/*) character combinations cannot appear anywhere in an operator name, as they will be interpreted as the start of a comment.

- A multiple character operator cannot end with a plus sign (+) or dash (-), unless the name also contains at least one of the following characters:

    — Tilde (~)

    — Exclamation mark (!)

    — At symbol (@)

    — Number symbol (#)

    — Percent sign (%)

    — Caret (^)

— Ampersand (&)

— Pipe (|)

— Backtick (`)

— Question mark (?)

— Dollar sign ($)

These restrictions on operator names let PostgreSQL parse syntactically valid queries without requiring the user to separate tokens with white space.

When you create an operator, you must include at least one LEFTARG or one RIGHTARG (as the operator must take an argument). If you are defining a binary operator (one which operators on a value to the left *and* right of the operator), *both* the LEFTARG and RIGHTARG must be specified. If you are creating a right unary operator, you will only need to define LEFTARG; likewise, when creating a left unary operator, you will only need to define RIGHTARG.

The function you specify as the *func_name* parameter when creating an operator must have been defined to accept the correct number of arguments for that operator.

For the query optimizer to correctly reverse the order of operands, it needs to know what the commutator operator is (if it exists). For some operators, a commutator should exist (or at least, the existence of one would make sense). For example, the commutator of the greater-than symbol (>) is the less-than (<) symbol, and it makes sense that these operators should be related to one another in this fashion. With this information, your operator order can easily be reversed, changing something like x < y to y > x if the query optimizer finds it to be more efficient.

In the same way that specifying the commutator operator can help the optimizer, so can specifying a negator operator (if one exists). The negator to the equals sign (=) is !=, signifying *not-equals* or *not-equivalent*. When a negator is specified, the query optimizer can simplify statements like this:

```
booktown=# SELECT * FROM employees WHERE NOT name = 'John';
```

This simplified form of this query, using the negator operator, is:

```
booktown=# SELECT * FROM employees WHERE name != 'John';
```

Note that you may technically specify an operator's commutator or negator operator to PostgreSQL before that operator actually exists. This is to allow you to create two operators which reference one another. Exercise care, however, in remembering to create the appropriate operator to fit the definition of your commutator or negator if it does not yet exist.

Use the HASH option to indicate to the query optimizer that an operator can support the use of a hash-join algorithm (usable only if the operator represents equality tests where equality of the type also means bitwise equality of the representation of the type). Likewise, use SORT1 and SORT2 to inform the optimizer that, respectively, the left and right side operators can support a merge-sort. These sorting operators should only be given for an equality operator, and when they are given they should be represented by less-than and greater-than symbols for the left- and right-hand data types, respectively.

The RESTRICT and JOIN parameters provide functions that assist the query optimizer with estimation of result set sizes. With some query conditions, it may be necessary for PostgreSQL to estimate the number of results an action with operators may produce; in these situations, the query optimizer will call the res_proc function with the same arguments passed to the operator, then use the number returned by that function to estimate how many results there will be. Because of this, the res_proc function must already be defined using CREATE_FUNCTION and must accept the correct arguments.

The function specified with JOIN is used to help with estimation of the size of a join when the operands of an operator are not constant values. The query optimizer uses the floating point number returned from join_proc to compute the estimated size of the result.

Examples

The following example defines a non-zero boolean operator for the integer type, using the is_zero function (see Chapter 7 for more on this function and its definition):

```
booktown=# CREATE OPERATOR !# (PROCEDURE = is_zero,
booktown(#              LEFTARG = integer,
booktown(#              RIGHTARG = integer);
CREATE
```

CREATE RULE — Defines a new rule on a table.

Synopsis

```
CREATE RULE name AS ON event TO object [ WHERE condition ] DO [ INSTEAD ]  action
action ::= NOTHING | query | ( query [; ...] ) | [ query [; ...] ]
```

Parameters

name

> The name of the new rule you are creating.

event

> The event that triggers the rule. This parameter should be one of: SELECT, UPDATE, DELETE, or INSERT.

object

> The name of a table, or the fully qualified name of a table column (e.g., *table_name.column_name*).

condition

> A SQL condition evaluating to a value of type boolean, which specifies when this rule should be used. This statement should not refer to a table; the only exception to this is that the condition *may* refer to the special new and old relations, which represent the existing rows, and any new row data provided, respectively.

INSTEAD

> The INSTEAD keyword; when used, the *action* is executed instead of the specified *event*. Otherwise, the *action* executes before the *event* does.

action

> The query (or queries) that define the action to perform when the rule is triggered, and the condition is met. The query (or queries) can be any valid SELECT, INSERT, UPDATE, DELETE, or NOTIFY statements. Supply multiple queries by surrounding them in parentheses.

> You may alternatively use the NOTHING keyword instead of a query. NOTHING will perform no action, and is only useful if you also specify the INSTEAD keyword.

Within the *condition* and *action* values, you are able to use the special new and old relations to access column values from both the referenced *object*, and from the data triggering the rule.

The new relation is available in an INSERT or UPDATE rule, containing the column values being inserted or updated, while the old relation is available in a SELECT, UPDATE, or DELETE rule, containing the row data being selected, updated, or deleted.

Results

CREATE

> The message returned when a rule is successfully created.

Description

Use CREATE RULE to create a rule. Rules allow you to define alternate actions to be taken upon table and class inserts, updates, and deletions. You can also use the PostgreSQL rule system to implement table views.

When SELECT, INSERT, DELETE, or UPDATE is issued, the rules for that event are examined in an unspecified order. If a WHERE clause has been specified by the rule, it is checked; if the specified condition is met, the rule's specified action is performed. If you specified INSTEAD when creating the rule, the action will be taken instead of the event; otherwise the action will be performed before the query is processed (the event itself). Be careful not to create what are known as *circular rules*; these are rules that reference other rules that in turn reference the original rule.

When using ON SELECT rules, you must pass the INSTEAD parameter. Essentially, this means that ON SELECT must always implement table views.

Examples

The following example shows the definition of a rule named sync_stock_with_editions that updates the stock table's isbn column automatically when the editions table is modified:

```
booktown=# CREATE RULE sync_stock_with_editions AS
booktown-#           ON UPDATE TO editions
booktown-#           DO UPDATE stock SET isbn = new.isbn
booktown-#                          WHERE isbn = old.isbn;
CREATE
```

CREATE SEQUENCE — Creates a new sequence number generator.

Synopsis

```
CREATE SEQUENCE seqname [ INCREMENT increment ]
        [ MINVALUE minvalue ] [ MAXVALUE maxvalue ]
        [ START start ] [ CACHE cache ] [ CYCLE ]
```

Parameters

seqname

The name of the new sequence.

increment

The value to be applied on each sequence increment. Specify a positive number to make an ascending sequence; specify a negative number to make a descending sequence.

minvalue

> The minimum value the new sequence will generate. The default minimum is 1 for an ascending sequence and –2147483647 for a descending sequence.

maxvalue

> The maximum value the new sequence will generate. The default is 2147483647 for an ascending sequence, and –1 for a descending sequence.

start

> The starting value of the sequence. By default, an ascending sequence will start at *minvalue*, and a descending sequence will start at *maxvalue*.

cache

> The quantity of sequence numbers that can be stored in cache memory. Using a cache value greater than 1 will speed up performance, because some calls for new sequence values will be satisfied from the cache. By default, the cache value is set at 1, which forces generation of one sequence number at a time (by default, *cache* is not used). Set it to a number higher than 1 to enable the use of caching.

CYCLE

> Use this keyword to enable wrapping. When wrapping is enabled, a sequence can wrap around past its minimum or maximum value and begin again at its minimum or maximum value. The direction of the wrap depends on whether a sequence is ascending or descending.

Results

CREATE

> The message returned when a sequence is created successfully.

ERROR: Relation '*seqname*' already exists

> The error returned if the sequence already exists.

ERROR: DefineSequence: MINVALUE (*start*) can't be >= MAXVALUE (*max*)

> The error returned if the sequence's minimum starting value is out of range.

ERROR: DefineSequence: START value (*start*) can't be < MINVALUE (*min*)

> The error returned if the starting value is out of range.

ERROR: DefineSequence: MINVALUE (*min*) can't be >= MAXVALUE (*max*)

> The error returned if the minimum and maximum values are incompatible.

Description

Use the CREATE SEQUENCE command to create a new sequence number generator in the database.

Examples

This example demonstrates the creation of the `shipments_ship_id_seq` sequence:

```
booktown=# CREATE SEQUENCE shipments_ship_id_seq
booktown-#                 START 200 INCREMENT 1;
CREATE
```

Once created, you can select the next number from a sequence with the `nextval()` function:

```
booktown=# SELECT nextval ('shipments_ship_id_seq');
 nextval
---------
     200
(1 row)
```

You can also use a sequence in an `INSERT` command:

```
booktown=# INSERT INTO shipments VALUES
booktown-#         (nextval('shipments_ship_id_seq'), 107, '0394800753', 'now');
```

CREATE TABLE — Creates a new table.

Synopsis

```
CREATE [ TEMPORARY | TEMP ] TABLE table_name (
        { column_name type [ column_constraint [...] ] |
          table_constraint }
        [, ...]
    )
    [ INHERITS ( inherited_table [,...] ) ]

column_constraint ::=
  [ CONSTRAINT column_constraint_name ]
  { NOT NULL | NULL | UNIQUE | PRIMARY KEY |
    DEFAULT default_value |
    CHECK (condition |
    REFERENCES foreign_table [ ( foreign_column ) ]
      [ MATCH FULL | MATCH PARTIAL ]
      [ ON DELETE action ]
      [ ON UPDATE action ]
      [ DEFERRABLE | NOT DEFERRABLE ]
      [ INITIALLY DEFERRED | INITIALLY IMMEDIATE ]
  }

table constraint ::=
  [ CONSTRAINT table_constraint_name ]
  { UNIQUE ( column_name [, ... ] ) |
    PRIMARY KEY ( column_name [, ... ] ) |
    CHECK ( condition ) |
    FOREIGN KEY ( column_name [, ... ] )
      REFERENCES foreign_table
```

```
        [ ( foreign_column [, ... ] ) ]
        [ MATCH FULL | MATCH PARTIAL ]
        [ ON DELETE action ]
        [ ON UPDATE action ]
        [ DEFERRABLE | NOT DEFERRABLE ]
        [ INITIALLY DEFERRED | INITIALLY IMMEDIATE ]
    }
```

```
action ::= { NO ACTION | RESTRICT | CASCADE | SET NULL | SET DEFAULT }
```

Parameters

TEMPORARY | TEMP

The keyword which defines a table as having a temporary lifespan. Such a table will be destroyed after the user's session has ended. Any table-related constructions (such as indices and constraints) will also be destroyed with the table at the end of the session.

If a temporary table is given the same name as an existing permanent table, only the temporary table will be accessible by the session which created it. This will cause problems, since it will implicitly take precedence over the permanent table within the current session until it is destroyed.

table_name

The name of the table you are creating.

column_name

The name of a column within the new table. Multiple column definitions are specified within parentheses, separated by commas.

type

The type of a specified column, immediately following a column name. This can be a standard type or an array of a standard type.

column_constraint

A complete constraint definition for a column. Here are the parameters available for a column constraint:

column_constraint_name

The optional name for a constraint clause.

NULL

The clause used to explicitly allow the column to contain NULL values. This option is set by default.

NOT NULL

The clause used to forbid the use of a NULL value for this column. You can accomplish this by using the CHECK (*column* NOT NULL) column constraint.

UNIQUE

The clause used to force all rows within a column to have unique values (unique within the table). This is enforced by the creation of a unique index on the column.

PRIMARY KEY

The clause used to set a column as a primary key for the table. Other tables rely on primary keys to act as the identifying column for each row. A primary key is effectively the same as a column created with the UNIQUE and NOT NULL clauses.

DEFAULT

The clause used to set a default value for a column. Such a value is used if an input value is not provided for the column by an INSERT statement. Without an explicit default_value, a column defaults to contain NULL.

CHECK

The clause used to have values checked against a specified condition. If the condition yields false on an INSERT or UPDATE, the statement will fail.

condition

An arbitrary conditional expression yielding a Boolean value, following the CHECK clause.

REFERENCES

The clause used to verify column values against the values of a column in another table. (See Chapter 7 for more on this creating and using this constraint.)

foreign_table

The name of a table you wish to be referenced by a foreign key constraint.

foreign_column

The name of a column in another table which you are referencing in a foreign key constraint. The column must reside within an existing table. If no column name is given, the database will use the referenced table's primary key.

MATCH FULL | MATCH PARTIAL

The MATCH clause affects what kind of NULL and non-NULL values are allowed to be mixed on insertion into a table whose foreign key references *multiple columns*. The MATCH clause is therefore only practically applicable to table constraints, though the syntax is technically valid in a column constraint as well.

MATCH FULL disallows insertion of row data whose columns contain NULL values unless all referenced columns are NULL. MATCH PARTIAL is not supported as of PostgreSQL 7.1.x. Not specifying either clause allows NULL columns to satisfy the constraint.

ON DELETE

The ON DELETE clause indicates that when a DELETE is executed on a referenced row in the referenced table, one of the following actions will be executed upon the constrained column, as specified by *action*:

NO ACTION

The NO ACTION clause produces an error if the reference is violated. This is the default if *action* is not specified.

RESTRICT

The RESTRICT keyword is identical to NO ACTION.

CASCADE

The CASCADE keyword removes all rows which reference the deleted row. Exercise caution with this action.

SET NULL

The SET NULL clause assigns a NULL value to all referenced column values.

SET DEFAULT

The SET DEFAULT clause sets all referenced columns to their default values.

Note that specifying CASCADE as the ON UPDATE action updates all of the rows which reference the updated row with the new value (rather than deleting them, as would be the case with ON DELETE CASCADE).

ON UPDATE

The ON DELETE clause indicates that when an UPDATE statement is performed on a referenced row in the referenced table, the same actions are available as with the ON DELETE clause. The default action is also NO ACTION.

Specifying CASCADE as the ON UPDATE action updates all of the rows which reference the updated row with the new value (rather than deleting them, as would be the case with ON DELETE CASCADE).

DEFERRABLE | NOT DEFERRABLE

The DEFERRABLE clause gives you the option of postponing enforcement of the constraint to the end of a transaction rather than having it enforced at the end of each statement. Use the INITIALLY clause to specify the initial point at which the constraint will be enforced.

The NOT DEFERRABLE clause indicates the enforcement of the constraint must always be done immediately as each statement is executed. This is the default.

INITIALLY DEFERRED | INITIALLY IMMEDIATE

The INITIALLY DEFERRED clause postpones constraint enforcement until the end of the transaction, whereas INITIALLY IMMEDIATE causes constraint checking to be performed after each statement. The INITIALLY IMMEDIATE clause is the default.

table_constraint

A complete table constraint definition for the table being created. A table constraint can affect multiple columns, whereas a column constraint only creates a constraint for a single column. Here are the parameters available for a table constraint:

table_constraint_name

The optional name for the constraint to be created.

column_name [, . . .]

The name of the column (or comma-delimited list of columns) to which the table constraint applies.

PRIMARY KEY | UNIQUE

The table constraint keywords that apply an implicit index. Use the UNIQUE keyword to have the specified column's value checked for duplicate values. Any attempt to insert new rows that do not contain a unique value for the specified column (or columns) will fail if this constraint is used.

Use the PRIMARY KEY keywords to both check for duplicate values, *and* to disallow NULL values on the specified column, or columns.

CHECK (*condition*)

The conditional CHECK constraint keyword. Use this keyword to check a value against the evaluated boolean *condition* before a new row is inserted; if the check fails (i.e., *condition* returned false), the row is not added.

FOREIGN KEY

The FOREIGN KEY constraint keyword. Use this keyword to identify a column in another table that will be referenced as a foreign key relation (see Chapter 7 for more on this constraint). The remainder of this clause is identical to the REFERENCES clause of a column constraint.

inherited_table

The name of a table from which the new table should inherit columns. If there are any column names inherited that match column names you've already specified as columns for the new table, PostgreSQL will display an error and terminate execution of the command.

Results

CREATE

The message returned when a table is successfully created.

ERROR: Relation '*table_name*' already exists

The error returned if a table named *table_name* already exists.

ERROR: CREATE TABLE: attribute "*b*" duplicated

The error returned a column name is listed twice.

ERROR: Unable to locate type name '*type*' in catalog

The error returned if a specified column *type* does not exist.

ERROR: Illegal class name '*table_name*'

The error returned if *table_name* begins with *pg_*.

Description

Use the CREATE TABLE command to add a new table to the database to which you are connected. After it is created, the new table will be completely empty, and its ownership will be set to the user who issued the CREATE TABLE command.

You must supply a name and data type for each column of which the new table will be comprised (except for inherited columns, for which this data will be derived from the parent table). The name supplied may be up to 31 characters in length, and will be folded to lowercase unless placed within double quotes. The data type can be a standard type (e.g., int4, char), or an array type (a standard type, followed by square brackets, such as float4[]).

You may set a variety of constraints on a column, such as the NOT NULL clause, which disallows NULL values from being inserted into the column.

 Tables cannot have the same name as existing data types; nor can they have the same names as system catalog tables, or even be pre-fixed with pg_, which is the reserved system table prefix.

A table can have a maximum of about 1,600 columns. Due to tuple-length issues, this number is lower in practice.

For more information about creating tables, see Chapter 4. For more information about column and table constraints in general, see Chapter 7.

Examples

The following example creates a table called shipments. It places the NOT NULL constraint and DEFAULT constraints on its id column:

```
booktown=# CREATE TABLE shipments (
booktown(#        id integer NOT NULL DEFAULT nextval('shipments_ship_id_seq'),
booktown(#        customer_id integer,
booktown(#        isbn text,
booktown(#        ship_date timestamp);
CREATE
```

CREATE TABLE AS — Creates a new table built from data retrieved by a SELECT.

Synopsis

```
CREATE TABLE table [ ( column [, ...] ) ]
          AS select
```

Parameters

table

The name of the new table to be created.

column

The name of a column to create; you can specify multiple columns by including their names in a comma-delimited list. There should be the same number of columns specified as are returned by *select*.

select

A valid SELECT statement. The number of targets selected must match the number of columns in the optional column list preceding the AS clause.

Results

SELECT

The message returned on successful creation of, and insertion of row data into, *table*.

ERROR: CREATE TABLE/AS SELECT has mismatched column count

The error returned if the optional list of *columns* in parentheses contains a different number of rows than the *select* statement returns.

Description

Use the CREATE TABLE AS command to create a table from the contents of result set, such as a query on a table that already exists within the database. Both the column types, and row data for the new table, come from the SELECT command specified by *select*.

Note that, as of PostgreSQL 7.1.x, if you specify the optional column list within parentheses, you cannot use the asterisk (*) in the *select* statement.

Example

The following example creates a backup table (aptly named book_backup) from all of the columns taken from the books table:

```
booktown=# CREATE TABLE book_backup
booktown-#            AS SELECT * FROM books;
SELECT
```

CREATE TRIGGER — Creates a new trigger.

Synopsis

```
CREATE TRIGGER name { BEFORE | AFTER } { event [ OR event ... ] }
       ON table FOR EACH { ROW | STATEMENT }
       EXECUTE PROCEDURE function ( arguments )
```

Parameters

name

The name of the new trigger.

table

The name of the table with which the trigger will be associated.

event

The event with which you wish to associate the trigger, that causes the trigger to fire. Valid events are: INSERT, DELETE, and UPDATE. A trigger may be associated with more than one event.

function

The name of the function you wish to link to the new trigger. When the trigger fires, the function is invoked. The function must return a variable of type *opaque*; the *opaque* type is used only by internal functions and such functions cannot be invoked directly from SQL.

arguments

The arguments to pass to the *function* when the trigger is called.

Results

CREATE

The message returned when a trigger is successfully created.

Description

Use the CREATE TRIGGER command to add a trigger to a database. When a trigger is added to the database, it is associated with the *table* specified in the ON clause. When the specified *event* "fires" the trigger, the function you specified will be executed.

 A trigger may only be created on a table by the table's owner, or by a superuser.

When you create a trigger, you must specify whether it is to be fired before or after the *event* is attempted (or completed). If the trigger is set to fire BEFORE one of those events, it may skip the operation for the current tuple, or change the tuple being inserted. If you have set the trigger to fire AFTER the event, it will be aware of all changes that were made during the event (including the last insertion, update, or deletion).

Examples

The following example defines a trigger that is invoked when an existing row in the authors table is updated:

```
booktown=# CREATE TRIGGER sync_authors_books
booktown-#             BEFORE UPDATE
booktown-#             ON authors
booktown-#             FOR EACH ROW
booktown-#             EXECUTE PROCEDURE sync_authors_and_books();
CREATE
```

The sync_authors_and_books() function is a PL/pgSQL function defined to update the value of the author_id column in the books table if the id value in the authors table is updated. It therefore keeps the books table in sync with the authors table. A similar effect could be achieved with a FOREIGN KEY constraint (see Chapter 7).

CREATE TYPE — Defines a new data type for use in the database.

Synopsis

```
CREATE TYPE typename ( INPUT = input_function, OUTPUT = output_function
    , INTERNALLENGTH = { internallength | VARIABLE }
  [ , EXTERNALLENGTH = { externallength | VARIABLE } ]
  [ , DEFAULT = "default" ]
  [ , ELEMENT = element ] [ , DELIMITER = delimiter ]
  [ , SEND = send_function ] [ , RECEIVE = receive_function ]
  [ , PASSEDBYVALUE ]
  [ , ALIGNMENT = alignment ]
  [ , STORAGE = storage ] )
```

Parameters

typename

> The name of the new type being created, which may be up to 30 characters in length. All type names must be unique within a database, and may not begin with an underscore (which is reserved for implicit array types).

internallength

> The internal length of the new type, in bytes.

externallength

> The optional external (displayed) length of the new type.

input_function

> The name of the new type's input function. You must have already defined the function using CREATE FUNCTION, and it must act to convert data of the type's external form into the type's internal form.

output_function

> The name of the new type's output function. This function must convert data of the type's internal form into its displayable form.

element

> The data type of individual array elements which this type addresses, if you intend to create an array type manually. The *element* must be fixed-length data type.

delimiter

> The value delimiter for the implicitly created array associated with the new type (*typename*[]).

default

> The default value for the new data type. If you do not specify a default, the default value for an unspecified column will fall back to either a table-level DEFAULT constraint or NULL.

send_function

> The name of the new type's send function. This function would convert data of the type into a form that can be transferred to another machine, but is not used by PostgreSQL as of 7.1.x, and can be omitted.

receive_function

> The name of the new type's receive function. This function would accept data of the form returned by send_function, and convert that into the type's internal form, but it is also not used by PostgreSQL as of 7.1.x, and can be omitted.

PASSEDBYVALUE

> The optional PASSEDBYVALUE keyword indicates that operators and functions that use this data type should be passed the argument by value, rather than by reference (the default). You may not use this option on types whose internal representation is more than four bytes in length.

alignment

> The storage alignment that this type will require. This must be either char, int2, int4, or double. If unspecified, int4 will be chosen by default.

storage

> The storage technique that will be used for the type. Set this to one of plain, external, extended, or main. If left unspecified, the storage type will default to plain.

Results

CREATE

> The message returned when a type is successfully created.

Description

Use the CREATE TYPE command to register a new, user-defined data type within the current database. The PostgreSQL user that issues the command becomes the owner of the data type.

For a type to be created, it must use two user-defined functions (written in C). These functions are the input and output functions of the data type. The input function converts the type's external representation into an internal representation that can be used by the system objects associated with the type. The output function converts the internal representation back to an external representation.

Both the input and output functions must take a single argument of the opaque type. The output function must return a value of type opaque, while the input function should return a value of the type you intend to create. Notice that this is done before the type is actually created.

You can set the type as either fixed or variable length. If you intend to create a fixed-length type, set internallength to set its numeric length, in bytes. If you intend to create a variable-length type, use the VARIABLE keyword instead of the *internallength* parameter, and the length will be handled in the same way as for the text data type. Specify the external length in the same way, using either a numeric value for *externallength*, or the VARIABLE keyword.

When a new type is created, PostgreSQL automatically adds an implicit array type for the new data type. Internally, this implicit array type is named *_typename* (with a leading underscore). Any reference to a data type called *typename*[] will automatically be translated to the internal array type (*_typename*).

If you wish to provide a delimiter character for the array type, use *delimiter* to do so. This is the character used to separate array elements within array constants passed to PostgreSQL (e.g., {1,2,3}). This is also the character used to separate elements in the external display of values for this array type. By default the delimiter is set to a comma.

If you choose to manually create an array data type, you may provide the PostgreSQL array_in and array_out functions as the input and output function, respectively. You may then use the ELEMENT keyword to specify the data type of the array elements.

To define a system-wide default value for insertion on a column of the new data type (which would ordinarily default to NULL, in instances where a value is neither provided by a user, or by a DEFAULT constraint), use the DEFAULT keyword. Note that, as of PostgreSQL 7.1.x, this must be the *internal* representation of the default value.

The *alignment* value dictates the internal storage alignment of the new data type. Data types created with a variable internal length must be either int4 or double.

The *storage* value determines the internal storage method. Data types with fixed internal length can only be set to plain. Data types with variable internal length can be set to plain, extended, external, or main.

The plain method causes data to be stored in an uncompressed, literal representation. This representation is subject to a maximum length of 8 kilobytes. The extended method allows values that go over this limit to be compressed, as well as to be stored outside of the physical location of the table if the size of the value goes over the physical limit through PostgreSQL's *TOAST* extension (*The Oversized Attribute Storage Technique*, coined by Tom Lane).

The external method is similar to the extended method, but does not attempt to compress the value before using TOAST to store values over the physical limit of the table. The main method is also similar to the extended method, in that it supports compression and TOAST, but it prefers to be maintained physically within the main table unless there is no other storage alternative.

Example

The following example demonstrates the creation of a new data type called zero, which is a numeric data type always set to 0. First, the input and output functions are created. Then, the type itself is created, referencing those functions, as follows.

```
booktown=# CREATE FUNCTION zero_out(opaque) RETURNS opaque
booktown-#                    AS '/usr/local/pgsql/lib/zero.so' LANGUAGE 'C';
CREATE
booktown=# CREATE FUNCTION zero_in(opaque) RETURNS zero
booktown-#                    AS '/usr/local/pgsql/lib/zero.so' LANGUAGE 'C';
NOTICE:  ProcedureCreate: type 'zero' is not yet defined
CREATE
booktown=# CREATE TYPE zero (internallength = 16,
booktown(#                  input = zero_in, output = zero_out);
CREATE
```

CREATE USER — Creates a new PostgreSQL database user.

Synopsis

```
CREATE USER username
    [ WITH
      [ SYSID uid ]
      [ PASSWORD 'password' ] ]
    [ CREATEDB | NOCREATEDB ] [ CREATEUSER | NOCREATEUSER ]
    [ IN GROUP groupname [, ...] ]
    [ VALID UNTIL  'abstime' ]
```

Parameters

username

> The name of the new user you intend to create.

uid

> The explicit user ID for the PostgreSQL user that you are creating; if left out of the CREATE USER command, the user ID will be automatically assigned.

password

> The new PostgreSQL user's password; if the database is setup to require password authentication, this must be set for the user to be able to connect. Otherwise, a defined password is not meaningful to PostgreSQL.

CREATEDB | NOCREATEDB

> The privilege to create new databases. Use CREATEDB, to give the user permission to create databases. Use NOCREATEDB to explicitly deny that permission (which is the default).

CREATEUSER | NOCREATEUSER

> The superuser privilege. The use of CREATEUSER allows access to both the CREATE USER and DROP USER commands, as well as makes the user a *superuser* (with universal rights across all databases). NOCREATEUSER is the default.

groupname

The optional name of a group to which the user is to automatically be added.

abstime

The timestamp that defines when a user's password expires. When the date and time that *abstime* defines has been reached, the user's defined password becomes invalid. If unset, the password never expires.

Results

CREATE USER

The message returned when a user is created successfully.

Description

Use CREATE USER to add new users to a PostgreSQL database. This command is only usable by database superusers. For more information about managing users and authentication, refer to Chapter 10, *User and Group Management.*

 You may also use the *createuser* script to add users to a database from the operating system command line. Use of the script is essentially the same as using this command.

Example

The following example demonstrates how to create a PostgreSQL user (david) in the accounting group that is valid until January 1, 2005 and has the specified password of *jw8s0F4*.

```
booktown=# CREATE USER david
booktown-#              WITH PASSWORD 'jw8s0F4' CREATEDB
booktown-#              IN GROUP accounting VALID UNTIL 'Jan 1 2005';
CREATE USER
```

CREATE VIEW — Creates a view on a table.

Synopsis

```
CREATE VIEW view AS query
```

Parameters

view

The name of the view to create.

query

The SQL query to provide the columns and rows of the view.

Results

CREATE

The message returned when a view is successfully created.

ERROR: Relation 'view' already exists

The error returned if a view with the name you supplied (view) already exists.

NOTICE create: attribute "column" has an unknown type

The notice returned if the data type for column in the query definition is of an ambiguous type.

Description

Use CREATE VIEW to define a new table view within the current database.

 Views are read-only as of PostgreSQL 7.1.x (the most current version as of the writing of this book).

Example

The following example creates a view of publishers whose names begin with H:

```
booktown=# CREATE VIEW h_publishers AS
booktown-#        SELECT * FROM publishers WHERE name LIKE 'H%';
CREATE
```

CURRENT_DATE — Returns the current date.

Synopsis

```
CURRENT_DATE
```

Parameters

This function does not accept any parameters.

Results

date

The current date. The returned data type is date.

Description

Use the CURRENT_DATE function to retrieve the current system date as an object of data type DATE. Use SET DATESTYLE to format the display of that date to your liking. See the section titled "Data Types" in Chapter 3, *Understanding SQL*, for more information on this variable and available options when setting it.

Examples

The following example retrieves the current date:

```
testdb=# SELECT CURRENT_DATE AS today;
    today
------------
 2001-10-29
(1 row)
```

CURRENT_TIME — Returns the current time.

Synopsis

```
CURRENT_TIME
```

Parameters

This function does not accept any parameters.

Results

time

> The current time. The return data type is time.

Description

Use the CURRENT_TIME function to retrieve the current system-recorded time in an object of data type TIME.

Examples

The following example retrieves the current time:

```
testdb=# SELECT CURRENT_TIME AS the_time;
 the_time
----------
 19:44:35
(1 row)
```

CURRENT_TIMESTAMP — Returns the current date and time.

Synopsis

```
CURRENT_TIMESTAMP
```

Parameters

This function does not accept parameters.

Results

timestamp

> The current date and the current time. The return data type is timestamp.

Description

Use the CURRENT_TIMESTAMP function to retrieve the current date and time in a data type of timestamp.

Examples

The following example displays the result of a call to CURRENT_TIMESTAMP:

```
testdb=# SELECT CURRENT_TIMESTAMP AS date_and_time;
     date_and_time
----------------------
 2001-09-04 19:48:21-08
(1 row)
```

CURRENT_USER — Returns the current database username.

Synopsis

```
CURRENT_USER
```

Parameters

This function does not accept parameters.

Results

This function returns the name of the current database user.

Description

Use the CURRENT_USER function to retrieve the name of the current user in a string of type *name* (a 31 character length non-standard type used for storing system identifiers).

Examples

The following example displays the current user logged into testdb:

```
testdb=# SELECT CURRENT_USER AS myself;
 myself
--------
 jlx
(1 row)
```

DECLARE — Defines a new cursor.

Synopsis

```
DECLARE cursorname
    [ BINARY ] [ INSENSITIVE ] [ SCROLL ]
    CURSOR FOR query
    [ FOR { READ ONLY | UPDATE [ OF column [, ...] ] } ]
```

Parameters

cursorname

The name of the new cursor.

BINARY

The BINARY keyword causes the cursor to fetch data in binary format, rather than in the default text format.

INSENSITIVE

The INSENSITIVE keyword specifies that all data retrieved from the cursor will be unchanged by updates from other processes (and other cursors). This option is unneeded when using PostgreSQL, as the database already encapsulates all cursor operations within transactions. This option exists for compatibility with other database systems.

SCROLL

The SCROLL keyword allows data to be retrieved in multiple rows per FETCH operation. However, specifying it will have no effect, as PostgreSQL already allows this functionality implicitly.

query

The SQL query that will provide the new cursor with rows. For information on how to construct this query, see the reference entry titled "SELECT."

READ ONLY

The READ ONLY clause indicates that the cursor will be used only to read data (read-only mode). Using this keyword has no effect, as PostgreSQL already only provides read-only access for use with cursors.

UPDATE

The UPDATE clause specifies that the cursor will be used to update tables; however, updates from cursors are not supported as of PostgreSQL 7.1.x (the current version at the printing of this book).

column

The columns to be updated; however, cursor updates are not currently supported as of PostgreSQL 7.1.x (the current version at the printing of this book).

Results

SELECT

> The message returned when a SELECT statement executes successfully.

NOTICE: Closing pre-existing portal "*cursorname*"

> The notice returned when a cursor with the name you specified has already been declared within the current transaction block. If this happens, the previously declared cursor is automatically discarded.

ERROR: DECLARE CURSOR may only be used in begin/end transaction blocks

> The error returned if you attempt to declare a cursor outside of a transaction block. You must be within a transaction block to use cursors.

Description

Use the DECLARE command to create a cursor within a transaction block, which can then be used to retrieve data from queries. Returned data can be in either text or binary format. The use of cursors is only supported within transaction blocks. You will receive an error if you attempt to use them without starting a transaction block.

 Use binary cursors with caution, as not all clients support their use.

PostgreSQL does not require you to explicitly open a cursor; the cursor is opened when you declare it. However, the use of explicit OPEN commands is supported by the preprocessor, *ecpg*, for use with embedded or interactive SQL applications.

Example

The following example declares a cursor named cur_publisher and then uses that cursor to fetch 2 rows. Used directly within *psql*, these results are immediately displayed:

```
booktown=# BEGIN WORK;
BEGIN
booktown=# DECLARE cur_publisher CURSOR FOR SELECT name FROM publishers;
SELECT
booktown=# FETCH FORWARD 2 IN cur_publisher;
         name
---------------------------
 Kids Can Press
 Henry Holt & Company, Inc.
(2 rows)
```

DELETE — Removes rows from a table.

Synopsis

```
DELETE FROM [ ONLY ] table [ WHERE condition ]
```

Parameters

table

The name of the table from which you are deleting rows.

condition

The condition that identifies rows to be deleted. This is just like the WHERE clause of a SELECT query; refer to the reference entry titled "SELECT" for more information on constructing conditions. Note that not providing a WHERE condition will cause *all rows* to be deleted from a table.

Results

DELETE *count*

The message returned when the command is executed. The *count* is the number of rows that were removed. If that number is 0, then either no rows met the specified condition, or there were no rows in the table to be removed.

Description

Use DELETE to remove rows from a table. Only rows that match a condition you specify will be deleted. To delete all rows from a table, do not specify a condition. Issuing a DELETE with no condition results in all rows being deleted from the target table. You will then be left with an empty table.

 Use TRUNCATE to empty a table more efficiently (and explicitly) than with an unconditional DELETE statement.

Use the ONLY clause to prevent the deletion of rows from tables that inherit from the target table. ONLY restricts the delete operation to only the target table. Otherwise, the delete operation will affect not only the target table, but all tables that inherit from it.

Example

The following syntax removes all shipped orders from the shipments table that were placed by customer ID 142, and that were shipped before August 7, 2001:

```
booktown=# DELETE FROM shipments
booktown-#        WHERE customer_id = 142
booktown-#        AND ship_date < '2001-08-07';
DELETE 1
```

DROP AGGREGATE — Removes an aggregate function from a database.

Synopsis

```
DROP AGGREGATE name type
```

Parameters

name

The name of the existing aggregate function you wish to remove.

type

The data type that the existing aggregate function accepts.

Results

DROP

The message returned when an aggregate function is dropped successfully.

ERROR: RemoveAggregate: aggregate '*name*' for '*type*' does not exist

The error returned if an aggregate function with the specified name and type does not exist.

Description

Use the DROP AGGREGATE command to remove an aggregate function definition from your database. As with other DROP commands, you must be the owner of the object that you are dropping.

Examples

The following example removes the sum aggregate for type text:

```
booktown=# DROP AGGREGATE sum text;
DROP
```

DROP DATABASE — Removes a database from the system.

Synopsis

```
DROP DATABASE name
```

Parameters

name

The name of the database you wish to remove.

Results

DROP DATABASE

The message returned when a database is dropped correctly.

ERROR: user 'username' is not allowed to create/drop databases

The error returned if you attempt to drop a database with a PostgreSQL user that does not have superuser privileges. You must have a user that was created with the CREATEDB privilege to drop databases. See the reference entry titled "CREATE USER" for more about this.

ERROR: dropdb: cannot be executed on the template database

The error returned if you attempt to drop the template1 database. This database cannot be dropped; it is a system database.

ERROR: dropdb: cannot be executed on an open database

The error returned if you attempt to drop a database to which you are currently connected. If you get this error, try connecting to the template1 database and then issuing the command to drop the database on which you were previously working.

ERROR: dropdb: database 'name' does not exist

The error returned if the database you are trying to delete does not exist.

ERROR: dropdb: database 'name' is not owned by you

The error returned if you attempt to delete a database that you do not own.

ERROR: dropdb: May not be called in a transaction block

The error returned if you attempt to issue the DROP DATABASE command from within a transaction block. You must finish any current transaction before dropping a database.

NOTICE: The database directory 'directory' could not be removed

The notice message displayed if the dropped database's data *directory* could not be removed. You will have to delete the data directory manually in order to complete the drop.

Description

Use the DROP DATABASE command to remove a database from the system. All data and catalog entries for the database are deleted when you drop a database. Attempting to use this command on a database you are currently connected to will result in an error; for this reason it may be more convenient to use the *dropdb* shell script.

Only the owner, or a superuser, may drop a database.

Examples

The following example permanently removes the `testdb` database:

```
template1=# DROP DATABASE testdb;
DROP
```

DROP FUNCTION — Removes a user-defined function.

Synopsis

```
DROP FUNCTION name ( [ type [, ...] ] )
```

Parameters

name

> The name of the existing function you wish to drop.

type

> Zero or more data types consisting of the function's arguments. The types combine with the name to uniquely identify the function.

Results

DROP

> The message returned when a function is successfully dropped.

ERROR: RemoveFunction: Function '*name*(*types*)' does not exist

> The error returned if the function *name* for the specified *types* does not exist in the current database.

Description

Use this command to remove C function references that are defined in a database. Specifying the parameter types that the function takes allows proper identification; this is necessary when dealing with the C language, as functions exist with the same name that only differ in the types of arguments they take.

 DROP FUNCTION does not check if any database elements rely on the function, or if removing it would cause any negative effects. You must check these things on your own.

Example

The following example removes the `title(integer)` function from the `booktown` database:

```
booktown=# DROP FUNCTION title(integer);
DROP
```

DROP GROUP — Removes a user group from the database.

Synopsis

```
DROP GROUP name
```

Parameters

name

> The name of group you wish to drop.

Results

DROP GROUP

> The message returned when a group is successfully removed.

Description

Use DROP GROUP to remove a group from the database in which you are working. This command is independent of the DROP USER command; as such, any users within the group that you drop will not be removed from the database.

Example

The following example drops the sales group:

```
booktown=# DROP GROUP sales;
DROP GROUP
```

DROP INDEX — Removes an index from a database.

Synopsis

```
DROP INDEX index_name [, ...]
```

Parameters

index_name

> The name of the index you wish to remove from the database.

Results

DROP

> The message returned if the index is removed successfully.

ERROR: index "*index_name*" does not exist

> The error returned if the specified index cannot be found within the database.

Description

The owner of an index may remove it from the database by using this command.

Example

The following example drops an index called `customer_id_idx` from the `booktown` database:

```
booktown=# DROP INDEX customer_id_idx;
DROP
```

The next example drops two indices simultaneously from the `booktown` database:

```
booktown=# DROP INDEX books_id_pkey, books_title_idx;
DROP
```

DROP LANGUAGE — Removes a procedural language from a database.

Synopsis

```
DROP [ PROCEDURAL ] LANGUAGE 'name'
```

Parameters

name

The name of the existing language you wish to remove from the database.

Results

DROP

The message returned if the language is successfully removed without error.

ERROR: Language "*name*" doesn't exist

The error returned if the language you specify does not exist within the database.

Description

Use the DROP PROCEDURAL LANGUAGE command to remove the definition of the procedural language named *name*.

 DROP LANGUAGE does not check to make sure that functions and triggers you have registered for use with this language have been removed. Be sure that no existing functions in your database rely on a language before dropping it.

Example

The following example removes the `plexample` language from the `booktown` database:

```
booktown=# DROP PROCEDURAL LANGUAGE 'plexample';
DROP
```

DROP OPERATOR — Removes an operator from the database.

Synopsis

```
DROP OPERATOR op
     ( { lefttype | NONE } ,
       { righttype | NONE } )
```

Parameters

op   The operator you wish to remove.

lefttype | NONE

The operator's left argument type (or NONE, if it does not have a left argument).

righttype | NONE

The operator's right argument type (or NONE, if it does not have a right argument).

Results

DROP

The message returned when a user is dropped successfully.

ERROR: RemoveOperator: binary operator '*op*' taking '*lefttype*' and '*right-type*' does not exist

The error returned if you specify a binary operator that does not exist.

ERROR: RemoveOperator: left unary operator '*op*' taking '*lefttype*' does not exist

The error returned if you specify a left unary operator that does not exist.

ERROR: RemoveOperator: right unary operator '*op*' taking '*righttype*' does not exist

The error returned if you specify a right unary operator that does not exist.

Description

Use the DROP OPERATOR command to remove an existing operator from the database. You can only drop an operator if you are the operator's owner or a superuser.

Removing an operator when there are access methods or operator classes that rely on it can cause problems; be sure you know what elements of your database rely on an operator before dropping it.

Example

The following example drops the binary `!#` operator for the `integer` data types:

```
booktown=# DROP OPERATOR !# (integer, integer);
DROP
```

DROP RULE — Removes a rule from a database.

Synopsis

```
DROP RULE name [, ...]
```

Parameters

name

> The name of an existing rule to drop. You may drop multiple rules by specify-ing their names in a comma-delimited list.

Results

DROP

> The message returned when a rule is dropped successfully.

ERROR: Rule or view "*name*" not found

> The error returned if the specified rule *name* does not exist.

Description

Use the DROP RULE command to remove a rule from a PostgreSQL database. When a rule is dropped, the change is effective immediately. A rule becomes unavailable as soon as it is dropped, and its definition is completely removed from the database system.

Example

The following example drops the `sync_stock_with_editions` rule:

```
booktown=# DROP RULE sync_stock_with_editions;
DROP
```

DROP SEQUENCE — Removes a sequence from a database.

Synopsis

```
DROP SEQUENCE name [, ...]
```

Parameters

name

The name of the sequence you wish to permanently remove. You may drop multiple sequences by specifying their names in a comma-delimited list.

Results

DROP

The message returned when a sequence is successfully dropped.

ERROR: sequence "*name*" does not exist

The error returned if the specified sequence *name* does not exist.

Description

Use the DROP SEQUENCE command to remove a sequence number generator from a database.

Example

The following example removes a sequence named shipments_ship_id_seq from the database:

```
booktown=# DROP SEQUENCE shipments_ship_id_seq;
DROP
```

DROP TABLE — Removes a table from a database.

Synopsis

```
DROP TABLE name [, ...]
```

Parameters

name

The name of an existing table you intend to drop. You may drop multiple tables by specifying their names in a comma-delimited list.

Results

DROP

The message returned when a table is dropped successfully.

ERROR: table "*name*" does not exist!

The error returned if the specified table or view *name* does not exist in the database.

Description

DROP TABLE removes tables from the database. You must be the owner of the table, or a superuser, in order to drop it.

 To empty a table (as opposed to completely deleting it), use either the TRUNCATE or DELETE command.

Deleting a table also destroys any indices that were placed on that table.

Example

The following command permanently removes the employees table from the book-town database:

```
booktown=# DROP TABLE employees;
DROP
```

DROP TRIGGER — Removes a trigger definition from a database.

Synopsis

```
DROP TRIGGER name ON table
```

Parameters

name

    The name of the trigger you wish to remove.

table

    The name of the table the trigger is on.

Results

DROP

    The message returned when a trigger is successfully dropped.

ERROR: DropTrigger: there is no trigger name on relation table

    The error returned if the trigger name does not exist on table.

Description

Use the DROP TRIGGER command to remove a trigger from the database. All references to the trigger are removed when you issue this command. You must be the owner of trigger in order to drop it.

Examples

The following command removes the sync_authors_books trigger from the authors table, in the booktown database:

```
booktown=# DROP TRIGGER sync_authors_books ON authors;
DROP
```

DROP TYPE — Removes a type from the system catalogs.

Synopsis

```
DROP TYPE typename [, ...]
```

Parameters

typename

> The name of a type you wish to remove. You may drop multiple types by specifying their names in a comma-delimited list.

Results

DROP

> The message returned when a type is dropped successfully.

ERROR: RemoveType: type '*typename*' does not exist

> The error displayed if the type *typename* is not found in the connected database.

Description

Use the DROP TYPE command to remove a type from the database system. Only the owner of a type, or a superuser, is allowed to do this.

If you are logged in as a superuser, you *will* be able to drop system types. However, doing so can cause extreme instability. Be careful!

The DROP TYPE command will not automatically remove any objects that reference the data type, or types, that you are dropping. Once a data type is removed, anything that uses it will most likely stop working. Be sure to remove objects that depend on types that you drop, and be sure not to drop types used by objects you wish to keep.

Examples

The following command removes the zero data type from the booktown database:

```
booktown=# DROP TYPE zero;
DROP
```

DROP USER — Removes a PostgreSQL user.

Synopsis

```
DROP USER name
```

Parameters

name

The username of the PostgreSQL user you wish to remove.

Results

DROP USER

The message returned when a PostgreSQL user is successfully removed.

ERROR: DROP USER: user "name" does not exist

The error returned if the specified PostgreSQL user cannot be found on the connected host.

ERROR: DROP USER: user "name" owns database "database", cannot be removed

The error returned if a database called database still exists when you attempt to drop the name user. Any owned databases must first be removed.

Description

Use the DROP USER command to remove a user from a database. You are not allowed to remove a user that owns a database. All database objects the user owned will continue to exist within the database.

To run this command from the command prompt, use *dropuser*, which is a wrapper application to the same SQL command (see Chapter 10 for more about this command).

Example

The following example permanently drops the PostgreSQL user named jonathan from the system:

```
template1=# DROP USER jonathan;
DROP
```

DROP VIEW — Removes an existing view from a database.

Synopsis

```
DROP VIEW name [, ...]
```

Parameters

name

The name of the view you wish to remove.

Results

DROP

The message returned when a view is successfully dropped.

ERROR: view "name" does not exist

The error returned if the view *name* does not exist in the current database.

Description

Use the DROP VIEW command to remove a view from a database. As with most objects, you must be the owner a view to remove it.

Example

The following example removes the h_publishers view from the booktown database:

```
booktown=# DROP VIEW h_publishers;
DROP
```

END — Ends the current transaction block and finalizes its modifications.

Synopsis

```
END [ WORK | TRANSACTION ]
```

Parameters

WORK | TRANSACTION

A pair of optional noise keywords. They can be ignored, or used to make your SQL more readable.

Results

COMMIT

The message returned when a transaction is successfully committed.

NOTICE: COMMIT: no transaction in progress

The notice returned if there is no transaction in progress for the END command to end.

Description

The END command is a synonym for COMMIT. Use it to end transactions the same way you would use the COMMIT command.

Example

The following example demonstrates how to commit a transaction using the END command:

```
booktown=# END WORK;
COMMIT
```

EXPLAIN — Shows the statement execution plan for a supplied query.

Synopsis

```
EXPLAIN [ VERBOSE ] query
```

Parameters

VERBOSE

> The optional verbose output keyword, which results in extra information being returned about a query plan.

query

> The query you intend to have explained.

Results

NOTICE: QUERY PLAN: plan

> The notice which will be followed by an explicit query plan sent from the backend.

EXPLAIN

> The message returned below the query plan, signifying that execution of the command is complete.

Description

Use the EXPLAIN command to view the execution plan for a query, generated by PostgreSQL's *planner* component. The planner component is the part of PostgreSQL that attempts to determine the most efficient manner in which to execute a SQL query. The execution plan details how tables referenced within your query will be scanned by the database server. Depending on the circumstances, tables might be scanned sequentially, or through the use of an index. The plan will list output for each table involved in the execution plan.

The EXPLAIN command is useful for determining the relative *cost* of query execution plans. This cost is measured literally in disk page fetches. The more pages needed, the longer it takes a query to run.

PostgreSQL does not attempt to equate this number of fetches into a meaningful unit of time, as this will vary widely from machine to machine based on the hardware requirements and load of the operating system. The cost of a query execution plan is therefore only meaningful to the relative cost of an alternative query.

Two numbers are associated with the cost, separated by two periods. The first number is the estimated cost of startup (the time spent before the first tuple can be returned). The second number is the estimated *total* cost that the query will incur to completely execute.

If you pass the VERBOSE keyword, EXPLAIN will display the internal representation of the plan tree. This is fairly indecipherable to the average user, and should only be used by developers familiar with the internal workings of PostgreSQL.

Example

The following example shows the results received when executing EXPLAIN for a query on the books table, in the booktown database:

```
booktown=# EXPLAIN SELECT * FROM books AS b (book_id)
booktown=#            NATURAL INNER JOIN editions;
NOTICE:  QUERY PLAN:

Merge Join  (cost=71.27..83.96 rows=150 width=64)
  -> Sort  (cost=1.44..1.44 rows=15 width=24)
       -> Seq Scan on books b  (cost=0.00..1.15 rows=15 width=24)
  -> Sort  (cost=69.83..69.83 rows=1000 width=40)
       -> Seq Scan on editions  (cost=0.00..20.00 rows=1000 width=40)

EXPLAIN
```

The next example shows a verbose explanation of a simpler query, with the VERBOSE keyword:

```
booktown=# EXPLAIN VERBOSE SELECT * FROM books;
NOTICE:  QUERY DUMP:

{ SEQSCAN :startup_cost 0.00 :total_cost 1.15 :rows 15 :width 24 :qptargetlist
({ TARGETENTRY :resdom { RESDOM :resno 1 :restype 23 :restypmod -1 :resname id
:reskey 0 :reskeyop 0 :ressortgroupref 0 :resjunk false } :expr { VAR :varno 1
:varattno 1 :vartype 23 :vartypmod -1  :varlevelsup 0 :varnoold 1 :varoattno 1}}
{ TARGETENTRY :resdom { RESDOM :resno 2 :restype 25 :restypmod -1 :resname title
:reskey 0 :reskeyop 0 :ressortgroupref 0 :resjunk false } :expr { VAR :varno 1
:varattno 2 :vartype 25 :vartypmod -1  :varlevelsup 0 :varnoold 1 :varoattno 2}}
{ TARGETENTRY :resdom { RESDOM :resno 3 :restype 23 :restypmod -1 :resname
author_id :reskey 0 :reskeyop 0 :ressortgroupref 0 :resjunk false } :expr
{ VAR :varno 1 :varattno 3 :vartype 23 :vartypmod -1  :varlevelsup 0 :varnoold
1 :varoattno 3}} { TARGETENTRY :resdom { RESDOM :resno 4 :restype 23 :restypmod
-1 :resname subject_id :reskey 0 :reskeyop 0 :ressortgroupref 0 :resjunk false }
:expr { VAR :varno 1 :varattno 4 :vartype 23 :vartypmod -1  :varlevelsup 0
:varnoold 1 :varoattno 4}}) :qpqual <> :lefttree <> :righttree <> :extprm ()
:locprm () :initplan <> :nprm 0  :scanrelid 1 }
```

NOTICE: QUERY PLAN:

Seq Scan on books   (cost=0.00..1.15 rows=15 width=24)

EXPLAIN

FETCH — Retrieves rows from a cursor.

Synopsis

```
FETCH direction
      [ count ] { IN | FROM } cursor

direction ::= { FORWARD | BACKWARD | RELATIVE }
count ::= { numrows | ALL | NEXT | PRIOR }
```

Parameters

direction

Use the optional *direction* parameter to specify the direction you want to fetch. It may be specified as any of the following keywords:

FORWARD

The keyword used to retrieve rows following the current position. This is the default, if the *direction* is not explicitly set.

BACKWARD

The keyword used to retrieve rows preceding the current position.

RELATIVE

A noise term made available for SQL92 compatibility. As of PostgreSQL 7.1.x, all cursors locate rows relative to the current cursor position, and this keyword therefore has no effect. Note that combining the RELATIVE keyword with a count of 0 will produce an error (see the "Results" section later in this reference entry).

count

This parameter takes the number of rows you wish to fetch. You can specify an integer constant here to have a specific number of rows fetched (*numrows*), or use any of the following keywords:

ALL

The keyword used to retrieve all rows.

NEXT

The keyword used to retrieve the row immediately following the current position.

PRIOR

> The keyword used to retrieve the row immediately preceding the current position.

cursor

> The name of an open cursor you wish to use for the FETCH.

Results

A successful FETCH command returns any query results generated by the specified cursor. If the query fails, one of the following messages will be displayed:

NOTICE: PerformPortalFetch: portal "*cursor*" not found

> The notice returned if the specified cursor has not yet been declared. Remember that you must declare a cursor within a transaction block before it can be used.

NOTICE: FETCH/ABSOLUTE not supported, using RELATIVE

> The notice returned if you attempt to use absolute positioning with the ABSOLUTE keyword in place of the RELATIVE keyword. PostgreSQL does not currently support absolute positioning of cursors (which would move a cursor to a specific row offset in a result set, rather than a row relative to the current cursor position).

ERROR: FETCH/RELATIVE at current position is not supported

> The error returned if you attempt to pass 0 as the number of rows to fetch, with the RELATIVE direction specified. This happens because the FETCH RELATIVE 0 FROM cursor syntax is defined within SQL92 as allowing a user to continually retrieve the row which is at the cursor's current position.
>
> PostgreSQL does not support the use of this syntax; used without the RELATIVE keyword, instead of returning the current position's row, the use of 0 indicates to the database that you wish to retrieve *all* rows. Used with the RELATIVE keyword, however, PostgreSQL assumes you are instead trying to use the SQL92 defined functionality and displays this error instead of fetching all rows.

Description

Use the FETCH command to retrieve a specified number of rows using a cursor. You always need to be within a transaction while using cursors, as the data they store is not independent of other users within the system. The number of rows you specify can be either positive or negative. A positive number will fetch from whatever direction you specify with the direction parameter (if you don't specify a direction, FORWARD will be used by default).

A negative number will take you in the opposite direction as that specified by the *direction* parameter. For example, specifying FORWARD –5 has the same effect as specifying BACKWARD 5. If the number of rows you specify is greater than the number of rows remaining to be retrieved, the FETCH command will return all those remaining.

 As of PostgreSQL 7.1.x, you cannot update data using a cursor.

Examples

The following examples assume a transaction and an already-defined cursor (named cur_employee) that returns rows from the employees table.

The following example fetches the first two rows in the cur_employee cursor:

```
booktown=# BEGIN;
BEGIN
booktown=# DECLARE cur_employee CURSOR FOR
booktown-#            SELECT first_name, last_name FROM employees;
SELECT
booktown=# FETCH FORWARD 2 IN cur_employee;
 first_name | last_name
------------+-----------
 Vincent    | Appel
 Michael    | Holloway
(2 rows)
```

The following example uses BACKWARD -2 (a double negative) to then fetch two rows in the forward direction:

```
booktown=# FETCH BACKWARD -2 IN cur_employee;
 first_name | last_name
------------+-----------
 David      | Joble
 Ben        | Noble
(2 rows)
```

The next example demonstrates how to actually fetch backwards in the cur_employee cursor:

```
booktown=# FETCH BACKWARD 3 IN cur_employee;
 first_name | last_name
------------+-----------
 David      | Joble
 Michael    | Holloway
 Vincent    | Appel
(3 rows)
```

GRANT — Grants access privileges to a user, a group, or to all users in the database.

Synopsis

```
GRANT privilege [, ...] ON object [, ...]
     TO { PUBLIC | GROUP group | username }
```

Parameters

privilege

The privilege you wish to grant. Valid privileges are:

SELECT

The privilege allowing the specified user or group to access all columns in a specific table or view.

INSERT

The privilege allowing the specified user or group to insert data into all columns of a specified table.

UPDATE

The privilege allowing the specified user or group to update all columns of a specified table.

DELETE

The privilege allowing the specified user or group to delete rows from a specific table.

RULE

The privilege allowing the specified user or group to delete rules from a specified table or rule.

ALL

A shorthand way to grant all of the previous privileges to the specified user or group.

object

The name of the object upon which you are granting privileges. Valid object types are tables, views, and sequences.

PUBLIC

The optional PUBLIC keyword indicates that privilege be granted to all users of the database.

group

The name of a group to receive the privileges that you are granting.

username

The name of a PostgreSQL user to receive the privileges that you are granting. You can use PUBLIC here to represent all users.

Results

CHANGE

The message returned when a target is successfully granted the specified privileges.

ERROR: ChangeAcl: class "*object*" not found

The error returned if *object* is not found in the connected database.

ERROR: aclparse: non-existent user "*user*"

The error returned if *user* does not exist.

ERROR: non-existent group "*group*"

The error returned if *group* does not exist.

Description

Use the GRANT command to set user and group permissions for objects you own. You can set permissions for specific users and groups, or you can set permissions for PUBLIC, which represents all users in the database. By default, no one but the object owner has access permissions to an object. Object permissions must be granted by an object's owner after an object is created.

To grant privileges to a only part of a table, create a view that constrains the result set to the columns or rows you wish to grant access to. To allow users access to those columns and rows, allow them access to the view.

Use *psql*'s backslash-z (\z) command to display permission information for existing objects.

Example

The following example grants all privileges on the publishers table to the user manager:

```
booktown=# GRANT ALL ON publishers TO manager;
GRANT
```

The next example shows how to use the \z *psql* command to view access privileges on the publishers table:

```
booktown=# \z publishers
Access permissions for database "booktown"
  Relation  |   Access permissions
------------+----------------------
 publishers | {"=","manager=arwR"}
(1 row)
```

INSERT — Inserts new rows into a table.

Synopsis

```
INSERT INTO table [ ( column [, ...] ) ]
              { DEFAULT VALUES |
                VALUES ( value [, ...] ) |
                query }
```

Parameters

table

The table into which you are inserting data.

column

A column for which a value will be specified. The name must match a column in the *table*, though these columns need not be listed in their literal order within the table.

value

A constant or expression to insert into a column within *table*. This value is associated with the corresponding column in the column list if a column list was specified (columns in the column list correspond in a one-to-one fashion with expressions in the value list). If the expression for each column is not of the correct data type, automatic type coercion will be attempted. If this fails, the INSERT will fail completely.

query

A valid SQL SELECT statement. The number of columns returned by the query must match the number of columns you are inserting, as well as be of a compatible data type.

Results

INSERT *oid 1*

The message returned if one row of data is inserted correctly. The *oid* is the object identifier of the newly inserted row.

INSERT *0 #*

The message returned if more than one row is inserted. The # symbol represents how many rows were updated in total.

Description

Use the INSERT command to add new rows into a table. This can be done either one row at a time, or in sets. Used with the VALUES keyword, an INSERT statement can only insert one row of data. To insert multiple rows, you can instead supply a query. Results from the query are then fed into the INSERT command's target table.

If an incorrect data type is provided for a field on insertion, PostgreSQL will attempt to automatically coerce it into the appropriate type. If it cannot, the INSERT will fail.

When inserting values into columns (instead of whole rows), the columns can be listed in any order; however, the values for those columns will need to be listed in the same order.

 If you leave out values for any fields in your table, the database will automatically do one of two things. Fields for which you have not specified a default value will be set to NULL. Fields for which you *have* specified a default value will be set to their defaults.

Examples

The following example inserts a single row into the employees table:

```
booktown=# INSERT INTO employees
booktown-#            VALUES (106, 'Hall', 'Timothy');
INSERT 3752064 1
```

Alternatively, you can insert only an ID number and last name, and not a first name, by specifying a target column list preceding the VALUES clause. This results in a NULL value for the first_name column in the new row:

```
booktown=# INSERT INTO employees (id, last_name)
booktown-#            VALUES (108, 'Williams');
INSERT 3752065 1
```

The next example inserts all 15 rows from the books table into the book_backup table by providing a query from which to insert data:

```
booktown=# INSERT INTO book_backup
booktown-#            SELECT * FROM books;
INSERT 0 15
```

LISTEN — Listen for a notification event.

Synopsis

```
LISTEN name
```

Parameters

name

The name of the notify condition for which you want the backend to listen.

Results

LISTEN

> The message returned when a command is successful, and the backend process is listening for notification.

NOTICE: Async_Listen: We are already listening on *name*

> The notice returned if the backend is already listening for the specified notify condition *name*.

Description

The NOTIFY and LISTEN commands work together to create a system for PostgreSQL components to communicate between themselves. Use the LISTEN command to start the backend process listening for a notification named *name*. Notifications are passed by the NOTIFY command, which is usually placed in rules related to changes of various database components; in this way, notifications are sent out to listeners when things are changed.

All running backend processes that are listening for a specific notification are sent that notification when a NOTIFY command is issued for it by any of the processes. When a backend process receives a notification, that notification is sent to the client application (such as *psql*), which then handles the notification in whatever manner it is written for. For more information about this method of IPC (inter-process communication), see the reference entry titled "NOTIFY."

You can use any valid string no longer than 31 characters for the name of the notification to listen for (this is also true for the NOTIFY command). To stop a backend process from listening for notifications, use the UNLISTEN command.

Example

The following example configures and executes a listen/notify sequence from *psql*:

```
booktown=# LISTEN publisher_update;
LISTEN
booktown=# NOTIFY publisher_update;
Asynchronous NOTIFY 'publisher_update' from backend with pid '16864' received.
```

LOAD — Dynamically loads object files into a database.

Synopsis

```
LOAD 'filename'
```

Parameters

filename

The name of the dynamic object file you wish to load.

Results

LOAD

The message returned when a dynamic object file was successfully loaded.

ERROR: LOAD: could not open file '*filename*'

The error returned if the specified file was not found. Make sure the PostgreSQL backend is permitted to access the file.

Description

Use the LOAD command to load an object file into the PostgreSQL backend. Once loaded, an object file provides the backend the required functionality for which the file was created. In this way, you can incorporate your own database components (such as types and functions) dynamically. If you do not explicitly load an object file, the backend will load it automatically when a function from the file is called. Currently, only C language object files are supported.

 You can also use this command to force the reloading of recently recompiled object files.

Example

The following example loads the object file */usr/local/src/lxp/libxpl.so* in the lx database:

```
lx=# LOAD '/usr/local/src/lxp/libxpl.so';
LOAD
```

LOCK — Locks a table within a transaction.

Synopsis

```
LOCK [ TABLE ] name
LOCK [ TABLE ] name IN lock_mode

lock_mode ::= { [ ROW | ACCESS ] { SHARE | EXCLUSIVE } |
               SHARE ROW EXCLUSIVE } MODE
```

Parameters

name

The name of the table you intend to lock.

lock_mode

There are seven valid lock modes that may be combined from the available keywords. Here they are, in order from least restrictive to most restrictive, along with the commands and modes they block:

ACCESS SHARE MODE

The ACCESS SHARE MODE lock is acquired automatically by a SELECT statement on the table or tables it retrieves from. This mode blocks ALTER TABLE, DROP TABLE, and VACUUM commands on the table on which it is placed.

This mode also blocks concurrent ACCESS EXCLUSIVE MODE locks from being acquired on the same table.

ROW SHARE MODE

The ROW SHARE MODE lock is acquired automatically by a SELECT statement that has a FOR UPDATE clause. It blocks ALTER TABLE, DROP TABLE, and VACUUM commands on the table on which it is acquired.

This mode also blocks concurrent EXCLUSIVE MODE and ACCESS EXCLUSIVE MODE locks from being acquired on the same table.

ROW EXCLUSIVE MODE

The ROW EXCLUSIVE MODE lock is acquired automatically by an UPDATE, INSERT, or DELETE command. This mode blocks ALTER TABLE, DROP TABLE, VACUUM, and CREATE INDEX commands.

This mode also blocks concurrent SHARE MODE, SHARE ROW EXCLUSIVE MODE, EXCLUSIVE MODE, and ACCESS EXCLUSIVE MODE locks from being acquired on the same table.

SHARE MODE

The SHARE MODE lock is acquired automatically by a CREATE INDEX command. It blocks INSERT, UPDATE, DELETE, ALTER TABLE, DROP TABLE, and VACUUM commands.

This mode also blocks concurrent ROW EXCLUSIVE MODE, SHARE ROW EXCLUSIVE MODE, EXCLUSIVE MODE, and ACCESS EXCLUSIVE MODE locks from being acquired on the same table.

SHARE ROW EXCLUSIVE MODE

The SHARE ROW EXCLUSIVE MODE lock is a special lock mode nearly identical to the EXCLUSIVE MODE lock, but which allows concurrent ROW SHARE MODE locks to be acquired.

EXCLUSIVE MODE

The EXCLUSIVE MODE lock blocks INSERT, UPDATE, DELETE, CREATE INDEX, ALTER TABLE, DROP TABLE, and VACUUM commands on the table on which it is acquired, as well as SELECT commands with a FOR UPDATE clause.

This mode also blocks concurrent ROW SHARE MODE, ROW EXCLUSIVE MODE, SHARE MODE, SHARE ROW EXCLUSIVE MODE, EXCLUSIVE MODE, and ACCESS EXCLUSIVE MODE locks.

ACCESS EXCLUSIVE MODE

The ACCESS EXCLUSIVE MODE lock is acquired automatically by a ALTER TABLE, DROP TABLE, or VACUUM command on the table it modifies.

This mode blocks *any* concurrent command or other *lock_mode* from being acquired on the locked table.

Results

LOCK TABLE

The message returned when a lock is successfully applied to a table.

ERROR: Relation '*name*' does not exist

The error returned if the table *name* does not exist in the connected database.

ERROR: Deadlock detected

The error returned if two LOCK TABLE commands result in a deadlock between two concurrent transactions.

Description

Use the LOCK TABLE command to manually *lock* tables during a transaction. Locking is a function of an RDBMS that temporarily blocks various kinds of access to a table (depending on the *lock_mode*). The session that locks the table retains normal access; the effect is only felt by concurrently connected users attempting to access the locked table.

Note that, in this context, *blocking* access is not the same as *denying* access. Any concurrently connected user attempting access which is blocked by a SQL lock will pause, but not fail, and wait until either the blocked command is terminated by the user, or until the table lock is released.

Several SQL commands implicitly acquire locks before they perform their work; in these cases, PostgreSQL will always choose the least restrictive lock necessary. A table lock immediately releases when a transaction is committed.

Using LOCK TABLE without an explicit locking mode causes the most restrictive mode (ACCESS EXCLUSIVE) to be used. You can specify less restrictive locking procedures by providing an explicit *lock_mode*.

You can only lock tables when working within a transaction. Using LOCK TABLE outside of a transaction will not display an error, but it will immediately autocommit, and release the lock, which serves no purpose. Use the BEGIN command to start a transaction, and the COMMIT command to commit your changes, and release the lock.

Deadlocks can occur when two transactions are waiting for each other to finish their operations. While PostgreSQL can detect them and end them with a ROLL-BACK, deadlocks can still be inconvenient. To prevent your applications from running into this problem, make sure to design them in such a way that they will lock objects in the same order.

Examples

The following example locks the books table within the booktown database in ACCESS EXCLUSIVE mode:

```
booktown=# BEGIN;
BEGIN
booktown=# LOCK TABLE books IN ACCESS EXCLUSIVE MODE;
LOCK TABLE
```

MOVE — Repositions a cursor to another row.

Synopsis

```
MOVE [ direction ] [ count ]
     { IN | FROM } cursor
```

Parameters

direction

The direction you wish to move the specified cursor. See the reference entry titled "FETCH" or more information about the different usable directions.

count

The number of rows you wish to move the cursor.

cursor

The cursor that you are moving.

Results

The MOVE command will return the same errors and messages as the FETCH command; however, it will not return rows. See the reference entry titled "FETCH" for more information on what messages you may encounter.

Description

Use the MOVE command to reposition a cursor. This command operates essentially the same as the FETCH command. However, unlike FETCH, it does not use the cursor to return the traversed rows after it is repositioned.

Examples

The following examples assume a transaction and an already defined cursor (cur_employee) that uses the employees table for data. Using the MOVE command, this example moves the cursor one row forward in the result set:

```
booktown=# MOVE FORWARD 1 IN cur_employee;
MOVE
```

The only output returned by using this command is the message MOVE. The next example uses the FETCH command to display the second row of the cursor, after moving:

```
booktown=# FETCH 1 IN cur_employee;
 first_name | last_name
------------+-----------
 Michael    | Holloway
(1 row)
```

NOTIFY — Signals all backends that are listening for the specified notify event.

Synopsis

```
NOTIFY name
```

Parameters

name

The condition to be signaled.

Results

NOTIFY

The message returned when a notification is sent out correctly.

Description

The NOTIFY command is the counterpart of the LISTEN command, which we covered earlier in this chapter. The two commands provide a simple interprocess communication (IPC) implementation that can often prove useful if used correctly.

Use NOTIFY to send out a notification with the specified name; if any frontends have issued a LISTEN command with the same notification name, they will be informed of the notification.

The behavior of a frontend process after receiving a notification sent by the NOTIFY command is dependent upon its implementation of the feature, so it may not respond immediately (or at all).

A notification is comprised of the notification's name and the issuing backend's process ID (PID). The original designer of the database specifies what notify condition names exist and how they function within the database.

The NOTIFY and LISTEN commands are most often used to provide a way to notify frontend processes that tables have been modified; as such, notification names are often set to the names of tables. This is the *common* use of this feature, but it is not required that notification names be table names.

Automatic notification of table modifications can be achieved by placing the NOTIFY command in a rule that gets triggered by table updates.

Transactions

It is important to note how NOTIFY behaves when used with transactions. Most importantly, any NOTIFY commands executed within a transaction will not be delivered until after the transaction is committed. This behavior prevents notifications from being sent out from aborted transactions.

Also important is that a backend will not deliver a notification to its connected frontend if a transaction is in progress. If a frontend process is currently within a transaction, the backend will wait to send a notification until that transaction has been terminated with either a COMMIT or ROLLBACK.

Multiple signals

The NOTIFY/LISTEN system works in a way that is very similar to that of Unix signals. Even if the same notification is signaled multiple times using multiple NOTIFY commands, that notification may only be sent to listening processes *once*, instead of however many times it was signaled.

Because of this design feature, you cannot use the number of received notifications as a counter or to track anything important within your database. The correct way to achieve tracking or counting would be to use NOTIFY with a sequence object (or something similar) to wake applications and track or count actions and events.

Example

The following example defines a notify event to listen for, and then notifies the backend process that the event was reached:

```
booktown=# LISTEN publisher_deletion;
LISTEN
booktown=# NOTIFY publisher_deletion;
Asynchronous NOTIFY 'publisher_deletion' from backend with pid '16864' received.
```

REINDEX — Rebuilds indices on tables.

Synopsis

```
REINDEX { TABLE | DATABASE | INDEX } name [ FORCE ]
```

Parameters

TABLE | DATABASE | INDEX

   The type of database object to be re-indexed.

name

   The name of the database object you wish to re-index.

FORCE

   The FORCE keyword forces the rebuilding of all specified indices. If this parameter is not given, the REINDEX command will rebuild only invalidated indices.

Results

REINDEX

   The message returned when a target object is successfully reindexed.

Description

Use the REINDEX command to rebuild any indices that have become corrupt. This is especially useful if system indices become corrupted. To fix them, shutdown *postmaster* and start it using the *-o "-O -P"* command-line parameter. This opens a standalone server that allows for re-indexing of system indices. Run the REINDEX DATABASE command once you are at the *psql* prompt.

Examples

The following example rebuilds all indices on the books table, within the booktown database:

```
booktown=# REINDEX TABLE books;
REINDEX
```

RESET — Restores runtime variables to their default settings.

Synopsis

```
RESET variable
```

Parameters

variable

> A runtime variable that you wish to reset to its default value. See the reference entry titled "SET" for more information on available variables.

Results

RESET VARIABLE

> The message returned when a specified variable is reset to its default value.

Description

Use the RESET command to return runtime variables to their original values. For more information about values allowed for these variables, and what the original values were, refer to the reference entry titled "SET."

You can also issue the following command to accomplish the same effect:

```
SET variable TO DEFAULT
```

Example

The following example resets a variable called SEED to its default value:

```
testdb=# RESET SEED;
RESET VARIABLE
```

REVOKE — Revokes access privileges from a user, a group, or all users.

Synopsis

```
REVOKE privilege [, ...]
    ON object [, ...]
    FROM { PUBLIC | GROUP groupname | username }
```

Parameters

privilege

> A privilege to revoke. Specify SELECT, INSERT, UPDATE, or DELETE to revoke the privilege to use the corresponding command. Use RULE to revoke the privilege to create rules on a table. Use ALL to remove all privileges on a table or other object.

object

> The name of the object from which you wish to revoke privileges. This object can be a table, view, or sequence.

group

The name of a group from which to revoke privileges.

user

The name of a PostgreSQL user from which to revoke privileges.

PUBLIC

The keyword that revokes specified privileges from all PostgreSQL users.

Results

CHANGE

The message returned when privileges are successfully revoked.

ERROR: Relation '*object*' does not exist

The error returned if *object* does not exist in the connected database.

ERROR: aclparse: non-existent user "*user*"

The error returned if *user* does not exist.

ERROR: non-existent group "*group*"

The error returned if *group* does not exist.

Description

Use REVOKE to remove privileges to an object of which you are the owner. You can revoke privileges from a specific user, from a group, or from all users (by specifying the PUBLIC keyword).

Example

The following example revokes INSERT privileges on the books table from a user guest:

```
booktown=# REVOKE INSERT ON guest FROM books;
CHANGE
```

ROLLBACK — Aborts the current transaction block and abandons any modifications it would have made.

Synopsis

```
ROLLBACK [ WORK | TRANSACTION ]
```

Parameters

WORK | TRANSACTION

A pair of optional noise keywords. They can be ignored, or used to make your SQL more readable.

Results

`ABORT`

The message returned when a transaction is aborted successfully.

`NOTICE: ROLLBACK: no transaction in progress`

The notice returned if there is not a transaction in progress to rollback.

Description

Use `ROLLBACK` to abort a transaction in progress and discard all changes either already made or queued to be made on `COMMIT`.

Example

The following example demonstrates how to rollback an accidental delete performed within a transaction block:

```
booktown=# BEGIN WORK;
BEGIN
booktown=# DELETE FROM shipments;
DELETE 36
booktown=# ROLLBACK WORK;
ROLLBACK
```

SELECT — Retrieves rows from a table or view.

Synopsis

```
SELECT [ ALL | DISTINCT [ ON ( distinct_expression [, ...] ) ] ]
    target_expression [ AS output_name ] [, ...]
    [ FROM from_item [ { , | CROSS JOIN } ...] ]
    [ WHERE condition ]
    [ GROUP BY aggregate_expression [, ...] ]
    [ HAVING aggregate_condition [, ...] ]
    [ { UNION | INTERSECT | EXCEPT [ALL] } select ]
    [ ORDER BY order_expression [ ASC | DESC | USING operator ] [, ...] ]
    [ FOR UPDATE [ OF update_table [, ...] ] ]
    [ LIMIT { ALL | count } [ { OFFSET | , } start ] ]

from_item ::= { [ ONLY ] table_name [ * ]
                  [ [ AS ] from_alias [ ( column_alias_list ) ] ] |
                  ( select ) [ [ AS ] alias [ ( column_alias_list ) ] ] |
                  from_item [ NATURAL ] join_type from_item
                    [ ON ( join_condition ) | USING ( join_column_list ) ]
               }

join_type ::= [ INNER |
                LEFT  [ OUTER ] |
                RIGHT [ OUTER ] |
                FULL  [ OUTER ]
              ] JOIN
```

Parameters

ALL | DISTINCT

> The DISTINCT keyword indicates that duplicate values found in two or more rows will not be shown after the first row. The ALL keyword explicitly reinforces the default to retrieve all rows regardless of uniqueness.

> Note that the ORDER BY clause sorts rows before the DISTINCT clause removes non-unique rows. Use these clauses together to ensure that the row found is the row you intend to retrieve.

DISTINCT ON

> The ON keyword, following the DISTINCT keyword, allows you to specify one or more *distinct_expressions* by which to judge uniqueness.

distinct_expression

> A column name within a *from_item*, or a valid expression, whose value is used by the DISTINCT ON clause as a basis for removing duplicate values.

target_expression

> A column name within a *from_item*, or a valid expression.

output_name

> An alternate name for an output column, following the AS clause. This name will then be used during display of the output and can be used to reference the column within ORDER BY and GROUP BY clauses in the same SELECT statement. However, this name does *not* apply to the WHERE or HAVING clauses; you will need to use the correct column name for them.

FROM

> The clause which is passed *from_items*, from which to retrieve rows.

from_item

> The name of a table, a subselect, or a JOINed set of *from_items* that you wish to retrieve data from.

{ , | CROSS JOIN }

> The comma (or formal CROSS JOIN clause) separates multiple *from_items*.

WHERE

> The clause that is passed *conditions* by which to constraint a result set.

condition

> An expression that yields either true or false, applied conditionally to non-grouped target expressions.

GROUP BY

> The clause that is passed *aggregate_expressions* to aggregate (group) rows together.

aggregate_expression

> A column name within a *from_item*, or a valid expression, to be used as a basis to aggregate (group) rows together.

HAVING

> The clause to which is passed any *aggregate_conditions* by which to constrain a result set.

aggregate_condition

> An expression that yields either true or false, applied conditionally to aggregated (grouped) target expressions.

UNION

> The clause that combines two result sets with compatible column structure into a single combined result set.

INTERSECT

> The clause that removes any rows from the initial result set *not* found in the following *select* statement's result set (resulting in the overlapping, or intersecting, set).

EXCEPT

> The clause that removes any rows from the initial result set that *are* found in the following *select* statement's result set (resulting in the difference set).

select

> A full *select* statement. The limitation on this form of subquery is that you cannot use any of the ORDER BY, FOR UPDATE, or LIMIT clauses unless the statement is enclosed in parentheses.

ORDER BY

> The ORDER BY clause sorts the retrieved result set by each *order_expression* provided.

order_expression [ASC | DESC | USING *operator*]

> A column name in the retrieved result set by which the ORDER BY clause sorts the results. The use of the ASC keyword explicitly defines the default of ascending sorting, while the DESC implies descending sorting. The USING clause defines an *operator* (e.g., >) to compare subsequent *order_expression* values with.

FOR UPDATE

> The locking clause that places an implicit ROW SHARE MODE lock (see the reference entry titled "LOCK") on the *from_item* table selected in the current transaction.

OF *update_table*

> A specific table to which to apply ROW SHARE MODE locking when multiple tables are selected in the FROM clause.

LIMIT

> The LIMIT clause constrains only a specified portion of the retrieved results.

ALL | *count*

> The ALL keyword explicitly specifies the default, which is to not limit the number of rows returned. The use of a numeric *count* value limits the number of rows in the retrieved result set to *count*.

{ OFFSET | , } *start*

> The OFFSET keyword (or informal comma, following the LIMIT clause) allows a result set to ignore the first *start* rows.

The following clauses and parameters are available within each *from_item*:

[ONLY] *table_name* [*]

> The name of an existing table or view from which you wish to retrieve rows. If you do not specify ONLY, all descendant tables will be searched as well. You can also add an asterisk (*) to indicate a wildcard after the table name to have descendant tables searched.

sub_select

> A sub-SELECT statement within the FROM clause of a SELECT statement; this creates a temporary table from which rows can be pulled for the duration of the command. Aliases must be provided for sub-SELECTs, and they must also be surrounded in parentheses.

[AS] *from_alias*

> The *from_alias* is a substitute name for a referenced table in the FROM clause.

column_alias_list

> A comma-delimited list of aliases for each column in the *from_alias* source preceding it. There may be fewer aliases listed in *column_alias_list* than there are columns in the *from_alias* source to which it applies.

join_type

> The join type, where the type is one of the following:

> - [INNER] JOIN
> - LEFT [OUTER] JOIN
> - RIGHT [OUTER] JOIN
> - FULL [OUTER] JOIN

NATURAL

> The optional NATURAL keyword indicates that the join will join the two *from_items* based on any identically-named columns they share. The use of this keyword precludes the use of explicit *join_conditions* or a *join_column_list*.

join_condition

> A join qualification condition following the ON clause. Functionally, this clause is the same as a WHERE clause, except that the condition will only be applied to the two objects being joined.

join_column_list

> A list of columns following the USING clause. This list is a shortened way of specifying the ON clause; it implies equivalence of columns within the FROM sources of a join that have the *same names* in the two joined sources.

Results

The primary result of a SELECT statement is a list of rows contained in the selected result set, followed by the number of rows retrieved. One of the following error messages may alternatively be encountered:

ERROR: Relation '*from_item*' does not exist

> The error returned if a specified *from_item* table or view cannot be found in the connected database.

ERROR: Table name "*from_item*" specified more than once

> The error returned if a *from_item* database table or view is specified twice without an alias. You can avoid this error by applying an alias to one of the named *from_item* sources with the AS clause.

ERROR: Attribute '*column*' not found

> The error returned if a specified *column* cannot be found in any specified *from_item*.

Description

Use the SELECT command to retrieve rows of data from a table, view, subquery, or any joined result set. Use the WHERE clause to set a condition that rows must meet in order to be retrieved; rows will not be retrieved if they don't meet the condition. If you do not specify any conditions using WHERE, all rows in the data source will be retrieved.

There are many clauses available within a SELECT statement. See the "Parameters" section of this reference entry for a listing of these clauses and their descriptions. See Chapter 4 for more detailed instructions on their use.

Examples

The following example selects all rows from the books table:

```
booktown=# SELECT * FROM books;
   id  |             title             | author_id | subject_id
-------+-------------------------------+-----------+------------
  7808 | The Shining                   |      4156 |          9
  4513 | Dune                          |      1866 |         15
  4267 | 2001: A Space Odyssey         |      2001 |         15
  1608 | The Cat in the Hat            |      1809 |          2
  1590 | Bartholomew and the Oobleck   |      1809 |          2
 25908 | Franklin in the Dark          |     15990 |          2
  1501 | Goodnight Moon                |      2031 |          2
   190 | Little Women                  |        16 |          6
  1234 | The Velveteen Rabbit          |     25041 |          3
  2038 | Dynamic Anatomy               |      1644 |          0
   156 | The Tell-Tale Heart           |       115 |          9
 41472 | Practical PostgreSQL          |      1212 |          4
 41473 | Programming Python            |      7805 |          4
 41477 | Learning Python               |      7805 |          4
 41478 | Perl Cookbook                 |      7806 |          4
(15 rows)
```

The next example selects only rows with an ID number higher than 5000 will be retrieved:

```
booktown=# SELECT * FROM books WHERE id > 5000;
   id  |         title         | author_id | subject_id
-------+-----------------------+-----------+------------
  7808 | The Shining           |      4156 |          9
 25908 | Franklin in the Dark  |     15990 |          2
 41472 | Practical PostgreSQL  |      1212 |          4
 41473 | Programming Python    |      7805 |          4
 41477 | Learning Python       |      7805 |          4
 41478 | Perl Cookbook         |      7806 |          4
(6 rows)
```

SELECT INTO — Construct a new table from the results of a SELECT.

Synopsis

```
SELECT [ ALL | DISTINCT [ ON ( distinct_expression [, ...] ) ] ]
    target_expression [ AS output_name ] [, ...]
    [ INTO [ TEMPORARY | TEMP ] [ TABLE ] new_table ]
    [ FROM from_item [ { , | CROSS JOIN } ...] ]
    [ WHERE condition ]
    [ GROUP BY aggregate_expression [, ...] ]
    [ HAVING aggregate_condition [, ...] ]
    [ { UNION | INTERSECT | EXCEPT [ALL] } select ]
    [ ORDER BY order_expression [ ASC | DESC | USING operator ] [, ...] ]
    [ FOR UPDATE [ OF update_table [, ...] ] ]
    [ LIMIT { ALL | count } [ { OFFSET | , } start ] ]
```

```
from_item ::= { [ ONLY ] table_name [ * ]
                  [ [ AS ] from_alias [ ( column_alias_list ) ] ] |
                ( select ) [ [ AS ] alias [ ( column_alias_list ) ] ] |
                from_item [ NATURAL ] join_type from_item
                  [ ON ( join_condition ) | USING ( join_column_list ) ]
              }

join_type ::= [ INNER |
                LEFT   [ OUTER ] |
                RIGHT  [ OUTER ] |
                FULL   [ OUTER ]
              ] JOIN
```

Parameters

Most SELECT INTO parameters are the same as for the SELECT command. The following two are the only parameters unique to SELECT INTO:

TEMPORARY, TEMP

The TEMPORARY (or TEMP) keyword indicates that the table is for temporary use; it will be destroyed when the session has ended.

new_table

The name of the new table created to hold the resulting rows of the query. This table will be created automatically and must not already exist before you execute this command.

Results

Refer to the reference entry titled "CREATE TABLE" and the reference entry titled "SELECT" for a list of possible results.

Description

Use SELECT INTO to execute a query and use the resulting rows to populate a new (automatically created) table. Each column's names and data type for the new table are derived from the rows resulting from the original query. This command is effectively the same as the CREATE TABLE AS command, and it is recommended that you use that syntax, due to the fact that SELECT INTO is non-standard and is also not interpreted correctly by PL/pgSQL.

Example

The following example will create a temporary employee table for employees with an identification number below 105:

```
booktown=# SELECT * INTO TEMP TABLE old_emp
booktown-#     FROM employees
booktown-#     WHERE id < 105;
SELECT
```

SET — Set runtime variables.

Synopsis

```
SET variable { TO | = } { value | 'value' | DEFAULT }
SET TIME ZONE { 'timezone' | LOCAL | DEFAULT }
```

Parameters

variable

The name of the runtime variable you are setting.

value

A new value for the specified variable. Use DEFAULT to reset the variable to its default value.

timezone

The time zone of the client. The following are a few valid time zone values:

PST8PDT

Pacific Standard/Daylight Savings Time (GMT offset by 8 hours).

EST5EDT

Eastern Standard/Daylight Savings Time (GMT offset by 5 hours).

NZST13NZDT

Standard/daylight savings time zone in New Zealand (GMT offset by 13 hours).

LOCAL

The clause to set the time zone to the local system's configured time zone.

DEFAULT

The clause to set a variable value, or a time zone value, to its default.

Results

SET VARIABLE

The message returned when a variable is successfully set.

ERROR: not a valid option name:(*name*)

The error returned if you try to set a variable that doesn't exist.

ERROR: permission denied

The error returned if you do not have adequate permissions to alter the specified variable.

ERROR: *name* can only be set at start-up

The error returned if you attempt to set a variable that can only set set upon startup.

Description

Use the SET command to modify PostgreSQL runtime configuration variables. The following variable can be altered:

CLIENT_ENCODING

> The multibyte client encoding scheme (if enabled in PostgreSQL).

DATESTYLE

> This variable sets the date and time representation style. When setting this variable, you can choose one format from the normal output styles, one of the two substyles, or both an output style and a substyle. Initialize the format by manually changing the PGDATESTYLE environment variable. You can also initialize the format using *postmaster* command options. For example, run *postmaster* using *-o "-e"* to set dates to the European format (see Chapter 9 for more about the options available to *postmaster*).
>
> The following are valid date and time output styles:

ISO

> The ISO-8601–style date and time formatting. Date and time are displayed as *YYYY-MM-DD HH:MM:SS*. This is the default style.

SQL

> The Oracle/Ingres–style date and time formatting. Despite this format's label, it is not the SQL default; SQL uses ISO–8601 style formatting.

Postgres

> The traditional PostgreSQL date and time formatting.

German

> The traditional German-style formatting. Numeric date representations are displayed as *DD.MM.YYYY*.

European

> The standard European-style formatting. This is a substyle of the *SQL* and *PostgreSQL* styles. Numeric date representations are displayed as *DD/MM/YYYY*.

NonEuropean, US

> The standard United States-style formatting. This is a substyle of the *SQL* and *Postgres* styles. Numeric date representations are displayed as *MM/DD/YYYY*.

SEED

> This variable sets the internal seed for the PostgreSQL random number generator, which is used by the random() function. Allowed values are floating point numbers between 0 and 1. The number you supply is then multiplied by 2^30.
>
> Alternatively, you may set the seed by calling the SQL setseed() function,

with a single argument of type double precision.

SERVER_ENCODING

The server's default multibyte encoding (if enabled in PostgreSQL).

Examples

The following example sets the DATESTYLE variable to use traditional PostgreSQL style formatting. It also sets the substyle to U.S., which uses additional United States-specific formatting.

```
booktown=# SET DATESTYLE TO Postgres,US;
SET VARIABLE
```

The next example sets the date and time formatting to ISO:

```
booktown=# SET DATESTYLE TO ISO;
SET VARIABLE
```

SET CONSTRAINTS — Sets the constraint mode for the current transaction block.

Synopsis

```
SET CONSTRAINTS { ALL | constraint [,... ] }
               { DEFERRED | IMMEDIATE }
```

Parameters

ALL

The keyword indicating that the mode you are specifying should be applied to all constraints within the current transaction.

constraint

The name of a specific constraint for which you wish to set the mode.

DEFERRED

The keyword indicating that constraints (or a specific constraint) shouldn't be checked until the transaction reaches a COMMIT.

IMMEDIATE

The keyword indicating that constraints (or a specific constraint) *should* be checked at the end of each statement within a transaction.

Results

SET CONSTRAINTS

The message returned when a constraint mode is set successfully.

```
ERROR: Constraint 'constraint' does not exist
```
The error returned if you attempt to change the mode of a *constraint* that does not exist.

Description

Use the SET CONSTRAINTS command to set the constraint mode for all constraints or for a single constraint within the current transaction block. You can choose to set the constraint mode to either IMMEDIATE or DEFERRED. Use of IMMEDIATE mode will force the checking of all constraints at the end of each statement within the transaction. In DEFERRED mode, constraints are not checked until a COMMIT command is issued.

PostgreSQL 7.1.x (the most current version as of the writing of this book) only supports the use of these modes with foreign key constraints, as both check and unique constraints are set to a constraint mode that is not affected by this command.

Example

The following example sets the constraint evaluation mode to IMMEDIATE for all constraints within the transaction:

```
booktown=# SET CONSTRAINTS ALL IMMEDIATE;
SET CONSTRAINTS
```

SET TRANSACTION — Sets the transaction isolation level for the current transaction block.

Synopsis

```
SET TRANSACTION ISOLATION LEVEL
    { READ COMMITTED | SERIALIZABLE }
SET SESSION CHARACTERISTICS AS TRANSACTION ISOLATION LEVEL
    { READ COMMITTED | SERIALIZABLE }
```

Parameters

READ COMMITTED

The clause that specifies that statements will be able to view changes to the database that were committed before the transaction began. This is the default.

SERIALIZABLE

The clause that specifies that statements will be able to view all rows that were committed in the database before the transaction's first DML statement is executed.

Results

SET VARIABLE

The message returned when the isolation level has been set successfully. To verify that it is correctly set, you can issue the command SHOW TRANSACTION ISOLATION LEVEL, which should then return the variable's setting (either READ COMMITTED or SERIALIZABLE).

Description

Use the SET TRANSACTION command to set the transaction isolation level for the current transaction. This change will affect only the current transaction; all other subsequent transactions must have their isolation mode explicitly set, otherwise the default of READ COMMITTED will be used.

You can only use this command before the first *DML* statement has been executed. A DML statement is one of SELECT, INSERT, DELETE, UPDATE, FETCH, or COPY.

To set the default transaction isolation level (as opposed to individual transaction), use SET SESSION CHARACTERISTICS and specify either READ COMMITTED or SERIALIZABLE. Issuing a SET TRANSACTION command from within a transaction can override this default setting.

When the isolation level is set to READ COMMITTED, all statements within the transaction view only the rows that were committed before the transaction was started. Setting the isolation level to SERIALIZABLE allows statements within the transaction to view changes made to the database before the first DML statement was executed within the transaction.

Examples

The following example sets the transaction isolation level to SERIALIZABLE for the current transaction:

```
testdb=# SET TRANSACTION ISOLATION LEVEL SERIALIZABLE;
SET VARIABLE
```

The next example demonstrates setting the default transaction isolation level for the current session:

```
testdb=# SET SESSION CHARACTERISTICS AS TRANSACTION ISOLATION LEVEL SERIALIZABLE;
SET VARIABLE
```

SHOW — Displays the values of runtime variables.

Synopsis

```
SHOW name
```

Parameters

name

The name of a runtime variable.

Results

SHOW VARIABLE

The message returned after the SHOW command returns.

ERROR: Option 'name' is not recognized

The error returned if the variable specified (name) does not exist.

ERROR: permission denied

The error returned if you do not have the permissions necessary to view this information.

NOTICE: Time zone is unknown

The notice returned if you request to show the TIMEZONE variable when the TZ or PGTZ environment variable is not set.

Description

Use the SHOW command to display the current settings for a specified runtime variable. The variables in question are specified using the SET command or automatically determined during server startup.

Examples

The following example displays the current transaction isolation level:

```
booktown=# SHOW TRANSACTION ISOLATION LEVEL;
NOTICE:  TRANSACTION ISOLATION LEVEL is SERIALIZABLE
SHOW VARIABLE
```

The next example displays the current date formatting style:

```
booktown=# SHOW DATESTYLE;
NOTICE:  DateStyle is ISO with US (NonEuropean) conventions
SHOW VARIABLE
```

TRUNCATE — Empties the contents of a table.

Synopsis

```
TRUNCATE [ TABLE ] name
```

Parameters

name

> The name of the table you wish to truncate. To truncate a table means to remove all rows from the table.

Results

TRUNCATE

> The message returned if the specified table is successfully truncated.

ERROR: Relation '*name*' does not exist

> The error returned if the specified table *name* does not exist in the connected database.

Description

Use this command to remove all rows of a specified table. It does not scan through the table before removing data, making it rather helpful when emptying large tables of data. In essence, it is a quicker form of the DELETE command.

Example

This example empties all of the rows in the temp_emp table:

```
booktown=# TRUNCATE TABLE temp_emp;
TRUNCATE
```

UNLISTEN — Stops the backend process from listening for a notification event.

Synopsis

```
UNLISTEN { notifyname | * }
```

Examples

notifyname

> The name of the NOTIFY condition you wish to stop listening for.

*

> Passing the asterisk symbol (*) as the name of the notify condition will stop the backend from listening for any currently defined conditions.

Results

UNLISTEN

The message returned when a UNLISTEN command is completed successfully.

Description

Use the UNLISTEN command to unregister a current NOTIFY registration matching the notify condition specified by *notifyname*. Alternatively, you can use the wild-card symbol (*) to remove *all* listener registrations for the current session. When a backend shuts down it will automatically issue UNLISTEN * to remove all listener registrations.

 If you are interested in seeing all of the notification events being listened for, you may query the relname column from the pg_listener system table.

More information about using the NOTIFY and LISTEN commands (which work together to form the simple interprocess communication or IPC system) can be found by referring to the reference entry titled "NOTIFY."

Example

The following example checks all notifications being listened for, and subsequently stops the backend process from listening for the publisher_update event:

```
booktown=# SELECT relname FROM pg_listener;
     relname
------------------
 publisher_update
 publisher_delete
(2 rows)

booktown=# UNLISTEN publisher_update;
UNLISTEN
booktown=# SELECT relname FROM pg_listener;
     relname
------------------
 publisher_delete
```

UPDATE — Modifies the values of column data within a table.

Synopsis

```
UPDATE [ ONLY ] table SET
                column = expression [, ...]
                [ FROM fromlist ]
                [ WHERE condition ]
```

Parameters

ONLY

The optional ONLY keyword indicates to only update the specified *table* (and not its inheriting child tables, if it has any).

table

The name of an existing table to update.

column

The name of a column to update in the table you specified.

expression

An expression or value that you want assigned to the specified column.

fromlist

A valid table, view, or other *from_item* as defined in the reference entry titled "SELECT." A PostgreSQL extension of the UPDATE command is the ability to use column values from other tables within the WHERE condition; to do this correctly, you must use this parameter to list the tables from which you will be pulling column values.

condition

The WHERE condition for UPDATE to use when determining what rows are to be updated. This can be any valid expression resulting in a value of type boolean.

Results

UPDATE *count*

The message returned when an UPDATE was successful. The *count* will actually be the number of rows that were modified as a result of the UPDATE. For example, if *count* is zero, it means that no rows were updated.

ERROR: Relation '*table*' does not exist

The error returned if *table* is not a table in the connected database.

ERROR: Relation '*table*' does not have attribute '*column*'

The error returned if a *column* that does not exist in the *table* is used in the SET clause.

ERROR: Cannot update a view without an appropriate rule

The error returned if an UPDATE is attempted on a view instead of a table, without a defined rule on how to handle the attempt.

Description

Use the UPDATE command to modify column values of all rows that match a WHERE condition that you specify. You can also use this command to update the values of array columns. For an array column, you can modify a single element, a range, or the entire array. To update only the table specified, pass the ONLY parameter: otherwise all sub-tables will be updated as well.

You must have write access to any columns you are attempting to modify, and read access to any columns referenced within your WHERE statement.

Example

The following example adds one to the total stock number for the book with the specified ISBN within the stock table:

```
booktown=# UPDATE stock SET stock = stock + 1 WHERE isbn = '0385121679';
UPDATE 1
```

VACUUM — Cleans and analyzes a database.

Synopsis

```
VACUUM [ VERBOSE ] [ ANALYZE ] [ table ]
VACUUM [ VERBOSE ] ANALYZE [ table [ (column [, ...] ) ] ]
```

Parameters

VERBOSE

The keyword that causes VACUUM to display an activity report for each table it operates upon.

ANALYZE

The keyword that causes VACUUM to update column statistics for the optimizer.

table

A table you intend to vacuum. If you do not specify a table, VACUUM will operate upon all tables.

column

The name of a column to analyze (used when updating statistics for the optimizer).

Results

VACUUM

> The message returned when a VACUUM successfully vacuums a database or table.

NOTICE: —Relation table—

> The notice returned when VACUUM begins cleaning a table (*table*) while in verbose mode.

NOTICE: Pages 1: Changed 1, reaped 1, Empty 0, New 0; Tup 12: Vac 39, Keep/
VTL 0/0, Crash 0, UnUsed 0, MinLen 52, MaxLen 76; Re-using: Free/Avail.
Space 7180/0; EndEmpty/Avail. Pages 0/0. CPU 0.00s/0.00u sec.

> The notice returned from the analysis on a table.

NOTICE: Index *indexname*: Pages 2; Tuples 12: Deleted 39. CPU 0.00s/0.00u
sec.

> The notice returned from an analysis of *indexname*.

Description

Use the VACUUM command to clean up records from rolled back transactions and to update system catalog statistics. Call it with the ANALYZE option to collect statistical information about data. Using this command periodically can increase the performance of your database.

Example

The following example displays the output of the VACUUM command when run on the books table with the VERBOSE keyword:

```
booktown=# VACUUM VERBOSE books;
NOTICE:   --Relation books--
NOTICE:   Pages 1: Changed 0, reaped 1, Empty 0, New 0; Tup 15:
          Vac 0, Keep/VTL 0/0, Crash 0, UnUsed 5, MinLen 52,
          MaxLen 76; Re-using: Free/Avail. Space 7108/0;
          EndEmpty/Avail. Pages 0/0. CPU 0.00s/0.00u sec.
NOTICE:   Index books_id_pkey: Pages 2; Tuples 15: Deleted 0.
          CPU 0.00s/0.00u sec.
```

Multibyte Encoding Types

Table A-1 lists the various multibyte encoding types supported by PostgreSQL, as of version 7.1.x. These encoding types are only available if PostgreSQL was configured with the *--enable-multibyte* flag (see Chapter 2, *Installing PostgreSQL*). A database can be created with a default encoding type if *SQL_ASCII* is not desired.

Table A-1. Multibyte encoding types

Encoding type	Integer	Description
SQL_ASCII	*0*	Plain ASCII format
EUC_JP	*1*	Japanese Extended Unix Code
EUC_CN	*2*	Chinese Extended Unix Code
EUC_KR	*3*	Korean Extended Unix Code
EUC_TW	*4*	Taiwan Extended Unix Code
UNICODE	*5*	UTF-8 Unicode
MULE_INTERNAL	*6*	Mule internal type
LATIN1	*7*	ISO 8859-1 (English, with some European languages)
LATIN2	*8*	ISO 8859-2 (English, with some European languages)
LATIN3	*9*	ISO 8859-3 (English, with some European languages)
LATIN4	*10*	ISO 8859-4 (English, with some European languages)
LATIN5	*11*	ISO 8859-5 (English, with some European languages)
KOI8	*12*	KOI8-R
WIN	*13*	Windows CP1251
ALT	*14*	Windows CP866

B

Backend Options for postgres

The *postgres* program is the actual backend server that processes SQL statements. It is generally not called directly, but invoked through the multiuser *postmaster* process. It can be helpful to know the options available to this program, however, as they can be called indirectly through the *postmaster*'s *-o* flag.

The following syntax diagram shows the options recognized by *postgres*:

```
postgres [ -A { 0 | 1 } ] [ -B buffers ] [ -c name=value ] [ -d debug-level ]
         [ -D datadir ] [ -e ] [ -E ] [ -f { s | i | n | m | h } ] [ -F ]
         [ -i ] [ -L ] [ -N ] [ -o file-name ] [ -O ] [ -P ]
         [ -s | -t { pa | pl | ex } ] [ -S sort_mem ] [ -W num ] database

postgres [ -A { 0 | 1 } ] [ -B buffers ] [ -c name=value ] [ -d debug-level ]
         [ -D datadir ] [ -e ] [ -f { s | i | n | m | h } ] [ -F ] [ -i ]
         [ -L ] [ -o file-name ] [ -O ] [ -p database ] [ -P ]
         [ -s | -t { pa | pl | ex } ] [ -S sort_mem ] [ -v version ] [ -W num ]
```

-A { 0 | 1 }

The run-time assertion check parameter. This enables debugging, if the debugging option was enabled during compilation of PostgreSQL. This parameter should only be used by knowledgeable developers working on PostgreSQL.

-B buffers

The number of shared-memory disk buffers that *postmaster* will allocate for use by the backend. By default, this is 64.

The *buffers* value passed to *-B* must be at least twice the number supplied for the *-N* parameter.

-c name=value

An arbitrary run-time configuration, setting *name* to *value*. Any configuration settings found in the *postgresql.conf* file (within the database cluster's data directory) may be over-ridden with this option.

-d debug_level

The debug level, which determines the amount of debugging output that will be logged by the backend. The default is 0. With a higher the *debug_level* number, more output will be generated. Values as high as 4 are reasonable for normal use, though this can log a great deal of information.

 Unless the standard output and standard error streams from *postmaster* are redirected to a file (e.g., from the shell, or with the *-l* option to *pg_ctl*) all debugging information will be displayed to the controlling terminal session of the *postmaster* process.

-D datadir

The data directory of the intended database cluster. If this is not supplied, *postmaster* will use either the value of the PGDATA environment variable, or the */data* path off of the path defined in the POSTGRESHOME environment variable. If neither environment variable is set, the default compile-time directory is used (e.g., */usr/local/pgsql/data*).

-e

The *European* date style parameter. This causes PostgreSQL to assume that dates such as 3/2/2001 are day-first rather than month-first. It also causes PostgreSQL to display the day before the month (e.g., *dd/mm/yyyy*) when displaying dates.

-E

The verbose echo parameter. Causes all passed statements to be output (e.g., to the controlling terminal session, or to the server log).

-f{ s | i | n | m | h }

The forbid parameter, which can forbid the use of certain scan and join methods. The following options may follow the *-f*:

s

Forbids sequential scans

i

Forbids index scans

n

Forbids nested loops

m

Forbids merge joins

h

Forbids hash joins

-*F*

The fsync-disabling option. Using this increases performance at the risk of data corruption in the event that the operating system or physical hardware crashes unexpectedly. Be sure you know what you are doing before you use this parameter!

-*i*

The -*i* parameter disables query execution, and causes PostgreSQL to only show the plan tree.

-*L*

The lock-disabling parameter. This turns off the ability to lock in PostgreSQL.

-*N*

The -*N* parameter disables the use of a newline as a statement delimiter.

-*O*

The -*O* parameter allows system tables to be modified.

-*p database*

The *postmaster* parameter, indicating that this *postgres* instance was started by *postmaster* connecting to *database*. This causes *postgres* to make different decisions about memory management and file descriptors.

-*P*

The -*P* parameter causes PostgreSQL to ignore system indices when scanning and updating system tuples. This option is required by the REINDEX command when indexing system tables.

-*s*

The statistics parameter. This causes PostgreSQL to display processing time and other statistics after each query, which can be helpful in benchmark tests, or for tuning the amount of buffers you make available with the -*B* parameter.

-*S sort_mem*

The amount of memory to be allocated for internal sorting and hashes before falling back on temporary hard disk files. *sort_mem* is a numeric value, in kilobytes, and defaults to 512. For complex statements, several sorts or hashes may run simultaneously; each one will be allocated up to the value specified by *sort_mem* before using temporary disk space.

-t { pa | pl | e }

The timing statistics parameter, specific to only one of the major *postgres* components. The following are the valid options that may follow the *-t* parameter:

pa

Times the parser component

pl

Times the planner component

e

Times the executor component

The *-t* and *-s* options are mutually exclusive.

-v version

The protocol *version* parameter. This option sets the internal version number of the frontend-to-backend protocol.

-W num

The wait parameter. Specifying this value causes *postgres* to wait for *num* seconds before starting up, allowing a developer time to attach a debugger.

C

Binary COPY Format

In addition to saving data in text format, PostgreSQL can also save COPY output in its own binary format. This is the format compiled programs are stored in, which is not readable by normal text editors.

The Header

The PostgreSQL binary file header contains 24 bytes of fixed fields, and a variable length header extension area. The fixed fields are as follows:

Signature Field

A 12-byte sequence, which is literally: PGBCOPY\nÿ\r\n\0

The signature is used to identify files that are malformed through a non-8-bit-clean transfer; it is changed by dropped NULL values, parity changes, newline translation filters, and dropped high bits.

Integer Layout Field

A 32-byte integer constant (0x01020304) in the source's byte order. This is to assist an application reading this file format in preventing byte-flipping of multi-byte values.

Flags Field

A 32-bit integer, which is the main storage point for file formatting information. Within this field, bits are ordered from 0 (least significant byte, or LSB) to 31 (most significant byte, or MSB). To hold backwards-compatibility formatting information, bits 0 through 15 are reserved. Bits 16 through 31 are used to flag critical file formatting information. As of 7.1.x, the only bit here that has a definition is bit 16.

BIT 16

If bit 16 is set to 1, object IDs are included in the file.

If bit 16 is set to 0, object IDs are *not* included.

Header Extension Length Field

A 32-bit integer describing the length, in bytes, of the remainder of the header (not including the header extension length field). In earlier versions, this was set to zero, and the first tuple immediately followed.

Tuples

The structure of tuples within the binary file is as follows: a 16-bit integer count of the fields within the tuple (this is the same within every tuple), a 16-bit integer *typlen* word, and the field data for each field. The available options for the *typlen* field are as follow:

0

NULL; this field contains no data.

>0

A fixed-length data type. The specified number bytes of data follow the *typlen* word.

-1

A *varlena* data type. The next four bytes are the *varlena* header, consisting of the value's total length (including the length of the header).

<-1

Reserved for possible future use.

To create a convenient way for an application reading this format to check the integrity of incoming binary data, all non-NULL fields have a *typlen* value, which can be compared against the *typlen* of the destination column before attempting to insert or update data within PostgreSQL.

A few formatting options were left un-implemented to improve the portability of binary file dumps. Primarily, extra data between fields is not possible (e.g., alignment padding), and there is no distinguishment between data types based on passes by reference, or passes by value.

If OIDs are included in a PostgreSQL binary file, they immediately follow the field count word. OIDs are not included in the field count.

Trailer

The PostgreSQL binary file trailer is a single 16-bit integer with a value of *-1*, followed by the end of the file. This is easily distinguishable from a tuple's initial 16-bit field-count, and can aid an application in staying in sync with the data.

D

Internal psql Variables

The *psql* client uses a variety of internal variables as special system variables to control aspects of the program. A few of the most notable variables are PROMPT1, PROMPT2, and PROMPT3, which store the prompts for the program. While running the program you can set and unset these variables at will using the \set and \unset commands. A list of all the special variables *psql* uses follows:

DBNAME

This variable holds the name of the database *psql* is currently connected to. This variable is set whenever *psql* connects to a database, either when starting up or when instructed to connect during program operation.

ECHO

This variable controls what gets displayed on the screen when executing commands from a file. To display all contents of a script file on the screen as it is parsed, set this variable to *all*. To display all queries as they are sent to the backend process, set this variable to *queries*.

ECHO_HIDDEN

This variable, when set to *true*, displays the queries used by slash commands from within *psql*. Such queries will be displayed before they are sent to the backend. To show the queries for slash commands without actually executing them, set ECHO_HIDDEN to *noexec*.

ENCODING

This variable holds the database's multibyte encoding scheme. You must have compiled PostgreSQL to support multibyte encoding; if you did not, this variable will contain *SQL_ASCII*.

HISTCONTROL

This variable sets methods of controlling the *psql* history buffer. Set this variable to *ignorespace* if you wish for the history to ignore all lines entered that were preceded by spaces. Set it to *ignoredups* to ignore any entries that matched the previous line entered. To ignore both lines beginning with spaces and lines that duplicate, use the value *ignoreboth*.

HISTSIZE

This variable sets the length of the history buffer; the default length is 500 lines.

HOST

This variable holds the hostname of the database server you are currently connected to. This value is set during startup and whenever a database connection occurs.

IGNOREEOF

This variable controls how *psql* handles EOF characters. Normally, when *psql* receives an EOF character the application terminates. This character is usually generated by pressing CTRL-D on the keyboard. Setting this option to any non-numeric value will inform *psql* that you wish to have the EOF character ignored until it is repeated more than 10 times. You may alternatively set this variable to a specific number; if you do so, *psql* will ignore that many EOF characters before terminating.

LASTOID

This variable contains the last object identifier (OID) set from an INSERT command, or lo_import() function call.

LO_TRANSACTION

This variable sets the action *psql* will take during large object operations. It may be set to one of the following values:

rollback

This causes any transaction you are currently working within to be rolled back if you attempt an operation on a large object (or a large object import). For maximum efficiency, large object operations should usually be placed within their own transactions; for this reason, LO_TRANSACTION defaults to *rollback*.

commit

This causes *psql* to commit any transaction you were in before you issued a large object operation.

nothing

This causes *psql* to execute the large object operation within the current transaction.

ON_ERROR_STOP

This variable, when set (to any value), causes *psql* to terminate the processing of a script that encounters an error (such as incorrect SQL syntax or misuse of a slash command), instead of continuing to process it. By default, scripts that have encountered errors continue to be processed by *psql*.

PORT

This variable holds the port number that you are currently connected to. This value is set automatically both when you start the program and when you manually connect to a database from the *psql* prompt.

PROMPT1, PROMPT2, PROMPT3

These variables hold character strings that directly control the prompt's structure within *psql*. Setting these will change the way each prompt is displayed within the program. See Chapter 6, *PostgreSQL Clients*, for information on how to set these variables.

SINGLELINE

This variable, when set (to any value), causes SQL input to *psql* to be executed when a newline is reached, without the need for a semi-colon or \g terminator. This mode can also be set by the command line option -*S*.

SINGLESTEP

This variable, when set (to any value), causes each statement to require confirmation before being executed.

USER

This variable holds the PostgreSQL username you are connected to the database with.

Index

We'd like to hear your suggestions for improving our indexes. Send email to *index@oreilly.com*.

About the Authors

Joshua Drake is the co-founder of Command Prompt, Inc., a PostgreSQL and Linux custom development company. He is also the current author of the Linux Networking HOWTO, Linux PPP HOWTO, and Linux Consultants HOWTO.

John Worsley is the co-founder and lead developer of Command Prompt, Inc., located in idyllic Portland, Oregon. His projects include the LXP Content-Management Apache module, a variety of DocBook-oriented XML utilities, and a host of custom PostgreSQL-based solutions.

Command Prompt was founded in late 1997 as an Internet application development firm, and functioned originally as an after-hours company working with PostgreSQL, Perl, and PHP. Since January 2000, when it became Command Prompt, Inc., the company has specialized in advanced web-based application development using PostgreSQL and languages such as PHP, C++, Perl, and Java. The firm's primary efforts are in the area of their PostgreSQL Application Server (included with this book) and specialized development, such as e-fulfillment systems,

Colophon

Our look is the result of reader comments, our own experimentation, and feedback from distribution channels. Distinctive covers complement our distinctive approach to technical topics, breathing personality and life into potentially dry subjects.

The animal on the cover of *Practical PostgreSQL* is a mammoth. Mammoths (of the genus *Mammuthus*) inhabited the Earth during the last Ice Age, which ended about 10,000 years ago. There are several types of mammoths, such as Colombian and Imperial, but the best known is the woolly mammoth. Mammoths resided on the tundra of Asia, Europe, and North America. They are believed to have migrated to North America over the Bering Strait land bridge.

Known for their large size, mammoths ranged from 12 to 15 feet tall at the shoulder and weighed as much as 6 to 8 tons. They had long, dense hair and under fur, long trunks, and large ears. Their most prominent features were long, curved tusks that measured up to 16 feet. Mammoths used their tusks for digging underneath the snow to find food, for protection, and in mating rituals. As herbivores, they ate leaves of willow, hornbeam, fir, hazel, and alden. They lived up to 60 years in age. Scientists attribute the mammoths' extinction to the climate changes that ended the Ice Age.

Sarah Jane Shangraw and Jeff Holcomb were the copyeditors for *Practical PostgreSQL*. Jane Ellin provided quality control.

Ellie Volckhausen designed the cover of this book, based on a series design by Edie Freedman. The cover image is a 19th-century engraving from the Dover Pictorial Archive. Emma Colby produced the cover layout with QuarkXPress 4.1 using Adobe's ITC Garamond font.

The print version of this book was created by translating the DocBook XML markup of its source files into a set of gtroff macros using a filter developed at O'Reilly & Associates by Norman Walsh. Steve Talbott designed and wrote the underlying macro set on the basis of the GNU *troff –gs* macros; Lenny Muellner adapted them to XML and implemented the book design. The text and heading fonts are ITC Garamond Light and Garamond Book; the code font is Constant Willison. This colophon was written by Linley Dolby.

Whenever possible, our books use a durable and flexible lay-flat binding.

More Titles from O'Reilly

Linux

Using Samba

By Peter Kelly, Perry Donham
& David Collier-Brown
1st Edition November 1999
416 pages, Includes CD-ROM
ISBN 1-56592-449-5

Samba turns a Unix or Linux system into a
file and print server for Microsoft Windows
network clients. This complete guide to
Samba administration covers basic 2.0 con-
figuration, security, logging, and troubleshooting. Whether you're
playing on one note or a full three-octave range, this book will
help you maintain an efficient and secure server. Includes a
CD-ROM of sources and ready-to-install binaries.

Managing & Using MySQL, 2nd Edition

By George Reese, Randy Jay Yarger & Tim King
2nd Edition January 2002 (est.)
504 pages (est.), ISBN 0-596-00211-4

This edition retains the best features of the
first edition, while adding the latest on
MySQL and the relevant programming language interfaces, with more complete reference information. The administration section
is greatly enhanced; the programming lan-
guage chapters have been updated—especially the Perl and PHP
chapters—and new additions include chapters on security and
extending MySQL and a system tables reference.

Linux Network Administrator's Guide, 2nd Edition

By Olaf Kirch & Terry Dawson
2nd Edition June 2000
506 pages, ISBN 1-56592-400-2

Fully updated, this comprehensive, impres-
sive introduction to networking on Linux
now covers firewalls, including the use of
ipchains and iptables (netfilter), masquerad-
ing, and accounting. Other new topics
include Novell (NCP/IPX) support and INN
(news administration). Original material on serial connections,
UUCP, routing and DNS, mail and News, SLIP and PPP, NFS, and
NIS has been thoroughly updated.

Understanding the Linux Kernel

By Daniel P. Bovet & Marco Cesati
1st Edition October 2000
650 pages, ISBN 0-596-00002-2

Understanding the Linux Kernel helps readers understand how Linux performs best and
how it meets the challenge of different envi-
ronments. The authors introduce each topic
by explaining its importance, and show how
kernel operations relate to the utilities that
are familiar to Unix programmers and users.

UNIX Power Tools, 2nd Edition

By Jerry Peek, Tim O'Reilly & Mike Loukides
2nd Edition August 1997
1120 pages, Includes CD-ROM
ISBN 1-56592-260-3

Loaded with practical advice about almost
every aspect of Unix, this second edition of
UNIX Power Tools addresses the technology
that Unix users face today. You'll find thorough coverage of POSIX utilities, including
GNU versions, detailed bash and tcsh shell coverage, a strong
emphasis on Perl, and a CD-ROM that contains the best freeware
available.

Linux Device Drivers, 2nd Edition

By Alessandro Rubini & Jonathan Corbet
2nd Edition June 2001
586 pages, ISBN 0-59600-008-1

This practical guide is for anyone who wants
to support computer peripherals under the
Linux operating system. It shows step-by-step
how to write a driver for character devices,
block devices, and network interfaces, illustrating with examples you can compile and
run. The second edition covers Kernel 2.4 and adds discussions
of symmetric multiprocessing (SMP), Universal Serial Bus (USB),
and some new platforms.

O'REILLY®

TO ORDER: **800-998-9938** • *order@oreilly.com* • *www.oreilly.com*
ONLINE EDITIONS OF MOST O'REILLY TITLES ARE AVAILABLE BY SUBSCRIPTION AT *safari.oreilly.com*
ALSO AVAILABLE AT MOST RETAIL AND ONLINE BOOKSTORES

Unix Basics

Learning the UNIX Operating System, 5th Edition

By Jerry Peek, Grace Todino & John Strang
5th Edition November 2001
176 pages, ISBN 0-596-00261-0

Learning the UNIX Operating System is the most effective introduction to Unix in print. The fifth edition covers Internet usage for email, file transfers, and web browsing. It's perfect for those who are just starting with Unix or Linux, as well as anyone who encounters a Unix system on the Internet. Complete with a quick-reference card to pull out and keep handy, it's an ideal primer for Mac and PC users of the Internet who need to know a little bit about Unix on the systems they visit.

Learning the Korn Shell

By Bill Rosenblatt
1st Edition June 1993
360 pages, ISBN 1-56592-054-6

A thorough introduction to the Korn shell, both as a user interface and as a programming language. This book provides a clear explanation of the Korn shell's features, including ksh string operations, co-processes, signals and signal handling, and command-line interpretation. *Learning the Korn Shell* also includes real-life programming examples and a Korn shell debugger (kshdb).

Learning the vi Editor, 6th Edition

By Linda Lamb & Arnold Robbins
6th Edition October 1998
348 pages, ISBN 1-56592-426-6

This completely updated guide to editing with vi, the editor available on nearly every Unix system, now covers four popular vi clones and includes command summaries for easy reference. It starts with the basics, followed by more advanced editing tools, such as ex commands, global search and replacement, and a new feature, multi-screen editing.

Using csh and tcsh

By Paul DuBois
1st Edition August 1995
242 pages, ISBN 1-56592-132-1

Using csh and tcsh describes from the beginning how to use these shells interactively to get your work done faster with less typing. You'll learn how to make your prompt tell you where you are (no more pwd); use what you've typed before (history); type long command lines with few keystrokes (command and filename completion); remind yourself of filenames when in the middle of typing a command; and edit a botched command without retyping it.

Learning GNU Emacs, 2nd Edition

By Debra Cameron, Bill Rosenblatt
& Eric Raymond
2nd Edition September 1996
560 pages, ISBN 1-56592-152-6

Learning GNU Emacs is an introduction to Version 19.30 of the GNU Emacs editor, one of the most widely used and powerful editors available under Unix. It provides a solid introduction to basic editing, a look at several important "editing modes" (special Emacs features for editing specific types of documents, including email, Usenet News, and the World Wide Web), and a brief introduction to customization and Emacs LISP programming. The book is aimed at new Emacs users, whether or not they are programmers. Includes quick-reference card.

UNIX in a Nutshell: System V Edition, 3rd Edition

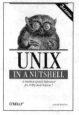

By Arnold Robbins
3rd Edition September 1999
616 pages, ISBN 1-56592-427-4

The bestselling, most informative Unix reference book is now more complete and up-to-date. Not a scaled-down quick reference of common commands, *UNIX in a Nutshell* is a complete reference containing all commands and options, with descriptions and examples that put the commands in context. For all but the thorniest Unix problems, this one reference should be all you need. Covers System V Release 4 and Solaris 7.

How to stay in touch with O'Reilly

1. Visit Our Award-Winning Web Site

http://www.oreilly.com/

★ "Top 100 Sites on the Web" —PC Magazine
★ "Top 5% Web sites" —Point Communications
★ "3-Star site" —The McKinley Group

Our web site contains a library of comprehensive product information (including book excerpts and tables of contents), downloadable software, background articles, interviews with technology leaders, links to relevant sites, book cover art, and more. File us in your Bookmarks or Hotlist!

2. Join Our Email Mailing Lists

New Product Releases
To receive automatic email with brief descriptions of all new O'Reilly products as they are released, send email to:
ora-news-subscribe@lists.oreilly.com
Put the following information in the first line of your message (not in the Subject field):
subscribe ora-news

O'Reilly Events
If you'd also like us to send information about trade show events, special promotions, and other O'Reilly events, send email to:
ora-news-subscribe@lists.oreilly.com
Put the following information in the first line of your message (not in the Subject field):
subscribe ora-events

3. Get Examples from Our Books via FTP

There are two ways to access an archive of example files from our books:

Regular FTP
- ftp to:
  ftp.oreilly.com
  (login: anonymous)
  password: your email address)
- Point your web browser to:
  ftp://ftp.oreilly.com/

FTPMAIL
- Send an email message to:
  ftpmail@online.oreilly.com
  (Write "help" in the message body)

4. Contact Us via Email

order@oreilly.com
To place a book or software order online. Good for North American and international customers.

subscriptions@oreilly.com
To place an order for any of our newsletters or periodicals.

books@oreilly.com
General questions about any of our books.

cs@oreilly.com
For answers to problems regarding your order or our products.

booktech@oreilly.com
For book content technical questions or corrections.

proposals@oreilly.com
To submit new book or software proposals to our editors and product managers.

international@oreilly.com
For information about our international distributors or translation queries. For a list of our distributors outside of North America check out:
http://www.oreilly.com/distributors.html

5. Work with Us

Check out our website for current employment opportunites:
http://jobs.oreilly.com/

O'Reilly & Associates, Inc.
1005 Gravenstein Hwy North
Sebastopol, CA 95472 USA
TEL   707-829-0515 or 800-998-9938
     (6am to 5pm PST)
FAX   707-829-0104

O'REILLY®

TO ORDER: **800-998-9938** • order@oreilly.com • www.oreilly.com
ONLINE EDITIONS OF MOST O'REILLY TITLES ARE AVAILABLE BY SUBSCRIPTION AT **safari.oreilly.com**
ALSO AVAILABLE AT MOST RETAIL AND ONLINE BOOKSTORES

International Distributors

http://international.oreilly.com/distributors.html • international@oreilly.com

UK, EUROPE, MIDDLE EAST, AND AFRICA (EXCEPT FRANCE, GERMANY, AUSTRIA, SWITZERLAND, LUXEMBOURG, AND LIECHTENSTEIN)

INQUIRIES
O'Reilly UK Limited
4 Castle Street
Farnham
Surrey, GU9 7HS
United Kingdom
Telephone: 44-1252-711776
Fax: 44-1252-734211
Email: information@oreilly.co.uk

ORDERS
Wiley Distribution Services Ltd.
1 Oldlands Way
Bognor Regis
West Sussex PO22 9SA
United Kingdom
Telephone: 44-1243-843294
UK Freephone: 0800-243207
Fax: 44-1243-843302 (Europe/EU orders)
or 44-1243-843274 (Middle East/Africa)
Email: cs-books@wiley.co.uk

FRANCE

INQUIRIES & ORDERS
Éditions O'Reilly
18 rue Séguier
75006 Paris, France
Tel: 33-1-40-51-71-89
Fax: 33-1-40-51-72-26
Email: france@oreilly.fr

GERMANY, SWITZERLAND, AUSTRIA, LUXEMBOURG, AND LIECHTENSTEIN

INQUIRIES & ORDERS
O'Reilly Verlag
Balthasarstr. 81
D-50670 Köln, Germany
Telephone: 49-221-973160-91
Fax: 49-221-973160-8
Email: anfragen@oreilly.de (inquiries)
Email: order@oreilly.de (orders)

CANADA

(FRENCH LANGUAGE BOOKS)
Les Éditions Flammarion ltée
375, Avenue Laurier Ouest
Montréal (Québec) H2V 2K3
Tel: 1-514-277-8807
Fax: 1-514-278-2085
Email: info@flammarion.qc.ca

HONG KONG

City Discount Subscription Service, Ltd.
Unit A, 6th Floor, Yan's Tower
27 Wong Chuk Hang Road
Aberdeen, Hong Kong
Tel: 852-2580-3539
Fax: 852-2580-6463
Email: citydis@ppn.com.hk

KOREA

Hanbit Media, Inc.
Chungmu Bldg. 210
Yonnam-dong 568-33
Mapo-gu
Seoul, Korea
Tel: 822-325-0397
Fax: 822-325-9697
Email: hant93@chollian.dacom.co.kr

PHILIPPINES

Global Publishing
G/F Benavides Garden
1186 Benavides Street
Manila, Philippines
Tel: 632-254-8949/632-252-2582
Fax: 632-734-5060/632-252-2733
Email: globalp@pacific.net.ph

TAIWAN

O'Reilly Taiwan
1st Floor, No. 21, Lane 295
Section 1, Fu-Shing South Road
Taipei, 106 Taiwan
Tel: 886-2-27099669
Fax: 886-2-27038802
Email: mori@oreilly.com

INDIA

Shroff Publishers & Distributors Pvt. Ltd.
12, "Roseland", 2nd Floor
180, Waterfield Road, Bandra (West)
Mumbai 400 050
Tel: 91-22-641-1800/643-9910
Fax: 91-22-643-2422
Email: spd@vsnl.com

CHINA

O'Reilly Beijing
SIGMA Building, Suite B809
No. 49 Zhichun Road
Haidian District
Beijing, China PR 100080
Tel: 86-10-8809-7475
Fax: 86-10-8809-7463
Email: beijing@oreilly.com

JAPAN

O'Reilly Japan, Inc.
Yotsuya Y's Building
7 Banch 6, Honshio-cho
Shinjuku-ku
Tokyo 160-0003 Japan
Tel: 81-3-3356-5227
Fax: 81-3-3356-5261
Email: japan@oreilly.com

SINGAPORE, INDONESIA, MALAYSIA, AND THAILAND

TransQuest Publishers Pte Ltd
30 Old Toh Tuck Road #05-02
Sembawang Kimtrans Logistics Centre
Singapore 597654
Tel: 65-4623112
Fax: 65-4625761
Email: wendiw@transquest.com.sg

AUSTRALIA

Woodslane Pty., Ltd.
7/5 Vuko Place
Warriewood NSW 2102
Australia
Tel: 61-2-9970-5111
Fax: 61-2-9970-5002
Email: info@woodslane.com.au

NEW ZEALAND

Woodslane New Zealand, Ltd.
21 Cooks Street (P.O. Box 575)
Waganui, New Zealand
Tel: 64-6-347-6543
Fax: 64-6-345-4840
Email: info@woodslane.com.au

ARGENTINA

Distribuidora Cuspide
Suipacha 764
1008 Buenos Aires
Argentina
Phone: 54-11-4322-8868
Fax: 54-11-4322-3456
Email: libros@cuspide.com

ALL OTHER COUNTRIES

O'Reilly & Associates, Inc.
1005 Gravenstein Hwy North
Sebastopol, CA 95472 USA
Tel: 707-829-0515
Fax: 707-829-0104
Email: order@oreilly.com

last system

Other books by

Natalie Savage Carlson

A BROTHER FOR THE ORPHELINES
Pictures by Garth Williams

CARNIVAL IN PARIS
Pictures by Fermin Rocker

THE FAMILY UNDER THE BRIDGE
Pictures by Garth Williams

THE HAPPY ORPHELINE
Pictures by Garth Williams

JEAN-CLAUDE'S ISLAND
Pictures by Nancy Ekholm Burkert

A PET FOR THE ORPHELINES
Pictures by Fermin Rocker

SASHES RED AND BLUE
Pictures by Rita Fava

THE SONG OF THE LOP-EARED MULE
Pictures by Janina Domanska

THE TALKING CAT
Pictures by Roger Duvoisin

THE TOMAHAWK FAMILY
Pictures by Stephen Cook

WINGS AGAINST THE WIND
Pictures by Mircea Vasiliu

THE ORPHELINES
IN THE
ENCHANTED CASTLE

THE ORPHELINES
IN THE
ENCHANTED CASTLE

BY

Natalie Savage Carlson

PICTURES BY

Adriana Saviozzi

HARPER & ROW, PUBLISHERS
NEW YORK, EVANSTON, AND LONDON

FOR SISTER EVANGELINE

THE ORPHELINES
IN THE
ENCHANTED CASTLE

Once upon a time there were twenty beautiful French princesses who were going to live in an enchanted castle with their fairy godmother and their thirty knights.

The princesses were really the twenty little *orphelines*, as the French call girl orphans, and their fairy godmother was plump, kindly Madame Flattot, the woman in charge of them. The noble knights were the thirty boy orphans who would share the castle with them.

And the castle was to be their new orphanage. It was in the forest of Fontainebleau, south of Paris, waiting for them to bring it to life again—as the prince had done in THE SLEEPING BEAUTY OF THE WOODS.

"Of course the castle will be enchanted," Madame Flattot assured the girls. "Everyone knows that the forest of Fontainebleau is full of fairies and witches. And the ghostly huntsman who rides with his pack of dogs."

Genevieve, the young girl who helped take care of the children, rolled her blue eyes fearfully. "There is a robbers' cave there," she stated, "and my godmother said that there are wolves in the forest."

1

"Bah!" scoffed Madame. "Who cares for wolves?" She tossed her false braid and lifted a corner of her apron. "In the forest of Fontainebleau even *I* shall be enchanting," she declared.

She danced a few steps of the stately minuet and ended with a deep curtsey to the moving man who was also bowing to her because he was carrying out a table on his back.

But, alas! The move to the enchanted castle was poorly timed. It came on St. Médard's Day, when it is said that even one drop of rain foretells forty days of wet weather.

St. Médard is the good saint who, in medieval times, answered the prayers of drought-stricken farmers, and he has never learned that one can get too much of his rain.

The long trip to the castle was made in a downpour, so the disappointed orphelines could see only a blur of green leaves and black tree trunks as they drove through the famous forest.

Madame Flattot sat in back of the autobus with Coucky on her lap. He was the little Arab baby who had been abandoned in the bread basket of the girls' orphanage. For a long anxious time it had looked as if he would be taken away from the girls and put in the boys'

2

orphanage. But now that both orphanages were to be combined, the orphelines did not have to worry about losing their littlest brother. And they could hardly wait to meet their thirty new brothers.

The girls squeezed against the windows. Genevieve wiped a round spot free of moisture on her pane and searched the great tree trunks and piles of gray rocks for the forms of fleeing wolves.

"I saw something running over the rocks that might have been a big dog," she said. "It really could have been a dog. Maybe it *was* a dog."

"I think it was a wolf," said Brigitte, tossing back her thick braid that was like a tassel of millet seeds. "And if you weren't in this autobus, you could be Little Red Hood and talk to him about your godmother."

She was the happiest orpheline and the first one to think of a new game or remember an old story.

Yvette, who was near Brigitte's age, tried to still Genevieve's fears. "If a wolf ever comes near you," she said, "our thirty knights will protect you. They will slay the wolf." Of course, Coucky wasn't old enough even to slay a beetle so they could not count him among their knights yet.

"I will be satisfied with the knights if they are obedient boys with clean faces and polite habits," said Genevieve. "I won't expect them to kill wolves."

"Perhaps the wolves will chase our cats," worried curly haired Josine, the youngest. She was worried about the ten cats the orphelines had adopted at a cat show in Paris.

"Do not worry about the cats," said Genevieve. "They have been sent to the castle's farm already, so they can live happily ever after in the barn."

Madame Flattot, with Coucky still in her arms, went forward to consult the driver of the autobus. She came back beaming.

"He says we are getting close to the castle now," she told the children. "First we will come to the village." She wiped the window with her handkerchief. "Oh, that St. Médard and his rain!" she exclaimed. "But in three days it will be St. Barnabé's Day, and if the sun shines even a minute, St. Médard's nose will be cut and we shall have good weather from then on through the summer."

"Will St. Médard's nose really be cut?" asked Yvette in a shocked voice.

"Of course not," replied Madame. "It is only the old-time way of saying that St. Barnabé will turn off St. Médard's rain."

The driver's information was correct because the road went out of the trees and wound through the narrow street of a village. It curled around the village square

5

with its rusty statue of a World War I soldier and past the church whose steeple was crumbling with age.

Then back into the trees went the autobus and in two jerks and a backfire they drew up to the castle.

It was small as castles are measured, and certainly nothing to compare with the royal palace of Fontainebleau, but it really looked as if it belonged in a fairy tale. On one side of the entrance was a squat round donjon with flat top and on the other a graceful pointed tower, like a saltshaker and pepper pot set precisely against a fluted soup tureen. A real moat circled the building, but in place of a drawbridge was a sturdy concrete bridge that led to the recessed entrance.

The orphelines clasped their hands and sighed with blissful delight, but Madame Flattot was not so charmed. "Oh, là!" she cried. "They haven't filled the moat yet. And already water is gathering in it from the rain."

"I will have to keep my third eye on the girls all the time," said Genevieve, because she feared drownings even more than wolves.

Madame Flattot had one consolation. "At least I have been assured that the furniture has arrived and been put in place," she comforted herself. "And Monsieur de Goupil told me that there are fine new desks in the classrooms—although that will be of no use to us now that it is summer vacation."

Monsieur de Goupil was the head of both orphanages so he had to think of everything. He had even thought of buying his brother-in-law's old deserted castle so the boys and girls could live together in one big family.

"I do hope my portrait of Napoleon wasn't damaged in the moving," fretted Madame, "that is, no more than it was when I bought it." She had purchased the oil painting at the Ham and Iron Fair in Paris, dickering with the dealer until he had lowered his price for the last time.

The painting had since hung in the place of honor in the orphanage parlor.

But the girls weren't interested in the furniture or Napoleon's picture.

"Have the boys come yet?" one of them asked as they rose from their seats and crowded the aisle. "Did our knights get here ahead of us?"

"I don't think so," said Madame as the autobus came to a stop by the footbridge. "Now don't worry about the boys. Worry about the rain. When the door is opened, everyone run for the castle as fast as possible. Pretend that Genevieve's wolves are chasing you and safety lies within the castle."

So, as soon as the door of the bus opened, the orphelines screamed shrilly and ran to the recessed door. And to hasten them even more, Genevieve ran behind them making growling noises.

When they entered the great hall, they fell silent with awe. There was an enormous fireplace at each end and over the stairway was mounted the head of a stag. To be sure, part of an antler had been broken off and the hair had been eaten by a century of moths, but he still served as a reminder that this had been one of the old hunting castles of the forest of Fontainebleau.

"Where's the rest of him?" asked Josine, because she

thought that the stag had thrust his head through the wall.

She promptly went running up the stone steps to find the room behind the stag's head which should contain his body.

Madame Flattot admired the great fireplaces. "It will be such a problem to decide over which one to hang Napoleon's portrait." She sighed. "Now would he prefer to look at the stag or would he have better light by the windows at the other end? I think he would do better in the light. But I am overlooking the most important thing. I must see the kitchen. Monsieur tells me that everything is new. There is even a modern gas stove." She saluted the spot where Napoleon's picture would hang. "You had your empire and I have mine," she announced to the picture that hadn't been hung yet. "My kingdom is my kitchen."

The kitchen was almost as large as the great hall and as dark. But a shiny chrome sink had been added to one corner and close to it was a new stove that gleamed silver and white. Over it hung rows and rows of bright new metal pots and pans.

Madame lifted a pan from its peg critically. She juggled it disapprovingly.

"Regard my battery of cooking pots," she said to

Genevieve. "Would Napoleon have sent his troops into battle with tin cannons?" She held the pot at arm's length. "It does not even bend my wrist," she complained. "It should be of iron or copper and almost too heavy to lift. And this omelette pan next to it. If I cooked eggs in this thin pan, the whites would burn or turn to rubber. I shall insist to Monsieur de Goupil that I get my old iron pots back."

"But these pans look so pretty hanging on the wall over the stove," said Genevieve. "And they make the castle more modern."

"I may live in a modern castle," pronounced Madame Flattot, "but I am an old-fashioned cook. That is why I can make cheap food taste so good."

She looked into the oven. She tried to light one of the burners. Nothing happened. She looked behind the stove.

"*Hélas*, Genevieve," she mourned, "we do not live in a modern castle yet. The stove is not connected. Now how can I get supper?"

The orphelines loved the discovery that the new-fashioned stove was not connected.

"The big fireplaces, Madame," cried Brigitte. "Since you are an old-fashioned cook, you can cook in one of them. It will be like the olden times in the castle."

10

"And where will the wood for the fireplace come from?" asked Madame. "Do you think we are living in one of your fairy tales where hands with invisible bodies will carry in logs for the fireplace and lay the cloth for a feast?"

It really seemed like living in a fairy tale because no sooner had Madame said these magic words than invisible hands began pounding on the heavy outer door.

"It's the boys," cried Brigitte excitedly. "The boys have arrived. They can look for some wood."

But it was not the boys. It was a man in dripping blue work clothes and muddy wooden shoes. Clinging to his hand was Josine. She was smeared with mud from her curly hair to her soaking shoes.

"I came to bring you the message that the boys will not arrive until after supper," explained the man. "Then I found this little one caught in the moat. I'm Hubert, one of the farm workers," he added hastily.

Madame Flattot was aghast. The orphelines opened their mouths in astonishment. The last time they had seen Josine she was running up the stairs to find the room behind the stag.

"I couldn't find the rest of the stag," said Josine, "so I looked out of the window and I saw a little snake in the moat. I didn't want him to drown so I found a back door and went out to save him."

"A snake!" shrieked Madame Flattot. "You tried to catch a snake?"

Hubert handed Josine to her. "It was only a harmless water snake," he explained, "and the water in the moat isn't deep enough to drown a child. But the sides were so slippery that she couldn't get out."

Madame Flattot began to marshal her forces after the first shock.

"Take her upstairs and try to find a bathroom," she said to Genevieve. "And pray that the water pipes are connected. If they are, give her a good hot bath. And if there is no hot water, give her a brisk rubbing down after you have washed off the mud. And if there is no water, we will have to set pots out in the rain to catch some. Those new ones should be good for that."

Then like the good general she was, Madame Flattot turned the disaster into victory. "Can you please bring us some wood, Hubert?" she asked the farm worker. "And build a roaring fire in the fireplace under Napoleon's picture."

Genevieve and Hubert quickly obeyed Madame's orders, although the farmer had to be shown which of the fireplaces was to be under Napoleon's picture.

Madame Flattot caught her breath and shook her finger at the orphelines. "And don't anyone dare go outside until the rain stops and the moat is dry," she commanded.

Hubert's wooden shoes clacked back and forth over the stone floors, leaving a trail of muddy footprints. Madame brought a mop from the kitchen and followed behind him as he carried in load after load of fire logs.

The orphelines were disappointed that the boys would not arrive for supper. But it was fun to watch Madame bustling around the fireplace like a cook of old. She filled the biggest pot she could find with the meat and vegetables she had had the foresight to bring along with them.

Soon a delicious smell was coming from the fireplace. The great logs crackled and the flames leaped higher and higher. Black soot gathered on the sides of the big pot. Madame's face grew redder and redder from the heat of the fire.

"It may not be breast of white peacock," she apologized, "but it will taste as good."

Then she ladled her stew into bowls she found in a cupboard and gave the children big spoons from a drawer. The orphelines and Coucky squatted on the stone floor with their bowls and didn't have to mind

their table manners. It was such a wonderful feast in the enchanted castle. They only regretted that the boys couldn't have shared the meal with them.

After they had carried out their dirty dishes and spoons, the orphelines decided to explore the castle since Madame had forbidden them to go outside. The first thing they wanted to explore was the tower. They followed its corkscrew steps to the very top. There they came to a barred door. What would they find when they opened it? A dwarf spinning straw into gold? A witch with a poisoned apple?

They were disappointed, because when they pulled the bolt and opened the door there was only an empty round room with tiny windows.

"Let's play Bluebeard," cried Brigitte. "I'll be Bluebeard's wife on the steps outside. Yvette, you be my sister Anne looking out of the window to see if my brothers are coming to rescue me. And the rest of you can just lie on the steps and be Bluebeard's murdered wives."

Of course all the orphelines understood the play without any more explanation. Yvette was to watch for the arrival of their brothers, the boy orphans.

Yvette went to a window and began her vigil. Brigitte banged on the door desperately. "Anne, Sister Anne," she cried, "dost thou see anyone coming?"

"I don't see anything but a lot of wet trees," answered Sister Anne. "It's still raining, and I bet it will keep on for forty days and we'll never get outside."

The murdered wives giggled.

Brigitte pounded on the door again. "Anne, Sister Anne," she besought, "dost thou not see anyone coming? Hubert said they'd get here after supper."

"I wish they had come in time to eat with us," said one of the murdered wives.

"Hush!" Brigitte reprimanded her. "You're dead and can't talk."

But some of the wives grew tired of being dead.

16

"This is dull," complained Marie. "We can't see anything."

"And Marie keeps sticking her foot in my face," whined Charlotte.

"These steps are so hard," Lucette joined in. "We should get some pillows so we can be comfortable while we're dead."

But at that point there was a cry of triumph from the tower room.

"They're coming! They're coming!" cried Sister Anne. "There's an autobus coming down our road."

The murdered wives came to life completely and

went running down the steps to see the boys. But Brigitte opened the door and joined Yvette in the tower room.

"I wish we could open these windows and lean out," said Yvette.

But they had to be content with flattening their faces against the small panes and watching the autobus halt by the bridge. It immediately exploded with boys. They came flying from both ends of the bus. They gathered in little groups, staring up at the castle while Monsieur Roger, who was in charge of them, talked to the driver.

Brigitte began tapping the window panes to attract their attention. Yvette waved wildly.

Soon one of the boys saw them because he was most interested in the tower. The girls watched him turn to some others. Soon all of the boys were looking up at them. Both girls waved their welcome.

"Our knights," cried Brigitte. "Our knights have come to rescue us from Bluebeard."

Two of the boys stooped and gathered something into their hands. Then they threw the somethings at the tower. There were soft ploppings below the window and mud speckled the panes.

"How craven!" declared Brigitte indignantly. "Our knights are throwing mud balls at us."

18

## CHAPTER TWO

It seemed to the orphelines that they never would
have a chance to get acquainted with the boys. Although they took their meals together in the dining hall,
the boys sat at two long tables and the girls at their own.

Monsieur Roger sat at the head of one of the boys'
tables. It was hard to think that he had ever been a boy
himself. It was much easier to imagine him as a tiny
man with a mustache who had popped out of a cabbage
head and grown to full size.

He disapproved of talking at table and cast many a
black look at the chattering orphelines. But he did not
need to be so strict because the boys seemed to be interested in nothing but their food anyway.

And immediately after the meal was over, they were
marched out of the dining hall to their wing of the
castle.

Monsieur Roger privately told Madame Flattot the
reason for his strictness.

"These boys should be in a reform school instead
of an orphanage," he declared. "That Pierre came to us
from the streets of Paris. Only yesterday he tried to set

19

the haystack on fire, but luckily it was too wet to burn easily. And all the others are trying to be like him because he is the biggest."

"Perhaps the girls will be a good influence on them," said Madame.

"I do not believe in mixing girls with boys," replied Monsieur Roger. "It is not proper."

"I don't see why," retorted Madame. "If the good God thinks it proper to mix them together in families, surely they should not be separated in this big family."

On St. Barnabé's Day the rain stopped. The orphelines immediately went in search of the boys. They found some of them playing hopscotch in the lane that led to the farm. They had scrawled squares in the dirt and at one end had scratched CIEL, which means "heaven" in French.

The boys showed little interest in them, especially the one who was hopping in the squares.

"May we play ciel with you?" asked Brigitte.

The boy with a cowlick over his forehead croaked twice like a frog. "We don't play with girls," he said.

"We play with boys," encouraged Yvette.

"We have a wonderful game to play with you," said Brigitte eagerly. "We're princesses living in the enchanted castle and you may be our knights. We shall have tournaments and you may joust for our favors."

20

"Listen to the little goslings, Pierre," said the boy with the cowlick to the biggest one, whose hair bristled like the quills of a hedgehog. "They want us to be their knights and joust for them."

Pierre scornfully put his finger against his nose. "They have rats in the head," he said. "When I grow up I'm going back to Paris and be the leader of a gang."

The boy with the cowlick looked disdainfully at the girls. "Who wants to be a knight on a horse?" he asked. "I'm going to have my own automobile when I grow up."

"And I'm going to be in Pierre's gang," said a little freckle-faced boy.

The orphelines were disappointed in their knights. But Brigitte did not give up.

"I'm a princess," she said dreamily. "I live in a castle with my nineteen sisters, and Madame Flattot is my loving fairy godmother."

Pierre hooted derisively. "You're just a poor orpheline without any parents or relatives," he told her. "You live in a moldy old castle that nobody else wants. Madame Flattot and Genevieve don't care about you really. They wouldn't bother with you if they weren't paid for it. Nobody has ever bothered with me unless he was paid."

Tears came into Brigitte's eyes at the boy's words.

Yvette put her arm around her shoulder. "Don't listen to him, Brigitte," she said. "You're a wicked boy," she told Pierre. "Some ogre cast a spell on you."

Pierre glanced at the small boy standing beside him. "Listen to these little goslings, Marcel," he said. He shoved the little boy toward the girls. "You can be their knight."

The little boy ran to Brigitte and made a clownish bow.

Josine immediately stepped behind him and gave him a shove that sent him sprawling in the dirt at Brigitte's feet. Marcel scrambled to his own feet and started for Josine. The littlest orpheline screamed as she ran for the safety of the castle, but she kept looking behind to see if Marcel was still following her. She stopped in the shelter of the doorway. "My knight has freckles all over his face," she taunted him, "and he can't catch *me*."

But Marcel had lost interest in her because he was needed by the other boys. Yvette had scraped out the hopscotch squares with the side of her shoe and Pierre was calling for help.

At his command the boys banded together and gathered rocks. They began throwing them at the girls.

Brigitte picked up a heavy clod and heaved it at Pierre. The other girls quickly followed her example.

When the jousting between the knights and their ladies was at its height, Monsieur Roger came hurrying down the lane.

"Stop!" he thundered, as a misdirected rock hit his ear. "Stop this scandal at once! Come here, you Pierre! Come here, all of you."

The boys sullenly shuffled toward him.

"They started it," accused Pierre. "We were just minding our own business and they came down here and started fighting us."

"We did not," declared Brigitte hotly. "We just came here and wanted to be friendly and play with them. They started it. They teased us."

"We did not," cried Marcel. "That littlest gosling pushed me into the dirt. She's an *enfant terrible*."

"Silence!" roared Monsieur Roger. "I have had enough. You boys go to the farm and help Hubert with the weeding. That is what you were supposed to be doing." He glared at the orphelines. "And you bold girls report to Madame Flattot immediately and tell her I have forbidden the boys to play with you."

The girls were very subdued as they returned to the castle. They told Madame Flattot their side of the trouble. They had asked the boys if they might play ciel with them, and the boys had immediately begun throwing rocks at them. "And we didn't do anything at all to them," said Marie.

"I pushed Marcel into the dirt," admitted Josine proudly, "and he chased me. I think he's a handsome boy. His face looks like a big round cookie full of chocolate drops."

Madame Flattot listened to all the complaints then gave her judgment. "They are very wicked boys," she said, "and you are foolish girls. I forbid you to speak to them unless they improve."

Brigitte still smarted from Pierre's words. Were they true? She knew that they were really orphelines and not princesses. But did Madame and Genevieve pretend to love them only because they were paid for it?

"One of them said that you don't really love us," said Brigitte. "He said you just take care of us because you're paid for it. If Monsieur de Goupil stopped paying you, would you still take care of us for nothing?"

"That makes a real question," pondered Madame Flattot. "I could not live without an income. How would I pay my social security and buy my safety pins? No, I would have to go and work in a café in Paris."

The orphelines' faces dropped.

Madame gaily tossed her braid to and fro. "But, ah, there would be my day off every week," she continued.

"On that day I would go back to the café as usual. But I would not cook a soup or toss a salad. I would gather together all the eggs and sugar and chocolate I could find. Then I would bake a giant chocolate cake. I would bring that cake here, and one day a week we would be a happy family again and eat chocolate cake all day long."

The orphelines were pleased with Madame's answer. Of course she really loved them. Wouldn't she spend her day off with them instead of going to the cinema or a park in Paris?

But there was still Genevieve. If her pay stopped, would she be willing to bake them a chocolate cake once a week and spend the day with them?

They looked for her through the great rooms and stairways of the castle. At last they found her hanging the bedding out of the windows. The sheets looked like white banners flying from the castle walls.

They gathered around her anxiously. "Genevieve, do you really love us, or do you only take care of us because you are paid for it?" asked Brigitte.

"Suppose you didn't get any money for working here," put in Yvette. "Would you stay with us anyway?"

"Oh, là!" exclaimed Genevieve. "I could not work

26

free. My godmother wouldn't let me do that because she wouldn't think it was fair. I would have to marry that stupid Jacques she is saving for me." The orphelines groaned with disappointment, but Genevieve's face brightened. "But only on one condition," she went on. "That we adopt all of you and take you on our honeymoon. And after that, we would all live together on his farm in Normandy."

"And once a week Madame would come to visit us with her chocolate cake," finished Josine. "I hope she'll bake that cake even if she still gets paid for taking care of us."

So the girls were satisfied with the answers that Madame Flattot and Genevieve had given them, but they were disappointed in the conduct of their knights.

"And we'll never, never have anything more to do with them until they apologize," decided Brigitte.

"Can't I even push Marcel so he'll chase me?" pleaded Josine.

One morning when mists veiled the old castle in a dream, a most unchivalrous thing happened to Josine's cat, Swan.

The littlest orpheline often went to the barn to play with him and usually ended up by smuggling him into the castle. It was so easy to hide a cat in the many passage-ways and rooms. And Swan walked with such light *peti peta* steps that he often went unnoticed for many hours.

Then Madame would say, "Take the cat outside, Josine. No cats in the castle. Monsieur de Goupil has forbidden it. After all, Swan is not the Booted Cat so he cannot expect to live in a castle."

Monsieur de Goupil had been very nervous about the cats ever since the time that Swan had jumped from the window onto his shoulder when he was holding a teacup in his hand.

But this day Swan came to the castle of his own accord. He came flying in a white streak with a small tin pan tied to his tail. Josine found him by the back door, mewing sadly and sitting on the edge of the pan.

28

At first she thought that Madame had tied the pan
to his tail, because it was one of the small light ones
she didn't like for cooking. But Madame had been gone
all morning.

Quick suspicion flashed into Josine's head. One of
those boys had done it–probably Marcel. She would
go and find out.

She loosened the pan from her cat's tail and took him
into her arms. She started down the graveled road that
led to the farm. Wait until she found that Marcel. Perhaps she would push him into the dirt twice.

Some of the boys were busy cleaning the fowlyard.
When they saw her coming they gathered their heads

together. Josine advanced upon them angrily, her eyes searching for Marcel.

"Somebody tied a pan on my cat's tail," she accused, "and I think I know who did it."

The boys immediately became sympathetic. "Poor cat," said Pierre. "It was that wicked ogre from the other side of the woods. You saw him do it, didn't you, Marcel?"

There was the little freckle-faced boy. He looked sufficiently frightened. "I ran away," he said. "I was afraid of that old ogre. He was tall as a church steeple and he had a fierce black beard."

Josine wasn't sure. "I think one of you did it," she maintained. "I think it was Marcel."

Pierre stepped up to Josine, indignantly tossing his bristly head. "And that isn't all," he said. "The wicked ogre has turned poor Madame Flattot into a hen. If you don't believe me, you can come and see for your-self."

Josine was worried. She went to the fence and looked through the wiring.

"It's that black and white hen with the chicks." Pierre pointed. "Madame tried to stop the ogre from tying the pan on the cat's tail, so he turned her into that hen. You saw it, Tintin."

"I told her to run," said Tintin, "but she wouldn't do it. Then the ogre tried to turn me into a dog." At these words a sudden spasm seized Tintin. He crouched down on all fours. "Ouaf, ouaf, ouaf," he began barking.

"*Hélas*, poor Tintin!" exclaimed Pierre. "You didn't get away fast enough. You're caught under part of his spell." He began to pat Tintin's head as the barking grew more ferocious. "Down, boy," he ordered. "Down, *toutou*."

But Josine wasn't interested in Tintin's plight. She was staring at the black and white hen surrounded by her yellow chicks. She did look something like Madame Flattot. She had the same bright eyes and plump figure. She even walked like Madame.

"Is it really you, Madame?" Josine questioned the hen.

Josine put the cat down. The partly bewitched boy immediately leaped at Swan with a fierce growl, and the cat dashed for safety.

Josine stood at the gate and watched the black and white hen. She was clucking fussily to her chicks. "*Glousse, glousse*," she clucked in Madame's anxious tone of voice. And when she cocked her red-combed head, gave Josine a sharp, bright look, and shook her wings fretfully, the little girl was sure that it was Madame Flattot.

"Poor, poor Madame," she cried. "Perhaps Brigitte will know what to do about you."

She caught the hen and turned back to the castle. Tintin flopped after her on all fours, barking and snapping at the hem of her skirt. Josine gave him a kick. "Bad dog!" she said. "Why didn't you bite the wicked ogre?"

As she carried the hen in her arms she tried to comfort her. "Never mind, Madame," she said. "I will take care of you. When I was littler than you, you took care of me. Now that you're the littlest, I'll take care of you." She patted the hen and asked, "How does it feel to be a hen? Do the feathers stick you?"

But the hen made no answer.

Josine couldn't find anyone in the girls' side of the castle. Perhaps Genevieve had taken them to gather cabbages on the farm. Another fright came over her. Perhaps the ogre had turned them all into cabbages.

She would take Madame Flattot to her room and try to make her comfortable. She punched a nest into the soft comforter on Madame's bed and eased the hen into it. "You can rest now," she told her. "You won't have to cook or scrub anymore. I'll do it for you."

32

Then she jumped as a deep voice at the door demanded, "Josine, what is that hen doing on my bed?"

Behind her stood Madame Flattot without feathers or red comb. The little girl quickly looked back to the bed. There was the black and white hen. For a few seconds Josine wasn't sure which was Madame Flattot.

Then she realized that the boys had played a trick on her.

"I thought the hen was you," said Josine sheepishly. "The boys said a wicked ogre had turned you into a hen."

Madame Flattot was angry at the boys for the trick

they had played on Josine. She was angry with Josine for being so taken in. She was angriest at the black and white hen. She raised her skirts and shook them at her. "Shoo! Shoo!" she scolded. "Out of here, impostor!"

"I thought it was true," persisted Josine. "Everybody is always talking about princesses and ogres and fairies. Sometimes I don't know what is real and what isn't."

Madame Flattot closed the door on the hen's tail. "It has all gone too far," she declared. "There will be no more fairy tales. The business must end before we all lose our minds." She gave Josine a quick henlike glance. "And if an ogre ever changed me into anything," she ended, "it would not be a hen. It would be a formidable creature such as a rhinoceros or a tiger."

After the incident had been discussed by Madame, Genevieve and Monsieur Roger—to say nothing of all the orphelines—it was decided that the boys should either make a public apology to Josine or be kept in the castle for a week. They decided on the apology.

The littlest orpheline insisted on wearing her blue and white Sunday dress and her biggest hair bow for the important event. Genevieve even loaned her red necklace. All the other girls cast envious looks at Josine as she stood between Monsieur Roger and Madame Flattot in the courtyard.

The boys advanced in a group. They looked ashamed and self-conscious. They tried to make themselves small as they marched to Josine with bowed heads and lowered eyes. All but Marcel. He was grinning as happily as if he were arriving for a fête.

Pierre, as the eldest, stepped from the group and approached Josine. He nervously plucked at the blond quills of his hair.

"We, the boys of the orphanage," he began, "humbly beseech your—your—"

"Pardon," prompted Monsieur Roger.

The boy began again in a surer voice, "We, the boys of the orphanage, humbly beseech your pardon, Mademoiselle Josine, for the trick we—we—"

"Perpetrated," pronounced Monsieur for him.

"On you," went on the boy.

"And we will never let it happen again," added Monsieur Roger for himself as well as the boys.

"And I'm sorry I tied the pan on your cat's tail," added Marcel, although Josine did not think that he looked sorry at all.

"It was a scandal," declared Monsieur Roger.

Josine airily perked her hair ribbon with one hand

and twisted the red necklace with the other. Madame Flattot nudged her. Josine remembered her speech.

"I forgive you," she answered graciously, "because we are brothers and sisters in one big family."

"And we should live together in peace and love," Madame finished for her.

Then Pierre made a clumsy bow to Josine because he didn't know how to end the ceremony. Marcel pinched Tintin. The delegation turned and slowly marched away. But as soon as the boys reached the edge of the cobblestones they took to their heels as if an ogre were really after them.

Brigitte whispered to Yvette, "Weren't they knightly? Perhaps they will be that way from now on."

Monsieur Roger said to Madame, "The girls are as bad as the boys. Their heads are full of elves and butter-flies."

Madame Flattot felt guilty too. "Oh, I know that the forest of Fontainebleau has bewitched all of us," she admitted. "Perhaps we should take the children on a tour of the royal palace so they will become interested in real kings and queens. And I have always wanted to see Napoleon's rooms."

"It would be good for the boys too," Monsieur Roger agreed. "It will keep them from forgetting their history during vacation. I shall make arrangements with Hubert to use the farm trucks." He added severely, "We will keep the boys and girls in separate groups."

Madame turned to the girls. "And I forbid you to speak to the boys or have anything more to do with them until they have proven their good intentions," she commanded. "They didn't look too remorseful to me."

Not all was play for the orphelines. They had many chores to keep them busy. They helped weed the farm gardens and gather in the vegetables.

One day they went with Genevieve to fill some sacks full of big onions which Madame planned to braid into garlands and hang in the tower room to dry.

Brigitte talked and dawdled so much that she was behind the others in her work.

"We will go back," said Genevieve, "and as soon as your bag is full, you may follow. Josine, perhaps you would like to stay to help Brigitte."

Josine agreed to stay, but she wasn't much help. She was trying her hand at braiding the onion tops, and Brigitte stopped pulling onions to show her how.

As they worked at the braiding Hubert's horse and cart came slowly down the road that cut through the field. Three of the boys were in the cart. It stopped near the girls. Hubert jumped out and started down the rows to take a look at the cabbages in the next field. The boys were left alone in the cart.

"Hé, if it isn't the little princesses braiding onion

tops," said Pierre. "Where are the others? At Prince Charmant's ball?"

Brigitte turned her nose into the air. "We can't talk to you," she informed him. "Madame forbade it."

"So the princesses can't talk," said Jean. "A witch must have their tongues."

Josine ran up to the horse. "We can talk to you," she told the heavy-hoofed beast. "Tell them that we are going to tour the palace of Fontainebleau sometime soon and if they are good, perhaps Madame will let us talk to them again."

"We're going too," said Pierre, "but we aren't going with you. Monsieur Roger said so. We are going to see Napoleon's hat and his sword."

Brigitte joined Josine. She addressed herself to the horse. "Tell those boys that the palace used to be a royal hunting castle long ago. I learned that in my history."

"We know that," retorted Pierre, "so we don't need a horse to tell us. And these woods were the royal hunting grounds."

Little Marcel spoke for the first time. "Maybe Hubert will take us rabbit hunting with him next fall," he said.

"May we go too?" asked Josine.

Brigitte warningly put her hand over Josine's mouth. "You can't talk to them," she reminded her. "You'll have to let the horse ask them."

"Of course you can't go," replied Jean, without waiting for the horse to repeat the question. "Girls can't go hunting."

Then Pierre leaned over the cart with a grin as wide as his face. "Maybe they would like to go on a cuckoo hunt," he suggested.

The other boys became enthusiastic at the idea. The girls abandoned the horse immediately because Madame had imposed silence on them only until the boys improved. That moment seemed to have arrived.

"How do you hunt cuckoos?" asked Brigitte. "Do you ride horses with hounds or shoot them with a gun?"

Pierre looked disgusted. "Maybe we shouldn't take them after all," he said, "because they're so stupid. You don't hunt cuckoos with guns or hounds," he informed Brigitte. "You have to get a big sack, like the one you have there, and go out in the woods. Someone has to hold the sack while we boys chase the cuckoos into it."

"Cuckoos are very shy birds," added Jean. "When they are chased, they fly into a dark hole to hide."

"I bet your Madame Flattot would make a wonderful cuckoo pie if we could catch enough of them," said Marcel. "I caught a sackful the first time the boys took me on a cuckoo hunt."

"I'll ask Madame if we may go," offered Brigitte eagerly.

"No, no," Pierre stopped her. "Why don't you make it a surprise? Think of how surprised she will be when we bring her a sack full of cuckoos for a pie."

"Why don't we go right now?" suggested Jean. "They have the sack and I heard some cuckoos calling in the woods beyond the barn."

Brigitte quickly emptied the onions from the sack while the boys hopped down from the cart. Hubert came back across the field, his wooden shoes stepping carefully between the rows of onions.

"We have to see Madame Flattot about something important," Pierre told him.

Brigitte was relieved. She really thought that they should ask Madame's permission to go hunting cuckoos. But as soon as Hubert had driven away, the boys began heading for the woods.

"Come on," they urged the girls. "Do you want the cuckoos to get away?"

"Shouldn't we tell Genevieve anyway?" asked Brigitte.

"No," refused Pierre. "If you tell her, all the other goslings will want to go. And such a crowd will scare the cuckoos away."

Brigitte said no more about it. She was happy that the boys were so friendly. They were really like brothers

42

now. Perhaps the time would come when they would be willing knights.

The children entered the mysterious forest. Great oak trees towered above them and hid the sky. It was very quiet and they could not hear any bird calls at all. They climbed over huge gray boulders sometimes, and at others their footsteps were deadened by the carpet of thick green moss.

At last the boys stopped in a thicket of pine trees.

"This is a good place," suggested Pierre. "We will chase the cuckoos here. They like pines."

He showed Brigitte how to hold the sack with its side resting on the ground and its mouth opened wide.

"Be sure to close it as soon as a cuckoo flies in," he explained. "And be very quiet. You'll have to be patient too."

The boys turned and went running through the woods. The girls waited expectantly. Brigitte kept adjusting the opening of the bag so it would look inviting to a cuckoo.

For a long time they waited patiently. Then Brigitte said, "My back's getting tired. Will you hold the sack for a while, Josine?"

The smaller girl took a turn at the sack, but her back tired more quickly than Brigitte's.

43

"When are the cuckoos going to come?" she whined.

"*Chut!*" warned Brigitte. "They will hear you."

More time passed. It was very, very still in the forest. The stillness was almost frightening.

"Perhaps they couldn't find any cuckoos," said Josine, and this time Brigitte didn't hush her.

"But I think we should wait for the boys to come back for us," she said uneasily. "It was so nice of them to take us on this hunt. We don't want them to think we are poor sports."

They waited a while longer.

Then Josine said, "I don't like cuckoo hunts. I want to go home."

Brigitte felt guilty at the thought of abandoning the hunt and disappointing the boys who had become so friendly. But Josine began to whimper, so Brigitte took her by the hand and started back through the woods. She hoped to come upon the boys and explain to them that Josine was such a little girl that she did not have much patience.

But there was no sign of the boys and every tree and rock seemed strange. They walked aimlessly, hoping to come upon some familiar landmark. Soon they reached a trail that led through leafy chestnut trees. But the trail was strange too.

At last Brigitte said, "We're lost in the woods like poor Little Thumb and his brothers."

"We should have brought some white pebbles and scattered them as we walked into the woods, like he did," said Josine. "Then we could find our way back."

"I wanted to bring pebbles," Brigitte began to imagine, "but I didn't have time. So I broke up bits of bread and dropped them along the way instead. But the birds have eaten them and now we can't find our way back."

"Perhaps we'll be lost all night," quavered Josine. "Perhaps we'll have to sleep under the leaves like Little Thumb and his brothers."

She began to gather leaves as she walked so she would have enough for a coverlet. There were floppy chestnut leaves like the feet of goblin geese, stubby oak leaves that seemed all thumbs, and clumps of pine needles to sew a witch's cape. One by one Josine dropped them into Brigitte's sack.

They heard something coming down the trail.

"The boys," cried Josine. "It's the boys coming after us."

But Brigitte quietly grabbed her by the hand and pulled her away from the trail. "It might be wolves," she whispered.

The two orphelines hid in the bushes. But it wasn't the boys or wolves. It was a dark man with a spade beard riding on a coal black horse. He had a riding whip in his hand, and a long-eared hound followed the horse's hoofs.

"The ghostly huntsman," whispered Brigitte. The girls crouched in the bushes like statues of cherubs in a palace garden. The specter passed on, although the dog gave an inquiring sniff toward the bushes.

Then Brigitte took Josine's hand and they left the trail for the open woods.

"We don't want to meet him again," said Brigitte.

They walked on and nothing looked familiar.

"I'm tired," whimpered Josine. "I don't want to be in the fairy tale anymore. I want to go home."

"We can't go home," said Brigitte. "We don't know where it is."

In a rocky gorge they came upon another trail, so they turned into it.

"It must go somewhere," said Brigitte.

As the gorge opened they came upon a strange sight. Ahead of them was a great cave where some figures were gathered around a campfire. Others were climbing the rocky cliff with the aid of ropes. They were in khaki shorts and had black neckerchiefs tied around their heads.

Brigitte's heart skipped. "The robbers' cave," she told Josine, "and those must be the robbers."

Josine began to wail. Brigitte didn't know whether to run or stand her ground when one of them came toward her. She then saw that he was only a big boy and that he had a friendly, sun-tanned face.

"What is wrong?" he asked. "Did the little girl hurt herself?"

"We're lost," quavered Brigitte. "We've been walking through the woods forever and we can't find our home."

A tall man in a green beret and khaki uniform like the boy's joined them. He had a friendly face, too, with smile wrinkles lightly drawn around his eyes and lips.

"Who hasn't done his good deed for the day?" he asked the boys. "What about you, Claude?"

"Please, *Chef*," the long-legged youth accepted, "let me take care of them. I'll take them to that old castle over the hill and ask the people there."

The girls silently followed the big boy. He led them back through the gorge and over a wild sandy waste. As they approached a grove of birch trees they heard the clopping of a horse's hoofs. The dark man came riding toward them.

Josine clutched Brigitte and Brigitte seized the boy's arm.

"The ghostly huntsman," she cried. "He is after us."

Claude looked at her with amusement. "It is only Monsieur Courcy," he said. "He is from Paris. He often comes out here to exercise his hunting dog."

Brigitte blushed with embarrassment at her mistake as the boy and the horseman saluted each other in passing. Then Claude continued, "Our troop is from Paris too, so we don't know much about this neighborhood. But the people in the castle should be able to help you."

They stepped from the birches into the sunlight of a clearing beside the road.

"If they don't know where you belong," said the boy, "you can wait there while they call the gendarmes."

They looked down the road. There was the old castle with its tower, donjon, and moat.

"That's our home," cried Brigitte joyfully. "We must have wandered around in a circle."

"People often do when they're lost," confirmed Claude. He raised his hand to his forehead in a salute. "At your service," he said.

But before they left him, Brigitte said, "There may be some boys looking for us in the woods. If they come to your cave, will you tell them that we are safely home? They must be worrying about us."

Claude waited to see that they reached the door of the castle before he turned away.

But when Brigitte told Madame Flattot about their adventure and their concern for the boys, she dashed their dreams.

"The boys are back here in the castle," she said. "You have been fooled by a very old trick. When I was a little girl in Provence, some of my schoolmates played it on me. Only they said we were going on a magpie hunt. They took me out in the cemetery and left me holding the sack while they ran home. But I can tell you that I was more patient than you two. Although night came, I still waited for them to chase a magpie into my sack."

"Weren't you frightened too?" asked Josine.

"If you think it was frightening in those woods," said Madame Flattot, "I can tell you it was worse in a dark cemetery among the tombs and cypress trees."

"But you gave up and went home at last, didn't you?" asked Brigitte.

"No," Madame proudly shook her head. "I did not go home until a searching party found me next morning."

Josine was impressed. "And if they hadn't found you," she said, "you would still be in the cemetery holding that sack."

Madame Flattot gravely nodded; then she frowned. "But those children were severely punished by their parents for the trick they played on me. And so shall it be for the boys. They will not be allowed to go on the tour of the palace."

Now that Brigitte realized the treachery of the boy orphans she was outraged.

"And we thought they had improved," she said. She turned to Josine. "It will take nothing less than magic to turn them into knights," she said. "*Strong* magic."

When the truck brought the orphelines in sight of the royal palace of Fontainebleau, they were too overcome by its magnificence to speak for a few minutes. It looked so proud with its sharp roofs and stone walls yellowed by the ages. They entered a courtyard where a double stairway, shaped like a horseshoe, rose to the main entrance.

"It looks big enough for all the orphans in France to live in," decided Brigitte.

She was carrying a loaf of stale bread under her arm because they had been promised a visit to a carp pond where sightseers fed the fish.

Madame Flattot made arrangements for a guide to take them through. He was a square, weary-looking man with sleepy eyes and a droopy mustache. When he saw the group of children, he looked sad. But he bravely shrugged his shoulders, then fastened his eyes on them.

"You must not touch anything and do not crawl under the ropes," he commanded. "Keep together and do not dawdle in the rear." His voice then became businesslike. "To the right we have the wing of the White Queens and to the left the Chapel of—"

"When do we see Napoleon's rooms?" interrupted Madame Flattot.

"When do we feed our bread to the carp?" asked Brigitte.

The guide gave them a scolding look and began again. "To the right we have the rooms of the White Queens," he repeated.

They went from room to room and the guide kept on talking as if he were reading a history lesson.

Brigitte yawned and Josine stopped to make faces at herself in a great mirror. Yvette sat down to rest on a fragile gilt chair.

The guide went on and on with his talk, "Napoleon once said—stop breathing on that mirror, little girl. And do not sit on the chairs. It is forbidden."

Josine jumped back from the mirror and Yvette sprang from the chair as obediently as if Napoleon himself had given the orders.

The orphelines followed the guide on tiptoe over many slippery inlaid floors. They wished that the guide wasn't with them so they could go coasting on the soles of their shoes.

They were hushed by the splendor of the great

crystal chandeliers, magnificent tapestries, and marble statues.

"I feel like I have died and gone to heaven," Yvette whispered to Brigitte. "Look at that big marble fire-place."

"Did the White Queens ever cook supper in it for Napoleon?" asked Josine.

They went on from room to room, and like a prince exploring a strange castle in a fairy tale, each room they entered was grander than the one before.

Then Josine asked, "When do we get to the fish?"

And Madame asked, "When do we see Napoleon's rooms? I am very loyal to him."

"He lives with us too," Josine told the guide. "He's over one of our fireplaces. But we live in a poor palace."

The guide was disappointed with his group. "If you don't want to see the ballroom, we can go to Napoleon's rooms immediately," he offered.

"I want to see the ballroom," said Brigitte.

"I want to see Napoleon's rooms," said Yvette, "and his hat."

"I want to feed the carp," insisted Josine.

The guide clapped his hands briskly. "*Eh, bien*," he said, "since everyone agrees, we will go to Napoleon's rooms."

So they trooped through more halls and rooms and bumped into other groups of sightseers.

"Oh, là, it is getting crowded," said Madame Flattot. "We must surely keep together. This place is so vast that we may get lost."

Brigitte remembered the time that she and Josine had been lost in the forest. She thought about Little Thumb in the fairy tale. She began picking off bits of bread from the loaf and dropping them on the polished floors as they walked along.

In Napoleon's apartments Madame Flattot was so

55

overcome with emotion that tears glistened in her eyes. At sight of his bed with its rich hangings, she burst into tears.

As Madame mourned over the bed the guide told the history of several vases and statues, although the orphelines did not listen to him.

"But where is the famous court where Napoleon told his soldiers farewell before he went into exile on Elba?" asked Madame, because she wasn't interested in hearing about the vases or statues either. "I must see the court."

The guide gave her his weariest look. "Madame," he said patiently, "that was the courtyard where you entered."

"Then we must go back to it while I am still in the mood," insisted Madame.

As they turned to leave, her tear-stained eyes bulged with horror. The guide turned white as a widowed queen. They both stared at Josine holding a rare Egyptian vase in her hands.

"Don't startle her," warned Madame in a loud whisper. "Don't make any sudden movement. She might drop it." Then she began talking to Josine in a voice that was almost calm, as if she were addressing a sleepwalker on a roof. "Put the pretty vase back, dear," she coaxed. "Just raise your arms carefully and put it back."

Josine obediently set the vase back in place. "It's all right," she assured them. "There was nothing in it to spill."

The guide put his hand over his heart, then sternly said, "The children must leave the palace at once. I had a foreboding of this when I first laid eyes on them. I will take you to the Court of Farewells immediately."

So they didn't get to see all of the palace. But Madame was satisfied when she stood again at the head of the horseshoe stairway where Napoleon had told his soldiers farewell before he went into exile.

"Imagine the sight that day, Madame," the guide addressed himself to her. He pointed into the cobbled courtyard. "The carriage is waiting for him. His soldiers are lined up below. The drums are beating and everyone salutes as he descends the stairway."

The guide stepped down three stairs. He raised his uniform cap in the air. "Soldiers of my old Guard, I bid you farewell," he cried in a choked voice. He returned the cap to his head sideways, thrust his hand into his uniform jacket, and bowed his head in grief. It was such a touching scene that Madame Flattot burst into tears again.

But Josine asked, "When are we going to feed the fish?"

The guide became himself once more as he held out

57

his hand for a tip. He explained how they could go around the long wing and get to the carp pond. "And keep those children out of the palace," were his own words of farewell to Madame.

They had to follow the square, cobbled paths out of the courtyard and go around the wing to reach the pond, but it was worth it. There lay the smooth expanse of water like a giant palace mirror reflecting the glory of the yellowed walls and the tall green trees.

Other visitors were feeding the fish. Brigitte divided the loaf as fairly as she could, and the orphelines leaned over the stone parapets and flung crumbs to the carp. The gray fish streaked through the water and fought each other for the crumbs. Their big mouths opened and closed at the surface.

"I have heard that some of them are a hundred years old," Madame told the orphelines. "King François I had golden necklaces put on them."

The orphelines strained their eyes to catch the flash of a golden necklace, but these carp were quite un-adorned.

When the bread was all gone, it took Madame some time to lure the girls away.

"Don't you want to visit the Garden of Diane?" she tempted them. "A lady says that it is just on the other side of that wing. We can rest on the grass."

With finger to lip, she led them to a doorway. She stepped inside and carefully looked up and down for any sign of the forbidding guide. Then she hurried them across the hall and through more rooms until they found a door on the other side.

The orphelines loved the garden with its sweeping lawns and curving paths. They feasted their eyes on the statue of the goddess Diane who was pulling an arrow from her quiver with one hand and resting the other on the antlers of a small deer.

"If we had some bows and arrows, we could fight the boys better," suggested Josine.

Madame Flattot was so tired that she spread herself generously over a stone bench and took off her shoes. The girls scattered to play and explore.

As Brigitte walked grandly across the grass, pretending that her fairy godmother had waved a wand and all of this great palace with its gardens belonged to her alone, she was surprised to see a familiar figure on one of the benches. It was the man whom the boys at the robbers' cave had called their chief.

She tripped over to him and made a regal curtsey. "Good day, Monsieur Chef," she greeted him politely. "Have you seen Napoleon's rooms?"

The man smiled and beckoned her to sit down beside

him. He was no longer wearing the khaki uniform but a trim dark suit.

"I hope you aren't lost again," he said. "You look like a pretty statue come to life in this garden. Have you been through the palace?"

There was something about his friendly manner that invited Brigitte's trust.

"We live in a castle too," she said. "We're really fairy princesses, but we disguise ourselves as orphelines."

The Chef's happy wrinkles deepened as he patted her hand understandingly. "Ah, yes," he said in a low voice, "one must be careful because grown-ups do not understand such things. Sometimes they even call it lying. Would you believe that I was once the Silver Knight of Burgundy and that I rode a white horse with blue and silver trappings? But I disguised myself as a little boy and my parents thought that my steed was a stick-horse."

Brigitte bubbled with laughter.

"Did you fight dragons?" she asked.

"I slew many, many dragons," he boasted, "and rescued many a fair maiden."

Brigitte's face sobered. "We want the boy orphans who live with us to be knights," she said, "but they

only tease us. They are very bad boys and weren't allowed to come on the tour with us today."

Then she told him about the cuckoo hunt in the woods and the evil spell which had changed Madame Flattot into a hen. "Do you have any boys?" she ended.

"More than I can count," answered the Chef. "You saw some of them at the camp."

"Are any of them as wicked as our boys?" asked Brigitte.

"No, indeed," said the man. "They are all knights of France. I know of a very strong magic that turns knavish boys into noble knights."

"And do they fight dragons?" asked Brigitte hesitantly, because she wasn't sure that they were still playing the fairy-tale game.

"Yes, we all fight dragons," he answered. "Of course the dragons today are much bigger than those of my childhood, and so many of them are invisible."

"Could you use the magic on our boys?" asked Brigitte eagerly.

"I have just that in mind," said her companion. "I am always looking for new boys. You say that you live in that old castle above the cave?"

"The castle is old, but we're new," said Brigitte. "We moved there in June, so our vacation started early."

The man rose slowly. "I must get back to my party," he said. "They will be waiting for me in the Gallery of François I."

Brigitte jumped up and he shook her hand.

"You'll really come and work your magic on our boys, won't you?" she asked anxiously.

"On the oath of the Silver Knight of Burgundy," he replied gravely. Then he gave her the same salute as the boy at the cave had used. He went up the path toward the place.

Brigitte hurried to find the other orphelines to tell them about her meeting with the Silver Knight of Burgundy who could slay dragons and work magic on bad boys. They were still discussing it as they walked back to the Court of Farewells where their truck would be waiting.

As the orphelines passed the horseshoe stairway they saw their guide lounging against the stone railing with a cigarette in his lips. They all waved to him and some of them called, "Farewell, Napoleon."

The orphelines were so excited about the magic that was going to turn the boys into knights that they expected the Silver Knight to arrive at their castle the very next day.

They took turns watching for him from the tower window between their chores.

"How will we know him?" asked Yvette. "What does he look like?"

Brigitte's eyes grew dreamy. "He will be wearing silver armor," she declared, "and he will be riding on a white steed with trappings of blue and silver."

So the girls eagerly awaited the arrival of the magical knight. Day after day they watched for him, but he did not come.

"Perhaps the dragon won the last fight," suggested Josine.

"Don't be foolish," said Brigitte. "The brave knights always conquer the dragons. Surely you've heard enough fairy tales to know that."

But the days passed and the orphelines talked less and less about the brave knight.

They had something new to talk about. Bastille Day was only a week away. That is the French Fourth of July and it falls on the fourteenth of that month. It is the day when the French Revolution began with the storming of the Bastille prison by the oppressed citizens.

"There will be speeches and fireworks in the village," said Madame Flattot, "and a wreath is to be laid at the statue of the soldier in the square."

The eyes of the orphelines sharpened with interest.

"Will we get to go?" asked Brigitte.

"Of course," answered Madame. "The mayor himself has asked for two orphans to lay the wreath. He wants a girl and a boy, so we have chosen Brigitte and Pierre. The others will march in the parade, so everyone will have a part."

But Pierre refused the great honor of laying the wreath.

"I won't lay a wreath with a girl," he flatly declared.

And if Pierre would not, neither would any other boy.

Monsieur Roger was so provoked that he spoke of dragging Pierre to the village in chains and handcuffing him to the wreath.

Madame Flattot did not believe in taking such extreme measures with children. "Perhaps Brigitte can carry the wreath alone," she said, "and we can find some other patriotic task for Pierre and the boys."

But Pierre and the boys thought up their own way of celebrating Bastille Day.

The result was that Monsieur Roger came dashing into the great hall to see Madame Flattot. He was so angry that he was chewing his own teeth. In his hands were an old tin can, a greasy rag, and some firecrackers.

"I caught Pierre and some of the boys trying to make a bomb with these," he announced.

"A bomb!" exclaimed Madame Flattot. "Why were they trying to make a bomb?"

"To blow up the castle on Bastille Day," explained Monsieur Roger ominously.

Madame clutched at her heart with one hand and Genevieve's shoulder with the other.

"Mercy on us all!" she cried. "They are dangerous. I now see that it was a great mistake to combine the orphanages. I shall call Monsieur de Goupil and tell him that the boys must be taken back to their old building. And before Bastille Day."

But Madame Flattot did not get to call the head of the orphanage because the Silver Knight arrived at the castle before she could reach the telephone.

He must have been in disguise because he came on a dark motor scooter instead of a white horse, and he was wearing his khaki uniform instead of silver armor. But he brought magic with him.

The orphelines gathered silently in the upstairs hall while he was in conference with Monsieur Roger and Madame Flattot under the portrait of Napoleon. They must have talked long and earnestly because the waiting orphelines became very impatient. And when the talk was over, the Silver Knight did not leave immediately. He went with Monsieur Roger to meet the boys and talk to them too.

Madame Flattot's face was sunny when she joined the orphelines.

"That should fix our boys and keep them out of mischief," she said. "The visitor in uniform is a chef of the Scouts of France. He is going to start what he calls a wolf cub pack with them."

The girls were uncertain about this magic club.

"You mean they are going to pretend that they are wolf cubs instead of knights?" asked Brigitte with disappointment in her voice.

"Là, there is much more to it," said Madame. "They will be playing a story, but it is one written by an Englishman, Monsieur Rudyard Kipling. It is called THE JUNGLE BOOK, and it is full of animals who are noble. Another Englishman, Lord Baden-Powell, got this wolf cub idea from it. The Chef gave me a copy of the book, and Genevieve can read some of it to you tonight before you go to bed."

The orphelines were sure that they would not like Monsieur Kipling's book if there were no knights and ladies in it.

Genevieve was not enthusiastic either. "But I have seen the scouts hiking," she admitted, "and they looked very polite and healthy."

"You will learn more about them, Genevieve," said Madame Flattot meaningly.

The orphelines were always ready to hear a story, though. Evening found them listening intently while

Genevieve read to them from the book. Even Madame Flattot lent an ear as she sat darning stockings. Coucky toddled around the group, although he was too young to understand the story.

It was happening in far-off India. It was happening to a small boy named Mowgli who was lost in the jungle after his village had been attacked by Shere Khan, a ruthless tiger.

The orphelines forgot that they were not going to like the book. They gathered closer around Genevieve, and soon they were in the story themselves. Monsieur Kipling had not written it that way, but when the kind wolf mother found the boy, there were twenty orphe-

lines with him. They were safe too when she persuaded Akéla, the wise gray wolf, to allow her to raise Mowgli with her own cubs.

Genevieve skipped around in the book because she wanted to reach the most exciting parts before bedtime. She read about Baloo, the wise bear who taught Mowgli and the orphelines the law of the jungle. She read about Bagheera, the powerful black panther, who taught Mowgli and the orphelines to hunt and to protect themselves.

When she reached the most exciting place, even Madame Flattot felt as if she were in the story too. There was a big meeting at the council rock. The evil young wolves led by Shere Khan were planning to seize Mowgli and the orphelines and Madame Flattot. Would Akéla be able to save them now? Would Mowgli and the orphelines and Madame Flattot be devoured by Shere Khan? The wolves were snarling and howling for them.

Suddenly Genevieve, although she was too busy reading the book to be in it, raised her head in alarm. She could hear the howls too.

"What's that?" she cried, for the noise was coming closer and closer. There was no doubt about it now. They really were hearing bloodcurdling howls.

Genevieve snapped the book shut as if to drive the

wolves back into its pages. Still they could hear the frightening sounds in the courtyard.

"The wolves have come out of the forest," cried Genevieve.

Madame Flattot's face turned white. "They have surrounded us," she cried. "Where is Akéla?"

The howls grew louder. But Madame Flattot showed great presence of spirit. She flung the half-darned stocking into a chair. She ran to the heavy oak door. First she pulled the big bolt, then the little one. She turned the key in the lock. She dropped the latch. She hooked the chain.

Genevieve had presence of spirit too. She grabbed Madame's sewing scissors in her trembling hand and pointed them at the door.

"You shouldn't have read that story," whimpered Josine, because she believed that somehow the wolves had escaped from the book.

Then Coucky, who would not have known a wolf from a poodle, began to bawl with the fright he had caught from the others.

Josine clutched him protectively. "Don't cry," she tried to console him. "I will let the wolves eat me first." Then at such a noble thought, she began to cry too. "But I don't want the wolves to eat me either," she sobbed.

There was a battering of blows upon the door.

"Go away, bad wolves," ordered Madame Flattot bravely. "Go away or I shall call the gendarmes and they will come with their pistols."

"Open the door, please," shouted a voice that did not belong to a wolf.

"Please open the door," pleaded another voice.

Madame Flattot slowly relaxed. "It is only the boys," she said. "This was one of their tricks. I shall give them a good scolding."

But it was quite a while before she could talk to the boys. First she had to raise the latch. Then she had to turn the key. She pushed first the small bolt, then the big one. But she left the chain on until she had opened the door a crack and one of her eyes could see that it really was the boys.

"Good evening, Madame," Pierre greeted her. "We have been practicing our wolf howls so we can be tender paws in the wolf cub pack. Don't you think we are very good at it?"

Madame Flattot unhooked the chain.

"You are too good," she complimented them. "You have scared the girls to death and Coucky has had a crisis of the nerves."

Pierre slipped inside. He raised two fingers to his forehead in a wolf's ear salute.

"I come to ask for the honor of laying the wreath with Brigitte on Bastille Day," he said. Then because he did not wish to appear weak in resolution, he added, "I really don't want to, but I have to do a good deed today. It is getting late and I can't think of anything else."

"And why must you do a good deed if it is such a strain?" asked Madame.

"Wolf cubs have to do a good deed every day," explained Pierre. "That's what the Chef said. And if we don't get to be wolf cubs, we can't go on camping trips. I have never been on a camping trip."

"And we're going to take overnight hikes," said Jean.

"And explore the forest," said Tintin.

"And blaze trails through it," added Pierre. "That is why I want to be a wolf cub so very much."

"I am sure that Brigitte will be delighted to lay the wreath with you if it will help you to become a wolf cub," said Madame Flattot to Pierre.

Brigitte hesitated because she did not think that Pierre's invitation was much of a compliment. Then she politely answered, "I shall be very happy to lay the wreath with you, Pierre–and I really shall be."

Then the pack let out such air-splitting howls that Genevieve dropped the scissors she was still holding.

It gave Madame Flattot a start too, but she recovered quickly. She invited the boys in for cookies. All of them were eager to accept the invitation but Pierre. He shook his head warningly at them. "Thank you, Madame," he said, "but we cannot accept rewards for doing good deeds. That's what the Chef said, too."

"We're having a meeting in the barn," Pierre stated. "It's our jungle."

Then the wolf cubs turned away and went howling over the bridge toward the farm.

So the orphelines thought that there might be some good in the Scouts of France after all as they munched on the cookies that had been sacrificed by the boys.

Bastille Day was all they had hoped for. They dressed in their polka-dot dresses, and Madame Flattot put a new bunch of artificial flowers on her big hat. The mayor sent two autobuses, one for the girls and the other for the boys. The buses were festooned with the tricolor flags of France, and the drivers wore their old army uniforms.

The mayor himself greeted Brigitte and Pierre. He led them to a florist's van where the wreath was waiting. The wreath was enormous. It was made of red tulips, white carnations, and blue cornflowers. And from it flut-

76

tered a gold ribbon with the words Liberty, Equality, Brotherhood, which make the motto of France.

The beautiful wreath was braced between Pierre and Brigitte and their arms were arranged so the gold ribbon wouldn't be hidden. They raised their heads high. They were proud to be French. They were proud to pay homage to the soldier in the square. Even though his statue was rusted and the bayonet broken off his gun, he still represented all the men and women who had given their lives for France.

The parade formed, led by the mayor and a soldier carrying a big flag. They marched around the square once, then the wreath was laid at the base of the statue.

There was a minute of silence when everyone bowed his head in respect for the dead patriots. And it was natural that in this secret little minute the orphelines thought of their own parents who were now in heaven with the brave soldiers. They were thankful for good Madame Flattot, but no one can take the place of a real parent. Little Josine squeezed Madame's hand as they stood together because she had never known any other mother.

Then the band struck up *La Marseillaise*, the national anthem, and its strong notes went marching through the square, past the trees, and over the golden wheatfields beyond.

There were speeches and dancing in the streets, although the dancing wasn't supposed to commence until evening. Some people lighted firecrackers and threw them at their friends, but Madame Flattot did not approve of such imprudence.

"There will be a gala display of fireworks in the village tonight," she told the children, "and we can watch it from our upstairs windows."

"Won't we get to dance in the streets?" cried Brigitte.

"Do we have to go home now?" asked Yvette.

"We have shown our patriotism," said Madame, "and the bus drivers are waiting. It won't be a holiday for them until they have driven us back."

So back to the bus trooped the disappointed orphelines.

But the fireworks display that night made up for everything else at the fête which they had missed.

"Oh," breathed Brigitte as a deep boom in the distance was followed by a burst of red, green, and yellow sparks in the sky. "It is enchanted confetti."

"Ah!" gasped Yvette as a single flame of fire tossed into the blackness burst into hundreds of glittering lights. "It is the rainbow on fire."

"Hé!" cried Marie as a cascade of blue and green fires fell toward the earth. "It is a fiery fountain."

"Ho, ho!" cried Madame after the last bright lights had colored the sky. "It is time to go to bed and dream that you are dancing in the streets."

Despite Pierre's noble act, the girls were still jealous and unhappy about the JUNGLE BOOK story in which they had no part.

It was only for Genevieve that a part had been found.

"The Chef and I have been talking it over," Madame Flattot told her, "and we have decided that you are to be the *cheftaine* of the wolf cub pack."

The young girl looked suspicious. "What is that?" she asked.

"Ah, it is a very noble position," explained Madame. "Every pack must have a young girl in charge–a chiefess."

Genevieve looked gloomy. Like the boys, she felt that joining this club was going to call for sacrifices.

"Do I have to start fires and swim rivers and build monkey bridges?" she asked. "I have heard that scouts do such things."

"You shall do more than that," said Madame. "You shall inspire the boys and strengthen their characters and tell them stories and bake cookies for them. All over France are young girls helping boys to grow up right. Would you shirk your duty?"

"I don't know how to inspire boys," said Genevieve desperately. "I've always taken care of girls."

But Madame firmly pressed a booklet into her hands.

"It is the handbook of the wolf cubs," she said. "Take it to the meeting next Thursday afternoon and read it to yourself and them. It will inspire all of you."

"What meeting?" asked Genevieve.

"The meeting at the council rock in the jungle, of course," said Madame. "Where else would future wolf cubs meet? And you are to conduct it."

"I know where it is," put in Brigitte. "The boys have been meeting in the barn and we've been spying on them."

"They're making a wooden standard with a wolf on top of it," added Yvette. "It's the only thing about the club that is knightly."

So that was the way that Genevieve who feared wolves so greatly became the wise wolf Akéla and head of the wolf cub pack.

The orphelines didn't have much time to spy on the boys because their chores kept them busy. They helped with the housework, and some of the older girls even did the washing and ironing as well.

Charlotte was learning to cook, although she was not as devoted to the heavy iron pots as Madame Flattot.

She sometimes went down into the dusty wine cellar and cast envious eyes at the bright new pans that had been put away "until the iron ones wear out," as Madame Flattot had explained to Monsieur de Goupil.

One day it was the turn of Brigitte and Yvette to sweep the courtyard. They chased their brooms over the cobbles and pretended that they were poor Cinderellas having to drudge at the housework. It made the sweeping more fun and less work.

As they swept away Jean and Tintin slowly approached them.

"May we sweep the courtyard for you?" asked Tintin.

Brigitte raised her broom threateningly. "You go away," she retorted. "We've had enough of your tricks and you aren't going to run away with our brooms."

"We won't run away with them," promised Tintin.

As he put out his hand for the broom Brigitte clubbed his head with it. The blow upset Tintin's balance and he fell to his knees. He covered his head protectively with his hands.

"Please let me sweep for you," he begged on bended knees.

"If you dare move, I'll hit you again," threatened Brigitte, standing over her victim.

"But we really want to do it for you," insisted Jean.

He leaped at Yvette and grasped her broomstick. Yvette gripped it fiercely and a tug of war ensued. Back and forth they tugged each other across the cobbles. Yvette stumbled and fell. But she still clung to the broom.

Then Brigitte ran to Yvette's assistance and began battling Jean with her broom. Tintin got up and ran to help his companion. But as he did so, Brigitte tripped him with her broom and he went sprawling on the cobbles again.

As they fought the battle of the brooms Genevieve hurriedly came out of the door.

"Stop it!" she cried. "Stop this fighting. I am ashamed of you, Jean and Tintin. Have you forgotten your wolf cub honor?"

Jean let go of Yvette's broom and Tintin rose from the cobbles.

"We only wanted to do our good deeds for the day," said Jean in an injured voice, "and the girls won't let us. They started fighting us."

"We offered to sweep the cobbles for them," said Tintin, rubbing his bruised elbow. "There's nobody else to do good deeds for. If we lived in the village, we could help old ladies across the street and give directions to strangers. They wouldn't hit us with brooms."

Genevieve straightened the matter out.

"That is right, girls," she said. "The boys must do a good deed every day if they are to become full-fledged wolf cubs. It says so in the book."

Brigitte and Yvette reluctantly surrendered to the good deeds, but they held onto their authority over the brooms.

"You're not sweeping between the cobbles," Brigitte called Tintin's attention.

"You're raising such a cloud of dust it'll get those clothes on the line dirty again," complained Yvette to Jean.

When the boys had finished their good deeds and gone on their way, the girls swept the places they had missed.

Even Marcel did a good deed. He came running to Josine one morning with something clutched in his fist.

"Hold out your hand," he ordered the littlest orpheline, "and I'll give you a surprise."

Josine immediately clasped her hands behind her. She said, "I think you're going to drop a spider into my hand."

"No, I'm not," persisted Marcel. "Please hold out your hand."

Josine shook her head stubbornly. "I think you've got a bee in your hand," she said, "and you want it to sting me."

Marcel lost patience.

"If you don't hold out your hand," he threatened, "I'll drop it down your neck."

"If you do, I'll scream," said Josine, "and Monsieur Roger will come out and spank you."

"No, he won't," said Marcel.

"Yes, he will," insisted Josine.

"He won't."

"He will."

"Won't."

"Will," persisted Josine, and she was a stubborn child who was bound to have the last word with Marcel. "Will, will, will," she added for good measure.

At last Marcel had to spoil the surprise by showing her what he had. It was a fuzzy brown caterpillar with bright black eyes.

"I really want it for myself," he admitted, "but I'm giving it to you for my good deed."

Marcel put the caterpillar into her open hand. It began to crawl over her fingers.

"It's wonderful," said Josine, "and it tickles. But Genevieve said you aren't old enough to be a wolf cub."

Marcel longingly watched his caterpillar curl up in Josine's palm. "I will be in two years," he said, "and I'm beginning to get ready so I can be in Pierre's group."

Josine rose to the occasion. "Thank you very much for the caterpillar," she said, "and I think you have beautiful freckles."

Marcel blushed under the freckles. "And tomorrow I'll dig a long worm for you," he promised, "and when I'm a big wolf cub and go camping, I'll catch a fish for your cat."

Although the boys had a hard time thinking up good deeds, Pierre chanced upon the idea for one without searching.

He had gone down to the old wine cellar to look for a basket when he spied the bright new pans stacked on a shelf. He was sure that Madame Flattot did not know about them or she wouldn't be using those old black pots. As a pleasant suprise for her and a good deed in the bargain, he waited until she went shopping in the village.

Then he crept into the kitchen and began gathering the old pots together. It took several trips up and down the dark winding steps to make the exchange.

Pierre proudly arranged the new pans on the stove. Then he awaited Madame Flattot's return.

Madame was shocked at sight of the pans which she had discarded. "Now who has done this?" she demanded.

"I did, Madame," announced Pierre proudly. "And I carried all those old ones down. It is my good deed for today. Genevieve—I mean, Akéla—says that I am a born leader and that if I always do my good deeds, I may carry the standard when we hike."

"Pierre." Madame Flattot sighed. "It is like the good deed done by Vincent Bernos when I lived in Provence. A poor widow's roof fell in, partly destroying her house. So the people of the parish came to her aid. This Vincent Bernos gave up a day's work and pay to repair her electric wires. There was much talk about Vincent's good deed and do you know what came of it?" Pierre slowly shook his head. "He was arrested and fined twenty francs for wiring a house when he didn't have an electrician's license."

"But he was doing a good deed," protested Pierre.

"So he was," admitted Madame, "and I will have to say to you what the judge said to Vincent, 'I congratulate you upon your good deed, but I must condemn your lack of prudence.'"

Pierre's face clouded. "I thought it was a good deed," he said in a disappointed voice. "I want to be a chef in the Scouts of France when I grow up."

Madame gave him a second look. Then she seemed to

be straining to do a good deed herself. She patted the boy's shoulder.

"And so it is, Pierre," she said. "I am the one who lacks prudence. You may leave the new pans here. I really should learn to use them and not be so old-fashioned."

At last the girls had a chance to take part in the wolf cub pack's activities. It was only as audience at the boys' reception into the pack, but the girls were grateful for that. They felt like princesses getting ready for a court of honor.

"There will be a big campfire in the courtyard," said Madame Flattot, "and we shall see ceremonies and hear speeches. It will be a grand sound-and-light spectacle."

The boys did more good deeds by gathering wood for the fire. Marcel reverently helped set up the wolf standard, even though he was not old enough to enter the pack yet and could be only a spectator like the girls. He was so full of the spirit of service that he even offered to take care of Coucky during the event.

All of them carried benches to set around for the honored guests. The village priest was among them because he was the chaplain of the pack, and it was said that even in his long black skirt he could outrun and outjump any of the boys.

The Chef came on his scooter because he was to make the big speech. He brought badges and more booklets with him.

Genevieve cut a fine figure in her new blue uniform with the brass buttons and the perky beret. But someone had to knot her kerchief for her because she still tied her fingers into fancy knots.

The boys in their uniforms of navy blue shorts and berets with sky blue shirts formed a circle around her. Each yellow neckerchief was tied with two correct knots, one at the throat and the other in the ends.

One by one, they stood up and took the scout oath after they had asked the chaplain's blessing.

"I promise to do my best, to be faithful to God, France, my parents, the law of the pack and to render service to someone each day," were the words of the promise. And Pierre said his with the sincerity which had been lacking when he made his apology to Josine in the same courtyard. He said it without the reluctance he had admitted in laying the wreath with Brigitte.

At the word "parents," Madame Flattot's face glowed as brightly in the firelight as if it burned with a flame of its own. And Monsieur Roger smiled be-nignly, which was not often his custom.

As each boy finished making his *promesse* his com-rades gave out a great wolf howl, but no one was fright-ened by it tonight.

Brigitte leaned across the bench to the orphelines in front of her. "Why, they are taking the oath of chiv-alry," she said in an awed whisper. "They really are knights."

Then the Chef made his speech about the ideals of the Scouts of France. He reminded the boys that their motto was "Our best."

"You must think of others before yourselves," he said, "have open eyes and ears and always be neat, speak the truth and be cheerful."

Madame, as the mother of the new wolf cubs, had memorized her speech. She walked to Genevieve, carry-ing a bulky package under her arm.

She said, "Cheftaine, I have thought that this cere-mony was a little like a scout baptism. So permit me to give this little package to all of you."

This little package was quite an enormous bag full of *dragées*, the candy-coated almonds that are so popu-lar at French baptisms, and everyone present shared in the gift.

It was a date to remember along with Bastille Day, 18 Brumaire, which brought Napoleon into power, and that St. Médard's Day when the orphelines had first come to their castle with high hopes and noble fancies about their knights.

The new wolf cub pack came marching down the lane. Genevieve, in her chic uniform, was taking her little wolves on a hike to the palace of Fontainebleau—the outing they had once missed because of their naughtiness.

Pierre walked at the head of the column carrying the wolf standard because he was the leader. But there was a heavy worry on his heart. He hadn't done his good deed for the day yet. Perhaps he wouldn't find time because of this trip to the palace. He doubted that there would be any disabled soldiers to be helped up the stairs or any children to be rescued from the carp pond.

As the pack approached the old stone wall he could see all the orphelines sitting on it to watch the departure. There was sisterly pride in the girls' faces.

A sudden inspiration came to the boy. As he passed the girls he dipped the standard gallantly.

"At your service, princesses of the enchanted castle," he called out in a clear, strong voice.

He had done his good deed. He had brought pleasure to the romantic orphelines.

The girls squealed with joy. In a chorus they shouted, "Bravo! Bravo!"

Brigitte was so bubbly with pride and happiness that
she squeezed Josine.

"Aren't our knights chivalrous?" she cried. "Now
we shall live happily ever after."